THE
COLLECTED LETTERS
OF
W. B. YEATS

VOLUME ONE
1865–1895

EDITED BY

JOHN KELLY

ASSOCIATE EDITOR

ERIC DOMVILLE

CLARENDON PRESS · OXFORD
1986

Oxford University Press, Walton Street, Oxford OX2 6DP
Oxford New York Toronto
Delhi Bombay Calcutta Madras Karachi
Kuala Lumpur Singapore Hong Kong Tokyo
Nairobi Dar es Salaam Cape Town
Melbourne Auckland
and associated companies in
Beirut Berlin Ibadan Nicosia

Oxford is a trade mark of Oxford University Press.

Published in the United States
by Oxford University Press, New York

British Library Cataloguing in Publication Data
Yeats, W. B.
The collected letters of W. B. Yeats.
Vol. 1, 1865–1895
1. Yeats, W. B.—Biography 2. Authors, Irish—
20th century—Biography
I. Title II. Kelly, John III. Domville, Eric
821'.8 PR5906
ISBN 0-19-812679-4

Set by Macmillan India Ltd., Bangalore
Printed in Great Britain at
The Alden Press, Oxford

ACKNOWLEDGEMENTS

Our thanks are due first and foremost to Anne Yeats and to Michael and Grania Yeats, without whose help and hospitality this edition would not have been possible. We also gratefully acknowledge the generosity of those who have allowed us to make copies of Yeats material in their possession: Seymour Adelman, Joann M. Andrews, Joan Linnell Burton, Francis Evers, James Gilvarry, A. B. Alan Haughton, Professor Richard M. Kain, Dr M. Radford, Dr D. F. Wall, Mrs Anne White.

This volume, and the edition as a whole, have been greatly assisted by grants and other financial help from the British Academy, the Canada Council, the Leverhulme Trust, the University of Kent at Canterbury, the University of Leicester, the President and Fellows of St. John's College, Oxford, and the Oxford English Faculty.

We are also indebted for help and advice to Terry Abraham, Washington State University Library; J. R. R. Adams, Ulster Folk and Transport Museum, Professor Bo Almqvist, University College, Dublin; Professor I. J. Austin, Cambridge University; B. J. Baldwin, University of Glasgow Library; Professor Conrad Balliet, Wittenberg University; Professor Robert Becker, Emory University; Professor Karl Beckson, City University, New York; John Bell; Robert J. Bertholf, Lockwood Memorial Library, Buffalo; Alan Bold; Professor George Bornstein, University of Michigan; Anne Marie Bouche, Mills College Library; Harry Bovenizer, Trinity College, Dublin Library; Louisa Bowen, Morris Library, Southern Illinois University; Professor Zack Bowen, University of Delaware; Kay Bridgwater; Hugo Brunner; Susan Brynteson, University of Delaware Library; Philip Bull, Bodleian Library, Oxford; Penelope Bulloch, King's College, Cambridge, Library; Lucy Burgess, Cornell University Library; Professor F. J. Byrne, University College, Dublin; P. M. Cadell, National Library of Scotland; Humphrey and Mari Carpenter; Philippa Casimir, the National Army Museum; Ann Cnudde-Knowland, Stefan Congrat-Butler; Professor Lester Conner, Chestnut Hill College; David F. Cook, The John Rylands Library, Manchester; G. R. Cowie; Gordon A. Cronin, Taurus Books; Aldo R. Cupo, Beinecke Library, Yale University; William T. Dameron, Chalmers Memorial Library, Kenyon College; Roy Davids, Sotheby & Co.; Rodney G. Dennis, Houghton Library, Harvard University; Alan Denson; Freda Domville; Professor Denis Donoghue, New York University; Maureen Duffany, Doheny Memorial Library,

California; Ellen Dunlap, Rosenbach Foundation; Michael Durkan, Swathmore College Library; J. A. Edwards, Reading University Library; Professor Richard Ellmann, Emory University; W. A. N. Figgis; Professor Benjamin F. Fisher, Hahnemann Medical College; Harry Fisher, Froebel Institute; Professor Richard Finneran, Tulane University; Professor Mary Fitzgerald, University of New Orleans; Professor Ian Fletcher, University of Arizona; Kathleen Foster, City of Manchester Library; Robin Gard, Northumberland County Archivist; Joan Gibbs, University of London Library; William A. Gifford, Norwood Historical Society; Phyllis M. Giles, Fitzwilliam Museum Cambridge; the late Professor Donald Gordon; Dr Warwick Gould, Royal Holloway College, London; Victor W. Graham, the Dublin High School and TCD; Fr. Aubrey Gwynn, S.J.; Dr J. T. Hall, Edinburgh University Library; N. Hardiman, Dublin Public Libraries; Professor George Harper, Florida State University; Fr. Eugene J. Harrington S.J., College of the Holy Cross; Janet Hart; Sir Rupert Hart-Davis; Joy Hawkins; Dr Barbara Hayley, Maynooth College; Patrick Henchy, National Library of Ireland; Cathy Henderson, Humanities Research Center, University of Texas; M. Hewson, National Library of Ireland; Audrey Hill; the late Pamela Hinkson; Mary S. Hodgson, BBC Archives; Sarah S. Hodson, Huntington Library; Michael Holroyd; Ann Hyde, Kenneth Spencer Research Library, University of Kansas; John E. Ingram, Brown University Library; Professor A. N. Jeffares, University of Stirling; Robert H. Jenkinson, Belfast Public Libraries; George M. Jenks, Ellen Clarke Bertrand Library, Bucknell University; Norma Jessop, University College, Dublin, Library; Professor K. P. S. Jochum, University of Bamberg; Kenneth W. Johnson, Trent University Library; Estelle Jussim; Lionel Kelly, Reading University; Revd G. Kivlehan, ONI; Dr G. Krishnamurti, The Eighteen Nineties Society; Professor Mary Lago, University of Missouri; James Laughlin, New Directions Publishing Co.; James Lawton, E. S. Leighton-Jones, Boston Public Library; Miriam M. Lennon, Norwood Historical Society; Jeremy Lewis; D. W. Liddle, Gateshead Borough Librarian; Professor Walt Litz, Princeton University; Kenneth A. Lohf, Columbia University Library; the late Professor F. S. L. Lyons; Claire McCann, University of Kentucky Libraries; Dr Bill McCormack; James McGarry; Fr. Fergal McGrath S.J.; Professor Roger McHugh; Dr B. McKenna, National Library of Ireland; Colin A. McLaren, Aberdeen University Library; Alf MacLochlain, National Library of Ireland; John McTernan, Sligo County Library; James Mahony, College of the Holy Cross; Stanley Mallach, Fromkin Memorial Collection, University of Wisconsin-Milwaukee; Charles Mann, Pennsylvania State University; Professor Augustine Martin, University College, Dublin;

David I. Masson, Brotherton Library, University of Leeds; Dr Colin Mathews, St Hugh's College, Oxford; Virginia Lowell Mauck, Lilly Library, Indiana University; Irene M. Moran, Bancroft Library, University of California Berkeley; Carole Munden, College of Psychic Studies; Professor William M. Murphy, Union College Schenectady; N. Frederick Nash, University of Illinois Libraries; Professor James Nelson, University of Wisconsin; L. M. Newman, University of Lancaster Library; Nora Niland, Sligo County Library; Professor Kevin Nowlan, University College, Dublin; Thomas F. O'Connell, Boston College Library; Professor William O'Donnell, University of Pennsylvania; Margaret Pamplin, University Library, Cambridge; Constance-Anne Parker, Royal Academy of Arts; Trevor Parkhill, Northern Ireland Public Record Office; J. Percival, University College, London, Library; M. R. Perkin, University of Liverpool Library; Sigrid P. Perry, Northwestern University Library; Jean F. Preston, Princeton University Library; Christopher Phillips; J. Richard Phillips, Stanford University Libraries; D. S. Porter, Bodleian Library, Oxford; Bernard Quaritch Ltd.; Princess Mary Rachewiltz; Kathleen Raine; Professor B. L. Reid, Mount Holyoke College; Dr Michael Rhodes, Westfield College, London; Isabel Richardson, Dr R. Robson, Trinity College, Cambridge; Bernard Rota Ltd.; Revd John Ryan; Professor Ann Saddlemyer, University of Toronto; Michael Saich, Merton Borough Librarian; Professor Christopher Salvesen, Reading University; Nicholas B. Scheetz, Georgetown University Library; Professor Ronald Schuchard, Emory University; C. D. W. Sheppard, Brotherton Library, University of Leeds; Elspeth Simpson, University of Glasgow Library; Anne Skally, University of Cork; John Slemon, Abbey Theatre, Dublin; Revd H. John Smith; Colin Smythe; Nicholas Spence; Professor Jon Stallworthy, Cornell University; Revd Thomas M. Steel; Joan Stevenson; John Studley; Sherry Sullivan; Lola Szladits, Berg Collection, New York Public Library; Saundra Taylor, Lilly Library, Indiana University; Roger Watson, Longman Group; Professor Robert Welch, University of Coleraine; Professor Trevor West, Trinity College, Dublin; Margaret M. Wright, University of Manchester Library; Thomas F. Wright, Clark Memorial Library, California; Marjorie G. Wynne, Beinecke Library, Yale University; Yeats Society, Sligo; Lela Ulrich, J. & S. Graphics; Dr Peter van de Kamp.

Special thanks are due to Alita Dusek who gave generously of her time and expertise in Irish genealogy; Catherine Carver who spent many hours helping to hammer the volume into unity; and to Frances Whistler who saw it through the press.

Photographs and pictures of W. B. Yeats and others are reproduced by kind permission of Anne Yeats, Michael Yeats, the National Gallery of Ireland, the Dublin Municipal Gallery, and the Ulster Museum. Despite strenuous efforts it has not proved possible to trace copyright holders in all cases.

CONTENTS

LIST OF ILLUSTRATIONS

CHRONOLOGY

1865   **13 June** William Butler Yeats (WBY), eldest child of John Butler Yeats (JBY) and Susan Mary Yeats (née Pollexfen), born at Georgeville, Sandymount Avenue, Dublin.

1866   **Jan** JBY called to the Irish Bar. **25 Aug** Susan Mary (Lily) Yeats (SMY) born at Enniscrone, Co. Sligo.

1867   **Late Feb/early Mar** JBY gives up the law and moves to London to enrol at Heatherley's Art School. **Late July** Susan Yeats, WBY, SMY, and Isabella Pollexfen (aunt) join JBY at 23 Fitzroy Road, Regent's Park.

1868   **11 Mar** Elizabeth Corbet (Lollie) Yeats (ECY) born in Fitzroy Road. **Summer** Family holiday in Sligo.

1869   **Summer** Family holiday in Sligo; children remain there until Dec.

1870   **27 Mar** Robert Corbet (Bobbie) Yeats born in Fitzroy Road. **Apr** WBY ill with scarlatina. **Summer** Family holiday in Sligo.

1871   **29 Aug** John Butler (Jack) Yeats born in Fitzroy Road. **Sept** Short family holiday in Sligo.

1872   **23 July** Yeatses leave London for Sligo where Susan Yeats and the children remain for more than two years, living at Merville.

1873   **3 Mar** Bobbie Yeats dies suddenly in Sligo. **Oct–Dec** JBY painting portraits at Muckross Abbey.

1874   **Winter-spring** JBY painting portraits at Stradbally Hall; rejoins his family in Sligo in the summer. **Late Oct** Yeatses move back to London, settling at 14 Edith Villas, North End (West Kensington).

1875   **29 Aug** Jane Grace Yeats born at Edith Villas.

1876   **6 June** Jane Grace Yeats dies of bronchial pneumonia; the same month, JBY's mother dies of cancer in Dublin. **Summer** Yeatses holiday in Sligo. JBY returns alone to London and, having decided to abandon portrait-painting for landscapes, spends extended periods at Burnham Beeches. **Autumn** WBY joins his father at Burnham Beeches, lodging with the Earles in Farnham Royal.

1877   **Jan** Susan Yeats and the other children return to Edith Villas. **26 Jan** WBY enrolled at the Godolphin School, Iffley Road, Hammersmith.

1879   **Spring** Yeatses move to 8 Woodstock Road, Bedford Park. **Summer** Family holiday at Branscombe, Devon.

1881   **Easter** WBY leaves the Godolphin School. **Summer** JBY's
chronic financial difficulties worsen; in the autumn he moves to
Dublin and rents a studio at 44 York Street. **Late autumn** JBY
brings his family (except Jack, who is living permanently in Sligo
with grandparents) to Ireland and they settle at Balscaddan Cottage
in Howth. WBY enrolled at the Erasmus Smith High School,
Harcourt Street, Dublin.

1882   **Spring** Yeatses move from Balscaddan Cottage to Island View,
Harbour Road, Howth. **Autumn** WBY meets his distant cousin,
Laura Armstrong, and is attracted to her.

1883   **20 Nov** Attends lecture by Oscar Wilde in Dublin. **Dec** Leaves the
Erasmus Smith High School.

1884   **8 Jan** Begins play, *Vivien and Time*, for Laura Armstrong. **Early
spring** Yeats family forced by financial considerations to leave
Howth for 10 Ashfield Terrace, in the south Dublin suburb of
Terenure. **May** WBY enrols as a student at Metropolitan School of
Art, Kildare Street, Dublin. **Sept** Laura Armstrong marries Henry
Byrne.

1885   **19 Jan** John O'Leary (JO'L) returns from exile in Paris; WBY
meets him a little later in the year. **Mar** WBY's first publications, a
poem later entitled 'Song of the Faeries' and 'Voices', in the *Dublin
University Review* (*DUR*). **Apr–July** *The Island of Statues* published in *DUR*. **2 June** Attends an evening meeting in C. H.
Oldham's rooms in TCD to discuss how to bring a national spirit
into *DUR*; Hyde, Gregg, and Coffey among those present.
16 June First meeting of Dublin Hermetic Society, WBY presiding. **Late June** Oldham introduces WBY to Katharine Tynan
(KT) at her house in Clondalkin. **Aug** Death of Matthew Yeats,
JBY's uncle and his agent on the Thomastown estate; JBY's money
problems increase. **21 Nov** Contemporary Club founded by C. H.
Oldham. **13 Dec** WBY at social evening at the Coffeys'. **18
Dec** Attends meeting of Young Ireland Society to hear paper by
Oldham, after which, in Oldham's rooms, spends three hours
talking to Douglas Hyde.

1886   Poems, plays, and literary articles appearing regularly in *DUR*, *Irish
Monthly*, and *Irish Fireside*. **Apr** Leaves the Metropolitan School of
Art. **10, 11 Apr** Hears William Morris lecture in Dublin and meets
him at the Contemporary Club. **Oct** *Mosada*, WBY's first publi-
cation in book form, privately printed in Dublin. Begins first part of
'The Wanderings of Oisin'. **24 Nov** At JO'L's house with Sigerson,
Rose Kavanagh, KT, George and Mrs Coffey. **4 Dec** Afternoon

with Hyde discussing their poetry and afterwards to a debate on the land question at the Contemporary Club. **7 Dec** Attends Roman Lipmann's conversazione at the Russell Hotel. **11 Dec** Discussion of historical drama with Hyde at the Contemporary Club.

1887 **10 Jan** Accompanies KT to a meeting of the Protestant Home Rule Association at which T. W. Rolleston is a speaker. **23 Jan** With Hyde to visit KT at Clondalkin. **30 Jan** At the Dowdens'. **15 Feb** Calls to ask KT for another sitting to his father for a portrait begun the previous summer. **2 Mar** Visits the Misses Gill at Roebuck House, Dublin. **3 Mar** JBY to London to arrange for family's return there. **6 Mar** WBY, SMY, and ECY at KT's. **3 Apr** WBY's last visit to KT before moving to London. **Early Apr** The family join JBY in England. SMY and ECY in Liverpool with Uncle John; Jack with Uncle Varley; WBY lodges at 6 Berkeley Road, Regent's Park, London, until the family house is ready. **Early May** WBY joins the family at 58 Eardley Crescent, South Kensington. **6 May** Attends debate at House of Commons. **May** Meets Ernest Rhys. WBY out of sorts; works on reviews, articles, and poems at the Art Library, South Kensington Museum. First visit to Mme Blavatsky (HPB), lately arrived in London. **19 June** Hears H. H. Sparling lecture on 'Irish Rebel Songs' at William Morris's house in Hammersmith; meets May Morris. Thereafter WBY regularly attends the Morris 'Sunday Nights'. **11 Aug** Arrives in Sligo to stay with his uncle, George Pollexfen, at Rosses Point; working on 'Oisin'. **Late summer** Susan Yeats has her first stroke. **Oct** WBY moves into Sligo town to stay with his grandparents. **18 Nov** Finishes 'Oisin'. **22 Nov** To Dublin where he stays with KT at Clondalkin. Sees much of the O'Learys and other Dublin friends; JO'L begins to organize subscriptions for WBY's book of poems. **11 Dec** WBY brings AE (George Russell) to Clondalkin to reintroduce him to KT; Hyde also there. **Dec** Susan Yeats and SMY go to stay with Elizabeth Pollexfen Orr at Denby near Huddersfield; Mrs Yeats suffers another stroke and falls down a back stair.

1888 **Jan** WBY experiences severe nervous disturbance at a Dublin seance. JBY decides to look for a house in Bedford Park. **26 Jan** WBY returns to London. **Feb** Commissioned by Rhys to edit a book of Irish folklore. **11 Feb** Meets a ruined relation in a London hotel. **12 Feb** Meets George Bernard Shaw at William Morris's house. **12 Mar** Takes MS of *The Wanderings of Oisin and Other Poems* to Kegan Paul, who accepts it but tells WBY he needs more subscribers. **21 Mar** First visit to the Southwark Irish

Literary Club where he hears Daniel Crilly, MP, lecture on Fanny Parnell. **24 Mar** Yeats family moves to 3 Blenheim Road, Bedford Park. Susan Yeats and SMY go there from Denby on 13 Apr. **Apr** WBY attending French lessons at the Morrises'. **28 Apr** At a Home Rule party given by the Hancocks. **Early May** Publication of *Poems and Ballads of Young Ireland*. **13 June** WBY lectures to the Southwark Irish Literary Club on 'Sligo Fairies'. **17 June** Attends performance of William Morris's play, *The Tables Turned*. **28 July** Meets Lady Wilde and becomes a frequent guest at her Saturday afternoon 'at homes'. **11 Aug** In Oxford copying out Caxton's edition of Aesop's *Fables* at the Bodleian. **6 Sept** First proofs of *Oisin* arrive. **18 Sept** John Davidson visits 3 Blenheim Road and argues with WBY over metaphysics. **Late Sept** *Fairy and Folk Tales of the Irish Peasantry* published. **13 Oct** At the Irish Exhibition; in the evening with Jack to a performance of *Dr Jekyll and Mr Hyde*. **30 Oct** With the other Yeats children to a performance of Barnes's *Prince Karl* at the Lyceum. **4 Nov** Edmund Russell, the Delsartian, to tea at the Yeatses'; in the evening WBY takes him to Morris's. **6 Nov** T. W. Lyster, the Dublin librarian, at Blenheim Road with May Morris, Sparling, and Todhunter. **18 Nov** WBY at the Arts and Crafts Exhibition with the other Yeats children. **Nov** Attacked by 'lunar influences'. Joins Esoteric Section of the Theosophical Society. **1 Dec** SMY begins work as embroidress at May Morris's. **12 Dec** WBY chairs a lecture by Sparling on 'The Literature of '98' at the Southwark Irish Literary Club. **Mid-Dec** Composes 'The Lake Isle of Innisfree'. **25 Dec** Spends Christmas Day with the Oscar Wildes in Tite Street.

1889 **2 Jan** Goes with Jack to a performance of Gilbert and Sullivan's *Yeomen of the Guard*. **c. 10 Jan** *Oisin* published. **22 Jan** First reviews of *Oisin*. **Late Jan** Yeats family financial problems particularly acute. **30 Jan** Maud Gonne (MG) visits Blenheim Road. **31 Jan** WBY dines with MG in London. **Feb** Begins *The Countess Kathleen*. **2 Mar** At a reception given by the novelist 'John Strange Winters' (Mrs Stannard). **3 Mar** Spends night at the Ellises', probably to discuss a proposed edition of *The Works of William Blake*. **Apr** Begins literary notes for the *Manchester Courier*. **1 May** In Oxford copying Blake's *The Book of Thel*. **6 May** Reads *The Countess Kathleen* to Florence Farr. **29 May** Lectures on Mangan to the Southwark Irish Literary Society. **2 July** KT at Blenheim Road; visits again 21–2 July. **6 Aug** WBY in Oxford copying an Elizabethan book for Nutt. **23 Aug** *Stories from*

Carleton. **1 Sept** WBY dines in London with Sir Charles Gavan Duffy. **15 Oct** Ellen O'Leary dies in Cork. **20–3 Oct** WBY sees JO'L in London. **17 Nov** Jack Yeats persuades WBY to shave off his beard. **Late Dec** Ellis and WBY discover Linnell's MS of Blake's *Vala*. **20 Dec** Meets with Annie Besant and other members of the Esoteric Section of the Theosophical Society to renew their pledges to HPB.

1890 **Early Jan** WBY ill with Russian influenza. **11 Jan** MG gives birth to a son, George, by Millevoye. **Jan** With Rhys, founds the Rhymers' Club. **7 Mar** WBY initiated into the Hermetic Order of the Golden Dawn in Moina Bergson's studio, 17 Fitzroy Street. **16 Mar** Sends off MS of *Representative Irish Tales*. **5 May** Attends performance of Todhunter's *A Sicilian Idyll* at the Club House in Bedford Park. **June** Meets Louise Imogen Guiney. **16 June** MacGregor Mathers marries Moina Bergson. **Aug** Ellis signs contract with Quaritch for publication of *The Works of William Blake*. **Sept** WBY meets Fred Holland Day. **11 Oct** First number of the short-lived *Weekly Review* to which WBY and other Rhymers contribute. **Mid-Oct** Asked to resign from the Esoteric Section of the Theosophical Society. **Autumn** In state of semi-collapse; a slight heart ailment is diagnosed. **18 Nov** Verdict in the O'Shea divorce case precipitates a political crisis in the Irish Party. **1–6 Dec** Irish Party debate on the leadership crisis ends in a split between Parnellite and anti-Parnellite factions.

1891 **Mar** *Representative Irish Tales*. **May** Gets to know Richard Le Gallienne. **8 May** HPB dies in London. **c. 17 July** WBY arrives in Dublin. **22 July** Meets MG in Dublin; his love for her revives. **23 July** At Ballykilbeg House near Downpatrick to stay with Charles Johnston for a week or ten days. **Early Aug** Returns to Dublin, to stay at various addresses while writing 'Rosy Cross Lyrics'. **10–16 Aug** Staying with KT at Clondalkin. **31 Aug** MG's son dies in Paris. **15 Sept** Inaugural Meeting of the Young Ireland League, organized by WBY and JO'L to unite various Irish literary societies. **7 Oct** Charles Stewart Parnell dies in Brighton. Funeral in Dublin on 11 Oct. **c. 21 Oct** WBY returns to London. **Early Nov** *John Sherman and Dhoya*. **28 Dec** Meeting at Blenheim Road to plan an Irish Literary Society.

1892 **Jan** WBY planning a new Library of Ireland. **13 Jan** Meeting at Clapham Reform Club formally decides to establish an Irish Literary Society in London. **17 Jan** Lectures on 'Nationality and Literature' to the Clapham Branch of the Irish National League. **Feb** *The Book of the Rhymers' Club*. **8 Feb** Fisher Unwin takes

over unsold stock of *Oisin* from Kegan Paul. **May** *Irish Fairy Tales.*
6 May Copyright performance of *The Countess Kathleen* at the
Athenaeum Theatre, Shepherd's Bush. **Mid-May** WBY arrives in
Dublin to found a central Irish Literary Society. **24 May** Attends
meeting at the Wicklow Hotel to consider the setting up of a
National Literary Society. **9 June** Public Steering Committee
meeting of the National Literary Society held at the Rotunda;
speeches from WBY, MG, Sigerson, Ashe King, and Count
Plunket. **14 June** WBY and MG appointed to the Libraries Sub-
committee of the National Literary Society. **30 July** Provisional
acting committee of the National Literary Society meet with Gavan
Duffy to discuss the publication of Irish national books.
8 Aug Public meeting at the Mansion House, Dublin, to discuss
the revival of Irish literature, the foundation of a publishing
company, and the circulation of books. **16 Aug** Inaugural Meeting
of the National Literary Society with Gavan Duffy in the chair;
address by Sigerson; WBY also speaks. **18 Aug** Provisional
committee of the National Literary Society formally elect a Council;
WBY elected a vice-president. **Late Aug** *The Countess Kathleen
and Various Legends and Lyrics.* **Early Sept** Newspaper controversy over proposed New Irish Library. **22 Sept** WBY appointed secretary of the Library Committee of the National Literary
Society. **Oct** In Sligo, where his grandmother, Elizabeth Pollexfen,
dies on 2 Oct; WBY asked to represent the family at the funeral. His
grandfather is also seriously ill. **6 Oct** Death of Alfred Lord
Tennyson. **29 Oct** Rolleston and Gavan Duffy begin negotiations
with Fisher Unwin over publication of the New Irish Library, thus
angering WBY and JO'L. **10 Nov** National Literary Society takes
rooms at 4 College Green, Dublin. **12 Nov** William Pollexfen dies
in Sligo. **20 Nov** WBY returns to Dublin from Sligo and takes
room at Lonsdale House, Clontarf. **25 Nov** Hyde inaugurates the
first lecture session of the National Literary Society with his
influential address, 'The Necessity for De-Anglicizing Ireland'.
Mid-Dec WBY goes to London to confer with the Committee of
the Irish Literary Society, London, and Fisher Unwin about the
rival schemes for the New Irish Library. **Late Dec** Preparing for
the Portal examination of the Golden Dawn.

1893   **20 Jan** Undergoes the Portal Ritual for entry to the Second Order
of the Golden Dawn at the Vault in Clipstone Street, London; he
also takes the 1st Point part of the $5° = 6°$ grade, the lowest grade of
the Second Order. **21 Jan** Takes 2nd and 3rd Points of $5° = 6°$
grade. **22 Jan** Arrives in Dublin. **23 Jan** Travels to Cork with

Hyde to promote the National Literary Society at a public meeting.
26 Jan WBY reads from *The Countess Kathleen* at a social meeting
of the National Literary Society. **27 Jan** Highly contentious
meeting of the Committee of the National Literary Society, to
discuss Gavan Duffy's proposals for the New Irish Library,
adjourned until 2 Feb. **Late Jan** Small-paper version of *The Works
of William Blake* ready. Large-paper version appears in mid-Feb.
Mid-Feb Brief visit to Sligo where he stays with George Pollexfen.
4 Mar Delivers the address at the National Club, Dublin, on the
anniversary of the birth of Robert Emmet; Arthur Griffith present.
21 Mar Formal agreement for publication of the New Irish Library
signed by Fisher Unwin and Gavan Duffy. **4 May** KT marries
Henry Albert Hinkson in London. **19 May** WBY lectures on
'Nationality and Literature' to the National Literary Society at the
Leinster Hall, Molesworth Street. **Late May** Returns to London.
30 May Attends a Council of Adepts at the Second Order of the
Golden Dawn, Clipstone Street, where he continues to pay regular
visits that summer until his return to Dublin in mid-Sept. **17
July** Lectures to the Chiswick Lodge of the Theosophical Society
on 'The Nature of Art and Poetry in Relation to Mysticism'. **31
July** Gaelic League founded in Dublin. **29 Aug** Begins small white
notebook in which many of the poems to be published in *The Wind
Among the Reeds* are drafted. **Mid-Sept** Returns to Dublin with
Lionel Johnson, to make plans for an Irish literary magazine; they
stay with J. P. Quinn at 56 North Circular Road. **4 Oct** WBY
present at Annual General Meeting of the National Literary
Society. **14 Oct** Speaks at the Commemoration of Thomas Davis
organized by the Young Ireland League at the National Club. **21
Nov** Lectures to the Belfast Naturalists' Field Club on 'Irish Fairy
Lore'. **Late Nov** *The Poems of William Blake*. **Dec** *The Celtic
Twilight*. **Late Dec** Returns to London.

1894   **7 Feb** Goes to Paris, staying with the Matherses. Sees MG and
Verlaine but fails to meet Mallarmé. **26 Feb** With MG, attends a
performance of Villiers de l'Isle-Adam's *Axel* at the Théâtre de la
Gaité. **c. 27 Feb** Returns to London. **Mar** Begins writing *The
Shadowy Waters*. **29 Mar** *The Land of Heart's Desire* produced with
Todhunter's *The Comedy of Sighs* at the Avenue Theatre, London,
until 14 Apr. **Apr** Meets Olivia Shakespear (OS). *The Land of
Heart's Desire* published, and on 21 Apr revived at the Avenue
Theatre with Shaw's *Arms and the Man* until 12 May. **June** *The
Second Book of the Rhymers' Club* published by John Lane.
16 July Attends unveiling of Keats bust at Hampstead Church.

6 Aug MG's daughter, Iseult, born. **23 Aug** Present at marriage of Jack Yeats to Mary Cottenham White at Emmanuel Church, Gunnersbury. **10 Oct** Arrives in Dublin, staying again with J. P. Quinn at 56 North Circular Road. **25 Oct** Goes to stay with George Pollexfen in Sligo. Spends much time revising poems and plays for collected edition, and writing *The Shadowy Waters*. **Mid-Nov** Stays at Lissadell and contemplates asking Eva Gore-Booth to marry him. Collects folklore and lectures on fairy tales.

1895   **Mid-Jan** Joins in a controversy with Edward Dowden over Irish literature. **27 Feb** Begins a controversy in the Dublin *Daily Express* over 'The Best 30 Irish Books'. **Late Feb** WBY and George Pollexfen ill with influenza. **Early Mar** *A Book of Irish Verse*. **27 Mar** Finishes revision of his poems for collected edition. **13 Apr** Leaves Sligo to visit Hyde at Frenchpark, Co. Roscommon. **16 Apr** Visits Castle Rock in Lough Key. Returns to Sligo on 1 May. **4 May** Leaves Sligo for Dublin *en route* to London. **19 May** Calls on Oscar Wilde to offer sympathy and support during his trial. **July–Oct** Four articles on Irish literature in the *Bookman*. **16 July** Visits Kent with OS. **10 Aug** Visits Henley in new black coat. **14 Aug** JO'L stays at the Yeatses'. **17 Aug** JBY suffering from an illness which is to persist for much of the autumn. **20 Aug** WBY receives an advance copy of *Poems*. **22 Aug** Meets Col. Maurice Moore, George Moore's brother. **3 Sept** OS calls at Blenheim Road together with Nora Hopper, Louise Imogen Guiney, Dora Sigerson, and Elkin Mathews. **4 Sept** WBY having his portrait painted by Faulks. **13 Sept** Aunt Agnes Pollexfen Gorman arrives at Blenheim Road, having escaped from a mental home. Her husband, Robert Gorman, summoned the next day, recommits her. **14 Sept** WBY goes to stay with Jack and Cottie Yeats at Chertsey. **Early Oct** Leaves the family house and takes rooms with Arthur Symons in Fountain Court, the Temple. **5 Oct** Delivers the address at a Parnell Commemorative Meeting at the Arbitration Rooms, Chancery Lane. **15 Oct** SMY leaves London for Hyères where she is to be a governess.

1896   **Late Feb** WBY moves from the Temple to rooms at 18 Woburn Buildings. Begins an affair with OS; starts work on *The Speckled Bird*. **Summer** Visits Aran Islands. **Dec** To Paris, where on 21 Dec he meets Synge.

1897   **Mid-Jan** Returns to London. **Mar** Visits Robert Bridges. **Apr** *The Secret Rose*. **May** In Sligo. **June** *The Adoration of the Magi*. **June** Visits Edward Martyn at Tillyra Castle. **Late July** To Coole to stay with Lady Gregory for two months; WBY collects folklore and they discuss the possibility of a 'Celtic Theatre'. **Nov–Dec** Returns to Dublin and thence back to London.

1898   Working at 'Celtic mysticism' with MG and members of Golden Dawn. **Jan** Synge calls on him in London. **Early Mar** Short visit to Dublin. **1 Apr** Meets Wilfrid Blunt. **Late Apr–May** Visits Paris to discuss Celtic mysticism with Mathers and MG. Successfully lobbies MPs to change theatrical licensing laws in Dublin. **May** Sits to Rothenstein for portrait. **8 June** To Dublin, and thence to Coole on 20th. **Mid-Aug** In London and Dublin for '98 banquets and celebrations. Controversy with AE and John Eglinton over 'Literary Ideals in Ireland' in Dublin *Daily Express.* **Sept–Nov** Staying with George Pollexfen in Sligo. **Late Nov** To Dublin, where MG tells him she has long been in love with him but cannot marry him.

1899   **Late Jan** Returns to London. **Feb** Short visit to Paris, where he again proposes to MG. Returns to London to arrange rehearsals of Irish Literary Theatre plays with Florence Farr, George Moore, and Martyn. **Late Mar** Martyn worried by supposed heresy of *The Countess Cathleen*, but is reassured. **Apr** *The Wind Among the Reeds.* F. H. O'Donnell attacks *The Countess Cathleen* with support of Cardinal Logue. **8 May** *Gountess Cathleen* performed at the Antient Concert Rooms as first production of Irish Literary Theatre. **May** Revised edition of *Poems.* At Coole until Nov except for short trips to Dublin and Belfast. **Late Oct** Begins collaboration with Moore on *Diarmuid and Grania*; **17 Nov** Returns to London.

1900   **3 Jan** Susan Yeats dies. **19–24 Feb** Second season of the Irish Literary Theatre. **Mar–Apr** Protests against Queen Victoria's visit to Dublin. **17–25 Apr** Mathers sends Aleister Crowley to seize the Golden Dawn headquarters but WBY evicts him and guards the rooms against him. **June** Takes on A. P. Watt as his literary agent. **23 June** To Dublin and thence to Coole. **14 Oct** Returns to London. Disputes with Moore over writing of *Diarmuid and Grania*; play finished on **12** Dec.

1901   **Jan** Contributes to *Ideals in Ireland*. **Feb** Trouble in Golden Dawn. WBY resigns from Irish Literary Society because Moore has been blackballed. **30 Mar** Impressed by stage scenery in Gordon Craig's production of *Dido and Aeneas*. **Late Apr** Visits Stratford. **9 May** To Dublin, and on to Sligo 20 May until late June. **July** At Coole, writing a series of poems on the Irish heroic age. **Late Aug** Attends Pan Celtic Conference in Dublin. Sees the Fays act. **29 Aug** Attends Galway Feis. **21–3 Oct** *Diarmuid and Grania* produced at Gaiety Theatre. **21 Oct–3 Nov** JBY's Dublin exhibition. **Mid-Nov** WBY returns to London; begins experiments with the psaltery.

1902   In Dublin, allows Fays to rehearse *Cathleen ni Houlihan*, and they produce it, with AE's *Deirdre*, on 2 Apr. **5 Apr** Meeting with Fays to discuss an Irish National Theatre. **9 Apr** Returns to London. **Spring and summer** Public lectures on the psaltery. **21 June** To Ireland, where he helps prevent the destruction of Tara. **8 Aug** Fays' company move into the

Camden Street Hall. **Aug** Meets John Quinn. **Late summer** Meets James Joyce. **Sept–Oct** Quarrel with Moore over *Where There Is Nothing*. **4 Oct** Lionel Johnson dies. **29 Oct–1 Nov** Irish National Theatre Society productions, including *A Pot of Broth*. **Late Nov** Dun Emer Press set up. **Early Dec** Meets Joyce in London and tries to find him reviewing work. Discovers Nietzsche.

1903   **21 Feb** MG marries John MacBride. WBY lecturing on the psaltery with Florence Farr. **Mid-Mar** To Dublin for plays by the Irish National Theatre Society. In London, helps to set up the Masquers theatrical society. **Early May** Irish National Theatre Society's first visit to London. **May** *Ideas of Good and Evil*. **June** At Frenchpark with Hyde; thence to Coole. **Aug** *In the Seven Woods*. MG and Hyde, with some actors, withdraw from Irish National Theatre Society in protest against the production of Synge's *In the Shadow of the Glen*. **4 Nov** WBY leaves for tour of USA. Arrives in New York on 11 Nov, lecturing there and in north-eastern states.

1904   **Jan–Feb** Lectures in New York, Midwest, and California, returning to New York by way of Canada. **9 Mar** Leaves USA for London. **Mid-Apr** In Dublin to help plan the design for the Abbey Theatre. **Late June** *Where There Is Nothing* produced by the Stage Society. **Aug** Abbey Theatre granted a patent. **27 Dec** First productions at the Abbey.

1905   **Jan** WBY learns that MG's marriage is breaking up. Supports Hugh Lane's plans for a gallery of modern art in Dublin. **Sept** Reorganizes the Irish National Theatre Society into a limited company with WBY, Synge, and Lady Gregory as directors. **Late Nov** Abbey company on tour to Oxford and Cambridge.

1906   Theatre business; lecturing. **Aug** Quarrel with ECY over books for the Dun Emer Press. **Late Sept** *The Poems of Spenser*. Reading Jonson, Donne, and Jacobean dramatists. **Oct** *Poems 1899–1905*.

1907   **Late Jan** Riots over Synge's *Playboy of the Western World*. **16 Mar** Death of JO'L. **May** WBY accompanies Lady Gregory and her son Robert on a visit to Italy. **Dec** Difficulties with the Fays. *Discoveries* published. **21 Dec** JBY leaves for New York where he is to remain for the rest of his life.

1908   **13 Jan** Fays resign from the Abbey company. **Spring** Affair with Mabel Dickinson. **Late June** Visits MG in Paris. **Sept–Dec** *Collected Works* published in 8 vols. **Nov** Mrs Patrick Campbell in *Deirdre* in Dublin and London. **Dec** WBY goes to Paris to work on *The Player Queen*.

1909   **Feb** Lady Gregory's illness causes concern. **24 Mar** Synge dies. **Aug** Quarrel with John Quinn. Dispute with Dublin Castle over production of Shaw's *Blanco Posnet*. **Late autumn** Plans for buying out Miss Horniman's interest in the Abbey.

1910   **May** Stays with MG in Normandy. **10 May** Abbey remains open on day of Edward VII's death, causing violent row with Miss Horniman.

June Jack Yeats moves from Devon to Ireland. **9 Aug** WBY granted a Civil List pension of £150 per annum. **Sept** George Pollexfen dies. **Autumn** Talk of WBY taking up Edward Dowden's TCD professorship. **Dec** *The Green Helmet and Other Poems.*

1911 **Late Jan** C. P. Scott offers to arbitrate in the dispute between Miss Horniman and the Abbey directors. **Mar** WBY meets Winston Churchill. **Apr** Visits Paris, where Ezra Pound calls on him. **May** Scott finds in favour of the Abbey directors. **26 July** *Synge and the Ireland of His Time.* **13 Sept** Accompanies the Abbey Players to USA. **23 Oct** Returns to London. **Nov–Dec** Helps Nugent Monck with the Abbey School in Dublin.

1912 **Jan** Abbey Players arrested in Philadelphia. **May** Third Home Rule Bill introduced. **June** Meets Tagore. **Aug** Stays with MG in Normandy. **Sept** Solemn League and Covenant in Northern Ireland. **Oct** WBY staying with the Tuckers in Devon. **Nov** Severe nervous indigestion. **13 Nov** *The Cutting of an Agate.* **Dec** Lady Gregory in USA with Abbey Players.

1913 **Jan** Home Rule Bill thrown out by House of Lords. **Spring** Visiting Mabel Beardsley in hospital. Active in getting support for Lane's Dublin Art Gallery. **4 Apr** Dowden's death renews WBY's interest in Chair of English at TCD. **May** Lady Gregory and Abbey Players return from USA. Ulster and National Volunteers organized. **Summer** Experiments in automatic writing with Elizabeth Radcliffe. **Oct** *Poems Written in Discouragement.* Rents Stone Cottage in Sussex with Pound as his secretary from Nov.

1914 **31 Jan** Leaves for American tour. **Mar** Resumes broken friendship with John Quinn. **Apr** Returns to London. **May** Investigates miracle at Mirabeau with MG and Everard Feilding. **25 May** *Responsibilities.* **July** Home Rule Bill passed but suspended because of European situation. **4 Aug** First World War begins. **Autumn** Begins his memoirs.

1915 **Jan–Feb** At Stone Cottage with Ezra and Dorothy Pound. Reading Wordsworth. **May** Hugh Lane drowned on the *Lusitania.* **Summer** WBY helps to obtain a grant for Joyce from the Royal Literary Fund. **Dec** Refuses a knighthood.

1916 **Jan–Mar** At Stone Cottage with the Pounds. **20 Mar** *Reveries over Childhood and Youth.* **Late Mar** Macmillans become his publishers. **4 Apr** *At the Hawk's Well*, first of WBY's Noh plays, produced at Lady Islington's. **24 Apr** Easter Rising in Dublin. **July–Aug** Stays with MG in Normandy and on 1 July asks her to marry him. Reads the modern French poets with Iseult Gonne and discusses marriage with her. **Oct–Dec** Lady Gregory and WBY begin campaign to have the Lane pictures brought to Dublin.

1917 **Jan** Quarrel with D. S. MacColl over Lane biography. **Late Jan** Elected to the Savile Club. **Late Mar** Buys the Tower at Ballylee from the

Congested Districts Board. **7 Aug** Arrives in Normandy to stay with MG; proposes to Iseult but is refused. **Late Aug** Lectures in Paris. **c. 24 Sept** Proposes to George Hyde-Lees and is accepted. **Early Oct** Visits Coole. **20 Oct** Marries George Hyde-Lees at Harrow Road Registry Office. Honeymoon in Ashdown Forest, WBY ill. **27 Oct** George Yeats (GY) begins the automatic writing that is eventually to form the basis of *A Vision*. **8 Nov** Moves to Stone Cottage with GY. **17 Nov** *The Wild Swans at Coole*. **20 Dec** After a short stay in London, Yeatses move to Ashdown Cottage to escape Zeppelin raids.

1918 **Jan–early Mar** Move to Oxford. **18 Jan** *Per Amica Silentia Lunae*. **23 Jan** Robert Gregory killed in action. **Mar–early Apr** To Ireland, to stay at Glendalough and Glenmalure. **6 Apr** Visit to Coole. **May–Sept** At Ballinamantane House, near Coole, to supervise restoration of Thoor Ballylee. **Late Sept** Move into Ballylee. In Dublin, WBY rents 73 Stephen's Green. **Nov** GY seriously ill with pneumonia. **11 Nov** First World War ends. **Late Nov** Quarrel with MG. **14 Dec** General Election, in which Sinn Fein scores resounding success.

1919 **Jan** *Two Plays for Dancers*. **26 Feb** Anne Yeats born. **9 May** WBY returns to England. **25 May** Stage Society produces *The Player Queen*. **25 June** Gives up 18 Woburn Buildings. Summer at Ballylee. **July** Invitation to Jápan. **Oct** Move to 4 Broad Street, Oxford. Guerrilla warfare in Ireland.

1920 **13 Jan** With GY, sails for USA on the *Carmania*; lectures in America until 29 May. **Aug** Invited to Ireland by MG to help resolve Iseult's marital problems. GY has miscarriage. **Oct** Gogarty removes WBY's tonsils. **Autumn** Guerrilla War in Ireland intensifies.

1921 **Feb** *Michael Robartes and the Dancer*. **17 Feb** WBY denounces British policy in Ireland at the Oxford Union. **Apr–June** Oxford house let; move to Minchin's Cottage, Shillingford. **May** Lectures for the Abbey Fund. **28 June** Move to Cuttlebrook House, Thame. **11 July** Truce in Anglo-Irish war. **22 Aug** Michael Yeats born in Thame; has operation in Dublin in Sept. **7 Oct** Return to Oxford. **28 Oct** *Four Plays for Dancers*. **Late Oct** Michael Yeats operated on in London. **Nov** WBY lectures in Scotland. **Dec** *Four Years*. Anglo-Irish Treaty debated by the Dáil.

1922 **7 Jan** Dáil ratifies the Treaty, leading to civil war in Ireland. **Mid-Jan** WBY and GY attend Irish Race Conference in Paris. **3 Feb** JBY dies in New York. **20 Mar** Move from Oxford to 82 Merrion Square, Dublin. **Mar–Sept** At Ballylee; civil war raging. **4 July** Honorary degree at TCD. **19 Aug** Ballylee bridge blown up by Republicans. **20 Sept** Return to Dublin. **Oct** *The Trembling of the Veil*. **3 Dec** Dines with T. S. Eliot in London. **11 Dec** Becomes a Senator. **24 Dec** Bullets fired into the Yeatses' house.

1923 **Jan–Feb** In London campaigning for Dublin's right to the Lane pictures. **12 Apr** First production of O'Casey's *Shadow of a Gunman* at Abbey. **July** To London to arrange a nursing home for SMY who is seriously ill with consumption. **Nov** Awarded the Nobel Prize. **27 Nov** *Plays and Controversies*. **Dec** In Stockholm for Nobel Prize ceremony.

1924   **6 May** *Essays*. **June–July** Helps with the short-lived publication *Tomorrow*. **11 July** Honorary degree at Aberdeen. **29 July** John Quinn dies in New York. **Aug** WBY attends the celebrations connected with the Tailteann Games. **Autumn** Suffering from high blood pressure.

1925   **Jan–Feb** Visit to Sicily and Rome. **11 June** Speech on divorce in Senate causes controversy.

1926   **15 Jan** *A Vision*. **Feb** *The Plough and the Stars* causes controversy at the Abbey. **Early Apr** WBY has slight rupture and measles. **19 May** Appointed chairman of the committee on coinage design. **July** Reads Spengler's *Decline of the West*. **5 Nov** *Autobiographies*. **Nov** In London seeing leading politicians and public figures about Lane pictures.

1927   **Jan–Feb** Violent attack of arthritis followed by influenza. **10 July** Assassination of Kevin O'Higgins. **Nov** Yeatses at Algeciras, Seville, and Cannes; WBY seriously ill with congestion of the lungs.

1928   **Jan** At Cannes. **14 Feb** *The Tower*. **17 Feb** To Rapallo to look for an apartment. **Early Apr** Return to Dublin. **Early June** Controversy over rejection by the Abbey of O'Casey's *The Silver Tassie*. **31 July** Sells 82 Merrion Square and moves to a flat at 42 Fitzwilliam Square. **Sept** Resigns from the Senate. **Nov** To Rapallo flat for the winter.

1929   **Early Jan** Visit to Rome. **Mar** Meets Gerhart Hauptmann and George Antheil. **Early May** Return to Dublin by way of London, where he meets Wyndham Lewis. **Nov** Haemorrhage of lungs delays departure for Rapallo. **Dec** Dangerously ill in Rapallo with Malta fever; makes an emergency will witnessed by Pound and Basil Bunting.

1930   **Jan–Mar** Slow convalescence at Rapallo. Reads Swift. **3 July** Leaves Italy by sea to arrive in Dublin, via London, on 17 July. **23 July–6 Aug** Portrait painted at Renvyle by Augustus John. **Sept–Oct** At Coole. **Early Nov** Visits Oxford where on 5 Nov Masefield organizes a recitation of his poems. Visits May Morris at Kelmscott and meets Walter de la Mare and Virginia Woolf at Garsington. **Nov–Feb 1931** Winter in Dublin.

1931   **Feb–May** Stays at South Hill, Killiney. **May** Cuala Industries in financial difficulties and bailed out by WBY. **26 May** Honorary D.Litt. at Oxford. **1 June** Delivers bulk of MS for proposed 'Edition de Luxe' to Macmillans. **July–Aug** Works on Berkeley with Mario Rossi. Lady Gregory in decline and WBY spends most of the autumn and winter at Coole. **Sept** Broadcasts for BBC Belfast.

1932   **Winter and spring** at Coole. **Feb** Reads the autobiography of Shri Poruhit Swami in MS. **16 Feb** General election, after which De Valera and Fianna Fail form government. **Early Apr** In London, WBY discusses setting up of an Irish Academy of Letters with Shaw. Acts as unofficial go-between in Anglo-Irish controversy over the oath of allegiance. **10**

Apr Broadcasts for BBC London. 22 May Lady Gregory dies at Coole. July Moves to his last Irish home, Riversdale, Rathfarnham, Dublin. Sept Foundation of Irish Academy of Letters. 21 Oct Sails from Southampton on last tour of USA. 26 Oct–7 Nov Lectures in New York and north-east. Nov Midwest and Canada. 14 Nov *Words for Music Perhaps*. Dec Lectures in New York to raise funds for Irish Academy of Letters.

1933   22 Jan Sails from New York. Mar Meets De Valera. June In London, Oxford, and Cambridge. July–Aug Becomes involved in the Blueshirt movement; their march in Dublin on 12 Aug banned. 19 Sept *The Winding Stair and Other Poems*. Nov *Collected Poems*.

1934   Jan–Mar In Dublin. 5 Apr To London for Steinach operation. June With GY to Rapallo to dispose of their flat. Oct Speaks on 'The Dramatic Theatre' at 4th Congress of the Alessandro Volta Foundation in Rome. Begins friendship with Margot Collis. Late Oct In London for discussions about the Group Theatre. 13 Nov *Wheels and Butterflies*. 30 Nov *Collected Plays*. 7 Dec To London to arrange for committee meetings of Group Theatre; preparing poems for *A Full Moon in March*. Late Dec Begins friendship with Ethel Mannin.

1935   11 Jan Returns to Dublin. Mid-Jan–early Mar Renewed congestion of lungs causes collapse and confinement to bed. Late Mar In London on Group Theatre business, suffers a further attack of congestion. Late Apr GY goes to London to look after him. 3–4 June Stays with Dorothy Wellesley in Sussex for the first time. 13 June Celebrations in Dublin for his 70th birthday, including a PEN dinner on 27 June. 17 July AE dies in Bournemouth; WBY attends his funeral in Dublin on 20 July. 14–23 Aug Visits Dorothy Wellesley with Anne Yeats. Early Sept Clerical attacks on the Abbey. 16 Oct Operation to remove a lump on his tongue. 27 Oct In London for special 'birthday' production of *The Player Queen* at the Little Theatre. 22 Nov *A Full Moon in March*. 28 Nov WBY sails from Liverpool for Majorca, where he and Shri Purohit Swami are to collaborate on a translation of the Upanishads. 9 Dec *Dramatis Personae*. From 12 Dec In Majorca working on the Upanishads and *The Herne's Egg*.

1936   Late Jan Severe collapse with heart and kidney ailments; GY, summoned by the doctor, flies to Majorca on 2 Feb. Feb–Apr Slow recovery from illness. Mid-May Margot Collis arrives unexpectedly *c*. 14 May, suffering from a temporary fit of insanity. Yeatses go to Barcelona to help her. On return to Majorca WBY sees Shri Purohit Swami off for India. 25 May Leaves by steamer for London. June In London and Sussex. Late Sept–early Nov In London for BBC broadcast and to arrange distribution of *Broadsides*. 19 Nov *Oxford Book of Modern Verse* causes controversy.

1937   1 Feb Broadcast of WBY's poems from Abbey stage by Radio Eireann not a technical success. 16 Feb Elected a member of the Athenaeum. Early

Mar–24 Apr In London. **2 Apr** BBC broadcast 'In the Poet's Pub'. Begins friendship with Edith Shackleton Heald. **18 Apr** *The Ten Principal Upanishads*. **22 Apr** BBC broadcast 'In the Poet's Parlour'. **26 May** Announces his retirement from public life. **8 June–21 July** In London. **3 July** BBC broadcast 'My Own Poetry'. **17 Aug** Irish Academy of Letters dinner for Patrick MacCartan and WBY's Irish-American benefactors. **9 Sept–1 Nov** In London, at Steyning and Penns in the Rocks. **7 Oct** Revised edition of *A Vision*. **29 Oct** BBC broadcast 'My Own Poetry Again'. **Nov–Dec** Planning *On the Boiler* and helping to reorganize the Cuala Press. **14 Dec** *Essays 1931 to 1936*.

1938 **8 Jan** Leaves Dublin for South of France, where GY joins him in Menton on 4 Feb. **23 Mar** Arrives in London; remains in England, visiting Steyning and Penns in the Rocks, until 13 May. **18 May** *New Poems*. **June** In Dublin to arrange affairs at the Cuala Press and the Abbey. **Early July–8 Aug** In England. **10 Aug** First production of *Purgatory* at the Abbey causes theological controversy. **3 Oct** OS dies. **Late Oct** WBY leaves Dublin for England. **26 Nov** With GY, leaves London for South of France.

1939 **28 Jan** Dies. Buried at Roquebrune. **10 July** *Last Poems and Two Plays*. **Sept** *On the Boiler*.

A NOTE ON
EDITORIAL PRINCIPLES

OUR ambition in this volume, as in the edition as a whole, is to give as accurate and yet readable a text as possible. In the case of Yeats this modest aim presents more difficulties than one might wish. As he wrote to Katharine Tynan in March 1888 when seeking employment, 'Todhunter says my bad writing and worse spelling will be much against me . . .' (p. 56). These faults, together with lack of punctuation and a failure to date his letters, are also much against editors who wish to be at once true to what Yeats wrote and tactful to the reader. The poet himself was eager that his letters should be emended when they appeared in print. He instructed Katharine Tynan to show him any of his letters that she intended to publish in her memoirs so that he could correct them, and as late as 1938 asked his wife, when passing on a letter to his daughter, to 'put spelling right & make it legible'. But to correct and regularize as he would have wished would be to lose much of the immediacy and personality of his correspondence and especially of the letters in this volume, written amid the doubts and uncertainties of his setting out on a poetic career. We should also have missed many unintentional felicities, as for instance 'woeman' for 'woman' (this even before he had met Maud Gonne), or 'write on' for 'right on', where the aspiring but procrastinating young poet converts a temporal phrase into a literary imperative. Besides, we could even argue that in our editorial practices we are following his lead, for in a letter to Edwin Ellis of February 1893, discussing the publication of Blake's poems, Yeats writes: 'I incline myself, to the irregular text on the ground that the "tincture" to quote the Lavatar Notes "has entered into the errors & made them physiognomic"'' (p. 353).

We have, therefore, attempted to reproduce the physiognomy of his letters, orthographic warts and all, but endeavouring always to hold back from an officious pedantry that would involve the reader in unnecessary confusion. To have marked with '*sic*' every misspelling or solecism would have been wilfully tiresome, and so errors in spelling and punctuation are silently reproduced. Any editorial emendations appear within square brackets—as, for instance, where we have supplied letters or sometimes whole words omitted through carelessness, when such an omission would be otherwise confusing or unprofitably irksome. Where Yeats has used a word obviously in error for another we have given, again in square brackets, the most likely intended reading—for example (p. 447), 'always [*for* almost]'. The poet's hand can be extremely difficult, and uncertain readings are preceded by a query in square brackets. Where proper names have been so grievously mangled as to be unrecognizable or misleading, we have supplied the correct form in square brackets. Careless repetitions and false starts are silently excised, as are directions (such as 'P.T.O.' or 'Second Page') no longer applicable to the form of the letter as printed. Significant cancelled passages, where they can be deciphered, are printed within angle brackets (⟨ ⟩). Words underlined once in the original are printed in italics, twice in small capitals, three times in full capitals. Yeats's use of superior letters— 'M ʳ', 'D ʳ', 'R ᵈ'—has been adhered to throughout. Punctuation follows the original, except that full stops have been supplied where clearly intended, and where their omission would cause confusion. Open or close brackets, and open or close inverted commas have also been supplied where Yeats has forgotten them; and single and double inverted commas have been regularized where they are mismatched in the original.

The format of the letters has been slightly standardized, in that addresses and dates, where present, are always placed at the top right regardless of where they occur in the MS, with vertical rules to indicate the original line-divisions. Printed and blind-stamped addresses are given in small capitals. Yeats's abbreviated complimentary closes— e.g. 'Sincly', 'Yrs trly'—have not been expanded. Postscripts are placed uniformly at the end of the letter (thus following the temporal sequence of composition), with a note in square brackets indicating their position in the original. Letters to newspapers and periodicals follow the original published form exactly except for the signature, which has been regularized.

Each letter is headed by a line giving the addressee, if known, and the date. Since Yeats rarely dated his letters in full, many of these dates, the most accurate we have been able to fix upon, are conjectural and appear within square brackets, often with a preceding query or '*c.*'. A line following each letter identifies the copy-text and describes it (ALS, TS, etc.; see List of Manuscript Sources for the abbreviations used), recording where possible the postmark and the address to which the letter was sent; gives its location; and lists the first and/or most significant instances of previous publication.

Yeats is an allusive correspondent, and so the footnotes attempt not only to identify individuals and to provide information on particular points or references but also to supply wider contextual material. Certain important correspondents and other individuals and institutions which figure largely in this volume are given fuller treatment in the Appendix at p. 479. References to Yeats's works (see List of Abbreviations) are to the original editions or, where a collected edition is in question, to the best text available at the time of this volume's preparation; *Variorum Poems* and *Variorum Plays*, together with the 2-volume *Uncollected Prose*, are cited where possible.

J.S.K.

LIST OF MANUSCRIPT SOURCES

INSTITUTIONS

Albany	Library, State University of New York at Albany
Amherst	Robert Frost Library, Amherst College, Amherst, Mass.
APH	Archivae Provincia Hibernia, S.J., Dublin
Belfast	City of Belfast Public Libraries
Berg	The Henry W. and Albert A. Berg Collection, New York Public Library
BL	British Library
Bodleian	Department of Western MSS, Bodleian Library, Oxford
Boston College	University Libraries, Boston College, Chestnut Hill, Mass.
Brown	John Hay Library, Brown University Library, Providence, R.I.
Bucknell	Ellen Clarke Bertrand Library, Bucknell University, Lewisburg, Pa.
Buffalo	Lockwood Memorial Library, State University of New York at Buffalo
Cambridge	University Library, University of Cambridge
Delaware	University Library, University of Delaware, Newark
Doucet	Bibliothèque Littéraire Jacques Doucet, Paris
Emory	Robert W. Woodruff Library, Emory University, Atlanta, Ga.
Fitzwilliam	Fitzwilliam Museum, Cambridge
Harvard	Houghton Library, Harvard University, Cambridge, Mass.
Holy Cross	Dinand Library, College of the Holy Cross, Worcester, Mass.
Huntington	Henry E. Huntington Library, San Marino, Calif.
Illinois	University Library, University of Illinois at Urbana—Champaign
Indiana	Lilly Library, Indiana University, Bloomington
Kansas	Kenneth Spencer Research Library, University of Kansas Libraries, Lawrence
Leeds	Brotherton Library, University of Leeds
McGill	McGill University Library, Montreal, Que.
Manchester	University of Manchester Library
NLI	National Library of Ireland
NLS	National Library of Scotland
Northwestern	Northwestern University Library, Evanston, Ill.
NYU	Fales Library, New York University, New York City
Penn State	Pattee Library, Pennsylvania State University, University Park, Pa.
Philadelphia	Philadelphia Historical Society, Philadelphia, Pa.

Princeton	Princeton University Library, Princeton, N.J.
Reading	University of Reading Library
Southern Illinois	Morris Library, Southern Illinois University at Carbondale
TCD	Trinity College Library, University of Dublin
Texas	Humanities Research Center, University of Texas at Austin
Toronto	University of Toronto Library, Toronto, Ont.
Tulane	Tulane University Library, New Orleans, La.
UCLA	William Andrews Clark Memorial Library, University of California at Los Angeles
Wellesley	Wellesley College Library, Wellesley, Mass.
Westfield	John Lane Papers, Westfield College, University of London
Yale	Beinecke Rare Book and MS Library, Yale University Library, New Haven, Conn.

PRIVATE OWNERS

Anne Yeats	Miss Anne Yeats, Dublin
MBY	Michael B. Yeats, Dublin

Other MSS designated 'Private' are in the hands of the following individuals:
Irene Dwen Andrews Collection, Yucatan, Mexico
Mr. Francis Evers, Villajoyosa, Spain
Mr. James Gilvarry, New York City
Mr. B. Alan Haughton, Cork
Professor Richard M. Kain, Louisville, Ky.
Dr. M. Radford, London
Dr. D. F. Wall, Dublin
Mrs. Anne White, Dublin

The following abbreviations are used in the description given with the provenance at the foot of each letter:

AD	autograph draft
ALS	autograph letter signed
APS	autograph postcard signed
MS copy	handwritten copy in another hand
TS copy	typewritten copy.

LIST OF ABBREVIATIONS
AND SHORT FORMS

WBY = W. B. Yeats

ECY = Elizabeth Corbet Yeats (Lolly)

JBY = John Butler Yeats

SMY = Susan Mary Yeats (Lily)

KT = Katharine Tynan (later Mrs Hinkson)

HPB = Helena Petrovna Blavatsky

MG = Maud Gonne (later Madame MacBride)

JO'L = John O'Leary

OS = Olivia Shakespear

Principal Sources Cited or Quoted
PUBLISHED

BY W. B. YEATS

Aut	Autobiographies (1955)
AV(B)	A Vision (1937)
CP	Collected Poems (1933)
E & I	Essays and Introductions (1961)
Expl	Explorations, sel. Mrs W. B. Yeats (1962)
LNI	Letters to the New Island (1934)
McHugh	Letters to Katharine Tynan, ed. Roger McHugh (1953)
Mem	Memoirs, ed. Denis Donoghue (1972)
Myth	Mythologies (1959)
Oisin	The Wanderings of Oisin, and Other Poems (1889)
PW	Poetical Works, 2 vols. (1906–7)
UP	Uncollected Prose, ed. John P. Frayne, 2 vols. (1970–5)
VP	The Variorum Edition of the Poems of W. B. Yeats, ed. Peter Allt and Russell K. Alspach (1957)
VPI	The Variorum Edition of the Plays of W. B. Yeats, ed. Russell K. Alspach (1966)
Wade	The Letters of W. B. Yeats, ed. Allan Wade (1954)

EDITED BY W. B. YEATS

BIV	A Book of Irish Verse (1895)
Carleton	Stories from Carleton (1889)
FFT	Fairy and Folk Tales of the Irish Peasantry (1888)
IFT	Irish Fairy Tales (1892)
RIT	Representative Irish Tales (1891)

OTHER WORKS

Bibl	*A Bibliography of the Writings of W. B. Yeats*, ed. Allan Wade, rev. Russell K. Alspach, 3rd edn. (1968)
Daly	Dominic P. Daly, *The Young Douglas Hyde 1874–1893* (1974)
Denson	*Letters from AE*, ed. Alan Denson (1961)
Hone	J. M. Hone, *W. B. Yeats 1865–1939*, rev. edn. (1962)
JBYL	J. B. Yeats, *Letters to His Son W. B. Yeats and Others*, ed. Joseph Hone (1944)
LWBY	*Letters to W. B. Yeats*, ed. Richard J. Finneran, George Mills Harper, William M. Murphy, with Alan B. Himber, 2 vols. (1977)
Middle Years	Katharine Tynan, *The Middle Years* (1916)
Murphy	William M. Murphy, *Prodigal Father: The Life of John Butler Yeats 1839–1922* (1978)
PBYI	*Poems and Ballads of Young Ireland* (Dublin, 1888)
Ryan	William P. Ryan, *The Irish Literary Revival* (1894)
SQ	Maud Gonne MacBride, *A Servant of the Queen* (1938)
25 Years	Katharine Tynan, *Twenty-Five Years: Reminiscences* (1913)

PERIODICALS

DUR	*Dublin University Review*
PSJ	*Providence Sunday Journal*

All other published sources are cited in full at the first mention. The place of publication is London unless otherwise indicated.

UNPUBLISHED

APH	Archiviae Provincia Hibernia, S.J., Dublin
Armagh	Armagh County Museum
Belfast	City of Belfast Public Libraries
Hinkson	Pamela Hinkson papers, Dublin
KPA	Kegan Paul account books, Reading University
LC	Library of Congress
MBY	Michael B. Yeats, Dublin
NLI	National Library of Ireland
Norwood	Norwood Historical Society, Norwood, Mass.
NYPL	New York Public Library
Princeton	Princeton University Library, Princeton, N.J.
Quaritch	Archive of Bernard Quaritch Ltd., London
Rylands	John Rylands Library, Manchester
Southern Illinois	Morris Library, Southern Illinois University at Carbondale
TCD	Trinity College Library, University of Dublin
Texas	Humanities Research Center, University of Texas at Austin
UCD	Archive, University College, Dublin

Other MS material in private hands is designated 'Private' when cited or quoted in the notes.

GENERAL INTRODUCTION

I

At a crucial moment in Yeats's early novel the eponymous hero, John Sherman, passes the time by piecing together a letter that has been torn up and strewn beneath the park bench upon which he is sitting. 'We do not mind spying on one of the crowd,' Yeats observes, 'any more than on the personages of literature.' The letters which are published in this and subsequent volumes are also scattered although, as the provenance lines will show, they are dispersed far further than the compass of a park bench. As first envisaged, *The Collected Letters of W. B. Yeats* was to have been in four volumes, because it was hoped that there might be as many as two thousand letters still extant. As the search progressed, however, nearly seven thousand letters came to light, distributed through five continents, and, since the plan is to print every page of correspondence that can be found, the project has stretched to at least twelve volumes. The justification for publishing at such length must be that Yeats is a great poet and the more we can know of him and his work the more we shall be able to appreciate his achievement in its entirety. The same might, of course, be said of all great writers, but in Yeats's case the correspondence is especially illuminating in that his work stands in a complex but inextricable relationship to the biography which provided its occasions. Life offered him unpurged images—those images that yet fresh images beget—which triggered a peculiarly Yeatsian process of poetic transformation, and his letters help us to identify the source and inspiration of much of his work. Thus, while the pleasures of Yeats's correspondence are many—its variety and vitality not least among them—the main value of the present volume, as of the project as a whole, lies perhaps in three directions: the letters offer an insight into a private self that was often hidden in public; they illuminate his literary development and the particular nature of his artistic genius and methods; and they chart the ways in which the larger intellectual, political and social forces of his age helped to mould his consciousness and his creativity.

II

When John Sherman finally manages to reconstruct the fragments of his letter he discovers that it was not written by a stranger at all but (for even great poets are sometimes reduced to such narrative stratagems) by his fiancée and that he himself is discussed in it at some length. The shock of recognition in reading Yeats's letters cannot be quite so intimate and yet, although he might now be described as one of the 'personages of literature' himself, his correspondence gives a sense of immediacy which reaches behind the pompous public role that this term implies to a vivid and living personality. In a letter to Katharine Tynan of August 1888 (p. 92) he says that he writes to her 'as if talking to myself' and this is a feeling that we get from many of his letters, especially those to his trusted women correspondents. During the severe emotional crisis that took place just before his marriage, for instance, he writes fully and frankly to Lady Gregory 'that I may keep nothing back', going on to tell her that 'the chief happiness & favour of my life has been the nobility of three or four women friends'. With Katharine Tynan, Olivia Shakespear, Lady Gregory herself, Mabel Dickinson, Mrs Yeats, Ethel Mannin, Dorothy Wellesley, and Edith Shackleton Heald, he could discuss personal and public matters with a revealing candour. We find in such letters a more vulnerable and human Yeats than the public was allowed to see.

The present volume reveals the poet as he begins to emerge from obscurity, from 'the distress/Of boyhood changing into man;/The unfinished man and his pain'; it ends with his moving from the family home to independent quarters. It was not until the spring of 1887 that Yeats became a serious letter writer, an occupation brought about by his exile from Ireland and his consequent home-sickness, loneliness, and uncertainty. Hitherto he had enjoyed a wide circle of friends in Dublin—the O'Learys, Douglas Hyde, Katharine Tynan, the Coffeys—all of whom liked and admired him. They met frequently together, at the O'Learys 'At Homes', at Katharine Tynan's farmhouse 'salon' in Clondalkin, in Hyde's College rooms, and at the Contemporary Club. Until he went to London Yeats would hardly have needed to write more than brief notes to these people, for he could talk to them whenever he wished, and, indeed, in a letter of March 1887 just before he left Dublin, he disclosed that he wrote 'not more than one or two letters in six months'. Now all this was to change. Not only did he begin a vigorous correspondence with his Dublin friends but grew impatient with them when they were dilatory in their replies. Although an inhabitant of what was then the largest, richest, and most powerful city in the world, he describes himself as 'Robinson Crusoe in this dreadful London' and begs for Irish news. If he desired news, he was also ready to impart it, and his letters give a detailed account of the impact upon him of London literary life. They also chart his own more gradual growth into maturity and self-confidence. In 1887 and 1888 he is still full of painful self-doubts. He is 'going about on shoreless seas. Nothing anywhere has clear outline'; it has been his misfortune 'never to have faith in success or the future', and when he contemplates his boxes of unpublished manuscripts he feels that he has 'built a useless city in my sleep'. Such moods of despair oscillate with adolescent bravura: 'I am no idle poetaster. My life has been in my poems. To make them I have broken my life in a morter as it were. I have brayed in it youth and fellowship peace and wordly hopes. . . . I have buried my youth and raised over it a cairn—of clouds.' In 1888 Alastor was alive and well and living in Bedford Park. And yet his troubles were real enough: the family's chronic lack of money, his mother's severe and persistent breakdown, his own ill-health and fatigue. Taxed by Katharine Tynan with being too bookish and inhuman, he replied that 'other things at present for many reasons make me anxious and I bury my head in books as the ostridge does in the sand. . . . On the rare occasions when I go to see any one I am not quite easy in my mind for I keep thinking I ought to be at home trying to solve my problems—I feel as if I had run away from school.'

By dint of hard work and application as well as of talent, things gradually began to improve. His editions of Irish folklore, fiction, and poetry made him better known to the London reviews and he cultivated American contacts. The preparation and negotiations for the publication of his first book of verse also taught him much, not only about his own identity as a poet but also about the practical workings of the book trade. The reception of *The Wanderings of Oisin*, especially in Ireland, disappointed but did not discourage him. 'I shall sell,' he told Katharine Tynan, 'but not yet. Many things my own & other folks have to grow first.' Moderate but palpable successes with *John Sherman*, *The Countess Kathleen*, and *The Celtic Twilight* helped his confidence, while repeated exposure to literary journalism had, by 1895, given him a sober but calculated estimation of his chosen audience and his own abilities: 'My new book is in the press,' he writes. 'I wonder how they will receive it in Ireland. Patronize it I expect & give it faint praise & yet I feel it is good, that . . . the coming generations in Ireland cannot but value what I have done.'

His experiences in public life had been just as painful and educational. He quickly saw that the crisis in Ireland after the fall of Parnell was no less one of national identity than of politics, and he set about founding literary societies in London and Dublin to take advantage of the new mood. His practical dealings with public meetings and committees taught him the value of argument, organization, and procedural niceties. Fundamental in this process was his quarrel with Duffy and Rolleston over the New Irish Library, a defeat from which he learned lessons that he was never to forget: indeed, his skill in managing the Abbey Theatre, the constitutional coup through which he transformed it into a limited company in 1905, and his adroit manipulation of the Irish Academy of Letters, may be traced to this frustrating but instructive event.

Emotionally, too, this was time of growth. The adolescent infatuation

with Laura Armstrong behind him, he fell as hopelessly but far more deeply
in love with Maud Gonne. After more than five years of unrequited passion
he met Olivia Shakespear, a beautiful and sympathetic married woman, and
after a series of clandestine trysts with her decided to leave his father's
house, a move that would give him greater personal freedom. On 4 October
1895 Lolly Yeats wrote to her sister in Sligo, 'WB has taken a room says he
can live on 10/– a week, let him try.' He not only tried but succeeded. The
previous nine years, since his arrival in London, had been full of
uncertainties, hardships and self-doubts. By a combination of genius and
dedication he was now consolidating his reputation as one of the leading
young poets in English. He could command sufficient if not large fees for his
articles. His sympathetic sister Lily, on her return from Ireland, reported in
her diary on 13 October 1895: 'Willy came full of his new start—very good
thing, I think.' And so it was.

III

After reading the unpublished correspondence of the minor poet John
Keegan, Yeats commented that he was 'always especially pleased to come
across anything that throws light on the personal side of Irish history or
literature in the way these Keegan letters do'. His own letters provide such a
personal insight and yet, in that he was so much the greater poet and a far
more complex man than the ill-fated Keegan, they also have a com-
mensurately deeper interest for us. Yeats was perpetually working at his art
and testing his literary ideas against experience. He was animated by a few
firmly held convictions and inspired by a few deeply influential 'sacred'
books. Many of these convictions and influences came to him early and the
process of his artistic life is the amplification, refining and redefinition of
certain seminal ideas. One could begin a satisfactory essay on Yeatsian
aesthetics by taking as a text the fourth letter in this volume, that to F. J.
Gregg, in which he attacks George Eliot and the nineteenth-century Realist
movement with which she was associated. The ideas he proclaimed here—
that art should be epic, extravagant, and imaginative—were expanded and
modified during his long and laborious work on Blake; we shall find them
undergoing a further revision in those letters in which he discusses his
reading of Nietzsche and yet again in the correspondence which preceded
the publication of *A Vision*.

As well as providing a running commentary upon the growth of his
literary ideas, Yeats's letters also gloss his practice and intentions as a poet.
This happens as early as 1884 when, in a precocious note to Mary Cronin (p.
7), he explains that his aim is directness and extreme simplicity, and it
continues through to those letters he wrote while correcting his last poems

and plays on his deathbed. In this volume many such comments are to be found in his correspondence with Katharine Tynan as he prepares his poems for publication in *The Wanderings of Oisin* and *The Countess Kathleen*, while the criticism he offers to Lily White (pp. 130–1) and Ernest Rhys (p. 284) on their poems shows his increasing mastery of the craft of verse. In later volumes he will discuss poetic technique with AE, Ezra Pound, Olivia Shakespear and Dorothy Wellesley, among others, as well as proffering advice and suggestions to a host of younger poets and playwrights.

Although the letters do not and cannot 'explain' the poetry in any simple or reductive way, they provide us with a fuller understanding of the context in which it originated and grew. And given the kind of imagination that Yeats possessed this endows them with a peculiar importance. As a late Romantic he was preoccupied with questions of identity and the nature of the self; as a Modernist he was concerned to escape the merely subjective. Much of his best poetry has its occasion in the exploration of these tensions. In this sense, his letters have a value beyond those of many other poets and writers, for they provide us in a direct way with the raw material out of which his art was composed. Yeats believed what was certainly true in his own case, that a 'poet writes always of his personal life', yet to express this personal life satisfactorily he must create out of 'the bundle of accident and incoherence that sits down to breakfast' a secondary 'artistic' personality. In providing the context for his art, in revealing the complex relationships between the man and his masks, the letters offer many insights into the workings of his imagination. They do this in a more authentic way even than his autobiographical writings, which are far more carefully structured and orchestrated. Shaped by hindsight, these lack the day-to-day immediacy of his correspondence.

IV

Revealing as the letters are in illuminating Yeats's biography and charting his literary development, they have yet a further interest. T. S. Eliot said that Yeats was 'one of those few whose history is the history of their own time, who are a part of the consciousness of an age which cannot be understood without them'. His letters mediate the area between the poetry and the period; they register his reaction both to passing historical events and to the deeper movements of thought that gradually shape and reshape the consciousness of an epoch. The first letter to have been traced was written in 1876, the last in January 1939, a few hours before his death. The intervening sixty-three years had altered the map of men's minds no less than of the world. In this volume Irish agitation for Home Rule, the fall of

Parnell, and the subsequent divisions in the Irish Party are urgent issues, while a broader sense of historical process is introduced by Maud Gonne's improbable reflections on the death of the heir to the Austro-Hungarian Empire and Yeats's interest in the possible Armageddon of a war between Britain and the USA. Armageddon was to come but not yet: later volumes will trace his reaction to the Great War, to the Irish 'Troubles' and Civil War, to the rise of Communism and Fascism, to the struggle in Spain, and to the events that he saw clearly were leading towards a Second World War.

These political and military upheavals were accompanied by far-reaching social changes. By the time this volume begins, Ireland was already embarked upon those policies and agitations that were to transfer the traditional power of Yeats's class to an emerging Catholic bourgeoisie. The last remnant of the Yeats estate was sold in 1888 through a scheme which was already breaking up many larger properties by enabling the tenant farmers to become freeholders. In these early years Yeats tried to identify himself with the popular and nationalist forces, but this proved to be more difficult than he had hoped. He lost the battle with Duffy's supporters in the National Literary Society, found his rural libraries scheme thwarted by young men he had supposed his friends and came under clerical disapproval in his attempts to define an Irish literary tradition. By the summer of 1894 he is even thinking of writing a book 'to be feirce mockery of most Irish men & things'. Ireland, mad or otherwise, would continue to hurt him into poetry and later volumes of his letters register his pain and defiance as the Abbey Theatre, the Lane Gallery and the Irish Academy of Letters all come under attack.

In literature and the arts, as much as in politics and society, this was a period of change. As a young man Yeats was, as he tells us elsewhere, a Pre-Raphaelite, and in the course of the present volume he encounters Wilde's aestheticism, Morris's craft socialism and Symons's reading of the French symbolists. His long collaboration with Edwin Ellis on the study of William Blake is a theme in many letters and was to have a lasting effect in shaping his own aesthetic. Inspired by Standish O'Grady's mythological histories and John O'Leary's library, as well as by the contemporary growth of interest in folklore and comparative mythology, he helped to create the movement that quickly became known as the Celtic Twilight, although even by 1895 he understood the dangers for his art of disembodied spirituality on the one hand and patriotic propaganda on the other. In later years his friendship with Synge, H. J. C. Grierson and Pound helped him to reshape his style, and he lived to see the rise of Cubism, Imagism, Futurism, and the politicized arts of the thirties. An ageing triton amid the streams of these new developments, he watched and commented in his letters upon their flow with a vigour that was certainly not diminished by his frequent disapprobation. As is indicated by his correspondence with Shaw, Joyce, Pound, T. S. Eliot, Synge, and O'Casey, as well as others, he numbered among his friends and acquaintances the men and women who were moving forces in the literary life of his time.

For Yeats there could be no divorce between his creativity and what he described as his 'philosophy'—an increasingly elaborate system, constructed both to defy the empiricist and materialist views he abhorred and to help him grasp at truth. In London in the late 1880s he frequented the Blavatsky Lodge of the Theosophical Society, although Madame Blavatsky herself always remained an enigma to him. From this he turned to the Golden Dawn, a more esoteric and structured society for the study of ritual magic. In both cases, as in his later psychical experiments, he was driven by the need, in a post-Darwinian world, to find a system of belief that would endorse the value and potency of mind and imagination over materialism. Eccentric and unfashionable though many of his ideas seemed, he pursued them with an energy and conviction that grew out of a deep personal concern, rounding upon the disparaging O'Leary (p. 303) to tell him that the 'mystical life is the centre of all that I do & all that I think & all that I write. It holds to my work the same relation that the philosophy of Godwin held to the work of Shelley & I have all-ways considered my self a voice of what I beleive to be a greater renaisance—the revolt of the soul against the intellect—now begining in the world.' His belief in the possibility of the new renaissance waned after the beginning of the century but his defence of his idealist position never lost its intensity. In 1902 he found an ally in Nietzsche; later on, in a friendly but combative exchange of letters with T. Sturge Moore, he attacked the prevailing trends in British philosophy, especially as stated by 'baldy pate' Bertrand Russell, marshalling upon his side Plotinus, Kant, Croce and Bishop Berkeley. His correspondence with Joseph Hone and Mario Rossi helped him to clarify further his thoughts on Berkeley, while, as a considerable correspondence shows, he could turn to F. P. Sturm for advice on more arcane philosophic points and to Shri Purohit Swami for enlightenment about Eastern thought.

V

If the main interest of Yeats's correspondence lies in the revelation of his personality, the relationship of his biography to the work, and the work to its age, we must also add that much of the pleasure of reading his letters derives from the sheer range and vitality of his interests. One of his predominating images was of the isolated artist in a lonely tower, but the correspondence presents him as gregarious, chatty, amusing, inquisitive, and even scandalous, alert to the world in its changing fashions as in its more profound movements. In the present volume, for all his praise of solitude and despite his frequent illnesses and breakdowns, he is already firing off letters to the press and, indeed, initiating and orchestrating newspaper controversies. Notwithstanding his diffidence and uncertainties, within a few weeks of his arrival in London he was in touch with many of the younger writers and soon a welcome guest of William Morris, Oscar Wilde, and W. E. Henley. An indefatigable organizer, a moving spirit behind the Rhymers Club and the various Irish literary societies, he also acted as unofficial agent for all the Irish writers he could discover. Over the years he appears in many roles: as theatre director, discussing scenery and staging with Gordon Craig and the Fays; as psychic researcher who creates consternation by raising ghosts in the Assyrian Department of the British Museum; as a gossip with a sure ear for anecdote—as in his wry report of Sparling's views on his fiancée, May Morris (p. 26): 'She is very beautiful. Morris you know says so'; as a rather more passionate fiancé himself: 'O my dearest I kiss your hands full of gratitude and affection . . . Am I not Sinbad thrown upon the rocks & weary of the sea?'; as a director of the Irish National Gallery, laying down the law as to which pictures may or may not be purchased; as a man about town, dining with Prime Ministers and Captains of Industry, unexpectedly meeting the Queen, and spending an evening with Winston Churchill; as unsuccessful suitor: 'I asked Maud to marry me a few days ago. She said that it would be bad for her work & mine, & that she was too old for me'; as an ardent lover, who, ecstatic at the start of some new affair, writes 'Wonderful things have happened. This is Bagdad. This is not London'; as the absent-minded traveller: 'My dear Dobbs [i.e. Mrs Yeats] I have four vests and no drawers except those on me'; as a Senator threatened with assassination but full of beans: 'I am having a tremendous day—10–11.30 verse, 11.30 to 1.30 upsetting Col. Moores apple cart at a committee to start a new party, 2 to 3 letters & 3 to about six senate. I am in high spirits . . .'

The very appearance of the letters endorses this sense of immediacy and personality. Nearly always untidy, mostly undated, misspelt and badly punctuated, they offer a striking contrast to the care with which he revised and re-revised his poems, stories and plays. For such a fastidious craftsman they show a rare spontaneity. On one occasion the enticing sound of dinner preparations brings a letter to an untimely close (pp. 188–9); at another (pp. 77–8) he races against the dying flame of a single remaining candle and is obliged to address the envelope by the light of a match; later we shall find letters interrupted by Zeppelin raids. It is to retain this spontaneity that the letters are reproduced with their misspellings uncorrected and their format unregularized. Refreshing though this immediacy can be, it can pose editorial problems. Twenty-two letters from 18, Woburn Buildings, dated simply 'Tuesday' offer their own challenge; no less perplexing are letters securely dated 'March' that clearly belong to May. And there must always be a question as to which month the letter dated 'Feb 31' (p. 446) properly belongs.

Yeats is constantly apologizing for his handwriting and has every reason to do so. More than one of his original recipients, in generously sending his letters for transcription, have begged for a spare typed copy that they may at last read what has hitherto been illegible. If Yeats's bad handwriting has one virtue it is that it disguises his even worse spelling. Indeed, in this respect legibility can sometimes let him down, and nowhere more notably than in a letter of 1911 sounding out the authorities at Trinity College, Dublin, about the possibility of his succeeding to Edward Dowden's professorship. Unhappily, the eager aspirant to a Chair of English contrives to spell the sought-after office 'proffesrship'.

VI

Nearly half of the letters in this first volume are printed for the first time, and the proportion of new material increases in every subsequent volume. Most of the previously published letters have appeared in Allan Wade's *The Letters of W. B. Yeats* (1954) and/or in Roger MacHugh's *W. B. Yeats: Letters to Katharine Tynan* (Dublin, 1953), two admirably edited collections, both now, alas, long out of print. The provenance line gives details of the first and, where appropriate, subsequent major publications of any letter that has been printed before, although, for reasons given above, the present edition departs from previous practice by reproducing Yeats's original spelling and punctuation.

Among the larger groupings of new letters in this volume are those to the publisher T. Fisher Unwin and to Douglas Hyde; later volumes will include a substantial number of hitherto unpublished letters to Mabel Beardsley, A. H. Bullen, Gordon Craig, Edmund Dulac, T. S. Eliot, St. John Ervine, William Fay, Gwyneth Foden, Lady Gregory, F. R. Higgins, T. W. Horton, James Joyce, the Macmillan Company, Harriet Monroe, Ottoline Morrell, Ezra Pound, John Quinn, Lennox Robinson, J. M. Synge, Clement Shorter, Shri Purohit Swami, Rabindranath Tagore, and Mrs Yeats. In locating this material, as well as many smaller collections, the edition is indebted to librarians in many countries, some of whom have gone to trouble well above and beyond the call of duty. Tracing letters in private hands is more difficult but most, although regrettably not all, of the individual collectors approached have been generous both with their time and material and the acknowledgement of their help repays but a fraction of the debt owed to them.

Some letters which would have appeared in the present volume seem to be irrecoverably lost. Maud Gonne's heirs have kindly allowed access to what remains of Yeats's correspondence with her but the great bulk of this was mislaid or destroyed in military raids on her house during the Irish Civil War. Unfortunately, T. W. Rolleston, a born organizer and one of the pivots of the Irish literary revival, destroyed his papers shortly before his death. Little has apparently survived of Magregor Mathers' possessions, and correspondence to other members of the Golden Dawn, apart from Florence Farr, has also proved elusive. Miss A. E. F. Horniman's niece arrived just too late to stop her aunt's literary executrix making a bonfire of her papers, and so perished letters from Shaw, Synge, and Lady Gregory, as well as from Yeats. The letters to Lionel Johnson loaned by his sister to a graduate student in the late 1940s and never returned are still missing despite strenuous efforts to trace them. Although few in number, they might have revealed something of Yeats's early development in the craft of verse. There were undoubtedly more letters to Ellen O'Leary, judging by her replies, but it is probable that these would have repeated much of the information that we find in the contemporary letters to Katharine Tynan. A letter to Edward Dowden about *The Wanderings of Oisin* and sold by Mr Norman Colbeck in the 1920s remains, alas, untraced.

Nearly all the letters published in this edition have been checked against the original manuscript. In the cases where this has not been possible the provenance line indicates that printed, typed, or manuscript copies have been used instead. Since a correspondence is a two-sided matter, it is often useful to be able to consult the replies to given letters. In this volume these are provided, where appropriate, in footnotes both for ease of reference and for economy of space. In later volumes, where the length and complexity of the letters involved make this an unwieldy procedure, both sides of an exchange will occasionally be printed, as will letters written on Yeats's behalf by amanuenses or agents.

Given Yeats's conscious monitoring of his own development and the way in which events, people, and places helped to extend and modify that development, it was clear that this edition should be arranged chronologically rather than according to recipient or theme. Chronologically the letters interweave to give the close texture of a full and creative life. Such a texture makes itself felt in the wealth of allusions and names with which the letters abound as he attempts to 'hammer' into unity apparently disparate but earnestly pursued interests. For this reason, it was also obvious that the edition must be amply annotated. For a writer who saw Unity of Being as a central goal it seems appropriate that passing references should not only be satisfactorily explained but also located in the wider context of his life and work.

THE LETTERS
1865–1895

My dear Lilly

        I have two
water lizards in
a jar a glass one
[image] They eat the
worms I gave
them first but they
spit them out
now– I had some
frogs too but I

An extract from W. B. Yeats's first letter, written to his sister Lily in the autumn of
1876. (*See pp. 3-4*)

1865–1887

To Susan Mary Yeats,[1] *[autumn 1876]*

[Farnham Royal][2]

My dear Lilly

I have two water lizards in a jar a glass one. [*drawing of newt in jar*] They eat the worms I gave them first but they spit them out now. I had some frogs too but I let them out because I did not know how to feed them   I put a little peace of wood on top for an island they go on it   I begun a letter in Uncle Alfreds alphabet[3] but I lost it   Mr Jemicen has begun a new picture of the common[4]   I am getting stilts   Mr Earls son[5] [*drawing of boy on stilts*] can go very well on them he was walking over a pool on them and they stuck in and he fell in   have you any frost yet we have a little. The kind of lizards I have got are called salamander lizards   have you any frogs we have lots of them   I will send Jacks other letters as soon as I can get them from

---

[1] Susan Mary ('Lily') Yeats (1866–1949) was the older of WBY's two surviving sisters, and particularly close to the poet. This, the earliest of WBY's letters to have come to light, dates from the autumn of 1876 when 'my father and I and a group of landscape-painters lodged at Burnham Beeches with an old Mr and Mrs Earle' (*Aut*, 28); the rest of the family were at Sligo with WBY's maternal grandparents. The letter is reproduced opposite.

[2] A small village in the south-east corner of Buckinghamshire, $3\frac{1}{2}$ miles north of Eton and Slough and close to the picturesque scenery of Burnham Beeches. John Butler Yeats (1839–1922; see Appendix) had given up a career as a lawyer to become a painter. Now, having decided temporarily to abandon portrait painting in order to refine his technique in landscape, he was lodging with WBY at Beech Villa, a guest house for visiting artists. The house was demolished some years ago to make way for the Woodgate Garage, which stands on the main road through the village.

[3] Alfred Edward Pollexfen (1854–1916), the 'stout and humorous' uncle (*Aut*, 10) who was a particular favourite of his nieces and nephews, was a lifelong bachelor. He worked for many years as a clerk in the offices of the family's Sligo Steam Navigation Company in Liverpool before returning to Sligo in 1910 to help run the family business. WBY's elegy, 'In Memory of Alfred Pollexfen' (*VP*, 360–1), written shortly after his uncle's death, was published in the *Little Review*, June 1917.

[4] Possibly James Arthur Henry Jameson (1856–1930), a land- and seascape painter born in Dublin, who held a number of exhibitions in Ireland between 1883 and 1923. He lived for much of his life in Kingstown (now Dun Laoghaire), near Dublin.

[5] Probably Alfred Frederick Earl (b. 1864), youngest son of Joseph Earl (1811–81).

home where I forgot them[6] Send me another copy of the alphabet Uncle
Alfred made as I lost the first one. I went to see the a meet of a deer hunt
which was near here They had the deer in a big van the people who were
looking on ran after the deer and shouted at it to make it jump It was a doe
although it was a poring wet day there were about fifty or sixty horsemen
there all in red cats there were some ladies[*drawing of a kitten*] I can walk on
stilts now can you get little folks at Sligo[7] Papa is going to town to day but
he will be back to morrow he has a little kitten to paint and it is running
about the roon purring one minute and crying another she has sumthing
wrong [*drawing of tail*] with her tail. My lizards walked off one night, Mrs
Earl came in one morning to cettle the books on the top of the cupboard on
which were the lizards but when she found them gone she was afraid to
touch the books lest she should put hand on them, we looked every where for
them but have not found them yet[8] Papa is reading out the Redgauntlet by
Sir W Scot when he has read them I lend them to Mr Earls second youngest
son[9] I have got your letter to day we have frightful weather so that papa
and Mr Jameson cant go out they get models to sit for them I an your
affectionate bother

W B Yeats

P S I recognized knocnoray[10]
[*drawing of sailing boat and lighthouse*]

ALS (black-bordered paper)[11] MBY.

[6] John Butler (Jack B.) Yeats the younger (1871–1957), WBY's surviving brother and the youngest of
the family, was to become a celebrated artist.

[7] *Little Folks*, a children's picture paper, ran from 1871 to 1933.

[8] WBY recalls this incident in *Aut* (28). Elizabeth Adlam Earl, née Davis (1821–88), the second wife
of Joseph Earl whom she married in 1849, was originally from Frome in Somerset.

[9] While at the Earls', JBY was educating his son personally and had bought him primers on physical
geography and chemistry. He described the routine in a letter to Susan Yeats (autumn 1876; MBY):
breakfast at eight; WBY worked until 1.30 or 2 p.m. and then took the afternoon off. In the evening JBY
would read to him until nine o'clock when WBY went to bed. The Earls' second youngest son, Joseph
George (1861–1946) became, like his father, a carpenter and builder.

[10] In a letter to WBY, now lost, SMY had presumably drawn a picture of Knocknarea, the limestone
mountain of 1,078 feet which lies a few miles to the south-west of Sligo; WBY mentions it in a number of
poems including 'The Hosting of the Sidhe' (*VP*, 140–1) and 'Red Hanrahan's Song about Ireland' (*VP*,
206–8). A picture of the mountain would be instantly recognizable because of the cairn of Queen Maeve
on the summit line.

[11] WBY's infant sister, Jane Grace (b. 1875), had died on 6 June 1876; a few weeks later his paternal
grandmother, Jane Grace Corbet Yeats (1811–76), had died of cancer in Dublin.

To Elizabeth Corbet Yeats,[1] *[autumn 1876]*

[Farnham Royal]

[drawing of a sailing boat]
MY DEAR LOLLY I AM MAKING THE PRICES OF MY CLUB[2]
LESS.   WE AR GOING TO HAVE RABE SOON *[drawing of house and
greenhouse]*   BOATS LIKE LILLIES WE WILL GIV A NIE BOAT AS
PRISE[3]   I WILL GEET A BOY TO RABE HER *[drawing of sailing
ship]*   THE   BOAT   IS   LIKE   THIS   I   AM   MAKNG   A
COLLECTON OF LEAVES   RIT TO ME IN THIS ALPABIT
SOME TIMES   *[drawing of bed]* WHEN I WENT TO SE THE
TREASURER HIS BROTHE AND SISTER WHO WARE PLAYING
WITH HIM HERD SOME WONE CALL THEM THAY WENT
UNDER THE BEED   MRS EARL GAVE A LIV BIRD TO HER CAT
TO DAY.   MRS EARLS CLOCK STRUCK 12 TO DAY[4]   ABOUT
THE CLUB ABOUT 15s   NOW GOOD BYE

W B YEATS

[drawing of three ships, one passing lighthouse]

ALS (black-bordered paper) MBY.

To Mary Cronin,[1] *[c. 1882]*

[Kilrock Road, Howth][2]

My Dear M ⟨Meary⟩ Cronan
    I send you the verses you asked for   I have very few poem under a great
many hundred lines but of those that I have this is the shortest and most

---

[1] Elizabeth Corbet ('Lolly') Yeats (1868–1940), WBY's second sister, was the third of JBY's surviving
children. The letter, reproduced on p. 6, is written in 'Uncle Alfred's alphabet' (see preceding letter),
and here transcribed as it stands; clearly WBY had only imperfectly mastered the code set out at its head.
[2] In *Aut* (28–9) WBY recalls his friendship with the local children at Farnham Royal.
[3] As a child WBY had a passion for boats; SMY recalls in her unpublished memoir 'Odds and Ends'
(MBY) that JBY bought him a splendid toy yacht when he was a child. In *Aut* (28–9) WBY describes
how he would wander 'round some pond imagining ships going in and out among the reeds and thinking
of Sligo or of strange seafaring adventures in the fine ship I should launch when I grew up'.
[4] Since this is an unremarkable diurnal event, one assumes that WBY meant to write a higher and
more astonishing figure, but was prevented from doing so by his inadequate command of Uncle Alfred's
alphabet.

[1] Possibly Mary Cronin (1832–1919), born in Cork, wife of a solicitor, Robert Barry Cronin, at this
time practising in Dublin. Shortly after this letter was written, the Cronins moved to Mitchelstown, Co.
Cork, where Robert Cronin died in 1885.
[2] For six months, from late 1881 until early 1882, the Yeats family lived in Kilrock Road, Howth, Co.
Dublin, in Balscaddan Cottage, 'a long thatched house' (*Aut*, 55).

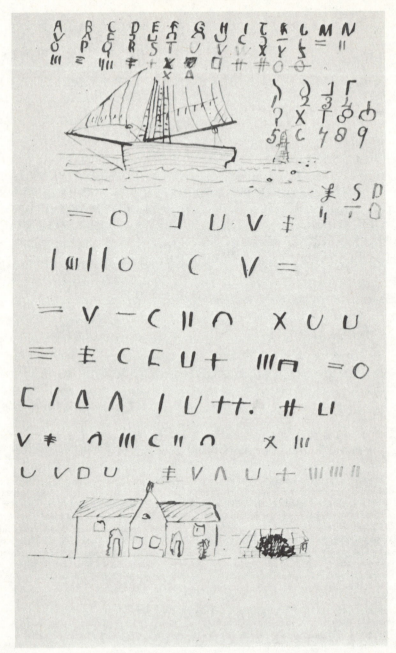

Letter to Lolly Yeats in Uncle Alfred's code (*See p. 5*)

most intelligible. its subject was sugested by ⟨my last visit to the Monday evening⟩ my last two visits to Kilrock.³ I am afraid you will not much care for it—not being used to my peculearitys which will never be done justice to and until they have become classics and are set for examinations.

Yours truly

W B Yeats

PS as you will see my great aim is directness and extreme simplicity.

> A flower has blossomed, the world heart core
> The petels and leves were a mo[o]n white flame
> A gathred the flower, the ⟨soul⟩ colourless lore
> The aboundant meadow of fate and fame
> Many men gathers and few may use
> T[he] sacret oil and the sacret cruse⁴

ADS (in pencil, on a leaf torn from an exercise book) MBY. Wade, 30.

*To F. J. Gregg,*¹ [*late summer 1886*]

Rosiss Point² | Sligo

My dear Gregg
I have only read four books of George Elliot's—Silas Marner—Romala—Spanish Gypsy—and a volume of selections³ I dont mean to read a fifth.
reasons why

³ Kilrock House, one of the principal residences in Howth, was occupied by Joseph and Sidney W. S. Wright, who were the Yeatses' landlords. Sidney Wright, a solicitor, had offices at 17 Westmorland Street, Dublin, close to Robert Cronin's at 45 Fleet Street, and it seems the two lawyers had struck up a friendship.

⁴ This poem, written on the verso of the draft letter and difficult to decipher, may not have been the one sent.

¹ Frederick James Gregg (1864–1927), a contemporary of WBY's at the Erasmus Smith High School in Dublin, was living at this time at 6 Eccles Street, Dublin, and preparing for the law examination at the Royal University. He published poems in the *Irish Monthly* and two were to be included in *Poems and Ballads of Young Ireland* (Dublin, 1888). Growing disillusioned with the political climate in Ireland, Gregg emigrated to the USA in 1891 and worked as a journalist on the *New York Evening Sun*. He became a close friend of John Quinn, WBY's American patron, who nicknamed him 'El Greggo', and also saw a good deal of WBY's father after the latter settled in New York in 1908; in February 1922 Gregg helped to arrange JBY's funeral.

² Rosses Point of Upper and Lower Rosses, on the east side of Sligo Bay: 'a little sea-dividing, sandy plain covered with short grass, like a green table-cloth, and lying in the foam midway between the round cairn-headed Knocknarea and Ben Bulben' (*Myth*, 88). WBY was staying with his uncle, George Pollexfen (1839–1910), who usually spent the summer in this seaside village in the parish of Drumcliffe, 5 miles from Sligo town.

³ Probably *Wise, Witty, and Tender Sayings in Prose and Verse Selected from the Works of George Eliot*, ed. Alexander Main (Edinburgh and London, 1872), in its 4th edn. by 1880 and the fullest and most readily available of such selections to appear before 1890.

firstly—

Tito, her most famous character, Is as interesting as a cat on the vivisection table. In him there is none of that beauty that Hugo gave to everything he touched not only to Esmeralda but to the hunchback. In literature nothing that is not beautiful has any right to exist. Tito is created out of anger not love.[4]

Secondly—

She understands only the conscious nature of man. His intellect, his morals,—she knows nothing of the dim unconscious nature the world of instinct which (if there is any truth in Darwen) is the accumulated wisdom of all living things from the monera to man while the other is at the very most the wisdom gathred during four score years and ten.[5]

Thirdly her beloved analysis is a scrofula of literature. All the greatest books of the world are synthetic, homeric—

Fourthly She has morals but no religion—

If she had more religion she would have less morals. The moral impulse and the religious destroy each other in most cases.

fifthly

I never met a George Elliotite who had either imagination or spirit enough for a good lie.

sixthly In the "spanish gypsy" there are seven arguments of about fifty pages each. This is the way she describes passion.

Seventhly. she is too reasonable. I hate reasonable people the activity of their brains sucks up all the blood out of their hearts.

I was once afraid of turning out reasonable myself. The only buisness of the head in the world is to bow a ceaseless obeisance to the heart.

Yours sincerely
W B Yeats

[*At top of first page*]
PS I am coming home next week

ALS Buffalo. Wade, 31.

---

[4] Tito Melema is the treacherous villain of *Romola* (1863), whom George Eliot, WBY complained in a 1901 essay, 'plucks . . . in pieces with as much assurance as if he had been clockwork' (*E & I*, 102); Esmeralda and the hunchback Quasimodo are characters in Victor Hugo's *Nôtre-Dame de Paris* (1831). Of his resistance to George Eliot at this period, WBY recalled (*Aut*, 87) that when Edward Dowden (1843–1913; see Appendix), Professor of English Literature at Trinity College, Dublin, urged him to read her he 'became angry and disillusioned . . . I had read all Victor Hugo's romances and a couple of Balzac's and was in no mind to like her.'

[5] A word introduced by Ernst Haeckel and used by the evolutionists to signify 'those forms of life standing at the lowest grade of organization' (*OED*). WBY had read Haeckel and the evolutionists while at Howth (*Aut*, 60). An undated document (MBY) signed by Gregg and Charles Johnston (1867–1931), another contemporary of WBY's at the Erasmus Smith High School, shows an evolutionary line extending from 'Monara' through various forms of organic life culminating in 'W.B.Y.'. WBY has crossed out his initials and redirected the line to the signatures of Gregg and Johnston. Perhaps it was the influence of Mme Blavatsky's optimistic evolutionism that led him to add a score to the Psalmist's span.

To an unidentified correspondent, 11 March [*1887*]

10 Ashfield Terrace | Harolds Cross[1]
March 11th

Dear Sir

Excuse me not having answered your letter before. At first I was of opinion that you were decidedly right on second thoughts I was not sure—Third thoughts that I was decidedly right—I meant by the two lines

"From the hills of Earth have pealed
Murmurs of her children talking"

that loud continuous confluence of murmurs that I have heard going up from a wooded mountain at dawn—[2]

As to the lion and whether a roar may be musical or not I think all uncivilized beast sounds have a certain cadence in them—[3] Prose and discord are in the main modern brain products not of the primeval world which had only a heart and no brain.

However I will keep your letter by me and consider these things when I reprint the two poems—

Have we not a common friend in T. Lister.[4] He tells me—if I am not mistaken in your identity—that you are an admirer of Walt Whitman—To me also Whitman is the greatest teacher of these decades.[5] So we have also a

---

[1] Early in 1884 financial difficulties had obliged JBY to move from Howth to Terenure, a suburb 2½ miles south of central Dublin. WBY describes 10 Ashfield Terrace (now 418 Harold's Cross Road) in *Aut* (83): 'We lived in a villa where the red bricks were made pretentious and vulgar with streaks of slate colour, and there seemed to be enemies everywhere.' In a letter to Lady Gregory of 1 Mar 1922 (MBY), he recalled with horror 'that Rathgar villa where we all lived when I went to school, a time of crowding & indignity . . .'.

[2] The lines are from 'A Dawn-Song' (*VP*, 705–6), which had appeared in the *Irish Fireside* on 5 Feb 1887. WBY never republished the poem. His correspondent had evidently drawn his attention to the incompatibility of 'pealed', 'murmurs', and 'talking'.

[3] A reference to line 9 of the poem, 'On Mr Nettleship's Picture at the Royal Hibernian Academy' (*VP*, 688–9), first published in *DUR*, April 1886, which describes the lion's roar as 'Low, long and musical . . .'. When WBY reprinted the poem, unrevised, in *The Wanderings of Oisin and Other Poems* (1889), a reviewer in the *Evening Mail*, 13 Feb 1889, also remarked on the inappropriateness of a musical roar.

[4] Thomas William Lyster (1855–1922), head librarian at the National Library of Ireland 1895–1920—he appears as the 'Quaker librarian' in Joyce's *Ulysses*—was the first to encourage WBY to write. He helped him in 1884 to revise the MS of *The Island of Statues*, taught him to correct proof sheets, and guided his reading in Elizabethan literature (cf. *UP* II. 470–2). WBY described him as 'the most zealous man I know' (*UP* II. 305) and later chaired the Lyster Memorial Committee.

[5] The popularity in Britain and Ireland of the poetry of Walt Whitman (1819–92) at a time when he was largely neglected in the United States is a curiosity of Anglo-American literary history. The scholarly criticism of Edward Dowden had been influential in establishing *Leaves of Grass* and had helped to make Dublin a centre of interest in Whitman; a number of WBY's Irish friends were admirers of the American poet.

common enthusiasm. If I can lay hands on a copy I will send you my poem
"Mosada" either in "University Review" or the reprint If you have not seen
it.[6]

Yours very sincerely

W B Yeats

PS—Please excuse this somewhat rudderless scrawl. I write not more than
one or two letters in six months and so to compose a more elaborate affair
would be a sort of alpine journey—

ALS Buffalo. Wade, 32–3.

To Katharine Tynan,[1] 27 [April 1887]

6 Berkley Road[2] | Regents Park Road
Wednesday 27th

My dear Miss Tynan

I hear Bale was much pleased with your article.[3] I suppose you have heard
from him.

I saw Todhunter he is busy writing a book of irish poems on something
the same plan as De Veres "Innisfail".[4] I feel more and more that we shall

---

[6] *Mosada*, a poetic drama (*VP*, 689–704), first appeared in *DUR*, June 1886. An offprint edition of 100
copies was published by Sealy, Bryers & Walker, Dublin, in the same year, and had been reviewed by
Katharine Tynan in the *Irish Monthly*, March 1887 (166–8).

[1] Katharine Tynan (1859–1931; see Appendix), poet and novelist, to whom WBY was introduced by
C. H. Oldham in June 1885. In a letter of 30 June 1885 to Mrs Pritchard (*Apex One* [1973], 23), KT said
she 'found him very interesting, he has the saddest, most poetical, face I ever saw; he looks a poet. . . .'
WBY often visited her at her father's house, Whitehall, in Clondalkin, Co. Dublin, and after his move to
London wrote to her frequently until her marriage in 1893 to H. A. Hinkson, after which the
correspondence became intermittent.

[2] A temporary address, at which WBY was lodging by courtesy of William Giles, a friend of JBY's
who had lived there from 1886.

[3] Edwin Bale (1838–1923) was art director for the publishers Cassell & Co. 1882–1907, and provided
JBY and later Jack Yeats with work during the late 1880s and early 1890s. A member of the Royal
Institute of Painters in Water Colours, he was the first chairman of the Imperial Arts League 1909–12
and editor of the League's *Journal* 1910–19.

In the week ending 7 Apr 1887, on a commission from Bale which came through WBY, KT had
written the first of three articles for Cassell's *Magazine of Art* under the title 'Irish Types and Traits'.
The articles, for which she was paid a guinea a page, were to accompany illustrations by H. Helmick; the
first two were published in November 1887 and February 1888; the third did not appear until April 1892.

[4] John Todhunter (1839–1916; see Appendix), a friend and later neighbour of the Yeatses who had
abandoned medicine for literature. In so far as his book *The Banshee and Other Poems* (1888) takes its
theme from Irish history, it resembles *Inisfail* (1861), which was intended as 'A Lyrical Chronicle of
Ireland'. But whereas most of Todhunter's poems deal with the mythological period, the prolific Irish
poet Aubrey de Vere (1814–1902) offers in *Inisfail* a consecutive account of Irish history from the
Norman invasion of 1170. WBY was perhaps thinking here of what he called the 'retrospective poems' in
Inisfail, those which looked back to the bardic period and which he thought 'full . . . of the spirit of these
stormy centuries' (*UP* I. 163).

have a school of Irish poetry—founded on Irish myth and History—a neo-remantic movement. I shall commence to morrow or next day my review of your book[5] for the "Gael". Have you seen the cover yet or will you see it before publication. I have written a couple of Ballads which will probably appear in the "Gael" did you care for my Fin article or has it appeared for I have not heard.[6] London is just as dull and dirty as my memory of it. I do not like it one whit better. You will see by the headding of this letter that I am in lodgings by my self our house being still in disorder. I like being by myself greatly. Solitude having no tongue in her head is never a bore. She never demands of us sympathies we have not. She never makes the near war on the distant.

Downey the publisher and author of "the House of Tears"[7] has seen and much admired one of your poems.

My sisters are still in Liverpool and Jack is still stopping with my uncle Varley[8] and my father is painting at Oxford[9] so you see we are a devided

---

[5] *Shamrocks*, KT's forthcoming collection of verse, which WBY was reading in page proof.

[6] No complete file now exists of *The Gael*, an eight-page penny weekly established in the spring of 1887 by the Executive of the Gaelic Athletic Association to be the quasi-official organ of the Association, under the editorship of P. T. Hoctor. Although devoted primarily to the promotion and reporting of Gaelic sports, the paper also, through the offices of its literary editor, John O'Leary, gave a great deal of space to literature, and published poems, stories, and articles by WBY, KT, Douglas Hyde, John Todhunter, T. W. Rolleston, and Ellen O'Leary.

A note 'To Our Readers' in the *Gael* for 16 Apr 1887 regretted that pressure of athletic news had crowded out WBY's 'Fin MaCumhaill', but hoped that it would be published the following week. The article, which was a retelling of the legends associated with Finn and the Fenians taken largely from the *Transactions* of the Ossianic Society, did appear in the *Gael* on 23 April (4–5), but WBY did not see it until at least a month later, for on 23 May 1887 JBY wrote (NLI) to John O'Leary, 'Willie . . . has not received the paper with the Fin MaCool article.' (The issue may have been sent to his temporary address in Berkley Road.) The article is of interest since it mentions Ossian (Oisin), whose adventures WBY was already drafting into his first extended poetical treatment of Irish myth:

And Ossian? He passed away to the island of Hy-Brazil, till longing after three hundred years to see Fin once more, he returned; but the moment his feet touched an earthly shore, his three hundred years fell on him, and his beard swept the ground, and his form bent double, and his eyes became blind. Patrick and his saints kept him with them, and tried hard to make him think of heaven, but the burthen of his cry was ever, 'better Hell with the Fini, than Heaven without them.'

'I wish', WBY went on, 'I could recommend you some poem concerning these events, but there is none of any importance.'

[7] Edmund Downey (1856–1937), son of a Waterford shipbroker, moved to London in 1878 and became a partner in the publishing firm of Ward & Downey; in 1894 he set up his own firm, Downey & Co. In 1906 he returned to Ireland to become editor and proprietor of the *Waterford News*. He published numerous books, some under the pseudonym 'F. M. Allen'; *The House of Tears*, a novel, was published anonymously in 1886.

[8] SMY and ECY would have broken their journey from Ireland to London with a visit to their sailor uncle, John Pollexfen (1845–1900), and his wife Mary Jane, who lived at Blundellsands, just outside Liverpool. John Varley (1850–1933), a painter of landscape and oriental subjects who exhibited frequently at the Royal Academy 1876–95, was a grandson of John Varley sen., the noted water-colourist and associate of Blake; he had married WBY's aunt, Isabella Pollexfen (1849–1938), and they were now living at Cheltenham in Gloucestershire.

[9] In a letter of 23 May 1887 (NLI) JBY told John O'Leary that he had been in Oxford painting the

family at present, and Rose is sullen and home sick[10]—this latter we are all a little I think. My father has a large water colour in the Academy that grey thing he did in Dublin of the Girl with the basket.[11]

Remembrances to everybody

Your friend ever
W B Yeats

ALS Huntington, with envelope addressed to Clondalkin; postmark illegible. McHugh, 25–6; Wade, 33–4.

To Katharine Tynan, 8 May [1887]

58 Erdley Crescent[1] | South Kensington
May 8

My dear Miss Tynan

I received the Firesides this morning your article on O'Shaughnessy[2] is admirable well written in every way.

Indeed you are right I ought to have crossed the line with you at Black-

portraits of two children. The commission was probably arranged through his friend, Frederick York Powell.

[10] Roseanna Hodgins (*c.* 1848–1930) joined the Yeats household as a servant in 1884 and remained with Lily and Lolly until her death, as 'our kind friend and confident servant all those years' (SMY, scrapbook, MBY). In *Middle Years* (31–2), KT describes her as

for years the presiding domestic genius, the homely guardian angel of a family too highly endowed with the gifts of the spirit to be very efficient in mundane affairs. . . . 'Rose is never afraid of us,' said Mr Yeats once, 'but we are very often afraid of her.' We used to say that his extravagantly good opinion of servants as a class was because he saw them through Rose-coloured spectacles.

Rose continued to be homesick for Dublin which, as JBY reported to John O'Leary 10 Jan 1888 (NLI), she regarded 'as a sort of lost Eden'.

[11] JBY's a painting *Going to Their Work* was exhibited at the Royal Academy in 1887. It had been shown at the Royal Hibernian Academy of Arts in 1885, and a reproduction appeared in the Illustrated Art Supplement to *DUR*, March 1885.

[1] JBY had now moved his family from Dublin to London for the second time, to 58 Eardley Crescent, in South Kensington. Situated behind the recently built Earls Court Exhibition Hall—where, at the time the Yeatses moved in, Buffalo Bill and his Indians were performing with much noisy gunfire—the house had more permanent drawbacks: JBY later described it (in a letter of 20 Mar 1888 to John O'Leary, NLI) as 'old and dirty and dark and noisy' and SMY thought it a 'horrible' house with 'a bit of cat-haunted sooty gravel' for a garden (scrapbook, MBY).

[2] 'Arthur O'Shaughnessy', *Irish Fireside*, 7 May 1887. O'Shaughnessy (1844–81), best known for his ode, 'We Are the Music Makers' (frequently quoted by WBY), published four volumes of poetry, most notably *An Epic of Women* (1870) with illustrations by John Nettleship. He worked in the Natural History Department of the British Museum.

rock.[3] I do not know why I did not. I was blaming myself for it afterwards. I am very sorry. I wrote two letters one to you and one to Miss O Leary[4] and then threw them aside meaning to rewrite them I think—but some one found the Miss O Leary note and posted it or else I did myself in shere absence of mind unless an eastern Mahatma carried it through the air travelling "on the pure cold wind, and on the waters wan".[5] I have written to Miss O Leary to find out whether he put a stamp on.

I am no more at Berkley Road by myself but here at Erdley Crescent. A few more paragraphs will finish the article on your book which may be ought [*for* out] any day now[6] I suppose—Rolleston acting on my suggestion prompted in my turn by Lister has sent a review of your book to the Academy but since I hear he does not like the religious poems and thinks "Dermot and Gania" not like Fergusson which is true and that therefore it not as good as it might be which is not true for all immitation is barren, I am sorry I made any suggestion in the matter. However he thinks "Aibhric" very good indeed, and altogeather the best thing you have ever done.[7]

I was in the house of commons last Friday night. Healey made a rugged passionate speach the most human thing I heard, I missed Dillon however.[8]

---

[3] WBY and KT had probably been to visit Richard Ashe King (1839–1932), for 38 years literary editor of the London weekly magazine *Truth*, who lived at 11 Waltham Terrace, Blackrock, Dublin. Ashe King, a retired Anglican curate, published several novels under his own name and under the pseudonym 'Basil'. He was president of the Irish Literary Society 1925–32. (For an account of him, his house, and the extended literary lunches he gave there, see *25 Years*, 282–3.) To reach Blackrock, KT would have travelled by train from Clondalkin; on this occasion WBY apparently neglected to see her to her seat on the return journey.

[4] Ellen O'Leary (1831–89), sister of John O'Leary whose nationalist politics she shared. She contributed poems to the *Nation* and other magazines in Ireland and America; her *Lays of Country, Home and Friends* (Dublin, 1891), ed. T. W. Rolleston, was published posthumously. In an undated letter to KT (Belfast) she described WBY as 'my special and first favourite among our young men'.

[5] An echo of KT's 'The Pursuit of Diarmuid and Grainne', the first poem in *Shamrocks*: ' 'Tis Angus the Magician—no son of mortal man; / He travels on the pure cold wind, and on the waters wan.' WBY is making a joke at the expense of the Theosophists A. P. Sinnett and A. O. Hulme, who in October 1880 found that through 'precipitation' they could exchange letters instantaneously between Madras and the Mahatmas Koot Hoomi and Morya in Tibet. Sinnett reported on the phenomenon in *Occult World* (1881), and the letters were published in full as *The Mahatma Letters*, ed. A. T. Barker (1923). AE had made a similar joke about his communication with WBY (see Denson, 5–6).

[6] *Shamrocks* was published 31 May 1887.

[7] Thomas William Hazen Rolleston (1857–1920; see Appendix), a disciple of John O'Leary and at this time regarded as a potential successor to Thomas Davis, leader of the Young Irelanders. He founded and edited *DUR* (published 1885–7), where WBY's early work appeared, had translated Epictetus into English and Walt Whitman into German, and was writing a life of Lessing. The review of *Shamrocks* prompted by Lyster and WBY (*Academy*, 9 July 1887, 19), while finding KT's 'Diarmuid and Grainne' 'somewhat disappointing', did not compare it with the work of Sir Samuel Ferguson (1810–86), whose poem, 'The Death of Dermid', had appeared in his *Lays of the Western Gael* in 1864. Rolleston did, however, praise 'The Story of Aibhric', KT's poem based on incidents in the early Irish tale, *The Fate of the Children of Lir*.

[8] On Friday, 6 May 1887, Timothy Michael Healy (1855–1931), nationalist MP for North Longford, spoke on the fourth and final night of a Commons debate as to whether an article in *The Times* of 2 May

Altogather I was delighted with Healey the others on both sides were sophisticated and cultivated in him there was a good earth power. I would be very glad to meet Mr Rankin.[9] I hear that Burne Johnes is a furious Home Ruler says he would be a Dynamiter if an Irishman.[10]

Your friend ever
W B Yeats

ALS Huntington. McHugh, 26–7; Wade, 34–5.

To J. G. Legge,[1] *[18 May 1887]*

58 Erdley Crescent | South Kensington

For J G Legge Esq
Miss Tynan wrote to me to leave these for you. A few pages at the end unhappily are missing[2]—Will send them if I find them. Sorry I missed you.

W B Yeats

ALS Bodleian. *TLS*, 6 Jan 1956.

(part of the notorious 'Parnellism and Crime' series) constituted a 'wilful falsehood . . . against John Dillon, Member for East Mayo', and was therefore a breach of privilege. The motion was initiated by the Conservatives in an attempt to embarrass the Irish Home Rule Party and Dillon (1851–1927), a leading figure in the 'Plan of Campaign' on behalf of Irish tenant farmers, by giving a wider airing to the supposed connections between Parnellism and agrarian outrage in Ireland. In his speech, Healy called for an inquiry by a Select Committee into the whole business, accused *The Times* of sensationalism to raise its flagging circulation, and ended with the declaration that while individual members of the Irish Party might come and go, the Irish cause would endure for ever. *Hansard* reports that Dillon, who had remained unobtrusive throughout the four nights of debate, entered the chamber some time after Healy had finished speaking. In spite of Healy's eloquence, the Conservatives gained a tactical victory when the House resolved that *The Times* article did not constitute a breach of privilege. Both Healy and Dillon opposed Parnell after the divorce scandal of 1890, and became rivals for the leadership of the anti-Parnellites.

[9] The critic and poet Boyd Montgomerie Ranking (1841–88) was at this time busy on KT's behalf; as she wrote to Fr. Matthew Russell on 12 May 1887 (APH): 'Mr Ranking is I think writing my *Morning Post, Graphic* and *Pictorial World* reviews from the proof sheets. . . .'

[10] Sir Edward Coley Burne-Jones (1833–98), a leader of the Pre-Raphaelite movement, was one of WBY's favourite painters. In *Memorials of Edward Burne-Jones* (1904) Lady Burne-Jones cites many examples of her husband's sympathy for Irish nationalism (see esp. II. 104); on a visit to the painter in 1892 Douglas Hyde found that he 'had almost every Irish book that was in print' (Daly, 151).

During the 1880s a dynamiting campaign in England had been organized by an Irish-American group of Fenians and attempts had been made to blow up London Bridge (1884) and the Houses of Parliament (1885) among other targets.

[1] James Granville Legge (1861–1940), eldest son of the Revd James Legge, Professor of Chinese at Oxford, entered the Civil Service after Queen's College, Oxford. At this time he was attached to the Admiralty, but in 1888 moved to the Home Office, where he rose to a senior position. KT records going to tea with him at his rooms in the Temple in the summer of 1889 (*25 Years*, 293). Legge published a number of books of criticism. WBY occasionally stayed with him in Liverpool (see WBY to unidentified correspondent, 1 Dec 1922, Princeton) after he became Director of Education there, and later a Liverpool councillor; he retired to Oxford in 1925.

[2] The pencil note is attached to a set of heavily corrected page proofs of KT's *Shamrocks* which WBY was using as an advance copy for his *Gael* review. Legge also needed the proofs for a review which KT had 'asked him to get into an Oxford mag.' (KT to Fr. Russell, 12 May 1887, APH). Pages 177–92 are missing from the proofs.

To Katharine Tynan, 18 May 1887

58 Eardley Crescent | South Kensington
May 18 /87

My dear Miss Tynan

I hoped to have heard from you but suppose you are busy. You do not know what a satisfaction a letter is. Any breath from Ireland blows pleasurably in this hateful London where you cannot go five paces without seeing some wretched object broken either by wealth or poverty.[1]

I have finished and sent off my review for the "Gael" and sent off likewise the proofs to Mr Legge.[2] I mean took them to him and finding him out thrust them through his letter box and heard them spreading out on the floor like a pack of cards.

I am horribly irritable and out of sorts.[3] Living over at Berkley Road by myself I tried experiments in cheep dinning—for a man if he does not mean to bow the knee to Bael must know all such things—making my dinner off vegitables and so forth—After some time I was gaunt and nervous and able to do little work and since then have had a variable asortment of coughs colds and headaches. All this I write not to weary you with any of my personal greviences against the Universe but because I fear it has wraught ill for the review. You would be astonished at the number of petulant pages against this man or that other I have chopped out of it. Though now as it stands it is a calm though not very brilliant exposition of your book.

I have met some literary men over here with the usual number of "bon mots" and absence of convictions that characterize their tribe. One however has no "bon mots" and several convictions—a welsh man Ernest Rhys editor of the "Camelot Classics".[4] I rather like him. I recommended your poems to him strongly. He knew your name but not your work. He tells me a

---

[1] cf. the lines (cited by McHugh) from 'Street Dancers' (*VP*, 731–3), a poem included in *Oisin*:

> London streets have heritage,
> Blinder sorrows, harder wage—
> Sordid sorrows of the mart,
> Sorrows sapping brain and heart.

[2] See preceding letter.

[3] JBY reported to John O'Leary on 23 May 1887 (NLI) that 'Willie has been I think very home sick & has many uneasy thoughts—he has not at all settled down—& looks not at all strong. . . .'.

[4] Ernest Percival Rhys (1859–1946; see Appendix), although of Welsh extraction, was born in London and took up a literary career after a period as a mining engineer. He wrote fiction and poetry but is best known as the editor of Everyman's Library. The Camelot Classics, also under his editorship, was a 64-volume series of classical and modern writings published from 1886 by Walter Scott, continued after 1891 as the Scott Library.

friend of his is editing for the "Canterbury" poets a book of Irish songs.[5] Knowing that the Irish Monthly had published at various times articles on Irish poets some little known of, I ventured to suggest that he should write to Father Russel[6] as I knew not in what numbers these articles or Miss Kavanaghs little poems[7] appeared. I wish I could get a copy of Sir Charles Gavan Duffies article on Miss O Learys songs[8]—I will get one some where and let him see it. Your poems Ernest Rhys will make sure are known to his friend.

I have sent two ballads to the 'Gael'. One I expect O Leary will like one not. You I think will like the one O'Leary will not and care less for the other and I will agree with you.[9]

I have been in several studios amongst others Smaltz'ses—a good hearted vain empty man. What a very small soul goes to a great peice of prosperity?

Todhunter has gone down to Oxford to see the performance of the Alcestis.[11] When he comes back he is to read me a long Irish legendary poem he has done—Those were fine "Shan Van Vocht" verses of his in "North and South". We may have them for the ballad book if we wish.[12] I suppose naught has changed with you except outer nature. The wild briar roses must be holding their festival through all your lanes. There! I have sent you a short letter and a longer one now in your turn post me a good many pages.

Yours forever
W B Yeats

ALS Huntington. McHugh, 27–9; Wade, 35–7.

[5] The anthology *Irish Minstrelsy*, edited by H. H. Sparling, appeared in the autumn of 1887 in the Canterbury Poets series, in which 104 volumes were published by Walter Scott, 1884–1922.

[6] A long-running series on Irish poets began in 1877 in the *Irish Monthly*, edited by Fr. Matthew Russell, SJ, with an article on Aubrey de Vere. From the 13th article onwards (June 1885), the pieces were published under the heading 'Our Poets', i.e. those poets possessing 'one or both of two qualifications—they are Irish or Catholic.'

[7] Rose Kavanagh (1859–91), a close friend of the O'Learys and KT, published numerous poems and stories in the *Irish Monthly* and other Irish and American periodicals. She edited the *Shamrock* and the *Irish Fireside*, and to the latter contributed a regular feature, 'Uncle Remus to his Nieces and Nephews', which was continued in the *Weekly Freeman* after the demise of the *Fireside* in 1889.

[8] 'A Celtic Singer' by Sir Charles Gavan Duffy (1816–1903; see Appendix), published anonymously in *DUR*, December 1886, was reprinted in Ellen O'Leary's posthumous *Lays of Country, Home and Friends*. The volume was dedicated to Gavan Duffy, one of the leaders of the Young Ireland movement in the 1840s, who had now returned to Europe after years of emigration in Australia.

[9] For the two ballads, see below p. 19.

[10] Herbert Gustav Schmalz (1856–1935), a London painter of portraits, oriental and biblical subjects, who exhibited regularly at the Royal Academy. He changed his German name during the Great War and was thereafter known as Herbert Carmichael.

[11] Euripides' *Alcestis*, performed in Greek by the Oxford University Dramatic Society 21–8 May 1887, was reviewed by Todhunter in the *Century Guild Hobby Horse* (July 1887); he had published his own English version of the play in 1879.

[12] Todhunter's long poem, 'The Doom of the Children of Lir', appeared in his forthcoming volume, *The Banshee*. His 'The Shan Van Vocht of '87' first appeared in the Dublin weekly *North & South*,

To Katharine Tynan, 31 May [1887]

58 Eardley Crescent | South Kensington
31 May

My dear Miss Tynan

"Shamrocks" arrived all right this morning the binding is very pretty.[1] Miss O Leary tells me you were pleased with my review. I must now do one for the Fireside.[2]

I want you to send me If you can some of the reviews in the irish papers— *Freeman*—*United Ireland* etc. I feel almost as anxious about it as if it were my own book. And tell me of any English notices and I will get the papers.[3]

I saw your friend Mr Legge breakfasted with him—he seems eager about literature and spent much time painting a french verse on his mantle piece— Ernest Rheis of the Camelot classics I have seen also a not brilliant but very earnest welsh man.

I am about to write some articles on Irish litterature for the "Leisure Hour".[4] I have no news. One day here is much like another day. I read every morning from 11 to 1.30 at the art Library South Kensington Museum[5] where I am now writing—a very pleasent place the air blowing through the open windows from the chesnut trees—the most tolerable spot London has yet revealed to me—I then dine and through the afternoon write or try to write as fate, and langour the distroyer, will have it and in the evening read out to my father who is afraid to task his eyes. Michels Jail Journal[6] has sufficed us for many days now.

---

23 Apr 1887. The 'Shan Van Vocht' (i.e. the 'Poor Old Woman', a traditional symbol for Ireland) poem was reprinted in *The Banshee*, but was not included in the collaborative anthology, *Poems and Ballads of Young Ireland*, being planned by WBY and his friends as 'another link, however small', in 'the long chain of Irish song that united decade to decade' (*LNI*, 121–2).

[1] A copy of KT's *Shamrocks* inscribed 'To dear Willie Yeats, with the belief in him and affectionate friendship of the writer May 30th 1887', is now in the Pearse Street Library, Dublin. The volume is bound in olive green paper over boards, with a dark green spine stamped in gold. The overall effect is of an elegant simplicity.

[2] On 29 May 1887 Ellen O'Leary wrote to WBY (Belfast) that KT (who had seen an advance proof of his review of *Shamrocks* for the *Gael*) 'was delighted with your article which she says is splendid'. For WBY's *Fireside* review see p. 26.

[3] *Shamrocks* was to be reviewed by nearly 40 journals and newspapers, in North America and Australia as well as in Britain and Ireland. Most of the notices appeared in July and August, including those in the *Freeman's Journal*, 29 July 1887, and *United Ireland*, 13 Aug 1887.

[4] Although much mentioned in subsequent letters, WBY's article, 'Popular Ballad Poetry of Ireland' (*UP* I, 146–62), did not appear in *Leisure Hour* until November 1889.

[5] Since 1899 the Victoria and Albert Museum.

[6] John Mitchel's *Jail Journal: or, Five Years in British Prisons* was first published in New York in 1854; there were several subsequent Irish editions. Mitchel (1815–75), a Young Irelander and editor of the *United Irishman* 1847–8, was tried on charges of sedition in 1848 and transported to Australia; in 1853 he escaped to the USA. WBY admired the *Jail Journal*, an account of Mitchel's trial and transportation,

I sent two ballads to O Leary for the "Gael". He does not like them—& he will not use them and if you care for them would you kindly send them to Father Russel for I M.

There is a socity at whose meetings Michael Field (Miss Bradley) is to be seen sometimes. It is called the "Society of the New Life" and seaks to carry out some of the ideas of Thoreau and Whitman. They live togeather in a Surrey village[7]—Ernest Reis is to bring me to a meeting. Michael Field is a bird of a another feather from these London literators whom I cannot but rather despise—

Now write me a letter much longer than this one I send you, and tell me much about every body and every thing and still more about your self.

Your Friend
W B Yeats

[*At top of first page*]
I have not got Russels adress but will write to Johnson for it.[8] Have forgotten to do so hitherto—but will write at once.

ALS Huntington. McHugh, 29–30; Wade, 39–40.

but thought the author too committed to 'his cause, to his opinions, to his oratories' to sustain or perfect his craft (cf. *UP* 1. 361).

[7] 'Michael Field' was the pseudonym adopted jointly by Katherine Harris ('Michael') Bradley (1846–1914) and her niece, Edith ('Henry') Cooper (1862–1913). WBY had written a favourable but unpublished review of their early plays, to which Edward Dowden had introduced him. The Fellowship of the New Life was based in Reigate, Surrey, where the Misses Bradley and Cooper lived. Founded by Thomas Davidson (d. 1900), a Dante enthusiast, in December 1883, the Fellowship had 'Vita Nuova' as its motto. In January 1884 some of the more practically-minded members seceded to form the Fabian Society. The Fellowship (not to be confused with the contemporaneous Brotherhood of the New Life) continued until 1898, its members including Olive Schreiner and Havelock Ellis.

[8] The poet and artist George William Russell ('AE'; 1867–1935; see Appendix), whom presumably KT wanted to invite to one of her Sunday literary gatherings at Clondalkin, was living at this time with his parents at 67 Grosvenor Square, Dublin; WBY's former schoolfellow, Charles Johnston, was a friend of AE's. This first visit seems not to have been a great success; but when WBY reintroduced them on 11 Dec 1887 Russell impressed KT with his genius. As she wrote to Fr. Russell on 12 Dec 1887 (APH), 'Yesterday there was a young artist named George Russell here, a friend of Willie Yeats and certainly even more of a genius than he is. I take his body to be inhabited by the soul of William Blake. He was here last year once, but then was very shy. He comes out wonderfully in the warmth of kindly interest.'

To John O'Leary,[1] [*13 June 1887*]

58 Eardley Crescent | South Kensington
Monday

My dear Mr O'Leary,

Thank you very much for the check. What you say about the style of the article[2] is I think true. And one of the ballads is certainly morbid (the woman about whom it is, is now in the Sligo madhouse or was there some while since). However I do not think the Howth one morbid though now on thinking it over I quite agree with you that neither are suitable for a newspaper.[3] I enclose a ballad on another Sligo story something like

[1] John O'Leary (1830–1907; see Appendix), President of the Supreme Council of the Irish Republican Brotherhood. After twenty years spent in prison and exile for his part in the Fenian movement, O'Leary had returned to Ireland in 1885 and was now living in Dublin with his sister Ellen. He exerted a profound influence on WBY through his uncompromising honesty, as well as through his library of Anglo-Irish literature, and was to become one of the poet's principal correspondents for the next eleven years.

[2] Although WBY had devoted the greater part of his review of *Shamrocks* in the *Gael* (11 June 1887, 5–7) to KT's Irish poems, he turned towards the end to her religious poems, almost certainly in an attempt to rebut Rolleston's criticism of them in the *Academy* (see p. 13), and found that

all in 'a child's day', and 'The Heart of a Mother', and 'St. Francis to the Birds' seems very right. . . . Miss Tynan's very highest note is a religious one, as in 'The Heart of a Mother' and some few lines in 'Death and the Man', and here and there in other places, but besides these dealing with the here and the hereafter there are others of the hereafter and the spiritual world, more exclusively such as 'Sanctuary'. Poems full of the passionate and sensuous religion of Italy and the South. In caring less for these I do so diffidently, knowing how much in the matter of one of them, I differ thereby from possibly the highest judge of sacred verse now living.

In a leading article, 'Miss Tynan's New Book', published in the same issue of the *Gael* and on the same page, JO'L criticized WBY's review:

Mr Yeates [*sic*] does not pretend to that judical [*sic*] frame of mind, which is generally assumed by the critic, and we do not know that his review is any the worse for its absence. Towards a poem or any other work of genius, the proper primary attitude is always one of admiration; criticism, involving more or less of censure, or at least limitation of praise, may easily enough come after. . . . We must, however, mark our dissent from Mr Yeates, and from 'probably the highest judge of sacred verse now living', whoever that may be, as to the value, poetical or other, of Miss Tynan's devotional verses. While admiring greatly 'St. Francis to the Birds', and in a lesser degree some of the other religious poems, we are very far, indeed, from thinking that 'Miss Tynan's very highest note is a religious one.' We merely put in our protest . . . our views on this point matter probably little to the world at large, and need matter less to Miss Tynan herself, while she has Mr Yeates, 'the possibly highest judge', and, no doubt, many others on her side.

[3] With his review of *Shamrocks* (see p. 15) WBY had sent JO'L two ballads, and on 23 May 1887 JBY told JO'L (NLI), 'Willie is very anxious to see proof sheets of article and ballads.' On 29 May Ellen O'Leary wrote to WBY (Belfast), 'John says your ballads are Irish in nothing but the name. He thinks them abnormal. . . . I think the Sligo one treated highly poetically though sad and painful.' This ballad, the 'morbid' one about a Sligo madwoman, is now lost; 'the Howth one' is presumably 'The Ballad of Moll Magee' (*VP*, 94–6), the story of which WBY said he took 'from a sermon preached in the chapel at Howth if I remember rightly' (*VP*, 843). In 1908 KT told Allan Wade that she thought 'The Ballad of Moll Magee' had appeared in the *Gael* (*Bibl*, 20); if so, it was in an issue after 20 Nov 1887, for on that day

Douglas Hide though not suggested by him[4] for I have long had it in my mind.

I think you mistake me about "the probably highest judge" (Miss Christina Rossetti). I did not quote her as an ally but as an opponent for the religious poems *she* likes—the Sanctuary & its tribe—I do not so much care for.[5] The religious poems *I* like being "St Francis", "Heart of a mother" & their tribe. In these poems more than in any of the others the form & matter seem to me in perfect unison & the simplicity greatest.

If you cannot use the two ballads I would be glad if you would send them [back] as I think I would like to send to Father Russell, at least one of them—though probably they will not suit him either. Is there any news from John Boyle O'Reilly. I hope the poems did not go astray, as I have only a rough copy & had made some important & radical changes—however I daresay I can partially remember them.[6] I hope you are all well. I will write soon to Miss O'Leary.

Yours very sincerely
W B Yeats

Ellen O'Leary wrote to WBY (Belfast), 'we shall do nothing to Molly Magee until you tell us.' Unless further copies of the *Gael* are discovered details of publication must remain conjectural.

[4] WBY's poem 'The Protestants' Leap. *(Lug-na-Gal, Sligo)*' was based on a legend that he later modified for his story 'The Curse of the Fires and of the Shadows' (*Myth*, 177–83). The poem, which did not appear in the *Gael* until 19 Nov 1887, is a dramatic monologue in which a sole surviving Cromwellian recounts how his companions were led over a precipice to their death by a Catholic Irish guide; the speaker escaped death because his horse fell just before the edge of the chasm. A long two-paragraph note to the poem, wrongly ascribed to 'Ed. Gael', explains that 'Lug-na-Gal is a very grey cliff overlooking that Glen-car lake, where Dermot and Grania had once a cranoque (whereof the remnants were found some years back)', and goes on to give the Protestant and Catholic versions of the legend. WBY explains that he had 'made the guide one whose incorruptable [*sic*] heart moved in a body corrupted by generations of famine, suffering, fear, and foiled projects. One of those whose fruitless lives have saved Ireland at any rate from the modern worship of success.'

Hyde's poem 'A Ballad of '98' (*PBYI*, 64–7) uses the same story as WBY's 'The Protestants' Leap', but transposes it to the time of the 1798 Rebellion and tells it from the point of view of the rebel guide. His poem was probably published in the *Gael* in June 1887, for on 29 May Ellen O'Leary wrote to WBY (Belfast), 'Douglas Hyde sent back his 98 ballad improved and shortened. . . .'

[5] *Shamrocks* was dedicated to Christina and William Michael Rossetti, whom KT first met in 1885, when Christina Rossetti wrote to her, of her first collection, *Louise de la Vallière* (1885), 'the piety of your work fills me with hopes far beyond any to be raised by music of diction' (*25 Years*, 150). Of 'Sanctuary!', a 10-stanza declamatory poem in which the protagonist implores Christ to take her dead companion into heaven, Miss Rossetti had written to KT, in a letter of New Year 1887 (Southern Illinois), that it had 'a very touching feeling, and may easily go to the reader's heart because I *think* it comes from the writer's'.

[6] John Boyle O'Reilly (1844–1890), editor of the *Boston Pilot*, was born in Dowth, Co. Meath. He joined the British Army as an IRB (Irish Republican Brotherhood) agent, was sentenced to death (1866), but was transported to an Australian penal colony, from which he escaped to the USA in 1869. In Boston, where he settled, he published a substantial amount of verse, and his novel about the convict settlements, *Moondyne* (1880), ran to 12 editions. Only one of WBY's poems, 'How Ferencz Renyi Kept Silent' (*VP*, 709–15), was published in the *Boston Pilot*, on 6 Aug 1887, but he was soon to contribute a regular 'Irish Letter' to the paper.

PS 1

On second thoughts the Sligo ballad of the mad woman was I fear not only morbid in subject but a little so in treatment. It was a mere experiment. PS2. The ballad I enclose I believe to be good. The copy I send you has many corrections my own has not, so please return it if you cannot make use of it. I wrote this letter yesterday morning but kept it back to finish the ballad.

Todhunter has a new poem that will suit our ballad book. Miss Tynan tells me she has done a new legendary poem. I wonder would it suit also. It is on an incident in the "Voyage of Maldun".[7] If enclosed ballad is suitable I will add a short note giving the story & saying where it took place. In one point you will see it differs from Hides—in mine the rebel goes over the cliff.[8] When you are sending the next Gael would you kindly send me one or two more copies of my article.

MS copy in D. J. O'Donoghue's hand, Belfast. Wade, 37–9.

To Katharine Tynan, 25 June 1887

58 Eardley Crescent | South Kensington
June 25/87

My dear Miss Tynan

I saw Mr Ranking on Thursday. He is decididedly interesting—seems much dissapointed and pathetically angry against every body and every thing modern and yet is withal I think kindly. He looks older than in your photograph and in his long dressing gown was not unlike a retired and somewhat sentimental old cavelry officer spending his latter days between a laugh and a tear. I fear dispondence and indifferent health have left him little energy for any good purpose. I asked him did he know Watsons work and recited

> In mid whirl of the dance of time ye start
> Start at the cold touch of Eternity
> And cast your cloaks about ye and depart
> The minstrils pause not in their minstralsy

[7] Todhunter's poem was probably 'Under the White-Boy Acts, 1800', and KT's 'Ronain on His Island', based on an episode in the early Irish *immrama*, *The Voyage of Maeldune*. Only the Todhunter poem was included in *PBYI*.

[8] See n. 4 above. In Hyde's 'A Ballad of 98' the rebel guide turns his horse sharply aside at the edge of the cliff but flings his lamp forward so that the soldiers follow it over the precipice. In WBY's 'The Protestants' Leap' both guide and troopers go over the precipice, the Cromwellian narrator alone surviving.

When I came to the third line he gave the queerest little shudder and looked down at his dressing gown and I changed the subject. He has written he says a lengthy review of your book for the Graphic.[1]

I met some while since Sparling Editor of "Commonweal", and Miss Morris's intended. He it is who is bringing out that Irish poem book I told you of.[2] A friend of yours he says, a Mr MacCall I think, is also a friend of his.[3] On the whole I hated Sparling at first sight

> "None ever hate aright
> Who hate not at first sight"[4]

but begin rather to like him now. London litterary folk seem to divide into two classes—the stupid men with brains and the clever ones without any. Sparling I fear belongs to the latter. Earnest Rheis and possibly Mr Ranking to the first. The latter is the most numerous—young men possesing only an indolent and restless talent that warms nothing and lights nothing. Indeed I find little good, with scarcely an exception, in any of these young litterary men—feel malignant on the whole subject and made myself uncivil I fear to young Sparling, however he seems to bare no malice and I begin to like him in a moderate sort of way. he lectured on Irish Rebel Songs last Sunday sympathetically and well. I was introduced to Miss Morris afterwards. She is decididly beautiful and seems very intelligent. Sparling knows and much admires your "flight of the wild Gease" from which I conclude it will figure in his poem book. Concerning our own ballad book would not your legend poem of the saint on his island be perhaps suitable

---

[1] Boyd Montgomerie Ranking (see p. 14), who had praised KT's *Louise de la Vallière* in the *Graphic*, 30 May 1885, was called to the Bar in 1886; he never practised, but turned his attention to literature, publishing several books of poetry and editing a number of texts and anthologies. He wrote for the daily and weekly press, helped edit *The Pen*, a short-lived periodical, and was later associated with *Time*. The favourable paragraph on *Shamrocks* which appeared in the *Graphic* for 2 July 1887, though unsigned, was undoubtedly by him.

WBY here slightly misquotes no. XXXI in William Watson's *Epigrams of Art, Life and Nature* (Liverpool, 1884); he cited the epigram again in a review of Watson's *Wordsworth's Grave*, *PSJ*, 15 June 1890 (*LNI*, 210).

[2] Henry Halliday Sparling (1860–1924), editor of the forthcoming *Irish Minstrelsy* (see p. 16), was William Morris's protégé and assistant. SMY described him as 'the queerest looking young man, very tall, thin, stooped, great round eyes and small chin' (SMY, scrapbook, MBY). May Morris (1862–1938) married him in June 1890, partly to spite her parents, but the marriage was not a success, and could not, understandably, recover from the irruption of George Bernard Shaw into the conjugal home (see GBS's 'William Morris as I Knew Him', in *Morris as a Socialist*, ed. May Morris, 1936). By June 1894 there was an official separation, and divorce followed in 1898.

[3] Patrick Joseph McCall (1861–1919), described by WBY (*Aut*, 203) as 'poet and publican of Patrick Street, and later member of the Corporation', published songs, verse, and humorous sketches under his own name and also under the pseudonyms 'Cavallus' and 'Droighneen Don'. He married Margaret Furlong, whose family were friends of KT's.

[4] cf. Marlowe, *Hero and Leander*, l. 176: 'Who ever loved, that loved not at first sight?'

W. B. Yeats in 1886 by J. B. Yeats

Portrait of W. B. Yeats in April 1889 by Henry Marriot Paget. (*See p. 159*)

after its appearance in Blackwood.[5] Todhunter has done two more ballads for us or rather a ballad and a story poem somewhat long but very vigorous dealing with marshal law times in Ireland. He will send them to me shortly to be sent on. Did I tell you that he read out a very fine "children of Lir" the other night his high watermark so far I think.[6] Some few days latter I read my "Oisin" which was very well received especially the second part the third remains still little more than commenced. When you see the O'Learys would you ask them to show you three ballads they have of mine, more especially "Lug Na Gal" and tell me how you like them.[7]

July 1—

I had thrown this letter aside and forgotton it except that occasionally I remembered just as the postman came that as I still owed you a letter I had no chance of one from you.

Last Sunday evening I had supper at Morris's—pictures by Rossetti all round the room and in the middle much socialistic conversation. Morris kindly asked me to write for the "commonweal" somewhat, on the irish question.[8] However though I think socialism good work I am not sure that it is my work.

Have there been any more reviews of "Shamrocks". Gregg's or any one elses. Did Miss Kavanagh tell you I sent one to the Fireside. I will send today "King Goll"[9] to Miss O'Leary and go and hurry up Dr Todhunter so that there need be no further delay.

I find this hot weather very trying and go about like a sick wasp feeling a

[5] In the event, Sparling chose 'Shamrock Song' as KT's contribution to *Irish Minstrelsy* (see p. 16), rather than 'The Flight of the Wild Geese', from her *Louise de la Vallière*. Her 'legend poem', 'Ronain on His Island', did not appear in *Blackwood's Magazine*; it was published in the *Catholic World* (New York), January 1888.

[6] 'Under the White-boy Acts, 1800', which Todhunter based on an article of the same name in the *Pall Mall Gazette* of 9 Apr 1887, tells of the horror of a young soldier on seeing his commanding officer cut down a blind fiddler. Because a Coercion Act was in force in Ireland in 1887, martial law and its abuses were a topical theme. Todhunter's 'The Doom of the Children of Lir', published in *The Banshee*, retells the Gaelic legend of Lir's four children who were changed into swans by a jealous stepmother, until released by the coming of Christianity. (KT, having based 'The Story of Aibhric' on part of the same legend, was using the theme again in her 'Children of Lir', published in *Ballads and Lyrics*, 1891.)

[7] WBY's long poem, 'The Wanderings of Oisin' (*VP*, 1–63), begun in 1886, was to occupy him in coming months and to give its title to his first book of verse. For the three ballads, see pp. 19–21.

[8] William Morris (1834–96), described by WBY (*UP* 1. 183) as 'poet, Socialist, romance writer, artist and upholsterer', was living at Kelmscott House, Upper Mall, Hammersmith, where the Socialist League heard lectures and held debates on Sunday evenings. 'I was soon of the little group who had supper with Morris afterwards. . . . We sat round a long unpolished and unpainted trestle table of new wood in a room where hung Rossetti's *Pomegranate*, a portrait of Mrs Morris, and where one wall and part of the ceiling were covered by a great Persian carpet' (*Aut*, 139–40). WBY never wrote for *Commonweal* (1885–93), Morris's socialist magazine.

[9] WBY's 'King Goll, An Irish Legend' (*VP*, 81–6; later retitled 'The Madness of King Goll'), which appeared in the *Leisure Hour*, September 1887, with a facing illustration by JBY, was included in *PBYI* and reprinted in *Oisin*.

sort of dull resentment against I know not what. I was introduced to Sharpe of the "sonnets of this century" and hated his red British face of flaccid contentement[10]—However it seems just possible that I may be able to get away to Sligo this summer going by Liverpool and on from there in a relations steamship for cheapness.[11]

I do not think I shall ever find London very tolerable—it can give me nothing. I am not fond of the Theatre—literary society bores me—I loathe crowds and was very content with Dublin though even that was a little too populous but I supose

> "Where ever in the ⟨worlds⟩ wastes of wrinkling ⟨heat⟩ sand
> Worn by the fan of ever flaming time
> Longing for human converse, ⟨man has⟩ we have pitched
> A camp for musing in some seldom spot
> Of not unkindly nurture, and let loose,
> To roam and ponder, those sad dromendaries
> Our dreams. The master of the pilgramage
> Cries, "Nay the caravan goes ever on
> The goal lies further than the morning stars."[12]

Now I want you to write and tell me about all that you are writing and doing—did that poem get into Blackwoods? Is your novelette finished? Have you done any thing for the ballad book? How are your dogs? do you see Miss O Leary often? is your book selling well?[13] do you see Miss Kavanagh and the Sigersons?[14] Is your Children of Lir commenced? Is it very hot in

---

[10] William Sharp (1855–1905), poet, novelist, biographer, and editor, published prolifically both under his own name and from 1894 as 'Fiona Macleod'. His edition of *Sonnets of This Century* appeared in 1884, with further editions in 1886 and 1887. WBY came to revise his opinion of Sharp: 'I feel that I never properly used or valued this man, through whom the fluidic world seemed to flow, disturbing all. . . . To look at his big body, his high colour, his handsome head with the great crop of bristly hair, no one could have divined the ceaseless presence of that fluidic life' (*Mem*, 128–9).

[11] WBY recalled (*Aut*, 49–50) leaving for Sligo from the Clarence Basin, Liverpool, 'upon the SS *Sligo* or the SS *Liverpool* which belonged to a company that had for directors my grandfather and his partner William Middleton'. William Pollexfen (1811–92) had entered into partnership with his wife's brother to form the Sligo Steam Navigation Co.

[12] These lines are untraced, and were probably composed by WBY for the occasion.

[13] KT was writing an article on Alice Meynell's poetry for the *Catholic World*. On 16 June 1887 she wrote to Fr. Russell (APH) that she had finished a story which was much more ambitious than her other prose, being 35 pages of small handwriting. The story, a romance, remained unpublished until the following year, when the *Christian World Magazine* accepted a shortened version which appeared under the title 'Queen Bee' in December 1888.

Kegan Paul's account books (KPA, II. 200–1) reveal that 278 copies of *Shamrocks* had been sold by the end of 1887; thereafter sales fell away sharply, and in June 1896 nearly half the edition of 1,000 was still unsold.

[14] This Dublin medico–literary family comprised Dr George Sigerson (1836–1925), his wife Hester, neé Varian (d. 1898), and their daughters Dora (1866–1918) and Hester (1870–1939). George Sigerson, born near Strabane, studied medicine in Cork and in Paris, where he was a pupil of Charcot (whose work

Ireland? being quite out of breath I bring my letter and my questions to an end.

Yours very affectionately

W B Yeats

On looking over what I wrote about Mr Rankin it seems all preamature and little to the point. I shall perhaps reverse it next time.

[*At top of first page*]

I am writing on Irish poets for Leisure Hour—also on Irish faeries.[15]

ALS Huntington. McHugh, 30–2; Wade ('Now I want you to write . . . reverse it next time' transposed), 40–3.

To Katharine Tynan, [*11 July 1887*]

58 Eardley Crescent | South Kensington

Monday

My dear Miss Tynan

I enclose your copy of the "Registar"[1] which I had forgotton before, also "Baron of Bray" with a few suggested emendations in the rhythm. I want you to find out would Mrs Sigerson mind there being made if you think them needful. I send them to you hearing the materials for the ballad book are now with you. My emendations are hurriedly made perhaps you or Mrs Sigerson herself could improve on them. but as it stood the rythm

on diseases of the nervous system he edited and translated), and practised for many years in Dublin, where he attended Maud Gonne in the 1890s. He published poems and essays as well as books on Irish history, land tenure, and political prisoners, and edited a number of anthologies, the most celebrated being *Bards of the Gael and Gall* (1897). He was later Professor of Botany and Biology at the Catholic University, and a Free State senator 1922–5. JO'L admired Sigerson's intellect, but WBY found him 'learned, artificial, unscholarly . . . but a friendly man' (*Aut*, 202) who typified a constricting form of provincial culture. Mrs Sigerson, author of novels, stories, and poems, took a motherly interest in WBY, who was, as Ellen O'Leary wrote to him (23 Apr 1887, Belfast), 'a special favourite of hers.' Dora Sigerson published her first book, *Verses*, in 1893; after her marriage in 1896 to Clement Shorter, editor of the *Illustrated London News*, she and her husband often entertained WBY in London. Her sister Hester contributed poems, reviews, and articles to a number of Irish, American, and English periodicals and was for many years on the staff of the *Weekly Freeman*, where she succeeded Rose Kavanagh (see p. 16) as 'Uncle Remus'. She married Arthur Donn Piatt, American Vice-Consul in Dublin, in 1900.

[15] The article on Irish poets became 'Popular Ballad Poetry of Ireland' (see p. 17); 'Irish Fairies' (*UP* I. 175–82) eventually appeared in *Leisure Hour* in October 1890.

[1] An unsigned review of *Shamrocks* appeared in the *Weekly Register*, a Catholic magazine edited by Wilfrid Meynell, on 4 June 1887 (729–30); the reviewer found in the book 'all the quality of its predecessor, with less manner and a more general restraint. . . . Miss Tynan's imagery is rather material and pictorial than thoughtful—rather fanciful than imaginative—but the fancy is of the most warm and brilliant quality.'

seemed to halt.[2] Perhaps you had better not show the ballads to Gill[3] until you have the whole of Todhunters contribution
Namely—

The marshal law story in blank verse
The Shan Van Vough—
The Coffin Ship—
And two songs and a short ballad the names of which I forget—[4]

These I sent a week ago to Miss O Leary but they do not seem to have arrived. I beleive my "Fireside" review of your book has come out but—I have not seen a copy. Could you kindly send me one? I hope you do not mind my fault finding. I was only allowed very little space and that made it very difficult to say all that should have been said. Many things I would have liked to praise I could not even mention. I saw no "proof" and so must have been sadly misprinted I fear.[5] I saw Mr Ranking's review in the "Graphic" and liked it and liked him also when I met him, do not mind what I said in that letter, I see every thing through the coloured glass of my own moods, not being I supose very sympathetic.

I was at Morrises again since I wrote and like Morris greatly though I find much in his philosophy of life altogather alien. He talks freely about everything, called the English the "Jews of the North" and seems realy worshiped by those about him by young Sparling especially who carries it so far, that when he was telling Rhys about his engagement to Miss Morris said "She is very beautiful. Morris you know says so" taking Morrises opinion as final in all matters as indeed the only opinion. Meanwhile Morris denounces Hero Worship, praising the northern Gods at the expense of the Greek,

---

[2] 'The False Baron of Bray' by 'H.S.' (Mrs Hester Sigerson), (*PBYI*, 30–3), in which the treacherous hero deceives and slaughters his guests, is in five-line stanzas. The rhythm, basically in the ballad form of alternating four- and three-footed lines, is a mixture of iambs and anapaests, but the number of hypermetrical lines and false quantities often produces an effect of awkwardness or bathos.

[3] Henry Joseph Gill (1836–1903), Dublin bookseller and publisher of *PBYI*. He had succeeded his father, Michael Henry Gill (1792–1877), as head of the firm of M. H. Gill and greatly expanded the business. He served as nationalist MP for West Meath 1880–3 and Limerick City 1885–8, and was High Sheriff of Dublin in 1892.

[4] Four poems by Todhunter were eventually published in *PBYI*: 'Under the White-boy Acts, 1800' (the 'marshal law story'), 'The Coffin Ship', 'Eileen's Farewell', and 'Aghadoe'—the last being one of Todhunter's best poems, which WBY selected for *A Book of Irish Verse* (1895 and 1900).

[5] Although he criticized the ending of 'The Sick Princess' as operatic, literary, and conventional, such fault-finding as occurs in WBY's *Irish Fireside* review of *Shamrocks* (9 July 1887) is at the expense of KT's earlier volume, *Louise de la Vallière*, whose 'pro-Raphaelite [*sic*] mannerism and alien methods of thought' he contrasts with the fidelity to nationality and 'things themselves' of *Shamrocks*. Apart from the amusing coinage 'pro-Raphaelite' the 500-word review (*UP* I. 119–22) contains few misprints; most occur in quoted extracts from KT's poems.

because they were so friendly feasting and warring with man, so little above him.

Your friend
W B Yeats

PS. 1

King Goll will not appear for a month yet I hear now.

PS. 2

I find Todhunter will not be able to let us have the "Banshee" wishing to print it in his own book this autumn—

PS. 3

When you ask Gill about the expense of the book ask also how much a cheap paper covered edition would cost?[6]

[*At top of first page*]
I have just read Rolleston review of Shamrocks[7] agreeing not at all.

ALS Huntington. McHugh, 33–4; Wade, 43–4.

To John O'Leary, [*12 July 1887*]

58 Eardley Crescent | South Kensington
Tuesday | July

My dear Mr O Leary

Have Dr Todhunter's MSS turned up as yet, I posted them a week ago. You have not said wheather you care for "Lug Na Gall" I hope you will let me see a proof especially as I have a rather important note to add. Miss O Leary speaks of it as from the other side than Hides. Of course that is not so, The Cromwellian being used dramatically alone. My note will state the old legend and point out the place of its happening.[1] Would you kindly let me have, the two poems you did not care for, back as *I did not keep a copy of either.*

I have just heard that "King Goll" will not appear untill September being crowded out of the August "*Leisure Hour*". I have seen no copy as yet of the

---

[6] A paper-covered edition of *PBYI*, price 6d, eventually appeared in 1890.

[7] Rolleston, in the *Academy* of 9 July, found KT's religious poems over-ornate; WBY's praise in his *Fireside* notice of such poems as 'The Heart of a Mother' and 'St. Francis to the Birds', as doing 'more to give the mind a holy and temperate thought than a great number of poems of the symbols and metaphors of religion', was perhaps another attempt to counter this criticism (see pp. 13 and 19).

[1] See p. 19. The setting of WBY's ballad, 'The Protestants' Leap', is Lugnagall ('Hollow of the Strangers'), a townland in Glencar Valley at the base of Cope's Mountain, in Co. Sligo.

Fireside. I hope Miss Tynan will like my review there in, and am glad to hear that her book is selling steadily have you heard any particulars.

I have just seen Rolleston's review in the Academy seems not much to the point though some of it is good—much to like the average "Academy" manner. I may be wrong though. I have been asked to edit an Irish or other volume in the "Camelot Classics" and have thought of Croker's "Irish Fairy Tales"[2] but fear the copy right has not lapsed—could you suggest me some book. I am working hard at my articles for the "Leisure Hour".

Dr Todhunter tells me that he wishes to reserve the "Banshee" for a new book of his own this autumn—so we will have to content us with the poems of his, I sent.

Yours sincely
W B Yeats.

ALS NLI. Wade, 45.

To W. M. Crook,[1] [*summer 1887*]

58 Eardley Crescent | South Kensington
Sunday

My dear Crook

Johnston writes to say you wish to see madame Blavatsky.[2] Would Wednesday suit you? We should start about 4 in the afternoon by Victoria.

---

[2] Thomas Crofton Croker (1798–1854) began collecting Irish legends and stories on walking tours as a boy; his *Fairy Legends and Traditions of the South of Ireland* (Part I, 1825; Parts II and III, 1828) was translated into German (by the brothers Grimm) and French, and marked a new departure in British folklore studies. Although WBY did not edit Croker's book, he used 12 extracts from the collection in *Fairy and Folk Tales of the Irish Peasantry* (1888), published as No. 32 in the Camelot Classics.

[1] William Montgomery Crook (1860–1945) was born in Sligo and read classics at Trinity College, Dublin. As classics master at Wesley College, Dublin, 1879–86, and member of the Contemporary Club, he got to know WBY, Hyde, and JO'L. Moving to London, he taught at Manor House School, Clapham, and lectured extensively for C. H. Oldham's Protestant Home Rule Association. This brought him to the attention of Liberal politicians and he was to stand unsuccessfully as a Parliamentary candidate for Wandsworth in 1892; he was secretary to the Home Counties Liberal Federation, 1902–31. In 1892 Crook helped WBY found the Irish Literary Society London. In later life he turned from schoolmastering to journalism: he was on the staff of the *Methodist Times* 1892–8, and editor of the *Echo* 1898–1900.

[2] Helena Petrovska Blavatsky (1831–91; see Appendix), co-founder of the Theosophical Society, had recently settled in England, and was staying with a follower, Mabel Collins (Mrs Keningale Cook), at Maycot, a small villa in Upper Norwood, in south-east London. WBY first called on her, bringing an introduction from Charles Johnston, in May 1887; he seems to have been alone on that occasion, recorded in *Aut* (173–4), and says that he did not see her again until after his return from Ireland early in 1888, so this planned visit with Crook may not have taken place.

Charles Johnston, in Dublin cramming for the Indian Civil Service examination, was corresponding with Crook in July 1887 about theosophical matters.

Let me know at once, if Wednesday will do as I will have to write to Madame. Where shall we meet? would you come hear as it is near Earls Court Station. We can go also by Clapham Junct perhaps that would be a better way? in which case I could meet you at the Junct or at your house.[3]

Yours truly
W B Yeats

ALS Bodleian.

To Katharine Tynan, [1 August 1887]

58 Eardley Crescent | South Kensington
Monday

My dear Miss Tynan

I enclose the review you asked for I hope it does not come to late. I take up your letter and see I should have sent it some days ago and also that ten lines was the needed length. But if necessary you or Ash King might shorten it.[1] I waited on hoping to get some more subtile or suitable words but they would not come. I have been thinking about the woemen of the poets but have not read the modern men for so long a time that I realy cannot help you at all I fear.[2] Swinburn's chief woemen creations are I suppose Queen Mary in "Chattelard" and Iseult in "Tristram of Lyonesse" (which I have read lately) resembling each other much—both passionate and gorgious animals

---

[3] Manor House School, where Crook was living, was at 1–5 Lydon Road, Clapham, SW, a few streets away from the suburban station on the line to Upper Norwood.

[1] *Shamrocks* was reviewed in *Truth* on 11 Aug 1887 (247), in an intermittent series, 'Letters on Books'. Although the letter was signed on this occasion by Barry O'Brien, the paragraph on *Shamrocks* was written by WBY, for it praised 'The Heart of a Mother' and 'St. Francis to the Birds' as he had done in the *Fireside* (see p. 27, n.7), and found the book 'full of gorgeous colour and rich music'. Moreover, KT wrote on 3 Aug 1887 to Fr. Russell (APH): 'Mr Yeats has written a bit about my book to go in Mr King's *Truth* letter. Mr K. wanted me to do it myself!!!!' (While very properly declining to contribute on this occasion, KT did write anonymously for *Truth*, and told Wilfrid Scawen Blunt on 18 Mar 1889 [Southern Illinois] that 'my friend Mr Ashe King, the reviewer allows me *sub rosa* to pronounce upon poetry in his bookletter: he claims to have no judgment of it'.)

[2] KT had been asked by Oscar Wilde to contribute to the *Lady's World* (which in *Middle Years* she confuses with the later *Woman's World*, also edited by Wilde) a series of articles on the treatment of women by various major poets, and she 'had asked Willie's help'. On 3 Aug 1887 she wrote to Fr. Russell (APH) that she 'troubled over that article for Oscar Wilde . . . as yet I have only about one fifth of it done. . . . I half wrote to him (O.W.) on Monday asking him for another subject but then I think it would be a pity to be troublesome over the very first article though it will be more pitiful still if I fail . . . '. On 16 September she told Fr. Russell (APH) that she had finished the article and sent it to Wilde 'long ago but have heard nothing'. In fact, none of the articles appeared in either *Lady's World* or *Woman's World*: 'Lord Tennyson's Women' was published in the *Nation*, 2 Aug 1890 and six articles, on the heroines of Tennyson, Longfellow, Keats, and Browning, appeared in *Sylvia's Journal* between March 1893 and January 1894.

one innocent the other malignent. Morris's chief woman I imagine is "Gudrun" but it is some years since I read the poem that I only dimly remember her. Morris has however I beleive a greater range of characterisation than Swinburn though he has done nothing perhaps as powerful as Queen Mary in "Chattelard". Do you not think there is considerable resemblence between the heroines of all the neo romantic London poets namely Swinburn, Morris, Rossetti—[3] and their sattelites for one thing they are essentially men's heroines with no seperate life of their own in this different from Brownings. Tennisons are I beleive less heroic than any of the others and less passionate and splendid but realized as far as they go more completely—much more like actual every day people witness "Mary Tudor" and the aristicratic young ladies in the Idyls of the King.[4] I have a notion but am not sure, that Rossettis are a more spiritual version of the same type as Swinburns and Morrises. These are only appologies for ideas on the subject and will help you little I fear.

I was greatly pleased with a little poem called "Outlaws" in the Gael by Hide I hope he is putting it in our ballad book.[5]

I was at Morris's last night. He says he makes only a hundred a year by his books all told, and denounces the british public because he says it only reads scandals and the newspaper.

Your friend ever
W B Yeats

I have not been reading Browning this long while but I imagine his heroines are actualized like Tennisons but are not so much tipes as his and are more of the brain than his, and less of the heart[6]—

---

[3] Swinburne's five-act tragedy *Chastelard* (1865) dramatizes the downfall and death of Pierre de Boscosel de Chastelard, courtier, poet, and lover of Mary Stuart; *Tristram of Lyonesse* (1882) is a treatment of the Tristan and Iseult legend. Gudrun, the tragic wife of Sigurd, is the heroine of William Morris's *Sigurd the Volsung* (1876), a poem WBY recalled (BBC radio talk, 10 Apr 1932) having heard Morris read on a visit to Dublin in 1886. In his essay of 1902, 'The Happiest of the Poets' (*E & I*, 53–64), WBY was to contrast Morris's heroines, whom he describes as 'good housewives', accepting Nature's fullness, both with Rossetti's women, who symbolise 'some immense desire' and impossible hope, and with Swinburne's Mary Stuart, who is 'in love with love for its own sake, with a love that is apart from the world or at enmity with it'.

[4] Mary Tudor is the heroine of Tennyson's play *Queen Mary* (1875). In an 1892 review (*UP* I. 252), WBY speaks of Tennyson 'now triumphing with "The Idylls of the King," and now failing dismally with "Queen Mary"'; and elsewhere, of the *Idylls*, 'no one will say that Lord Tennyson's Girton girls do not look well in those old costumes of dead chivalry. . . . Yet here [in Ferguson's *Deirdre*] is that which the Idylls do not at any time contain, beauty at once feminine and heroic' (*UP* I. 95).

[5] None of the five poems by Douglas Hyde included (under the pseudonym 'An Craoibhin Aoibhinn') in *PBYI* deals with the theme of outlaws. McHugh suggests (159) that the poem in the *Gael*, now lost, may have been an English version of Hyde's 'An Dibirteach' (The Outlaw).

[6] Although his 1889 obituary notice of the poet (*LNI*, 97–9) praised Browning's absorbing interest in life, WBY later thought him a dangerous influence, and the 'psychological curiosity' (*Aut*, 313) of the poetry too obtrusive.

The heroines of the neo romantic school are powerful in conception shadowy and unreal in execution—Brownings and Tennisons poor in conception perfectly realized in execution.

[*At top of first page*]
I send you Morrises Socialist poems[7] in case you have not seen them.

ALS Huntington. McHugh, 34–5; Wade, 45–7.

To John O'Leary, [5] August [1887]

58 Eardley Crescent | South Kensington
Friday | August 4[1]

My dear Mr O Leary,

I heard from Miss Kavanagh this morning & return John Boyle O'Reilly's letter.[2] I have I find a copy though an imperfect one of my poem.[3] Will I, as Miss Kavanagh suggests work it up & send it to you. Or will we wait to see if the old copy turns up. I enclose a poem from the Gaelic made from a prose version given by Walsh in the introduction to his book of poems. It might be suitable for the "Gael"[4] if so might I see a proof as a miss print in a short lyric is quite ruinous & as I am always especially unfortunate in that way. Douglas Hide's two poems are very good indeed.[5] My father was greatly delighted with "Outlaws". I hope it is for our ballad book which same book need surely be delaid no longer. Miss O Leary I find by her letter

---

[7] *Chants for Socialists* (1885).

[1] A misdating for 5 August, which in 1887 was a Friday.

[2] See p. 20. The letter probably told JO'L that his protégés' poems had arrived safely and that O'Reilly would publish them. WBY's 'How Ferencz Renyi Kept Silent' appeared in the *Boston Pilot* on 6 August 1886; Rose Kavanagh had poems published there on 30 July and 1 October.

[3] Presumably 'The Protestants' Leap'; see pp. 20 and 27.

[4] WBY's 'Love Song' (*VP*, 717) is adapted from Edward Walsh's translation, in his *Irish Popular Songs* (Dublin, 1847, 1883), of a stanza from 'Edmund of the Hill' by Edmund O'Ryan, of which WBY said that he knew 'nothing more impossibly romantic and Celtic' (*UP* I. 153). Walsh (1805–50), a penurious school-master at Cork and later to the convicts on Spike Island, contributed poems to the *Nation* and made many translations from the Irish, sometimes introducing Gaelic forms into English for the first time. Besides *Irish Popular Songs* he published *Reliques of Irish Jacobite Poetry* (Dublin, 1884). 'Love Song' was almost certainly published in the *Gael*, as Ellen O'Leary told KT (early 1888, Belfast) that JO'L thought it 'one of the best he ever did'.

[5] In her letter of 29 May 1887 (Belfast), mentioning Hyde's Ballad of 98' (see p. 20), Ellen O'Leary told WBY that Hyde had also sent 'the little one Heine-ish[?] which you like so well, John O'Mahoney's Death Lament and a new one'. Since there seems often to have been a lag between the time the *Gael* received MSS and their publication, it is possible that two of these are the poems referred to here. On 1 July 1887 Hyde wrote 'My grief on the sea', one of his best-known translations, and he may have sent this to JO'L.

thinks "King Goll" put off indefinitely—that is not so for I hear it will be out in a fortnight.

My article on Irish ballads for "Leisure Hour" is now merely to be copied out. It has been a long job. I have seen the "Union" sent by a conservative relative & read in it much about the "Gael" & the athletic etc.[6] I have been a great many times at William Morris's lately. Tell Miss O'Leary that he thinks Moore much underrated nowadays[7]—tell her also that the editor of the Irish poem book about to appear in "Canterbury Poets" will include one or two of hers quoted in *Dublin University Review*.[8] He suggests by the way that we should allude to each others ballad books in our prefaces (are we to have a preface?) which I fear is 'log-rolling'. However if his book is a good book I see no objection.[9] The next time you hear from me I will be at Sligo I hope, for I start possibly next Tuesday. I shall be there some few weeks & return possibly by Dublin. I have an article on the stocks for the Gael but have laid it aside for the present.

Yours sincerely

W B Yeats

Miss Tynan tells me she has not shown poems to Gill yet, but waits for Todhunter.

MS copy in the hand of D. J. O'Donoghue, Belfast. Wade, 47–8.

[6] *The Union*, an Ascendancy paper which ran from 29 Jan 1887 to 5 Apr 1890 (continuing thereafter until 12 July 1890 as *England and the Union*) was constantly on the look-out for treason. In July and August 1887 it ran a series of articles denouncing the Gaelic Athletic Association as 'an institution for drilling and preparing the manhood of Ireland for insurrectionary purposes' (9 July). JO'L as patron of the GAA, and the *Gael* as an organ of the Association, also came in for attack (15 August). WBY's Conservative relative was almost certainly his uncle, George Pollexfen.

[7] After enormous popularity in the earlier part of the century, Thomas Moore (1779–1852), friend of Byron and author of *Moore's Melodies, Lalla Rookh*, etc., was at this time losing favour, especially among the younger nationalists. See *Aut* (207–8), and Stephen Dedalus's jibe that Moore 'was a Firbolg in the borrowed cloak of a Milesian' (*A Portrait of the Artist as a Young Man* [1968] 183). JO'L criticized Moore for what he considered to be his spurious patriotism, and in his lecture 'What Irishmen Should Know', delivered at Cork in February 1886 and later reprinted, said: 'Moore has, I think, been at first somewhat overrated, then in the Young Ireland period—for natural causes enough—somewhat underrated and is now, I fancy fairly estimated.' It is probable that Ellen O'Leary concurred with her brother's judgement; WBY, in his review of her poems, wrote: 'They are all written according to the Davis tradition, rather than the more elaborate one of Moore and his imitators' (*LNI*, 126).

[8] Those quoted by Gavan Duffy in his December 1886 *DUR* article, 'A Celtic Singer', (see p. 16, n. 8). Only one poem by Ellen O'Leary, 'To God and Ireland True', was published in Sparling's *Irish Minstrelsy*.

[9] Sparling did not, in fact, mention *PBYI* in his Introduction to *Irish Minstrelsy*.

To Katharine Tynan, [*13 August 1887*]

Rosses Point | Sligo
Saturday

My dear Miss Tynan

You will see by the top of this letter that I am down at Sligo. I reached hear Thursday morning about 2 °ᶜ having come by Liverpool[1] but will return by Dublin perhaps.

Have been making search for people to tell me fairy stories and found one or two. I hope to get matter enough for an article or so. Have you heard about your story yet[2] I too am resolved to try story writting but so far have not made a start I will send my first to the "Gael". I got the last number with Todhunter's "Lament of Ailleen" which seems to me no good and possibly should not be included in our ballad book[3] especially as we will have three or four from him without it. In so small a book every thing should be good. My "king Goll" ought [to] be out in a day or two a week at most.

I fear the few rambling thoughts on poetic woemen I sent, will not have helped you or the review scrap.[4] I hope you did not feel bound to this last but if it was not suitable got some one else to touch it up or rewrite it.

I saw Mr Rankin just before I left London and found him very friendly and pleasent he was much irritated by Rolleston's review in the Atheneum.[5] I had almost forgotten what I should have sead at the beggining that Aubrey De Vere sent me his last book[6] I have been busy reading it and find it wonderfully pleasent and kindly and beautiful. Have you seen it? It came through Father Russell.

It is a wonderfully beautiful day the air is full of trembling light. The very feel of the familiar Sligo earth puts me in good spirits. I should like to live here always not out of liking for the people so much as for the earth and the sky here, though I like the people too. I went to see yesterday a certain cobler of my acquaintance and he discoursed over his cat as though he had walked out of one of Kickhams novels "Cats are not to be depinded upon" he said and told me how a neighbours cat had gone up the evening before to the top of a tree where a blackbird used to sing every night "and pulled him down" and then he finished sadly with "cats are not to be depinded upon".[7] I have

---

[1] Boats of the Sligo Steam Navigation Co. (see p. 24, n. 11) left Liverpool every Tuesday and Sligo every Friday.

[2] Presumably the novelette ('Queen Bee') mentioned at p. 24.

[3] Todhunter's three-stanza poem, 'The Lament of Aidheen', was published in the *Gael*, 6 Aug 1887. The poem was reprinted in *The Banshee* as 'The Lament of Aideen for Oscar', but was not included in *PBYI*.

[4] His notice of *Shamrocks* for *Truth*; see p. 29.

[5] WBY means the *Academy*, where Rolleston's review of *Shamrocks* had appeared on 9 July.

[6] Probably his *Legends and Records of the Church and the Empire*, which appeared in June 1887.

[7] In a report of WBY's recollections published in the *Irish Booklover*, April 1925 (20), is one of an old

been reading Philip Bourke Marstons stories.[8] Some of them are good—
very good but the most idifferent and all a little feverish. You'll remember
wont you your promise to send me the reviews of Shamrocks to read as soon
as you have them all stuck in a book.

Your Friend
W B Yeats

Write soon and more than one sheet if possible.
PS—Monday
I enclose these trivial verses the first fruits of my fairy huntings.

The Fairy Docter

The fairy docter comes our way
    Over the sorrel covered wold
Now sadly, now unearthly gay
    A little withered man and old

He knows by signs of secret wit
    The man whose hour of death draws nigh
And who will moan in the under pit
    And who foregather in the sky

He sees the fairy hosting move
    By heath or hollow or rushy mere
And then his heart is full of love
    And full his eyes of fairy cheer

Cures he hath for cow or goat
    With fairy smitten udders dry;
Cures for calf with plaining throat
    Staggering with languid eye;

Many herbs and many a spell
    for hurts and ailes and lovers moan—
For all save he who pining fell
    Glamoured by fairies for their own.

man in the neighbourhood of Sligo who had 'told him why the cats were a people in themselves. In the
beginning of the world every cat had ninepence. He gave threepence to be able to see in the dark,
threepence to have nine lives, and the last threepence to have a plate of milk every day. Hence no
gratitude might be expected from a cat. They were merely carrying out a contract.'
    At this period WBY viewed the Fenian writer Charles Joseph Kickham (1828–82) as the 'most
rambling and yet withal most vivid, humorous, and most sincere of Irish novelists' (*UP* I. 161). Later he
found him conventional and idealizing, and resented the picture of Irish life Kickham's novels
presented, for it blinded people to the true originality of J. M. Synge (see *Expl*, 234–5).
    [8] Philip Bourke Marston (1850–87), poet and short-story writer who had died on 14 February, was a
brother-in-law of the poet Arthur O'Shaughnessy. Marston's *For a Song's Sake and Other Stories*, had
been published in March with a memoir by William Sharp.

> Greet him courtious, greet him kind,
> Lest some glamour he may fold
> Closely roud us body and mind—
> The little withered man and old.[9]
> W B Yeats

You must tell me whether you like it. I will maybe have the editing of Crockers Fairy tales for the Camelot Classics but have been this long time waiting for Rheis to decide.

How does your article[10] go on? I wish it were an Irish article, though at the comencement one I supose cannot chose ones own subjects always; but remember by being as Irish as you can you will be the more origonal and true to your self and in the long run more interesting even to English readers.

I am going now to a farm house where they have promised me fairy tales so I can write no more.

ALS Huntington. McHugh, 35–8; Wade, 48–51.

To H. H. Sparling,[1] *10 September* [*1887*]

Rossis Point | Sligo
September 10

My dear Sparling

You asked me to find out for you the date of Miss O Learys birth and the place where she was born. I have just heard from her it was in Tipperary 23 of October 1831. She says you are a very ungallant editor but is very glad to have one of her ballads taken and would like to know which it is. I fear this may be too late but really it is ungallant to print all the ladies ages and so it will be no harm at all if it be late. Miss Mulhollads I do not yet know—I asked Father Russel about both Miss O'Leary and Miss Mulholand some weeks ago but he remained descreetly silent.[2]

---

[9] 'The Fairy Doctor' (*VP*, 716–17), published in the *Irish Fireside* 10 Sept 1887, was included in *Oisin*, but not afterwards reprinted by WBY.

[10] KT's article on women in poetry; see pp. 29–30.

[1] See pp. 22, 26.

[2] Rosa Mulholland (1841–1921), daughter of a Belfast doctor, spent a good deal of her early life in the west of Ireland. Charles Dickens encouraged her early attempts at writing and she contributed to his *Household Words* and *All the Year Round*. Although she wrote some poetry, she is more noted as a prolific novelist and short-story writer; her work is Catholic and national in sentiment. In 1891 she married the historian John T. Gilbert (1829–98), who founded the Dublin Public Record Office and was knighted in 1897. Fr. Russell's discreet silence was fitting in a relative: his brother Charles, later, Lord Russell of Killowen (1832–1900), was married to her sister. No date of birth is given for Rosa Mulholland, whose 'Shamrocks' and 'Song' are included in *Irish Minstrelsy*. Ellen O'Leary's birth date is recorded there; the poem of hers Sparling included was 'To God and Ireland True'.

In last Fireside there was a complementary allusion to you in which I recognize Miss Kavanaghs hand. Have you seen it? if not I will send it. the allusion commenced an article on Miss O'Brien.[3] On same page was a trifle concerning a "fairy docter" by me—full of mistakes though. I got no proofs and had put some things down to be altered in proof not yet being sure of the improved versions.[4] I have been busy gathering fairy tales in the cabins. And have many new and curious. Have written like-wise a short romance of ancient Ireland—somewhat over dreamy and florid but quite readible any way and now commence another of latter day Ireland.[5]

You I suppose are trampling in the wine-press—I mean speaking in the open air and cursing the capatalists.[6]

I hear from Miss Tynan she is busy about many things—written a story, & some irish poems, concerning fairies one of them, another on the children of Lir, has finished some articles likewise.

I am deep in antiquities trying to grubb up some pearls out of that muddy well of clan squabbles that made up our Sligo history[7]—nothing there though, as epic as the mob yesterday soaking, for momentos, their handkerchiefs in the blood of the men the police shot.[8]

Your sincerely
W B Yeats

[At top of first page]
P.S. write and say if you want that Fireside.

ALS Brown.

[3] In an unsigned review of Charlotte Grace O'Brien's *Lyrics* (1887) in the *Irish Fireside*, 10 Sept 1887 (581), Sparling is described as a 'distinguished English writer, at present editing a volume of Irish poetry for the Canterbury Series . . .'. The review is almost certainly the work of Rose Kavanagh. Grace O'Brien (1845–1909), daughter of the Young Ireland leader William Smith O'Brien, wrote novels as well as verse. Sparling included one of her poems, 'Song', in *Irish Minstrelsy*.

[4] WBY's 'The Fairy Doctor' (see preceding letter) was printed immediately above the reference to Sparling in the 10 Sept *Irish Fireside*. The variants between the version printed there and that in *Oisin* are recorded in *VP* (716–17).

[5] The first mention of *Dhoya*, WBY's story set in the Sligo countryside, of the lonely and violent giant who loses his fairy lover in a game of chess. JBY had suggested that WBY should write a story to make some money, 'and, partly in London and partly in Sligo, where I stayed with my uncle George Pollexfen, I wrote *Dhoya*, a fantastic tale of the heroic age. My father was dissatisfied and said he meant a story with real people . . .' (*Mem*, 31). The second, more orthodox, tale was at first set in the eighteenth century, but later became the contemporary story, *John Sherman*.

[6] The *Commonweal*, vol. III (1887), advertises a number of socialist lectures by Sparling at this time, especially in Clerkenwell.

[7] Probably a reference to Fr. Terence O'Rorke's *History, Antiquities, and Present State of the Parishes of Ballysadare and Kilvarnet in the County of Sligo* (Dublin, 1878), a 'learnedly and faithfully and sympathetically written history' (*FFT*, 324), the source for 'The Ballad of Father O'Hart' (*VP*, 91–3) which WBY was composing at this time.

[8] In the so-called 'Mitchelstown Massacre' of 9 Sept 1887, large crowds who had gathered in Mitchelstown, Co. Cork, for the trial of the nationalist MP William O'Brien under the Conservatives' Crimes Act, held a meeting in the course of which they attacked a police shorthand writer. In the ensuing violence the police shot one man dead and wounded four others, two mortally.

To Katharine Tynan, [*17 or 24 September 1887*]

Rosses Point | Sligo
Saturday

My dear Miss Tynan

I was very glad to get the Liverpool review of "Shamrocks" it ought to greatly help.[1] I see the reviewer picks out my own favourite "The Heart of a Mother". I will keep the paper safely for you but wish to keep it by me for a few days yet.

My plans are very hazey just now depending on the weather—Miss O Leary has asked me to stop at Rathgar Road for a few days if I reach Dublin before Mr O Learys return.[2] But I hardly know when I leave as I wish greatly to finish "Oison" first. but the weather breaking might send me off any time as my uncle stops here only so long as it is fine.

"Oison" goes a head famously the country helps one to think.

I went last Wednesday up Ben Bulban to see the place where Dermot died,[3] a dark pool fabulously deep and still haunted—1732 feet above the sea line, open to all winds. Tracks of sheep and deer and smaller tracks of hares converging from all sides, made as they go to drink. All peasents at the foot of the mountain know the legend, and know that Dermot still haunts the pool, and fear it. Every hill and stream is some way or other connected with the story.

Have you heard about your story yet. The one you sent, to "Household Words" I think.

I lived some days in a haunted house a little while ago, heard nothing but strange knockings on the walls and on the glass of an old mirror. The servent one evening before I heard anything heard the stamping of heavy feet the house being empty.[4]

---

[1] *Shamrocks* received a highly laudatory review of over 30 column inches in the *Liverpool Daily Post* of 14 Sept 1887 (7). The reviewer quoted several poems, including 'The Heart of a Mother', and claimed that 'there is not a dull poem in the volume', and that many were 'full of that rarest possession of all now-a-days, "the vision and the faculty divine" '; he predicted that if KT's blank verse turned out to be equal in power to her lyrics 'she will take rank not far from the highest among English poets'. The review was unsigned, but in her scrapbook (Hinkson Archive) KT identified it as being by E. R. Russell, i.e. Edward Richard, later 1st Baron Russell, editor of the *Daily Post* from 1869.

[2] The O'Learys had moved in 1886 to 134 Rathgar Road, Dublin, and remained there until late 1887 when they went to 30 Grosvenor Road. In the event, WBY remained in Sligo until after JO'L's return, as Ellen O'Leary informed KT in an undated letter of later this autumn (Belfast): 'I told Mr. Yeats in writing just now that we had not a place for him to stay since John returned but that we'll be happy to have him dine with us any and every day he comes to town. . . . John is looking well after his travels. He was staying in Manchester with a College friend of Davis's. . . . '

[3] The site would have been of particular interest to KT, whose 'The Pursuit of Diarmuid and Grainne' was the chief poem in *Shamrocks*. WBY was to use the place as the setting for Act III of *Diarmuid and Grania* (*VP I*, 1208) and he mentions it in *Dhoya*.

[4] Elsinor Lodge at Rosses Point, which had belonged to WBY's great-uncle William Middleton

Jack has gone home a few days now but I sent on the "Alley Sloper".[5]
I think I have no other news.

Am as usual fighting that old snake—revery to get from him a few hours
each day for my writing.

Your friend
W B Yeats

ALS Huntington. McHugh, 38–9; Wade, 51.

To Katharine Tynan, 25 October [1887]

Charlemont[1] | Sligo
25th of October

My dear Miss Tynan

Dont be angry with me for not having written—I will like better to stop at
White Hall[2] than anywhere else. Strewn about my desk are the first pages of
at least three different letters started on various dates to you. And all left
only started, on various excuses. firstly because—and this is something
more than an excuse—I wanted to be able to tell you when I would start
from this. And my start has depended on two things. I want to finish Oison
before I leave, and he has been very obdurate had to be all rewritten once—
the third part I meen—but has gone very well today I may finish this
week—and also I did not fix a day until I heard from home and now I hear
they wish me not to go home just yet. Lilly, you see, is not well yet of her bad
suppressed rheumatism attack and Mamma is not well either.[3] However I

(1820–82). WBY visited his cousin George Middleton there and recalled (*Aut*, 15–16) that there were
'great cellars under the house', for it had been the house of a smuggler, John Black, a hundred years
before, 'and sometimes three loud raps would come upon the drawing-room window at sundown, setting
all the dogs barking: some dead smuggler giving his accustomed signal. One night I heard them very
distinctly and my cousins often heard them, and later on my sister.' Later the house passed to the
eccentric recluse Henry Middleton (1862–1932) of whom WBY writes in the second of 'Three Songs to
the One Burden' (*VP*, 606–7): 'My name is Henry Middleton, / I have a small demesne, / A small
forgotten house that's set / On a storm-bitten green.'

[5] *Ally Sloper's Half-Holiday* was a popular English comic paper for children. In a letter to KT, dated
'Thursday' and illustrated with a huntsman on a horse and cowboys, Jack Yeats wrote: 'thank you very
much for the Ally Slopers it is very kind of you to send them. The weather here is very cold just now. I
remain your sincerely Jack Yeats' (Southern Illinois).

[1] In 1885 WBY's Pollexfen grandparents had moved from their big house, Merville, to Charlemont,
'a tall, bare house overlooking the harbour' (*Aut*, 67). The house is now a nurses' home.

[2] KT's father's house at Clondalkin, near Dublin.

[3] WBY's mother, Susan Mary Yeats, née Pollexfen (1841–1900), suffered a stroke in the summer of
1887 and remained an invalid for the rest of her life. SMY, her namesake, had been taken ill before this
and remained in poor health for much of her life. Not until 1930 did she learn the cause of her trouble:

dare say a week longer here is all I shall stay—But it is very hard for me to fix a day for certain Oison being unfinished.

I suddenly remember that perhaps my putting off longer my visit to Dublin may inconvenience you as you may wish to go to England you had some such plan—If so tell me and I will start in a few days. But if not I will wait till Oison is finished and one or two other odds and ends.

I had thought to have left when my uncle left Rossis Point but I am now with my Grandfather so my address is

c/o William Pollexfen Esq

Charlemont

Sligo

Write and tell me what you are doing and what you have done of late. I am as hungry for news as Robinson Crusoe.

I must now go for my walk having but an hour till teatime.

Your friend alway

W B Yeats

I enclose an advertisement of Sparlings book[4]—which he sent me.

ALS Huntington. McHugh, 39–40; Wade, 52.

To Katharine Tynan, [? 30 October 1887]

Charlemont. Sligo

Sunday—

My dear Miss Tynan

As to the place of my birth—I was born in Dublin at Sandymount[1] and as to that sonnet here it is—

'My thyroid gland is abnormally low down & has sent down a lobe for eight inches down behind my breast bone—it is pressing on my wind pipe & makes it difficult for me to breath [*sic*] & also presses on nerves & gives me incessant pain in my chest. The condition was quite unknown till I produced it.' (Family Book, 1930, MBY)

[4] *Irish Minstrelsy*, which was about to be published.

[1] In 1865, when WBY was born, the maritime village of Sandymount, which lies on Dublin Bay three miles south-east of the centre of the city, was becoming a suburb of Dublin. The grandly named Sandymount Castle, an eighteenth-century country house to which had been added Gothic battlements, a clock tower and a cloister, and which stood in its own extensive grounds, was owned by WBY's great-uncle, Robert Corbet, who later went bankrupt and committed suicide in 1872 by jumping overboard from a ferry crossing the Irish Sea. WBY was born at Georgeville, now 5 Sandymount Avenue, about half a mile from the Castle; this recently built six-room, semi-detached house, although a substantial dwelling, was regarded with disdain by Robert Corbet, who called it 'The Quarry Hole'.

KT, who persisted in supposing that WBY had been born at Sandymount Castle, was seeking the information on behalf of her American friend, John James Piatt (see n. 5 below), who intended to lecture on contemporary Irish poets during a visit to the USA. She provided him with facts about Rose Kavanagh and Rosa Mulholland as well as WBY.

She who dwelt among the sycamores

A little boy outside the sycamore wood
Saw on the wood's edge gleam an ash grey feather;
A kid, held by one soft white ear for teather
Trotted beside him in a playful mood.
A little boy inside the sycamore wood
Followed a ringdove's ash-grey gleam of feather;
Noon wrapt the trees in veils of violet weather,
And on tip-toe the winds a whispering stood.
Deep in the woodland pause they, the six feet,
Lapped in the lemon daffodils; a bee
In the long grass—four eyes droop low—a seat
Of moss, a maiden weaving. Singeth she
"I am love Lady Quietness, my sweet,
And on this loom I weave thy destiny".

But would not "Stollen Child" or "Medditations of Old Fisherman" be
more widely understandible[2] or if you wish him to quote—for in this matter
I leave myself wholly in your hands—from my more *litterary* work that song
commencing

Oh wanderer in the southern weather
Our isle awaits us, on each lea
The peahens dance, in crimson feather
As parrot swaying on a tree
Rages at his own image in the enameled sea.

rather a favourite of my own. You will remember it in one of the final
DUR's.[3] I cannot recall the whole correctly. Enough of all this however!
  Lately between a severe cold and cough and that savage greybeard Oison
I have had a bad time of it. Between them very sleepless! But now am much
as usual. The dog cart you speak of will do beautifully for my Town ward
excursions—I will shortly let you know when I start but still have no exact
dates—dates are the first born of Satan mainly. "Old chaos" was the only
person old or young ever extant who understood freedom properly.[4]

  [2] All three poems had appeared in the *Irish Monthly*, 'She Who Dwelt among the Sycamores' (*VP*,
715–16) in September 1887, 'The Stolen Child' (*VP*, 86–9) in December 1886, and 'The Meditation of
the Old Fisherman' (*VP*, 90–1) in October 1886. The last two became part of the canon, but 'She Who
Dwelt . . .', although included in *Oisin*, was excluded from later collections.
  [3] These lines were originally the opening of 'An Indian Song', which appeared in *DUR*, December
1886, and was included in *Oisin*. Later heavily revised and retitled 'The Indian to His Love', the poem
(*VP*, 77–8) became part of the canon.
  [4] WBY apparently brings together memories of Milton's *Paradise Lost*, where (ll. 757–60) Satan's
first-born is Sin, and where (l. 543) the satanic forces made such an uproar that they 'Frighted the Reign
of Chaos and old Night'.

Lilly I beleive spells her name with a y and two l's and is better—quite well now almost.

Will you thank Mr Piat[5] for intending to mention my work though I dare say I ought to thank you rather but you know I am not unthankful.

I must finish to catch the post.

Your Friend
W B Yeats

ALS Huntington. McHugh, 40–1; Wade, 53–4.

To Katharine Tynan, [*18 November 1887*]

Charlemont | Sligo
Friday.

My dear Miss Tynan

Oison having come to an end—nothing now remaining but the copying out, if quite convenient to you I will be with you Tuesday next by the train that reaches the Broadstone[1] at 4.15 in the afternoon—This finishing of Oison is a great releaf—never has any poem given me such a trouble—making me sleepless a good deel, it has kept me out of spirits and nervous—the thing always on my mind—these several weeks back. It seems better now than when I was working it out. I suppose my thinking so badly of it was mainly because of colds and head aches mixing themselves up with the depression that comes when one idia has been long in the mind, for now it seems one of my successes. Two days ago it seemed the worst thing I ever wrote. A long poem is like a fever—especially when I am by myself as I am down here. This to me is the lonliest place in the world. Going for a walk is a continual meeting with ghosts for Sligo for me has no flesh and blood attractions—only memories and sentimenttalities accumulated here as a child making it more dear than any other place.

I was going along the side of the river a few days ago when a man stopped me and said "I think I should know you sir". I found out he knew me well as a child. He asked me to go for a row with him saying "come we will tell old yarns" and with old yarns mainly fairy yarns collected round about here I have filled two note books. You shall hear the best when we meet.

[5] John James Piatt (1835–1917), poet and journalist, was US Consul at Queenstown (now Cobh) 1882–93. His wife, Sarah Morgan Piatt, née Bryan (1836–1919), was also a poet, whose complete poems appeared in two volumes in 1894. Piatt, who had worked on a number of papers in Ohio, was acquainted with William Dean Howells and Walt Whitman. The Piatt family became friends of KT and the Sigersons, whose younger daughter, Hester (see p. 24, n. 14), married one of their sons.

[1] The Midland Great Western Railway's terminus on the Phibsborough Road in north Dublin.

Did I tell you Lolly is writing a story—a good one papa says.[2] I wish Lilly had some such thing on hands especially now that she may not go out. She will find things very dull this winter with that disponding temperment of hers. My mother is somewhat better—is to come down here, if well enough to travel, which I fear is doubtful—Jack is going to South Kensington school of art and sent me a good drawing the other day which I enclose. I had spelt metre wrongly hence the drawing which is a recognisable likeness enough.[3]

You have not told me this long while what you are writing—so when I see you you may expect many questions on that head. I myself have nothing to read you but Oison, Dhoya and some few scraps, but have much to tell of. You have many poems to read I hope.

Your friend
W B Yeats

Say if Tuesday is convenient.

ALS Huntington. McHugh, 41–2; Wade, 54–5.

To the Editor of The Gael,[1] 23 November 1887

23rd November, 1887.

DEAR SIR—I write to correct a mistake. The curious poem in your issue of the 19th inst. was not by me, but by the compositor, who is evidently an imitator of Browning. I congratulate him on the exquisite tact with which he

[2] On 10 Jan 1888 JBY wrote to JO'L (NLI) that 'Jack is at art school & Lolly is making experiments in tale-writing. She belongs to a mutual improvement society of 7 girls who in reference to their numbers call themselves the Pleiades & meet at regular intervals & read their stories & criticize them.' The girls produced an elaborate home-made magazine, *Ye Pleiades*, to the Christmas 1887 number of which ECY contributed 'A Story Without a Plot'.

[3] WBY spelt 'metre' variously: 'meter', 'meater', etc.; Jack's drawing has not been traced. He was admitted in 1887 to the National Art Training School, situated in the then South Kensington Museum; in 1896 the school became the Royal College of Art.

[1] Although no copy has come to light of the issue of the *Gael* in which this letter appeared— presumably that of 26 Nov 1887—the letter was reprinted some four years later in the *Irish Monthly*, with the explanation that WBY had 'contributed a poem to a clever but peculiar journal, *The Gael*, which has ceased to appear. Many misprints occurred in the poem, owing (as the editor meekly explained afterwards) to "imperfect editorial supervison of the proofs". Instead of any angry remonstrance, showing that he belonged to the "genus irritabile", the poet pretended not to recognise his own verses through the disguise of so many printer's blunders . . . .' The *Gael* ceased publication in January 1888, having become involved late in 1887 in an acrimonious controversy with its direct rival, the *Celtic Times*, established by Michael Cusack (1847–1907) in January 1887, over its sporting contributions; both publications were suspended by a newly elected executive of the GAA from which JO'L's friends had been ousted.

has caught some of the confusion of his master. I take an interest in the matter, having myself a poem of the same name as yet unpublished.[2]

Yours faithfully,
W B Yeats.

Irish Monthly, July 1891, 385. Wade, 55–6.

To John O'Leary, 13 December [1887]

White Hall | Clondalkin[1]
Dec 13

My dear Mr O Leary

I see by the paper the "Gael" will come out as a Xmas number. I repent me of the idea of sending Dhoya elsewhere and send it to you hoping it may suit for the Xmas number for some number anyway[2]—

Miss Tynans cold is much better[3] otherwise no news to speak of.

Yours sincerely
W B Yeats

ALS NLI. Wade, 56.

[2] WBY's poem 'The Protestants' Leap' (see p. 20) as it appeared in the *Gael* for 19 Nov 1887 (5) has some grievous misprints both in the text and punctuation. The first stanza in the weekly reads:

> Mat formed our guide as from a failing tribe
> Hurried and starved as suits earth crazy rust,
> Tiller of sordid cliffs, the strong man's jibe,
> All over grey from sitting in the dust.

In a fair copy of part of the poem in the Yeats archive (MBY), this stanza appears as:

> Malformed he seemed as from a failing tribe
> Harred and starved as suits earth's crazy rust,
> Tiller of sordid cliffs, the strong man's jibe
> All grey from sitting in the scorching dust.

The fifth stanza in the *Gael* reads in part:

> The bubbles from the ebbs arose, and slipped
> Poolward dull frogs luxurious in the slow;
> Water his flame the grey guide, whispering, dipped.

In a letter to WBY of 20 Nov 1887 (Belfast) Ellen O'Leary explained: 'To my great annoyance and John's they put your poem in "The Gael" without letting us know, deeming it better without consulting John to leave out some article. In they stuck the ballad with all its misprints. 'Tis too bad and this has been going on this long time owing to the pig headedness with regard to things those in the office know nothing of.'

[1] The Tynans' house, Whitehall, was 'a small cottage building with little windows under immense overhanging eaves of thatch and a hall door within a porch of green trellis' (*25 Years*, 31). The village of Clondalkin is 4½ miles south-west of Dublin, on the Grand Canal.

[2] Without a complete file of the *Gael*, it is impossible to tell whether *Dhoya* was first published there.

[3] On 12 Dec 1887 KT wrote to Fr. Russell (APH) telling him that she had spent the previous week in bed with a bad cold and inflamed throat.

1888

To Stephen Gwynn,[1] *[24 January 1888]*

White Hall | Clondalkin
Tuesday

My dear Gwynn

Please excuse my not writing somewhat earlier. I have not been very well so have let all letters stand over—

Many thanks for your name for four copies and your offer to try and get me other names.[2]

The book will have for longest poem "The Wanderings of Oisin". As you see, an irish poem of some length and about my best. The remainder will be made up of short lyrics and ballads—irish a good many of them,—and a few dramatic sketches & a few philosophical quatrains. So far as I see this will be the selection but when I get back to London—I start to morrow[3]—and begin sorting things, I may modify it indefinately.

Mr R B O Brien[4] has sent me his name for two copies. Many thanks for telling him about it.

Very faithfully yours
W B Yeats

ALS Emory.

[1] Stephen Lucius Gwynn (1864–1950), journalist, novelist, critic, poet and nationalist politician. Born in Co. Dublin, a grandson of William Smith O'Brien, Gwynn remembered a time when 'Some of us were recognised as counting for something and likely to count for more. But every one of us was convinced that Yeats was going to be a better poet than we had yet seen in Ireland; and the significant fact is that this was not out of personal liking.' (Hone, 46.) At this time teaching classics, Gwynn in 1896 gave up schoolmastering to become a free-lance journalist in London. In 1904 he returned to Ireland where he was elected MP for Galway City, 1906–18. He published a number of biographies and books on Irish travel, literature, and society, as well as a volume of *Collected Poems* (1923) and an autobiography, *Experiences of a Literary Man* (1926).

[2] It had been decided, almost certainly at JO'L's suggestion, to bring out a book of WBY's poems by subscription. Orders were taken before a publisher was found, but later Kegan Paul, Trench & Co. took over the volume and issued it, as *The Wanderings of Oisin*, in January 1889.

[3] Jack Yeats's diary for 26 Jan 1888 (MBY) recorded: 'Willie came home this morning.'

[4] The Irish barrister, historian, and journalist Richard Barry O'Brien (1847–1918), born in Co. Clare,

To John O'Leary, [after 26 January 1888]

58 Eardley Crescent | South Kensington
Saturday

Dear Mr O Leary,

I don't remember about the other post card. I have been looking for it, but I suppose I must have got it & forgotten.

I got one from Miss O Leary & will write soon. I have just heard from Sparling who asks me to make suggestions about improving his book as an edition de luxe is coming out. I fear it wants so much that it is not improvable. Have you or Douglas Hide or anybody noticed any little points that will help him.[1] The book has been a wonderful success.

I was at Madame Blavatsky's.[2] She abused me over the spiritualistic affair.[3] A second sighted person there, who is rather a fool otherwise, told me true things about myself—such as that I had had rheumatism in the arms & shoulders lately, & tried to mesmerise me but Madame Blavatsky stopped him. Anyway he was having no effect. They all look to Ireland to produce

was called to the Irish Bar in 1874 and the English Bar in 1875 and practised for a short time as a barrister in England before moving into politics and literature. He was on the editorial staff of the *Speaker*, a Liberal weekly paper published in London to which WBY occasionally contributed. Following the split in the Irish Party in 1890, O'Brien remained loyal to Parnell and for a period acted as his unofficial private secretary; his 2-vol. *Life of Charles Stewart Parnell* was published in 1898.

[1] The 'de luxe' edition of *Irish Minstrelsy* (1888), much enlarged and revised, did not supersede the first edition, but seems to have been aimed at a more prosperous readership. The two forms of the book went into a number of parallel editions. Douglas Hyde, who in a letter to KT of 30 Dec 1887 (Southern Illinois) called the anthology 'a good and painstaking collection', commented in an otherwise favourable review in the *Irish Monthly* (March 1888, 175–9), that there was too much of Walsh and not enough of Mangan, that two poems 'from the Irish' were bogus, and that Davis's nationalist poetry should have been preferred to his love poems; Hyde also wanted more of Thomas Irwin and lamented 'the utter exclusion of Joseph Brennan'.

Sparling did not act upon these suggestions, but in his Introduction to the new edition, dated 'London March 17 1888', he says that has 'received counsel and encouragement from many sources', mentioning Fr. Matthew Russell and Sir Charles Gavan Duffy in particular, and 'Irish folk everywhere', to whose suggestions he has 'given anxious thought' and 'embodied all I could'.

[2] In the autumn of 1887 Mme Blavatsky removed to 17 Lansdowne Road, Holland Park, the 'romantic house' leased and furnished by her disciples, at which WBY used to visit her (*Aut*, 173–82).

[3] 'There have been private spiritualistic seances in Dublin lately,' wrote George Russell (AE) to Carrie Rea in an unpublished letter *c.* 17 Jan 1888 (Armagh); 'I would like to have gone to one, but [Charles] Johnston thinks it would be bad for me. Willy Yeats has not recovered from the effects of one which he attended.' At the seance, to which he had gone with KT shortly before his return to London in January 1888, WBY had been frightened by a violent impulse that ran through his nerves. He tried to pray but because he could not remember any prayers, recited the opening lines of *Paradise Lost*. 'For years afterwards I would not go to a séance or turn a table . . . ' (*Aut*, 103–5; see also *25 Years*, 208–9). HPB had engaged in a great number of 'spiritualistic affairs' in the USA and India, but had recently been exposed as a fraudulent medium by Richard Hodgson (see *Report of the Society for Psychical Research*, June 1885). Thereafter she admonished her followers against spiritualism: 'Beware of mediumship,' she told WBY; 'it is a kind of madness; I know, for I have been through it' (*Aut*, 177).

some great spiritual teaching. The ark of the covenant is at Tara, says the second-sighted person, but he's a fool.[4]

Things seem better here—my father's drawings a little more in request.[5] I am busy at an article of Folklore & have almost finished it.

I have sent no forms to Rolleston. Could he get me any filled up do you think, if so let him have those I sent you, or some of them, if not send them back as I have only a few.[6] I send a few old book catalogues. I hope they are the sort of things you want. Will send many more in time. My sister Lolly has written a really good little story[7]—she will do well in time, lives on the right mental plain for that sort of work.

Yours very sincerely

W B Yeats

MS copy in D. J. O'Donoghue's hand, Belfast. Wade, 56–7.

To John McCall,[1] *4 February 1888*

58 Eardley Crescent | South Kensington

February 4 1888.

Dear Sir

I did not write to you before as I was waiting to hear from my Authority Archdeacon O'Regan[2] but I have just heard he sometimes does not open his letters for a month togeather—

[4] In 1902 a group from the British-Israelite sect actually began to dig up the Hill of Tara in a quest for the Ark of the Covenant and WBY, George Moore, and Douglas Hyde wrote to *The Times* protesting against this destruction of a national monument (*UP* II. 294–5).

[5] Jack Yeats's diary for 10 Feb 1888 (MBY) records that JBY was doing some hunt sketches for Edwin Bale, presumably for one of the Cassell's magazines.

[6] The subscription forms for *Oisin* (see preceding letter) were printed by Sealy, Bryers & Walker of Dublin. WBY later recalled that JO'L had found 'almost all the subscribers' (*UP* II. 509).

[7] The February 1888 number of *Ye Pleiades* contained 'Love Me Love My Dog', a story in two chapters by E. C. Yeats.

[1] John McCall (1822–1902), father of the poet P. J. McCall (see p. 22), was a native of Clonmore, Co. Carlow, but moved to Dublin at the age of seventeen and remained there for the rest of his life. He kept a public house in Patrick Street, in the Liberties, and became an expert on the oral traditions of Dublin. He was also a student of nineteenth-century popular Dublin journals, almanacs, and chapbooks, and was particularly interested in the poet Mangan (1803–49), whom he had known by appearance. In 1882 he published serially in *Young Ireland* a long article on the poet which was subsequently issued as a pamphlet, *The Life of James Clarence Mangan*, in 1883.

[2] John O'Regan (1818–98), Archdeacon of Co. Kildare, was born in Ennis and appears on the books of TCD as early as 1833. He took his BA in 1846, was ordained the following year, and held various livings in the diocese of Dublin until he was appointed Archdeacon in 1862.

He knew Mangan somewhat, but knew the Stackpools well.[3] I have written for leave to refer you to him and will write when I hear.[4]

Yours faithfully

W B Yeats.

ALS Private. Reproduced in John M'Call, *The Life of James Clarence Mangan* (repr. Blackrock, 1975), facing p. 2.

To Katharine Tynan, 12 February [*1888*]

58. Eardley Crescent | South Kensington
February, 12.

My dear Miss Tynan.

I have not written for some time now for I have been very busy—have written a long article, nearly 50 MSS pages long of Folklore and copied out most of my poems for the book—and so often when I wished to write in the evening was somewhat too tired.

Rhys has written from America asking me to bring out in the Camelot series a book of selected Folk Lore.[1] I am trying to get some sort of regular work to do however, it is neccessary, and better any way than writing articles about things that do not interest one—are not in ones line of

---

[3] McCall in his pamphlet had referred (15) to speculation upon the identity of the woman with whom Mangan had had an unhappy love affair: 'All we know of the fickle deluder is that her name was Frances, and that she was far above her suitor in social position.' When WBY, in an article in the *Irish Fireside*, 12 Mar 1887, claimed that the woman in question was 'a Miss Stackpoole (now for the first time named) of Mount Pleasant-square, one of three sisters' (*UP* I. 116), McCall demanded evidence. WBY knew that his source, O'Regan, was unreliable, but Gavan Duffy, who had seen Mangan's letters, later confirmed the story. (Duffy's daughter, however, told Louise Imogen Guiney that the Miss Stackpoole in question was not Frances but Margaret; cf. *James Clarence Mangan: His Selected Poems*, ed. Guiney [1897], 16.)

Mangan, whom WBY described (*Aut*, 396) as 'our one poet raised to the first rank by intensity', lived a miserable life, working first as a law scrivener and later as a cataloguer in the TCD Library. He wrote for Davis's *Nation* and other Dublin journals under his own name and a variety of pseudonyms, translated much from the German, and, although he knew no Irish, rendered many Gaelic poems into English with the help of Irish scholars. His main publications include the two-volume *German Anthology* (Dublin, 1845) and *Poets and Poetry of Munster* (Dublin, 1850). Worn out by work, poverty, alcohol, and probably opium, he succumbed to the cholera epidemic of 1849. WBY published eight of his poems in *BIV*, including his most famous one, 'Dark Rosaleen'.

[4] In the book into which he copied this letter, McCall noted: 'W. B. Yeats did not write again—I never got Archdeacon O'Regan's address, or leave to write to him, and the only other reply I received from Mr Yeats was that contained in his second article on Mangan which appeared in United Ireland a long time afterwards.' This was 'Clarence Mangan's Love Affair, *United Ireland*, 22 Aug 1891 (*UP* I. 194–8), in which WBY told the story of his claim, and cited Gavan Duffy's corroboration.

[1] The selection, *Fairy and Folk Tales of the Irish Peasantry*, replaced the edition of Croker WBY had thought of preparing for the Camelot Classics (see p. 28). Ernest Rhys had gone to America in December 1887 and stayed until June 1888, visiting Whitman among other literary men and journalists.

developement—not that I am not very glad to do the Folklore book or any thing that comes to my hand. The hope of regular work may come to nothing. As soon as the copying out of Oisin is over I set to work at a short romance.[2] To me the hope of regular work is a great thing for it would mean more peace of mind than I have had lately but Papa sees all kinds of injury to me in it. It makes him quite sad.[3] perhaps the loss of mental liberty entailed in routine is always harmful. On the other hand it would save me from the insincerity of writing on all kinds of subjects, of writing on other men's truth. And I am anxious to look about me and become passive for a while too. I have woven about me a web of thoughts I wish to brake through it, to see the world again—Yesterday I went to see—in a city hotel—an acquaintence who has had sudden and great misfortunes, come in these last few days to a crisis. I knew this but was not able to let him know that I did, I was sent by his family who were anxious about him. We talked of all manner of things, of the theatres, of politics, of Ghosts, meanwhile I saw his hands and eyes moving restlessly and that his face was more shrunken than when I saw him some months before.[4] Of course all this pained me at the time but I know, now that he is out of my sight, that if I heard he was dead I should not think twice about it. So thick has the web got. An accident to one of my MSS or a poem turning out badly would seem of more importance. Yet I do not think I am an egotist. there are a few, whose welfare I think is more to me than my own. It is all the web. If I had routine work for a time I could break it. The web has grow[n] closer lately, perhaps because I have not had as good health as usual. I must often have seemed dreadful to you as I sometimes did to myself. You used to say I had no heart—that is all the web.

Lilly writes often, from Yorkshire, most delightful letters full of humour. She has developed quite a talent that way. Lolly works industriously at her stories. Jack draws as usual—Mamma is much better. We are still looking for a new house at Bedford Park.[5] We must leave this at the end of March.

[2] JBY, disappointed with the mythological fantasy, *Dhoya*, had urged WBY to make some money by writing 'a story with real people'. The longer, strongly autobiographical *John Sherman* was the result.

[3] WBY recalled (*Mem*, 31) that at this time he was eager to do something to help the family's precarious financial state and York Powell 'offered to recommend me for the sub-editorship of, I think, [the] *Manchester Courier*. I took some days to think it over; it meant an immediate income, but it was a Unionist paper. At last I told my father that I could not accept and he said, "You have taken a great weight off my mind."' WBY did however contribute paragraphs of literary gossip to the *Courier*; see pp. 158, 172.

[4] In *Aut* (42, where the episode is placed ten years earlier) WBY recalls 'a hotel sitting-room in the Strand, where a man is hunched up over the fire. He is a cousin who has speculated with another cousin's money and has fled from Ireland in danger of arrest. My father has brought us to spend the evening with him, to distract him from the remorse that he must be suffering.'

[5] In late December 1887 Susan Yeats had gone with SMY to stay with her sister, Elizabeth Anne ('Lolla') Pollexfen (1843–1933), wife of the Revd Alexander Barrington Orr, vicar of Denby, near Huddersfield. On 11 Feb 1888 Jack Yeats began a series of sketches for *Pictorial World*, which he delivered to their offices on 18 February. Jack Yeats's diary (MBY) records that 'Papa decided on house

Rhys mentions in his letter that Whitman is a great admirer of Samuel Fergusson.[6]

The little deformed lady at Atalanta talked with enthusiasm of your poetry, and praised the poem you sent them.[7]

Sparling is going to put "Father John O Hart" in the "Edition de luxe" of his book.

I went to see Madame Blavatsky on Wednesday but found she had gone away for her health but sent the Countess Weirchmeister to look after her study with orders to sleep there even, so close must she watch over the sacred MSS. When she heard I had been to a spiritulistic sceance, she told me she had gone to many till Madame Blavatsky told her it was wrong. So you need not fear for spiritulistic influence coming to me from that quarter. She told me of horrible things she has seen or beleives she has seen at sceances. She has seen the medium thrown down by a spirit and half stifled, the marks of fingers coming on his throat and finally his clothes set on fire. She declares she has seen distant places in mirrors and crystals. Being rich it seems she has travelled much in search of magic in its many forms. Is a clairyoyant likewise has seen many visions some beautiful. Has more titles than talent but is interesting on the whole.[8] A sad accident happened at Madame Blavatskys lately I hear. A big materialist sat on the astral Double of a poor young indian. It was sitting on the sofa and he was too material to be able to see it. Certainly a sad accident![9]

I saw Todhunter yesterday (Sunday for I am finishing this letter on

---

at B. Park' on 13 January, but there followed some weeks of negotiation before JBY managed to knock the rent on 3 Blenheim Road down below £50 per annum.

  [6] Whitman had in fact been introduced to Ferguson by WBY's own article, 'The Poetry of Sir Samuel Ferguson' (*DUR*, November 1886), which he had read with close attention and approval. See Horace Traubel, *With Walt Whitman in Camden* (Pennsylvania 1953), IV, 347–50.

  [7] *Atalanta*, a successor to *Every Girl's Magazine* and aimed at the same young, female, middle-class readership, began publication in October 1887. It was edited until 1898 by Mrs L. T. Meade, with, for its first year, Alicia Amy Leith—probably the person WBY refers to here. KT's 'A Dream Garden' appeared in the issue for August 1888.

  [8] Countess Constance Georgina Wachtmeister (1838–1910), HPB's devoted companion, was assistant corresponding secretary of the Theosophical Society in London and a contributor to its periodical, *Lucifer*. Born in Florence, the daughter of a French diplomat, she was sent to England at the age of four to be educated under the care of an aunt. In 1863 she married Count Carl Wachtmeister, her second cousin, then Swedish Ambassador in London, who died in 1871. She later travelled widely in Europe, taking an interest in psychic research and attending many seances. She met HPB in London in 1884 and subsequently stayed with her at Würzburg and Ostend, returning to London with her in 1887.

  [9] A rather different, and allegedly eye-witness, account of this incident is given by Archibald Keightly in his article 'Reminiscences of H. P. Blavatsky', *Theosophical Quarterly*, October 1910 (118):

On the sofa sat a distinguished Hindu, in full panoply of turban and dress. The discussion proceeded and apparently our distinguished guest was much interested, for he seemed to follow intelligently the remarks of each speaker. The President of the Lodge arrived that night very late, and coming in looked around for a seat. He walked up to the sofa and sat down—right in the middle of the distinguished Hindu, who promptly, and with some surprise, *fizzled and vanished*!

Monday). He has finished *Deirdre* and begins soon the *Children of Tourien*.[10]

Last night at Morrises I met Bernard Shaw who is certainly very witty. But like most people who have wit rather than humour, his mind is maybe somewhat wanting in depth—However his stories are good they say.[11]

Both Papa and Edwin Ellis—the only people who have seen it—say that the last part of Oisin is much the best—Edwin Ellis praises the whole poem much.[12] Lolly has the clasp you gave her on, it looks very well indeed, quite beautiful. Jack has gone to the meeting in Hyde Park for the reception of the Irish members.[13]

It is a great pleasure to write to you therefore I have prolonged this letter beyond my news. But you must write me a good long letter and tell me what you are doing and so forth. I feel like Robinson Crusoe in this dreadful London.

I am very anxious about this search for regular work. Neither I nor papa know well how to set about it but I imagine Mr Bale will help us. Papa spoke to him. I am hurrying on with the copying out for the book. As judging by something Mr Trail said[14] that might help in the matter, if the immediate hope of something brakes down. Papa wants me to write a romance, all I suppose in the vain hope that in the eleventh hour this regular employment he thinks such an evil might be unnescessary.

[10] Todhunter's 'The Fate of the Sons of Usna', which retells the Deirdre story, appeared in his *Three Irish Bardic Tales* (1896). 'The Lamentation for the Three Sons of Turann' (which had never before been rendered into English verse) was included in *The Banshee*.

[11] George Bernard Shaw (1856–1950) was at this time, as WBY recalls in *Aut* (147, 134), 'an obscure man, known only for a witty speaker at street corners and in Park demonstrations'. Recoiling from the mechanistic views of this 'notorious hater of romance, whose generosity and courage I could not fathom', WBY shared ambiguous attitudes towards him: 'we all hated him with the left side of our heads, while admiring him immensely with the right side.' Although never able to resolve these conflicting emotions, WBY came increasingly to delight in 'Shaw, the formidable man', for, while they had not the same friends, they had the same enemies, and Shaw 'could hit my enemies . . . as I could never hit.' Shaw's novel, *Love Among the Artists*, was currently being serialized in Annie Besant's *Our Corner* (November 1887–December 1888). Shaw noted in his Diary for 12 Feb that he had dined with 'an Irishman named Yeats?'

[12] Edwin John Ellis (1848–1916; see Appendix), painter, poet, and an old friend of JBY's, had recently returned to London from Italy. WBY disliked Ellis's painting but found some of his verse memorable. He had been four when they first met (and when WBY asked him if he was related to 'Cinder Ellis'); now Ellis was to exert a seminal influence on him: 'I owe to my discussions with this man, who was very sane and yet I think always on the border of insanity, certain doctrines about the Divine Vision and the nature of God which have protected me for the search for living experience, and owe to him perhaps my mastery of verse' (*Mem*, 30).

[13] On Monday, 13 Feb 1888, a meeting organized by various Liberal and Home Rule associations took place in Hyde Park to present an address of welcome and sympathy to T. D. Sullivan and the other Irish MPs who had been imprisoned under the Conservatives' Crimes Act. The attendance was estimated at 50,000.

[14] Henry Duff Traill (1842–1900), a barrister turned journalist and man of letters, was writing at this time for the *Pall Mall Gazette* and *Saturday Review* and in September was to be offered the editorship of the *St. James Gazette*. He wrote a number of literary and historical biographies, edited *Social England* (6 vols., 1893–7), and was editor of *Literature* from 1897 to his death.

"United Ireland" has not yet paid me, bad luck to it, when it does I meen to pay my debts. They must wait until then.

I have sent two poems to Boyle O Reilly.

By the way did Father Russel like the poem I sent him.[15]

Has Mr Griffen come to town yet.[16] I have a book of his to send him when I hear where he is.

Your Friend

W B Yeats

[*At top of first page*]

You would be quite pleased with me if you knew how industrious I have been lately. Dont say anything to any one about my hope of getting some employment. It may come to nothing.

ALS Huntington. McHugh, 43–6; Wade, 57–60.

To Katharine Tynan, [*? 20 February 1888*]

58 Eardley Crescent | South Kensington

Monday

Dear Miss Tynan

I write again without waiting for your letter because I heard at the Bales the other day that they will want a third and last article on Irish peasent life from you,[1] and fear they may not have told you remembering they did not do so before.

Mr O Leary sent me a lot of filled up forms[2] the other day I have 90 copies promised for, at least, now. And so hope to publish this spring season. I will be ready as far as copying out goes before the end of the month easily.

When I last wrote I was out of spirits what with fatigue and being somewhat unwell—Whenever I write you a letter so full of myself and my sensations you may know that I am tired or unwell. Then one is either like a sick wasp or a cat going about looking for someone to rub itself against.

---

[15] WBY's 'The Prose and Poetry of Wilfrid Blunt' (*UP* I. 122–30) had appeared in *United Ireland* on 28 Jan 1888, the first of many articles he was to contribute to this Dublin nationalist weekly. No poem by him appeared in Boyle O'Reilly's *Boston Pilot*, nor in the *Irish Monthly*, edited by Fr. Russell, in 1888.

[16] Montagu Laurence Griffin (1860–1924) came from Killarney, Co. Kerry. He had been a pupil of Edward Dowden's at TCD in the early 1880s and was now studying medicine there, but his studies were interrupted by his ill health and by his father's impecuniousness. Greatly under the influence of Ruskin and Newman, he contributed poems, and articles on painting, to the *Irish Monthly*. After taking his medical degree in 1892, he moved to England and spent most of his professional life in or near Plymouth, where he died.

[1] The third article remained unpublished for some years; see p. 10, n. 3.

[2] i.e. subscription forms for *Oisin* (see p. 44).

It is pleasent to think that this letter will go away out of this horrid London and get to the fields and rattle along in the basket with the letters from Clondalkin to White Hall. I wish I could fold my self up and go in it. A ghost they say, you know, can hide in a diamond, or any such small thing.

I suppose the buds are all coming out with you. Here there is snow on the ground.

Any news of our ballad book. Will it be soon out. Did I tell you that Rhys says Whitman is a great admirer of Fergusson. By the way I read Fergusson almost every evening for a short while. Are there any other of his books out since the "Lays of the Western Gael" at a 1/–.[3]

Your Friend
W B Yeats

ALS Huntington. McHugh, 46–7; Wade, 60–1.

To Father Matthew Russell,[1] 6 March [1888]

58 Eardley Crescent | South Kensington
March 6

My dear Father Russel

Many thanks—a great many—for you[r] list of names. Getting my MSS in order has taken all my time and thought—hence all my letters have remained unanswered—under the circumstances I hope you will forgive this long delay. I have been much hurried over the MSS fearing to miss the spring season. The book will make I immagine about 140 pages.[2] Todhunter, who is himself printing a volume of irish poems on Dierdre, the children of Lir, and such, will speak to Keegan Paul today for me.[3] I have

[3] A paperback edition of Ferguson's works, at 1/– a volume, was issued by George Bell & Sons in London and Sealy, Bryers & Walker in Dublin. *Lays of the Western Gael*, first published in 1865, appeared in this form early in 1888 and was noticed in the *Nation* on 25 February.

[1] Fr. Matthew Russell, SJ (1834–1912) younger brother of Lord Russell of Killowen, was educated at Maynooth and joined the Society of Jesus in 1857. In 1873 he founded the *Irish Monthly*, which he continued to edit until his death, and through which he hoped to foster an Irish national and Catholic literature. A man of tolerant and liberal outlook, he opened the magazine to Protestant as well as Catholic writers, and published a number of poems by WBY in 1886–7.

[2] *Oisin* had 156 pages.

[3] Todhunter's *The Banshee* was published in the spring of 1888 by the firm of Kegan Paul, Trench & Co. Charles Kegan Paul (1828–1902) was the son of a clergyman and took the cloth himself, but his High Church leanings towards ritualism and his radical politics (he was associated with F. D. Maurice, Tom Hughes, and the Christian socialist movement) brought him into conflict with some sections of the Anglican hierarchy, and in 1874 he gave up his living and moved to London to pursue a literary career. In 1877 he took over the publishing house of Henry Samuel King and in 1881 Alfred Chenevix Trench (b. 1859), third son of Richard Chenevix Trench, Archbishop of Dublin, joined the new company as a

about 110 names so far and will want a hundred and fifty or more but they will come in, in time.

I sent some while since a long article on Fairies to a London magazine but have not heard as yet. Faires are not popular this side of the water, are considered unscientific. There will be half a dozen poems about them in my book.

What a horrid place this London is? I wonder at that water for overflowing and drowning all those poor Chinamen busy with their opium dreams,[4] and leaving this horrid black place alone.

Dr Todhunters book will be out about the same time as my own and will be called he thinks "The Banshee or the Three sorrows of story telling" the whole in long unrhyming lines—alexindrines I think you call them[5]—

Yours sincerely
W B Yeats

March. 13—

Correcting MSS has so filled my mind that I find I forgot to post this. Yesterday I brought my MSS to Keegan Paul who says I will need about 200 subscribers or 180 any way. I have about 130 or so but will get the others without doubt. Every one is so kind in the matter. O'Leary has just sent me a lot of names including Justin MaCarthy, Stopford Brook. Gavan Duffy.[6] He has worked wonderfully for me indeed I could not have managed without him.

ALS APH. Wade, 61–2.

partner. The firm prided itself on lending 'a helping hand to any young authors in whom we saw promise', but, with the exception of Blunt, Coventry Patmore, and Morris, Kegan Paul found 'no one now worthy of being called a poet' and thought that literature was not in itself a profession (*Memories* [1899], 278).

[4] In late February 1888, 4,000 coolies and three mandarins who were supervising them were drowned while attempting to repair the banks of the Yellow River which the previous autumn had flooded large parts of Honan Province, with massive loss of life and property.

[5] Todhunter used a form of the alexandrine, without conspicuous success, in his renderings of the 'Children of Lir', and 'Sons of Usna'.

[6] JBY in a letter of 20 Mar 1888 to JO'L (NLI) apologized for not having acknowledged 'the subscription for 18 copies of Willies book which I duly recd & handed to him'. Justin McCarthy (1830–1912), journalist, man of letters, and from 1879 the Irish Party Member for Longford, was to become leader of the anti-Parnellites in December 1890. Stopford Augustus Brooke (1832–1916), a Dublin-born divine and man of letters, became a fashionable London preacher and Chaplain in Ordinary to Queen Victoria, before seceding from the Church of England in 1880 because he could no longer believe in the Incarnation; he published a number of influential critical books. He had returned a signed subscription form for *Oisin* to JO'L on 22 Feb 1888 (NLI) saying, 'I shall be glad to have his poems.'

To Katharine Tynan, 14 March [1888]

58 Eardley Crescent | South Kensington
14th of March.

Dear Miss Tynan

My poems have at last gone in, to Keegan Paul. He says I will want about 180 or two hundred subscribers, I have 130 or there abouts, also that I should publish at 3/6 not 5/0 as a 3/6 book is cheeper to get up, but as this matter is not yet settled—he putting the decision off—we must I suppose get names on the old understanding. Of course a given number of names go for less if 3/6 be the price that will have to be weighed against the cheeper estimate. Which can only be done when I hear from him—I dont much take to him. Coffey[1] and Todhunter had spoken of me, so he proffesed much interest in all my doings. I gave I fear very monosylabic answers, not much liking his particular compound of the superciliousness of the man of letters with the oiliness of a tradesman. That was on Monday. Yesterday I spent answering letters for they had all been neglected while working at the MSS—Pat Gogarty sent me, by the way, a really fine story[2]—But I put off writing to you till today that I might write at leasure. I have much improved Mosada by polishing the verse here and there.[3] I have noticed some things about my poetry, I did not know before, in this process of correction, for instance that it is almost all a flight into fairy land, from the real world, and a summons to that flight. The chorus to the "stollen child" sums it up[4]—That it is not the poetry of insight and knowledge but of longing and complaint—

[1] The Dublin antiquarian and archaeologist George Coffey (1857–1916), later Keeper of Irish Antiquities in the National Museum of Science and Art, 1897–1914. He published *The Origins of Prehistoric Ornament in Ireland* (1897) and *The Bronze Age in Ireland* (1913), and had a keen interest in drama and literature. He was probably an acquaintance of Kegan Paul's partner, Alfred Trench.

[2] Pat Gogarty (*c.* 1849–91), whom KT describes in *Middle Years* (8–9) as 'a village genius who used to come to see me in those days. He was not a genius, by the way, but only a village shoemaker, tremendously interested in literature. The need to talk would send him rushing over the couple of miles from the village to Whitehall, still wearing his leather apron.' Shortly after Gogarty's death, she contributed a sketch of him, 'A Village Genius', to the *Speaker*, 6 Feb 1892 (reprinted in her *A Cluster of Nuts*, 1894), in which she recalled him as 'a spare man, with hair greyer and thinner than it should have been, regular pale features, eager eyes that jumped at you when you gave an advice or an explanation, a high bulging brow that might have given warning of the brain disease he was to die from. . . . He made his way to France and remained long enough to learn the language, so as to get at the French writers.' For WBY's description of him see *LNI* 73–4.

[3] See p. 10, n. 6. WBY's revisions to the play before reprinting it in *Oisin* were fairly light, and he did a little pruning.

[4] The chorus to 'The Stolen Child' (see p. 40) appeared in *Oisin* as:

Come away, O human child!
To the woods and waters wild
With a fairy, hand in hand,
For the world's more full of weeping than you can
understand.

Laura Armstrong ('Vivien'), Yeats's first love. (*See p. 155*)

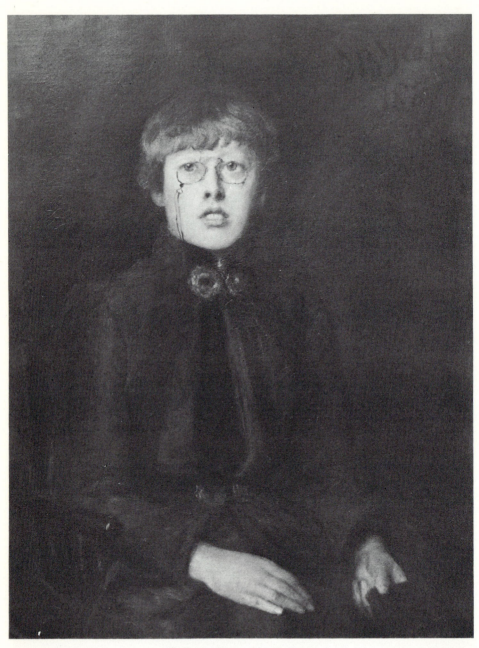

Katharine Tynan by J. B. Yeats

the cry of the heart against neccesity. I hope some day to alter that and write poetry of insight and knowledge.

Todhunter's book has gone, or is about to go to Keegan Paul. It will contain "Children of Lir", "Children of Toureen" and some shorter Irish poems. His "Dierdre" will not be ready in time. The books may help each other by drawing attention to the subject of old celtic romance—which Keegan Paul assures me is not popular. And by drawing attention to it, draw attention to each other.

I have a couple of poems that may suit the Providence Journal, one being the Phantom Ship. Would you kindly send me the Editors address?[5] I suppose their is plenty of time for them to appear before the book comes out. I sent two to the "Pilot" but have not heard. I wrote, by the way to United Ireland some ten days or a week ago but have not been paid yet.

I have met Miss Skeffington Thomson twice lately, once at her sisters Mrs Rae's, and like her much. She tells me—or her sister, I forget which—that she has been canvassing. Edwin Ellis—who is publishing a volume of drawings and poems this year—praises her last novel,[6] and he is rather an exacting judge I immagine. I shall see her again soon when I hope to find out more about the inside of her mind. She is so little opinionative that she makes it a hard task.

Mr Mongomery Rankin has changed his lodgings some time, the landlady says, and she does not know where he is—Do you? I suppose a note addressed to the Graphic office would find him out.

I was at a sort of Socialist tea meeting at Kelmscot house of late and talked a long time to Mrs Cunningham Graham—a little bright American.[7]

Fahy I saw one day in the British Museum Reading Room, Sparling

---

[5] WBY's 'A Legend of the Phantom Ship' (*VP*, 718–19) appeared in *PSJ*, 27 May 1888. The editor of the *Journal* 1884–91 was Alfred Mason Williams (1840–96), author of *The Poets and Poetry of Ireland* (1881) and other books. He had toured the poorer parts of Ireland as a journalist in 1865–6, and met KT in 1887 on a return visit to Dublin.

[6] Emily Skeffington Thompson, born in Canada in 1845, was the granddaughter of John Foster, the last Speaker of the Irish House of Commons. She was living at this time with her married sister, Catharine Jane Alicia Rae (b. 1837), wife of the Arctic explorer, Dr John Rae, near the Yeatses at 4 Addison Gardens, Kensington. Miss Thompson and her sister, both ardent Irish nationalists, had together founded the Southwark Junior Irish Literary Club, to educate London Irish children in Irish history and culture. They would have been canvassing for R. K. Causton, who retained West Southwark for the pro–Home Rule Liberals at a by-election on 17 Feb 1888. Miss Thompson's novel *Moy O'Brien* (Dublin, 1887), a romantic story set against the political and social life of contemporary Ireland, had first appeared serially in the *Weekly Freeman's Journal*, 1878–9. Edwin Ellis's *Fate in Arcadia*, which contained poems and drawings, did not appear until 1892.

[7] Gabriela (sometimes Gabrielle) Cunninghame Graham, née de la Balmondière (1861–1906), supposedly the orphan daughter of a Chilean merchant of French descent, married R. B. Cunninghame Graham in 1878. She published some verse and a biography of St. Theresa. WBY probably thought of her as American because, apart from her Chilean origins, she spent a good deal of time in North and South America after her marriage.

introduced us. A very brisk cordial neat little man—Asked me down to his Irish Litterary Club. Seems a king among his own people and what more does any man want. I hear they—that is the members of the club—sing his songs and have quite a Fahy cult.[8] Wish we had him in our ballad book, which comes out when? Gill seems slow about it.

We go to our new house 3. Blenheim Road. Bedford Park on the 25th of this month—a fine roomy house which by good luck we have got very cheep.[9] Bedford Park is the least Londonish place hereabouts—a silent tree filled place where every thing is a little idylic except the cockcroaches that aboud there. The quantity of new wood brings them—and the old wood brings a stray nightingale now and again, says rumour, & certainly thrushes and black birds in almost country plenty. I will have a study to myself with one of those white wooden balconies native to that part of the world.

Your Friend Always
W B Yeats

PS—
Mamma & Lilly do not come home 'till after the move.

PS—   15th of March
No news yet about any regular work. Todhunter says my bad writing and worse spelling will be much against me but thinks I may get some thing to do in the way of an assistant librarianship. Meanwhile he says my book is likely to succeed, says good Irish reviews, in the present state of English opinion may do much, and a successful book may help me in the other matter.

Writing articles seems not very satisfactory. I have two long ones still waiting the decision of Editors. One has been a month waiting the other 9

---

[8] The meeting with Fahy took place on 23 Feb, and on 27 Feb 1888 Fahy reported to D. J. O'Donoghue (UCD), 'I saw Sparling at the British Museum on Thursday where he introduced me to Yeats. Both looked different to what my fancy painted them.' Francis Arthur Fahy (1854–1935), poet, song-writer, and humorist, was born in Galway. After joining the Civil Service he moved to London, where in 1883 he helped found the Southwark Irish Literary Club. Later he became a member of the Irish Literary Society, London, and president of the London Gaelic League. He contributed poems and sketches to a number of Irish periodicals, sometimes under the pseudonym of 'Dreoilin', and is best known for his poem 'The Ould Plaid Shawl'. His *Irish Songs and Poems* had been published in Dublin in 1887 by M. H. Gill & Son.

[9] JBY, WBY, ECY, and Jack Yeats moved into 3 Blenheim Road on Saturday, 24 Mar 1888, and Susan Yeats and SMY returned there from Yorkshire on 13 April. JBY told JO'L in a letter of 20 Mar 1888 (NLI) that it was 'an admirable house, large and airy, with plenty of room' and that the rent was £45 p.a. WBY recalled it as 'a red-brick house with several mantelpieces of wood, copied from marble mantelpieces designed by the brothers Adam, a balcony and a little garden shadowed by a great horse-chestnut tree'. The family had lived in Bedford Park (see Appendix), at 8 Woodstock Road, from spring 1879 to mid-1881 (see *Aut*, 42–4), and WBY felt disappointed that the architecture seemed less romantic now than when 'as a schoolboy of twelve or thirteen I had played among the unfinished houses'. Nevertheless 'it had some village characters and helped us to feel not wholly lost in the metropolis'. (*Aut*, 113–14.)

months. ⟨And⟩ besides a few odd poems waiting here and there. Sorry I did not begin beseiging Editors a year or two ago, but it has been my misfortune never to have faith in success or the future. I have a few more things to do for the book—a few lines to add. Then I begin an Irish story, I do not beleive in it, but it may do for some Irish paper, and give me practice. Todhunter found Keegan Paul, on Tuesday, reading my poems, but no verdict of course yet from that quarter.

There is a robin singing the dirge of yesterdays rain outside my window—the most cheerful creature I have seen these many days, and I see only the rain that is coming.

ALS Huntington. McHugh, 47–9; Wade, 62–5.

To Katharine Tynan, 22 March [1888]

58 Eardley Crescent | South Kensington
22 March

Dear Miss Tynan

I send you the only forms I can find.

Mr O Leary told Seeley Bryers & Walker to send on 50 to me, but they never came.[1] I dare say you could get some from Mr O Leary. I will write to him about it tonight. I cannot write much now to you—as I am writing in Horne's office (Horne of the "Hobbey Horse").[2] He may be hear any time— I have been busy these last two days making up material in the British Museum reading room for a story about Father John O Hart.[3]

Horne has just come in and tells me that your poem will be in next "Hobby Horse"[4] —

[1] JBY complained to JO'L on 20 Mar 1888 (NLI) that 'Willie's forms are all exhausted—he says you told the printer to send him some long ago but they have never sent him any. . . .'

[2] Herbert Percy Horne (1864–1916), architect, art historian, and poet, was from 1887 to 1891 editor of the *Century Guild Hobby Horse* (later *The Hobby Horse*), a quarterly founded in 1883 and dedicated to the restoration of crafts and fine art; its offices were in Tooks Court, Chancery Lane. Horne designed a number of buildings, including the Church of the Redeemer in the Bayswater Road, and went on to become an authority on Italian art and especially Botticelli. WBY admired him 'for his knowledge and his taste' (*Aut*, 317) but suspected him of a leaning towards the eighteenth century and later regretted that his own youthful prejudice against that century had prevented their becoming close friends. Horne, who was later a member of the Rhymers Club, published a volume of poems, *Diversi Colores*, in 1891.

[3] This story, taken from Fr. T. O'Rorke's *History . . . of Ballysadare and Kilvarnet* (see p. 36, n. 7), 199–210, resolved itself into the poem eventually entitled 'The Ballad of Father O'Hart', published twice in 1888, in the de luxe edition of H. H. Sparling's *Irish Minstrelsy* and in *FFT*, under its first title, 'The Priest of Coloony'.

[4] KT's 'In a Cathedral' appeared in the June 1888 *Hobby Horse*.

I was at the Southwick Literary Club last night—Crilly lectured on Miss Fanny Parnell.[5]

I must finish now as I want to talk to Horne.

Your Friend

W B Yeats

I got £2 from "United Ireland" as soon as I get it changed I will send your father the 5/– I borrowed.

ALS Huntington. McHugh, 49–50; Wade, 65.

To Katharine Tynan, 11 April 1888

3 Blenheim Road | Bedford Park

April 11. 1888

My dear Miss Tynan

I send the 5/– I owe you[r] father. I was about to send it sometime ago when paid by United Ireland but their was a sudden call for money—we were changing houses—and so I have had to wait 'till now. Give him my apologies.

Last night Todhunter read out the latter part of his Dierdre. It will not be in his coming book being too long he says.[1] Which book will be out before mine. I go again to Keegan Paul this week he is away at present. My difficulty is the need of some 80 more subscribers 3/6 being the price per copy unless I take Todhunters suggestion of sending my subscribers 2 copies for their 5/– instead of one. In that way turning 200 copies at 5/– into 400 at 2/6   2/6 being about the ordinary price of a 3/6 book when you take the

---

[5] Of this, WBY's first visit to the Southwark Irish Literary Club, W. P. Ryan recalled (*The Irish Literary Revival* [1894], 29), that 'on the occasion of Mr Crilly's lecture . . . a young man found his way to the Club, who was just beginning a highly remarkable Irish literary career, and who found in the Club's proceedings an attraction which brought him over miles of London many a time afterwards, till gradually he became one of ourselves. . . . In appearance he was tall, slight, and mystic of the mystical. His face was not so much dreamy as haunting: a little weird even. . . . He spoke in a hushed, musical, eerie tone: a tone which had constant suggestions of the faery world. . . . His name was W. B. Yeats.'

Daniel Crilly (1857–1923), journalist, poet, and Irish Party Member for North Mayo 1885–1900, had recently been on trial for his part in the 'Plan of Campaign', but the jury failed to reach a verdict. Fanny Parnell (1849–82) was the favourite sister of Charles Stewart Parnell (1846–91; see Appendix), leader of the Irish Party, over whom she had a considerable influence. In the 1860s she had contributed patriotic verse to the Fenian *Irish People* over the pseudonym 'Aleria'. She was a fervent supporter of the Land League, for which she wrote in 1880 her best-known poem, 'Hold the Harvest', described by Michael Davitt (1846–1906), the League's founder, as 'the *Marseillaise* of the Irish peasant'. She died suddenly, probably of a heart attack, in Boston where she had been living for some years.

[1] i.e. 'The Fate of the Sons of Usna'; see p. 50. Todhunter explained in *The Banshee* (vii) that the poem, 'being longer than the others, and more epic in character, would rather overweight this little book'.

discount off. Not quite the price but 3 ᵈ under—Mrs Mead of Atalanta² once did much the same she says: which comforts me for I feared it somewhat unceremonius as well as a losing arrangement exausting my whole edition but 100. I may manage otherwise. Keegan Paul seems to think June time enough to be out. So can wait a bit. perhap[s] I will reduce the size of the book. At any rate 3/6 is likely to be the price. A 5/– book should be over 200 pages. I will decide this week and write after seeing Keegan Paul. Whatever be decided on I will submit to O'Leary for his opinion he having got so many names for me. If it comes to lightening the ship I will hardly know what to throw over board—the "*Seaker*" for one thing I fear & "*Farencz Renyi*" the Irish poems must all be kept, making the personality of the book—or as few thrown over as may be.³

I am reading up for my romance—Eighteenth century all day long. I should dream of it only I do not dream much. I am very cheerful over it. Making my romance I have so much affirmative in me that even that little wretch Sparling with his atheisms and negations does not make me meloncholy or irritable when I meet him in the British Museum. I have gone there every day for some time. Today I did not go feeling tired after Todhunters. After breakfast I got out on the roof under the balcony and arranged a creeper that climbs over it. Every thing seemed so delighted at the going of the east wind—so peaceful and delighted. It all most seemed that if you listened you could hear the sap rising in the branches—bubble bubble. Later on I read Mitchel. I must have my mind full of that century.⁴ Tomorrow I read old magazines of the period I have a long list of them.

Jack had his first printed drawing the other day in the "Vegetarian" a drawing of Fairies. There will be another this week. I will try and get you a copy. He has also a gossipy paper sent him to illustrate—on a country house⁵—

I send you a copy of Morris' play it is a little soiled as it is one of the copies

---

² Elizabeth Thomasina Toulmin Smith, née Meade (*c.* 1844–1914), a prolific author of children's books under the name of 'L. T. Meade', was born at Bandon, Co. Cork; she married Alfred Toulmin Smith, a solicitor, in 1879. WBY probably made her acquaintance through his father who illustrated a serial by her for *Atalanta* (see p. 49), of which she was co-editor.

³ 'The Seeker. A Dramatic Poem—in Two Scenes' (*VP*, 681–5) had been published in *DUR*, September 1885; both it and 'How Ferencz Renyi Kept Silent' were eventually included in *Oisin*—whose price remained 5s—but not afterwards reprinted by WBY.

⁴ John Mitchel's *History of Ireland from the Treaty of Limerick to the Present Time* (New York, 1868; London, 1869) would have given WBY a great deal of information about Irish politics in the eighteenth century—although his romance, *John Sherman*, was finally set in the late nineteenth century.

⁵ Jack Yeats had been introduced to the *Vegetarian* on 26 Mar 1888 by his friend Rolly Hall (Jack Yeats's diary, MBY), and began sketching for the paper then. His illustrations to 'The Elves' Polo Match' appeared in the *Vegetarian's* 'Children's Corner' on 7 Apr 1888 (13). An occasional series, 'Diary of Diogenes Dustbin, F. R. S., While Staying in a Country House in the Year 1887', which he illustrated, first appeared in the *Vegetarian* on 16 June 1888; there were further instalments on 30 June and 25 Aug.

used by the actors—no others being to be had. He is writing another—of the middle ages this time.[6] Horn of the *Hobby horse* tells me that Christina Rossetti has a wonderfully high opinion of your poetry, and also says your poem will come out next *Hobby horse*.

As to the matter of the copy of the picture. I will try or get my father to make a sketch of me. But wait till this reading is over.

On Thursday Mamma & Lilly come home.

I met John Burns & his wife at Morris's sunday evening—a fine black bearded man full of zeal—A sailor once—denounced Leightons pictures. The reason came out after a bit. The paddle of the boat in the *Arts of peace* at South Kensington was much too large.[7]

I will write no more now as I meen to let you know when I have seen Keegan Paul.

Yours Affectionately

W B Yeats

PS. Todhunters *Dierdre* is fine in everything but Dierdre herself. He has made her too querulous and complaining and modern—No ancient placidity of nerves about her at all.[8]

ALS Huntington. McHugh, 50–2; Wade, 66–7.

[6] William Morris's *The Tables Turned; or, Nupkins Awakened: a Socialist Interlude*, first performed at the Hall of the Socialist League on 15 Oct 1887, was published the following week. His play of the Middle Ages was never written.

[7] John Elliot Burns (1858–1943), an ebullient orator and working-class leader, became one of the first Labour MPs and was President of the Board of Trade in 1914. He had served six weeks' imprisonment earlier in 1888 for his part in the demonstration in Trafalgar Square on 'Bloody Sunday', 13 Nov 1887, on behalf of free speech and in protest at coercion in Ireland, and at this time was weakened by this experience and by the imminent prospect of dismissal from his engineering job because of his political views. He had never been a sailor as such, but had spent some time in Africa with the Niger Company and had travelled widely on river craft. His marriage in 1882 to Martha Charlotte ('Pattie') Gale (1860–1936), the daughter of a shipwright, may have enhanced his view of himself as a nautical man. The fresco, *The Industrial Arts of Peace*, by Sir Frederic Leighton (1830–96), President of the Royal Academy, shows a classical Greek house opening on to a waterfront where a highly decorative skiff, with two large paddles resting athwart it, is secured by an ornate looped chain. The fresco, with its companion, *The Industrial Arts of War*, filled large lunettes in the central court of the then South Kensington Museum.

[8] WBY is perhaps suggesting that Todhunter's conception of Deirdre is based upon his second wife, Dora Louisa Digby (*c.* 1853–1935), who seems to have shared these characteristics. Todhunter had married this ardent feminist, according to JBY (letter to SMY of 14 Nov 1916, MBY) a 'she-dragon of contention', in 1879. She had been a student, 1868–72, at Alexandra College, Dublin, where he was Professor of English from 1870 to 1877.

To D. J. O'Donoghue,[1] *17 April* [*1888*]

3 Blenheim Road | Bedford Park
17 April

My dear O Donoghue

I did not write before as it was not possible to answer your questions without seeing Keegan Paul, who I was to have seen some days ago, however he has been out of town till yesterday, when I saw him. Nothing very definite is yet decided 3/6 as far as I can see, will be the price. Things are still somewhat hazy. Keegan Paul will most likely be my publisher—even that you see is not certain. I will not know till I get his estimate which he promises in a few days. In the meanwhile subscribers names should be sent to me. I have had some subscription forms printed I send some. The 3/6 will not be asked for 'till the book is out—a month or six weeks hence, if all goes right.

The contents of the book will be in a great part Irish in matter—old legends and such like, mixed with a good many poems on general subjects. A great many thanks for your kind offer of a subscriber or two. I hope to see more of your Southwick Club but am somewhat occupied these present evenings.

Yours Sincerely
W B Yeats

ALS Private.

To Katharine Tynan, 20 April 1888

3 Blenheim Road | Bedford Park
20th April 1888

My dear Miss Tynan

I saw Keegan Paul on Monday. 3/6 as the price seems decided on. However nothing is decided on, until I get his final estimate which he promises in a few days. Also he has to read through the poems which it

---

[1] David James O'Donoghue (1866–1917), born in London of Cork parents, was at this time a leading light in the Southwark Irish Literary Club, and was evidently drumming up subscriptions for *Oisin* among the members. In 1892 he was to help WBY set up the Irish Literary Society, London, and in the same year produced the first edition of his compendious *Poets of Ireland*. At that time he was described in *United Ireland*, 23 Jan 1892 (1), as 'short and stout . . . He talked businessly [*sic*], brusquely, bluntly. I was not surprised . . . to learn that he was a self-educated man, and that by his own marvellous energy he has lifted himself from the position of an artisan to that of a litterateur and a scholar'. In 1896 O'Donoghue moved to Dublin, where he set up as a bookseller. He published biographies of William Carleton (1896) and Robert Emmet (Dublin, 1902), and a *Life and Writings of J. C. Mangan* (1897).

seems he has not yet done. If I act on that suggestion of giving three copies to the two copy people for their 10/– and so on with the four copy people &c I have close on sufficient copies subscribed for.

If Keegan Paul and I do not come to terms I may miss the season though I should be printed cheaper elsewhere I am told.

Last night I went with Mrs Todhunter to a meeting of a woman's political association. An invitation I accepted in sheer absence of mind. Having no knowledge of the fact till Mrs Todhunter told me of it. However I there heard your friend Tom Gill making a speach.[1] He is not much used to speaking I imagine. his sentences come out rustily. I talked for a few minutes to another friend of yours—Miss Mabel Robinson. But too short a time to learn anything of herself or her opinions. I hear a novel of hers called *Disillusion* much and often praised by Mrs Todhunter.[2] I have not so far been able to get you any of Jack's drawings in the *Vegetarian* but will order them today at the Railway bookstall. He has had a great many taken, only three have yet come out.[3] Tuesday I had one of my collapses having done over much walking and over much reading lately I suppose—I walk much of the way to the British Museum. I stoped therefore at home that day and being under orders to do little reading, planted seeds in pots all round the balcony, sweetpeas, convolvolus, nastertums, and such like—an[d] in the garden a great many sun flowers to the indignation of Lilly & Jack who have no love for that modest & retiring plant. Do you remember how they used to mock at me because years ago when we were hear before, I said I would have a forest of sunflowers & an underwood of *Love Lies Bleeding* and there were only three sunflowers after all. Well I am having my revenge. I planted the forest and am trying to get the *Love Lies Bleeding* & they say they dont like *Love Lies Bleeding* a bit. I thought I was in for a considerable collapse. but it wore off. I could only speak with difficulty at first. I was the same way only worse when finishing *Oisin*. How the robins & sparrows in the virginia creeper are singing away. When you read this—if you read it in your study—your robins will be singing away likewise may be and the sparrows chirping. Mine are all busy making their nests carrying away small twigs from off the balcony and sometimes tugging at a grass blade in the garden

[1] Thomas Patrick Gill (1858–1931), journalist and politician, born in Tipperary. He had been editor of the *Catholic World* in New York, to which KT contributed, before becoming Irish Party Member for South Louth, 1885–92. A man of moderation, Gill retired from politics following the Parnellite split. In the late 1890s he edited the Dublin *Daily Express* with flair, and from 1900 to 1923 was Secretary of the Department of Agriculture and Technical Instruction for Ireland.

[2] The novelist Frances Mabel Robinson (b. 1858) was interested in Irish affairs, and under the pseudonym 'William Stephenson Gregg' published *Irish History for English Readers* (1886). Her novel, *Disenchantment* (not '*Disillusion*') appeared in 1884. Her more successful sister, Agnes M. F. Robinson, married James Darmesteter, the French scholar.

[3] See p. 59, n. 5. Two further sketches, one signed 'Jack', were printed in the *Vegetarian* on 14 Apr 1888 (24, 28).

underneath. I wonder what religion they have. When I was a child and used to watch the ants running about in Burnham Beeches I used often to say "what religion do the ants have?" They must have one you know.[4] Yet perhaps not. Perhaps like the Arabs they have not time. Well they must have some notion of the making of the world. I must now go to work. Write me a long letter as much about your self and your thoughts and your work as you can.

Your Friend
W B Yeats

Many thanks for the forms.

ALS Huntington. McHugh, 52–4; Wade, 68–9.

To Ellen O'Leary,[1] 1 May [1888]

3. Blenheim Road | Bedford Park
1st of May

Dear Miss O Leary

When your letter came I had just been considering the question whether I had or not, acknowledged the latest batch of forms. I could not for the life of me remember nor can I now. I have—if I adopt the suggested arangement with the 2 & 3 copy people—close on a sufficiency but cannot say for certain until I get Keegan Pauls final estimate. He is very dilatory about it.

The English Illustrated has refused my Fairy article[2] bad luck to them. I shall try elsewhere, where I do not yet know.

I read the "proofs" of Todhunters book yesterday—the "Children of Lir" and "Sons of Turann" are quite wonderful all most like Fergusson. They will become Irish classics I beleive. Our ballad book should be ready be this surely. Will they send me my six copies—six is it not?—or must I write for them?[3] I am very anxious to see it. Have been watching the post, there for, these last days.

---

[4] For Burnham Beeches see p. 3; and cf. 'The Indian upon God', *DUR*, October 1886 (*VP*, 76–7).

[1] See p. 13.

[2] Apparently the article 'nearly 50 MSS pages long' (see p. 47) which was later to appear in the *Leisure Hour*.

[3] Count Plunkett dated the copy of *PBYI* that he gave to his wife '1 May 1888' (*Bibl*, 254), the earliest recorded date for the book. In a letter to WBY of 25 Mar [1888] (Belfast), Miss O'Leary had explained that Plunkett and Rolleston 'think twould be better have the expense of printing [*PBYI*] share and share alike & to have every contributor have the privilege of sending names for six copies to be sent to friends, or whoever one wishes. Any further copies contributors must pay for. That is all fair I think the system of paying according to the amount of space one occupies would hardly work, twould be confusing.'

I was at a big "Home Rule" party at a Mrs Hancoks Saturday. Mrs Gladstone was there and made a speach, a very short one, likewise Stransfield, Justin Macarthy, & Lord Aberdeen made speeches long or short.[4] All these good English Home Rule people how they do patronise Ireland and the Irish. As if we were some new sort of deserving poor for whom bazars and such like should be got up. Yet they are really in earnest on this Home Rule question I think.

I have been twice at the french class at Morrises.[5] A queer jumble its is of all sorts of scholors from Sparling who does'nt know a word of French to one or two quite instructed. William Morris himself has not joined us yet but may be expected next time or next after. It is rather amusing every one tries to talk French whether they know any or not. [*Last line and signature crossed out*]

AL Harvard. Wade, 69–70.

[4] At a political conversazione held at the residence of Mr and Mrs Charles Hancock, 125 Queens Gate, South Kensington, on 28 Apr 1888, Mrs Gladstone, the principal guest, conveyed in a short speech her husband's regrets at not being able to attend owing to fatigue, and spoke of his delight at the Liberal victory in the Mid-Lanarkshire by-election. Sir James Stansfeld (1820–98), Liberal MP for Halifax, 1859–95, a Lord of the Admiralty 1863–4, Under-Secretary for India in 1866, and a Lord of the Treasury 1868–9, was reported as having made some vigorous remarks on the present position of the Liberal Party. In his speech Justin McCarthy said that the Irish 'would be content with nothing short of managing their own domestic and national affairs for themselves without interfering with imperial matters'.

The other speaker mentioned by WBY, Sir John Campbell Hamilton-Gordon, Earl (later Marquess) of Aberdeen (1847–1934), had been Lord-Lieutenant of Ireland from January to July 1886. His brief was to carry out a policy of Home Rule, and he was extremely popular in Ireland until the fall of Gladstone's Government cut short his appointment. He subsequently became Governor-General of Canada (1893–8) and was again Lord-Lieutenant of Ireland, under less happy circumstances, from 1905 to 1915.

About 300 people were present at the conversazione, including WBY's future publisher, Charles Kegan Paul, W. M. Rossetti, T. P. Gill, and Mr and Mrs Oscar Wilde. The host, Charles Hancock, a cousin of Lord Castlemaine, was killed a month later by being thrown from a sidecar.

[5] In *Aut* (143–4) WBY recalls that soon after he began to attend lectures at Morris's, 'a French class was started in the old coach-house for certain young Socialists who planned a tour in France, and I joined it, and was for a time a model student constantly encouraged by the compliments of the old French mistress.' Then his sisters joined the class and he lost his enthusiasm, being once more but 'a figure in the comedy of domestic life' (*Mem*, 20). He continued his attendance until at least 18 Jan 1889 when ECY recorded in her diary (MBY):

went to French . . . Willie's dramatic intence way of saying his french with his voice raised to telling distinctness & every pronounciation wrong as usual, seemed to amuse Mr. Sparling more than ever, he simply doubled up when Willie commenced. Willie of course divided it up into any amount of full stops where there were not any so Madame said "Mr. Yagtes you dont read poetry like that do you."

"Yes he does Yes he does" volounteered Mr. Sparling & in truth he was rather like his natural way of reading.

To Katharine Tynan, [early] May [1888]

3 Blenheim Road | Bedford Park
May

My dear Miss Tynan

I enclose list of *errata* in Todhunters poems. He wishes if possible to have it printed on a slip of paper and gummed in the books. I have added one mistake in King Goll.[1] It is a pity to give you so much trouble but I do not know who it should be sent to else. I offered to send it as I was writing. Every body praises the book. Todhunter, Edwin Ellis York Powel the historien, Stevens of the Leisure Hour,[2] are the most notable I have heard speak of it. York Powell when I saw him, the day after I think he had been given his copy by Todhunter, had read it all and had written the names of the contributors after the names of poems in the "Contents" which shows interest.[3] You and Douglas Hyde seem to have interested him more especially. Your "Shameen Dhu" pleased him much. He also praised "The Story of Clessamnor" as did Todhunter who is greatly pleased with the book. "St Michans Churchyard" Todhunter praised also. Of course the dedicatory poem is liked by every one. I read out Rollestons "Dead at Clonmacnoise" to Edwin Ellis who said it was like "Victor Hugo".[4] Poor Dr Sigersons

[1] An errata slip inserted in some copies of the first edition of *PBYI* and in the reissue of 1890, listed corrections in Todhunter's 'Under the White-Boy Acts, 1800' and one in WBY's 'King Goll' (where 'lilt' had been printed for 'lift').

[2] Frederick York Powell (1850–1904), a don at Christ Church and Regius Professor of Modern History at Oxford University from 1894, lived at 6 Priory Gardens, Bedford Park, 1881–1902, and contrived to spend as much time there as his Oxford duties would allow. His wife had recently died and he was left with a small daughter. He quickly became friends with JBY who saw him (*JBYL*, 79) as 'a winged and aspiring Celt captured and put into the cage of an Oxford Donship'. WBY (*Aut*, 117–18) describes him as 'a broad-built, broad-headed, brown-bearded man clothed in heavy blue cloth and looking, but for his glasses and the dim sight of a student, like some captain in a Merchant Service'; unlike his father, WBY found himself 'too full of unfinished speculations and premature convictions to value rightly' Powell's conversation.

William Stevens (d. 1900), editor of the *Leisure Hour* 1888–1900, also edited *Sunday at Home* and was the author of *The Truce of God and Other Poems* (1879). 'Mr Stevens', wrote JBY to WBY on 3 Sept 1900 (MBY), 'was your first employer, and he has been a wonderful friend to me'; and later (to WBY, 20 Dec 1900, MBY): 'he is really so broadminded and loves ideas more than anybody I ever met.'

[3] Of the poems in *PBYI*, 5 were by Hyde; 4 each by WBY, Todhunter, and Rolleston; 3 each by KT, Rose Kavanagh, and Ellen O'Leary; 2 by F. J. Gregg; and 1 each by George Sigerson ('Patrick Henry'), Mrs Sigerson, Charles Gregory Fagan, and George Noble Plunkett.

[4] In KT's dialect poem, 'Shameen Dhu' (*PBYI*, 40–3), an Irish countryman recalls his old friend, evicted and obliged to leave home and sweetheart, to be heard of no more. The poem was republished in the *Boston Pilot* 8 Mar 1890. 'The Story of Clessamnor', a ballad by Charles Gregory Fagan (1860–85), tells how an Irish chieftain fights and kills his own son before realizing who he is. KT had probably sponsored its inclusion in *PBYI* after the early death of its author, whom she first met in 1882 at the Irish Exhibition. He had fascinated KT, who saw much of him during her trip to England in the spring of 1884, before he went out to India as a schoolmaster and died there the next year. She remembered him as 'full of poetry and all manner of artistic impulses . . . Of a life which might have been tranquil, he made storm and stress. He was over-wrought and too much unlike the pushing thronging world to be at his ease

"Exiles Return" is least cared for perhaps yet there are one or two good lines only it is a little confused. The book is certainly interesting. My remaining copy has been much read, it is continually in some ones hands, my fathers more especially. He praises your landscape bits in "Michael Dwyer". He says you describe beautifully rich arrable land such as lies about your own house. he objected a little to the word "amethyst" which you use, thinking I suppose that it spoilt the simplicity[5]—I need not say I admire the book and your choice in binding. If there is anything I object to, it is the conventional and badly drawn little harp in the corner & I do not object much to that.

Will you let me see the reviews. I will show them to Todhunter. How many copies do we get. Miss O'Leary said six I only got three as did Todhunter.

I have not seen the Irish Monthly, nor have I since leaving Dublin. I would much like to see it, for your poem's sake,[6] and also because it always interests me in itself. I hope you will give or lend me a copy. Your recent poems have been beutiful, any you send me, so full of calm and temperence as well as the old qualities of energy and beauty. I think you will be right to make your ballad Irish, you will be so much more origonal—one should have a speciality. You have yours in Ireland and your Religion. I cannot now think of a subject but will be on the look out—perhaps in the Sarsfield age their was something. There are many in Hayse's Ballads—which you will remember are printed according to the dates of their events. You might rehandle one of them.[7]

in it.' (*25 Years*, 152.) 'St. Michan's Churchyard', by Rose Kavanagh, a description in *terza rima* of the Dublin graveyard where Robert Emmet was laid without epitaph, is one of her most accomplished poems. The anonymous dedicatory poem, 'To John O'Leary', has been identified as being by T. W. Rolleston (see C. H. Rolleston, *Portrait of an Irishman* [1939], 141). WBY republished 'The Dead at Clonmacnois', a translation from the Irish of Enoch O'Gillan and Rolleston's best poem, in *BIV*.

[5] KT's 'The Grave of Michael Dwyer' (*PBYI*, 7–11), first published in the *Nation*, 9 Jan 1886, is a lament for the rebel of the 1798 rising who died, exiled from Ireland, and is buried in Sydney, Australia. KT imagines Dwyer restless in his grave because it is set in an alien landscape, and recalling the Irish countryside:

> The air blew soft from the late-mown meadows
>   Faint with the fragrant hay;
> Clear the blackbird piped in shadows,
>   And all in the twilight, dewy and grey,
>   The thrush was singing her heart away.
>
> The hills stood up in the summer weather,
>   Veiled with a fiery mist;
> Gold and purple blent on the heather,
>   Rose and silver and amethyst,
>   On the mystic peaks that the sunlight kissed.

Her use of the word 'amethyst' suggests the poetic influence of AE, of whom she had been seeing a good deal at this time.

[6] KT's 'St. Francis and the Wolf' appeared in the *Irish Monthly*, May 1888.

[7] Poems about Patrick Sarsfield (*c.* 1650–93) would have combined KT's Irish and Catholic interests,

"Evelyn Pyne" has turned up as a writer of poems in Lucifer they think no end of "Mr Pyne" as they call her. One man on the staff is quite enthusiastic has bought both her books and compares her metre to Swinburne. Has had quite considerable corrispondence with her, never dreaming she was not "Evelyn Pyne Esq". He is the Editor of the new Wagner journal the "Meister".[8]

I also am writing a short story—it goes on fairly well the style quite sane and the theme modern, more character than plot in it.[9] Because of this I have not been going into the Museum of late but will do so shortly—tomorrow most likely. So absorbed have I been I really forgot about Miss Probyn 'till this moment.[10]

The little poem—I should have come to it before—is beautiful. My father is also delighted with it. I think you have made a new start foreward lately, as for me I am stationary or advancing only on the side of prose.

I hope all your people are well. What fine weather this is—all green leaves coming out.

Yours Ever
W B Yeats

ALS Huntington. McHugh, 54–5; Wade, 70–2.

since he led James II's Irish troops against the Protestant William of Orange and successfully defended Limerick against him. The 2-vol. *Ballads of Ireland* (1855), collected and edited by Edward Hayes, is divided into 10 sections and the poems in the 'Historical' section, though by different hands, are arranged in the chronology of their historical subject matter. KT did not take up WBY's suggestion and, although many of the poems in her next book, *Ballads and Lyrics*, have Irish themes, none are set in Sarsfield's age.

[8] 'Evelyn Pyne' was the pseudonym of Evelyn May Noble (b. 1853), daughter of a nurseryman, who took her *nom de plume* from her address, The Pines, Bagshot, Surrey. KT had begun a correspondence with her early in 1885, having got to know her through a friend of Charles Fagan, and went to stay with her in November 1885; thereafter she contributed many poems to the *Irish Monthly*, and reviewed KT's *Louise de la Vallière* there in July 1885. On 15 Apr 1888 the Theosophical Society monthly, *Lucifer*, edited at that time by HPB and Mabel Collins, published three poems by 'Evelyn Pyne', and an unsigned article in the same issue gave an enthusiastic notice to her first book, *A Dream of the Gironde and Other Poems* (1877), but referred to her throughout as 'Mr Pyne'. The article did not in fact compare her to Swinburne (WBY may have associated her pseudonym and address with The Pines, Putney, where Swinburne was now living under the care of Theodore Watts-Dunton) but to Shelley: 'We are often forcibly reminded, in reading these lines, of the greatest nature poet, Shelley' (167). The writer was evidently Dr William Ashton Ellis (d. 1919), MRCS, LRCP, a member of the London Lodge of the Theosophical Society and the biographer and translator of Richard Wagner. *The Meister* was the quarterly journal of the London branch of the Wagner Society, published February 1888–November 1895.

[9] *John Sherman* had now become a story on a 'modern' theme.

[10] Some months before, on 22 Sept 1887, KT had written to Wilfrid Meynell (Hinkson): 'Can you tell me how to get at Miss May Probyn's poetry—or at herself if you don't know about the poetry? A visitor I have just had, Mr Alfred Williams, editor of the Providence *Journal*, a huge ten-sheet American daily, has just given me an order for some literary articles for his Sunday issue; the first to be on *Preludes*, the second Miss Probyn, and the rest according to my pleasure.' May Probyn (1856–1909), born in Wales, the daughter of an Anglican clergyman, and educated in Brussels, was converted to Catholicism in 1883 after reading Newman's *Discourses to Mixed Congregations*. Thereafter she devoted much of her time to

To D. J. O'Donoghue, 19 May [1888]

3 Blenheim Road | Bedford Park
May 19.

Dear Mr O Donaghue

I shall be very glad to lecture. I have a never delivered lecture on the "Folk lore of the West of Ireland" already written; so I am ready for any date you name.[1]

My book owing to a mistake of Keegan Pauls has been delayed too long for this spring season, it will not come out till early autumn.

The little ballad book you mention, is a joint matter got up by a dozen or so of us; Rolleston, Duglas Hyde ("An Chraoibin Aoibhinn") Miss Tynan, Dr Sigerson ("Patrick Henry") and a few more. Dr Todhunter also contributes some good poems. By the way I shall bring him down to one of your meetings I think. He is very Irish and interests himself much in the early romances, is bringing out a volume with poems on "Children of Lir" Etc.

I saw Sparling last night he had not yet heard from you, but I mentioned to him your intention to ask him to lecture. He will do so gladly.[2]

I shall be down at meeting you mention most likely.

Yours
W B Yeats

PS. Sparling is I beleive to edit Mangan. I have some intention of doing "Folk Lore" book as you say. But the editor of series is in America and I wait his return to decide some matters about it.[3] He asked me some while since but I am waiting to talk over details.

ALS Buffalo. Wade, 73–4.

placing orphaned children in convents. An invalid and a recluse, she moved from Devizes to South Street, Park Lane, London, to be near her spiritual adviser; KT was to call upon her there in June 1889, and the two struck up a literary friendship which led to a joint collection of poems, *Christmas Verses*, published by the Catholic Truth Society in 1895. KT did not publish an article on Miss Probyn in *PSJ*, although her article on Alice Meynell's *Preludes* (1875) had appeared there on 12 Feb 1888.

[1] WBY's lecture at the Southwark Irish Literary Club took place on 13 June 1888.

[2] Sparling replied to O'Donoghue's invitation in a letter of 3 June 1888 (Private): 'I shall be most happy to lecture for the Club on the 27th inst on "Irish Minstrelsy" and count it an honour to be asked to do so. Next Wednesday I have promised to attend Mr Yeats' lecture if I can, but rather fear that I shall have to go elsewhere.' In fact he spoke twice to the Club in this year, for on 12 Dec 1888 WBY chaired his lecture on 'The Literature of '98'.

[3] Sparling did not produce an edition of Mangan, but O'Donoghue himself was to publish a useful 'Centenary Edition' of Mangan's poems in 1903. Ernest Rhys, editor of the Camelot Classics, returned from America in June.

To Katharine Tynan, 19 May [*1888*]

3 Blenheim Road | Bedfor[d] Park
May 19

Dear Miss Tynan

I send at last Miss Probyns publishers names. I could not send it before as my father was very anxious for me to go on with my story, so I was not in town at all.

This is the list.

> A Ballad of the Road and other poems.   1883
> > W Satchell & Co. London.
>
> Who Killed Cock Robin (a tale)   1880
> > Literary Production Committee   London.
>
> Robert Treselian (a story)   1880
> > The Sea Side Annual.
>
> Once! Twice! Thrice! and Away! (a novel)   1878
> > Remington & Co. London.[1]

I saw Mr Ranking at last. He wished to be remembered to you. I showed him the ballad book. He will review it[2] but has not yet got it. I suppose it will be sent.

By the way. A few people like Aubrey de Vere, Gavan Duffy &c might perhaps be sent copies from the common stock. Do you not think so? As we have each so few. "St Francis & the Wolf" is beautiful—most beutiful—it is one of your very best it has all the beuties of your new manner like "St Francis to the Birds". My father, and indeed we all are, is delighted with it. It is so temperate and *naive* and simple. Like "St Francis to the Birds" & "Fianula" it has a peculiar kind of tenderness[3] which I think you only among contempories understand. It comes from your religion I suppose, yet

---

[1] See p. 67. *A Ballad of the Road* contained poems written before Miss Probyn's conversion, and she subsequently withdrew and burned the edition because of what she felt to be slighting references to Catholic priests in one of the poems.

[2] An unsigned notice in the *Graphic*, 9 June 1888, praised *PBYI* as a 'small, but almost superlatively charming volume', and singled out the poems of WBY 'who ought to have a future before him', and those of Rolleston, Todhunter, and KT whom 'it is a treat to meet with . . . again' (611). This review, evidently by Ranking, led JO'L, writing to WBY on 8 Sept 1888 (NLI), to hope that future British reviewers of the book would not be 'such horrible logrollers as Graphic fellow, who saw nobody in book but his three acquaintances and saw them far too well. The praises of you might in a sense pass but laudation of Miss T induces lows. Her things there have little or no merit: she only gave you her tenth best—or worst.'

[3] 'St. Francis and the Wolf', one of several poems KT wrote about the saint, tells how St. Francis tamed in Christ's name a wolf that had been terrorizing the town of Agobio. Fionnuala was the daughter of Lir; in KT's poem 'The Children of Lir' (to which WBY is presumably referring) she acts as mother to her brothers after they have all been changed into swans by their stepmother. WBY was to include both 'St. Francis and the Birds' and 'The Children of Lir' in *BIV*.

I do not find it in other Catholic poetry. Even in your poetry, I think, it has only come this last year or so.

My story goes well the plot is laid mainly in Sligo. It deels more with charecter than incidents. Sparling praised it much thinks my skill lies more in charecter drawing than incidents.

I have been asked to Lecture on Irish Folk Lore at the "Southwick Litterary club" in June.

I had almost forgot to tell you that through a mistake of Keegan Paul's my book will have to wait till Autumn worse luck.

I sent a short while ago an article on Allingham to Providence Journal.[4] I hope they will return it if not suitable. I think it is moderately good.

I read your little Eighteenth Century poem to Mr Ranking. He liked it I think, as did my father. Did I speak of it in my last letter. It is a very pretty little song.[5]

Good wishes to all

Yours Ever
W B Yeats

Sparling reviews Ballad Book in "Commonweal".[6]

ALS Huntington. McHugh, 56–7; Wade, 72–3.

To Katharine Tynan, [c. 15] June [1888]

3 Blenheim Road | Bedford Park
June

My dear Miss Tynan

I have got that book of selected fairy tales to do for the Camelot Classics. It must be done by the end of July.[1] The time is too short to make a really good book I fear. I hope to get Davis to edit in Canterbury Poets.[2] I have not

---

[4] 'The Poet of Ballyshannon', WBY's review of *Irish Songs and Poems* by William Allingham (1824–89), appeared in *PSJ*, 2 Sept 1888. Allingham, who served for many years in the customs service and after his retirement edited *Fraser's Magazine*, 1874–9, became a friend of Tennyson, Patmore, and the Pre-Raphaelites. He published several volumes of verse, including *Day and Night Songs* (1854), and a long poem on the Land Question, *Laurence Bloomfield in Ireland* (1864).

[5] 'The Blackbird', mentioned in an earlier letter (see p. 67).

[6] Apart from an occasional item, 'Literary Notes', which dealt with socialist writings, the *Commonweal* carried no book reviews.

[1] *FFT* was published in late September 1888.

[2] Thomas Osborne Davis (1814–45), poet, leader of the Young Irelanders, and founder in 1842 with Charles Gavan Duffy and John Dillon of *The Nation*, which rapidly became an influential voice of nationalist opinion. JO'L was a disciple of Davis's and had introduced WBY to his work. As WBY's recent article on Allingham (see above) shows, he at this time valued Davis for the nationalism of his

yet asked but will if this fairy book looks well when done. All this—the fairy book & plans for Davis book—is not much liked by my father who does not wish me to do critical work. He wants me to write stories. I am working at one as you know. It is almost done now. Their is some good charecter drawing I think, but the construction is patchy and incoherent. I have not much hope of it. It will join I fear my ever multiplying boxes of unsaleable MSS—work to[o] strange at one moment and to[o] incoherent the next for any first class Magazine and too ambitious for local papers. Yet I dont know that it is ambition for I have no wish but to write a saleable story. Ambitious no—I am as easily pleased as a mouse in the wainscot and am only anxious to get along without being false to my literary notions of what is good. I shall only get seven guineas for this fairy book but it is very pleasent working for a certainty. Can you send me any suggestions? I am at present extracting tales from Croker, Carleton and Kennedy. Do like a good Katherine search up suggestions for me. I have written to Rolleston for Lady Wildes book. Do you know any others or of any odd tales anywhere? There was a book of Irish fairy tales announced about a month ago in the Pell Mell do you remember its name &c?[3] My lecture on Sligo fairies at the Southwick Irish Literary Club went off merrily. Todhunter took the chair. Lady Wilde, not being able to come herself, sent a folklore specialist a big placid clergiman called Ponsonby Lyon.[4]

poetry; soon he was to find him too propagandist and so careless in technique as to be a dangerous model, although he always respected his magnanimity and honesty. No edition of Davis's poems appeared in the Canterbury Poets, but in 1890 T.W. Rolleston edited the prose writings for the Camelot series.

[3] The Irish novelist William Carleton (1794–1869) was best known for his *Traits and Stories of the Irish Peasantry* (Dublin, 1830; 2nd series, 1833), and for the later *Tales and Sketches, Illustrating the Character . . . of the Irish Peasantry* (Dublin, 1845). The Dublin bookseller and folklorist Patrick Kennedy (1801–73), born in Wexford, sometimes used the pseudonym 'Harry Whitney'; his most popular collections were *Legendary Fictions of the Irish Celts* (1866) and *The Fireside Stories of Ireland* (Dublin, 1870). Lady Jane Francesca Wilde (1824–96), mother of Oscar Wilde, had contributed much ardently nationalist verse to the *Nation* in the 1840s under the name 'Speranza'. The book WBY had asked for was her 2-vol. *Ancient Legends, Mystic Charms, and Superstitions of Ireland* (1887). On 7 Apr 1888 the *Pall Mall Gazette* announced (3) as forthcoming Oscar Wilde's *Five Fairy Tales*, and WBY, who had not yet met Wilde, probably assumed that any tales by the son of two distinguished Irish folklorists would have been taken from Irish tradition. Although he had now forgotten that the book was by Wilde, the mention of Lady Wilde in the previous sentence had perhaps awakened a subliminal association.

[4] Ryan (29–30) describes the occasion: 'Some of us thought till then that we had a very tolerable acquaintance with the ways and doings of the Irish fairies, but Yeats's lecture (of course it was on the good people) was something of a revelation to us—in fact he spoke as one who took his information first-hand. His only error was to speak unduly of the *soulths* and *sheogues* of his own county, but the South had a sturdy champion in John Augustus O'Shea, who gave it as his experience that there were more fairies on a square foot of Knockshegowna [in Tipperary] than in all the County Sligo.'

Todhunter Ryan remembered as 'a gifted Irishman . . . destined to be a comrade later on'. The Revd Ponsonby Annesley Lyons (1829–95) was an antiquarian and an editor of the 'Master of the Rolls' series. WBY does not seem to have known that Lyons was a friend and correspondent of KT's, having met her during her first visit to London in 1884.

I must write in this letter no more bookish news as I know you think me too little interested in other things. The real fact of the matter is that the other things at present for many reasons make me anxious[5] and I bury my head in books as the ostridge does in the sand. I am a much more human person than you think. I cannot help being "Unhuman" as you call it, these times. On the rare occasions when I go to see any one I am not quite easy in my mind for I keep thinking I ought to be at home trying to solve my problems—I feel as if I had run away from school. So you see my life is altogeather ink and paper. But it is hard to go on industriously writing for the MSS boxes. It tends to bring about a state of things when one is too idle to be industrious and too industrious to idle. However I am exemplery at present. I really do at most times a fair amount of work I think, & have written lately everything with a practical intention. Nothing for the mere pleasure of writing, not a single scrap of a poem all these months.

We have a little cousin staying with us Gereldine by name[6] she & Jack keep up a continual joking together. At dinner they have to be kept quiet almost by force. At the end of our garden is a pleasent shady place between a beech tree & a chesnut. Jack has put up a hammock there.

He has another batch of drawings in the Vegetarian and is going next Saturday to a picnic given by the Vegetarian Society I think, to make sketches for the paper.[7]

I have nothing new about Miss Noble (is she married yet?) not having seen my informant of Lucifer, except that the first of two articles on her poetry came out in a late number. I dont know whether I told you that the very simple minded musician who reviews and is so enthusiastic about her blushed when he was told "Mr Pyne" was a lady. Her poems in Lucifer are quite long.[8] I have not read them.

Father Fitzpatrick[9] has not yet turned up I shall be delighted if he does.

In looking over your letter I see you are in hot water with Miss Johnston

[5] His mother's illness and the chronic shortage of money in the house were two reasons for WBY's anxiety.

[6] This was Geraldine Elizabeth Mary Orr (*c.* 1876–1940), eldest daughter of WBY's aunt Elizabeth Pollexfen Orr.

[7] The first instalment of the 'Diogenes Dustbin' illustrations (see p. 59) appeared in the *Vegetarian* on 16 June 1888. Jack Yeats records (diary, MBY) going on *Vegetarian* picnics on 16 June and on 30 June 1888.

[8] Although a further article on 'Evelyn Pyne's' poetry had been promised in the *Lucifer* of 15 Apr 1888 (see p. 67), none was published. A long poem by her, 'Mary Merivale', appeared in two parts in the issues of 15 May and 15 June 1888, along with a shorter piece, 'At Sunset', on 15 May. Thereafter she was a regular contributor to the journal.

[9] The Revd John Fitzpatrick (1859–1929) of the Oblate order was a minor poet and translator who contributed to the *Irish Monthly* and the *Nation*, sometimes under the pseudonyms of 'A Priestman' and 'Smaragdus'. After 1889 he worked at the English Martyrs Church, 26 Prescot Street, Tower Hill, London, and died at Lee-on-Solent.

you should remind her that George Elliot liked nothing so much as a talk about dress.[10]

I am delighted about your "Good Words" poem.

Send me all news about Ballad book, and "Irish Monthly" when it reviews us.[11]

By the bye Russel is not so much a Theosophist as you call him as a mystic of medieval type. You must not blame him for that it gives origonality to his pictures and his thoughts.[12]

What are you writing now? How goes your story?[13]

Yours always
W B Yeats

ALS Huntington. McHugh, 57–9; Wade, 74–6.

To Katharine Tynan, [20] June [1888]

3 Blenheim Road | Bedford Park
June

My dear Miss Tynan

My father wants me to get him a copy or two of ballad book. How much are they? And would it do for you to get me, next time you are at Gills, three copies, and get them to add the price to my share in the expenses of book? or must I send the money?

Did you see the attack in United Ireland on Taylor last week.[1] My father

---

[10] In *25 Years* (252), KT gives an account of the 'hot water' she got into with Georgianna Audley Hay Johnston (1864–1904), sister of Charles Johnston: 'Miss Johnston started a debating society of an appalling dullness. She was quite ready to give me prominence in it; but at the first meeting—the subject under discussion being something that could not possibly interest any human creature—I sat at the back of the meeting and displayed Liberty patterns to some I had led astray. After this lightness the society left me severely alone.' The society may have been the Ethical Society; Miss Johnston was also a member for a time of the Dublin Lodge of the Theosophical Society (although KT would not have attended their meetings). After her marriage in 1893 to John Brereton she went to live in Scotland, where she died at Alloa.

[11] For KT's poem see p. 74, n. 3. An anonymous review of *PBYI* appeared in 'Notes on New Books' in the *Irish Monthly*, June 1888 (376–7).

[12] 'AE is always the visionary and the poet,' WBY was to write of his friend (*UP* I. 357), 'like all purely creative forces, [he] is unanalysable and incalculable.' See also 'A Visionary' (published in the *National Observer*, 3 Oct 1891, as 'An Irish Visionary', and reprinted in *The Celtic Twilight*, 1893).

[13] Probably 'Queen Bee' (see p. 24, n. 13), which KT was now revising for publication in the *Christian World Magazine*.

[1] John F. Taylor (1850–1902) was a barrister, journalist, and 'obscure great orator' whose eloquent defence of the study of Irish is quoted both in *Aut* (96–7) and the Aeolus episode in *Ulysses*. Although a nationalist, he detested William O'Brien and the politicians involved in agrarian agitation, and was

is anxious to see it and tried to get a copy yesterday in the Strand without success. If any day you are in town you could get me a copy I would be glad. I am afraid you will not thank me for these two requests. I do not want you to go out of your way for them, merely if you are in town and near Gills and Abbey St.[2]

We heard about Taylor from Miss Pursur who is sketching Lilly in the next room at this moment. She went yesterday to "Good Words" with the drawing for your poem. They have not yet decided but seem to think her "Mermaid" would shock their readers.[3] They had a mermaid once before and got letters about it.

I was at the east end of London on Sunday to see Morris act in his Socialist play. He really acts very well. Miss Morris does not act at all but remains her self most charmingly throughout her part. She acts Mary Pinch. Morris tells me he is writing a romance about the ancient Romans. He is going to abuse them he says.[4]

Do you know who the Miss Maclintock is or was who wrote articles in the old Dublin University mag about 1878 on 'Folk lore in Ulster". I want to quote from her articles and must first get her leave I suppose.[5] I suppose Dr Sigerson could tell me.

consequently often attacked in *United Ireland*, which O'Brien edited. On 16 June 1888 the paper, nettled by Taylor's disparaging remarks about O'Brien and Dillon in a recent *Manchester Guardian*, made what was in Irish terms the very grievous allegation that 'when the last Coercion Act was in full swing, this pure-souled and disinterested patriot begged for, received, and accepted a very petty Crown Prosecutorship under a Coercion Government'. Taylor rebutted these charges in the same issue and in the next (23 June), when JO'L and Michael Davitt, among others, also wrote in his defence.

² M. H. Gill & Son had offices in Sackville (now O'Connell) Street, Dublin; the *United Ireland* offices were in Abbey Street.

³ *Good Words*, a monthly magazine edited by the Revd Donald Macleod, DD, one of Queen Victoria's chaplains for Scotland, had a strongly religious and family slant. A number of its contributors were eminent clergymen, and the editor wrote a regular series, 'Sunday Readings', on religious topics. KT's poem 'The Dead Mermaid', accepted at this time by the magazine, did not appear until May 1889—and even then without the illustration by Sarah Purser.

Miss Purser (1848–1943), the Irish painter, wit, and patroness of the arts, was a family friend of the Yeatses. She took up painting after her father's business failed in 1873, studied at Julien's in Paris, and after a commission to paint Constance and Eva Gore-Booth, she 'went through the British aristocracy like the measles'. Although she appreciated WBY's talents as well as those of his father and brother, he was less friendly towards her than were the other members of the family, describing her (*Mem*, 43–4) as 'so clever a woman that people found it impossible to believe that she was a bad painter . . . though kind and considerate when her heart was touched,[she]gave currency to a small, genuine wit by fastening to it, like a pair of wings, brutality.' Later a trustee of the National Gallery of Ireland, and instrumental in the establishment of the Dublin Muncipal Gallery of Modern Art, Sarah Purser died as the result of a seizure brought on by rage at the sight of the bad design of a new postage stamp.

⁴ *The Tables Turned; or, Nupkins Awakened* (see p. 60) was given at the International Club, 23 Princes Square, Cable Street, on 17 June 1888. Mary Pinch is a labourer's wife falsely accused of stealing three loaves of bread and sentenced to eighteen months' hard labour after a farcical trial. During the trial a successful revolution inaugurates the new socialist era, so turning the tables on Judge Nupkins who is set to digging potatoes and making everyone happy. Morris played the Archbishop of Canterbury, a witness for the defence, with great gusto. He never wrote a play about ancient Romans.

⁵ Letitia McClintock, (b. 1835), minor novelist, published two articles with the title 'Folk-Lore of the

When I wrote last I was in bad spirits and tired and talked about myself of course and talked gloomily.

My story is going well another chapter will finish it. It is rather a curious production for me—full of observation and worldly wisdom or what pretends to be such.

Yours Ever
W B Yeats

[*At top of first page*]
Now you must send me a long letter about your doings and your thoughts.

ALS Huntington, with envelope addressed to Clondalkin; postmark 'LONDON JU 20 88'. McHugh, 59–60; Wade, 76–7.

To Dr William Frazer,[1] *23 June* [*1888*]

3 Blenheim Road | Bedford Park
June 23rd

My dear Dr Fraser

I enclose the MSS you asked for. It is the first of the poems of mine in "Poems and Ballads of Young Ireland 1888".[2] The local names are from County Sligo.

Yours very sincerely
W B Yeats

[*Enclosure*]

The Stolen Child
by W B Yeats

Where dips the rocky highland
Of Slewth Wood in the lake
There lies a leafy island
Where flapping herons wake

County Donegal' in the *Dublin University Magazine*, the first anonymously in November 1876, the second in February 1877. Her 'Folk Lore of Ulster' appeared anonymously in the issue for June 1877. WBY selected five passages from the first two articles for *FFT*.

[1] William Frazer (1824–99) lectured on Materia Medica at Carmichael School, Dublin, and published 'Treatment of Disease of the Skin' in 1864. He lived at 20 Harcourt Street, not far from the Yeatses' former residence in Harold's Cross, and gave WBY critical advice on his early writing. In 1885 WBY had sent Frazer an MS of *The Island of Statues* (now at King's School, Canterbury) for his comments.

[2] 'The Stolen Child', of which WBY encloses a fair copy, had first appeared in the *Irish Monthly*, December 1886, and recently been reprinted in *PBYI*. Slewth (from *slios*, meaning 'sloped') Wood is on the lower side of the Killery Mountains, at the edge of Lough Gill; for Rosses, see p. 7.

The drowsy water rats;
There we've hid our fairy vats
Full of berries
And of reddest stolen cherries.
Come away, O human child
To the woods and waters wild
With a fairy hand in hand
For the worlds more full of weeping than
    You can understand.

Where the wave of moonlight glosses
    The dim grey sands with light
Far off by furthest Rosses
    We foot it all the night,
Leaning softly out
  From ferns that drop their tears
    Of dew on the young streams.
Come O human child
To the woods and waters wild
With a fairy, hand in hand,
For the worlds more full of weeping than
    You can understand.

Away with us he's going
    The solemn-eyed—
He'll hear no more the lowing
    Of the calves on the warm hill-side
Or the kettle on the hob
    Sing peace into his breast
Or see the brown mill bob
    Round and round the oatmeal chest
For the comes the human child
To the woods & waters wild
With a fairy hand in hand.
For the worlds more full of weeping than
    he can understand.

ALS UCLA, with enclosure.

To Katharine Tynan, 2 July [*1888*]

3 Blenheim Road | Bedford Park
July 2nd

My dear Miss Tynan

I have to finish my folk lore book by the end of the month. It would greatly help if I could come across Lady Wilde. John O Leary writes to say that he does not know her but that you do he thinks. Could you give me an introduction? I have read her book[1] and mean if she gives me leave to quote several stories. If you can give me an introduction it would make several matters clear. How much I may quote for instance also she would be able to clear up one or two difficulties perhaps. As I dare say she knows Irish folk lore literature well. Having so short a time I fear I have not found all the authorities. Lady Wilde sent a friend of hers to hear my paper on folk lore at Southwick.[2]

I cannot write much of a letter this time for we have run short of candles and I have only a little peice now about, going to come to an end. It will only last about five minutes at most and you know what a slow writer I am.

Do you like Todhunters "Children of Lir"? To me it seems wonderfully bardic. Dowden does not like the metre. Gladstone in acknowledging a copy that was sent him said he had read it all through and praised the metre especially.[3]

How does the Ballad book sell? Miss O'Leary sent me the Nation review and two Tipperary ones.[4]

It has been raining all day I could not get in to the Museum and so lost my day.

When I wrote you that despondent letter I had one of my dreadful despondent moods on—partially fatigue. To keep happy seems like walking on stilts. When one is tired one falls off and comes down to the clay.

---

[1] *Ancient Legends . . . of Ireland* (see p. 71).

[2] The Revd Ponsonby Lyons (see p. 71).

[3] William Ewart Gladstone (1809–98), the great Liberal statesman—at this time Leader of the Opposition—took a keen interest in poetry throughout his life. Todhunter's 'The Dream of the Children of Lir', in *The Banshee*, was in alexandrines (see p. 53) made up of mixed iambic and anapaestic feet arranged in irregular stanzas.

[4] The *Nation* review (9 June 1888, 3) of *PBYI* noted that 'The crowning poem in the volume, to our mind, is Miss Katharine Tynan's "Grave of Michael Dwyer" '. However, KT's 'Shameen Dhu' was criticized for its maladroit use of 'patois'. WBY's 'The Stolen Child' was described as 'a charming poem'. In a generally unenthusiastic review in the *Clonmel Chronicle, Tipperary and Waterford Advertiser* on 16 June 1888 (3), the reviewer ('J.D.') lamented the lack of humour and gaiety in the book and concluded by asking, 'Has Paddy really become as grave and saturnine as his friend John Bull?' The second Tipperary review was almost certainly in the *Tipperary Nationalist and Southern Irishman*, published in Clonmel, the file of which is now incomplete; the paper was recommended by JO'L to KT, 10 June 1888 (Texas), in a list of Irish provincial papers where *PBYI* might be reviewed.

The wick of the candle has tilted over on its side and will be out in a moment.

Your friend
W B Yeats

I light a match to address the envelope.

ALS Princeton. (Partly in Wade, 77–8).

To Father Matthew Russell, 5 July [1888]

3 Blenheim Road | Bedford Park | Turnham Green
July 5

Dear Father Russel

D. R. McNally's book is not in the Museum catalogue. Do you know when it came out? Is it an origonal collection or a compilation?[1] Do you know any one who has a copy they could lend for a week or two? I have many stories about the fairies but am hard up for Banshee and Pooka stories and also for stories of the "headless coach" type. I would add a section about Giants but only know by way of material Carletons "legend of Knocmany".[2] I am anxious to have a section on Irish Saint stories and wish to give the prophesies of St Columnkille. The peasentry know them well. Their was a book published some years ago in Dublin I am told containing them.[3] Do you know anything about it? I have only to do with Irish tales.

The books and articles I shall use are these

Kennady's books

Crokers "legends of the South of Ireland"

---

[1] Presumably WBY failed to locate David Rice McAnally's *Irish Wonders* (London and Boston, 1888) in the British Museum catalogue because he looked under 'McNally' (he misspells the name thus in an article written at this time though not published until 1890; see *UP* I. 180); the BM copy of the US edition is date-stamped '11 April 1888'; the British edition, published in London by Ward, Lock & Co., '19 July 1888'. *Irish Wonders* was 'an original collection'; although WBY does not mention the book in *FFT*, he reviewed it the following year both for the *Scots Observer* (30 Mar 1889; *UP* I. 138–41) and *PSJ* (7 July 1889; *LNI*, 192–204).

[2] WBY explained in *FFT* that the banshee (*ban* = woman; *shee* = fairy) cry at deaths, while the *púca* was an animal spirit connected with *poc*, a he-goat. The 'coach-a-bower' (*coiste-bodhair*), an omen that sometimes accompanies the banshee, is a black hearse drawn by headless horses driven by a Dullahan or headless phantom. 'It will go rumbling to your door, and if you open it a basin of blood will be thrown in your face' (*FFT*, 108). Stories of these types were gathered under the general heading 'The Solitary Fairies'. *FFT* contains only two stories about giants: Carleton's 'A Legend of Knockmany', from his 1845 *Tales and Sketches*, and 'The Giant's Stairs' from Croker's *Fairy Legends*.

[3] Probably *The Life of St. Columb-kill . . . Together with his prophecies respecting lands etc.* (Limerick, 1827; subsequently reprinted twice in Dublin, probably in the 1850s and 1860s). *FFT* does have a section on Irish saint stories, but this does not contain any prophecies of St. Columbkille. In the Introduction to *FFT* and in *Myth* (5) WBY recalls hearing tales of Columbkille told by Paddy Flynn of Balisodare.

Lady Wilde "Ancient legends of Ireland"[4]

various articles in Dublin University Review[5]

Mrs Crowes "Ghost stories &c" from this I take the story of
        Castlereagh and the "Radient Boy"

Careltons "Traits and Stories"

Lovers "Legends & Stories of Ireland"[6]

The Folklore Journal & Folklore Record

Hibernian Tales.

Mrs S. C. Halls. Ireland[7]

I shall make extracts from all the above.

I have yet to look through The Dublin Penny Journal and other Dublin Magazines & Barringtons "Recollections" for the Banshee tales.[8]

The book must be finished by the end of month.

Many thanks for your suggestions.

Yours very Sincerely

W B Yeats

I am most anxious about stories of the Croker type that is to say stories about Fairies Ghosts Banshees &c. I hardly know if I will have space to include any of what they call "Household Tales" that is to say stories ⟨about kings

---

[4] WBY took 4 stories for *FFT* from Patrick Kennedy's *Legendary Fictions of the Irish Celts* and 2 from his *Fireside Stories of Ireland*, as well as citing 3 further Kennedy volumes as 'Authorities on Irish Folk-Lore'. He took 12 stories from Croker, 9 of them from *Fairy Legends*, and 4 extracts from Lady Wilde's volume (see p. 71).

[5] A slip of the pen for *Dublin University Magazine* (1833–77), a Conservative and Protestant monthly started by young lecturers and undergraduates at TCD, among them WBY's grandfather, the Revd William Yeats, Isaac Butt, Samuel Ferguson, and the Revd Caesar Otway. From the *Magazine* he took 7 legends: 2 from the issue for October 1839 and 5 from the issues of November 1876 and February 1877 (not, as he says in the notes to *FFT*, from the [non-existent] 1878 volume; see p. 74).

[6] From Mrs Catherine Crowe's *Ghosts and Family Legends, A Volume for Christmas* (1859), WBY took the legend that Lord Castlereagh had seen, as a young man, the apparition of a shining boy which betokened a successful life ending in a violent death. He used no stories from Carleton's *Traits and Stories of the Irish Peasantry* but took 6 extracts from his work, 5 of them from his later *Tales and Sketches*; from Samuel Lover's *Legends and Stories of Ireland* (Dublin, 1831; 2nd series, London, 1834) he took 2 stories.

[7] The *Folk-Lore Record*, founded in 1878, became the *Folk-Lore Journal* in 1883. From the *Folk-lore Record*, vol. II, WBY took 'The Story of Conn-eda', translated by Nicholas O'Kearney from the Irish of Abraham McCoy, which had first been published in the *Cambrian Journal*. He confuses *Hibernian Tales*, ed. James M'Cormick (Dublin, 1845) with *The Royal Hibernian Tales* (Dublin, n.d.), a chap-book from which Thackeray quotes in ch. XVI of *The Irish Sketch Book* (1843) and from which WBY took the stories of 'Donald and his Neighbours' and 'The Jackdaw'. *Ireland: Its Scenery, Character, Etc.* by Mr and Mrs S. C. Hall (1841–3) is an amalgam of history, geography, travelogue, statistics, and folklore from which WBY took a short extract, 'The Witch Hare'.

[8] The *Dublin Penny Journal* (1832–7), first edited by the Revd Caesar Otway and George Petrie, and from August 1833 by Philip Dixon Hardy, included articles on folklore, antiquities, and music as well as original fiction. WBY took no material from it, nor from Jonah Barrington's *Personal Sketches and Recollections of his Own Time* (1827, 3rd vol. 1832), though he recommended the latter for banshee stories.

& queens and fair princesses 〉 of the Cinderella kind. I will include some if possible but fear want of space.[9]

This letter is very badly written but I have to hurry away to the Museum.

I wonder how I could find out McNally London publisher. Though likely enough the book would be too expensive.

PS. 2.

I have just got your note with count Plunckets[10] most valuable suggestions for which thanks to him and you. I shall look up the books he speaks of to day.

Do you know the date of D R McNally's book? I could find out the London publisher if I had that.

In my search for matter I have come on much strange literature—notably a Dublin magazine of 1809 devoted to ghost stories and such like,[11] I have looked through several histories of Magic. In the various lists of folklore books given at the end of English and foreign folklore authorities there is hardly any mention of Irish books unhappily.

I looked up the Columbkille prophesies but did not find the picturesque ones I heard down in the country. Must look again.

I am afraid I have bothered you with a great many questions. I fear you are busy and these questions are a trouble. If so do not mind about them. I can get along with present material.

ALS APH. Wade, 78–80.

To Douglas Hyde,[1] *11 July* [*1888*]

3 Blenheim Road | Bedford Park | Turnham Green
July 11

My dear Hyde

Can you help me in the matter of Folk Lore? I am editing a volume of selected Irish Folk Lore for Walter Scot and Co's Camelot series.

---

[9] The stories in the last section of *FFT* fall into this category.

[10] George Noble Plunkett (1851–1948), created a papal count in 1884 by Leo XIII, was a barrister who contributed poetry, often under the name of 'Killeen', to a number of periodicals and anthologies. His *God's Chosen Festival* had appeared in 1877, and he had edited the short-lived but enterprising magazine *Hibernia* in 1882. He subsequently served as director of the Science and Arts Museum in Dublin and, later still, as Minister of External Affairs and of Fine Arts after the formation of the Irish Free State. His son, Joseph Mary Plunkett, was one of the leaders of the 1916 Easter Rising.

[11] *The Supernatural Magazine for 1809: containing ancient and modern supernatural experience in testimony to the truth of Revelation* (Dublin, 1809).

[1] Douglas Hyde (1860–1949; see Appendix), poet and translator, founder of the Gaelic League (1893) and first President of Ireland (1937–45), was one of the foremost workers in the attempt to revive the Irish language and to preserve Gaelic folklore. He had learned to speak Irish, and was for many years WBY's link with the oral traditions of Gaelic Ireland.

There are one or two little books I have not been able to do more than hear of. Little books of fairy tales to be found in peasent cottages brown with turf smoke. I have got one of the kind "Hibernian Tales" a chap book published by Duffey.[2] These books never reach the British Museum. Do you know how I could get at them—

The books I am using are

Crokers books

Kennedy's books

Carleton's "traits and stories"

Lady Wilde's "Ancient Traditions" &

Sir W Wildes "Irish superstitions"

Mrs S C Hall's "Ireland"

Lovers "Legends & Stories"

O'Hanlan's (Laginiensis) "Old Irish Folk Lore".[3]

besides these I have gone through a pile of Dublin Magazines and got nothing except from the Dublin University Magazine. "The Folk Lore Journal" like wise turns out useless, for scientific people cannot tell stories—[4]

There is a magazine of 1820 or 1830 called the London & Dublin Magazine contain[ing] according to Sir William Wilde the best Irish fairy tales every published. Do you know anything about it? there is no copy in the British Museum.[5] Do you know any one who could lend it to me or some friend who would make extracts.

My book is divided as follows

Section 1—Fairies

2—Changlings

3—Leprehauns

4—Banshee

5—Ghosts, headless horsemen, etc

6—Tier-na-oge.

7—Witches

---

[2] See preceding letter, n. 7.

[3] See preceding letter. WBY did not finally use anything from *Irish Popular Superstitions* (Dublin, 1852) by the Dublin surgeon and antiquarian Sir William Robert Wills Wilde (1815–76), father of Oscar; nor from *Irish Folk Lore: Traditions and Superstitions of the Country; with Humorous Tales* (Glasgow, 1870) by 'Lageniensis', the pseudonym of Canon John O'Hanlon (1821–1905), best known for his 10-vol. *Lives of the Irish Saints* (1875–1903).

[4] The *Folk-Lore Journal*, published by Alfred Nutt, was the organ of the Folk-Lore Society.

[5] 'The best of all our fairy tales are, perhaps, the "Superstitions of the Irish Peasantry," in the volumes of the "London and Dublin Magazine" [*sic*],' wrote Sir William (*Irish Popular Superstitions*, 17); his transposition of the cities in the name of the *Dublin and London Magazine*, published 1825–8, may explain WBY's inability to find it in the British Museum catalogue, where it is correctly listed. He quickly discovered his mistake, for he reprinted the tale 'Loughleagh' from it.

          8—Fairy docters
          9—Saints
          10—The devil

Do you know is the story of the Devil and the Tinker any where in print?[6]
My stories have of course to be tolerably short. Most of the Dublin
Magazine stories take up half a dozen pages to[o] many.

I have to finish by the end of month.

There will be several poems of Callanans, Allinghams, Walsh's, etc
scattered up and down most likely—[7]

Do you know anything about the "Newry Magazine"—Sir W Wilde said
in a note to "Irish Superstitions" that it contained fairy tales.[8]

                                         Yours very sincerely
                                            W B Yeats

Your poems in ballad book every one likes. York Powell a proffessor and
writer on history a neghbour of ours, praises especially your John O Mahony
lament. I like the 98 ballad greatly. I hope you will collect them into a book
these and your other poems. Their was a poem of yours in the "Gael" called
"Outlaws". I wish we had had it in our book. It was a very beautiful little
affair.

I wonder how that ballad book of ours is selling?

There is a story in Lefanu somewhere, about a supernatural bird alighting
on a dying man and waiting there till he died. Do you know what book of his
it is in?[9]

Could you let me know about this and other matters shortly. I have so
little time.

[6] Although WBY did not use this story, Hyde subsequently published it in *Legends of Saints and
Sinners* (1915) under the title 'Shaun the Tinker'. Carl Marnstrander's essay, 'Deux Contes irlandais', in
Miscellany Presented to Kuno Meyer, ed. O. Bergin and C. Marnstrander (Halle, 1912), 371–486, gives an
exhaustive account of the many European versions of the tale, tracing it back to a pagan germanic origin.
Fr Peter O'Leary used it as the basis of his *Séadna* (Dublin, 1907).

[7] The poet and collector of ballads and legends Jeremiah Joseph (sometimes John) Callanan (1795–
1829) was one of the first to introduce, through his translations from the Irish, a Gaelic influence into
Anglo-Irish poetry; WBY printed his poem 'Cusheen Loo' in *FFT* (33–4), together with three poems by
Allingham and Edward Walsh's 'The Fairy Nurse' (51).

[8] The *Newry Magazine; or Literary & Political Register* (1815–17), mentioned by Sir William Wilde
in *Irish Popular Superstitions* (17) as containing 'much interesting information' on the subject, is cited in
FFT (326) as an authority on Irish folklore.

[9] In a note on 'Omens' WBY recalls (*FFT*, 321–2), 'Some families are attended by phantoms of
ravens or other birds. When McManus, of '48 celebrity, was sitting by his dying brother, a bird of vulture-
like appearance came through the window and lighted on the breast of the dying man. The two watched
in terror, not daring to drive it off. It crouched there, bright-eyed, till the soul left the body. It was
considered a most evil omen. Lefanu worked this into a tale.' J. Sheridan LeFanu's story was 'The
Watcher', in *Ghost Stories and Tales of Mystery* (Dublin, 1851). WBY also mentions the incident in *Aut*
(98), where he says he heard it from Ellen O'Leary.

What think you of the Pan Celtic Society? they have sent me a notice and a newspaper cutting in which I see Grave's name—[10]

I let the first page of this get into some salid oil please excuse my not rewriting it.

[*Across top of last page*]
Since writing this I have found the name of Lefanus Story.

ALS Private.

To Douglas Hyde, [*mid-July 1888*]

3 Blenheim Road | Bedford Park | Turnham Green

My dear Hyde

I forgot to mention the Pookha section. I have two stories

The Kildare Pooka—Kennedy

A Pooka story (humerous) from "Leneniensis".[1]

On second thoughts I inclose list of all stories chosen. The stories of the Gilla Rua type come under the last heading of all. Any kind of story that does not come under preavious headings come under this—[2]

I will be very thankful for any stories. The more the better—I have just discovered my book to be 60 or 70 pages short. Could you send me the version you know of the ⟨ pedlar ⟩ Devil & Tinker.[3] You will see by list I am

[10] The Pan Celtic Society was founded in Dublin on 1 Mar 1888 by a medical student from Ballinasloe, Cornelius Gerald Pelly (1865–1901), who wrote poetry and sketches of Connacht life under the pseudonym 'Gerald' or 'G. Cieppe', in collaboration with A. F. Downey and M. D. Wyer. The Society was to be 'non-political and non-sectarian, but *National* in the broadest sense of the word', and was open to all 'who have published a poem, essay, tale or sketch in an Irish magazine or newspaper, or who have a literary knowledge of the Celtic tongue'. Its membership at this time included Hyde, the O'Learys, the Sigerson girls, KT, and Todhunter. A report of the meeting of the society published in the *Nation* 16 June 1888 announced that the poet and anthologist A. P. Graves (then living near Taunton) had been elected a member, and presumably WBY had been sent a cutting of this, together with a prospectus.

[1] WBY published three stories concerning the Pooka in *FFT*: 'The Kildare Pooka' (105–7), taken from Kennedy's *Legendary Fictions of the Irish Celts*; 'Daniel O'Rourke' (97–105), from Croker's *Fairy Legends and Traditions*; and 'The Piper and the Puca' (94–7), translated by Hyde presumably in response to this letter. WBY did not in the end use the 'Lageniensis' (O'Hanlon) pooka story 'Lackeen Castle, O'Kennedy, and the Phooka'.

[2] See p. 80, n. 9.

Gilla rua, 'The red-haired fellow or lad', acts as the benevolent *deus ex machina* in a number of Irish fairy stories, coming to the rescue of the mortal hero in perilous situations. He often appears (as in Hyde's story, 'Neil O'Carreg', of which WBY may be thinking) in tales of the 'grateful dead' type, returning unrecognized from the grave to help a human benefactor. No stories of this kind are included in *FFT*.

[3] See preceding letter, n. 6.

hard up for pooka stories. I shall of course be delighted to get notes on Leprehauns Banshee Etc. I will [write] but a short introduction before each section. I am dreadfully pressed for time. Only a week now. Could you let me have the stories as soon as possible. I will give your book of tales in Irish a few words if you will tell me its name.[4]

The poems given in list are as yet very incomplete. Joyce & Graves & De Vere (for Saint tales) will have to be looked up.[5]

My poems come out in Autumn some time.

Excuse my not writing more now. I will shortly.

Yours very sincerely

W B Yeats

[*Enclosure*]

Contents of Folk Lore book.

Fairies—

⟨Fairies Allingham⟩

Frank Martin & the fairies—	Carleton
† The rival Kempers—	Carleton
† Lanty M'Clusky—	Carleton
Paddy Corcorans Wife—	Carleton
† Childs Coffin—	Carleton

(the above are short stories taken from the Article called "The rival Kempers" and "Frank Martin")

Legend of Knocgrafton—	Croker
Priests Supper—	Croker
† Legend of Bottle Hill—	Croker
† Confession of Tom Burke—	Croker
Scalded Fairy—	Miss MacClintock
White Trout—	Lover
† Fairy Guest—	Sligo Chronicle
† Legend of Innis Sark—	Sir William Wilde
Poems	
Fairy Well of Lagnany—	Fergusson
† Fairy Struck—	Rolleston
Fairy Thorn—	Ferguson
Cusheen Loo—	Callinnan
Fairies—	Allingham

---

[4] In his Introduction to *FFT* WBY wrote (xvi) of the 'volume of folk tales in Gaelic' Hyde was now preparing (eventually published as *Leabhar Sgeulaigheachta*): 'He is, perhaps, most to be trusted of all. He knows the people thoroughly. Others see a phase of Irish life; he understands all its elements. His work is neither humorous nor mournful; it is simply life.'

[5] WBY published A. P. Graves's 'Song of the Ghost' in his section on 'Ghosts' (134–6), but included nothing by P. W. Joyce or Aubrey De Vere in *FFT*. He did however publish Joyce's 'Fergus O'Mara and the Air-Demons' in *Irish Fairy Tales* (1892).

Changlings
      Brewery of Egg shells—   Croker
      † Young Piper—   Croker
      Deaf and Dumb Girl—   Miss McClintock
      Poems
      The fairy nurse—   Walsh
      Stollen Child—   Yeats
The merrow
  The soul cages—   Croker
  ⟨Birds of⟩
  Flory Cantillons Funeral—   Croker
Leprehaun, Clearicaun, Fir Darrig.
      ⟨Leprehaun—   Allingham⟩
      Master & Man—   Croker
      † Clearicaune   Croker
      † The Three Wishes—   "Lageniensis"
                                    (O'Hanlon)

      Poem:
      Leprehaun—   Allingham
The Pooka—
      Kildare pooka—   Kennedy
      † Lackeen Castle, O'Kennedy & Pooka— "Legeniensis"
The Banshee
  Banshee (From Tom Connally & Banshee)   Todhunter
  Banshee of Macarthy—   Croker
Ghosts.
      Radient Boy and Castlereagh—   Mrs Crow
      Frank MacKenna—   Carleton
      The Black lamb—   Lady Wilde
          Poem
             Legend of Tyrone—   Miss O Leary
                † The Geraldines Daughter—
Hy Breasil—
      † Oisin and Tier-nan-Oge   Joyce
      Legend O Donahue   Croker
          Poem
         Hy Brazil—   Griffen.
Fairy Docters, Witches, Wizards, Spells.
      Pudding bewitched—   Carleton
      Witch turned hair—   Mrs S C Hall
      † Priest and Witch—   Dublin Univ Rev
                                    1839

Witches Excursion	Kennedy
† Butter Bewitched—	Kennedy
† The horned Woemen—	Lady Wilde
Saints	
† St Kevin and Goose, by—	?
† Saint turned hermit—	Hibernian Tales
(This section ⟨very⟩ incomplete as yet)	
The Devil—	
The three wishes—	Carleton
The Countess Kathleen O Shea—By—	?
The Long Spoon—	Kennedy.
The Demon Cat—	Lady Wilde.
Giants.	
Legend of Knocmanny—	Carleton
(section incomplete).	

Kings Queens Princesses & Other Tales
Section incomplete[6]

ALS Private, with enclosure.

To John O'Leary, 27 July [1888]

3 Blenheim Road | Bedford Park | Turnham Green
27 July

Dear Mr O Leary

I am so buisy over Folk lore I have no time to write a letter, merely this note. The story I spoke of would I find come in useful, it is in the same volume as the Ossianic Tales of Kennedy it [is] a witch tale about the origin of some lake or other a very wild american indianish tale.[1] I have to get my book into Walter Scot and Co's[2] hands by Monday or Tuesday.

---

[6] Those items preceded by a † were not included in the published volume, whose arrangement and contents departed widely from this provisional list.

[1] No such tale appears in *FFT*; but as WBY apparently used 'American indianish' as a general category (cf. below, p. 194) rather than having to do with racial origin, the description here could be applied to any of the tales about lakes in Kennedy's *Legendary Fictions of the Irish Celts* (which has a section of Ossianic tales).

[2] The firm of Walter Scott & Co. was headed by Walter (later Sir Walter) Scott (1826–1910), a Cumberland businessman who, as proprietor of Tyne Brass and Tube Manufacturing Co. and chairman of Walter Scott & Middleton Ltd., had constructed the first electric tube railway in London. The publishing company which he subsequently owned (built up by a clever manager after Scott had acquired it as a bad debt) specialized in cheap series such as the Camelot Classics, and reprints of the classics.

I have some more old book lists for you, will send them in a day or two.

I have been unable to find time to write to Miss O Leary lately but will do so first thing when this book is off my hands.

Yours always
W B Yeats

The Magazine is not in British Museum.[3] ⟨Have you Joyce's Irish Legends⟩

ALS NLI. Wade, 81.

To Katharine Tynan, 28 July [1888]

3 Blenheim Road | Bedford Park | Turnham Green
28 July

My dear Miss Tynan

A great many thanks for the introduction. I am going to Lady Wildes reception this afternoon. She was not visable—being not yet up needing as the servent put it "a great deel of rest" when I called last sunday afternoon. I wonder if I shall find her as delightful as her book—as delightful as she is certainly unconventional.[1] My folk lore matters wind up next Monday or tuesday for the present. My introduction and most likely the last few sections of book not going in till later. In the meanwhile I shall go for a few days to Oxford perhaps to copy an MSS or some such thing in the Bodlian for a friend of York Powells[2]—a very pleasent little job if it comes to anything.

Are you ever going to write to me? Do you know it is two months all but two days since you wrote? and I generous minded person am writing to you now to heep coals of fire—your letter when it comes will have to be very long or——

I am writing in the British Museum and the man has just brought me Sir William Wildes Irish Popular Superstition from which I have to make and extract[3] so this note must wind up presently.

---

[3] Possibly the *Journal of the Royal Historical and Archaeological Association of Ireland*, which had published 'Ancient Lake Legends of Ireland' (ser. 4, vol. I, pt. i, 1870, 94–110).

[1] KT called on Lady Wilde when in London, having been introduced in the spring of 1884 by Emily Skeffington Thompson, and had provided WBY with an introduction. Hereafter he often attended Lady Wilde's Saturday afternoon 'at homes' at 146 Oakley Street, Chelsea. He was sometimes accompanied by SMY, who marvelled at the many cameo brooches worn by their hostess, greeting her guests at the door of the reception room. Red-paper-covered lamps gave 'a kind of lowering twilight', and tea was handed round by two elderly Irish maids who knew everyone, Lady Wilde having an antipathy to smart English servants (scrapbook, MBY).

[2] York Powell's friend was Joseph Jacobs (1854–1916), author and journalist; he edited a number of collections of fairy tales.

[3] See p. 81, n. 3.

Walter Scott is going to print my Fairy book at once so it will be out in a month or two—it has been a very laborious buisness but well worth doing, for all the material for poetry, if for nothing else. You and I will have to turn some of the stories into poems. Russel copied out some folk tales not to be got at this side of the channel, in the National Library.[4] It was very good of him as he has not much time these days. You see him sometimes I suppose. Jack is drawing "Menu" cards and "Race" cards. Miss Pursur has sold a good many for him they are very witty little cards some of them.[5]

What is Miss Kavanagh doing? And what is the ballad book doing in the way of sale? About your self! have you any new ventures in hands? My story waits for its last chapter and will have to wait till immediate work concludes.

Your friend Always
W B Yeats

When you write remember I want to hear much about yourself.

ALS Huntington. McHugh, 60–1; Wade, 80–1.

To Douglas Hyde, 6 August [1888]

3 Blenheim Road | Bedford Park | Turnham Green
6 August

My dear Hyde—

You must excuse my not having thanked you before but all last week I was most terribly buisy I had not a single moment and these last two days I have been recovering simply from the effects. It was a great strain. I had not enough energy to write the shortest note yesterday.

Your three stories will be of course included. The one about the corpse is one of the most magnificent things in all Irish Folk Lore, it is the treasure of the book. Will you be even more generous still and consent to look through my proofs so as to give me some short notes.[1] I shall be desperately

[4] The tales copied out in Dublin by George Russell were probably those in *Royal Hibernian Tales* (see p. 79, n. 7), which was not available in the British Museum. WBY dedicated *FFT* 'to my Mystical Friend, G. R.'

[5] Jack Yeats's diary (MBY) records that he saw Sarah Purser on 28 July 1888 and she evidently commissioned him to design and illustrate various series of cards to serve as menus and race cards. Since he was leaving for Sligo three days later, he had no time to execute this order before the autumn; but on 25 Nov 1888 ECY noted in her diary (MBY): 'Jack sent off menus to Lady Gore Booth.' Miss Purser, as a friend of the Gore-Booths of Lissadell, Co. Sligo, had almost certainly suggested Jack to them. In January 1889 he made £5 for another series of menu cards which he sold through Colin Trotter, and on Feb 20 1889 (diary, MBY) he 'got sorter order for half doz cards' from Van Ingen & Co.

[1] In the Introduction to *FFT* (xviii) WBY thanks Hyde 'for his three unpublished stories, and for valuable and valued assistance in several ways'. The three stories, translated from the Gaelic, were 'Teig O'Kane and the Corpse' (16–31), which WBY thought 'the best told folk-tale in our literature' (*LNI*, 102), 'The Piper and the Puca', and 'Munachar and Manachar' (296–9). Hyde subsequently published all three in Irish in his *Leabhar Sgeulaigheachta* (Dublin, 1889).

⟨pushed⟩ hurried about them especially as my general introduction has yet to be written. The introductions to sections are of course finished and with the printer. In addition to all, I have a job in Oxford an old edition of Esope to copy in the Bodlean next week—am indeed pelted by the devils of bother, the little spirits no larger than flies, which according to the opera, are the worst of all. Though indeed the Oxford affair is a most delightful job in itself. I am to stop in the rooms of one of the dons—history proffessor York Powell and should have a good time of it only for these damned "Camelot" people and their hurry.[2]

When will your Gaelic book be out?

I have some notes done—not many—and was reading for others today they will come at end of book.

Mean to give account of some Irish peasent authorities on fairies, of my acquaintance, in introduction.[3] Sligo men! Shall also discuss the virtues and ⟨failings of⟩ faults of Irish Folk Lore collectors, Croker Kennedy & the rest.[4] Notes are my present bother.

Yours gratefully
W B Yeats

ALS Private.

To Douglas Hyde, [c. 25 *August 1888*]

3 Blenheim Road | Bedford Park | Turnham Green

My dear Hyde

I send you the first batch of proofs. I have only just been able to glance through them. I have a duplicate set. Would you kindly send me any note that may occur. I want to put four or five pages of such at end of book. Do

---

[2] WBY began copying out Caxton's edition of Aesop at the Bodleian on 11 Aug. The work was for Joseph Jacobs (see p. 87, n. 2), whose edition of *The Fables of Aesop* 'as first printed by William Caxton in 1484 with those of Avian, Alfonso and Poggio, now again edited and induced by Joseph Jacobs', was published in 1889 in 2 parts by the firm of David Nutt.

[3] WBY devotes more than a page of the Introduction to *FFT* (xii–xiii) to a description of Paddy Flynn, the 'most notable and typical story-teller of my acquaintance . . . living in a leaky one-roomed cottage of the village of B[allisodare], "The most gentle—*i.e.*, fairy—place in the whole of the County Sligo," he says'.

[4] 'The various collectors of Irish folk-lore', WBY wrote in his Introduction (xiv–xv), 'have, from our point of view, one great merit, and from the point of view of others, one great fault. They have made their work literature rather than science. . . . Croker and Lover, full of the ideas of harum-scarum Irish gentility, saw everything humorised. . . . What they did was not wholly false; they merely magnified an irresponsible type . . . into the type of a whole nation, and created the stage Irishman.' Croker, he said, 'is touched everywhere with beauty—a gentle Arcadian beauty', while Kennedy, with 'far less literary faculty, . . . is wonderfully accurate, giving often the very words the stories were told in'.

not put any note on the page of proof unless so short as to be got in by printer without disturbing the paging. Would you make any suggestions about my notes to sections etc. My general introduction is not yet in print.

I am busy copying out Esope these days for David Nutt from the old black letter of Caxton which take all my time.

Please correct any mistakes you find in my notes. Gaelic words look for one thing, missprinted.

"Tieg and Ghost" best thing in book.

Yours very sincerely
W B Yeats

You will hurry will you not with proofs?

Very good of you to take on your self so much trouble.

There are several gaelic words wanting notes I think such as "a sluagh shee airy" on page 51.[1]

[*On verso and not apparently part of the letter*]

shingawn. pisheóg

The Irish Echo
  187 Washington St
    Room 7. Boston

legend of white trout.

Douglas

ALS Private.

To Katharine Tynan, 25–30 August [*1888*]

August 30

My dear Miss Tynan

I have just heard from the Sigersons who were hear last night, that Fluffy is dead and that you have written a beautiful elegy there on. I am really sorry about Fluffy and look forward to reading the poem in the "Monthly".[1] The

---

[1] The words '*a sluagh shee airy*' occur in the third stanza of Walsh's poem 'The Fairy Nurse' (*FFT*, 51) and are correct, though a hyphen has been added between '*sluagh*' and '*shee*'. In his article on 'Irish Fairies' in the *Leisure Hour*, October 1890, WBY noted that '*A sluagh shee* means "fairy host", and "airy" is the peasant's way of saying "aery"' (*UP* I. 178).

[1] KT's 'A Lost Friend', an elegy for her pet dog, Fluffy, which died on 9 Aug 1888, appeared in the *Irish Monthly*, October 1888. The issue for November 1888 included a further poem, '"Fluffy" Athanatos' by 'N.N.R.', whom KT identified (letter to Fr. Russell, 1 Apr 1889, APH) as Douglas Hyde.

younger Miss Sigerson thought it a very good poem indeed, in your later style, and tells me of some other on the stocks.

She is greatly enthusiastic about Henleys little book which would be really a wonderful affair if it was not so cobwebby—I have not read the Hospital part yet. He had his leg cut off there.[2] Should like him greatly but for the journalists who flock about him. I hate journalists. There is nothing in them but tittering jeering emptiness. They have all made what Dante calls the Great Refusal. that is they have ceased to be self centred have given up their individuality.[3] I do not of course meen people like O'Brien who have a message to deliver[4] but the general run especially the sucessful ones. The other night I sat there without a word out of me trying to pluck up resolution to go,[5] but Henley wanted to see me about something and so I waited. The shallowest people on the ridge of the earth.

---

[2] The opening section of the *Book of Verses* (1888) by W. E. Henley (1849–1903; see Appendix) is a sequence, 'In Hospital: Rhymes and Rhythms', the main part dated 'The Old Infirmary, Edinburgh, 1873–75'. Henley had had a foot amputated early in his life because of tubercular arthritis; on a recurrence of the disease he sought the help of Joseph Lister, and from August 1873 to April 1875 underwent protracted treatment under Lister's supervision at the Royal Edinburgh Infirmary, in the course of which there was a further amputation. 'With the exception of some early poems founded upon old French models,' WBY wrote later of Henley (*Aut*, 124–5),

I disliked his poetry, mainly he wrote in *vers libre* . . . and filled it with unimpassioned description of a hospital ward where his leg had been amputated. I wanted the strongest passions, passions that had nothing to do with observation, and metrical forms that seemed old enough to have been sung by men half asleep or riding upon a journey. . . . I used to say when I spoke of his poems, 'He is like a great actor with a bad part; yet who would look at Hamlet in the grave scene if Salvini played the grave-digger?' and I might so have explained much that he said and did.

[3] Henley lived at 1 Merton Place, Chiswick, not far from the Yeatses. In *Aut* (128) WBY recalls meeting at his house 'of a Sunday night Charles Whibley, Kenneth Grahame, author of *The Golden Age*, Barry Pain, now a well-known novelist, R. A. M. Stevenson, art critic and a famous talker, George Wyndham, later on a Cabinet Minister and Irish Chief Secretary, and now or later Oscar Wilde . . .'. For 'the great refusal' (*il gran rifiuto*) see *Inferno*, III. 60.

[4] William O'Brien (1852–1928), at this time nationalist MP for Cork North-east, was one of Parnell's principal lieutenants, and a leader of the 'Plan of Campaign'. He had started his career as a journalist on the Cork *Daily Herald* (1868–76), moved to the *Freeman's Journal* (1876–81), and from 1881 to 1890 edited *United Ireland*, the influential and outspoken Parnellite weekly. He was imprisoned with Parnell from October 1881 to April 1882, but was to side with Dillon against Parnell after the split in the Irish Party.

KT had met O'Brien through her activities in the Ladies' Land League and he published her work in *United Ireland* throughout the 1880s. In an article on him which she was probably writing at this time, and which appeared in the *Catholic World*, November 1888 (151–61), she compared him to the prophet Ezekiel, praising his 'style picturesque, fervid, and full of colour and life' and 'the passionate fervour and devotion—one had almost said saintliness—which mark him out pre-eminently as a Christian soldier'.

[5] See *Mem* (252), where WBY remembers that 'When I was twenty or a little more, I was shocked by the conversation at Henley's. One day I resolved if the conversation was as bad again, I would walk out. I did not do so, and next day I reasoned over the thing and persuaded myself that I had thought of walking out from vanity and did not do so from fear.' Compare stanza III of 'The Hawk' (*VP*, 349).

Please do not mind my writing these opinions to you. I like to write to you as if talking to myself.

[*At top of first page*]
Enclosed letter has lain on my table this long while.

[*Enclosure*]
                    3 Blenheim Road | Bedford Park | Turnham Green
                                                        August 25

My dear Miss Tynan

I have at last found time to write. Such work as I have had lately! These last two days I have had to take a rest quite worn out. There are still a hundred pages of Esope.[6] When they are done I shall get back to my story in which I pour all my grievances against this meloncholy London—I somtimes imagine that the souls of the lost are compelled to walk through its streets perpetually. One feels them passing like a whif of air.[7] I have had three months incessant work without a moment to read or think and am feeling like a burnt out taper. Will you write me a long letter all about your self and you[r] thoughts. When one is tired the tendril in ones nature asserts itself and one wants to hear about ones friends.

Did I ever tell you that a clairvoyant, who had never seen me before,[8] told me months ago that I had made too many thoughts and that for a long time I should have to become passive. He told me besides in proof things he had know way of hearing of. Most passive I have been this long while, feeling as though my brain had been rolled about for centuries in the sea, and as I look on my piles of MSS, as though I had built a useless city in my sleep. Indeed all this last six months I have grown more and more passive ever since I finished Oisin and what an eater up of ideals is passivity for every things seems a vision and nothing worth seeking after.

I was at Oxford but was all day buisy with Esope. I dined two or three times with the fellows and did not take much to any one except Churten Collins who as you remember attacked Gosse so fiercely—he was there for a few days like myself[9]—a most cheerful mild pink and white little man full of the freshest unreasonablest enthusiasms.

---

⁶ See p. 89.

⁷ In *John Sherman* (85), the hero reflects: 'Never had London seemed to him so like a reef whereon he was cast away. In the Square the bushes were covered with dust; some sparrows were ruffling their feathers on the side-walk; people passed, continually disturbing them. The sky was full of smoke. A terrible feeling of solitude in the midst of a multitude oppressed him.' Throughout the book London is compared unfavourably to Sherman's native Ballah (Sligo).

⁸ This may have been Monsey, one of the mediums associated with the Esoteric Section of the Theosophical Society. See pp. 45, 48.

⁹ John Churton Collins (1848–1908), journalist, editor, and, from 1904, Professor of English at

I wonder any body does any thing at Oxford but dream and remember the place is šo beautiful. One almost expects the people to sing instead of speaking. It is all—the colleges I meen—like an Opera.

I will write again before long and give you some news. I merely write to you now because I want a letter, and because I am sad. My fairy book proofs are waiting correction.

Yours Always
W B Yeats

I saw Keegan Paul lately he will go on with my book now.

ALS Huntington, with enclosure. McHugh, 61–3; Wade, 81–3.

To Katharine Tynan, 6 September [*1888*]

3 Blenheim Road
Sept 6

Dear Miss Tynan

You told me some time ago that some of your subscribers for my book were 3/6ˢ. Could you remember who? As the price will have to be 5/–. However 3/6 will be all asked in cases where that is the arrangement and where one does not like to ask the people to become 5/– folk. Any body you do not think would mind would you ask? Only at 5/– can I get sufficient I fear. The difference in case of the 3/6ˢ I will pay myself by getting more names—I have several sure.

I got the first "proof" today so you see there is no time to loose. So would you kindly let me know. Do you think this will cause much confusion? Fortunately almost all names were got under the old arrangement.[1]

I am not very hopeful about the book. Somewhat inarticulate have I been I fear. Some thing I had to say. Dont know that I have said it. All seems confused incoherent inarticulate. Yet this I know I am no idle poetaster. My life has been in my poems. To make them I have broken my life in a morter as it were. I have brayed in it youth and fellowship peace and worldly hopes.

Birmingham, was a champion of English studies at the universities. Insistent upon precision in literary criticism, he published in the *Quarterly Review* of October 1886 a devastating review (subsequently collected in his *Ephemera Critica*, 1901), of *From Shakespeare to Pope* (1885) by the critic and biographer Edmund Gosse. Gosse (1849–1928; see below p. 476) replied in the *Athenaeum* of 23 Oct 1886 but was unable to refute many of the charges of inaccuracy levelled against him, and his reputation suffered as a result of the controversy.

[1] The early subscriptions to *Oisin* had been set at 5s. When Kegan Paul agreed to publish he suggested a price of 3s 6d (see p. 58), and a few more subscriptions had been got on that basis; now, to WBY's embarrassment, the publisher had announced that the higher price would have to apply after all.

I have seen others enjoying while I stood alone with myself—commenting, commenting—a mere dead mirror on which things reflect themselves. I have buried my youth and raised over it a cairn—of clouds. Some day I shall be articulate perhaps. But this book I have no great hopes of—it is all sluggish incoherent. It may make a few friends perhaps among people of my own sort—that is the most. Do what you can for it.

As to what you say of "a third manner" a return to early colouring. Certainly your colouring is a great power but you should be careful to make it embody itself, I think, in easily recognizable natural ladscapes is [?as] in your "Children of Lir" and keep it always secondary to the theme never being a colourist for the mere sake of colour. Average little read people will say the reverse perhaps to you, but do you not think I am right. The poem you send has that naivety you know how to use so well, The earliest verses are very good indeed it is all a good little poem not so good though as the St Francis one in a late "Irish Monthly".[2]

Coffey sent me a post card quoting "Ireland under Coercian" about the "Stollen Child". Very favourable. Something about "The spirit of Henrich Heine singing by moonlight on a silvan late [*for* lake]". To which spirit the author compared. To what or whom he compared the rest of us I know not as I did not see the rest. He appears to have written on the ballad book politically likewise.[3]

Your friend ever
W B Yeats

ALS Huntington. McHugh, 63–4; Wade, 83–4.

[2] KT had evidently sent a copy of the poem about her dog Fluffy (see p. 90). For 'St. Francis and the Wolf' see p. 66, n. 6.

[3] In *Ireland under Coercion* (2 vols., 1888), an account by the American William Henry Hurlbert (1827–95) of 'a series of visits to Ireland between January and June 1888', the author comments (II. 296–7) on 'the literary merit of these *Poems and Ballads of Young Ireland*': 'One exquisite ballad of "The Stolen Child", by W. B. Yeats, might have been sung in the moonlight on a sylvan lake by the spirit of Heinrich Heine.' Politically Hurlbert (like JO'L and Rolleston) was anti-land agitation—a fact which earned his own book hostile reviews in the nationalist press—and welcomed the political attitudes in *PBYI*: 'the spirit of all the poems it contains,' he said, 'is the spirit of '48, or of that earlier Ireland of Robert Emmet.' Born in Charleston, South Carolina, Hurlbert worked on the *New York Times* and the New York *World*, becoming proprietor of the latter paper in 1876. After selling his interest in the *World* in 1883 he moved to London, where he remained until April 1891 when he gave great joy to the Irish nationalists he had criticized by becoming implicated in a particularly sensational breach-of-promise case that involved a clergyman's daughter turned actress, a vanishing confidential clerk, French casinos, allegations of blackmail, supposedly mistaken identities, and a claim for £10,000 damages. Although the jury found in Hurlbert's favour on a legal technicality, much doubt remained as to his moral position. He left London for Italy and spent what was left of his life in an obsessive attempt to clear his name.

To Katharine Tynan, [? 22–28 September 1888]

3 Blenheim Road | Bedford Park | Turnham Green

Dear Miss Tynan

Last time I wrote if I remember correctly I left many things unanswered. I wrote I think in much hurry about "forms" for Oisin. (By the way I imagine Keegan Paul will charge full 5/–).

I will go and see Ranking as soon as ever I have a day at present the folk lore still is not quite off my hands—the folk lore and the Esope. Ranking lives now at the very other side of London.

You ask about the Esope. Nutt the publisher is bringing out a reprint of a very scarce copy of Esope published by Caxton. And I am making a copy for the printers. York Powell who got me the job, made a mistake and thought the only copy was at Oxford in the Bodlean. And so I had a very pleasent week in his rooms down there.[1] I am now—when folk lore gives me time— finishing it in the British Museum. Where by the way I saw Renan wandering about yesterday, looking very like an old fat priest.[2]

I have not done very badly these last few months. And it has been lucky as my father's finishing the story in Atalanta has left him, once more dependent on stray drawings.[3] Not that I have done well exactly. However I have had as much work as I could do—only badly paid. Did you read my article in Providence journal. I got £5 for Esope only but will get about another £1. I do not yet know what fairy book will bring I have had £5 as an instalment. I forgot to ask you if you read the phantom ship in Providence Journal. I mean to review Todhunter there.[4] The worst of me is that if my work is good it is done very very slowly—the notes to folk lore book were done quickly and they are bad or at any rate not good. Introduction is better. Douglas Hyde gave me much help with footnotes etc.

I had almost forgotton to say how gladly I will do some sort of a sketch of you and your doings for the american friend.[5] But please tell me some more

---

[1] See p. 89. The *DNB* describes York Powell's 'pleasant rooms in the Meadow Buildings of Christ Church, with their stacks of books and Japanese prints . . . '.

[2] Ernest Renan (1823–92), French philosopher and historian, published his *Essai sur la poésie des races celtiques* in 1854. He had in fact trained for the priesthood, but lost his faith and went on to write *Vie de Jésus* (1863), which was fiercely attacked by the Catholic Church. He was probably doing research at the British Museum for his *Histoire du peuple d'Israël* (1887–94).

[3] JBY illustrated several episodes of Mrs L. T. Meade's *The Lady of the Forest*, serialized in *Atalanta*, February–September 1888. The story, complete with illustrations, was published in book form in January 1889.

[4] WBY's article on William Allingham, 'The Poet of Ballyshannon', had appeared in *PSJ* on 2 September, and his 'Legend of the Phantom Ship' on 27 May; his review of Todhunter's *The Banshee* was published there on 10 Feb 1889.

[5] Probably the American poetess Sarah Morgan Piatt, wife of John James Piatt (see p. 41). Mrs Piatt's cousin, Colonel Donn, was connected with *Belfort's Magazine*, where she may have hoped to place the sketch.

about it. Am I to describe your house and surroundings and your self just, or do a general sketch of your literary life. Will you not tell me in any case come [*for* some] of the things you want said and should I do it at once? I shall have more time shortly. Could you tell me of any article of the kind you wish. Or shall I go my own road. I would sooner go yours. There must be several things you wish said. And have you any dates that are land marks in your literary life and development? How long should it be?

The other day I met a most curious and interesting man—I do not wish to say yet whether he be of interest in himself but his opinions are—At Madame Blavatsky's where I go about once every six weeks. Do you remember an interview in the Pall Mall with a man called Russel an American who came over to England with his wife to teach gesture according to the systim of some French philosopher? That was the man. We left Madame's at 11 and walked up and down Notting Hill till 1 oc in the morning talking philosophy. He was going to stop with the Shelley's for a while on his return I shall see more of him. The interesting thing about him is, that he is a dandy as well as a philosopher. A perpetual parodox. He is naturally insignificent in looks, but by dint of elaborate training in gesture has turned himself into quite a striking looking person. There was a sketch of him in the Pall Mall.[6] He is the most interesting person I have met at

---

[6] On 4 Feb 1886 the *Pall Mall Gazette*, quoting an unnamed American paper, revealed that ' "beautiful Edmund Russell" ', the 'new apostle of aestheticism', said to be leaving America for Europe in the spring,

enters the lecture-room with a halo of golden waving locks about his head and with a little hammer in his hand. With the hammer he demolishes the vases and the other objects of false art that his teachings have caused his hearers to despise. . . . Mr Russell teaches what he calls 'the beautiful' in dress, in home surroundings, in weddings—even in funerals. When he seats himself before his canvas he is clad in a Grecian robe. . . . (4)

The article was illustrated with a profile of Russell's head, and two sketches, 'The Meeting of Oscar and Edmund' and 'I Paint with a Peacock's Feather', showing him in his Grecian robe. On 2 Aug 1886 *Pall Mall* announced (3–4) that

'Beautiful Edmund Russell' is among us, but Mr Oscar Wilde has nothing to fear. It is only in the reflected light of Mrs Russell that this gentleman appears attractive at all; he is a species of propriety padding, and his share in Saturday afternoon's 'Illustration of Expression of Harmony and Motion' . . . may be dismissed with that remark. Mrs Russell is a much more serious person. She represents that large section of Americans who really study elocution—or try to—and gesture and the general philosophy of physical expression.

The Russells, who later settled in Paris, were disciples of François Delsarte (1811–71), who formulated nine laws of gesture, by which the soul expressed itself, as the basis of a teaching method. Russell, like WBY a member of the Esoteric Section of the Theosophical Society, contributed 'As I Knew Her', personal reminiscences of HPB, to the *Herald of the Star*, 11 May 1916 (197–205); he remembered WBY saying to him, 'Yes, she is wonderful, but when she is gone the fellow who opens the door will think he can take her place.'

ECY's diary (MBY) for 4 Nov 1888 records: 'Willie's American friend generally called the "beautiful Theodore" here to tea very amusing but I do *not* think beautiful he is a lecturer on Art decoration etc.' In

Madames lately as a rule one meets the penitent frivilous there. Still frivilous only dull as well. She devours them as she herself says like the locust in the Apocalyps.

Lately I have read much of George Merrideth's poems. They are certainly very beautiful. And have far more suavity and serenity than I had expected. Henley is very cobwebby after them, and not very spontanious. To me Henleys great fault is his form. It is never accidental but always preconceived. His poems are forced into a mold. I dislike the school to which he belongs. A poem should be a law to itself as plants and beasts are. It may be ever so much finished. but all finish should merely make plain that law. Read Merrideth's "Love in a Valley".[7] It is full of a curious intricate richness.

I enclose a couple of lyrics of my own for your opinion. One is made out of three lines of verse I picked up in Sligo—old Irish verse.[8]

I have had a great deal of trouble over the folk lore the publishers first making me strike out 100 pages on the ground that the book was too long and then when two thirds was in print add as many pages of fresh matter because they had made a wrong calculation and I had to set to work copying out and looking over materiel again as the pages struck out had to do with the section already in type. It is however at last off my hands or almost.[9]

I hear the ballad book has been reviewed in the Saturday but whether favourably or Saturdayishly I know not.

You would have been much amused to have seen my departure from Oxford. All the while I was there one thing only troubled my peace of mind—the politeness of the man servent. It was perpetually "Wine sir, coffey sir, any thing sir". At every "sir" I said to my self "that means an extra shilling in his mind at least". When I was going I did not know what to give him, but gave him five shillings. Then suddenly thought I had given too little. I tried a joke. My jokes had all been failures so far with him. It went explosively. And I departed sadly knowing I had given too much.

I have corrected the two first parts of Oisin. The second part is much

the evening WBY and Russell went to one of Morris's Sunday evenings. This was probably after Russell, who had a taste for cultivating the famous, had been to stay with Percy Florence Shelley, son of the poet, at Boscombe Manor, near Bournemouth.

[7] George Meredith's 'Love in the Valley' first appeared in *Poems* (1851) but was greatly expanded in 1878.

[8] KT notes (*Middle Years*, 46) that these were 'To an Isle in the Water' (*VP*, 89) and 'Down by the Salley Gardens' (*VP*, 90). The latter, based on the Sligo ballad 'Going to Mass last Sunday my True Love passed me by', was originally titled 'An Old Song Re-sung'; in a footnote WBY described it as 'an attempt to reconstruct an old song from three lines imperfectly remembered by an old peasant woman in the village of Ballysodare, Sligo, who often sings them to herself.'

[9] ECY recorded in her diary for 15 Sept 1888 (MBY): 'nothing by the post but proofs for Willie of "Folk Lore" he went to Madam Lvatskys.' The British Museum copy of *FFT* is date-stamped 27 Sept 1888.

more coherent than I had hoped. You did not hear the second part. It is the most inspired but the least artistic of the three. The last has most art. Because I was in complete solitude—no one near me but old and reticent people—when I wrote it. It was the greatest effort of all my things. When I had finished I brought it round to read to my uncle George Pollexfen, and could hardly read so collapsed I was. My voice quite broken. It really was a kind of a vision it beset me day and night. Not that I ever wrote more than a few lines in a day. But those few lines took me hours. And all the rest of the time, I walked about the roads thinking of it. I wait impatiently the proofs of it. With the other parts I am much disapointed—they seem only shadows of what I saw. But the third must have got itself expressed—it kept me from my sleep too long. Yet the second part is more deep and poetic. It is not inspiration that exhausts one, but art. The first parts I felt. I saw the second. Yet there too perhaps only shaddows have got them selves onto paper. And I am like the people who dream some wonderful things and get up in the middle of the night and write it, and find next day only scribling on the paper.

I have added to the book the last scene of the *Island of Statues* with a short argument to make all plain. I am sure the Island is good of its kind. I was then living a quite harmonius poetic life. Never thinking out of my depth. Always harmonius narrow, calm. Taking small interest in people but most ardently moved by the more minute kinds of natural beauty. Mosada was then written and a poem called Time & Vivien which you have not seen—it is second in my book. Every thing done then was quite passionless. The "Island" was the last.[10] Since I have left the "Island" I have been going about on shoreless seas. Nothing anywhere has clear outline. Everywhere is cloud and foam. Oisin and the Seaker are the only ⟨coherent⟩ ⟨intelligible⟩ readable result. In the second part of Oisin under disguise of symbolism I have said severel things, to which I only have the key. The romance is for my readers, they must not even know there is a symbol anywhere. They will not find out. If they did it would spoil the art. Yet the whole poem is full of symbols—if it be full of aught but clowds. The early poems I know to be quite choherent and at no time are there clouds in my details for I hate the soft modern manner. The clouds began about 4 years ago. I was finishing the Island. They came and robbed Nachina of her Shaddow[11] as you will see, the rest is cloudless narrow and calm.

---

[10] *The Island of Statues* (*VP*, 644–79), 'An Arcadian Faery Tale—in Two Acts', appeared in serial form in *DUR*, April–July 1885; the final instalment (Act II, sc. iii) was reprinted in *Oisin*, prefaced by a 'Summary of Previous Scenes'. 'Time and the Witch Vivien' (*VP*, 720–2), a short dramatic poem, was first published in *Oisin*.

[11] Naschina, the shepherdess heroine of *The Island of Statues*, successfully breaks the power of an Enchantress who has turned her lover, Almintor, into a statue. This victory is not, however, won without cost: the Enchantress had warned Naschina, 'Thou shalt outlive thine amorous happy time, / And dead

I ment to wind up this so long letter before this, but in order to propitiate you for all this literaryness must add a more human sheet or half sheet. Charley Johnston was at Madame Blavatsky's the other day with that air of clever insolence and elaborate efficiency he has ripened to such perfection. The before mentioned penitent frivilous delight in him. If you only saw him talking French and smoking ciggeretts with Madame's neice. He looked a veritable peacock. Such an air too of the world worn man of society about him. As if he also were one of the penitent frivilous instead of a crusading undergraduate.

You will have to read straight through my book of Folk lore. It was meant for Irish poets. They should draw on it for plots and atmosphere. You will find plenty of workable subjects. I will expect to hear as soon as you get the book your opinion of my introduction a very few pages it is too. Hyde is the best of all the Irish folklorists—His style is perfect—so sincere and simple—so little literary. I have been looking out in vain for the longer review of Todhunter in the Irish Monthly. Has the Freeman reviewed him yet, or the Nation.[12] What of the Pan Celtic? they sent me a prospectus. Should I join? Would it help my book or could I be of any use as a member living over here—[13]

When I see Atalanta with your poem[14] you will hear from me again.

Your Friend Always
W B Yeats

The "Saturday" *has* reviewed us Saturdayishly. Henly says he had nothing to do with it. Have not seen review yet.[15] Went to Henley's (where heaven knows there is little inducement to go) to find out for Miss O Leary[16]—and

---

as are the lovers of old rime / Shall be the hunter-lover of thy youth', and at the apparently happy ending of the play the light of the rising moon reveals that Naschina is 'shadowless', indicating that she has lost her soul and humanity.

[12] A brief notice of Todhunter's *The Banshee* appeared in the *Irish Monthly*, July 1888, and the *Nation* reviewed it at some length on 25 Aug 1888. The *Freeman's Journal* did not review the book.

[13] See p. 83. WBY did not join the Society, and in *Mem* (55) recalls that he 'had almost from the first the enmity of these poets, and had probably earned it by some needless criticism at a moment of exasperation'. Though flourishing in the late 1880s, the Society went into decline in 1891.

[14] KT's 'The Children of Lir' appeared in *Atalanta* in October 1888, with illustrations by E. Wilson.

[15] The *Saturday Review*, to which Henley was a frequent contributor in the 1880s, was an outspoken opponent of Irish nationalism, and might have been expected to notice *PBYI* in a hostile way. Its brief paragraph on 28 July 1888 (119) read:

The title of *Poems and Ballads of Young Ireland*, and an enthusiastic reference to the 'clarion' (*lege* 'tin trumpet') of Thomas Davis need not too much startle the timid Saxon. Except one or two inanities of Mr John Todhunter's, and a harmless effort from a young lady who probably cherishes a lock of 'Speranza's' hair, there is little or nothing that has even a snatch of sedition, and there is some very fair verse in the florid Hibernian fashion, after which the Harp of Erin (may it have no worse occupation!) is very welcome to discourse its not unsweet music.

[16] On 8 Sept 1888 Ellen O'Leary had evidently sent WBY a poem and in the covering letter (Belfast) asked, 'Would Mr Henley publish the enclosed do you think? Does he pay for verses?' The poem, which

heard the interesting question of the thickness of steaks at various parts of the world discussed at great length. Every one is very kind there but the Lord deliver us from Journalists. I met Sladen the australian poet and liked him—He much admires your poems.[17] Henley praises St Francis thinks it the best of yours he has seen—His book has been a great success. The expenses were very heavy as a large number of copies were printed expensively on japanese paper at Midsummer he had made twopence profit. There has been a good sale since. This very long letter has grown bit by bit. Several times I thought I had come to the end—but there being no stamps in the near neighbourhood, each time adding a bit. When my story which I am once more at work on came to a check at any time I took up this letter and added a bit.

Outside my window the balcony is all covered with whirls of fire-red leaves from the virginia creeper. To day it is raining and blowing and they are flying hither and thither or gathered in corners sodden with wet. How saddening is this old age of the year. All summer the wooden pilasters of the balcony have been covered with greenest leaves and pinkest sweet-pie flower. Now even the horse chesnut has begun to wither. The chesnuts fall every now and then with quite a loud rustle and thud, and the whole house at the garden side is covered with a crimson ruin of creeper and the sunflowers are all leening down weighted by their heavy seeds.

Has Ash King reviewed the ballad book? A review in Truth would hept [*for* help] it.[18] Has it sold at all well? I see it for sale at Irish Exhibition. A copy should be sent to British Museum.[19] Irish publishers are careless about this as I found in Folk lore hunts.

---

she does not name, is no longer with the letter; Henley apparently declined it, for neither the *Saturday Review* nor the *Scots Observer*, which was soon to be launched and of which he later became editor, published any verse by her.

  [17] Douglas Brooke Wheelton Sladen (1856–1947) was in fact born in London and educated at Oxford. He spent five years in Australia, was appointed to the first chair of Modern History in the University of Sydney, and published *Australian Lyrics* (1882), *Poetry of Exiles* (1883), and *A Summer Christmas* (1884). In 1888 he edited three anthologies of Australian poetry, of which his *Australian Ballads and Rhymes* was said to have had a very large sale. In his *Twenty Years of My Life* (1915), he recalls evenings at Henley's; in the early 1890s WBY was regularly to attend the Sladens' 'at homes' at 32 Addison Mansions. Sladen did not actually meet KT until after her marriage but they were in correspondence and she gave him at this time introductions to Louise Imogen Guiney and other American writers, since he was about to set off for an extended tour of the USA.

  [18] A brief notice of *PBYI* appeared in the column 'Letter on Books', over the name of 'Desmond B. O'Brien' (Richard Ashe King) in *Truth*, 15 Nov 1888 (878). The volume was commended for 'a sincerity which is most refreshing in these days of over-elaborated verse'; KT and Todhunter were mentioned as contributors 'known to fame already', and WBY's 'Stolen Child' singled out as having in it 'something of Shelley's music and much of "the native magic of the Celt".'

  [19] An exhibition held at Olympia, Kensington, 4 June–27 Oct 1888, displayed 'Products and Manufactures of Ireland' and 'Irish Arts and Antiquities'. *PBYI* had not yet been sent to the British Museum, where the copy—perhaps the result of this letter—is date-stamped '23 FE 89'.

PS. 2.

Just got your letter. Could you send me the sketch of you in Nation? The description of your own which you refer to. it would much help.[20]

Certainly I will try and get to see Mr Ranking as soon as I can.

Proofs I will send one of these days with pleasure just now I am going through them with Todhunter. Tomorrow or next day I will send them or the first batches the rest after.

I have an amusing piece of news you may not have heard. Charles Johnston has followed Madame Blavatsky's niece to Moscow and will there be married to her. He will be back in London with his wife on October the 8th. They told nobody about it. The girls mother—says Madame—cries unceasingly and Madame herself says they are "Flap doodles". Johnston *was* in the running for Mahatmaship and now how are the mighty fallen. Theosophy despairs, only the young wife of the dandy philosopher of gesture throws up her eyes and says "oh that beautiful young man and how wicked of Theosophy to try and prevent people from falling in love". Madame covers them with her lambent raillery. The future Mrs Johnston is very nice decidedly pretty with a laugh like bells of silver and speaks several languages and is not older than Johnston. If you only heard Madame Blavatsky trying to pronounce Ballykilbeg.[21]

Your poem on Fluffy is very good full of unstrained naivety but will write about it when I see "the Children of Lir". Want to catch post now and get some afternoon tea which I hear clattering below.

This letter is none of your "cock-boats" but a regular "three decker" of a letter.

ALS Huntington. McHugh, 65–71; Wade, 84–90.

[20] KT had presumably told WBY of an article to appear on 3 Nov 1888 in the *Nation*, the first in a new series 'Living Irish Literary Celebrities', devoted to her as 'a writer, not old in years, but of sufficient merit in achievement to have made a distinct place for herself in the literary history of our generation'. The article went on (3–4) to identify genuineness of feeling, as opposed to depth of thought, as KT's chief quality and praised the Irish inspiration of her work. The 'description of your own', her account of *Shamrocks*, was quoted verbatim: 'It is little imitative and in it I think I have gone far toward finding myself, whatever that self may be. While retaining the love of colour, which would have been my distinguishing characteristic in any case, it has outgrown, at least consciously, Pre-Raphaelite inspiration, and has acquired simplicity, which must be a gain.'

[21] HPB permitted less dedicated theosophists to marry, but those 'determined to tread that path of discipleship which leads to the highest goals' were instructed to remain celibate: 'Can a man serve two masters?' she asked in *The Key to Theosophy* (1889), 'No! Then it is equally impossible for him to divide his attention between the pursuit of Occultism and a wife. If he tries to, he will assuredly fail in doing either properly. . . . ' Charles Johnston, having been groomed for Mahatmaship, should have remained single; nevertheless, he and Vera Vladimirovna de Zhelikhovskaya (d. 1922), HPB's niece, were married on 14 Oct (o.s.) 1888. The Johnston family home was at Ballykilbeg, Co. Down.

To Ernest Rhys[1], [? early October 1888]

3 Blenheim Road | Bedford Park

My dear Rhys

I see by the paper for the day before yesterday that Folk Lore Book is out. Would you kindly get me some copies and suggest to Scott that he send copies for review to the following Irish papers and magazines *Irish Monthly* (sure of a good review) *Freeman* (have a friend who does the books on it) *Irish Times, Evening Mail, Express United Ireland, Nation.*[2]

Most of these papers have reviewed favourably things of mine more than once, as they came out in magazines. Probably Scott would have sent to these in any case. But I want him to send to the two following Sligo papers if he thinks fit, the *Sligo Chronicle & Sligo Independent.* The book is full—at least my part of it is—with yarns about Sligo in addition Sligo is my native place—considering which they will probably blow trumpets to some small extent[3] and sell some copies as well as helping the sale down there of my poems now being printed.

Please rattle up Scott in the matter of copies for me. ⟨You will send me two extra⟩ I had almost forgot to say that if they send a copy to *Lucifer* (of Duke St Adelphi) Madame Blavatsky will review it.[4] Will you be able to get me one of these days what remains due to me for book. I or rather we are cleared out at present.[5] Make plain to the mind of Scott that I have taken much trouble about book and that there is *origonal matter of value which no one else could have got*, that is to say Douglas Hydes stories—one of them the

---

[1] See p. 15.

[2] The item of 'day before yesterday' is untraced; *FFT* was not announced in the *Pall Mall Gazette*, the paper the Yeatses took, until 15 Oct 1888. Of the Irish papers listed, only two published reviews of the book: the *Irish Monthly* (November 1888, 687–8) and the *Nation* (27 Oct 1888, 4). The friend who reviewed for the *Freeman's Journal*—probably Richard Ashe King, whose regular column, 'In Bookland', was published there for some years under the pseudonym 'Fergus'—seems not to have obliged.

[3] Both Sligo papers reviewed *FFT* on the same day, 13 Oct 1888. The *Chronicle's* review (3) was composed largely of quotations from the book, and also mentioned WBY's favourable remarks on Fr. O'Rorke, the historian of Sligo. The *Independent* (4) quoted at even greater length from the book, commenting that *FFT* was deserving of notice in its pages 'on two grounds—the numerous references to Sligo throughout its pages; and the author, Mr Yeats, being a Sligoman', remarks that may have echoed a covering letter of WBY's. (Since WBY had been born in Dublin, he was an adopted rather than a native son.)

[4] No review of *FFT* appeared in *Lucifer*.

[5] ECY in her diary (MBY) recorded the onset of 'another crisis' on 17 Sept 1888, with 'only 2 pence in the house'. The 'crisis' continued until 6 Oct; on 21 Sept she wrote that 'the family between them all couldn't make up a farthing.' They lived meagrely on credit and, as the entry for 27 Sept shows, entertaining guests called for special ingenuity: 'Dr & Mrs Todhunter came to tea the amusing thing about it was that Willie borrowed 3/– from them which they little knew was destined to purchase tea sugar butter & marmalade for their tea.' It was almost certainly Scott's payment to WBY that relieved the situation, for on 10 Oct ECY was able to pay overdue tax 'out of Willie's money', so saving JBY from the threat of prosecution.

finest thing in the book almost[6]—and some gathering of my own besides in notes &c. Likewise I have copied much. York Powell says[7] you should give me 12 copies such being the usual, however I suppose Scott has is [*for* his] own custom in this matter.

My poems will be soon out now—proofs are mostly all to hand.

Am buisy writing a story and otherwise, on days I cannot get to the British to finish Esope for Nutt.

Will you soon be in Town—by the way that Folk lore book gained very greatly from the help of Hyde. I sent the proof sheets to him in most cases and he made a number of notes on gaelic words etc. The proof sheets of some of the additions and also of footnotes in some cases, were not seen by me at all; As there was so little time, Scotts printer revised them himself. Feel curious about them.

The address of *Irish Monthly* is Rev Matthew Russel. St Francis Xaviers Upper Gardeners St. Dublin. I have not the address of Sligo papers but the names of the papers and no other address than Sligo would reach. If they send me two additional copies I will dispatch them to Sligo myself If they like, with some sort of a note most likely.

Yours very Sincerely
W B Yeats

Please criticise book when you write.

ALS BL. Partly in Wade, 90–1.

To John O'Leary, 8 October [1888]

3 Blenheim Road | Bedford Park | Turnham Green
Oct 8

My dear Mr O'Leary

I quite let the acknowledgement of those forms and checks slip out of my mind. Your letter to day for the first time brought them to memory. I suppose they were crowded into forgetfulness by the telegrams wherewith Walter Scott's printer was pelting me at the time—however that matter is over and the book out, I send this post or next a copy to Miss O'Leary—I brought "forms" to Keegan Paul and one of the checks. The one pound check I had to borrow for a few days but will send amount to Keegan Paul tomorrow or next day when paid for Folk Tales book. Rhys (editor of Camelot Classics) is much delighted with Folk Tale book: says it is one of the half dozen books of his series he is proud of.

[6] See p. 88.
[7] ECY mentions in her diary (MBY) for 2 Oct 1888 that 'Mr York Powell called saw Willie.'

The Article on Allingham is all you say most likely as well as much misprinted.[1] I find it hard not to think of somebody like Sparling when writing prose and writing at them. I have some notion of doing Todhunter for Providence Journal also Proffessor Rhys' (not Camelot Rhys) book on ancient Celtic religion.[2] My novel or novelette draws to a close. The first draft is complete. It is all about a curate and a young man from the country. The difficulty is to keep the characters from turning into eastern symbolic monsters of some sort which would be a curious thing to happen to a curate and a young man from the country.

There is little news. Charles Johnston is gone to Russia to get married to Madame Blavasky's neice who is pretty and simple—Madame Blavatsky and her sister (the girl's mother) do not much like it. The sister weeps & Madame covers them with lambent railery —she likes Johnston very much but then he was intended for a Mahatma. The lodge Blavatsky despairs. He is the last failure. Only one member of the lodge is happy a young lady[3] who turnd up her eyes and said "oh that beautiful young man. How wicked of Theosophy to try and prevent people from falling in love."

We are all well. I am writing to Miss O Leary.

Yours very sincerely
W B Yeats

[*At top of first page*]
Keegan Paul cannot make out enclosed three forms[4] no more can I. I send them in hopes you will remember the names.

ALS Berg. Wade, 91–2.

[1] 'The Poet of Ballyshannon' (*LNI*, 163–74), WBY's review of William Allingham's *Irish Songs and Poems* (1887) in *PSJ*, 2 Sept 1888, is important for his early views on the relationship of nationalism to symbolism; JO'L may have objected to what he saw as its mystical tendencies, or to WBY's criticism of Allingham's long poem, *Laurence Bloomfield in Ireland*.

[2] WBY read *Lectures on the Origin and Growth of Religion as Illustrated by Celtic Heathendom* (Hibbert Lectures 1886, published 1888), by Professor Sir John Rhys (1840–1915), Principal of Jesus College, Oxford, soon after its appearance and although he did not review it, he mentions Rhys in a number of articles after January 1889. For a time he was influenced by Rhys's solar interpretation of bardic myth and said (*UP* II. 119) that *Celtic Heathendom*, together with Henri d'Arbois de Jubainville's *Le Cycle mythologique irlandais et la mytholigie celtique* (Paris, 1884) and Alfred Nutt and Kuno Meyer's *The Voyage of Bran* (1895, 1897), were 'the three books without which there is no understanding of Celtic legends'. He later used part of Rhys's book as a source for *The Only Jealousy of Emer* (1919).

[3] Mrs Edmund Russell (see p. 96, n. 6).

[4] The forms in question are no longer with the letter.

To John O'Leary, [after 13 October 1888]

3 Blenheim Road | Bedford Park | Turnham Green

Dear Mr O'Leary

The enclosed order form is not very legible Keegan Paul cannot make it out. The trouble is in the name I imagine.

One of the Sligo papers has given two culumns of quotations from Folk Lore book. They quoted all the parts about Sligo, including my two poems. This is the first review yet.[1]

What Irish American papers should I tell Walter Scott to send to, besides Boston Pilot.[2]

I have had a letter from Russel lamenting over what he calls "that detestable rumour" about C Johnston. He is very amusing on the subject. Never will he make any one his ideal again &c. Miss Tynan he says will crow over him.[3]

Yours very Sincerely

W B Yeats

ALS NLI. Wade, 91.

To Douglas Hyde, 9 November [1888]

3 Blenheim Road | Bedford Park | Chiswick

Nov 9

My dear Hyde

Can you tell me anything about a fairy called Fear-shee translated "Man of peace" by McNally? I ask you because I have an article on the ⟨cataloguing⟩ classification of Irish spirits on hand. Are there many forgotton to be mentioned in my notes of fairy tale book?[1]

---

[1] See p. 102, n. 3. It was evidently the *Sligo Independent* of 13 October that had reached WBY, for the review in that paper quoted his two poems with Sligo settings, 'The Stolen Child' and 'The Priest of Coloony' ('The Ballad of Father O'Hart'). The *Independent*, being the more Unionist and Protestant of the two papers, was probably the one George Pollexfen took and consequently the first to be sent on.

[2] An anonymous review of *FFT* appeared in the *Boston Pilot* on 17 Nov 1888 (4). No other American notices have come to light.

[3] The Dublin theosophists were supposed to remain chaste and unmarried, so Johnston's defection was a falling away in AE's eyes. KT, who confessed that she 'had an irreverent attitude towards Theosophy, which must have been a bit trying to my friends', upon hearing of Johnston's marriage 'was the first to convey the staggering news to George Russell. He looked on it as an invention of the enemy. It was really a shock to him; and for the first and only time he did not beam at me.' (*25 Years*, 252.)

[1] McAnally asserts in *Irish Wonders* (110) that 'The Banshee is quite distinct from the Fearshee or Shifra, the Man of Peace, the latter bringing good tidings and singing a joyful lay near the house when unexpected good fortune is to befall any or all its inmates.' In his article on 'Irish Fairies, Ghosts,

I hope you got the copy I sent you some while since?[2]

William Morris praises your folk tales much—thinks you are the best writer in the book by a great deal. I hope you will give us copious folk tale gatherings some of these days, in English of [*for* or] if in Gaelic with translations though indeed there is little doubt what gaelic you publish will someday be translated.

Is there any immediate liklihood of collected ballads by you. I regret you did not more largely contribute to ballad book. How does that book sell I wonder?[3]

Would you mind letting me know shortly anent *Fear-shee* and other fairy question. I hope you will forgive my bothering you.

Yours very sincerely

W B Yeats

ALS Private.

To Katharine Tynan, 14 November [*1888*]

3 Blenheim Road | Bedford Park | Chiswick

Nov 14

Dear Miss Tynan

I send you the remainder of the proofs.[1] They came this morning.

I will at once now—this week at any rate—start that sketch of you and your surroundings.[2] My father will help me at it. I would have done it before this but on reading my story to Edwin Ellis Saturday week he suggested alterations of much importance on which I am still at work and it is quite needful for me to get this story in some editors hands at once as we have not been doing very well lately. I think however three days will quite finish it

Witches, etc.' in *Lucifer*, 15 Jan 1889, which attempts to classify Irish spirits, WBY, probably on Hyde's advice, ignores this and argues instead that the Farshee [Fear-sidhe] was a man fairy, and the male equivalent of the ill-omened Banshee (UP I. 136). 'People are beginning now to run all the various spirits together in their own minds,' Hyde had told WBY in an undated fragment (MBY), probably in reply to this letter; 'the old distinctions are being forgotten . . .' He would, Hyde went on, 'much like to see your article when you have written it.'

² It had arrived, for in his reply (see n. 1 above) Hyde thanked WBY 'for all your kindly mention of me in your notes, you shd not have done it for I gave you no assistance worth mentioning.'

³ In the undated fragment Hyde replied: 'As to our little Ballad Book I asked Miss O'Leary how it was selling the other day but she said she did not know, only no one had been as yet called on to pay [see p. 63, n. 3] which was a good sign, she said' (MBY).

¹ WBY had sent KT the first batch of proofs of *Oisin* in early October and she had sent them on to Fr. Russell on 16 Oct (APH).

² See pp. 95–6.

and I will be able to do that sketch of you on Saturday or at least Sunday. I hope you will forgive this great delay. Please tell me one or two dates—they may be useful. Though indeed I think I will want little in the way of dates—but when did you first write, when first publish & where? Any others that may occur to you would be guides. I think I can do a good little article on you.

Please tell me what pleases you best and least in these proofs I send. What of the lyrics? York Powell curiously likes Moll Magee best so far as he has read, that is to about page 90.³ Tell me also taking the book as a whole what seems best.

I am trying to get work on the dictionary of National Biography. Henley reccomended me to Seeley.⁴ he tried to get me the writing of a life of Mitchell in the "great writers" series of Scotts but the editor Marzials (a very poor writer and shallow man judging by his life of Hugo) thought nothing of Mitchell and only knew him as the author of the "History of Ireland" the worst of his books.⁵ I shall edit another Camelot but am waiting to see Rhys on the matter. Selected translations of old Irish epics—Dierdre &c occurs to me.⁶ By the way have you read the Fairy Tales yet. There are some that would do for ballads I think. I shall some day try my had [*for* hand] at "Countess Kathleen O Shea" and the "Devil and the Hearth Money man" the first in some more elaborate way than a ballad perhaps. It is a subject that would suit you I think—do you feel inclined to try it?⁷ I wait impatiently the Xmas paper with your "Kinsale" ballad—You will send it me when it appears will you not? Also your story or tell me where I can get it.⁸

³ WBY obviously thought it odd that the future Regius Professor of History at Oxford University should prefer a rather sentimental ballad to the title poem and 'Time and the Witch Vivien' (which precede it in *Oisin*)—especially since both the O'Learys had been outspoken in their dislike of 'Moll Magee'.

⁴ Possibly a mishearing for S. L. Lee (1859–1926), later Sir Sidney Lee, sub-editor of the *DNB* at this time and editor 1891–1917. (Could Henley have said, 'See Lee, Yeats, he's your man'?)

⁵ Sir Frank Thomas Marzials (1840–1912), a civil servant who entered the War Office during the Crimean War, and was to serve as Accountant-General of the Army 1898–1904, when he was knighted. He acted as co-editor of Walter Scott's Great Writer series, producing lives of Dickens (1887) and Victor Hugo (1888) for it, and wrote for a number of reviews and magazines. WBY did not write a life of John Mitchel, nor was one published in the series.

⁶ WBY did not edit any selected translations of old Irish epics; instead he selected and introduced *Stories from Carleton*, No. 48 in the Camelot series, published by Walter Scott in 1889.

⁷ WBY did not again use the story of the devil and the hearth money man (taken from Kennedy's *Legendary Fictions* and entitled 'The Long Spoon' in *FFT*), but the legend of Countess Kathleen O'Shea became the basis of his play, *The Countess Kathleen*, begun in early 1889. KT's poem 'The Charity of the Countess Kathleen', illustrated by Gordon Browne, appeared in *Atalanta*, February 1891, and was reprinted in her *Ballads and Lyrics* with a note of acknowledgement to WBY.

⁸ KT contributed 'The Ballad of Courcey of Kinsale', to the 1888 *Weekly Freeman Christmas Sketch Book and Uncle Remus's Christmas Gifts*, a 6d illustrated Christmas supplement edited by Rose Kavanagh. The 32-stanza ballad was illustrated with a detailed drawing of Kinsale harbour. The story was KT's 'Queen Bee' (see p. 24), soon to appear in the *Christian World Magazine*.

I am reading Tolstoi—great and joyless.[9] The only joyless man in literature so different from Tourganeef. He seems to describe all things whether beautiful or ugly painful or pleasent with the same impartial, indifferent joylessness.

Also I have just read Merideth's "Diana".[10] He makes the mistake of making the reader think to[o] much. One is continually laying the book down to think. He is so suggestive ones mind wanders. The really great writers of fiction make their readers' minds like spunges.

How I long for your opinion on this little story of mine. A very quiet plotless little story.

But all this is too bookish—But really I have no news except that "Daniel O Connell" our black kitten having eaten to[o] much melon is sleeping it off at my feet.

Yours Always
W B Yeats

PS—
What of poor Ranking?[11] Did you write?

ALS Huntington. McHugh, 71–2; Wade, 92–4.

To W. M. Crook, [c. 15 November 1888]

3 Blenheim Road | Bedford Park | Chiswick

My dear Crook
    Hydes address is

Frenchpark
Co Roscommon.[1]

Johnston has departed for India and is married. His wife is the daughter of some Russian general or other and a neice of Madame Blavatsky's. The whole affair was very sudden.[2]

---

[9] SMY borrowed *Anna Karenina* from May Morris on 9 Nov 1888 and both ECY and WBY read it. In *Aut* (193) WBY recalls that he had hoped the book might be a sign that literature was turning away from modern abstraction to create a more medieval unity of being: 'I had lately read Tolstoy's *Anna Karenina* and thought that where his theoretical capacity had not awakened there was such a turning back. . . .'

[10] *Diana of the Crossways* (1885), with whose heroine WBY was later to associate Maud Gonne.

[11] News that Ranking was now seriously ill had presumably reached KT. He died on 1 Dec 1888.

[1] Crook must have written almost immediately upon getting this address, for Hyde, a friend from his TCD days, replied from Frenchpark on 20 Nov 1888 (Bodleian): 'I could hardly believe my eyes at getting your letter this morning.'

[2] Charles Johnston was posted to India soon after his marriage (see p. 101), arriving in January 1889 and serving there until June 1890, when he returned to England on medical leave.

Come out here on Monday evening—we have tea at 6.30. come then—
and I will recount the whole matter. You will meet a friend or two of a
political turn—home rulers.

Madame Blavatsky is now at

17 Lansdowne Road

Notting Hill

and receives friends as usual. Let us arrange a pilgrimage thither some
Saturday when there is always a little knot of usually interesting people to be
found there.[3]

Yours very sincerely

W B Yeats

You will find it quite easy to find us—we are a few hundred yards from
Turnham Green Station—

Please excuse this blotty letter.

ALS Bodleian.

To John O'Leary, [19] November [1888]

3 Blenheim Road | Bedford Park | Chiswick

Nov

Dear Mr O Leary

Walter Scott has written asking me to advise him as to the best Irish
newspapers to advertise the "Fairy and Folk Tales" in. Could you give me
some suggestions. What Cork papers for instence?[1] Which of the Dublin
papers? I suppose Irish Times, Freeman, Express. I am thinking of writing
to Miss Kavanagh for some particulars of Northern papers.

Todhunter is giving a lecture at a school near this next Friday on Irish
Fairy Tales and will use my book largely I think.[2]

The poems should be out in a month at most—I have sent off some days
the last "proofs".

Things are much as usual with us. My Father sent his story to Harpers

---

[3] Crook (see p. 28) may have been the 'T.C.D. man' whom WBY mentions, in an interview (*UP* 1.
300) in the *Irish Theosophist*, 15 Oct 1893, as having accompanied him on a visit to HPB at Lansdowne
Road.

[1] The list of provincial papers JO'L had sent to KT earlier in the summer (see p. 77, n. 4) had
included the *Cork Daily Herald*; presumably he recommended the same paper to WBY.

[2] On Friday, 23 Nov 1888, ECY recorded in her diary (MBY): 'Went to Dr Todhunters lecture on
Irish fairy tales—he read the stories very well but his speaking is very hesitating & hard to follow some
of the stories were splendid, he read a good many from Willie's book, & said that "no well brought up
child ought to be without it".' The lecture was probably given at the Bedford Park High School.

and has begun another short one³. These stories of his are quite poetical affairs. The new one deels with the west of Ireland. My own tale is at present being rewritten in the latter parts.

I am expecting Crook here this evening. You will remember Crook.⁴ He is settled at Clapham now—

What is Douglas Hyde doing? I wrote to Frenchpark twice and have not heard—the last letter only five days since however—So suppose he must be in Dublin or some other where out of Rosscommon and busy.⁵ William Morris praises much Hydes stories in Folklore book.

I have to get to work at my story—the *motif* of which is hatred of London—So please forgive this lean and short letter and forgive my troubling you about the newspapers.

Yours very sincerely
W B Yeats

I hope Miss OLeary is keeping better.⁶

ALS NLI. Wade, 94–5.

To Katharine Tynan, 4 December [1888]

3 Blenheim Road | Bedford Park | Chiswick
Dec 4

Dear Miss Tynan

I send you at last that sketch of you & your surroundings. If you can think of anything further you would like me to say send it back to me with your notes for alterations. I wrote it yesterday the first clear day I had. I would have done it long ago but thought it would be a work of several days. However my practice over "Sherman" has made my prose come much more easily. I am now setting to work on an article on Todhunters book.

I hope this sketch of you will please you. As your friend wants to use it

---

³ JBY was trying to make money by writing ghost stories which he dictated to ECY. He left a story at *Harper's Magazine* on 7 Nov 1888 but heard three weeks later (ECY diary, 28 Nov 1888, MBY) that it had been rejected.

⁴ JO'L did remember Crook, whom he would have met at the Contemporary Club, for Hyde wrote to Crook 20 Nov 1888 (Bodleian), 'I was dining with John O'Leary the other night and he was mentioning you as the only Prot. Home Ruler he knew who was in any way an orator. He was asking about you.'

⁵ 'At present,' Hyde wrote in his letter to Crook of 20 Nov 1888, 'I am in my native wilds shooting wild fowl, talking treason in guttural Gaelic and drinking illicit whisky hot from the still, as usual. Indeed I find it for a variety of reasons hard to get away and drifted off on my own hook, but I suppose I must launch myself free some of these days.' In fact Hyde was trying to decide whether to take orders in the Church of Ireland and grappling with Strauss, Renan, Mill, and Herbert Spencer to 'read the worst they could do'. Whatever they did, he decided not to become a clergyman.

⁶ Ellen O'Leary was suffering from cancer of the stomach.

with something of her own, if I remember rightly, I was afraid to make it longer. Was it Curran or another who lived once at Whitehall?[1] Do not forget to correct it if I have put the name wrong. Indeed make any alterations you like.

Do you know anything about the best Irish papers for literary advertisments? Walter Scott wrote to me some time since to ask where they should advertise Folklore book. I wrote & asked O Leary & Miss Kavanagh (she being the only journalist of my acquaintance) but have not heard.

There is little news to tell—the best is that Lilly is working embroidery with Miss Morris every day. She is to be a kind of assistant of hers. She has for a fellow worker a Miss Mason daughter of the celebrated painter of the "Harvest Moon".[2] She likes it greatly they make cushion covers and mantle piece covers without end. She dines at the Morrises every day. Morris is greatly disturbed by little boys who insist in playing under his study windows. He rushes out every now and then & drives them off. There is a parrot in the house that keeps up a great noise whistling and sneizing and holding conversations with itself. He is used to the parrot and does not mind it. The parrot's favourite is one of the servents. It likes her because she makes so much noise and hopes [*for* hops] all over the house after her copying every noise she makes.

This letter is very short but do not be led astray by it send me a very long one in answer.

                                                    Yours always
                                                    W B Yeats

[*at top of first page*]
I saw your article on William O'Brien it was copied in Sligo paper[3]—Very good in many ways—More about it next letter.

ALS Huntington. McHugh, 72–3; Wade, 95–6.

[1] In *25 Years* (31), KT notes that her house 'had once belonged to Curran, the great Irish lawyer and patriot, whose daughter, Sarah, should have married Robert Emmet'. John Philpot Curran (1750–1817) was famous for his defence of prisoners in the trials following the 1798 rebellion. Emmet was engaged to Curran's daughter, but was executed before they could be married.

[2] Lily began embroidery work at Morris's on 26 Nov 1888, initially at 10 s per week (ECY diary, MBY). Lily Mason was the daughter of George Heming Mason (1818–72), noted for his treatment of sunsets and moonlight and whose painting *The Harvest Moon* had been exhibited at the Royal Academy in 1872. Her mother took her away from Morris's because she was neglecting 'her social duties' and she later married and moved to China. (Murphy, 166).

[3] KT's 'William O'Brien, M.P.: A Sketch' (see p. 91) appeared in the *Sligo Champion* of 1 Dec 1888, reprinted from the *Catholic World* of November 1888.

To Douglas Hyde, [*13*] *December* [*1888*]

3 Blenheim Road | Bedford Park | Chiswick
Dec

My dear Hyde

A great many thanks for your folklore letter. Would you do some thing for me? There is an artist here called Nash chief man on the *Graphic* who is painting a picture for next years Academy to illustrate Todhunters story of "Tom Connolly and the Banshee". He is most anxious, by the way, to illustrate "Teig O'Kane" but for the present has the Banshee on his hands. He wants an irishman's suit of cloaths particularly the *Caubeen*. Do you know any where they could be got—either second hand or new, second hand prefered? Do you know any old peasent who would sell his cloathes? It might be a service to the peasent as well as to Nash. If you think you could get such things or as much as possible of such; *caubeen* being particularly needed, Mr Nash could give you *carte blanch* in the matter of the price. I enclose a sketch ⟨by him⟩ of what he wants.[1] Are the shoes anyway unusual in make? if not they do not matter the same is true of the stockings. I hope you will not think this troubling you too much but I know not another to write to on the matter.

Do you know any thing about a spirit called the *sowlth* and a spirit called the siabra and what is ꞅıabꞃa cꞃuıc written in english? Do you know *badhbh* or *bowa* as a name for the Banshee.[2]

I was down at Southwick Irish Literary club last night. Fahy author of songs published by Gill lately thinks your story of Teig the best in book.[3] I wrote a letter to you sometime ago but found it on my table unposted unless I sent a copy. In that letter I asked you had you read Todhunter's "Banshee and Other poems". It contains a very fine children of Lir and Sons of Turren. If you have not got it I can get you a copy from Todhunter. When does your gaelic work come out? Will it be mainly, or wholy, or only in part, folktales? I hope it will be translated into English. You seem to me far the best hand at

[1] Joseph Nash (1838–1922) the younger, son of Joseph Nash, Pugin's assistant, lived at 36, The Avenue, Bedford Park. Best known as an illustrator on the *Graphic*, he was a member of the Royal Institute of Water-colourists from 1886, and was particularly noted for his drawings of ships. In 1894 he was to accompany WBY to a number of occult meetings. The sketch that accompanies this letter was evidently drawn and labelled by him. He did not exhibit the picture mentioned here at the Academy.

[2] The *sowlth*, WBY later noted (*VPI*, 1287), is 'A formless, luminous phantom for which Father O'Hanlon was, I think, my authority.' The Gaelic, transliterated, is *siabhra cruic* which may be translated 'a mountain fairy wind', from *siabhra* (fairy wind) and *cruic*, gen. sing. of *cruc*, Connacht Irish for *cnoc*, meaning 'hill'. In the Appendix to *IFT* (232–3) WBY explains that 'The Banshee is called *badh* or *bowa* in East Munster'.

[3] For Francis Arthur Fahy see pp. 55–6. WBY chaired H. H. Sparling's lecture, 'The Literature of '98', at the Southwark Irish Literary Club on 12 Dec 1888.

Irish folktales that has written on the subject. William Morris thinks your tales best told of all in my book. I wish you would publish a book of Irish folklore in English retelling all the old tales of Crohur and others if need be.[4] What a great work you might make it. Is there any hope of a volume of poems from you soon?

Yours very sincerely
W B Yeats

[*At top of first page*]
My "Oisin" should be out very soon some time since I corrected the last "proof".
[*Enclosure*]
[*Recto: A sketch, presumably by Nash, of an Irish peasant, the relevant items of his clothing labelled* 'Caubeen', 'Tail coat or great coat', 'Breeches', *and at the bottom,* 'The older the better', *in a hand not WBY's. Verso:*] The things are wanted rather soon but not so soon as to endanger their being got right.
WBY

ALS Private, with enclosure.

To Douglas Hyde, 15 December [*1888*]

3 Blenheim Road | Bedford Park | Chiswick
Dec 15

My dear Hyde
　　My father will ask Nash to night about all matters converning the peasent dress. Nash has made a series of very fine preliminary drawings, without models as to yet, to illustrate Teig & the Corpse. He meens to exhibit the series at some exhibition next spring.[1]
　　I have just heard a version of Shule *Aroon* different from the one given by Sparling. Henley the man on the Saturday Review heard it long ago from his mother who heard it from an old chartist. Can you tell me anything about it? ⟨The first line began⟩
　　It is as follows. I underline the parts different from Sparlings version.

> I would I were on *Portstown hill*,
> Tis there I'd sit and cry my fill,
> And every tear would turn a mill

---

[4] Hyde's *Beside the Fire* (1890), containing translations of some of the folktales from his *Leabhar Sgeulaigheachta*, includes no tales of Crohur (Conchubar).

[1] If Nash completed the drawings, there is no evidence of his having exhibited them either singly or as a series.

For Willy among the rushes O!
   Suibhail, suibhail Etc

I'll sell my rock, I'll sell my ⟨wheel⟩ reel,
I'll sell my only spinning-wheel,
To buy for my love a sword of steel,
For Willy among the rushes O!
   Suibhail, suibh Etc

I will die my petticoats red,
And round the world I'll beg my bread,
And my old folk shall wish me dead
For Willy among the rushes O!
   Suibhail suibhail Etc.

And here it ended. This version he says goes better to the tune and is I think
more romantic and musical. "Willy among the rushes O" seems to me
Scotch in manner but is so beautiful I hope we can claim. The two further
Stanzas given by Sparling (who by the way, now that I think of it only
quotes from Duffy) seem to me by a different hand.[2]

Can you tell me is there any translation of "the book of invasions" quoted
by Keetinge?[3]

---

[2] The anonymous eighteenth-century ballad 'Shule Aroon', in which a girl laments her sweetheart's
absence in France where he is seeking 'his fortune to advance', presumably in the French army, was
printed both in Sparling's *Irish Minstrelsy* (232–3) and in WBY's *BIV* (231–2), where the title is
translated as 'Move O Treasure'. Sparling had taken the poem from Charles Gavan Duffy's anthology,
The Ballad Poetry of Ireland (Dublin, 1845), and reprints verbatim Duffy's headnote about it. In
Sparling's version the repeated line 'For Willy among the rushes O!' is 'Is go de tu mo murnin slàn'
(Mayest thou go, my darling, safe!). For 'Portstown hill' Sparling reads 'yonder hill'; for 'I will dye my
petticoats red' has 'I'll dye my petticoats, I'll dye them red', and for 'And my old folk shall wish me dead'
gives 'Until my parents shall wish me dead'. In R. L. Stevenson's *The Master of Ballantrae* (1889), in the
section entitled 'Persecutions Endured by Mr. Henry', the Master, as part of the attempted seduction of
his brother's wife, sings a version of stanza 3 close to, but not identical with, that quoted here by WBY:
'O, I will dye my petticoats red / With my dear boy I'll beg my bread, / Though all my friends should
wish me dead, / For Willie among the rushes, O!' Writing at the end of 1889 apropos the ballad and
Stevenson's novel ('Chevalier Burke and Shule Aroon', *Boston Pilot*, 28 Dec 1889), WBY noted that 'Mr.
Stevenson puts into the mouth of the Chevalier a curious version of Shule Aroon, which he seems to
suppose the correct one. Before the publication of *The Master* I heard from a common friend that he
would use this version, and wrote at once to a well known authority on Irish songs about it and got the
answer I expected, that it was a Scotch or North of Ireland variation, and certainly much later than the
words given by Gavan Duffy. It is a corruption, but a pretty one. . . . "For Willie among the rushes,
O!" is beautiful. I wish we could claim it.' (*LNI*, 91–2.) Henley's mother was Emma Morgan (1828–88),
a descendant of Joseph Warton. Henley himself, although at this time editor of the *Magazine of Art*, had
contributed regularly to the *Saturday Review* throughout the 1880s; it was doubtless he who told WBY of
Stevenson's use of this form of the ballad.

[3] *Leabhar Gabhála* (The Book of Invasions) is a fictitious history of Ireland from the earliest times to
the coming of Christianity, but was considered as authoritative by Geoffrey Keating (*c.* 1570–*c.* 1645),
priest, poet, and one of the most influential Irish historians, who repeats much of it in the early parts of
his *Foras Feasa ar Eirinn* (History of Ireland), written between 1629 and 1631. The book as such was not

Since I wrote the above my father has seen Nash about the cloaths. He only wants a caubeen a tail coat and trowsers and the older the better. Indeed new ones would not be at all so good. If they are so old as to be quite worn out so much the better. He seemed to think £3 or £4 pounds a good deel. He thinks you may find some ragged peasent ready to sell his rags cheap. I will ask Todhunter to night for a copy of his book for you.

By the way do you know any other mention of the pooka in the old books beside that one in "Mac-na-Michomhairle". I ask you this because in reading Rhys Celtic Heathendom his resemblence to the celtic Dis represented as a goat & a bull etc struck me.[4]

Yours Very Sincerely

W B Yeats

Can you tell me any thing about a gaelic speaking poet of the last century called William Heffernan or more usually William Dall or Blind William. He lived in Shronehill in county Tipperary and abused in verse Damer the usurer. I know Walshs account both in "Irish Popular Songs" and "Irish Jacobite Poetry" but their are no dates. Could you tell me of any other authorities who speak of him? I know, by the way, Hardiman quotes him. Do the peasentry still remember his name and verse in Tiperary or elsewhere—

On page 15 and 16 of Walsh's Irish Jacobite Poetry are some pieces of untranslated Irish of two and four lines each. I am afraid I will have to ask you to translate them for me. Have you the book if not I will lend you my copy. I hope you will not mind my giving you all this trouble but the fact is I

---

translated into English until R. A. S. Macalister published part of it in 1916, and the English version most easily available in 1888 would have been the opening portions of John O'Donovan's edition of *The Annals of the Four Masters* (Dublin, 1848–57), although this is a summary of the contents of the book rather than the text itself.

[4] In his note on the Pooka (*FFT*, 94) WBY writes:

'In the MS story, called "Mac-na-Michomhairle", of uncertain authorship,' writes me Mr. Douglas Hyde, 'we read that "out of a certain hill in Leinster, there used to emerge as far as his middle, a plump, sleek, terrible steed, and speak in human voice to each person about November-day, and he was accustomed to give intelligent and proper answers to such as consulted him concerning all that would befall them until the November of next year. And the people used to leave gifts and presents at the hill until the coming of Patrick and the holy clergy." This tradition appears to be a cognate one with that of the Púca.'

In his *Lucifer* article on Irish fairies (see p. 105) WBY argued that the Tuatha Dé Danann were gods of the light corresponding to Jupiter, and that the Celtic dark gods corresponded to the Saturnian Titans: 'Among the sociable fairies are many of the light gods; perhaps, some day, we may learn to look for the dark gods among the solitary fairies. The Pooka we can trace, a mysterious deity of decay, to earliest times. Certainly, he is no bright Tuatha-de-Danan. Around him hangs the dark vapour of Domnian Titanism.' (*UP* I. 137) Sir John Rhys in his *Celtic Heathendom* (see p. 104) had identified Domnu, a female deity, as the Celtic Dis.

want to write an account of Hefernan for the Dictionary of National Biography.[5]

Dont trouble about these Hefernan questions until you hear from me again as I do not yet know whether I will get the job. I have written asking for it. Henley recommended me.

Yours very sincerely
W B Yeats

ALS Private.

To Katharine Tynan, 21 December [1888]

3 Blenheim Road | Bedford Park | Chiswick
Dec 21.

My dear Miss Tynan

Would you kindly send on the enclosed letter to Prof'. Joyce. I cannot recall his address. You should read it as it is about the old song *shule Aroon* and may interest you. Prof' Joyce is as you know the great authority on Irish songs.[1] Do you often see him?

---

[5] The Gaelic poet William Dall Heffernan (the Blind) (*c.* 1700–60) was the author of 'Caitilin ni Uallachain' (translated by Mangan as 'Kathleen-Ny-Houlahan') and other poems. In 'The Voice of Joy' and elsewhere he attacked Joseph Damer, or Demer (1630–1720), an Englishman who, having fought for the Parliamentarians in the Civil War, fled to France after the Restoration and subsequently moved to Ireland where he set up as a money-lender in Dublin. Damer also purchased a large estate near Heffernan's home in Tipperary, and was a representative for the poet of all that was vulgar and offensive in English rule. Jonathan Swift wrote a mordant elegy and epitaph on Damer's death at the age of ninety—a rare eighteenth-century example of a Gaelic and an Anglo-Irish poet sharing a common theme.

In his *Irish Minstrelsy* (2 vols., 1831) James Hardiman (1790–1855) publishes Heffernan's poem 'Cliodhna na Carraige' (Cliona of the Rock) and a short biographical and critical note on the poet. WBY would have picked up this reference from Edward Walsh's *Irish Popular Songs* (Dublin, 1847), 28–9, which quotes from Hardiman at some length. The 2nd edn. of *Reliques of Irish Jacobite Poetry*, edited by John Daly with verse translations by Walsh (Dublin, 1866), also contains a sketch of Heffernan (11–17) in which two autobiographical quatrains by him are quoted. Although no entry on Heffernan appears in the *DNB*, WBY did translate, on the flyleaf of a copy of his *Poems* (1899) inscribed to Lady Gregory (Emory), one of these quatrains:

The Song of Heffernan the Blind: a translation

I often am in Shronehill, in Conroy is my bed,
I grind an old quern, I grind it for my bread,
And Teig and Nora with me, no other souls than these;
I grind an old quern & them I do not please.
W B Y

[1] Patrick Weston Joyce (1827–1914) was professor at a teachers' training college in Dublin; he published extensively on Irish history, folk-songs, and place-names. WBY was writing to him—perhaps on Hyde's recommendation—for information on the ballad (see preceding letter) which he later used in his review of Stevenson's *The Master of Ballantrae*.

I am writing an article on an old blind gaelic poet of the last century called Hefernan for the *National Dictionary of Biography*. He wrote the origonal of Mangan's Kathleen Ni Houlahan. If this article does I shall most likely do other Irish writers for them. Henley also has reccomended me to *Chambers Cyclopedia* for Irish subjects.[2] I should rather like such work for the present. My great wish being to do no work in which I should have to make a compromise with my artistic conscience. When I cannot write my own thoughts—wishing never to write other peoples for money—I want to get mechanical work to do. Otherwise one goes down into that whirlpool of insencerity from which no man returns. I am to write a series of articles on the deference between Scotch and Irish fairies for some new paper. These articles are to be done on approval but Henley feels small doubt of placing them.[3] All will go well if I can keep my own unpopular thoughts out of them to be mechanical and workmanlike is at present my deepest ambition. I must be careful in no way to suggest that fairies or something like them do veritably exist—some flux and flow of spirits between man an[d] the Unresolvable Mystery. Do you know that passage in De Veres "Legends of the Saints" on the hierarchy of the angels? It is the most Miltonic passage written this long while.[4] Not that fairies are angels. I am going to tell you a spiritulistic story. Do not be angry? I tell it you because it is pretty and because it is about Mrs Anna Kingsford. After her death Maitland went down to her tomb and entreated her for days in his mind, to make some sign that all was well with her. No sign came. The other day he handed a letter to a friend of mine who knew Mrs Kingsford and asked whose writing it was. My friend at once recognized Mrs Kingsford's writing. He asked her to look at the date. It was dated sometime in November last, long after Mrs Kingsfords death. This was the letter

"My dear Caro" (or some such name)

---

[2] No article by WBY appears in any volume of the *DNB*; nor did he contribute to *Chambers's Cyclopaedia of English Literature*, a 4th edition of which was in preparation.

[3] Henley was apparently commissioning articles on a sale-or-return basis for the *Scots Observer* (after 1890 the *National Observer*), which he was to edit from January 1889. The magazine, intended to have a nation-wide appeal, had been set up by some wealthy Edinburgh friends of Henley's, and began publication under the editorship of James Nicol Dunn on 24 Nov 1888. The first issues sold badly, and in late December 1888 Henley was invited to move to Edinburgh and become editor (Dunn remaining as managing editor); he filled the post with outstanding journalistic, though not financial, success until February 1894 when the ownership changed hands.

[4] WBY probably had in mind the following lines, from 'How Saint Cuthbert kept his Pentecost at Carlisle' in Aubrey de Vere's *Legends of the Saxon Saints* (1879):

> Yea, and in heaven itself, a hierarchy
> There is that glories in the name of 'Thrones':
> The high cherubic knowledge is not theirs;
> Not theirs the fiery flight of Seraph's love,
> But all their restful beings they dilate
> To make a single, myriad throne for God—

You are loosing your faculties you could not hear my voice—I cannot speak to you through mediums"
The letter came from a young Scotch girl who had known Mrs Kingsford so slightly that it is thought she had not even seen her writing. One night in the dark she had felt impelled to get writing materials and under some influence wrote this letter. She was then living in the Highlands I think. Her family said she was possesed by devils and have sent her to very strict relations in Ireland. I met Maitland at Lady Wildes last week he talked much of Mrs Kingsford I could hear her name in every conversation he held. He is an old man with a shrunken chest. He praised her continually. Madame Blavatsky says there were two Mrs Kingsfords "A good woman and a woman of the world who dyed her hair. She was good" she added "but her progress came more from intelligence." It was quite pathetic to watch Maitland that day at Lady Wildes. For the first time Mrs Kingsford interested me. She realy must have been good to have inspired so many people with affection.[5]

I have one of my "collapses" on.[6] I have had it these last three or four days. It is a very uncalled for "collapse" as I have given up going out in the evenings to see any one in order not to get tired out. I find a single vigerous conversation, especially if any philosophic matter comes up, leaves me next day dry as a sucked orange.

Today Tuesday I take up this letter to finish it the collapse is done thank goodness. I got the Xmas "Weekly Freeman" with your long ballad (Miss Kavanagh sent it me) and read it to papa. He objects to your describing the whole of England as in greif because of this French knight. It would only have affected the nobility. He also objects to the queen and her ladies going down the Thames from Windsor to bring from the Tower the Lord of Kinsale. The line he likes best is "Her grave would call me from all lands". I like the ballad myself in all the latter parts best & think there is a deel of fine

[5] Anna Kingsford, née Bonus (1846–88), the progressive wife of a Shropshire clergyman, went to Paris in 1874 to study medicine and so further the anti-vivisectionist cause in which she was deeply involved. Since her husband could not leave his parish, she was accompanied by Edward Maitland (c. 1824–97), a failed priest who became her devoted admirer and amanuensis. In Paris she began to experience prophetic dreams and with Maitland's help used these to expound an esoteric doctrine which drew heavily on neo-Platonism, Gnosticism, and above all, the Hermetists. She became an MD in 1880 and in 1883 was appointed president of the London Theosophical Society, but was unhappy about its leaning towards Buddhist rather than Christian tradition. In 1884 she founded the Hermetic Society, while still keeping strong links with the Theosophists. She died of pulmonary consumption, which developed, or was accelerated, as the result of a cold caught on a visit to Louis Pasteur's laboratory. Maitland dedicated the rest of his life to her memory and her teaching and his two volumes, *Anna Kingsford: Her Life, Letters, Diary and Work*, appeared in 1896. The 'spiritualistic story' told here by WBY is given in more detail in vol. II (415–18) of that work.
[6] In WBY's MS book, begun 25 Nov 1899 (NLI), he records that he was attacked by 'lunar influences' in November 1888.

romantic energy about it; but do not think it one of your very best I meen it
is not as good as "Heart of a Mother" & "St Francis to the Birds" or
"Children of Lir". I am not very fond of retrospective art. I do not think
that pleasure we get from old methods of looking at things—methods we
have long given up ourselves—belongs to the best literature. Your St
Francis was not retrospective the St Francis within you spoke. Neither was
the "heart of a mother" retrospective. I do not mean that we should not go to
old ballads and poems for inspiration but we should seach them for new
methods of expressing our selves. I think your work has gained much from
study of old ballads but this time you have tried to express feelings quite
different from those habitual with you, and have as a result described things
from without—more picturesquely than poetically. Your old knight
however I think is very fine[7]—but as to the rest you have sacrafised all things
to colour. In the last ballad before this "the Children of Lir" the colour is
most rich but it is not put in for its own sake—the rich greys and glimerings
of sunset round the four swans seeming in some mysterious way full of
affection and spiritual meening. Your love of colour too was made to serve a
real vision of a scene such as we all have known, the same was true though in
a less degree of "Aibric". Your best work—and no woman poet of the time
has done better—is always where you express your own affectionate nature
or your religious feeling, either directly, or indirectly in some legend; your
worst—that which stands in your way with the best readers—where you
allow your sense of colour to run away with you and make you merely a poet
of the picturesque.

I am afraid you will be angry with me first because I told you a spiritulistic
story secondly because I critizise in this way your last ballad. The latest—
the youngest—is I know always the best loved. The want of your poetry is, I
think, the want also of my own. We both of us need to substitute more and
more the landscapes of nature for the landscapes of Art. I myself have
another and kindred need—to substitute the feelings and longings of nature
for those of art. The other change—a less important one—you perhaps need
most. It is curious—do forgive me all this—that your other fault that of
sometimes a little overstating the emotion is only present when your
landscapes are those of Art. We should make poems on the familiar
landscapes we love not the strange and rare and glittering scenes we wonder
at—these latter are the landscapes of Art, the rouge of nature—Maybe I

---

[7] KT's 'The Ballad of Courcey of Kinsale' (see p. 107), based on the same story as WBY's 'The Ballad
of Earl Paul' (*VP*, 739–42; written in April 1893), tells how the imprisoned John de Courcey, Earl of
Kinsale, was released from the Tower to fight an overweaning French champion. After defeating the
Frenchman the Earl returns to Kinsale, having been granted the request that he and his descendants
shall be allowed to wear their hats in the presence of the King. An old Devonshire knight, 'The wisest
knight there is', first suggests to the King that de Courcey is the only knight capable of defeating the
French champion.

should not say these things as all poets get plenty of hostile criticism without getting it from their friends but then I think, I know your work better than any newspaper man. Now no more bookishness I had long arrears of critiscism to make up for.

Lilly—as you know—goes every day to William Morris's to embroider. So far she gets about thirteen shillings a week but will get more as she learns. She dines there every day and likes going very much. Did I tell you about the parrot who loves one of the servents because she makes so much noise? It follows her all over the house imitating every noise she makes.[8] Sweeps it has a deadly fear of. If one appears at the end of the road it trembles; when one is in the house it almost dies.

Lolly had a story taken by the Vegetarian. They gave it to Jack to illustrate. I send you a number with drawings of Jacks to a poem of mine.[9] Do not forget to send me the *Nation* with the article about you.

I met an american Lady the other day, a Miss Burn who met you in Dublin and intends to recite some of your poems.[10]

I hear that Lipman is teaching in Dublin. Have the Coffeys seen him?[11]

Hear are two verses I made the other day. There is a beautiful Island of Innis free in Lough Gill Sligo. A little rocky Island with a legended past. In

[8] 'The cook at Morris's', SMY recorded in her scrapbook (MBY), 'had a gray parrot she said he was eighty years old. He lived in a big cage in the kitchen window in the front of the house, but for one day, Boat race day, when he was moved to the back window, as the cook said he spat and swore for days after the race, and she could not put up with it.'

[9] ECY's 'Scamp; or Three Friends', with illustrations by Jack Yeats, was serialized 9, 16, and 23 Feb 1889 in the 'Children's Corner' section of the *Vegetarian*. WBY's 'A Legend' (*VP*, 724–5), written out and illustrated in a Regency style by Jack Yeats, was published in the same paper on 22 Dec 1888 on two full pages. The poem appeared in *Oisin* but was not afterwards reprinted by WBY.

[10] Unidentified; apparently an actress or performer who gave recitations of poetry.

[11] Roman Ivanovitch Lipmann (1866–96), who appeared in Dublin in 1886, was according to one account the son of a Greek Orthodox priest and born at one of the Russian border posts; he claimed to have been involved in an insurrection while at the University of Kiev as a result of which he was obliged to flee from Russia. He may, however, have been related to the Lithuanian Jew Reuben Robert Lipman, born at Kovno, Russia, *c.* 1868, who attended the Rathmines School with AE. In Dublin Roman Lipmann registered as a law student at TCD (to qualify himself for writing a future Russian constitution) but could not pay the fees and apparently went into the clothing business. He attended meetings of the Contemporary Club, where his knowledge of European affairs made a favourable impression and where he became known as the 'professional Nihilist'. He lived for a time at a temperance hotel run by T. W. Russell on Stephens Green, and KT in *25 Years* (245), recalling him as 'a little Russian, with a small, wistful Calmuck face', gives an amusing account of him and WBY in the rain. Lipmann's flamboyant article, 'The Progress of Socialism', appeared in *DUR*, April 1886, and his translation of Lermontov's *A Hero of Our Time* was published in the same year. Late in 1886 he absconded from Dublin, according to AE, 'with the proceeds of two forged bills, several odd sums of money which he had borrowed, the books and ideas of his friends' (Denson, 4). In London he associated with the Nihilist émigré Stepniak, but, losing favour with him because of some dishonesty, returned to Dublin in the winter of 1887–8 and took up residence in the Shelbourne Hotel. He neglected to pay his bill, and was finally arrested on a charge of obtaining money under false pretences from a pawnbroker and sentenced to a year's imprisonment in Mountjoy Gaol. Before his arrest, some of the lecturers at TCD had tried to help him financially by finding him work as a tutor and lecturer on European politics. It seems WBY had heard of this, but not of his imprisonment.

my story I make one of the charecters when ever he is in trouble long to go away and live alone on that Island—an old day dream of my own. Thinking over his feelings I made these verses about them—

I will arise and go now and go to the island of Innis free
And live in a dwelling of wattles—of woven wattles and wood work made,
Nine been rows will I have there, a yellow hive for the honey bee
And this old care shall fade.

There from the dawn above me peace will come down dropping slow
Dropping from the veils of the morning to where the household cricket
    sings.
And noontide there be all a glimmer, midnight be a purple glow,
And evening full of the linnets wings.[12]

I write this letter today hoping it will be in time for Xmas and close it with many good wishes.

Yours always
W B Yeats

ALS Huntington. McHugh, 73–8; Wade, 96–100.

---

[12] This poem, 'The Lake Isle of Innisfree' (*VP*, 117), was not published until 13 Dec 1890, when it appeared, heavily revised, in the *National Observer*. It was destined to be the most popular of WBY's poems, a fact that gave him some embarrassment later in life. It seems to have inspired the opening of KT's 'To Inishkea' which appeared in her *Ballads and Lyrics* (60–1): 'I'll rise and go to Inishkea, / Where many a one will weep with me . . .'.

1889

To Katharine Tynan, 13 January [1889]

3 Blenheim Road | Bedford Park | Chiswick
Jan 13

Dear Miss Tynan

I found enclosed letter to Proffessor Joyce on my desk to day so, unless I posted a copy, must have forgotton to enclose it in my last letter to you. Please send it to him. Read it first the version of *Shule aroon* may interest you.[1]

You will have got the book by this. Were you a subscriber or was it your father? If you were not, or even if you were if you like, I will send you a copy from myself.[2] Just this moment I have not one by me, except those which have to be posted to one or two people who paid me instead of Keegan Paul. And I know that either you or your father have a copy. I shall be slightly uneasy until the 3/6 people have all paid up their 5/,'s however there were but few such and O Leary thinks none of them will mind.

I am anxious to hear what you think of the third part of Oisin and of the rest of book. What you like best therein. Does Mosada or Oisin please you most Etc—[3]

I have not yet decided as to what papers it had best be sent to. I want information especially about American ones & have applied to O Leary. Could you also give some suggestions theron?

I sent a long article on Todhunters book to the "Providence Journal" and a shorter one to the "Nation".[4] About this last I have not yet heard. If you

---

[1] See pp. 113–4.

[2] 500 copies of *Oisin* were issued in January 1889 and presumably KT's or her father's volume had arrived by 11 January, when other copies reached Ireland. WBY did not send her 'a copy from myself' at this time but presented her with one when she came to London in the summer of 1889.

[3] In her reviews of *Oisin* KT devoted far more space to 'The Wanderings of Oisin' than to *Mosada*, his early verse drama set in fifteenth-century Spain.

[4] In his review of Todhunter's *The Banshee* (*PSJ*, 10 Feb 1889; reprinted as 'The Children of Lir', *LNI*, 174–92), WBY announced that 'Dr Todhunter no longer comes to us as an art poet: he claims recognition as one of the national writers of the Irish race . . . everywhere is a wild and pungent Celtic

happen to be in town would you ask about it as I forgot to tell them to return it if not suitable. There was an article on my fairy book, I am told, in the "Nation" some while since. Could you get me a copy? I am also anxious to see that article about your self you spoke of.[5]

Todhunter is trying to get the reviewing of me for the Academy. It will be good luck if he does get it. Have you heard of the new American serial "The Review of Poetry" a Mr Moulton edits it. I am to do a sketch of Todhunters life for it.[6] Dr Todhunter wrote to the editor giving names of Irish poets, yourself myself Etc—He sent copy of my book.

My prose is coming much more easily I have finished this week a long article on McNallys "Irish Wonders"—A somewat unfavourable review for "Providence Journal" and am looking about for some other paper that I can review same book in now that my mind is full of the subject. Do you think the "catholic World" would take an article from me?[7]

Did I tell you that Henley praised your St Francis to the Birds he had seen it quoted I think as he did not know the book.

Yours Always
W B Yeats

Lilly likes going greatly to the Morrises.[8] Morris Miss Morris says once tried to do embroidery himself. He was going away somewhere and made Miss Morris thread him several hundred neadles as that was he said the hardest part of the work. He gave it up however. The other day he said their would soon be nobody in the world but Jews and Irish. Lilly asked him which would he be. He said certainly not a jew. Every day he has some little Joke. The other day he said "all hands talk French" and then he began the most comic mixture of French and English.

ALS Huntington. McHugh, 79–80; Wade, 100–1.

flavor.' His review, 'almost the best I have done', of the same book was not printed or even acknowledged by the *Nation*.

   [5] In a lengthy unsigned review of *FFT* in the *Nation*, 27 Oct 1888 (4), the reviewer praised the editor for succeeding 'wonderfully in conveying, under a light and pleasing form, the fullest explanation of the subjects of the text. In fact when he comes to deal with the more mystical forms of primitive belief, he fairly revels in his theme.' For the *Nation's* article on KT, see p. 101.

   [6] For Todhunter's *Academy* review of *Oisin*, see below, p. 158. The *Magazine of Poetry*, a quarterly edited by C. W. Moulton from Buffalo, N.Y., 1889–95, published WBY's sketch in April 1889 (143–4; reprinted McHugh, 152–4) along with a selection from Todhunter's poems.

   [7] WBY's review of D. R. McAnally's *Irish Wonders* in *PSJ* on 7 July 1889 (see p. 78, n. 1) criticized McAnally for faulty dialect and inaccuracies of fact and detail: 'Mr McAnally', it began, 'does not treat his material with sufficient respect; he is too eager to embroider everything with humor, to steep everything in a kind of stage Irish he has invented. All this is very disappointing.' WBY also reviewed the book anonymously for the *Scots Observer* (*UP* I. 138–41) on 30 Mar 1889, complaining there of its 'poor slatternly patchwork of inaccurate dialect and sham picturesqueness.' See p. 160, n. 3.

   The *Catholic World* never published anything by WBY, although KT was a frequent contributor.

   [8] This was not to last. In her scrapbook (MBY) SMY describes the Morris house as 'gloomy' and May Morris as 'the Gorgon': 'Then the Morris temper hung over all like a thundercloud. . . . Morris hated most things and many people and May hated every one.'

To John O'Leary, 16 January [1889]

3 Blenheim Road | Bedford Park | Chiswick
Jan 16

Dear Mr O Leary

Would you kindly send back the extra five copies to Keegan Paul, unless
Miss Tynan could dispose of them, she once said, I think, that she might be
able to dispose of some when the book was out, if she had copies. I send you
your "form" with Keegan Pauls note. You will see that considering the way
the five is written the mistake was not unnatural.[1] I have written to Keegan
Paul explaining matters.

Could you tell me what American papers I should get review copies sent
to or American people.[2] I suppose the Dublin papers and perhaps a couple
of Irish non Dublin papers are all needeful in Ireland. Miss Tynan says, not
unless their are special reasons, should I send to Irish provincial papers—
What do you think?[3]

Dr Todhunter has got leave from the editor of the Academy to write two
columns therein on book.

Yours very sincerely
W B Yeats

We are all well. Lilly enjoys her embroidery work at Morrises much—
[*In ECY's hand*]
I said I thought only five copies are for you. You seem to have asked 10.
ECY[4]

ALS NLI.

[1] Kegan Paul had evidently misread '5' for '10' on JO'L's subscription form for *Oisin*. The O'Learys
were perplexed by the extra copies, as Ellen O'Leary wrote on 12 Jan 1889 to WBY (Belfast): 'We got by
parcel post yesterday 10 copies addressed to John. Are these our own 5 and what friends are the others
for.' The erroneous form has not survived.

[2] *Oisin* was eventually noticed in the *Boston Pilot* (by Rolleston), on 4 May 1889, in *PSJ*, 12 May, and
the *Magazine of Poetry*, 4 Oct, (both by KT), in the *Nation* (New York), 9 May, the *Boston Evening
Transcript*, 30 July, and the *Boston Daily Evening Traveller*, 17 Aug.

[3] WBY seems to have taken KT's advice, for there were few Irish provincial notices of *Oisin*. It was
reviewed in the *Sligo Independent*, 16 Feb 1889 (4) and the *Clonmel Chronicle*, 23 Feb 1889 (4).

[4] It is evident from her diary (MBY) that ECY kept the family accounts; she had probably been
helping WBY with his subscription lists.

To Katharine Tynan, 16 January [1889]

3 Blenheim Road | Bedford Park | Chiswick
Jan 16

Dear Miss Tynan

Keegan Paul tells me that Father Fitzpatrick has gone to the Orange States for his health[1] and asks me should he cancel the order or send on the book to the Orange States. Would you advise me in the matter.

Dr Todhunter has got leave from the Editor of the Academy to write two collumns on my book therein. Is not this great luck?

I cannot write more now as I have got to go in to the British Museum.

Yours Always
W B Yeats

ALS Huntington. McHugh, 80.

To John O'Leary, 24 January [1889]

3 Blenheim Road | Bedford Park | Chiswick
Jan 24

Dear Mʳ O'Leary

It was Miss Tynan not you I meant to ask about Father Fitzpatrick. I must have sent a note meant for her to you by mistake. Was a letter to be forwarded to Prof Joyce included? Were there also some questions about "Nation" newspaper?[1] Would account for her not writing.

When I brought your checque to Keegan Paul yesterday I found two sums of £1 and 10/– respectively credited to you as paid in October and November. Last night I looked up your letters and found the inclosed. I had evedently (in fact I remember doing so) mistaken second checque mentioned for instalment for your own copies. Who was Dʳ. F. or L? I underline in letter the part I was mistaken about. The 10/– remains a mystery.[2] Whose two copies did it pay for I wonder?

In looking over this September letter of yours I see you ask about reviewers for Ballad Book. Dowden I could not ask well—especially as the book is a nationalist book. Lyster is too West British. Sparling long ago

---

[1] The Revd John Fitzpatrick (see p. 72), whose Oblate order had a number of missions in the Orange Free State. The trip seems to have restored his health, for he was back in London by the following June, when KT reported to Fr. Russell (*c.* 8 June 1889, APH) that he 'looks pretty well'.

[1] See letters to KT pp. 122–3, and above.

[2] On the first page of the accounts for *Oisin* Kegan Paul has scrawled, 'Note we hold 10/– belonging to some subscriber whose name he cannot remember' (KPA, XV. 215).

promised a review but has not done so. I will write this post to Miss Tynan to get me a copy (I have not a single one) and give it to Ernest Rhys. He is going to do an article on my book, called "New Celtic poetry" and I do not see why he should not say a good word for the ballad book—Besides it would just suit him to discover a school of writers—he is always seaching for schools in the most unlikely places, especially Celtic ones being a most truculent Welshman.[3] Has Miss Sigerson's article come out?[4] I hope somebody will lend me a copy. I wonder how it has sold—

As to my own book. Morris is greatly pleased with "Oisin", and says he will review it in the "Commonweal." His aproval is very pleasent as he knows probably more about that kind of writing and story than any otherbody. Oscar Wilde will I think review in Pall Mall at least if they let him but he says they are much afraid of logrolling and always suspect it when he asks for a book. (He has reviewed Fairy book in "Womans World" for February. I have not yet seen it)[5] Fairy book I heard yesterday has sold very well and publishers are highly delighted & I am going to talk over with Rhys the possibility of my editing for him a selection of translations of the old Irish bardic tales—Deirdre Children of Lir Etc. He is negociating with Standish O Grady, for the publication of his "History of Ireland" in series.[6]

No copies of my book have been sent to papers as yet. I am sending list to

[3] Rhys did not notice *Oisin* in the letter on 'London Literary Life' which he contributed to the *Boston Evening Transcript* on 11 Jan 1889, nor did he publish an article on 'New Celtic Poetry' or on *PBYI*. (Indeed, it is doubtful whether Rhys saw a copy of *PBYI* before 1890 as in *Wales England Wed* (93) he recalls that WBY 'gave me a little brown-papered-covered book—*Songs and Ballads of Young Ireland*— in which some of his earliest poems had appeared.' This was evidently the cheaper version not issued until June 1890.) The *Boston Transcript* did, however, publish a review of *Oisin* on 30 July 1889, in a column entitled 'Literary London' signed by Dexter Smith, who observed (6): 'Among the new English poets giving promise of future greatness is Mr W. B. Yeats, whose book, "The Wanderings of Oisin and Other Poems," has just come from the press.'

[4] JO'L had written to WBY on 8 September 1888 (Belfast): 'Dora or Hester Sigerson has had review of it [*PBYI*] accepted by that American paper of Williams'. The review, by Hester Sigerson, appeared in *PSJ* on 26 Aug 1888.

[5] Although no review appeared in *Commonweal*, an article entitled 'Three New Poets', in the *Pall Mall Gazette* for 12 July 1889 (3), did include a notice of *Oisin*, 'Books of poetry by young writers', observed the anonymous reviewer, clearly Oscar Wilde, 'are usually promissory notes that are never met. Now and then, however, one comes across a volume that is so far above the average that one can hardly resist the fascinating temptation of recklessly prophesying a fine future for its author. Such a volume Mr Yeats's "Wanderings of Oisin" certainly is.' The wit, playwright, and poet Oscar Fingal O'Flahertie Wills Wilde (1856–1900) had yet to produce the work for which he is best known, but he had already acquired a reputation as the leader of the Aesthetic Movement. WBY who had met him at Henley's house in September 1888 and had just spent Christmas with his family at Tite Street, was fascinated by his conversation, self-possession, and personal courage. For Wilde's review of *FFT* see below, p. 136.

[6] Neither WBY's proposed edition of bardic tales nor the *History of Ireland* (1878–80) by Standish James O'Grady (1846–1928; see Appendix), which had done much to lay the foundations of the Irish literary revival, was published in the Camelot Classics series.

day—Miss Tynan promises to review me in "Providence Journal" and "Catholic World."[7]

I was delighted to hear about Miss O Learys book. When will it be out.[8]

We are all much as usual. Lilly going to Morrises & Lolly doing the housekeeping. And a story occasionally.

Yours very sincerely
W B Yeats

I do not remember getting the note, about American papers, you refer to but may have. I am sorry to have bothered you about it but know no otherbody who knows.

ALS Texas.

To Katharine Tynan, 24 January [1889]

3 Blenheim Road | Bedford Park | Chiswick
Jan 24th.

My dear Miss Tynan

I think I must have sent a letter about Father Fitzpatrick and other matters to O Leary by mistake, instead of you—As he writes to say Father Fitzpatrick was not one of the names he got me, and as you have not written—The letter also inclosed a note to Prof' Joyce. I have asked O'Leary did I send it to him—Only thus can I explain his allusion to Father Fitzpatrick—Keegan Paul[1] has gone to the Orange States for his health and Keegan Paul ask me should they cancel the order or send the book to Orange States? Which do you think?

---

[7] KT reviewed *Oisin* in *PSJ*, 12 May 1889 (2), and mentioned it in her sketch of WBY, published with a selection of his poems in the October 1889 *Magazine of Poetry* (454–6). No review appeared in the *Catholic World*, but she contributed a notice to the *Weekly Freeman's Journal*, 9 Mar 1889 (11).

[8] On 12 Jan 1889 Ellen O'Leary had written to WBY (Belfast):

I know you'll be pleased to hear I'm collecting my own poems for publication. Tis the gentlemen, at least a good many of the members of the Contemporary Club who are organizing the thing. The prime mover has been Mr Oldham. He has taken a good deal of trouble and has been very active and with quiet delicacy and tact even never let us know anything about it until he had already got subscriptions for 20£. Was it not wonderfully kind of them all. He said they were not only willing but anxious to get out the book. John and I had often wished to publish a small book but could not afford the expense. They are to have a short history of us in the beginning he thinks in connection with Fenianism also our portraits of that time and I believe Sir G. Duffy's article as an appendix.

The book, *Lays of Country, Home and Friends*, was not published until after her death. The lawyer and economist C. H. Oldham (1860–1926), founder of the Contemporary Club (see Appendix) and its secretary, was also the founder in 1886 of the Protestant Home Rule Association.

[1] A slip for 'Father Fitzpatrick'; see p. 125.

William Morris is greatly pleased with "Oisin" and is going to review it for "Commonweal". I met him yesterday in Holburn and he walked some way with me and talked of it.[2] Rhys promises a review also an article entitled "New Celtic Poetry" thereon. I do not see why, when he does it, he should not say a good word for the rest. So could you get me a copy of ballad book? I have not one—gave only copy to Sigersons for some problematical French journalist.[3] Rhys is an ardent Welsham and might be persuaded to consider us all as a school of "New Celtic" poets. Especially as his mind runs in the direction of schools. The book would have to be got at once I think. I wonder how ballad book has sold—

Would you ask Collis to review my poems off his own copy for express and whatever other paper he writes for? Unless some one else offers. I have not given names of Express & Irish Times to Keegan Paul as you suggested Collis[4]—Did I tell you that Todhunter has done me for "Academy".

Not a soul have I yet heard from about the book. Even you have only written— and that an age since when all was in proof—about first two parts of Oisin. Rolleston sent merely a short note to say he would review in Pilot and that he could have spared some of "Oisin" for the sake of "Island of Statues".[5] I was getting quite out of conceit with "Oisin" until I met Morris.

Fairy book is reviewed in February "Womans World" by Oscar Wilde who promises to try and get reviewing of poems for Pall Mall. I have not yet

---

[2] WBY elaborates on this encounter with Morris in *Aut* (146):

I had sent my *Wanderings of Oisin* to his daughter, hoping of course that it might meet his eyes, and soon after sending it I came upon him by chance in Holborn. 'You write my sort of poetry', he said, and began to praise me and to promise to send his praise to the *Commonweal*, the League organ, and he would have said more had he not caught sight of a new ornamental cast-iron lamp-post and got very heated upon that subject.

Despite Morris's enthusiasm no review appeared in the *Commonweal*.

[3] Probably Mme Juliette Adam, née Lamber (1836–1936), who founded *La Nouvelle Revue* in 1879 and edited it until 1899. She was a friend of Sigerson's and was in correspondence with him at this time on Irish affairs and the question of political prisoners.

[4] Ramsay W. Colles (1862–1919) a Dublin author and journalist, was at this time a frequent visitor of KT's at Clondalkin, where he had often met WBY. He contributed to a number of Conservative Dublin papers, particularly the *Daily Express*, which was owned by his friend James Poole Maunsel. Colles later became proprietor and editor of the *Irish Figaro*, in which capacity he was allegedly horsewhipped by Arthur Griffith for a libel on Maud Gonne (but see his account in *In Castle and Courthouse* [1911], 51–3). An unsigned review of *Oisin* appeared in the *Irish Times*, 4 Mar 1889, but none was published by the Dublin *Daily Express*.

[5] Rolleston's review of *Oisin* in the *Boston Pilot*, 4 May 1889 (2), was in the form of a Wildean dialogue, in which 'Lucius' offers several adverse criticisms. 'Leonard' is much more enthusiastic, but it is Lucius whose views prevail: 'If I said that [WBY's] poetry was perverse, affected, luxurious, wanting in intellectual substance and in the sense of form, I should say something that had a good deal of superficial truth in it. Only superficial, mind you, but he needs patience. . . . He needs a philosophy of life. He needs to interest himself in realities.'

seen "Woman's World". The Fairy book has been a great success Rhys tells me—

Yours Always
W B Yeats.

ALS Huntington. McHugh, 81–2; Wade, 102–3.

To [? *E. Scull*],[1] *30 January* [*1889*]

3 Blenheim Road | Bedford Park | Chiswick
Jan 30

Dear Sir

I have long had it in my mind to answer you[r] note. Please excuse delay. Your liking for "Time and Vivien" pleases me, the substance of it was written before any thing else in book and like most things old has pleasent associations gathered about it.[2] "Oisin" seems to divide my readers more than anything else. Prof Dowden likes it best[3] so does William Morris (who intends some sort of review I beleive) the rest for the most part do not take to it—finding it, I imagine uncouth. No reviews that matter as yet. Review copies being but just gone out. Two friendly ones that do not matter there have been[4]—one likes "Oisin" best other does not.

Yours very Truly
W B Yeats.

ALS Huntington. McHugh, 81–2; Wade, 102–3.

---

[1] This letter is tipped into a copy of the 1889 edition of *Oisin* which is inscribed to 'E. Scull from her brother Jan 11 1889'. The book was later acquired by Sir Hugh Walpole and carries his bookplate. E. Scull is unidentified.

[2] 'Time and the Witch Vivien', the second poem in *Oisin*, recounts how Vivien, the enchantress of Merlin, dies after losing games of dice and chess to Old Father Time. WBY never republished it. The MS notebook (MBY) containing the drama, *Vivien and Time*, from which the poem is taken, is dated 'January the 8th 1884'. The lines dealing with Vivien's encounter with Time are torn out—presumably for use as printer's copy.

[3] Edward Dowden had written to WBY on 28 Jan 1889 (*LWBY* I. 4) from Dublin praising *Oisin*: 'I do not think there is a page in it which has not its own beauty, & there is also a kind of unity in the whole book. . . . I decidedly think the "Wanderings of Oisin" the best thing in the volume. . . . '

[4] Unsigned notices of *Oisin* had appeared in the *Manchester Guardian*, 28 Jan 1889 (1) and in the *Newcastle Chronicle*, 22 Jan 1889 (8), both of which WBY received on Tuesday, 29 Jan.

To Elizabeth White,[1] *30 January* [*1889*]

3 Blenheim Road | Bedford Park | Chiswick
Jan 30

Dear Miss White

I have in the first place to apologize for slight damage to your MS. My study window was open and the wind blew your MS into the fender where a red hot coal somewhat charred one corner—

The poems seem to me musical and pleasent[2]—There are some really poetic phrases such as "breathing light" in the blank verse lines and what the "Merrow"[3] says about "The land fields, dark and still" and that other line about the sea lying dim—("dim" and "hill" by the way are too nearly rhymes without being so, to come so close together as they do in this verse.)[4] I very much like the verse on the trees that saw naught beyond autumn "and breathed half timidly soft love songs through their crimson-stainéd leaves".[5] It is the most poetic of your details perhaps, but I like the "Merrows lament" best as a whole. Blank verse is the most difficult of all measures to write well. A blank verse line should always end with a slight pause in the sound—words like "for", at the end of eigth line of "A mothers dream" and "who" at the end of second line on the next page are not good final words—such words have no natural pause after them. They belong really to the next line.[6] There are not however more than two or three such lines in the poem.

[1] Elizabeth (Lillie) White (1868–91) was born at Castlecaufield, Co. Tyrone, but spent most of her life at Magherally, near Banbridge, Co. Down, where her father was rector. Always in delicate health, she was educated at home, but later studied for short periods at art schools in Dublin and Belfast. Her younger brother, H. O. White, who was to become Professor of English at TCD, later recalled (TCD MS) 'at the age of three or four . . . being read to sleep by a sister long since dead with the "Madness of King Goll"'. She had published some of her poems in the *Banbridge Chronicle* of 4 Mar and 24 June 1882.

[2] MS versions of the three poems to which WBY refers are in the White papers at TCD: 'A Mother's Dream', a blank-verse poem, in which a recently widowed mother imagines her sleeping son grown to manhood with all his father's virtues; 'The Merrow's Lament', a three-stanza lyric in which a mermaid meets, is wooed, and abandoned by a human lover; and 'Slumber Song', a three-stanza lullaby in which a mother, coaxing her baby to sleep, recalls a similar evening on which the child's father died.

[3] In *FFT* (61) WBY gives the etymology of this Anglo-Irish word for mermaid as deriving from the Irish *moruadh* (*muir* = sea + *oigh* = maid).

[4] The passages in question are: 'Oh breathing light and living life without! / And dreary death and growing gloom within!' ('A Mother's Dream'); 'On a pale, pale eve when the sea lay dim, / From the rath that crowned the hill / Came a strange, wild sound, through the shadows round / The land-fields, dark and still . . . ' ('The Merrow's Lament').

[5] The second stanza of 'A Mother's Dream' tells how certain trees fear the approach of autumn while others ' . . . gazing on her sickly-beauteous face / Saw nought beyond, and breathed half timidly / Soft love songs through their crimson-stained leaves . . . '.

[6] The lines are: 'not as Sorrow counts them, for / In her dark journal we shall find the days / called months . . . ' and 'whereon was laid he, who / Had been to her all that a high-souled man / Can be to a true woman. . .'.

You should send these poems to the *Irish Monthly* the editor is the Rev Matthew Russel. St Francis Xaviers. Upper Gardener St. Dublin. The *Monthly* is the only literary Magazine in Ireland and there is quite a bevy of poets gathered about it. The editor is a catholic priest of a most courtious, kindly, and liberal mind. I should think the "Slumber Song" would suit him admirably and also the "Merrows lament" if he has not lately risen in arms against the fairies. I always have suspected him of thinking them unchristian creatures. He has himself published some little books of verse.[7] Of course the *Monthly* does not pay for its verse. How few magazines do. But if you send there you will be in good company—All Irish writers of poetry, no matter of what persuasion, sooner or later seem to find their way thither.

You will find it a good thing to make verses on Irish legends and places and so forth. It helps origonality and makes one's verses sincere, and gives one less numerous compeditors. Besides one should love best what is nearest and most interwoven with ones life.

Yours very Truly
W B Yeats

PS. I see that your letter dates from near Banbridge. My grandfather was rector there years ago.

[*On envelope flap*]
My grandfather was rector of *Tullylish* near Bambridge[8]

WBY.

ALS TCD, with envelope addressed 'Magherally Rectory, Bambridge, Co Down', postmark 'CHISWICK JA 31 89'. Wade, 103–4.

[7] None of Miss White's poems were published at this time in the *Irish Monthly*, although some appeared as part of an obituary notice on her in the issue of September 1893. Her short story, 'A Summer Idyll', was printed in the August 1893 number.

Fr. Russell printed his own poems from time to time in the *Monthly* over the initials 'M.R.' In 1889 his collection, *Emmanuel: Eucharistic Verses*, went into its 7th edition, and his *Madonna: Verses on Our Lady and the Saint* into its 2nd. He published four further collections, one of which appeared posthumously. His poems are characterized by the orthodoxy of their themes and by an undemanding lyrical fluency.

[8] WBY's paternal grandfather, the Revd William Butler Yeats (1806–62), was rector of Tullylish, near Portadown, Co. Down, from 1836 until his death. Previously he had been a curate in the parish of Moira, Co. Down. Reputedly the best jockey in Ireland in his youth, he is celebrated in WBY's poem 'Are You Content' (*VP*, 604–5) as 'That red-headed rector in County Down, / A good man on a horse . . .'

To Father Matthew Russell, 31 January [1889]

3 Blenheim Road | Bedford Park | Chiswick

Jan 31

My dear Father Russel

A great many thanks for your kind review of poems.[1] Curious enough for a long time I got no criticisms at all on book and then on the same day came the first reviews *Irish Monthly Manchester guardian, Manchester chronicle* and letters from Dowden and your self. *Manchester Guardian* very favourable, likewise *Manchester Chronicle*[2] though this last too short for any purpose. Dr Todhunter has written review in Academy. It has not yet appeared. I was greatly pleased with Montagu Griffen's criticism. Dr Todhunter praised it much thought it the most thoughtful yet. I do not expect any very immediate popularity for any of my poems. They are too remote from common life.[3] Oisin is more liked than I expected. Dowden thinks it, as do I, the best poem in book by a great deal, but I expect people generally will think it a little mad. By the way I got a lot of verses from a stranger, sent me for an opinion the other day, a Miss L White who lives in Co Down—The verses were somewhat artless but musical and sincere and having often really pretty phrases. She asked me could I tell her of any paper or Magazine to send them to. I reccomended yours. So I dare say you will hear from her. I dare say you will not thank me for sending another writer of verse to knock at your gate. But then, you know, you keep a kind of College

---

[1] Fr. Russell reviewed *Oisin* in the *Irish Monthly*, February 1889 (109–10). His notice was enthusiastic, although he clearly preferred the dramatic poems to 'The Wanderings of Oisin', which he thought needed 'a special training' to be appreciated fully and might require a further review. He was confident that no sensitive reader of the book could 'doubt that Ireland can boast of another true poet in William Yeats'.

[2] i.e. the *Newcastle Chronicle* (see p. 129, n. 4); WBY persistently confused this paper (whose editor, Joseph Cowen (1831–99), was a great friend of JO'L's) with the *Manchester Chronicle* which had in fact ceased publication at this time.

[3] Griffin wrote to Fr. Russell on 24 Jan 1889 (APH) from The Priory, Killarney:

I must say my first glance at 'The Wanderings of Oisin' disappoints me; but I shall not form an opinion yet. . . . There are some charming lyrics up & down the work. I think that 'Time & the Witch Vivien' of the longer poems seems to me the most powerful. But there is no doubt as to the originality of the writer's mind; he has a different way of looking at things from the general run of men. And he has a gift of introducing the common-place with startling effect in his pictures and to me it seems that he does it with great power and charm. I think that I will see more in the book when I know it better. At present the style is so new to me that like Irving's acting I feel I must grow accustomed to it before I can get at the good which it contains.

The remoteness of WBY's poetry from real life was remarked upon by a number of his Irish reviewers. It was, wrote the *Nation's* reviewer (Robert Donovan), on 25 May 1889 (3), 'this sense of unreality, of remoteness from living interests which makes the general effect of Mr Yeats's poetry pall'; the *Evening Telegraph* (see p. 144) noted 'that sense of remoteness characteristic of his verse'; and KT in *PSJ* observed that the 'human role and the modern note are almost absent from the volume . . .'.

of the bards. By the by I found a wonderful account of the old bardic colleges in a life of Clanricarde published in 1722, how the building was commonly in a garden remote from the world and without windows, and how the bardic pupils composed, on set themes, in perfect darkness that nothing might distract there minds.[4]

Have you given me the whole of Father Dillons address?[5] I[t] seemed meagre for so great a distance.

Yours very sincerely
W B Yeats

ALS APH. Wade, 104–5.

To Katharine Tynan, 31 January [1889]

3 Blenheim Road | Bedford Park | Chiswick
Jan 31

Dear Miss Tynan

I got the first criticisms of my book all on the same day. On Tuesday came Dowdens letter, Father Russel's quoting a capital criticism of Montagu Griffens, The *Manchester Guardian's* and *Manchester Chronicles* notices, and also I forgot to say the *Irish Monthly* notice enclosed in Father Russels letter. So far all favourable Guardian finds me rough but praiseworthy and likes me better than any other writer on Irish myth except Tennyson in "voyage of Maeldune", but at the same time seems to know nothin[g] of Irish writers on Irish myth as Aubrey de Vere is taken as typical of the tribe. On the whole I should say *Guardian* does not like me much. *Chronicle* favourable but too short for any purpose.[1] Dowden very favourable, likes

---

[4] The *Memoirs of the Right Honourable The Marquis of Clanricarde, Lord Deputy General of Ireland*, ed. Ulick Bourke (1722), is largely an account of Clanricarde's dealings with Charles II and the treaty between the Duke of Lorraine and the Irish Commissioners 1650–3; but it is prefaced by a Dissertation on Keating's History of Ireland and a Digression upon the education of the 'ancient Irish Fillim, or Poets', in the latter of which is found (clviii–clix) the passage to which WBY refers:

It was likewiſe neceſſary the Place ſhou'd be in the ſolitary Receſs of a Garden, or within a Sept or Incloſure, far out of the reach of any Noiſe, which an Intercourſe of People might otherwiſe occaſion. The Structure was a ſnug, low Hut, and Beds in it at convenient Diſtances, each within a ſmall Apartment. . . . No Windows to let in the Day, nor any Light at all us'd but that of Candles, and theſe brought in at a proper Seaſon only.

[5] Possibly Fr. Patrick Dillon (*c.* 1848–1909), who had been a priest in Longford and Dublin but who had recently moved as a missionary to the United States. He wrote some verse and became a popular preacher. He died in Chicago.

[1] The *Manchester Guardian* notice (see p. 129) spoke of WBY as 'a rough and a sometimes rather inharmonious bard' but continued: 'The chief poem . . . is very unequal. No one has handled these extraordinarily fascinating Irish legends thoroughly well yet in English verse except the Laureate in his

Oisin very much the best, wants me to set to work on a poetic drama for Ellen Terry.[2] I will enclose Father Russels note for sake of Griffens criticism if I can find it. Miss Gone (you have heard of her no doubt) was here yesterday with introduction from the O Learys[3] she says she cried over "Island of Statues" fragment but altogether favoured the Enchantress and hated Nachina. Did I tell you that William Morris likes the book greatly and intends, if he has time, to review me in the "Commonweal". Such are all criticisms so far. Todhunters article is not yet out.

In looking over an old letter of yours I see you reccomend me to send a copy to a Miss Whiting. What address? Should I send to Mrs Alexander Sullivan and if so what is her address?[4]

wonderful "Voyage of Maeldune". But Mr Yeats comes next, we think, and is far above the smooth but rather nerveless verse of Mr Aubrey de Vere. And nearly all his work, though the roughness is seldom absent long, is full of promise.' (Tennyson's 'The Voyage of Maeldune [Founded on an Irish Legend A. D. 700]' was published in 1880.) The *Newcastle Chronicle* notice, less than 50 words long, merely mentioned the full name and length of the title poem, and listed three of the shorter poems as 'very pretty and graceful'.

 [2] Dowden had written (see p. 129): 'What I should like you to do would be to write a poetical play specially for Ellen Terry. . . . The field for the poetical drama seems virtually open at present. For Ellen Terry it should not be tragic & it should end happily.' The actress (1848–1928) was at this time at the height of her fame as Henry Irving's leading lady at the Lyceum Theatre in London; Tennyson had written verse dramas specially for the pair.

 [3] 'I gave Miss Gonne a new lady friend of ours and new convert to love of Ireland a letter of introduction to your father,' wrote Ellen O'Leary to WBY on 12 Jan 1889 (Belfast). 'I'm sure she and you will like each other an artist and a poet could not fail to admire her. She is so charming, fine and handsome. Most of our male friends admire her.' Maud Gonne (1866–1953; see Appendix) visited Blenheim Road on 30 Jan 1889, as ECY records in her diary (MBY), ostensibly to call upon JBY but really to see WBY, who recalled the occasion in both *Mem* (40–3) and *Aut* (123):

Presently a hansom drove up to our door at Bedford Park with Miss Maud Gonne, who brought an introduction to my father from old John O'Leary, the Fenian leader. She vexed my father by praise of war, war for its own sake, not as the creator of certain virtues but as if there were some virtue in excitement itself. I supported her against my father, which vexed him the more, though he might have understood that . . . a man young as I could not have differed from a woman so beautiful and so young . . . she seemed a classical impersonation of the Spring, the Virgilian commendation 'She walks like a goddess' made for her alone. Her complexion was luminous, like that of apple-blossom through which the light falls, and I remember her standing that first day by a great heap of such blossoms in the window.

The apple blossom was perhaps apocryphal, for January, and other members of the family were less impressed: SMY (notebook, MBY) hated MG's 'sort of royal smile' and noticed (ECY diary) that, for all her airs, 'she was in her slippers.'

 [4] An anonymous review of *Oisin*, probably by Lilian Whiting, which appeared in the *Boston Daily Evening Traveller*, 17 Aug 1889(2), described the book as 'a volume of verse that is not only satisfying to an unusual degree, but which indicates future work which shall take rank with the best English living poets. . . . It is a new vien [*sic*] of poetry that Mr Yeats is working, in the old Celtic traditions and legends of flood and field and wood, and while his verse leaves much to be desired in the way of finish and of music power, it has still qualities that tend to greatness.' WBY's poem, 'A Legend of the Phantom Ship' (see p. 55), was published in the same issue of the newspaper and 'King Goll' was published there on 25 Aug. Lilian Whiting (1859–1942), a descendant of the New England divine, Cotton Mather, was for ten years, 1880–90, literary editor of the *Traveller*. Later editor-in-chief of the weekly *Boston Budget*, she devoted herself after 1893 to freelance journalism and the campaign for women's suffrage.

 The address of the American journalist Mrs Alexander Sullivan, née Margaret Buchanan (*c.* 1847–

My ideas of a poem have greatly changed since I wrote the Island. Oisin is an incident or series of incidents the "Island of Statues" a region. There is a thicket between three roads, some distance from any of them, in the midst of Howth. I used to spend a great deal of time in that small thicket when at Howth.[5] The other day I turned up a poem in broken metre written long ago about it. That thicket gave me my first thought of what a long poem should be, I thought of it as a region into which one should wander from the cares of life. The charecters were to be no more real than the shadows that people the Howth thicket. There mission was to lesson the solitude without destroying its peace. The other day Edwin Ellis read me an Arcadian play he has written. In it every thing is care worn, made sick by weariness. I told him it was the garden of Eden but the garden when Adam and Eve have been permitted to return to it in their old age. Yes he said and they have found the serpent there grown old too and regretting their absence and nibbling there initials on a tree. Which was quaint. He is the most enthusiastic reader of my poems and takes greatly to Oisin. I wish you could see some of his own poems his Arcadian play contains this beautiful line describing the heroine
　　　　"Seven silences like candles round her face"
meaning she was so calm and stately and awe inspiring.[6] But on the whole his verses lack emotional weight. Still he will have, I beleive, a small nitch some day.

I got, did I tell you, a bundle of verses, for an opinion on them, from a stranger the other day. Some lady in Co Down.[7] I spent a long time trying to say some thing pleasent about them, without saying to[o] much. They were not very good—though sincere and musical. You I suppose often get such letters. It was my first. How this letter rambles on in a rudderless way. In the old letter, I mentioned, of yours there is a little poem. I forgot, I think, to tell you at the time that it is very pretty.[8] I eny[*for* envy] your power of writing stray snatches of verse. I cannot do it at all. With me everything is

1903), would presumably have been c/o the *Chicago Chronicle.* Born in Ireland and possessed of what KT described (*25 Years,* 186) as 'a very masterful and self-assertive manner', she was the wife of one of the leading Irish-American Fenians. She visited Ireland in 1886 to report on political developments, and covered the opening of the Universal Exposition in Paris in 1889. At her first meeting with JBY she reprimanded him when he began to speak of art and its mission: 'Sir, your patrons would tell you that you had not to consider your mission, but your commission.' After her return from Ireland in 1887, Mrs Sullivan had commended KT's poetry to Lilian Whiting, who wrote a warm appreciation of it in the *Chicago Inter-Ocean,* June 1887.

　[5] In *Aut* (63) WBY recalls boyhood adventures at Howth, including living in a cave and trying to cook food: 'At other times, I would sleep among the rhododendrons and rocks in the wilder part of the grounds of Howth Castle.'

　[6] Ellis's play 'Fate in Arcadia' eventually appeared in his volume of that title in 1892. The line 'Seven silences as candles round her face' is spoken by the Knight to the Woodman in sc. iii of the play.

　[7] Elizabeth White; see p. 130.

　[8] Apparently her 'The Blackbird', the 'little eighteenth-century poem' referred to in letters of May 1888; see pp. 67, 70.

premeditated for a long time. When I am away in the country and easy in my mind I have such inspiration of the moment never here. I have written no verse for a long time.

In the same old letter I see you ask about my Mother. She is as usual, that is to say feable and unable to go out of doors, or move about much.

Our little black cat Daniel O Connel ate some mice that had been poisoned and he died last Sunday.

On second thoughts I enclose Dowdens letter and the *Manchester Guardian* review. Ellis says my poems are not rough but the style is one people will have to get used to. Montagu Griffen says much the same and contrasts with Irvings acting. Please return D's letter and review.

Yours Always
W B Yeats

[*At top of first page*]
In Women's World for Feb is long and friendly notice of Fairy book.[9]

ALS Huntington. McHugh, 82–4; Wade, 105–7.

To John O'Leary, 1 February [1889]

3 Blenheim Rd | Bedford Park | Chiswick
Feb 1

Dear Mr O'Leary,

Keegan Paul writes to me that the copies for J R Eyre & J A Fox were wrongly addressed—I dare say some one at the Contemporary will know where Eyre is. Did I get Fox's name from you? I do not know him, I think.[1] If I did not get his name from you, I must, I suppose, hunt round until I find out where I got it. I will ask Miss Tynan this post. Miss Gone came to see us

[9] Oscar Wilde's notice of *FFT* in *Woman's World*, February 1889 (221–2), observed that 'Mr Yeats has a very quick instinct in finding out the best and the most beautiful things in Irish folk-lore.'

[1] Both these subscribers proved elusive, and their copies were returned to Kegan Paul in the autumn of 1891 (KPA, xv. 215). John Richard Eyre, Dublin journalist and author, was described by WBY in September 1891 (*LNI*, 141) as the 'very clever editor' of the *Irish Monthly Illustrated Magazine*; he had been a fellow member with WBY of the Young Ireland Society, a contributor to the *DUR*, and was to be one of the founder members of the National Literary Society in 1892, when he lived at 37 South Frederick Street. He published a number of pamphlets on Irish affairs, and a guidebook to Kingstown. In *Justice or Coercion?* (Dublin, 1886) he described himself (4) as 'an Irishman and a Nationalist—the descendant of . . . a "Norman filibuster"—loyal to the Crown, and anxious for the maintenance of the British Empire . . .'. J. A. Fox, author of the pamphlet *Why Ireland Wants Home Rule* (Dublin, 1887), had probably met JO'L at the Contemporary Club.

the day before yesterday. I dined with her & her sister & cousin last night.[2] She is not only very handsome but very clever. Though her politics in European matters be a little sensational:—she was fully persuaded that Bismarck had poisoned or got murdered the Austrian King or prince or what was it? who died the other day.[3] It was pleasant, however, to hear her attacking a young military man from India who was there, on English rule in India. She is very Irish, a kind of "Diana of the Crossways".[4] Her pet monkey was making, much of the time, little melancholy cries on the hearthrug—the monkeys are degenerate men, not man's ancestors, hence their sadness & look of boredom & old age[5]—there were also two young pigeons in a cage, whom I mistook for sparrows—It was you, was it not, who converted Miss Gone to her Irish opinions.[6] She herself will make many converts.

[2] In 'Adam's Curse' (*VP*, 204–6) WBY celebrates MG's younger sister, Kathleen (1868–1919), as 'That beautiful mild woman for whose sake / There's many a one shall find out all heartache / On finding that her voice is sweet and low . . .' He was to be touched by her devotion to MG during the break-up of the MacBride marriage. Her own marriage foundered and she helped MG and her daughter Iseult with their nursing during the First World War. The cousin was May Gonne (1863–1929; later Mrs Bertie Clay), who was not only MG's cousin but her close friend and confidante. The belaboured military man from India was Captain (later Major General) Thomas David Pilcher (1858–1928), who was to marry Kathleen Gonne in December of this year. He had been serving with the 2nd Battalion of the Northumberland Fusiliers at Rawalpindi but was in process of transferring to the 1st Battalion, stationed at Colchester.

WBY recalled this and other dinner parties in *Mem* (40–1): MG asked him
to dine with her that evening in her rooms in Ebury Street, and I think that I dined with her all but every day during her stay in London of perhaps nine days, and there was something so exuberant in her ways that it seemed natural she should give her hours in overflowing abundance. She had heard of me from O'Leary; he had praised me, and it was natural that she should give and take without stint. She lived surrounded by cages of innumerable singing birds and with these she always travelled, it seemed, taking them even upon short journeys, and they and she were now returning to Paris where their home was.

[3] On 30 Jan 1889 the body of Crown Prince Rudolph (1858–89), son of the Emperor Franz Joseph, had been found, with that of his mistress, Baroness Maria Vetsera, in his hunting lodge at Mayerling. The authorities' efforts to hush up the scandal gave rise to many suspicions—especially since Rudolph had offended the Austrian establishment by his friendships with artists, liberals, and Jews—but the fact that the Prince died of severe gunshot wounds in the head makes MG's suggestion of poison somewhat less than plausible.

[4] See p. 108. Although MG had been born in England, to identify her with Meredith's dashing and beautiful Celtic heroine, Diana Merion, was clearly irresistible.

[5] In *Isis Unveiled* [1877], II. 278–9 HPB noted that an (unnamed) Hanoverian scientist had demonstrated

that Darwin was wholly mistaken in tracing man back to the ape. On the contrary, he maintains that it is the ape which has evolved from man. . . . This is a purely Brahmanic Buddhistic and kabalistic philosophy. His book . . . says that the gradual debasement and degradation of man, morally and physically, can be readily traced throughout the ethnological transformation down to our time . . . one portion has already degenerated into apes. . . .

HPB agreed that 'apes descend from man' (*The Secret Doctrine* [*1888*], I. 185), but only up to a certain point in her system of reincarnation. Fortunately, modern man has, it seems, reached the stage at which degeneration is no longer possible. See below, p. 468.

[6] In fact MG's conversion to Irish nationalism was caused by a variety of factors: her father's military

Dowden wrote me about my book the other day & urged me to write a poetic drama with a view to the stage. I have long been intending to write one founded on the tale of "Countess Kathleen O'Shea" in the folk lore book. I will probably begin one of these days.[7] No reviews except *Manchester Guardian* & *Irish Monthly* thus far. Both good. *Monthly* of course so. William Morris will I hope review in *Commonweal*.

I hope Miss O'Leary & yourself are keeping well. I enclose a receipt for your 2-10-0 sent me this morning by Keegan Paul. I explained to them the mistake about the 20/- & the 10/- as far as I knew it.

Yours always sincerely
W B Yeats

MS copy in D. J. O'Donoghue's hand, Belfast. Wade, 107–8.

To John O'Leary, 3 February [1889]

3 Blenheim Road | Bedford Park | Chiswick
Feb 3

My dear M^r O'Leary

"Tincture" and "Cincture" are used by me quite correctly. See Webster's dictionary it says tincture primeraly is "A tinge or shade of colour; as a *tincture* of red" and cincture is "that which encompases or encloses".[1] The Freeman reviewer is wrong about peahens they dance throughout the whole of Indian poetry. If I had Kalidasa by me I could find many such dancings.[2] As to the poultry yards, with them I have no concern—The wild peahen dances or all Indian poets lie.

posting to Dublin; her sympathy with evicted Irish families; her affair with the Boulangist Millevoye (1850–1918); and an ambition to become the Irish Joan of Arc. JO'L, however—whom she made, as Ellen O'Leary noted (letter to WBY, 12 Jan 1889, Belfast), 'her Irish philosopher and friend'—was the first to direct her enthusiasm, after she had failed to impress Michael Davitt (*SQ*, 85–92).

[7] It seems that WBY's meeting with MG had had as much to do with his beginning *The Countess Kathleen* (*VPl*, 1–169; from 1895 *The Countess Cathleen*), as the letter from Dowden (see p. 134): 'She spoke to me of her wish for a play that she could act in Dublin. . . . I told her of a story I had found when compiling my *Fairy and Folk Tales of the Irish Peasantry*, and offered to write for her the play I have called *The Countess Cathleen*' (*Mem*, 41). He worked at the play consistently during the spring and summer of 1889 and, as he wrote, it expanded in conception; it was not finished in its first version until October 1891. Published in *The Countess Kathleen and Various Legends and Lyrics* (1892), it was radically revised thereafter.

[1] JO'L had evidently criticized the couplet (ll. 45–6 of the first version) in 'The Wanderings of Oisin':

Her hair was of a citron tincture,
And gathered in a silver cincture

In spite of his defence of the lines here and in the following letter, WBY replaced them in all later versions with the present (*VP*, 3) l. 24: 'A citron colour gloomed in her hair.'

[2] An unsigned notice in the *Freeman's Journal*, 1 Feb 1889 (2), was more critical of *Oisin* than other reviews had been, finding that the book did not live up to the promise of *Mosada*. In particular the

About the checques! The only one that now perplexes me is one for 10/– payed about a month after the first. It is credited to you in Keegan Paul's book. I have no remembrence of any sum of 10/–. I am very sorry to have given so much trouble. The mistake about D r Fitzgerald's checque was wholy my fault.[3]

About the American papers! Your letter from Tipperary I received all right of course and acted on it and sent also to all American papers mentioned in the list you sent D r Todhunter so you need not trouble about them any more—I do not remember the letter, "a couple of months since", about American papers, though I do remember one about that date, which you very kindly sent me, on the subject of Irish provincial papers for Walter Scott to advertise the folklore book in.[4] I am very sorry indeed for giving you all this trouble.

That Freeman review will do no harm—It is the kind of criticism every new poetic style has received for the last hundred years. If my style is new it will get plenty more such for many a long day. Even Tennyson was charged with obscurity,[5] and as to charges of word torturing etc; the first thing one notices in a new country is its outlandishness, after a time it's dress and customs seem as natural as any others. I sent no copy to "Irish Times" or "Mail" as I wait to see if any one Collis or another will come forward.[6] I asked Miss Tynan to hunt up Collis (she suggested him for Irish Times & Mail). I am very sorry indeed to have given you so much trouble.

Your[s] always sincerely
W B Yeats

ALS NLI. Wade, 108–9.

---

reviewer urged WBY to 'rid his mind of the delusion that obscurity is an acceptable substitute for strenuous thought and sound judgement' and was 'tempted to wish that he would study the ways of poultry' since peahens did not dance—an allusion to line 3 of 'An Indian Song' (see p. 40): 'The peahens dance, in crimson feather.' There are, as WBY maintains, a number of descriptions of peahens dancing in the poems of Kalidasa, the great Sanskrit poet of the fifth century, especially in *The Passing Cloud*, and WBY retained the line, slightly amended, in *Poems* (1895) and thereafter.

The *Freeman* review, almost certainly by J. F. Taylor, continued to rankle. As KT remarked (*25 Years*, 255), 'I can see now the red-headed, red-bearded reviewer . . . a man with real knowledge this time, to whom the indiscretions of foolish over-praise would be impossible. "This fellow thinks too much of himself," said he, with that precious first volume in his hand, "and I'm going to slate him." And slate him he did.'

[3] See p. 125. Dr Charles Edward Fitzgerald (1843–1916) was Surgeon Oculist in Ordinary to the Queen in Ireland and in 1889 was a widower living at 27 Upper Merrion Street. He was a close and generous friend of JBY, who painted portraits of him and his children.

[4] See p. 109.

[5] This was particularly true of *Poems* (1832) and *Maud* (1855).

[6] KT evidently found her quarry, for *Oisin* was reviewed by both the *Irish Times* (4 Mar 1889, 6) and the Dublin *Evening Mail* (13 Feb 1889, 4).

To Ellen O'Leary, 3 February [*1889*]

3 Blenheim Road | Bedford Park | Chiswick
Feb 3ʳᵈ

My dear Miss O'Leary

You will see by my letter to Mʳ O Leary that I still hold to "cincture" and "tincture" and have inrolled Webster on my side. Words are always getting conventionalized to some secondary meaning. It is one of the works of poetry to take the truants in custody and bring them back to their right senses. Poets are the polecemen of language they are always arresting those old reprobates the words. "Tincture" is such an old fellow he ought to know better than to have hidden in a medecine bottle for so long.[1]

You ask me what is the meaning of "she who dwelt among the sycamores".[2] She is the spirit of quiet. The poem means that those who in youth and childhood wander alone in woods and in wild places, ever after carry in their hearts a secret well of quietness and that they always long for rest and to get away from the noise and rumour of the world. Here is a little poem written last night with something of the same feeling. It is not very good but then you know the youngest is always the best loved—hence I quote it.

Come and dream of kings and kingdoms,
Cooking chesnuts on the bars;
Round us the white roads are endless,
Mournful under mournful stars.

Whisper or we too may sadden—
Round us herds of shadows steal;
Care not if beyond the shadows
Passes Fortune's flying wheel.

Kingdoms falling, kingdoms rising,
Bowing servants, pluméd wars,
Weigh them in an hour of dreaming
Cooking chesnuts on the bars.[3]

Did I tell you how much I admire Miss Gonne? She will make many converts to her political beleif. If she said the world was flat or the moon an

---

[1] See preceding letter. WBY's affection for this word persisted and it became a key term in *A Vision* where he notes (*AV*[*B*], 72) that it is 'a common word in Boehme'.

[2] See p. 40.

[3] A revised version of this poem, entitled 'In the Firelight' (*VP*, 737), was published in the *Leisure Hour*, March 1891; WBY never republished it.

old caubeen tossed up into the sky I would be proud to be of her party.

I am very sorry to hear how ill you have been lately. You need not trouble to answer this. I will write shortly at greater length.

Yours Always
W B Yeats

ALS Berg. Wade, 109–10.

To Katharine Tynan, 6 February [1889]

3 Blenheim Road | Bedford Park | Chiswick
Feb 6th

Dear Miss Tynan

I have just heard from Keegan Paul. The copy was sent some little while since to "United Ireland". Would you ask them again? A great many thanks for your good offices in that direction.[1] I have both written and sent a copy to Miss Whiting.

The Freeman review of my book must have been done by some person of old fashioned tastes. He seemed to have suspected me of A'stheticism. Peahens do dance. At least they dance through out the whole of Indian poetry. The reviewer was evidently friendly but disgusted. Oisin will rouse much opposition because it has more immaginative energey than any other poem in the book. To many people nothing seems sincere but the commonplace. The "Monthly" speaks of an other review of Oisin. I hope Father Russel will have one[2]—Oisin needs an interpriter. There are three incompatable things which man is always seeking—infinite feeling, infinite battle, infinite repose—hence the three islands. If I can sell the 200 copies or so that remain of my book in anything like decent time I shall care little about reviewers likings or dislikings. I would then have made things simple for my second book. Griffen writes me that his father who knows well the old legends says my "Oisin" gave him a better idia of the mingled nobility and savagery of the ancient heroes than MacPhersons "Ossian".[3]

Yours Alway[s]
W B Yeats

[1] A review of *Oisin* appeared in *United Ireland*, 23 Mar 1889 (6).

[2] The notice of *Oisin* in the February 1889 issue of the *Irish Monthly* promised a 'further study' of WBY's poetry, and this duly appeared in May 1889, in the form of an article by Rosa Mulholland, reprinted from the *Melbourne Advocate*.

[3] See p. 132. This letter, now lost, was sent via Fr. Russell (for correct addressing) on 29 Jan 1889. In an accompanying letter (APH), Griffin told Fr. Russell that 'my father who is well up in the legends etc of the Ossianic period thinks a lot of the first poem in the book. He has had only time to read the first poem so far. It *is* poetry as you say.' Griffin's father, Laurence T. Griffin (1834–1906), a doctor in Kerry, was to be appointed Resident Medical Superintendent at Killarney Mental Hospital later this year.

All most every poem in book has been liked better than the rest by somebody—a good sign.

[*At top of first page*]

I did not send copies to Irish Times or Mail hoping Collis might do me from his copy or some one else come forward.

ALS Huntington. McHugh, 84–5; Wade, 111.

To George Russell (AE),[1] *8 February* [*1889*]

3 Blenheim Road | Bedford Park | Chiswick
Feb 8th

My dear Russel

I got the paper you sent with the "Oisin" review—very many thanks. Do you know who wrote it?[2] There have been no very satisfactory notices yet—though all except Freeman have been favourable. *Manchester Chronicle* and *Manchester Guardian Telegraph* & *Freeman* and *Irish Monthly* (preliminary notice) is the list of them. *Freeman* stupid and wrong about facts. Did you see it, says Peahens dont dance which they do; and that horses dont scream which they do. They scream when in terror or in pain—says also wet earth does not bubble. Dowden wrote me that "not a page is without some peculiar beauty" and that Oisin is far the best thing in book. A man down country who know[s] well all old Irish legends finds "Oisin" gives better idia of mingled savagery and nobility "of ancestral Irish" than McPhersons Ossian.[3] William Morris also much pleased with Oisin and promises to review it himself in *Commonweal*, Otherwise people seem to take most to the shorter poems. D[r] Todhunter who likes best *Mosada Island of Statues Stollen Child* Etc has done a longish review for *Academy* which has not yet appeared.

Write and tell me what you like best and what worst and what the other students[4] who got copies think. The people of my own age are in the long run the most important. They are the future. I am starting a new drama founded on an Irish Folk-tale. The best plot I ever worked on. So much

---

[1] See p. 18.

[2] Probably the Dublin *Evening Telegraph*, whose unsigned review of *Oisin* on 6 Feb 1889 (4) was by George Coffey (see below, p. 144).

[3] See preceding letter. James MacPherson's *Works of Ossian* (1765) drew, like WBY's 'The Wanderings of Oisin', on the Fenian legends, though MacPherson had notoriously claimed his versions to be a direct translation of Ossian (Oisin) himself.

[4] Members of the Dublin Hermetic Society, 'that met near the roof in York Street' (*Aut*, 90); WBY had helped found the Society in 1885 with the purpose of discussing and studying occult religions. Many of its members were to join the Dublin Lodge of the Theosophical Society.

about my self. What are you doing? You have not written lately. Where is Hughes? Is he your companion in that projected American trip. Is it still projected. I have heard many regret your coming departure and one named Hughes as your probable fellow travellor. Are any dates or other matters decided on.[5]

I am sorry that the whole of the "Island of Statues" is not in my book. It would have increased the book in size too much. It will be printed later on, in some future volume.[6]

Do you see Miss Tynan often? She has several times mentioned your name.

Yours very sincerely
W B Yeats

ALS Indiana. Partly in Wade, 111–12.

To Douglas Hyde, 9 February [*1889*]

3 Blenheim Road | Bedford Park | Chiswick
Feb 9

My dear Hyde

A great many thanks for the clothes. The parcel post man was much amused by the contents of the banbox. He had been able to see the old hat through the crack. Nash says that the hat & trowsers and stockings are perfection. The coat was almost to[o] "domesticated" but will do I think. A great many thanks.

Nash is anxious to know what he is to send you for the old fellow—He would rather over do it than under do it. Should he send clothes as well as money. He seems to think so. Should he send tobacco or what should he send.

Lady Wilde spoke to me the other day of your stories in my book. She spoke most enthusiasticly. She said your style is wonderful; that she never

---

[5] WBY and AE had met John Hughes (1865–1941), later a well-known Irish sculptor, at the Metropolitan School of Art in Kildare Street, where he was one of the 'elder students who had authority among us' (*Aut*, 80). Hughes at this time was attending morning and evening classes at the School, and living in Lennox Street, Dublin. AE's admiration for Whitman and Emerson had turned his thoughts towards the New World and although he was not to make the first of his four visits to the USA until 1928, the prospect of such a journey remained with him. On 10 Apr 1898 he wrote (Denson, 28), 'I feel all my old yearning to tramp through America come on me, and if I get a chance I think I will go.'

[6] Not only did WBY not reprint the whole of *The Island of Statues* in a future volume, he even dropped from subsequent collections the single scene published in *Oisin* (see p. 98). AE continued to admire the play, and in December 1899 published a further 53 lines from Act I in *A Celtic Christmas* (the Christmas number of the *Irish Homestead*), which he edited.

read anything like it, for truth to Irish idiom and manner—when will your book be out? will there be any translations in it?

Yours very sincerely

W B Yeats

As to "Fairy and Folk Tales" there is an Article in *Athenaeum* for Feb 9 by a scientific folklorist (David Nutt I suspect) a long article—he praises your tales—[1]

ALS Private.

To George Coffey,[1] *14 February* [*1889*]

3 Blenheim Road | Bedford Park | Chiswick

Feb 14

My dear Mr Coffey

A great many thanks for the review. I am pleased at your liking "jelousey" and the lyrics in it. You are wrong though to dislike my demon. He is the best animal in my whole managery. Most people have taken to that demon. You and Douglas Hyde are the only people who have mentioned "A girl's song".[2] It is a favourite of my own.

The man in "Freeman" was certainly stupid—Peahens *do* dance—I have the best authority for saying it. Wet earth *does* bubble. His other comments were equally stupid. The sunset simile is certainly good. He was plainly one of those old fashioned critics to whom only the commonplace seems natural. As to what he says about riddles—a great deal of poetry must always be difficult. He seemed friendly however.

---

[1] 'The one [*sic*] story here given from Mr. Hyde's collection, "Teig O'Kane and the Corpse", is of first-rate merit,' observed the reviewer of *FFT* in the *Athenaeum*, 9 Feb 1889 (174–5), 'and encourages the reader to expect at his hands a worthy pendant to Campbell's great work. Let us entreat him to follow Campbell's example, and print both Irish and English.' A number of features of this unsigned review suggest that it was written by the distinguished Celtic scholar Alfred Trübner Nutt (1856–1910), who traded as a publisher under the name of his father, David Nutt (d. 1863), with whom WBY is here evidently confusing him. The publishing house (see p. 95), which was later to issue Hyde's *Beside the Fire*, was noted for its folklore and anthropology lists as well as for its educational and foreign-language books; Alfred Nutt himself was a founder member and from 1897 president of the Folk-Lore Society, and co-editor with Kuno Meyer of *The Voyage of Bran*.

[1] See p. 54.

[2] In his unsigned review of *Oisin* in the Dublin *Evening Telegraph* of 6 Feb 1889, Coffey found the title poem 'the least satisfactory. . . . The second part especially . . . is too unsubstantial to be readily acceptable, and, we confess, the demon, with whom Oisin wages an ever-recurring battle in this Isle of Victories, is by no means up to the mark.' He went on to quote Anashuya's song from 'the charming dramatic sketch, "Jealousy"' (*VP*, 70–5; later retitled 'Anashuya and Vijaya'), which 'will attract attention', and to praise the lyric, 'Girl's Song' (*VP*, 723; not afterwards republished). (Hyde's comment on the latter was presumably in a letter to WBY, now lost, as he seems not to have reviewed *Oisin*.)

As yet there are no reviews except yours, the *Freeman* one, the *Manchester Guardian* (very favourable) and the *Irish Monthly*—The book went to the subscribers some time before the papers got it. Hence delay—I know of several written but not published yet. William Morris will review it in *Common weal* but is busy at present. He was won by *Oisin* about which he talked much to me. Hatton Chambers, author of *Captain Swift* the new play of which every body has been talking for some months now, is enthusiastic for the third part of *Oisin* likes it better than any other poem in book[3]— Dowden also likes *Oisin* best. Rolleston however, and to a great extent Todhunter, are of your opinion and prefer the shorter poems and the *Island of Statues*. I know nothing as yet about the sale, if any.[4]

I am preparing to start at once on a play founded on an Irish folk tale. The plot will be the best I have yet worked on—being both fantastic and human—human enough to rouse peoples sympathies, fantastic enough to wake them from their conventional standards. It will be about the same length as the *Island of Statues*. The *Atheneum* had a long review $3\frac{1}{4}$ collumns on my book of fairy tales—praised my introduction and blamed the unscientific nature of my selection. These people will not see that fairy tales must always exist mainly as literature. That science is quite secondary in the matter, their origonal purpose being literature. The *Atheneum* says I should have made the tales representative of the peasent in his stupidity as well as his cleverness. I should have been "beware above all of picking out only what strikes us as picturesque or humorous or profound". I wonder who would have read the book had I done so—not even the *Atheneum* man I think.[5] Oh these folklorists! and what have they done—murder a few

---

[3] Charles Haddon Chambers (1860–1921), born in Sydney, Australia, of Irish stock, settled in England in 1882 and took up journalism and play-writing. Shaw described him as 'a rough and ready playwright with the imagination of a bushranger', but with *Captain Swift* he provided Beerbohm Tree, who had just taken over the management of the Haymarket Theatre, with his first great success. The play had a long run in 1888 and was revived at both the Haymarket and the Grand Theatre in 1889. In a letter to Chambers's brother of 29 Aug [1923] (Texas) WBY recalled meeting Haddon Chambers 'in 1889 or 1890, when he was a handsome young man. Edwin Ellis introduced me.'

[4] *Oisin* sold 174 copies between January and June 1889. Of these, 146 copies went to subscribers and 28 were sold on the open market (KPA, XV. 215).

[5] The main objection of the *Athenaeum* reviewer of *FFT* (9 Feb 1889; see preceding letter) is not so much that WBY is unscientific as that this has led him to take literary, and often inferior, versions of stories instead of the genuine folk tradition. The book thus 'has but little of the tone and accent of the peasant'. The review questions WBY's easy dismissal of the folklorist as a mere scientist,

for the objects which Mr Yeats avows are the very objects of the folk-lorists. They . . . long to reach and grasp the life of the people; but to do that they must know what it is the people really tells and believes; they must sit at its fireside, listen to its every word, watch its every act. Above all, they must beware of picking out only what strikes them as picturesque, or humorous, or profound; they must refrain from any added touch that colours or distorts tradition. . . . In especial we believe that conscious literary art is as damaging to the genuine products of folk-fancy from an aesthetic as it is from a scientific point of view. . . . When we would transform we only vulgarize it.

innocent fairy tales. Invent a few theories worthy of inextinguishable laughter. Perhaps the fairies exist. Certainly an assumption of their existence is the only fit theory to build a selection of fairy tales on. The *Atheneum* man praises my poems but does not think I could give chapter and verse for all I say in them about the fairies. Oh these scientists. Rhys, editor of the series, is however delighted, it is a long time since any *Camelot* has been reviewed so seriously and at such length. I am writing articles for a Scotch paper on the strange diferences between Scocth and Irish fairy tales. The *Atheneum* man sees so little diference that he blames me for not printing Scotch tales among the Irish.[6] There is not much difference in the *substance* which a scientist understands; in the *mood* of the story teller their is the most extrordinary diference. The mood belongs to literature.[7]

We are all as usual. My father doing black and white drawings. Lilly going to the Morrises each day to do embroidery with Miss Morris.

Many thanks again for your kind review. Todhunter has done me for *Academy*. It has not yet appeared.

Yours very sincerely
W B Yeats

Good wishes to Mrs Coffey.[8]

ALS Texas.

[6] The first of WBY's articles (see p. 117) was soon to appear in the *Scots Observer*. The *Athenaeum* reviewer of *FFT* admonished WBY to bear in mind 'the substantial unity of mythic practice and narrative between the Gael of Ireland and Scotland, so that it is always allowable to illustrate the Highland folk-tales by the older Irish mythic literature, and conversely, where modern Irish tradition has run dry, to turn to the deeper and wider Scotch stream. . . .'

[7] WBY was to find the term 'mood' increasingly useful during the mid-1890s in accounting for the unanalysable qualities of literature over scientific writing and in establishing the peculiarly Irish quality of Anglo-Irish literature. See *UP* 1. 367 and his poem 'The Moods' (*VP*, 142).

[8] Jane Sophia Frances L'Estrange (*c.* 1847–1921), daughter of Sir George Burdett L'Estrange of Lisnamandra, Co. Cavan, had married George Coffey in September 1885.

To W. M. Crook, 15 February [*1889*]

3 Blenheim Road | Bedford Park | Chiswick
Feb 15

My dear Crooks

Will you come here on Wednesday next between 7 & 8 to meet Sparling and Miss Morris? Would you, if you can come, arrange with Gill and bring him with you?[1] Please let me know.

Yours very Sincerely
W B Yeats

ALS Bodleian, with envelope addressed 'Manor House, Clapham', postmark 'CHISWICK FE 15 89'.

To Katharine Tynan, [*after 27*] *February* [*1889*]

3 Blenheim Road | Bedford Park | Chiswick
Feb.

My dear Miss Tynan

⟨I enclose *Evening Mail* review[1] as you may not see it.⟩ I got the first substantial gain from my book yesterday—The editor of *Leisure Hour* sent five pounds as an instalment for an article of mine which he has been trying to make his mind up about for a year. At the same time writing to me about *Oisin* "every line almost every word is alive". I do not beleive he would ever have taken the article but for *Oisin*.[2] I got my proof sheets of an article on the difference between Scotch and Irish Fairies from Henleys new paper the *Scots Observer* the day before yesterday. I am to do other papers on same subject for him. I also have two articles with editor of *Providence Journal*. So

[1] ECY's diary for 26 Feb 1889 (MBY) records: 'Miss Morris Mr Sparling the Nashs Mr York Powell & Mr Crook spent an evening here last week, hope they didnt find it dull.' The evening would have been 20 Feb. ECY makes no mention of T. P. Gill (see p. 62), but had earlier recorded (diary, 7 Feb 1889, MBY) having gone to a Home Rule drawing-room meeting at Mrs John Rae's house and met the Irish Party MP: 'Mr Gill is *very thin* with a hooky nose pince-neys & rather prominent white teeth & he swayed himself gently backwards & forwards while he spoke . . .' Todhunter and Edwin Ellis were also present but she does not mention WBY, who it seems had not yet met Gill. Crook presumably knew the MP through his political associations (see p. 28, n. 1).

[1] A review of *Oisin* which appeared in the Dublin *Evening Mail*, 13 Feb 1889, and was reprinted in *The Warder and Dublin Weekly Mail*, 16 Feb 1889 (6), found the book uneven, and thought that the title poem did not 'reach the heights which much less assuming work attains'. Describing the volume as a 'remarkable' first book, the reviewer praised WBY's originality and promise but hoped that he would revise the poems and turn from infantile creatures of the fancy, such as fairies and goblins, to 'the joys and sorrows, hopes and fears, of humanity'.

[2] Despite his advance payment, William Stevens (see p. 65) was to hold WBY's article, 'Popular Ballad Poetry of Ireland', for a further eight months before publishing it in *Leisure Hour* in November 1889.

you see I am doing better than usual and feeling sounder financially.[3] That miserable *Nation* however has never acknowledged an article—almost the best I have done—on Todhunters book.

What I want to tell you about is my new poem. A drama founded on the *Countess Kathleen O Shea* in Folklore book (did you see the long and *naively* scientific review of Fairy book in *Atheneum*. Oscar Wilde says I should have replied—but I was too lazy—there was $3\frac{1}{4}$ collumns—Delighted Rhys by being so much longer and more serious than *Camelots* get mostly). This new poem of mine promises to be my most interesting poem and in all ways quite dramatic I think. I shall try and get it acted by amateurs (if possible in Dublin) and afterwards try it perhaps on some stage manager or actor. It is in five scenes and full of action and very Irish.[4]

Did you read that delightful Saint story in *Irish Monthly* called the "*Rapt Culdee*"—If not do, and write a poem about it. He lived in your own neighbourhood at Tallaght a great many poems should be written on him. I may do a drama about him some day.[5] Do not forget him. He is charming.

All this note is without news or thought but I have to get in to British Museum. I write mainly to persuade you to write to me—do you know, wretch, that your letters grow few and fewer or else I think they do.

Yours Always
W B Yeats—

[*At top of first page*]
Cannot find *evening mail* will find it again.
I read your poem on the wood carver in an old *Hobby horse* and think it most beutiful—Have things to say about it but no time now.

PS.
I wrote enclosed letter some days ago and forgot to post it. What I wished to say about your Hobby Horse poem is that it is one of your very best. Your

---

[3] WBY's article, 'Scots and Irish Fairies' (reprinted as 'A Remonstrance with Scotsmen for having Soured the Disposition of their Ghosts and Faeries'), appeared in the *Scots Observer*, 2 Mar 1889. Three more such pieces were published in the paper in the course of 1889: 'Village Ghosts' on 11 May; 'Kidnappers' on 15 June; and 'Columkille and Rosses' (reprinted as 'Drumcliffe and Rosses') on 5 Oct. All four were collected in *The Celtic Twilight* (1893). *PSJ* had already published his review of *The Banshee*, on 10 Feb 1889 (though the copy would probably not have reached him before the end of the month); his review of D. R. McAnally's *Irish Wonders* did not appear until 7 July (see pp. 78, 123).

[4] WBY was eager to let KT know that he had found what he thought was an Irish theme for a play because, as he recalled in a letter to her of 28 Aug 1906 (Harvard), 'you were the first person who ever urged me to write a play about Ireland—I had showed you some wild thing I had called Spanish'.

[5] 'The Rapt Culdee', an article by 'S.A.' in the *Irish Monthly*, January 1889 (21–35), concerns St. Aengus (*c.* 750), known as 'Angus Kélé Dé' (servant or lover of God), who composed a famous metrical 'Festology of the Saints'. (Tallaght, at this time a small village, is situated a few miles south of Clondalkin and in the same barony of Uppercross.) KT did write a poem on the saint, and WBY wrote, not a poem or a drama about him, but a short story, 'Where There Is Nothing, There Is God' (*Myth*, 184–90), which first appeared in the *Sketch*, 21 Oct 1896.

great gift of colour never in this poem overloads and smothers the feeling—
everything is harmonious and tender. It is full too of beautiful single lines.
But it seemed to me the moment I read it that it had been better perhaps
without the last two verses. I read it to my father without comment he made
the same criticism. It is not that the idea of these two verses is not pleasent.
To me it is an especially pleasent one but without them I think there had
been more unity and a better climax. Neither are the two verses so
condensed and magical in expression as the others.[6]

I brought your book to Rhys the other day that he might include you in
his article on new celtic poetry. He is anxious for the *ballad book*[7] did you tell
Gill to send one?

Lolly is doing embroidery now as well as Lilly. She works at home in
spare moments.[8] She cannot go with Lilly because of the house keeping
which is all on her hands, as my mother has a long time been unable for it.
My father has done a large portrait of Lilly that he probably will send to the
Academy.[9]

We have seen Legge once or twice. One evening he and Crooks were
here[10]—Last night I met him at Horne's ("Hobby Horse" Horne). He had
been in the *Commission Court* when Piggott escape was annonced. And
descripes it as a great scene. Poor Piggott![11]

[6] KT's 'In a Cathedral', published in the *Century Guild Hobby Horse*, June 1888 (114–5), describes the
life work of an anonymous carver in a medieval cathedral. The last two stanzas concern the continuation of
the workman's career in heaven, and WBY and his father were perhaps disconcerted by the bathos of the
concluding lines (which, with the penultimate stanza, were omitted in subsequent printings):

> My carver shapes with happy care
>   The lovely visions of his dream;
> And earns perhaps for fullest meed
> God's praise,—'the work is good indeed!'

[7] See p. 126, n. 3.

[8] ECY recorded in her diary (MBY) that she had begun some background embroidery for May
Morris on Wednesday, 27 Feb 1889: 'it is an immence screene when it will be finished I cant tell terribly
monotonous work the one stitch & colour all the time worked at it all Thursday & Friday . . .' The
background was to a design of rose leaves by Morris. She continued with the work through the following
week.

[9] On 11 Oct 1888 ECY recorded in her diary (MBY): 'Papa began new portrait of Lilly today very like
& very pretty so far the greeny blue dress harmonising well with the like blue grey background.'
Painting continued throughout the month and on 27 Oct ECY wrote: 'Papas new portrait of Lilly is a
great success very like.' The portrait was not exhibited at the Royal Academy and is now in Michael
Yeats's collection.

[10] This was 19 Nov 1888, when ECY recorded in her diary (MBY): 'Mr Legge & Mr Crookes came in
the evening stayed till eleven. We had supper, melon, grapes, cheese, apples & pears. Papa, Willie &
they had great talk & argument, politics, art etc. L & I felt dreadfully out of it. . . . They are all Home
Rulers so they got on well together.'

[11] Richard Piggott (*c.* 1828–89) had been editor of *The Irishman*, a paper of extreme nationalist views,
but was at this time acquiring notoriety because of forgeries he had composed implicating Parnell and
others in various agrarian murders and outrages. (They were the subject of the series of articles,
'Parnellism and Crime', in *The Times* in early 1887.) A Commission of three judges was established by

Do not forget to consider the "Rapt Culdee". You could make a poem out of him quite as charming as your St Francis poems. Indeed considering that he lived so near you—A poem upon him is clearly your duty.

Where is that story of the Lord of Kinsale to be found?[12]

The Piggott affair must have been a blow to our Dublin Unionist friends. I wish I were back amongst them to see what change is in their opinions or what loophole they have found—But here I am stranded for I know not how long, in this London desert. As soon as ever I find my work beginning to sell somewhat I shall be away out of this, to where there is something of green to look at.

> Yours Always
> W B Yeats

Did I tell you I dined at the National Liberal Club with T. P. Gill MP?[13] Coffey introduced me. I like him greatly.

[*in margin of first page of postscript*]

I found both this PS and letter stamped addressed and unposted in my pocket to day (March 8)

ALS Huntington. McHugh, 86–8; Wade, 113–15.

To Katharine Tynan, [*8 March 1889*]

> 3 Blenheim Road | Bedford Park | Chiswick
> Feb[1]

Dear Miss Tynan

I enclose another letter to Prof Joyce. I sent his letter to me, to Henley so have not got his address. Forgive my bothering you. It is another question about a song.

Enclosed are two reviews of no particular interest but please return them with the others some day, in case I want to advertize at any time they would be needful—The St James's Budget one is good considering source.[2]

Parliament to investigate the truth of the accusations, and on 22 Feb 1889, Piggott broke down under cross-examination by Sir Charles Russell (see p. 35, n. 2), counsel for Parnell. On the 26th he failed to appear in court and fled to Madrid. There he was traced by police to the Hotel Los Embajadores where, on 28 Feb, as they entered his room to arrest him, he shot himself.

[12] KT had perhaps found the source for her 'Ballad of Courcey of Kinsale' (see p. 107) in a short article, 'Privilege of the Earls of Kingsale [*sic*]', which appeared in *North & South*, 14 May 1887. WBY may already have been thinking of his own 1893 poem on the subject.

[13] See preceding letter.

[1] The reference to Piggott being hunted down (see preceding letter) suggests that this letter was written in March 1889—apparently, from WBY's explanation below (p. 153), on the 8th—not February.

[2] A short, highly favourable anonymous notice of *Oisin* appeared in the Conservative weekly *St. James's Budget*, 16 Feb 1889 (15): 'the quality of his work is undeniably good.' The title poem was singled out for particular praise: 'a happier endeavour to reproduce the music of Ossian's song for English ears has never been made.'

John O'Leary by J. B. Yeats

Douglas Hyde by J. B. Yeats

Todhunters *Academy* notice has not yet appeared, though it has been some time in print. The book is having some sale how much I do not know.—little I expect.

You will be surprized to hear what I am at besides the new play—A comentary on the mystical writing of Blake. A friend is helping me or perhaps I should say I am helping him as he knows Blake much better than I do, or any one else perhaps. It should draw notice—be a sort of red flag above the water's of oblivion—for there is no clue printed anywhere to the mysterious "Prophetic Books"—Swinburne and Gilchrist found them unintelligible.[3]

Poor Pigott! One really got to like him there was something so frank about his lies. They were so completely matters of busness not of malice. There was some thing pathetic too in the hopeless way the squallid latter day *Erinnyes* ran him down. The poor domestic minded swindler!

Write. You have been silent a long time—Your last letter was on the 26th of January.

Yours Always
W B Yeats

PS.

Henley liked my article and asks for others.

O Donahue (a little clerk of much literary ardour) is to read a paper on

---

[3] WBY, speaking of the beginning of his collaboration with Edwin Ellis on *The Works of William Blake* (1893), recalls (*Aut*, 161) that Ellis

had a passion for Blake, picked up in Pre-Raphaelite studios, and early in our acquaintance put into my hands a scrap of notepaper on which he had written some years before an interpretation of the poem that begins—

> The fields from Islington to Marybone,
>   To Primrose Hill and Saint John's Wood,
> Were builded over with pillars of gold,
>   And there Jerusalem's pillars stood.

The four quarters of London represented Blake's four great mythological personages, the Zoas, and also the four elements. These few sentences were the foundation of all study of the philosophy of William Blake that requires an exact knowledge for its pursuit and that traces the connection between his system and that of Swedenborg or of Boehme. I recognized certain attributions, from what is sometimes called the Christian Cabbala, of which Ellis had never heard, and with this proof that his interpretation was more than fantasy he and I began our four years' work upon the 'Prophetic Books' of William Blake. We took it as almost a sign of Blake's personal help when we discovered that the spring of 1889, when we first joined our knowledge, was one hundred years from the publication of *The Book of Thel*, the first published of the 'Prophetic Books', as though it were firmly established that the dead delight in anniversaries.

In his *William Blake* (1868), Swinburne had acknowledged (194) that although the Prophetic Books 'have qualities great enough to be worth finding out', no one should 'conceive that each separate figure in the swarming and noisy life of this populous daemonic creation has individual meaning and vitality'. Alexander Gilchrist (1828–61), Blake's first biographer, had earlier confessed his bewilderment in the case of particular poems: 'More apart from humanity even than the *America*, we are baffled in the endeavour to trace out any distinct subject, any plan or purpose, in the *Europe*, or to determine whether it

"Oisin" at the "Southwick Literary club".⁴ That wretched not ill meant *Freeman* notice is only unfavourable review yet. On 15ᵗʰ *Lucifer* will have very favourable review from Dʳ Carter Blake. It will be thoughtful certainly, old fashioned probably, excentric perhaps.⁵

ALS Huntington. McHugh, 85–6; Wade, 112–13.

To Katharine Tynan, 9 March [1889]

3 Blenheim Road | Bedford Park | Chiswick
March 9.

Dear Miss Tynan—

You know how to praise. What a good untiring friend you are? I got the article to day and write at once to thank you. It is a most generous article¹—

By the same post came the *Scots Observer* with a splended article by Henley headded "A new Irish Poet". Strange that the best articles yet, should come by the same post. Henley after "Oisin" praises "King Goll", "Song of the last Arcadian" "old Fisherman" and "Island of Statues". "Last Arcadian" is he says more subtle than any other poem in book. *Kanva on God* also he praises. He is most enthusiastic through out. I have just heard by this post that their is a "capital review" in *Saturday* of this week, but have not seen it of course. I will send you *Scots Observer* shortly.²

mainly relates to the past, present, or to come' (*Life of William Blake: pictor ignotus* [1863], I. 128). In the preface to their edition of Blake, Ellis and WBY praised Swinburne, Gilchrist, and the Rossetti brothers for 'having brought Blake into the light of day' but complained (viii) that 'though whatever is accessible to us now was accessible to them when they wrote . . . not one chapter, not one clear paragraph about the myth of Four Zoas, is to be found in all that they have published.'

⁴ No reports of O'Donoghue's paper on *Oisin* have come to light.

⁵ An anonymous review in *Lucifer*, 15 Mar 1889 (84–6), commended *Oisin* as 'a book of wholesome, ringing verse, which often illustrates the theosophical principle that Karma, Nemesis, or Destiny, attends all manifestations of life, and is an inseparable concomitant of every thought, word, and action. Mr Yeats is never so graceful, never so deeply devout, as when expressing the higher mysteries of the theosophical philosophy.' Charles Carter Blake (1840–1897), formerly a civil servant, was a zoologist, Hon. Sec. of the Anthropological Society of London, and published a number of scientific papers.

¹ KT's signed review of *Oisin* in the *Weekly Freeman's Journal*, 9 Mar 1889 (11), extends over 24 column inches, praises WBY for his originality, quotes liberally and approvingly from the book, and concludes 'that this young book of a young Irishman has rare performance and still rarer promise'.

² Henley's enthusiastic review appeared anonymously in the *Scots Observer* for 9 Mar 1889 (446–7). After praising 'The Wanderings of Oisin', Henley commends the scene from *The Island of Statues*,

which Mr Yeats has written under the charm of the Shelleyan manner and music, and which . . . proves him to have dramatic fire and dramatic insight, as well as the gift of telling a story in mellifluous verse. . . . The best of his lyrics are 'King Goll', with its haunting refrain; 'Kanva', which conveys a keen criticism of life in its flowing and daintily turned couplets; 'The Song of the Last Arcadian', the subtlest in thought of all the pieces in the volume; and the simple lilt of the old fisherman. . . .

What a jumble of letters I sent you yesterday.[3] I was taking the letter to the post when I found in my pocket a letter stamped and all, which I thought had gone to you long ago. I opened the letter I had just written, and added the other without having time even to read it. I fear the two letters between them contain too much mere personal news, the fortunes of articles, the book etc. But then you know I have little more to write about especially when as at present I am deep in lengthy MSS—the portcullis is down I am looking for dramatic thoughts. I do not know what is going on in the house, and what is the good of writing gossip of the people one meets one moment and forgets the next.

Hey ho I wish I was out of London in order that I might see the world. Here one gets into ones minority, among the people who are like ones self— mystical, literary folk, and such like. Down at Sligo one sees the whole world in a days walk, every man is a class. It is too small there for minorities.[4] All this bloodless philosophical chatter is poor substitute for news but then I have none. "You must not go to pear trees for apples" as our Allingham said,[5] or me for news. Again a great many thank-yous for your generous article.

Yours always
W B Yeats

ALS Huntington. McHugh, 88–9; Wade, 115–16.

The *Saturday Review's* notice, also on 9 Mar 1889 (293), was similarly enthusiastic: 'Mr W. B. Yeats is impelled to the heroic past by a poet's truest instinct. . . . He draws on the primitive sources of song, and proves them to be not yet exhausted. Heroes and giants, magic and fairy lore, are his themes, and his song is like that of a singer of old for freshness and force and buoyancy.' The anonymous reviewer praised the title poem for its 'entrancing' pictures, 'impressive imagery and dramatic close', and observed: 'Rare, indeed, in a modern poet is the entire absence of pose or self-consciousness. The absorption of the poet in his poetry is complete.'

[3] See the two preceding letters, pp. 148, 150.

[4] In *John Sherman*, the hero remarks (13) about Ballah (Sligo): 'In your big towns a man finds his minority and knows nothing outside its border. He knows only the people like himself. But here one chats with the whole world in a day's walk, for every man one meets is a class.'

[5] This line does not occur in Allingham's work. WBY seems to be confusing Publius Syrus's proverbial 'You should go to a pear-tree for pears not to an elm' (*Sententiae*, 674), with the sentiments of Allingham's untitled poem 'I'm but a lowly gooseberry / Hanging on my native tree . . . Mister Critic,—did I say, / Ever say I was a peach?' (*Evil May-Day* 1882, 86). By adding an apple to this fruit salad WBY arrived at his quotation.

To John O'Leary, 21 March [1889]

March 21

PS. Forgot to post this letter[1] somehow. "Saturday" notice[2] was very good indeed.

Lolly is going to teach at a Kindergarton school in Bedford Park. She has been going there every day to learn the system etc.[3] Her teaching begins next week.

AL NLI

To Katharine Tynan, 21 March [1889]

3 Blenheim Road | Bedford Park | Chiswick
March 21

Dear Miss Tynan

I send you the "Saturday" & "Scots Observer reviews" also the number of the "Hobby Horse" you asked for. I wonder would Father Russel draw attention to *Saturday* notice in "Monthly". I beleive that notice will help me a great deal[1]—

Who told you that I am "taken up with Miss Gonne". I think she is, "very good looking" and that is all I think about her. What you say of her fondness for sensation is probably true. I sympathize with her love of the national idia rather than any secondary land movement but care not much for the kind of red Indian feathers in which she has trapped out that idea. We had some talk as to the possibility of getting my "Countess O Shea" acted by amateurs in Dublin and she felt inclined to help, indeed suggested the attempt herself if I remember rightly. I hardly expect it will ever get outside the world of plans. As for the rest she had a borrowed interest, reminding me of Laura

---

[1] As the previous letter to JO'L is dated 3 Feb [1889] (see pp. 138–9), and an absent-mindedness of six and a half weeks is excessive, even for WBY, it is probable that this postscript is to another letter to JO'L, now lost.

[2] See previous letter, n. 2.

[3] ECY began work at the Bedford Park kindergarten in the spring of 1889, having enrolled for a certificate course in the Froebel method of teaching. Mrs Dorothy Rhodes, daughter of the Yeatses' neighbour H. M. Paget, recalled (interview, 1973) that the kindergarten 'was a private school in a private house and we went there to learn our ABC and then went on to the High School later.' The house, at 7 Queen Anne's Gardens, belonged to Thomas Matthews Rooke (1842–1942), most prominent among the many artists resident in Bedford Park at that time and now best known for the architectural drawings he made for Ruskin, 1878–93. He was married to Leonora Jane Jones, whose sister, a Miss Jones, ran the kindergarten.

[1] The *Irish Monthly* for April 1889 quoted (224) from the *Saturday Review*'s notice of *Oisin*.

Armstrong without Laura's wild dash of half insane genius. Laura is to me always a pleasent memory she woke me from the metallic sleep of science and set me writing my first play. Do not mistake me she is only as a myth and a symbol. Will you forgive me having talked of her—She interests me far more than Miss Gonne does and yet is only as a myth and a symbol. I heard from her about two years ago and am trying to find out where she is now in order to send her "Oisin". "Time and the Witch Vivien" was written for her to act. "The Island of Statues" was begun with the same notion though it soon grew beyond the scope of drawing room acting. The part of the enchantress in both poems was written for her. She used to sign her letters Vivien.[2]

What a nice neat letter you write and what a ragged affair is this of mine.

Do you ever see Lipman about now? Do any of the old set speak to him? Mrs Coffey Etc. I saw his book for sale the other day—a new edition apparently.[3]

Did you ask Gill to send me a copy of the ballad book for Rhys? I am afraid of his doing the article without it. I gave him your book. He has written something on my book which I have not seen. Lolly is teaching at a Kindergarton School in Bedford Park but will get no payment for a year

[2] Laura Armstrong (b. 1862), youngest and reputedly the prettiest daughter of Sergeant Richard Armstrong, was a distant cousin of WBY's through the Corbets. He first became infatuated with her when he saw her driving a dog cart at Howth, her red hair blowing in the wind. W. K. Magee ('John Eglinton') remembered her playing Vivien in the play WBY wrote for her, *Vivien and Time* (see p. 129), in an amateur performance at the house of Judge Wright (presumably Kilrock House; see p. 7) in Howth in the early 1880s (Ellmann, *Yeats: The Man and the Masks* [1948], 36). A letter from Laura Armstrong to WBY, dated 10 Aug 1884 from 60, Stephen's Green, Dublin, survives at MBY:

My dear Clarin,

What can I say to you for having been so rude to you—in not being at home when you called and I had asked you? I am really very sorry about it. I hope you will forgive me. It so happened that I was positively obliged to go out at the hour I had appointed for you to come but it was only to a house quite close here—and I told our maid to send me over word when you *came*—she did so—(but I find since it was just before you *went!*) and I was rising to leave the room. I looked out of the window and to my great disappointment—saw my Clarin leaving No. 60. It was too bad—and I am indeed sorry I missed you.—I like yr poems more than I can say—but I should like to hear you read them—I have not nearly finished them. Could you come some aft:—and read a little to me, I shall be in all Tuesday afternoon. *I promise*! so can you come? I should have written to you sooner but I have been away from home. Pray excuse my silence. Trusting to see "the poet"—! and with kind regards—Believe me

                Ever yrs
                "Vivien"

This letter was written barely a month before her marriage on 17 Sept 1884 to Henry Morgan Byrne, a Dublin solicitor and later barrister. That marriage apparently ended in divorce, and in 1915 JBY heard in New York (letters to SMY, 24 Dec 1915, and to WBY, 12 Feb 1916, MBY) that she had married again, a Welsh gardener—a 'very decent and intelligent man' whom she so henpecked that he was forced to leave her, allowing her £120 a year, though she told everyone she was a widow with two children. Laura Armstrong, JBY told John Quinn (letter of 3 Dec 1917, NYPL), served as a model for Margaret Leland in *John Sherman*, the 'wicked heroine in Willie's only novel'.

[3] Presumably a reissue of R. I. Lipmann's translation of Lermontov (see p. 120). He may have been socially ostracized in Dublin because he had been in prison for fraud.

which seems hard however she is learning the system which is some thing. She has not been well lately but seems better now. Lilly enjoys the embroidering much. These last few days she has had the teaching of two new assistants of Miss Morris's. Miss Morris was not there yesterday (they have moved to a house a little way from the Morris'es)[4] as Sparling is ill somewhat seriously I am afraid. At present I know no more than the fact of his illness.

I notice by your letter that you see Russel now and then. Tell him to write to me—Tell him myself and a friend are writing a book on Blake and perhaps he will send me a letter with some Blake criticisms.

Do you ever see Allen? "Lucifer" folk sent him my fairy tale book for review and he makes no sign.[5] Finds I suppose unpaid "Lucifer" articles thankless jobs.

What have written lately? What poetry? What prose? I always like details on these matters.

You have never sent me the "Nation" article on yourself[6] you promised.

I must wind up this letter presently, and get to work on the "Countess O'Shea" that my mind may be full of it when I go for my walk an hour hence. It is a wild windy night, the sky full of ravelled clouds and patches of greasey blue—the sort of night that stimulates thought and I must out.

Yours always
W B Yeats

Do not forget to send me all news of your prose and poetry.

PS. Saturday.

I got your note just now. Will send on 9/1 if possible next week. 275 was a very fair sale[7] considering all things. Has the sale ceased and if so *how many of the remaining copies are bound*? Dr Todhunter agrees with me that as soon as the sale of the 1/6 copies *is at an end*, the rest should be bound in some cheap way (brown paper he suggests as cheap and curious) and sold for a few pence each. I suggested 6^d he says that is too much and that 3^d would be enough. In this way the book would get distributed. Of course it would not be well to do so until the 1/6 sale ends certainly. What do you think of this

[4] May Morris and Sparling had moved to 8, Hammersmith Terrace, not far from Kelmscott House; they were joined for a time there by George Bernard Shaw.

[5] Fred J. Allan (d. 1937), a Fenian who had been charged with treason and felony in 1884 and who was now working on the *Freeman's Journal*, had been present at the Dublin seance in January 1888 (see p. 45) at which WBY had his 'spiritualistic' experience. Allan remained loyal to Parnell, becoming business manager of the Parnellite *Irish Daily Independent* after 1891; he was later a member of Sinn Fein and after the Treaty of 1922 an executive member of Cumann na nGaedheal. The review of *FFT* in *Lucifer* (see p. 102) failed to materialize.

[6] See p. 101; n. 20.

[7] i.e. of *PBYI* in its original edition. The 9s 1d was evidently WBY's share of the costs unrecovered after the sales had been reckoned.

scheme we would reach a class quite out of reach of the 1/6 book and might sell among the ballad books in small county towns. The brown paper covers might be labeled second edition (I suppose it would be fairly enough second edition) or cheap edition. A few 1/6 copies should be kept—as many as are now bound. This would be better than letting the books go to loss. You will remember that at the very beginning I proposed this cheap edition. I do not think any copies bound as at present should be cheapened.

I do not send "Saturday" notice of Oisin as you have seen it but enclose— "Scots Observer" one. "Atalanta" promises review in May number.[8] No American reviews as yet. I have stuck all yet received into a book which I will let you see when they wind up. 22 thus far mostly all praise my dramatic sketches most after *Oisin Time & Vivien* seems liked.

I am delighted to hear about the "Culdee". How do you treat it? Will you bring in local scenery—I hope you will do that. It would be a fine thing to write a poem that always would be connected with Tallah in peoples minds.[9] All poetry should have a local habitation when at all possible. Some day we shall have to publish another ballad book containing the best of our national and local songs & ballads. By "ours" I mean yours and mine. You were not quite at your best in "Balld of Young Ireland 1888" at least not always at your best. Though York Powell greatly likes your *Michael Dwyer*. Did I ever tell you that?

[*At top of first page of postscript*]
Have heard from Father Russel he will quote *Saturday* notice would you kindly let him see *Scots Observer* one.

[*On back of envelope*]
I see in Father Russels letter about Miss Wynne's good fortune. How did Andrew Lang come across her poems?[10]

This letter has [lain] unposted some days (March 25)

[8] An anonymous notice of *Oisin* appeared in *Atalanta*'s 'Notes on Books' in the May 1889 issue (552). 'It would be difficult,' the reviewer commented of the title poem, 'to find anything of its kind fresher or more replete with fairy colour than this old-world romance. . . . There is so far an element of absolute genius in this poem that the writer is completely forgotten in his theme.'

[9] KT's poem on the 'Rapt Culdee' (see p. 148), 'The Hiding Away of Blessed Angus' (*Ballads and Lyrics*, 121–6), refers directly to the village of Tallaght when she describes how Angus 'came barefoot, with tattered gown, / To Tallaght, nigh to Dublin town'. She makes no detailed use of local scenery, although she introduces a generalized setting: 'The low hills tender as the dove / Girdled the bright fields round with love.'

[10] Frances Alice Wynne (1863–93) published poems in a number of magazines and produced one volume of verse, *Whisper!* (1890), which WBY was to notice in *PSJ* (*LNI*, 127–8). KT, whose close friend she was, presents a lively portrait of her in *25 Years*. Her 'good fortune' was to have poems of hers accepted for publication in the prestigious column, 'At the Sign of the Ship', which the poet and novelist Andrew Lang (1844–1912) conducted in *Longman's Magazine*: her 'Sweetheart Daisy' appeared there in June 1889; 'Meadow-sweet' in August 1889; and 'In March the world was bare' in September 1890.

Would you kindly let Miss O Leary see *Scots Observer* notice she would perhaps send it on to Father Russel. In a letter just received she asks to see it (March 26)

ALS Huntington, with envelope addressed to Clondalkin, postmark torn off. McHugh, 89–92; Wade, 116–20.

To Katharine Tynan, 10 April [1889]

3 Blenheim Road | Bedford Park | Chiswick
April 10

Dear Miss Tynan

Lolly has gone to Dublin to stay with the Wellington Road people.[1] She started this morning. I gave her a book of Montagu Griffens to give you for him—She has not been very well; compined house keeping and kindergarten anxieties have been too much for her perhaps.

I enclose Dr Todhunters Academy review[2] which please return as I have no other copy.

I cannot just now send you the money for Gill. I thought to send it last week but the money I was expecting—£3.10 from Scots Observer—was all absorbed by pressing house expenses. Which I fear will be the same with a small amount I expect to morrow from *Leisure Hour*. However I will have it soon. I must brake of [f] this letter—only written to tell you about Lolly— very presently, to write an article on *Village Ghosts* for *Scots Observer* that will bring in a couple of pounds. I have also some notes to do for *Manchester Courier*. A man came yesterday morning and asked me to do literary gossip for it so please send me any news about literary persons and books you may hear and that is fresh.[3] Any Dublin doing of the kind you may know of. What books is Miss Mulholond busy about and what do you yourself intend? I can trumpet such things now and then perhaps.

[1] ECY left for Dublin on 10 Apr 1889, Jack Yeats seeing her off from the station (Jack Yeats diary, MBY). WBY's uncle, Isaac Butt Yeats (1848–1930), lived at 50 Wellington Road, Dublin, with his sister, the widowed Mary Letitia Wise (? 1841–95), and her daughter Edith (1863–1938).

[2] In his long-awaited review of *Oisin* in the *Academy*, 30 Mar 1889 (216–17), Todhunter described the book as 'a remarkable first volume; not merely full of promise in the aggregate, but containing a few poems of distinct achievement'. Although he found some flaws in execution, he praised the adventurousness, originality, and variety of the poems. He devoted a good deal of space to the title poem but thought that WBY was 'seen at his best in his shorter pieces' and commended the plays for their underlying thought and symbolic meanings. He also found that 'in the main, Mr Yeats has the true poet's instinct for imaginative diction and musical verse, musical both in rhythm and sound.'

[3] See p. 48. WBY contributed anonymous literary notes to a column headed 'From Our London Correspondent' in the Conservative daily, the *Manchester Courier and Lancashire General Advertiser*, at least until May 1890. During the winter and spring of 1889–90 he earned an average of 6s a month from this source. His contributions have been identified (*Bibl*, 11), as, e.g., a paragraph on 22 Apr 1889 (3) about two recent paintings by J. T. Nettleship (see below).

Walter Paget and my Father are using me as a model and are doing two portraits in competition against each other. Paget is Cassels chief illustrater—[4] so far my father['s] portrait is beyond all comparison the best.

Yours Always

W B Yeats

I enclose a letter from Nettleship[5] which please keep safe as I value it much.

ALS Huntington, with envelope addressed to Clondalkin, postmark 'LONDON W AP 11 89'. McHugh, 92–3; Wade, 120–1.

To Katharine Tynan, 21 April [1889]

3 Blenheim Road | Bedford Park | Chiswick

April 21

Dear Miss Tynan

Have you any novels of Carletons beside the short stories? I have them but am trying to borrow some where, one or two of his longer tales such as "Willy Reily" or "Valentine M'Clutchy" or indeed any of them. The Scots Observer people have asked me to write an article on him apropo[s] of the "Red-Haired Man's Wife" the posthumous tale of his discovered somewhere and printed the other day by Seeley Bryers & Walker.[1] Could you beg borrow or steal any Carletons for me? I am afraid I shall have to buy them if you have none, and my finances are low these times. Tract Society are full

---

[4] WBY has apparently mixed up Walter Stanley ('Wal') Paget (1863–1935) with his older brother, Henry Marriot Paget (1856–1936). Both were artists and book illustrators, as was another brother, Sidney Edward Paget (1860–1908). H. M. Paget, whose portrait of WBY (now in the Belfast Municipal Art Gallery) is dated 6 Apr 1889, was a friend and neighbour of the Yeatses in Bedford Park.

[5] The letter John Trivett Nettleship (1841–1902), solicitor, author, and painter friend of JBY, had written to WBY on 2 Apr 1889 (*LWBY* I. 5) in praise of *Oisin*: 'There can be no doubt that the title poem of your book is a new birth in poetry; it has come at the right time, because it had to come; criticism of it would be futile, because it is a real creation which must stand or fall by its own nature, and not by any outside supports or blows.' In *Aut* (155–6) WBY describes Nettleship as seeming

about sixty, had a bald head, a grey beard, and a nose, as one of my father's friends used to say, like an opera-glass, and sipped cocoa all the afternoon and evening from an enormous tea-cup that must have been designed for him alone. . . . I brought him an admiration settled in early boyhood, for my father had always said, 'George Wilson [see below, p. 351] was our born painter, but Nettleship our genius', and even had he shown me nothing I could care for, I had admired him still because my admiration was in my bones.

[1] William Carleton was the author of some 18 full-length novels besides his collections of short stories (see p. 71, n. 3). Although his review of *The Red-Haired Man's Wife* (1889; see below, p. 172) did not appear in the *Scots Observer* until October 1889, WBY was probably already beginning to collect material for his *Carleton* (see p. 107), published in August 1889. For *Valentine M'Clutchy, the Irish Agent; or, Chronicles of the Castle Cumber Property* (Dublin 1845; see below, p. 174); *Willy Reilly and his Dear Colleen Bawn: A Tale, Founded upon Fact* (1855), a sentimental romance set in the anti-Catholic Penal Law days of the eighteenth century, WBY later described (*UP* I. 397) as 'readable but empty melodrama'.

up with drawings and as a result my father has sold but little lately.[2]
Accordingly the family "swalley whole", to use a Sligo term, is unusually
gready. I have been doing rather well fortunately. I told you about the man
who came and asked me to do literary notes for the *Manchester Courier*.
They give me very little trouble and are fairly profitable. I got £7 for an
article in *Leisure Hour* and have had two in *Scots Observer* and sent off
another.[3] The Scots Observer pays well about £1 a column. These matters
have made the "Countess" fare but badly fortunately my constitutional
indolence brings my thoughts swinging perpetualy back to it by their own
weight. I am not half industrious enough to drive my thoughts. They go
their own road and that is to immaginative work. I shall have a day at the
"Countess" to morrow. To me the dramatic is far the ⟨easiest⟩ pleasentest
poetic form. By the way I have written two sets of verses to illustrations sent
me by the tract society. I quote one to show you how orthodox I can be—
[*Across top of page*]
The illustration was a wretched thing of a girl in church.

> She prayes for father, mother dear,
>   To Him with thuder shod,
> She prays for every falling tear,
>   In the holy church of God.

[*Vertically in margin*]
The spiritual church of course

> For all good men now fallen ill,
>   For merry men that weep,
> For holiest teachers of His will,
>   And common men that sleep.

> The sunlight flickering on the pews,
>   The sunlight in the air,
> The flies that dance in threes & twos,
>   They seem to join her prayer.

> Her prayer for father, mother dear,
>   To Him with thunder shod,

---

[2] The Religious Tract Society, founded in 1799, produced tracts and books for various Protestant
denominations throughout the world. Among the magazines it sponsored in the cause of cheap and
wholesome literature were the *Girl's Own Paper*, the *Boy's Own Paper*, and the *Leisure Hour*. William
Stevens was one of the editors of the Society at this time and commissioned drawings from JBY and Jack
Yeats as well as poems (see n. 4 below) from WBY.

[3] The *Leisure Hour* article was 'Popular Ballad Poetry of Ireland', which appeared in November 1889,
but for which WBY had been paid in advance. The two articles in the *Scots Observer* (see p. 148, n. 3) were
'Scots and Irish Fairies' (2 Mar 1889) and 'Irish Wonders' (30 Mar 1889), an anonymous review of D. R.
McAnally's book (see p. 78). The article he had sent off, 'Village Ghosts', was to be published on 11 May.

A prayer for every falling tear,
     In the holy church of God.[4]

You see how proud of myself I am for having been so business like. I have been making amends to myself by doing little else than plant sunflowers and marigolds all afternoon.

I saw Coffey & Mrs Coffey last week. I dined at Mrs Lawrences—that Miss Ramsey (now Mrs Butler) who was senior wrangler the other year—the papers talked a lot about her—sat next. Do you know it is possible to be a senior wrangler and yet have only the most common place idias. What poor delusiveness is all this "higher education of women". Men have set up a great mill, called examinations, to destroy the immagination. Why should women go through it, circumstance does not drive *them*. They come out with no repose no peacefulness—their minds no longer quiet gardens full of secluded paths and umbrage circled nooks, but loud as chaffering market places. Mrs Todhunter is a great trouble mostly. She has been through the mill and has got the noisiest mind I know she is always denying something—To return to Miss Ramsey (Mrs Butler) she is about 23 and is married to a man of 60, he being the only senior wrangler attainable—He is master of Trinity and very chatty & pleasent and quite human.[5] He seemed enormously interested in Mrs Coffeys baby.[6] Talked much too about Ireland.

Lady Wilde spoke the other day of some prose of yours (she said you sent it her I think). She said "every sentence was so beautifully poised". She thinks you should write a good deal of prose—I hope rather you are doing plenty of poetry. How goes the Rapt Culdee. Though indeed it were a good

[4] 'In Church' (*VP*, 735–6) appeared in the *Girl's Own Paper*, 8 June 1889, facing an illustration with that title; a second 'set of verses', 'A Summer Evening' (*VP*, 736–7), was published in the issue of 6 July 1889, facing an illustration entitled 'An evening presence fills the place'.

[5] Mrs Coffey's sister, Emily Mary L'Estrange (1845–1925), had married in 1873 Henry Waldemar Lawrence (1845–1908), younger son of Sir Henry Montgomery Lawrence who fell at the siege of Lucknow; they were now living at Alenho, Ridgway, Wimbledon. Henry Lawrence, a barrister and JP, became 3rd Bt. Lawrence of Lucknow when he succeeded his nephew in 1898. The 2nd Bt. was a neighbour of KT's in Clondalkin, and she was a regular visitor at his house, Belgard.

Agnata Frances Ramsay (1867–1931), third daughter of Sir James Henry Ramsay, Bt., of Bamff, Perthshire, went up to Girton College, Cambridge, in 1884 and in 1887 obtained the only First Class in Classics awarded by the University in that year. Gerald du Maurier celebrated this achievement with a cartoon in her honour in *Punch*, 2 July 1887. She remained a fourth year at Girton with a view to editing Herodotus, and in August 1888 married, as his second wife, the Revd Henry Montagu Butler (1833–1918), from 1886 Master of Trinity College, Cambridge, and formerly headmaster of Harrow School, Chaplain to the Queen, and Dean of Gloucester. The term 'wrangler' is usually only applied to mathematicians who have gained first class honours at Cambridge.

The feminist Dora Digby Todhunter, who had been through the educational 'mill' of Alexandra College, Dublin (see p. 60, n. 8), was 'a tiresome woman,' SMY recalled in a letter to Hone (21 Feb 1942, Texas); '—she contradicted every thing anyone said—York Powell said once about her—that "in a healthy state of society something would have been put in her tea."'

For WBY's view of bluestocking women, see 'Michael Robartes and the Dancer' (*VP*, 385–7).

[6] The Coffeys' son Diarmid was born 24 Dec 1888.

thing if your prose stories do well. They help the immagination I think. You have told me nothing lately about that story you had taken. Has it come out?[7] I know I gained greatly from my experiment in novel writing. The hero turned out a bad character and so I did not try to sell the story any where. I am in hopes he may reform.

You will have seen Lolly by this and heard all news.

There has been a great row in the Theosophical society. Madame Blavatsky expelled M[rs] Cook (Miss Mabel Collins) and the president of the Lodge for flirtation (M[rs] Cook has a husband living) and M[rs] Alicia Cremers an american for gossiping about it. As a result Madame Blavatsky is in high spirits.[8] The society is like the "happy family" that used to be exhibited round Charing Cross station—a cat in a cage full of canaries. The Russian cat is beginning to purr now and smoothen its furr again—The canary birds are less by three—The faithful will be more obedient than ever.

Jack has just arrived from his volunteering at Brighton.[9] He has made many sketches & gives an amusing account of everything. He enjoyed himself much.

Your friend
W B Yeats

Do not be disgusted at these trite verses for the tract society. I shall never do any more I think.

---

[7] Lady Wilde, as an 'ardent admirer' of Sarah Piatt (see p. 41), had written to KT on 27 Mar 1889 (Southern Illinois) asking if she could borrow an article, 'Poets in Exile: Mr and Mrs John J. Piatt', which KT had published in *PSJ* 3 Mar 1889. KT's poem on the 'Rapt Culdee' (see p. 157, n. 9) was finished by 3 May 1889, when she told Fr. Russell (APH) that it was under consideration by *Atalanta*. At the same time she had been trying her hand at short stories; 'A Girl's Stratagem' had appeared in *Merry England* in March and 'A Marsh-Marigold', which she had sent to the *Catholic World* in late March, appeared there in June 1889.

[8] Mabel Collins (1851–1927) was the daughter of the poet and novelist Mortimer Collins (1827–76), known as 'the King of the Bohemians'. In 1871 she had married the writer Keningale Robert Cook, but is usually known by her maiden name, under which she wrote a great number of novels and books of occult instruction, including *Light on the Path* (1885), which greatly influenced AE. In *Aut* (177) WBY describes her as 'a handsome clever woman of the world' who thought herself a penitent, and recalls that during this incident

there was much scandal and gossip, for the penitent was plainly entangled with two young men who were expected to grow into ascetic sages. The scandal was so great that Madame Blavatsky had to call the penitent before her and to speak after this fashion: 'We think that it is necessary to crush the animal nature; you should live in chastity in act and thought. Initiation is granted only to those who are entirely chaste'; but after some minutes in that vehement style, the penitent standing crushed and shamed before her, she had wound up, 'I cannot permit you more than one.'

The expulsions seem to have taken place in the first week of February, for after that date Mabel Collins was no longer advertised as co-editor of *Lucifer* and T. B. Harbottle, president of the Blavatsky Lodge, was replaced by W. Kingsland. Mrs Cremers is unidentified.

[9] Jack Yeats had joined the 20th Middlesex (Artists') Rifle Volunteer Corps in January 1889 and had spent many evenings during the spring drilling with them. From 18 to 23 Apr 1889 (when this letter was finished, presumably) he went to an Easter camp with the Volunteers at Shorncliffe on the south coast.

Have you heard anything of this new novel of Carleton's? Do you know if it has been touched up by anyone (as I rather fear from the preface)?
[*On back of envelope*]
I have the "Traits & Stories of Irish Peasentry" of course.

ALS Huntington, with envelope addressed to Clondalkin, postmark 'CHISWICK AP 23 89'. McHugh, 93–6; Wade, 121–4.

To John O'Leary, 7 May [*1889*]

3 Blenheim Road | Bedford Park | Chiswick
May 7.

Dear M^r O Leary

I should have thanked you before for the Carleton's but the day I got them I started for Oxford and only returned the day before yesterday. Down there I had no time to write letters at all, what with copying out in the Bodlean all day[1] and dining with dull college dons—friends of York Powell with whom I stoped or regular diners at Commons—in the evening. Met one or two people of interset however. A student on the ground floor had got my book—he was of interest of course—they have it too, in the Oxford Union.[2]

I have started reading Carleton's "Miser" and will write to the Coffeys about what Carleton's they have as soon as I hear of their return to Dublin. My father will ask the Butts about him. They or their father knew him well of course.[3]

I have been busy with Blake. ⟨I told you⟩ You complain about the mysticism. It has enabled me to make out Blake's prophetic books at any rate. My book on him will I beleive clear up that riddle for ever. No one will call him mad again. I have evidence by the way to show that he was of Irish

---

[1] WBY had gone to Oxford on 1 May to copy out the first edition of William Blake's poem, *The Book of Thel* (1789), at the Bodleian.

[2] The senior membership of Christ Church consisted of 28 dons (called 'Students' at that college), 6 canons, and the Dean. Among the more senior dons at this time was the Revd C. L. Dodgson ('Lewis Carroll'). York Powell shared WBY's views on the dullness of his colleagues. 'Commons' (from 'the common table') is a term used in Oxford for the evening meal.

The copy of *Oisin* in the library of the Oxford Union, a debating society and social club, was stolen in 1906.

[3] *Fardorougha the Miser; or, the Convicts of Lisnamona* (Dublin, 1839). Isaac Butt (1813–79), a friend and contemporary of WBY's grandfather, the Revd W. B. Yeats, had been editor of the *Dublin University Magazine* (see p. 79), in which a number of Carleton's stories and novels (including *The Miser*) first appeared. JBY worked for Butt in the 1870s and painted two portraits of him, one of which now hangs in the National Gallery of Ireland. Butt's four surviving children were living at this time in Oakley Street, London, where JBY was a frequent visitor. Butt's daughter Rosa (*c.* 1838–1926) was a particular friend of his.

extraction—his gradfather was an O'Neal who changed his name for political reasons.[4] Ireland takes a most important place in his mystical system.

You need not be afraid of my going in for mesmerism. It interests me but slightly. No fear of Madame Blavatsky drawing me into such matters—she is very much against them & hates Spiritulism vehemently—says mediumship and insanity are the same thing.[5]

By the way their has been a stir lately among the faithful. Madame Blavatsky expelled M[rs] Cook (Mabel Collins) a most prominent theosophist writer and daughter of Mortimer Collins, and expelled also the president of the lodge, for flirtation; and expelled an american lady for gossiping about them. Madame Blavatsky is in great spirits she is purring and hiding her claws as though she never clawed anybody. She is always happy when she has found a Theosophist out and clawed him. She thinks she is the most long suffering person. One day she said "forty thousand theosophists all gushing away, I try to stop them, then they scratch". According to her there are about half a dozen real theosophists in the world and one of those is stupid (Olcott I imagine). The rest she clasifies under the head "flapdoodles". Come to see her when you are in London. She is the most human person alive, is like an old peasent woman, and is wholy devoted, all her life is but sitting in a great chair with a pen in her hand. For years she has written twelve hours a day.

I have no theories about her. She is simply a note of interrogation. "Olcott is much honester than I am" she said to me one day "he explains things. I am an old Russian savage" that is the deepest I ever got into her riddle.[6]

---

[4] WBY's assertion about Blake's genealogy was as fanciful as his belief that he had for ever cleared up the riddle of the Prophetic Books. He and Ellis put forward this view with great gusto in vol. I of *The Works of William Blake*, where they argued (2–4) that Blake's grandfather, one John O'Neil, having got into debt, married Ellen Blake, the owner of a Rathmines shebeen, and took her name.

But if the old O'Neil origin was hidden, the wild O'Neil blood showed itself strongly. . . . William Blake, as we call him, was, before all things, an O'Neil. . . . The very manner of Blake's writing has an Irish flavour, a lofty extravagance of invention and epithet, recalling the *Tain Bo Cuilane* and other old Irish epics, and his mythology brings often to mind the tumultuous vastness of the ancient tales of god and demon that have come to us from the dawn of mystic tradition in what may fairly be called his fatherland.

Although WBY repeated these remarks, in an abbreviated form, in his Introduction to *The Poems of William Blake* (1893), he confessed in May 1900 that there was 'a good deal here & there in the biography etc. with which I am not in agreement'(*Bibl*, 217).Modern commentators dismiss the idea that Blake had Irish ancestry; WBY had apparently taken the notion from C. Carter Blake (see *BIV*, 255).

[5] Cf. p. 45, n. 3.

[6] Col. Henry Steel Olcott (1832–1907), an American who served in the Civil War, had met HPB in the autumn of 1874 and investigated a number of cases of psychic phenomena with her. In 1875, with William Quan Judge, they founded the Theosophical Society, and in 1878 sailed for India together to set up the Society's headquarters at Adyar, Madras. Apart from occasional visits to Europe, Olcott spent the rest of his life in India.

I read a scene of my new play to an actress yesterday she seemed to think it suitable in all ways for the stage. I think you will like it. It is in all things celtic & Irish.[7] The style is perfectly simple and I have taken great care with the construction made two complete prose versions before writing a line of virse.

Miss O Leary wished to keep the reviews of my book she had. I return those of which I have duplicates.

My father is delighted with Miss O Learys poem in the *Irish Monthly*[8] and so am I. It is most simple, delicate, and tender. I shall write to her very presently. I have to go out now—have been un-well these last two days (through want of exercise I suspect) but am nearly all right again now still do not care to write much—

Forgive me all this chatter about Madame Blavatsky.

Yours very sincerely

W B Yeats.

I hope Miss O'Leary's health will feel the benefit of this good spring weather.

ALS Berg. Wade, 124–6.

In *Aut* (173, 175) WBY describes HPB as 'a sort of old Irish peasant woman with an air of humour and audacious power. . . . A great passionate nature, a sort of female Dr Johnson . . . she seemed impatient of the formalism and the shrill abstract idealism of those about her, and this impatience broke out in railing and many nicknames: "O, you are a flapdoodle, but then you are a Theosophist and a brother." '

[7] The actress was Florence Beatrice Farr (1860–1917; see Appendix), later a close friend of WBY's. Her marriage in 1884 to the actor Edward Emery (1861–1938) was dissolved a decade later, after his emigration to America in 1888. Mrs Emery's sister Henrietta ('Etta') Paget (b. 1852) was the wife of the Yeatses' Bedford Park neighbour, H. M. Paget.

Though at this time WBY thought *The Countess Kathleen* 'in all things Celtic & Irish', a note in the 1927 revised edition of *Poems* (1895) reveals that he had been mistaken: 'I found the story of the Countess Cathleen in what professed to be a collection of Irish folklore in an Irish newspaper some years ago. I wrote to the compiler, asking about its source, but got no answer, but have since heard that it was translated from *Les Matinées de Timothé Trimm* a good many years ago, and has been drifting about the Irish press ever since. Léo Lespès gives it as an Irish story . . . ' (*VPl*, 176). A letter to the *Star* by the Irish journalist and author, John Augustus O'Shea, on 3 Sept 1892 (4), and reprinted in *United Ireland* on 10 Sept, reveals that he had

adapted it from the French more than 20 years ago. Mr Yeats . . . told me he heard it in the west of Ireland. That would be a surprising coincidence were it not for the possible explanation that I had it printed in the *Shamrock*, of Dublin [6 Oct 1867], which largely circulates among Irish people, previous to the Franco–German war. Singularly enough, it was reprinted in the same periodical at a comparatively recent date. To my small share in the work Mr Yeats is heartily welcome . . . but I question if a production concocted as a pot-boiler by a student in an attic from the French of Timothee Trimm, of the *Petit Journal*, can be labelled as genuine, unsophisticated, Irish folk-lore.

From this letter it appears that WBY knew of the non-Irish source of the story long before 1927.

[8] 'My Own Galtees', *Irish Monthly*, May 1889; the Galtees are a range of hills in Ellen O'Leary's native Tipperary.

To Katharine Tynan, 9 May [1889]

3 Blenheim Road | Bedford Park | Chiswick
May 9th

Dear Miss Tynan

That you are coming to London is the best news I have heard this long time. I shall work hard at the "Countess" that it may be finished when you come. The Meynalls are not so very far from us by good luck. An easy tram-ride away.[1] You will see Bedford Park at its best. All the trees and flowers in their full dress. There will be quite a number of people to bring you to see. Todhunter and York Powell who both admire your work are near at hand.[2]

Jack & myself begin painting a design on my study ceiling to day. We have had it long in our minds to do it. We have been putting it off. Now we set to work to have it done when you arrive.[3]

I wrote last night to Henley and asked him to send me the *Scots Observer* with your poem when it come[s] out.[4] I do not see the paper except when it contains some contribution of my own.

Lolly is home again of course. And looking very well. She tells me odd scraps of news about you all. Jack says she is on her good behaviour but that she will get "a fling in her tail" soon.[5]

---

[1] KT arrived in London on 27 May 1889 and stayed in England until the end of September. Although she also visited Oxford, Cambridge, Sussex, and Norfolk, she spent most of the time in London, staying in June, and again for part of July and for most of September, with the Meynells.

Alice Christiana Gertrude Thompson (1847–1922), essayist, poetess, and journalist, had been converted to Catholicism in 1872; in 1877 she married the poet, biographer, and editor Wilfrid Meynell (1852–1948), who in 1885 had helped arrange the publication of KT's first volume of poems, *Louise de la Vallière.* For many years the Meynells jointly edited the Catholic periodical the *Weekly Register,* to which KT often contributed, and the more light-hearted *Merry England.* At this time they were living temporarily at 65 Linden Gardens, Bayswater, but were to move into a new house near by, at 47 Palace Court, in July of this year. KT had visited them on previous stays in London; she devotes a chapter of *Memories* (1924) to Alice Meynell.

[2] Even for such an indefatigable seeker-out of the great as KT, this visit was impressive. She met, among many others, William Morris, Thomas Hardy, Nettleship, William Sharp, Todhunter, York Powell, Parnell, Cardinal Manning, and Christina Rossetti, as well as attending a Ladies' Literary Dinner and a hearing of the Parnell Commission.

[3] It seems that this task was postponed yet again, for not until Sunday, 26 May, does Jack Yeats's diary (MBY) announce: 'Willy and I did his ceiling.' Accompanying the entry is a sketch of WBY precariously perched on a pile of furniture painting the ceiling blue and splattering himself and the rest of the room in the attempt. Jack Yeats is attempting to shelter behind another pile of furniture. In the *Sketch,* 29 Nov 1893 (256), KT describes the map of Sligo painted on WBY's ceiling.

[4] On 18 Apr 1889 KT wrote to J. N. Dunn of the *Scots Observer:* ' "The Blackbird" has the metre and title of a Jacobite song: if the poem were to be printed I should duly acknowledge my indebtedness' (Hinkson). On 3 May 1889 she told Fr. Russell (APH), 'I have had an Irish poem—a new variation on the old "Blackbird"—very cordially accepted by Mr Henley's Scots Observer, which refused a Franciscan poem with regret, it being too long.' Her poem, 'The Blackbird (A new song with an old burden)' (see pp. 67, 70), was published on 1 June 1889.

[5] ECY resembled WBY temperamentally and there was often friction between them. In a letter to Dorothy Wellesley of 17 Dec 1937 (Private) WBY observed that 'my sister Elizabeth & I quarrelled at the

About Carleton. John O Leary has sent me some novels of his. I have not yet done much on the subject for I am only just home from Oxford in addition to which I have not been well the first days of this week but am all right again. Had a pleasent time at Oxford. Dined a good deel with the Fellows and did not enjoy that much but found the evening at York Powells with an occasional friend of his very pleasent. I found a student there who had bought my book. They have got it at the Oxford Union.

Your friend Alway[s]
W B Yeats

ALS Huntington, with envelope addressed 'to Clondalkin, postmark 'CHISWICK MY 10 89'. McHugh, 96–7; Wade, 126–7.

To Katharine Tynan, 28 [June 1889]

3 Blenheim Road | Bedford Park | Chiswick
July[1] 28

Dear Miss Tynan

We shall be all delighted to have you with us. I shall be at Paddington at 5.25 on Monday.

I have not yet written about Ibsen. The article still waits for the duello, to get done.[2]

I have seen a good deal of Mrs Alexander Sullivan. She is looking much better than when I wrote last & seems to have quite recovered her spirits. She is coming this evening to meet York Powell, Sydney Hall[3] & Miss Purser—I wrote an article for her a day or two ago—some thing about

edge of the cradle & are keeping it up to the grave's edge'. Always assertive and wilful, ECY was to suffer severe emotional problems later in life and in a letter to WBY of October 1904 (MBY), JBY confessed that he had 'often had my own dread that Lollie may lose her wits'. A more lighthearted account of inter-family teasing occurs in JBY's letter to SMY of 26 June 1894 (*Letters from Bedford Park* [1972], 10–12), which concludes 'You can always get a rise out of Lollie.'

  [1] Evidently—as the postmark confirms—a mistake for 'June'. KT had been staying in Oxford since 10 June, initially with the Legges (letter to Fr. Russell of 23 June 1889, APH), and would return to London via Paddington Station (see below). At the end of July she was in Norfolk, making WBY's dating an impossibility.

  [2] WBY's only article on Henrik Ibsen, 'The Stone and the Elixir', a *Bookman* review of a translation of *Brand* (*UP* I. 344–6), did not appear until October 1894 and cannot be what is referred to here. Perhaps WBY was worsted in his 'duel' with the Norwegian and never completed this article.

  [3] Sydney Prior Hall (1842–1922), a great friend of the Yeatses, was a painter and illustrator who contributed many drawings to the *Graphic*. After a distinguished career at Oxford, he became special artist of the *Graphic* during the Franco-German War, 1870–1, and subsequently accompanied a number of royal tours throughout the Empire, most notably that of India in 1875–6 by the Prince of Wales (later Edward VII).

D ^{r} Cronin. She is not yet sure that he is dead at all—He seems to have been a great rascal. It was really a very becoming thing to remove him—if he be dead and the man found at Chicago be not some one else. A spy has no rights.[4]

There! you will be angry with me for all these dreadful sentiments. I may think the other way to morrow.

Do you know who I heard from? Miss Little (you remember her?) sent me M ^{rs} Bryant's address who wishes me to call on her, also her own.[5]

Yours always
W B Yeats

ALS Huntington, with envelope addressed 'c/o D ^{r} Legge, 3 Keble Terrace, Oxford', postmark 'CHISWICK JU 28 89'. McHugh, 98; Wade, 131.

[4] In *25 Years* (293) KT recalls:

Again there came to London Mrs Alexander Sullivan [see p. 134] of Chicago, in great trouble this time because her husband had been arrested for the murder of Dr Cronin. We were all sympathetic and set out to be very consolatory, but after the first she brightened up so much that we concluded she knew everything and believed that he would be soon released, which he was. I think she had the deliberate intention at that time of appearing everywhere she could and meeting as many people—of facing the music, so to speak, and confuting by her presence those who might have believed her husband guilty.

The Irish-American Alexander Sullivan (*c.* 1847–1913), a lawyer, had settled in Chicago in 1872, where he became involved in Fenian politics and joined the Clan na Gael. As a member of the Triangle, the triumvirate which dominated the Clan during the 1880s, he encouraged terrorist activities in England and provided money for the Dynamiters. In June 1889 Sullivan had been arrested on suspicion of murdering Dr. P. H. Cronin, presumably in the course of a power struggle within the Clan, though Cronin was alleged to have been a British spy. Although Sullivan was never charged with the murder and was subsequently released from custody, the allegations of his involvement in it weakened his position in the Fenian hierarchy.

WBY's article on Cronin has not come to light and in the controversy following the murder, may never have been published.

[5] Sophie Bryant, née Willock (1850–1922), whose address at this time was 2 Anson Road, Tufnell Park, London, was born in Dublin. She spent a good deal of her childhood in Co. Fermanagh, where her father, the Revd W. A. Willock, DD, played a prominent part in the Irish National Education movement, before she moved to London to become a student at Bedford College. At the age of nineteen she married Dr William Hicks Bryant. When he died a year later, she resumed her studies, at the same time becoming mathematics mistress at the North London Collegiate School for Girls, and headmistress of the school in 1895. In 1884 she became the first woman to take the degree of Doctor of Science in Moral Science at the University of London. Subsequently she served on a number of educational bodies, and published widely on Irish and educational topics. Her book, *Celtic Ireland*, appeared in 1889.

Miss Little was probably Lucy ('Lizzie') Mary Little (1864–1909), author of *Persephone and Other Poems* (Dublin, 1884), who lived at 5 Claremont House, Lithos Road, Hampstead and who was teaching at the South Hampstead High School for Girls, Maresfield Gardens, N. W., at this time. She was one of three daughters of Joseph Bennett Little (b. 1820), an improvident Irish squire who had gambled away his Roscommon estate. The youngest daughter, Grace, was to marry Ernest Rhys in 1891.

To J. N. Dunn,[1] 28 [June 1889]

3 Blenheim Road | Bedford Park | Chiswick
July 28[2]

Dear Mr Dunn

I suddenly remembered to day that I had not answered your note about M[rs] Bryant's "Celtic Ireland". Please forgive me. The sudden turning up of an American friend[3] has driven every thing out of my head these last few days.

If you have not made other arrangements through not hearing from me, I should be very glad to review the book.[4]

Your[s] Truly
W B Yeats

ALS Texas.

To John O'Leary, 10 July [1889]

3 Blenheim Road | Bedford Park | Chiswick
July 10th

My Dear M[r] O Leary

I send herewith the Catalogues—I papered them up for posting a week ago. Had a kind of notion I might get more. I have sent all from the shops I pass going to the Museum.[1] I dare say however they will have new ones out by this—I will try any way. I am very seldom in town these days however. I will be one day this week I think.

Miss O Leary tells me that Carletons best are the "Nolans" & "Father Connel". Do you know any one who could lend them me? If not perhaps you

---

[1] James Nicol Dunn (1856–1919), a Scottish journalist who in 1888 was appointed managing editor of the *Scots Observer* (after a brief period as editor—see p. 117) in association with W. E. Henley. Dunn remained with the paper after it changed its name to the *National Observer* and moved to London, resigning in 1893 to become news editor of the *Pall Mall Gazette*. He went on to edit a number of other important papers, including the *Morning Post* (1897–1905), *Manchester Courier* (1905–10), and the Johannesburg *Star* (1911–14).

[2] Evidently, as in the preceding letter, a mistake for 'June 28'.

[3] Mrs Alexander Sullivan; see preceding letter.

[4] WBY's review, 'Bardic Ireland', appeared in the *Scots Observer*, 4 Jan 1890 (*UP* I. 162–6). He was generally in favour of Mrs Bryant's book, which gives an account of the history and social customs of the Irish Celts, but criticized the author for taking too historical a view of the Celtic legends, thus neglecting their imaginative mythological dimension.

[1] JO'L, an indefatigable book-collector, had evidently renewed his request of 1888 (see p. 46) for London booksellers' catalogues.

might chance on copies at some old book stall. I would send you the amount. I am also in need of a novel or two of Banims—his best.[2] Carleton I shall read all through probably the others only in their best work. Yet I dont know that I shall read all Carleton that depends on my getting or not getting books, & so forth. I must read one or two of his period of decadence however. My introduction though mainly of couse busy with Carleton will touch on all the chief Irish novelists of peasent life I hope—Banim & Kickham in chief.[3]

I am delighted to hear you will be in London soon.[4] There are several people in Bedford Park anxious to meet you—notably York Powell the translator of Sagas, and ⟨general⟩ historian.

Coffey's notice of my book was very good barring that he slighted my demon in the second part—a great favourite of mine. Miss Mulholand's notice in Irish Monthly also very good—I mean that I am pleased with her liking for the little Indian Scene.[5]

Miss Tynan was with us for a short time: she has got stouter & looks very well, looks indeed in every way better than when I saw her in Dublin.

After I have finished the Carleton book I may possibly or probably rather,

[2] Having heard WBY was now compiling a selection from Carleton for the Camelot Classics, Ellen O'Leary had written to him on 7 July 1889 (Belfast): 'I am glad you are doing Carleton, if only that it makes you read him yourself. John and I think *The Nowlans* and *Father Connell* his best novels. *The Nowlans* is certainly a very powerful and pathetic though a most unpleasant story.' She had, however, mixed up Carleton with the Banims, for *The Nowlans* (1826) was written by John Banim (1798–1842), and *Father Connell* (1842) by Michael Banim (1796–1874), probably in collaboration with his brother John.

At this juncture in his reading WBY seems to have been unaware that there were two novelists called Banim. Born in Kilkenny, John Banim studied art in Dublin but after some years as an art teacher in Kilkenny took up a literary life in London, where Macready produced his verse tragedy *Damon and Pythias* (1821). Under the influence of Sir Walter Scott he persuaded his brother Michael, who had remained in Kilkenny keeping the family shop, to collaborate with him (using the pseudonym 'Barnes O'Hara') on a series of novels which would 'insinuate, through fiction, the causes of Irish discontent'. These were published as *Tales by the O'Hara Family* (1st ser., 1825; 2nd ser., 1826) and were followed by a number of historical novels. Unfortunately John's chronic ill health grew worse and in 1835 he returned to Kilkenny as an invalid. Michael Banim produced little of value after his brother's death.

[3] Like JO'L a Tipperary man and the son of a prosperous shopkeeper, Charles Joseph Kickham (see pp. 33–4) took part in the Young Ireland movement, and joined the Fenians in 1860. In 1864 he formed, with JO'L and T. C. Luby, the three-man Executive in control of the Fenian organization. They were all arrested in 1865, and Kickham was sentenced to 14 years' penal servitude. While in prison he published *Sally Cavanagh* (Dublin, 1869), written some time before. Released after four years because of ill health, he subsequently published his best-known novel, *Knocknagow* (Dublin, 1879), a series of detailed pictures of Tipperary life, in which the Land Question is a major theme. His *For the Old Land* was published in Dublin in 1886.

[4] In her letter of 7 July (see n. 2 above) Ellen O'Leary had written that 'John will probably be in London some time in August and from thence will go for a while to Paris.'

[5] Rosa Mulholland's article on WBY and *Oisin* appeared as no. 23 in the series entitled 'Our Poets' (see p. 16, n. 6), in the *Irish Monthly*, May 1889 (365–71); it was reprinted from the *Melbourne Advocate* (to which she contributed a regular column) of 9 Mar 1889. She quoted from and praised 'the little floating cloud of pure poetry, named "Jealousy"' in which she found 'prisoned lightning'.

do a volume of old celtic romances for the series—reprints of various translations.[6] They will take me to Dublin I imagine.

I will write to Miss O Leary soon again.

Yours very sincery
W B Yeats

ALS NLI. Wade, 127–8.

To Father Matthew Russell, 13 July [*1889*]

3 Blenheim Road | Bedford Park | Chiswick
July 13

My dear Father Russel

A very great many thanks for printing Miss Mulholonds very kind notice of my book. I left the copy of the monthly with that little poem about my book at Oxford so did not know the name of the author, or I would have written to thank him. If you happen to be writting to him at any time you might say I mentioned it to you. Quite apart from my natural liking for the subject I think it was a very pretty little poem.[1]

I enclose a poem by a friend which I hope you may find suited to your magazine. Miss Tynan & I both think it a beautiful sonnet. Edwin Ellis the author is not a young man but a kind of a genius who has kept himself buried away for years in Italy, painting & reading Dante.[2]

I am writing an introduction to Carleton Traits & Stories for the Camelot series & intend contrasting him with Kickham & Banim. Miss Tynan says you could perhaps lend me Kickham's "Knocnagow". I know his other novels. It is laborious doing all the reading needful. What a voluminous creature Carleton was? I have still close on 15 novels to get through[3]—

[6] This project did not materialize.

[1] 'To William B. Yeats, Author of "The Wanderings of Oisin"', a poem by Robert Reilly (*Irish Monthly*, May 1889, 277), describes the author's delight in the natural magic of WBY's poetry. Reilly (1862–1893) was a doctor who contributed poems and articles to a number of Irish periodicals and newspapers.

[2] 'The Chosen' by Edwin Ellis, a sonnet in which the lily and the rose dispute their claim to be the Virgin Mary's flower, appeared in the *Irish Monthly* in September 1889.

[3] In his Introduction to *Carleton* (xvi–xvii) WBY wrote:

He is the great novelist of Ireland, by right of the most Celtic eyes that ever gazed from under the brows of storyteller. His equals in gloomy and tragic power, Michael and John Banim, had nothing of his Celtic humour. One man alone stands near him there—Charles Kickham, of Tipperary. . . . But, then, he had not Carleton's intensity. Between him and the life he told of lay years in prison, a long Feinian [*sic*] agitation, and partial blindness. On all things flowed a faint idealising haze. His very humour was full of wistfulness.

There 'is no wistfulness in the works of Carleton,' WBY goes on to say, but 'a kind of clay-cold melancholy'.

leaving Banim out of count. What do you think is Banim's best? I must take merely a few specemin nibbles at him.

In all ways I am a deel busier than I care to be—am reviewing Carleton's *Red Haired Man's Wife* for Scots Observer by the way. Do you know from what source it came & whether any body has added to or altered it?[4]

I have a play on the old Irish folktale, "the Countess Kathleen O Shee" half written. It is wholly my best poem I imagine, and is meant for the stage if possible.

I have been trying to persuade Miss Tynan to write a Miracle play. It would be a new poetic form for her & a new form often means a new inspiration.[5]

It is very good of you to send the Irish Monthly. I enjoy it always greatly—That article on the "Rapt Culdee' in a recent Number was one of the most charming articles I know. Miss Tynan has written a poem on the culdee and I shall probably do another.

Yours very sincerely
W B Yeats

Miss Tynan was staying with us lately for a week but she has now gone to another friends.[6] She is greatly in request.

If this little poem of Edwin Ellis happens to suit you I could bring him the proof sheet, if you would sent it me, or you could send direct to Edwin J. Ellis Esq. 40 Milson Road. Addison Road. Kensington London.

ALS APH. Wade, 128–9.

WBY is unlikely to have read all of Carleton's books. In the Introduction he refers chiefly to *The Miser*, *The Black Prophet*, *Valentine M'Clutchy*, *The Emigrants of Ahadarra*, and *Traits and Stories of the Irish Peasantry*, though he had also read *Tales and Sketches of Irish Life and Character*, *The Red-Haired Man's Wife*, and *Tales of Ireland*.

[4] *The Red-Haired Man's Wife* (Dublin, 1889) had first appeared in the *Carlow College Magazine*, May 1869–April 1870, and its authorship is in parts doubtful. An item in the *Manchester Courier's* column, 'From Our London Correspondent', for 27 Apr 1889 (6), presumably contributed by WBY (see *Bibl*, 11), notes: 'Judging by its rather vague preface, I imagine it is not all by the great Carleton, but that additions have been made by another hand in place of some lost pages'. In his review of the book in the *Scots Observer*, 19 Oct 1889 (which is prefaced by a one-sentence notice of his own *Carleton*), WBY observes (*UP* I. 141–6): 'From the preface about a "serious mishap" and "a literary friend", and from internal evidence, we gather that only a portion is by Carleton, the first two-thirds are his anyway.' D. J. O'Donoghue reports (*Life of Carleton* [1896], II. 321) that part of the original MS was destroyed by fire and the missing portions written by a Mr MacDermott after Carleton's death.

As a Catholic priest, Fr. Russell's attitude to Carleton was at best ambivalent. He found *The Red-Haired Man's Wife* better in book form than he had remembered it in the *Carlow College Magazine* but was reluctant to accept it 'as a representative Irish novel' (*Irish Monthly*, June 1889, 334).

[5] KT took his advice, although not for some years. Her first miracle play, *The Resurrection*, was included in *Cuckoo Songs* (1894), and the six-part sequence, *Miracle Plays: Our Lord's Coming and Childhood*—plays in simple rhyming octosyllabics, dramatizing episodes from the Annunciation to the Finding in the Temple—appeared in 1895.

[6] After leaving the Yeatses' KT went to stay with Mrs Pritchard and her family in Highgate, then to visit Wilfred Scawen Blunt in Sussex for a few days around 17 July; at the end of July she went for three weeks to the family of her dead friend Charles Gregory Fagan (see p. 65, n. 4) at Great Cressingham, Norfolk.

To Katharine Tynan, 16 July [1889]

3 Blenheim Road | Bedford Park | Chiswick
July 16

Dear Miss Tynan—

Where were you on Sunday, you sinner. I went to Miss Hickeys[1] giving up another engagement and one I was anxious to keep, for the purpose. Miss Little[2] was there to meet you.

I want you to come here next Saturday to meet Nettleship. I saw him to day & he can come. If you cannot, let me know in time to put him off.[3] He will be with us at 8 oc. Come you, for tea at 6.30 and as much earlier as you like. Stay the night if you can. As to Mrs Pritchard![4] do as you like about her. We shall be of course glad to see her.

I have got "Fairy and folk tales" for you. I am busy with Carleton; have got to have "copy" for book ready in three days & introduction in ten.

I just remember that you wish to show M rs Pritchard Bedford Park. Do not forget to come early so as to have day light. Would M rs Pritchard's coming necessitate your going home very early. If that is so you had better arrange to bring her another day & stay the night on Saturday.[5] I will try to get York Powell & it is no easy job to get him at any early hour & I somewhat misdoubt the punctuality of M r Nettleship.

Papa & Lilly have gone to Burnham Beeches for today & tomorrow.

Yours Always
W B Yeats

ALS Huntington. McHugh, 97–8; Wade, 129–30.

[1] Emily Henrietta Hickey (1845–1924) was born in Co. Wexford; the daughter of a Church of Ireland clergyman, she later converted to Catholicism. She took a First at Cambridge through correspondence classes and for many years taught English at the North London Collegiate School for Girls. In 1881, with F. J. Furnivall, she co-founded the Browning Society and in the same year her first book, *A Sculptor and other Poems*, was published. She continued to publish both poetry and prose, often on religious themes, up until her death. In the 1880s she lived at Clifton House, South End Green, Hampstead. If KT missed her on this occasion, she met her soon afterwards, for on 27 July 1889 she wrote to Fr. Russell (APH) that she had 'come to know Emily Hickey'.

[2] See p. 168.

[3] It seems probable that KT did keep this appointment, for Nettleship invited her to call upon him (as KT reported to Fr. Russell in a letter of 19 Aug 1889, APH) when she returned from Norfolk in late August.

[4] Mrs James Pritchard (b. *c.*1856), of 446 Camden Road, Highgate, with whom KT was staying at this time. Her husband was a cattle dealer who had business contacts with KT's father, Andrew Tynan. Flossie, one of Mrs Pritchard's daughters, spent the summer of 1884 with the Tynans at Clondalkin during her mother's confinement and illness in London, and the following year KT stayed with the Pritchards in London. In the 1880s KT wrote a series of letters to Mrs Pritchard (*Apex One*, 1973), one of which recounts her first meeting with WBY.

[5] KT seems to have stayed the night of Saturday, 20 July 1889, with the Yeatses, since on the following day WBY inscribed and dated a copy of *FFT* 'To my good friend Katharine Tynan', and a copy of *Oisin* 'To my dear friend Katharine Tynan' (both Berg).

To Father Matthew Russell, [? after 15 July 1889]

3 Blenheim Road | Bedford Park | Chiswick

My dear Father Russell

A great many thanks for the book which I will return as soon as I have read it.[1] Many thanks also for the promise of the poem book. Anything that any body may be doing in the way of Irish poetry interests me greatly. The Young Ireland impulse seems to have died out and one is always on the watch for any sign of a new start. I imagine it will be something much more complex than any thing we have had in Ireland heretofore and that it will appeal to, and draw its material from more numerous classes than young Ireland did. These are the bubbles I blow about it any way.[2]

I have to finish Carleton in a hurry to try and get the editor of the series out of a scrape, and may after all be unable to discuss Kickham as much as I had wished but shall take the matter up in articles.[3]

By the way I think you are unjust to Carleton he has drawn beatifully many entirely Catholic forms of life and virtue, and what ever he has said against the priests is mild indeed in comparison to his forocious attacks on the clergy of the protestant church in say Valantine McClutchy. He has drawn the charecters of several catholic clergimen most sympathetically and beautifully. His heart always remained Catholic, it seems to me. I may be wrong for their are still a good number of his novels I have had no time to read, but what anti-catholic feeling he ever had seems to have died out after the first few years. Unhappily "the traits and stories" were written in those years.[4] "Fardaroga the Miser" seems his best novel. I wish it were reprinted.

---

[1] Presumably Kickham's *Knocknagow* which he had asked to borrow (see p. 171).

[2] The book, *Songs of Remembrance* (Dublin, 1889) by 'Alice Esmonde' (Margaret Mary Ryan), which WBY was later to review (see below, p. 200), was not the new start he looked for. Nor had the impulse of the Young Irelanders, the group of writers and patriots who had gathered around Thomas Davis and the *Nation* newspaper, and whose anthology, *The Spirit of the Nation* (Dublin, 1845), went into numerous editions, died out, as WBY was to discover when he tried to break its hold over the Irish imagination. He had himself joined the Dublin Young Ireland Society, of which JO'L became president on his return from exile in 1885, but was to object later to the slipshod style and too-blatant political and moral purpose of Young Ireland poetry. WBY was to blow more of these 'bubbles' in his Introduction to *Representative Irish Tales* (2 vols., 1891); see I. 15–16.

[3] WBY did not write further about Kickham in articles but gave an extract from *For the Old Land*, prefaced by a biographical note, in *RIT*, II. 243–80. Here (245) his growing reservations about Kickham's art are obvious: 'One feels through all he wrote that in him were much humor and character-describing power of wholly Celtic kind, but marred by imperfect training. His books are put together in a hap-hazard kind of way—without beginning, middle, or end.'

[4] As a young aspiring writer, Carleton had been converted to Protestantism and was taken up by the rabidly anti-Catholic editor, the Revd Caesar Otway, for whose publication, the *Christian Examiner and Church of Ireland Magazine* (1825–69), he wrote some of his most violently anti-Catholic stories. As his reputation became more firmly established he began to tone down the anti-Catholic feeling in his tales and he frequently revised his work to this end. *Valentine M'Clutchy* (first published 1845), his most national and anti-Protestant book, follows the career of M'Clutchy, a rapacious and corrupt land agent,

M'Clutchy contains the best scenes almost of any but as a whole it seems less artistic—too much caracture and so forth.[5]

I must finish this now as I have to write my introduction to day.

Yours very sincerely

W B Yeats

ALS APH. Wade, 130–1.

To John O'Leary, [late July 1889]

Thursday

P S.[1]

I wonder how Dowden likes the crown of martyrdom. You heard I dare say that he did not get the Scotch Proffessorship he tried for. The reason was that all the unionists wanted him so the other side ran a scotch man named Knight. Lord some body or other, who had the chair in his gift, said as they were both party men he would have neither and put in a young man who had not yet taken any side.[2] I am sorry to hear about Miss Kavanagh not being so

and satirizes the sanctimonious hypocrite Solomon M'Slime, a religious attorney, and the Revd Mr Lucre, a Church of Ireland absentee clergyman and proselytizer. In the preface to this novel dated December 1844, Carleton even made a public recantation of his earlier bigotry: 'within the last few years, a more enlarged knowledge of life, and a more matured intercourse with society, have enabled me to overcome many absurd prejudices with which I was imbued. . . . I published in my early works passages which were not calculated to do any earthly good; but, on the contrary, to give unnecessary offence to a great number of my countrymen.' Fr. Roche in *Valentine M'Clutchy* and Fr. Moran in *The Red-Haired Man's Wife* are sympathetic characters, and Carleton dedicated *Art Maguire*, a temperance tale, to Fr. Theobald Matthew. Nevertheless, many of the *Traits and Stories* (e.g. 'The Station' and 'Denis O'Shaughnessy') present crude caricatures of priests and these were not forgotten in Ireland.

[5] 'In *Fardorougha*,' WBY wrote in the *Scots Observer*, 'there is none of the fierce political feeling that degraded some of Carleton's later novels into caricature. The book has a perfect unity . . .' (*UP* I. 144). Most critics concur with WBY in finding this the best of Carleton's novels. A new edition appeared in 1895, when it was also serialized in *United Ireland*.

WBY mentions the scenes with Raymond the madman in *M'Clutchy* both in his Introduction to *Carleton* and his review of *The Red-Haired Man's Wife*: '*Valentine M'Clutchy*, where half the characters are devils, would be intolerable but for its wild humour and the presence of the village madman, in whose half-inspired and crazy oratory Carleton seems to pour himself out' (*UP* I. 145). But he was later to describe the book as 'formless and unjust' (*UP* I. 383).

[1] The letter to which this postscript belongs has not survived.

[2] On 27 July 1889 the *Scots Observer* announced that the chair of English at Glasgow University, made vacant by the retirement in 1889 of John Nichol (1833–94), had gone to Andrew Cecil Bradley (1851–1935), who was later to write celebrated critical studies on Shakespeare's Tragedies and Tennyson's *In Memoriam*. The 'scotchman', William Angus Knight (1836–1916), was Professor of Moral Philosophy at the University of St. Andrews, 1876–1902; he published copiously, especially upon Wordsworth and the Lake Poets. The chair was in the gift of the Crown and on this occasion that perogative was exercised by Schomberg Henry Kerr, 9th Marquis of Lothian (1833–1900) as Secretary of State for Scotland from 1887 to 1892. The source of WBY's gossip was probably Henley, whose leading article, 'Glasgow and

well, & glad to hear of her going to Paris. Does she write anything now—I wish she would make her Uncle Rhemus children hunt up folktales. She might make one or two of her weekly competitions on the matter. She got a couple or so from the children at Xmas & they were very interesting.[3] I could give any help needful in the matter of course.

I am taking a few day[s], having finished Carleton, at my play the "Countess". When that is done I mean to write a series of Irish ballads—folk tales from Sligo set into rhyme & things out of history & so forth. You will like the "Countess" its Irish right through

[*no signature*]

APS Berg. *Irish Book Lover*, November 1940 (247).

To the Editor of The Spectator, *29 July 1889*

3 Blenheim Road, Bedford Park, Chiswick
July 29th

Sir,—In a kindly notice of my volume of poems, your reviewer asks where I got the materials for "The Wanderings of Oisin."[1] The first few pages are developed from a most beautiful old poem written by one of the numerous half-forgotten Gaelic poets who lived in Ireland in the last century. In the quarrels between the saint and the blind warrior, I have used suggestions from various ballad Dialogues of Oisin and Patrick, published by the Ossianic Society.[2] The pages dealing with the three islands, including your

English Literature', in the *Scots Observer*, 29 June 1889 (148–9), mentioned Dowden's candidature but hoped that Andrew Lang might apply for the post. Lang was, in fact, offered it but declined on grounds of ill health.

[3] Rose Kavanagh ran competitions of an educational nature in her 'Uncle Remus' column in the *Weekly Freeman*. In the 1888 Christmas Supplement (see p. 107) she edited for the paper, some of the entries had consisted of folktales collected by the children. MG had invited her to stay in Paris.

[1] In an unsigned notice of *Oisin, Spectator*, 27 July 1889 (122), asking about WBY's source for 'this somewhat strange poem', the reviewer was particularly curious to know whether the descriptions of the 'phantoms dread'—the hornless deer, phantom hound, maiden with apple of gold, and pursuing beautiful young man—were 'wholly the writer's own', and whether WBY had invented the encounter with the old man when Oisin returns to Ireland. The review concludes: 'That the story is Irish we know, for Oisin tells the story to St. Patrick. Mr Yeats goes to other fountains for his inspiration. What he gives us has always something fresh about it. His volume is a refreshing change from the commonplace of much modern verse.'

[2] In *Poems* (1895), WBY explains (*VP*, 793) that 'The poem is founded upon the Middle Irish dialogues of Saint Patrick and Oisin and a certain Gaelic poem of the last century.' WBY took much of his material from the *Transactions of the Ossianic Society* (1854–63), in vol. I of which is an account of the Battle of Gabhra, translated by Nicholas O'Kearney; vol. III contains Standish O'Grady's translation of 'The Lament of Oisin after the Fenians', and John O'Daly's rendering of the 'Dialogues of Oisin and Patrick' appears in vol. V. The eighteenth-century poem was Michael Comyn's 'The Lay of Oisin in the Land of Youth', published in vol. IV of the *Transactions*.

reviewer's second quotation, are wholly my own, having no further root in tradition than the Irish peasant's notion that *Tir-u-au-oge* (the Country of the Young) is made up of three phantom islands.—I am, Sir, &c.,

W B YEATS

Printed letter, *The Spectator*, 3 August 1889 (143). Wade, 132.

To Laurence Housman[1], *1 August* [*1889*]

3 Blenheim Road | Bedford Park | Chiswick

August 1

Dear Sir

Many thanks for your letter. I am glad you like my poems. I am sorry that I have no present intention of publishing an illustrated edition of any of them. Such things cost in everyway much money.

Two or three of the shorter poems, by the way, were written to illustrations of my fathers which were printed with them in one or two magazines.[2]

Yours Truly
W B Yeats

ALS Bryn Mawr

To Katharine Tynan, [*after 6 August 1889*]

2 St Johns Villas | St Johns Road | Oxford.

Dear Miss Tynan—

I am down here at Oxford & shall be, until the end of next week at earliest, copying a thing in the Bodlean.[1] I copy six & a half hours each day, then go

[1] Laurence Housman (1865–1959), dramatist, novelist, poet and illustrator was the younger brother of A. E. Housman. He had finished his training at the South Kensington Art School in 1887 and was now looking for commissions for book illustrations. Although he was to illustrate a number of books, his failure to find success at this period led him to take up literature and in 1893 he was to produce his first book, *Selections from the Writings of William Blake*. Thereafter, in the course of a long life he was to publish 'more books than I should have done had I given more time to second thoughts' (*Back Words and Fore Words* [1945] p. 7). His greatest commercial success was with *An Englishwoman's Love-Letters* (1900) and his play, *Victoria Regina*, attained wide popularity when it was produced during the abdication crisis in 1936. Although never a close friend of WBY's the two met occasionally.

[2] JBY had contributed a frontispiece to *Mosada* in 1886 and illustrated 'King Goll' when it appeared in the *Leisure Hour*, September 1887.

[1] On 6 Aug WBY had gone to Oxford to copy out an anonymous 1592 translation (possibly by Robert Dallyngton) of part of an Italian Renaissance prose allegory, published by David Nutt in 1890 as *The Strife of Love in a Dream*, 'being The Elizabethan Version of the First Book of the *Hypnerotomachia* by Francesco Colonna; A new Edition by Andrew Lang, M.A.'

for a walk until tea time making up lines for "the Countess" the while. After tea I read Kickham (for a couple of volumes of slections from the Irish novelists I shall probably be doing for Puttenham the Boston Publisher)[2] but on the whole am too tired after tea to do much good at anything. So you see the poem for East & West will have to elbow out "the Countess". I will begin thinking on the matter tomorrow and probably may get started on Sunday.[3]

I am in Lodgings here & do not know a soul (the Hunts[4] have left for a month). I lodge in the same rooms Vigusson (the Icelander who died the other day—a friend of York Powells) lived in. The landlady is a good woman with a pale ungenial English face & their is a big engraving on the wall called "the Soldier's Dream" and two more (the Bartololzzi school) of children being led through the sky by a couple of guardian angels with pointed noses.[5] I am always glad to get away by myself for a time & should be contented enough here but for the miserable aligory I copy out for Nutt. I am sorry to have had to come thither the very day John O Leary started for London (he stays a month however) and sorry too to have missed Pat Gogorty who by strange ill luck called the very day I left. He has been a month in Paris and is now on his way homeward.[6]

Of course we shall be delighted to have you with us, any time you come. I hope you will stay a good while.[7] You can, if you like always have my study or the drawing room to work in. And have them to your self if you like. Apropo[s] of which; M rs Stanard said she cannot work unless all her family are in the room with her. She once tried to work alone but cried from sheere lonliness.[8]

[2] WBY's anthology, *Representative Irish Tales*, was eventually published in March 1891 by G. P. Putnam's Sons, Boston, in their Knickerbocker Nuggets series.

[3] WBY's 'The Ballad of the Old Fox-hunter' (*VP*, 97–9), based on an incident in Kickham's *Knocknagow*, appeared in *East and West*, November 1889.

[4] KT had stayed with the family of Bertram Hunt, a doctor who lived at 39 St. Giles, Oxford, from 22 to 29 June 1889.

[5] WBY was lodging in St. John's Villas with Mrs George Smith. The distinguished Icelandic scholar Gúdbrandr Vígfússon (1828–89), for whom a Readership in Icelandic was created in 1884 by Oxford University, had died not 'the other day' but on 31 Jan 1889. Engravings of the school of the Italian Francesco Bartolozzi (1727–1815), frequently featuring putti and cupids, were popular in the nineteenth century.

[6] According to KT's 1892 article on him in the *Speaker* (see p. 54 n. 2), Gogarty had 'made his way to France and remained long enough to learn the language, so as to get at the French writers'.

[7] When KT returned to London from Norfolk, on 26 Aug, she stayed again with the Meynells, in their new house in Bayswater (see p. 166). She was reluctant to leave there, and wrote to Fr. Russell on 12 Sept 1889 (APH): 'I ought to stay awhile at the Yeats' to sit for a water colour but I grudge going . . . because I am so happy here.'

[8] Henrietta Eliza Vaughan Stannard, neé Palmer (1856–1911), wife of Arthur Stannard, a civil engineer, wrote under the pseudonym of 'John Strange Winter' a prolific number of stories and novels, mainly on army life. Her novel, *Bootles' Baby* (1885), sold two million copies and brought her temporary fame. In 1893 she became the second woman to be elected a Fellow of the Royal Society of Literature. She had four children and probably made the remark about the necessity of her family's company to WBY on 2 Mar 1889 when, as ECY recorded in her diary (MBY), 'Willie went this evening to a reception

I cannot well send a copy of my poems to the French lady,[9] I fear, until I get home. I shall have to go to Keegan Paul for a copy—

I have a good deal of work to do at present, more than I can manage. All at Irish literary subjects—which is as it should be. I wish you had made up the Irish novelists and folkloreists. You with your ready pen would find plenty to say about them. There is a want for a short book (about 150 pages or 200) on Irish literature—Lives & criticism of all the writers since Moore. It would sell largely, I hope, and do good I am sure. Some day you or I must take it in hands. There is a great want of a just verdict on these men and their use for Ireland. I have often thought of setting about such a book and may when I have got on more with the novel writers.[10] The worst would be, one's necessity of blaming so many whose use is not yet exausted. Blake is likely to be I dare say the one big prose matter I shall try just yet however. By big I mean not articles, merely. Though Blake book will be truly a biggish book.

What a downpore it has been this afternoon. I have written this letter instead of going for a walk. Now it is clearing up and a sparrow is beginning to chirp.

Yours Always
W B Yeats.

Write again soon & let me know about your plans.

Lilly & Jack are in Ireland (I suppose you know) at least Jack is and Lilly has either started or is about to do so. Lolly is housekeeping or will when she comes back from Hazelmere, where she is staying for a few days with the Nashes.[11] She will be home in a day or two now.

I must go for my walk now.

ALS Huntington. McHugh, 98–100; Wade. 132–4.

of John Strange Winters (Mrs Stannard) at Putney. She is a nice woman he says . . . he met some interesting people there & stayed to supper not coming home till twelve.'

[9] In *25 Years* (286–8), KT recalls: 'Among the editors I was writing for just then was a certain mysterious "M. Bertram", who lived in Paris and ran a magazine called *East and West*. No magazine could have been run in a more unbusiness-like fashion, but the payments were all right, and they were always made in Bank of England notes. Someone printed and published the magazine in London, and I may say that the production was scandalous.' Ward & Downey were the publishers of *East and West*, which began monthly publication in June 1889. 'M. Bertram' turned out to be the assumed name of a lady with literary aspirations; she was not, in fact, French but an aunt of Imogen Guiney.

[10] Although WBY never published such a book, his frequent articles on Irish literature, especially those on 'Irish National Literature' in the *Bookman*, July–October 1895, and the Introduction to *BIV*, were clearly prompted by the same feelings. To create a mature and independent Irish criticism was one of his chief ambitions, and he had written in *DUR* in November 1886, in his second published article (*UP* 1. 88): 'If Ireland has produced no great poet, it is not that her poetic impulse has run dry, but because her critics have failed her, for every community is a solidarity, all depending upon each, and each upon all.'

[11] Jack Yeats's diary (MBY) records that on 30 July 1889 he 'went to Liverpool and caught the steamer for Sligo'. SMY it seems left a little later. Haslemere was the holiday home of the artist Joseph Nash (see p. 112), the Yeatses' neighbour in Bedford Park, whose daughters were the same ages as SMY and ECY.

To John O'Leary, [8 August 1889]

2 St John's Villas | St John's Rd | Oxford
Thursday

Dear Mr O'Leary,

Two days ago I heard from Miss O'Leary that you were on your way to London. Here am I down in Oxford, by evil fortune, & will be for the next nine days I foresee. I am copying out for Nutt the publisher who like all his race is in a hurry a dull old aligory about love written by an Italian, who deserved to be forgotten long ago, & translated into fairly good English & published in a book full of misprints by an Elizabethan who wrote well enough to have known better.[1] However the thing may be good enough but then I copy $6\frac{1}{2}$ hours a day at it, never taking pen from paper except for a dip of ink. Covering so much paper gives one a fellow-feeling for the wandering Jew. Certainly he covered miles & years & I but foolscap sheets but then he walked fast & the years did not matter to him.

Papa writes to me that there is an MP one Atherley Jones—a Bedford Parkite & tepid Whig or some such thing—very anxious to meet you.[2] Indeed there are many most anxious, notably York Powell, who is away now for a week or two.

Pat Gogarty, the Clondalkin shoemaker called to see me I am told the very day I came down here—he is over for a few days. He has really sent one or two capital studies of peasant life as far as substance & sincerity go but written in an old fashioned clumsy way.

I am reading "Knocknagow" here in the evening & have Banim's "Croppy" to begin next.[3] However, I am rather too tired at night—I take a longish walk when the library closes—to read much. When walking I go on with my Irish play "The Countess Kathleen". I always find it pleasant being alone & would be quite happy but for the Italian & his aligory.

Yours very sincerely
W B Yeats

MS copy in D. J. O'Donoghue's hand, Belfast. Wade, 134–5.

[1] Francesco Colonna's *Hypnerotomachia* (see p. 177, n. 1).

[2] Llewellyn Archer Atherley-Jones (1851–1929), who lived at 1 Priory Gardens, Bedford Park, was a barrister on the North Eastern circuit and at this time Liberal MP for North Durham, a seat that he held until his appointment as a Judge in the City of London in 1914. He published a number of books on law, contributed articles to the *Nineteenth Century* and the *Edinburgh Review*, and wrote an autobiography, *Looking Back* (1925). Tepid he may have been, but Atherley-Jones was certainly no Whig: his father, Ernest Jones, had been imprisoned for his Chartist activities, and he himself was on the radical wing of the Liberal Party and opposed to the Whiggish element in it. He was probably eager to meet JO'L because in 1867, while still at school, he had been secretary of a committee to seek clemency for the 'Manchester Martyrs'. He and JO'L also had a common friend in Joseph Cowan, editor of the *Newcastle Chronicle*.

[3] Michael Banim's *The Croppy: A Tale of 1798* (1828) is a love story set against the violence and excesses of the 1798 rebellion in Ireland.

To Katharine Tynan, [14 August 1889]

2 St Johns Villas | St Johns Road | Oxford.
Wednesday

Dear Miss Tynan.

I find I shall be able to leave this on Friday afternoon. My work will then be finished. Are you coming to us this week if so when & would you like me to meet you at any railway station & help with the luggage, if it be after Friday afternoon.

This is a most beautiful country, about here—I walked sixteen miles on Sunday—going to the places in Matthew Arnolds poems—the ford in "the Scholour Gipsey" being the furthest away & most interesting.[1] How very unlike Ireland the whole place is—like a foreign land (as it is). One underſtands (a long S, I notice, has got in here out of the book I am copying) English poetry more from seeing a place like this. I only felt at home once— when I came to a steep lane with a ſtream in the middle. The rest one noticed with a foreign eye, picking out the strange and not as in ones own country the familiar things for interest—the fault by the way of all poetry about countries not the writers own. The people, I notice, do not give you "a fine day" or answer yours, as in Ireland. The children seem more civil I think—(perhaps however generations of undergraduates have scared them into good behaviour).

It is just possible but unlikely (very) that I shall not get away from this until Saturday morning.

O'Leary was at Blenheim Road, I hear, on Sunday.

You will have plenty of time to write when you come as every one has left Town by this.

Let me know your intentions in matter of arival.

Have started poem for you[2] but made little progress.

Yours Always
W B Yeats

ALS Huntington, with envelope addressed to Great Cressingham Rectory, Walton, Norfolk, postmark 'OXFORD AU 14 89'. McHugh, 100–1; Wade, 135.

[1] 'The stripling Thames at Bab-lock-hythe' (1. 74)—the ford at Bablock Hythe is some 6 miles west of Oxford by road, but WBY evidently took a circuitous route.
[2] i.e. the poem for *East and West* (see p. 178).

To Douglas Hyde, [23 August 1889]

3 Blenheim Road | Bedford Park | Chiswick

My dear Hyde.

I hear from O'Leary that your only reason for not printing with your long expected folklore collection, an English translation, is a question of expense.[1] I have good reason to beleive that Nutt, the publisher would be delighted to print at his expense a translation. Such would not, I imagine, injure the usefulness of your gaelic version & would be of great importance. For I firmly beleive, and I think he does the same, that you are the one great Folklorist Ireland has produced. York Powell said to me last week—'there was never a Folk lorist like him'. *Teig O Kane* alone is worth in my mind all the Folk lore journal since the commencement of the thing[2] (why is newspaper English supposed to ⟨resemble the⟩ reproduce the thoughts and speach of peasents. I found the phrase "Eternal Rome" in a scientists folktale a while since). Lady Wilde has again praised your style. You alone, it seems to me, preserve accuracy & the flavour of life—Lady Wilde says much the same I forget her words. In the name of Don of the Ocean Vats and all other kings of *Sidhe* country,[3] offer Nutt a translation (you will be elf shoot some fine day if you do not) or origonal folk book, and save our fairy tales from the newspaper English of science on the one hand and the ramshackle towrow dialect of men like ⟨McNall⟩ McAnally on the other.

Let me know what you think.

I have asked York Powell to let Nutt know that I am writing to you on the matter.

Nutt has taken an Irish folk book from David Fitzerald—who as a writer is nobody but seems devoted to the matter.[4] Nutt said to Powell something about you—almost ⟨committed⟩ as good as offering to take a book from

---

[1] This, apparently, was not the reason, for in a note to *Leabhar Sgeulaigheachta* (212) Hyde defends his decision not to give English versions as part of his campaign to restore the use of Irish:

It seems ridiculous that we cannot publish a book in our own language without introducing more or less of English into it. I had determined to publish these stories just as they are, without any commentary, such seeming to me unnecessary; but certain friends pointed out to me the advisability of adding some explanatory observations on the text, which should prove useful to any who may use this book to learn Irish.

[2] WBY was often to repeat this praise of 'Teig O'Kane and the Corpse'; cf. his letter to the *Academy* of 2 Oct 1890 (p. 229).

[3] A reference to Donn, the Sidhe god of the dead, who is said to live in Tech Duinn ('Don's House'), an island off the coast of Kerry.

[4] In his letter to the *Boston Pilot*, written 7 Sept 1889 and published on 28 Sept (*LNI*, 76–82), WBY announced that Nutt was to publish a book by David Fitzgerald (1843–1916), whose 'articles in La Revue Celtique promise well for his volume, some of the stories being most curious and weird, though spoiled a good deal by the absence of any attempt to give the native idiom they were told in. They are written more from the side of science than literature.' Fitzgerald had contributed three articles to the

3, Blenheim Road, Bedford Park, where the Yeatses lived from late March 1888

Maud Gonne

you—regretted that you had an idia of only writing in Gaelic—a notion he picked up from me I fear & I picked ⟨it⟩ up heaven knows where.

By the by I have just finished editing a volume of tales from Carleton for Walter Scott & am know [*for* now] at work on a proposed two volume selection of Irish stories of peasent life for Puttenham of Boston. Banim, Carleton, Edgeworth etc make up list. Have you done any thing that way—under 40 pages or 50 at very most—or know of any such. I am rather ignorant of the Irish prose writers. When I want to read up a subject I get a book to do there on. I write to read & never merely read to write.

Did I ever tell you my good fortune in finding out that William Blake—on whose Mystic System myself & a friend are ⟨working on a⟩ making a big book—the devil take all this prose—was an O'Neal. His grandfather was a Cornelious O'Neal who changed his name to Blake. Ireland makes much noise in his Mystic System & always holds a high ideal place.

Did they tell you our intentions of binding remaining Ballad of Young Ireland 1888 in paper covers and selling as a cheep edition at 3ᵈ or 6ᵈ? Todhunter, Miss Tynan, myself & probably Miss O'Leary will print at the end advertisements with press opinions of our books. Perhaps you might do likewise with your gaelic book. We want to let people know that there is a little school of us. At present there is no hurry about your deciding as we are waiting untill the fifty or so bound copies sell out. The book is still selling.

Yours very sincerely
W B Yeats

My Carleton is out today I find.[5]

ALS Private.

To Ernest Rhys, [*c. 29 August 1889*]

3 Blenheim Road | Bedford Park | Chiswick

My dear Rhys

Could you hurry up Scott do you think in the matter of paying me.[1] Funds are running rather low and he makes no sign and also ask him to send on my four copies still due.

Revue Celtique, two on 'Popular Tales of Ireland' in tom. IV, 1879–80, the other on 'Early Celtic History and Mythology' in October 1884. Not everyone found him as scientific as WBY; in the *Revue Celtique*, mai 1888 (370), the distinguished Irish antiquarian Whitley Stokes attacked the article on Celtic history and mythology as a 'farrago of bad Irish, doubtful English, mythological guesswork and impossible etymology'. This onslaught perhaps dulled Fitzgerald's appetite for publication, as he produced no more articles and no books, although he remained a life-long member of the Folklore Society.

[5] *Stories from Carleton* was announced as one of the day's publications in the *Pall Mall Gazette* on 23 Aug 1889 (7).

[1] The payment was for *Carleton*: 'I edited for a popular series the stories of Carleton and a volume of Irish fairy tales—getting I think seven guineas for the Carleton, I think twelve for the fairy stories' (*Mem*, 32).

I am very sorry to trouble you.

When will you be here in London again²—I am to dine with Gavan Duffy next Sunday. He praised you to me last week. He promises me unpublished letters of Clarence Mangans and I have written to an Irish publisher to ask him to let me edit for him a volume of Mangans poems in order to make use of them—the letters touch on Mangans very mournful love adventure.³

M ʳˢ Besant, you may not have heard, has turned theosophist and is now staying with M ᵈᵐᵉ Blavatsky.⁴ She is a very courtious & charming woman. John O'Leary is now in London & I can write no more now as I am due at his lodgings in an hours time and they are some distance off.⁵

Yours very sny
W B Yeats

Of course Scott will send book to *Irish Monthly* & other Irish papers Etc.

ALS BL. Partly in Wade, 137.

To John O'Leary, [? 30 August 1889]¹

Friday. 2ᵒᶜ

Dear Mʳ O Leary—

I was sorry to miss you last night. & am sorry to miss you again to day. Lolly told me you said something about my calling at 2ᵒᶜ as you would be writing letters until then. She gave the message wrong I supose.

---

² Rhys was living at this time at 1 Mount Vernon, Hampstead, London N.W., but was apparently away on holiday.

³ See p. 47, n. 3. The Irish publisher was probably M. H. Gill, who had brought out Mangan's *Irish and Other Poems* in 1886. Perhaps for this reason nothing came of the proposal.

⁴ Mrs Annie Besant, née Wood (1847–1933), was, with Charles Bradlaugh, one of the most outspoken atheists of the Victorian period and held office in the National Secular Society. Her dramatic conversion to theosophy took place in the spring of 1889 when W. T. Stead gave her HPB's *The Secret Doctrine* to review for the *Pall Mall Gazette*. Having read the book, she called upon HPB who implored her to 'come among us'. After some hesitation she joined the Theosophical Society on 10 May 1889 but did not announce this publicly until late June. Her two lectures on 'Why I Became a Theosophist', delivered on 4 and 11 Aug 1889, received wide press coverage. WBY was to work with her in the Esoteric Section of the Society in the autumn and winter of 1889–90 (see *Mem*, 281–2). After HPB's death the Society split into rival groups and Mrs Besant became leader of one of these.

⁵ JO'L was probably at the Bedford Head Hotel, in Bayley Street, Bedford Square, where he often stayed, close to his old friend and fellow Fenian, Dr Mark Ryan (1844–1940), who lived at 15A Gower Street.

¹ From WBY's letter of 7 May 1889 (see p. 164) it is clear that JO'L had not met HPB before 1889. This proposed visit to her (see below) must have been arranged while JO'L was staying in London in August and early September on his way to Paris.

I thought to arrange about Madame Blavatsky[2] but can on Sunday evening.

Yours very truly
W B Yeats

ALS NLI.

To Douglas Hyde [c. *1 September 1889*]

3 Blenheim Road | Bedford Park | Chiswick

My dear Hyde

I enclose a note of York Powell's who writes for Nutt, to accept your offer of Folk book.[1]

By the way I have not seen Pan Celtic book & would be glad to do so, I did not answer a note the sec of society sent me a while since, through sheer procrastination, and fear he may be offended with me. I must write to him now, or review him & his society, or some way make my peace with him.

I should be very glad of a copy of Pan Celtic book. Please tell me also ⟨anything⟩ about your Gaelic folk book—how many pages Etc. I am doing an Irish literary letter for Boston Pilot and will give some pars to you, also to Pan Celts. My Pilot letter should get itself written within two or three days.[2]

---

[2] JO'L wrote to his sister Ellen on 'Wednesday' [?4 September 1889] (NLI) that WBY

took me to Madame Blavatski's last night. She seems at first sight a terrible termagant, but at bottom is, I think, a good-natured old woman enough. She is certainly a person of strong will, and I should say that is the secret of the power she has over her surroundings, rather than any depth in her thought, which, however, to do it justice is broad enough. Said surroundings, as visible to me, not impressive. Most of the men being to my mind far more of women than their hostess, and the women more slavish parrot-like echoes of the big woman . . .

[1] In a note dated 30 Aug 1889 (Private) York Powell told Hyde: 'Mr Nutt would be glad to print the translations of the Book of Stories you have published together with an appending of such subsequently collected stories and translations as you think it worth (from folk-lore point of view) preserving.' He urged Hyde to let him have the MS as soon as possible 'as we cd then print at once'.

[2] In his letter to the *Boston Pilot* published on 28 Sept 1889 (see p. 182 n. 4) he prophesied that Hyde's book [eventually published as *Beside the Fire* in 1891] would be 'the most Irish of all folk-lore' since Hyde understood 'perfectly the language of the people and writes it naturally, as others do book-English. . . . He is surely the most imaginative of all Irish scholars, and I believe these wild and sombre stories of his will make some noise in the world.' Hyde was also a contributor to *Lays and Lyrics of the Pan-Celtic Society*, edited by Andrew Russell St. Ritch (Dublin, 1889), about which he wrote to KT, a fellow contributor, on 25 Aug 1889 (Southern Illinois): 'The editing of it is execrable but the pieces in it are better than I expected.' WBY included a mention of the Pan-Celtic anthology in his *Boston Pilot* letter, finding that Hyde's contributions to this 'new and very unequal' volume were 'full of true Gaelic flavor' (*LNI*, 80).

The introduction to Carleton you will hardly find of much interest, it was done in a great hurry to fill a gap and get Rhys out of a scrape.

Yours very sincerely
W B Yeats

ALS Private.

To Father Matthew Russell, [? week of 2 September 1889]

3 Blenheim Road | Bedford Park | Chiswick

Dear Father Russel

I shall at once send Irish Monthly to Edwin Ellis[1] who by the by is writing to gether with me a book on William Blake's hitherto never made out "Prophetic books". Blake's Grandfather I have found out by chance was a Cornelious O Neal who took the name of Blake to dodge his creditors. So we may almost claim Blake for an Irish poet.

You ask in your book notes for some one to translate Hyde's Folk lore book. He is going to do so himself. Only today I sent on a note from a publisher over here offering to take a book from him. The publisher (Nutt) had read his stories in my fairy book. It will be a great event I beleive. He is the best of all Irish folklorists & may do for us what Campbell did for Scotland.[2] I wonder when he will give us a volume of ballads by the by.[3]

I am up to the ears in Irish novelists making up the subject with view of a probable two volume selection of short stories of Irish peasent life for

---

[1] Ellis's poem 'The Chosen' (see p. 171) had appeared in the current number of the *Irish Monthly*.

[2] In a notice of Hyde's *Leabhar Sgeulaigheachta* in the *Irish Monthly*, September 1889 (498–9), Fr. Russell had lamented that the book was 'a fountain sealed for most of our readers' since, except for the notes, it was entirely in Irish. He went on to ask, 'Will not the author, or someone else, enable outer barbarians to enjoy some of the good things that must crowd the 212 pages which precede the notes?' Hyde translated some, but not all, of these stories for *Beside the Fire*.

Descended from Highland chieftains, John Francis Campbell of Islay (1822–85), the famous collector of Scottish folklore, was educated at Eton and the University of Edinburgh, but had mixed with the people as a boy on Islay and had learned Gaelic. Convinced that the Scottish folk tales were fast disappearing, he not only set out to record them himself but organised a team of trained, Gaelic-speaking collectors to help him. His 4-vol. *Popular Tales of the West Highlands* (Edinburgh, 1860–2) provided rich material for folklorists and anthropologists. Campbell always insisted that the tales should be taken down exactly as they were told, and WBY came to regard Hyde as superior to him since, 'Unlike Campbell of Islay, he has not been content merely to turn the Gaelic into English; but where the idiom is radically different he has searched out colloquial equivalents from among the English-speaking peasants' (*UP* I. 188).

[3] Hyde, who for some years had been publishing poems and ballads in newspapers and periodicals, produced a collection of translations from the Irish, *The Love Songs of Connacht*, in 1893; a selection of his Irish poems, *Ubhla de'n Chraoibh*, was published in Dublin in 1900, and *The Religious Songs of Connacht* in 1906.

Puttenham's *Knickerbocker Nuggat* series. Do you know of any off the general track of Carleton, Banim, Griffen Lover Etc. Any whose copywrites have lapsed or who would give leave to reprint (In America where leave is hardly needed).[4] It would be some what of an advertisement. The thing may not come off however I am dayly expecting a final clinching of the matter. The stories I am giving range from 20 to 80 pages (in a few cases of important people). You will have got my Carleton by this.[5] The introduction was done very hastily to get Rhys out of a difficulty made by some one or other not being up to date.

Miss Tynan is in London once more & staying with the Meynells. She goes about every where & seems much in request. She has got a monthly letter to do for *East & West*.[6] Do not forget that you promised me a copy of "Alice Esmonde's" poems. I saw advertised in the Monthly a while since a book called "Lays of South Sligo". Was there any good in the book? or any

[4] Gerald Griffin (1803–40), born in Limerick of middle-class Catholic parents, went to London in 1823 to eke out a living in hack journalism. After four years his collection of regional tales, *Holland-Tide*, brought him some success, and he returned to Ireland where he produced a number of stories and novels set in Munster. The best-known of these, *The Collegians* (1829), was described by WBY as 'the most finished and artistic of all Irish stories' (*RIT*, II. 162). Troubled by an unrequited love for the wife of a Limerick Quaker and increasingly uncertain about the morality of writing fiction, Griffin decided in 1838 to join the Christian Brothers and destroyed almost all of his unpublished work. In 1839 he became a teacher at the North Monastery, Cork, and died there the following year of typhus fever. His *Life and Works* appeared in 8 vols., 1842–3, and his *Poetical Works* in 1851. Griffin was an early voice of the emerging Catholic middle class in Ireland, a class with which WBY never felt great affinity and which he was later to attack. Thus, while he praised Griffin for his polish and art, he placed him (*RIT*, I. 14) with those novelists who 'cloak all unpleasant matters, and moralize with ease. . . . Their main hindrances are a limited and diluted piety, a dread of nature and her abundance, a distrust of unsophisticated life.' He published an extract from *The Collegians* and Griffin's short story, 'The Knight of the Sheep', in *RIT* (II. 167–204).

Samuel Lover (1797–1868), Dublin novelist, dramatist, song writer and painter, one of the founders of the *Dublin University Magazine*, is best known for his novel, *Handy Andy* (1842), which popularized a variant of the stage-Irishman type, the amiable, clumsy buffoon. He also enjoyed a considerable success with his play, *Rory O'More* (1837); WBY took material from his *Legends and Stories of Ireland* (Dublin, 1831, 1834) for both *FFT* and *RIT*.

If Fr. Russell made any suggestions, WBY evidently did not include them, for in July 1891 the *Irish Monthly* complained (379) 'That Mr. Yeats has not thus consulted best for the tastes of even his least Irish-hearted readers is manifest. . . . ' WBY was criticized for including the anti-Catholic story 'Father Tom and the Pope' and for wrongly ascribing it to William Maginn: 'The same mistaken notion of "representativeness" has, I think, spoiled almost the whole selection, in which the rollicking, savage, and droll elements are much too largely represented.' Fr. Russell, while applauding the inclusion of Rosa Mulholland, noted disapprovingly that she was the only living Irish writer chosen. The question of copyright in the works selected had little bearing on publication in America, for until 1891 American copyright was obtainable only by citizens or residents of the United States.

[5] If this was a hint that *Carleton* might be reviewed in the *Irish Monthly*, Fr. Russell ignored it.

[6] In a letter of 19 Aug 1889 to Fr. Russell (APH), KT told him that Mrs Bertram of *East and West* wanted her 'to contribute a monthly brick-a-brac thing to come at the end of the magazine'. In the event, no such series by KT was published, although her article, 'Ireland', appeared in the second number (July 1889), her poem, 'Prince Connla with the Golder Hair', in the fourth (September 1889), and her unsigned story, 'Lady Anne's Wraith', together with her poem, 'Queen's Roses', in the seventh number (December 1889).

legend even. All things about Sligo interest me & if you have a copy by you (you noticed it I beleive) I should like to see it.[7]

Miss A I Johnston verses in last Monthly are very pretty.[8]

Yours very Sincely

W B Yeats

ALS APH. Wade, 136–7.

To Douglas Hyde [early September 1889]

3 Blenheim Road | Bedford Park | Chiswick

Dear Hyde

Powell says you should write to Nutt and make the best terms you can about the matter of a pro-sheat—[1]

I am sure Nutt would make no difficulty about notes preface Etc.

I enclose his address on a slip of paper with a few words from York Powell on the matter of Gaelic origonals Etc.

By the by surely you would loose the flavour of the tales if you left out aphorious rhimes etc.[2]

---

[7] M. H. Gill & Sons advertised *Lays of South Sligo, a few Wild Flowers of National Poetry*, by John O'Dowd, as one of their new publications on the back page of the *Irish Monthly* from December 1888 to February 1889. Fr. Russell's brief notice of the book (*Irish Monthly*, February 1889, 114) was less than enthusiastic: 'We do not know what difficulties have been overcome by Mr John O'Dowd . . . but, taking the verses on their own merits, we can hardly give them credit for more than a good spirit, good intentions, and considerable rhythmical fluency.'

John O'Dowd (1856–1937), a farmer's son, was born in Goldfields, Co. Sligo; he became a dealer in agricultural goods. He wrote poems over the pseudonym 'Adonis' for the *Sligo Champion* and the *Shamrock* and, after his imprisonment under the Coercion Act 1881–2, used the pen name 'A Sligo Suspect'. He spent a short time in the USA and from 1900 to 1918 was nationalist MP for Sligo South. He appears to have shared Fr. Russell's opinion of his poems, for, in a Dedicatory Verse as disarming as it is accurate, he describes them as 'Of merit devoid, strung together, / Unpolished by beauty or art, / They're nought save the simple outpouring / Of one honest Irishman's heart . . . '

[8] 'The Sailor's Children' by A. I. Johnston (*Irish Monthly*, September 1889) is a mother's lament over her children's attraction towards the sea which has drowned their father. Anna Isabel Johnston (1866–1902), who often used the pseudonym 'Ethna Carbery', was the daughter of the Belfast Fenian William Johnston, a friend of JO'L. Born in Ballymena, Co. Antrim, she wrote verse, much of it in the patriotic style of Young Ireland, for the *Nation* and *United Ireland*, and with Alice Milligan edited the Belfast periodical *Shan Van Vocht*. Shortly before her death, she married Seumas MacManus (1868–1960), the Donegal writer and dramatist. A posthumous collection of her poems, *The Four Winds of Erinn*, appeared in 1902, and collections of her short stories, *The Passionate Hearts* and *In the Celtic Past*, followed in 1903 and 1904 respectively.

[1] Hyde wrote on 4 Sept 1889 to KT (Southern Illinois) that 'Willie Yeats informs me that Mr. Nutt the publisher is willing to publish a translation of my stories at his own expense, so I am preparing one for him. Whether I get any of the hypothetical proceeds or not, I have not heard, or whether he is merely activated by pure love of folk-lorery.'

[2] Alfred Nutt contributed a Postscript of 8 pages to Hyde's *Beside the Fire*, and a number of additional notes set out in square brackets. Although Hyde included translations of 15 rhyming riddles, some of

Powell whom you ask about is an historian and great authority on the Sagas. He has translated many together with Viggusson. He does a good deal of work for Nutt and edits a series of books published by him.[3] He is a folklorist though not of the same school as Nutt.

I am anouncing your book in my Boston Pilot book letter.

I have a theory about the Firbolg's etc that I will ask your opinion on some day. The theory of a good Occultist who beleives in every thing.[4]

I immagine, by the by that Nutt may find many things good stories that seem nothing to you & me. He looks on things, you see, with folklorists eyes—what would please him most perhaps would be a tale full of little hooks, as it were, to hang theories on. ⟨However I dare say he meens you to use your own discretion about what you⟩

I hear the dinner knives & forks being laid & so must end this as I have another note to write before dinner.

Yours
W B Yeats

ALS Private.

To Katharine Tynan, [*10 October 1889*]

3 Blenheim Road | Bedford Park | Chiswick

My dear Miss Tynan (I wonder if it would matter if I put your christian name, by the by)

I enclose order for 10/– as what is due from me for Ballad book. I have not your letter by me but think 9/8 was the amount[1] & I owe you 3 or 4 pence likewise if it was more—if either debt was more—let me know. Could you get Gill to send me three copies of the book (one for Lilly)—I can get them I

---

which had appeared in *Leabhar Sgeulaigheachta*, he did not publish any of the aphoristic 'Ranta agus Ceathrama' (Quatrains and Lines) from that volume.

[3] Frederick York Powell and Gúdbrandr Vígfússon edited or wrote together *Sturlunga Saga* (Oxford, 1878), *An Icelandic Prose Reader* (Oxford, 1881), *Corpus Poeticum Boreale* (Oxford, 1883), and the *Grimm Centenary: Sigfried-Arminius and other Papers* (1886). York Powell edited 8 vols. of the series 'English History by Contemporary Writers', published by Nutt in 1887.

[4] The Firbolgs were the descendants of Nemed who, according to the *Book of Invasions* (see p. 114), had colonized Ireland only to be defeated, after the death of Nemed, by the Formorians. The remnants of the clan fled to Greece where they were enslaved and forced to carry earth in bags to stony places, and so took the name *firbolg* (men of the bags). After 200 years they returned to Ireland which they held in peace until defeated by the invading Tuatha Dé Danann at the First Battle of Moytura. The Firbolgs were small and dark, the Tuatha tall, fair, and magical, thus reinforcing WBY's dichotomy, drawn in his 'Irish Fairies, Ghosts, Witches, etc.' (*Lucifer*, 15 Jan 1889; see p. 115), between the Celtic 'gods of the light' and 'gods of the great darkness' (*UP* I. 137).

[1] See p. 156; the amount owed was in fact 9s 1d.

suppose now that all is paid—I have not a single copy. Do you remember
O'Leary's suggestion (he thought I should remind you) that the book be
now published in paper at 6ᵈ and in cloth (of some cheep kind) at 1/– (I
mean the 1/– copies were O'Leary's suggestion) say 100 1/– copies—

Enough of mere mercantile matters. I am in the magazine of Poetry but
have not seen it[2]—have been waiting for funds to write for a copy—will to
morrow.

I have not with my whole heart forgiven that subediting Tablet man for
going off to the Train with you in the remaining cab seat and he with so
many sins already on his soul—those Pall Mall verses in chief & the way he
got them published.[3]

Your letter to my father was very interesting & all that about your dog in
chief so. With us there is nothing to tell other than that Jack has come home[4]
with a number of sketches of Sligo. I have got one framed for my room. He
keeps shouting mostly, Sligo nonsense rhymes (he always comes home full
of them) such as

> You take the needle & I'll take the thread
> And we'll sow the dogs tail to the Orange man's head.

You must be settling down by this though indeed you seem at home and
comfortable at all times (unlike me, the sole of whose foot is uneasy). You
must be settling down—writing and that kind of thing—not minding much
this dripping autumn. Do not forget that I am expecting a letter and do not
make it short merely because there is no news in this of mine—I have none
but Blake news, for that matter goes on well. The book may be done by
January if this Puttenham affair does not take all my time.

I have just—this moment—got a letter from Le Galleon's publisher
asking for an experimental dozen of Oisin sale or return of course and
promising to advertize me—with press opinions, in his catalogue—which
reminds me that I want to advertize—as will Todhunter, Miss O Leary,
Douglas Hyde—at end of the 6ᵈ and 1/– ballad books. When Gill is ready
let me know and we will send in.

---

[2] KT's article on WBY (see p. 127, n. 7) appeared in the *Magazine of Poetry* in October 1889.

[3] Vernon Blackburn (1867–1907) was sub-editor of the *Tablet* at this time, and later its Rome
correspondent; he was subsequently on the staff of Henley's *National Observer*, and music critic of the
Pall Mall Gazette. The 'verses' in question, 'To Cardinal Manning', a sonnet by 'S.H.', which appeared
in the *Pall Mall Gazette*, 16 Sept 1889, were reprinted in the *Tablet* on 21 Sept at the conclusion of an
article, 'The Cardinal's Hand in the Strike', dealing with Manning's part in the prolonged London dock
strike now in progress.

[4] KT's letter had arrived on 2 Oct 1889 and contained a cheque for £3 in payment for the portrait JBY
had done of her. In replying on the same day, JBY wrote (Southern Illinois): 'I was very glad to get your
letter independently of its contents as it put me so strongly in mind of Whitehall & the country about you
steaming with autumn mists. . . . Had Pat [KT's dog] been the most astute of Flatterers he could not
have hit on a more delicate way of welcoming you home.' Jack Yeats returned to London from Sligo the
same evening, 2 Oct.

Le Galleons publishers reader seems confident that publisher will sell *Oisin*.[5] I have no faith that way nor have had. I shall sell but not yet. Many things my own & other folks have to grow first.

When you write always tell me what you are writing especialy what poems, the journalism interests me more dimly of course, being good work for many people but no way, unless on Irish matters, good work for you or me, unless so far as it be really forced on us by crazy circumstance. At least I think this way about it, not with any notion of poets dignity of course, but because so much in the way of writing is needed for Irish purposes. You know all this as well as I do however. Much may depend in the future on Ireland now developing writers who know how to formulate in clear expressions the vague feelings, now abroad—to formulate them for Irelands not for Englands use. Well! One could run on endlessly in this kind of way and you who love men and women more than thoughts would soon grow indignant.

Yours Always
W B Yeats.

ALS Huntington, with envelope addressed to Clondalkin, postmark 'CHISWICK OC 10 89'. McHugh, 101–3; Wade, 137–9.

To John O'Leary, [? 19 October 1889][1]

3 Blenheim Road

Dear M^r O'Leary

If you come to Blenheim Road tomorrow evening there will be no one but ourselves.

[5] Elkin Mathews (1851–1921) had set up as bookseller and publisher at the sign of the Bodley Head in Vigo Street, London, in October 1887; Richard Le Gallienne's *Volumes in Folio* (1889) was the first book to bear the Bodley Head imprint. Mathews was soon to move to Bedford Park, where he became a neighbour of the Yeatses; however, WBY's hopes that he would take over from Kegan Paul the unsold stock of *Oisin* were disappointed, nor does he seem to have advertised the book in his catalogue.

The Bodley Head reader was John Lane (1854–1925), Mathews's unofficial partner and an active member of the firm which he had helped to found, although still employed at this time as a clerk in the Railway Clearing House.

[1] Ellen O'Leary died in Cork on 15 Oct 1889, while staying with her nephew, and was buried a few days later in the family plot in the old cemetery, Tipperary, behind her childhood home. JO'L was in Paris visiting a dying friend, J. P. Leonard, and was unable to get back to Ireland in time for the funeral. He arrived in London on Saturday, 19 Oct, having written to WBY from Paris. WBY probably sent this reply to JO'L's London lodgings on the 19th to arrange the meeting which took place on Sunday the 20th. JO'L was in Tipperary by 2 Nov.

It is no way needful for me to say how much I sympathize with you in your great calamity.[2]

Yours always
W B Yeats

If you brought the poems with you tomorrow or sent them I could correct & return them at once. Though they will in all liklehood need no correction of any kind. They will I beleive be a long lasting memorial.[3]

ALS NLI.

To Katharine Tynan, 23 October [1889]

3 Blenheim Road | Bedford Park | Chiswick
Oct 23rd

My dear Miss Tynan

I want you to tell me anything you know about poor Miss O Learys death. When did she die and so forth? I know nothing but the vagest rumours. Last week O Leary wrote to me from Paris saying "A horrible calamity has come, and the light of my life has gone out". He said nothing more definite. On Sunday and yesterday, I saw him, (he came Saturday from Paris). He gave me Miss O Learys proof sheets saying that she had wished me to correct them. He is evidently grieving very much. He makes constant indirect illussions to his trouble but says nothing definite. I would not be certain of her death at all only that on Monday I heard by chance that Miss Gone was in London and rushed off at once and saw her for about five minutes or less. She was just starting for Paris. She knew no more than that Miss O Leary died at Cork some few days ago. Do you know whether there was any kind of a public funeral? Were there any notices in any papers.[1]

---

[2] Since WBY was not absolutely sure at this point that Ellen O'Leary had died, he uses JO'L's own vague phrase, 'great calamity'.

[3] Plans for a collection of Ellen O'Leary's poems had been in the air since at least the beginning of the year (see p. 127, n. 8) and she had been correcting the proofs shortly before her death, writing to her niece (Belfast) that 'I was sick yesterday while correcting my proofs and I could not see any beauty or poetry in my poor verses. However tis to be hoped others may.' She was in a hurry to finish the proofs so that they might catch JO'L on his way through London 'for I wished John and W. Yeats to put their heads together over them. W. Yeats has a good eye for little verbal alterations and a good ear for harmonious sounds.'

[1] MG had returned unexpectedly to London to nurse her sister Kathleen, and, as she explained in a letter to JO'L written from Paris in late October (NLI), this had led to a breakdown in communications:

I did not answer your letter to me from Paris because when it arrived all my time was taken up nursing my little sister who I found very ill with congestion of the liver. When she was a little better & I had time you had left Paris & I had not your address. I only got it from Mr Yeats who came to see me the very evening I was starting for Paris. I put it in a pocket book which I lost on the journey so have to send this direct to Doctor Sigerson to be forwarded.

By the by, did you get my last letter enclosing 10/– for Gill in payment of my share of ballad book expenses. I corrected proofs of East & West ballad[2] so I dare say next number will contain it.

You will probably see me in Dublin next Spring Or before. O Leary asks me to stay with him for a while if I pass through on my way to Sligo.

Yours Always
W B Yeats

ALS Huntington, with envelope addressed to Clondalkin, postmark 'CHISWICK OC 23 89'. McHugh, 103; Wade, 139.

To Douglas Hyde, 25 October [*1889*]

3 Blenheim Road | Bedford Park | Chiswick
Oct 25th

My dear Hyde

How about the book of fairy tales? I have not seen Nutt this long while nor have I heard from you & am all anxiety to hear how you have got on with the matter. Has Nutt given you any kind of decent terms in the matter of profit. David Fitzgerald has also a book coming out with Nutt—you will beat him easily I doubt not for he is damnably scientific. When will your's get its self ready.[1]

My Blake book goes on and all difficulties in prophetic books clear up at ever increasing pace. It is the quearest and wildest and most facinating of philosophies. We (my colaberateur E J Ellis & myself) have found out things about his pictures also. At present I am trying to unravel his symbolic way of using colours.[2]

As to other plans—have some thoughts of getting Scott to let me edit a

Ellen O'Leary's death was announced in the *Cork Examiner*, 16 Oct 1889, and in the *Nation*, 26 Oct. *United Ireland* for 26 Oct said that her death had been mentioned at the weekly meeting of the Pan-Celtic Society, of which she had been a member, and on 9 Nov 1889 KT published a long obituary of her in the *Boston Pilot*, stressing her heroic nature, patriotism, devotion to her brother John, and her central place in Dublin literary life. The *Nation* printed extracts from KT's tribute in its issue of 23 Nov.

[2] 'The Ballad of the Old Fox-hunter' (see p. 178), which did appear in the November issue of *East and West*.

[1] *Beside the Fire* was not published until the week ending 24 Jan 1891.

[2] In an undated letter written at this time, Hyde told KT: 'I also had a letter from Willie Yeats wanting to know what about my folklore and saying that the more he progresses with his work on Blake (the madman and poet) the plainer the meaning of his rhapsodies appear, which I am inclined to doubt, and I await with interest this new key to his works of which I am very fond' (Texas). WBY interprets Blake's use of colour in 'The Symbolism of Colour', Part XI of his essay, 'The Symbolic System', in *The Works of William Blake*, I. 309–14.

"Verse Chronicle of Ireland" made up from Fergusson De Vere Mangan Etc.[3]

Heard a peice of Rosscommon folklore the other night. At some village or other, they lay pipes full of tobacco on the graves of the new burried in case they may like a draw of the pipe. A wild American indian kind of buisness it seems.

Yours

W B Yeats

PS—

I heard a fine Irish folk tale a couple of days since from a young artist who has been staying in Donegal at *Glen Collumbkille*. He was shown a large hole in a stone rath called *Cahel enore* and was told it was the place the three Byrnes dug for treasure in. While he was looking at the hole, one day, a ragged long haired, shoeless man came up & began digging. He spoke to him. The man shook his head; he only knew Gaelic. My friend asked someone about him "that is the third Byrne" was the answer. The treasure was under a ban. Three Byrnes had to catch sight of it one after another & die before it could be found. The first had just seen it when a huge dog came down the mountain & ⟨killed h⟩ tore him to pieces. The second saw it and immediately some terrible apperition appeared what was never known, & he died then. Now the third is working at the whole [*for* hole]. Some day he will see it & die but the treasure will be found and belong to his family. You might look the man up and get it from his own lips if ever in that direction.[4]

What did you think of Olcotts lecture. I have seen no reports nor heard anything. He is probably quite right about the real existence of these Irish goblins. At least I never could see any reason against their existence.[5] Blake saw them—I live in hopes.

How sad Miss O Leary's death has been. O'Leary is visibly greatly affected by it.

ALS Private.

[3] WBY had taken this idea from Thomas Davis, who had proposed 'A Ballad History of Ireland' in the *Nation*, 30 Nov 1844. Although nothing came of the idea, it remained with WBY for several years.

[4] WBY made a great deal of this story, probably told him by George Russell (AE), in his letter to the *Boston Pilot* dated 31 Oct 1889 and published 23 Nov (*LNI*, 84–5). He returned to it in his article 'Irish Fairies' in the *Leisure Hour*, October 1890, and in *The Celtic Twilight* (129–33) under the title 'The Three O'Byrnes and the Evil Faeries'.

[5] Col. Olcott had recently given two lectures in Dublin, the second, referred to here, on 'Irish Fairies', at the Antient Concert Rooms on 19 Oct 1889. WBY, mentioning this lecture in his letter published in the *Boston Pilot* on 23 Nov 1889, said Olcott 'asserted that such things really exist, and so strangely has our modern world swung back on its old belief, so far has the reaction from modern materialism gone, that his audience seemed rather to agree with him' (*LNI*, 83). Hyde had attended both lectures, and thought that the first, on 'Theosophy', 'wasn't very good at all, and I, having wined and dined well, kept dozing off ali the time' (Daly, 101). But on the second occasion he listened with care to Olcott's

To Katharine Tynan, 6 [November 1889]

3 Blenheim Road | Bedford Park | Chiswick
Oct 6ᵗʰ[1]

My dear Katey

I send you a Leisure Hour with an article on Irish ballad writers written more than two years ago.[2] It is very incomplete. You are not mentioned at all. The reason is that when I wrote it I intended to deel with contemporary writers in a seperate article. The Leisure Hour people however, having an Irish Story and other Irish things running were afraid of so much Ireland. My ballad is in East & West. I was almost forgetting the thing I am writing about—I knew there was some thing and could not think what.

A great many thanks for your pleasent little notice of me in the Magazine of Poetry. It is good as possible. There are just one or two little matters you were in error about. It is quite true that I used constantly when a very small child to be at Sandymount Castle but it was not my birthplace. I was born at a house in Sandy-Mount Avenue. A little house which my old Uncle looked on which scorn and called even on the outside of his letters "the Quarry hole" because he remembered there being, when he was a young man, a quarry hole where it was afterwards built.[3] The place that has really influenced my life most is Sligo. There used to be two dogs there—one smooth haired one curly haired—I used to follow them all day long. I knew all their occupations, when they hunted for rats & when they went to the rabbit warren. They taught me to dream maybe—Since then I follow my thoughts as I then followed the two dogs—the smooth & the curly—where ever they lead me.[4]

Our black little cat caught a mouse the other day. Since then she is not half so amusing. Lolly says she feels the responsibility of life and is always thinking. She has suddenly grown up.

examination of 'Irish fairy lore in the light of theosophic science' and used his description of Indian jugglers—men who could 'bring a person under their power so as to make him imagine that he saw whatever the juggler wished him to see'—in the notes to *Beside the Fire* (190).

[1] Evidently, from the postmark, a mistake for 'Nov 6th'; the references to the November numbers of both *Leisure Hour* and *East and West* make an October dating impossible.

[2] WBY's long article, 'Popular Ballad Poetry of Ireland' (see p. 17), finally appeared in the *Leisure Hour*, November 1889.

[3] In her biographical sketch of WBY in the October 1889 *Magazine of Poetry*, KT had noted (454) that he was born at Sandymount Castle, 'a quaint, castellated house, in a park full of beautiful forest trees, and containing within its limits a lake and an island . . . an ideal home for a dreamy imaginative child'. The Castle was in fact the home of his great-uncle Robert Corbet (see p. 39, n. 1), scorner of 'the Quarry hole' but KT repeated her error as late as October 1893 in a sketch, 'W. B. Yeats', in the *Bookman*, which began: 'William Butler Yeats was born at his grandfather's residence, Sandymount Castle, near Dublin, June 13th, 1865.'

[4] See *Aut* 13.

There is really nothing to record in the way of news other than this mouse. I have one of the drawings Jack made in Sligo framed & hung up in my study.

I will write about Miss O'Leary in the Providence Journal but perhaps I should wait until her poems are out. They cannot be long now.

I have just seen, Lady Wilde sent it me, your article on the Cardinal. A very good article it is. Am very glad to hear of the *Culdee* coming out in Xmas East & West.[5] My little Fox hunter ballad seems liked—Jack with his horse loving tendency likes it best of my short poems. A friend of Ellis's meditates a picture on the subject to be called "the march past". Hounds & horse being led past their dying owner.[6]

I have met lately an amusing musical & literary family. The Miss Keelings. One sings one writes novels some of which have been most successful. The novel maker has just published a clever sentimental book called "In thought land & Dream land". I had tea with them yesterday & they told me a good story of their childhood. One day they went into the store room—to see what they could see. There was a box full of apples. They knew it would be very wicked to take one, so instead they bit a peice out of each one & then turned the good sides up. There mother knew which had bitten each apple because one had lost one tooth one another. They used to live in the same house we lived in at Earls Court when we came to London two & a half years ago. Mrs Weeler was full of tales of them. The novel maker has described the Earls Court house in her last book.[7]

Yours Always
W B Yeats

ALS Huntington, with envelope addressed to Clondalkin, postmark 'CHISWICK NO 6 89'. Mc Hugh, 104–5; Wade, 140–1.

[5] KT's article, 'A Visit to Cardinal Manning', appeared in the *Boston Pilot,* 26 Oct 1889. The December 1889 *East and West* in fact included, not her poem on the 'Rapt Culdee', but 'Queen's Roses' (see p. 187, n. 6).

[6] WBY's poem would have been attractive to the landscape and genre painter Edward Brice Stanley Montefiore (b. 1855), who worked in London and at Newnham, Glos. Particularly fond of rustic subjects, he exhibited 10 works at the RA.

[7] WBY was to come into contact with the Dublin-born Keelings again in 1916, through an occult experience connected with the death of their younger sister, years before in Russia (WBY to SMY, mid-February 1916, MBY). Eleanor D'Esterre-Keeling, who was later a concert artist, edited *The Music of the Poets: A Musician's Birthday Book* (1896), the 'Introduction' to which is dated 'Kensington, November 1889', making it contemporaneous with this letter. The 'novel-maker' was the schoolmistress and teacher of elocution Elsa D'Esterre-Keeling (d. 1935), in whose *In Thoughtland and in Dreamland* (1890) the house at 58, Eardley Crescent is described, in the section 'Sary, The Door-Stepper' (68–70). (Mrs Wheeler was the owner of the house.) The book was reviewed unfavourably by WBY in the *Boston Pilot,* 23 Nov 1889 (*LNI,* 88–90). Elsa D'E.-Keeling was to review WBY's *BIV* in the *Academy,* 27 Apr 1895 (349–50).

To John O'Leary, 9 December [*1889*]

3 Blenheim Road | Bedford Park | Chiswick
Dec 9th

Dear M^r O'Leary

A great many thanks for the two Pilots. The reason I said so little about Miss O Leary was not at all that I did not wish to say a great deal but that Miss Tynan wrote to me and said that she was writing a notice for the Pilot and asking me if I were writing anything to let it be for the *Providence* Journal (an article I have put off until I come to do the poems) and so I felt bound not in any way to forestall her but in my next "Pilot" letter (one that has not yet been printed) I wrote a long paragraph which I hope you will like and wrote to Boyle O'Reilly at the same time asking leave to review the poems for him, as soon as they are published.[1] When I saw how meagre the notice in the Pilot letter you saw, was (I happened to see another copy) I felt sorry, very sorry, that I had taken care not to forestall Miss Tynan (The Pilot assuardly would not have minded two notices). Will the book be soon out? I hope to write all I can about it.

By the by I have found those "Christian Examiner" stories of Carletons I had mislaid.[2] I am working away at this American book of Irish stories and

---

[1] WBY had made a brief reference to Ellen O'Leary's death in the opening paragraph of an article (*LNI*, 83), dated 'London Oct 31', published in the *Boston Pilot*, 23 Nov 1889: 'We have all been saddened by Miss O'Leary's sudden death on the fifteenth of this month. The death of this heroic woman who lived ever, in the words of her own song, written of another, "to God and Ireland true," has left a sore place in numerous hearts. Everywhere sympathy is felt for her brother, Mr John O'Leary, whose lifelong friend and ally she was.' JO'L had evidently felt that these remarks were too brief but was, perhaps, mollified by the 'long paragraph' WBY had written on 5 Dec, and which appeared in the *Boston Pilot*, 28 Dec 1889. It concluded (*LNI*, 96) with the tribute:

All that was most noble and upright in Irish things was dear to her. The good of Ireland was her constant thought. As a friend she ever drew from one best one had. She, like her brother, was of the old heroic generation now passing away, the generation whose efforts for Ireland made the present movement possible. Our movement may surpass theirs in success; it will never equal it in self-sacrifice. She had the manner of one who had seen something of great affairs and shared in them, yet under all was a heart ever delighted with simple things, a heart from which rose a little wellspring of song. Her poetry had in its mingled austerity and tenderness a very Celtic quality. It was like a rivulet flowing from mountain snows. She was her brother's lifelong friend and fellow-worker. One thinks of him now sitting among his books in the house at Drumcondra.

WBY does not seem to have mentioned Ellen O'Leary in *PSJ*, but he reviewed her poems in the *Boston Pilot* when they eventually appeared, in 1891.

[2] Carleton published 13 stories in the anti-Catholic magazine the *Christian Examiner* (see p. 174), edited by the Revd Caesar Otway; all but one were reprinted, usually heavily revised, in his *Traits and Stories* or in *Irish Tales*. WBY, it later appears, had made his own compilation of the stories in their original form.

intend writing one for it myself, if I can get up the needful resolution and dialect.

Yours very sincerely
W B Yeats

Did you loose a sleave link (or part of one) when here one evening? We have found one.

ALS NLI. Wade, 141–2.

To Katharine Tynan, [? 10 December 1889]

3 Blenheim Road | Bedford Park | Chiswick
Tuesday.

My dear Katey

Please remember you owe me a letter. I am not going to confirm you in your sins by writting one until I get it. This is merely a note to tell you that I am reading for that book of Irish Tales and that you promised me a story of Miss Mulholds & one or two others.

Do not let Gill bring out the cheep editon of "Young Ireland" ballad book before getting from me and Hyde advertizements of our books.

I have a lot of things to say but will say nothing.

Write to me
Write to me
Write to me

till then I am dumb. It is about six weeks since your letter was due.[1]

Yours
W B Yeats

ALS Huntington. McHugh, 105–6; Wade, 142.

To Father Matthew Russell, [early] December [1889]

3 Blenheim Road | Bedford Park | Chiswick
December

My dear Father Russel

A great many thanks for the two Monthlys with Miss Mulholonds stories. They are very pleasent & pretty. I think I will use Bet's Match making but will not decide yet. It is not quite in my scheme I am trying to make all the

---

[1] i.e. in answer to WBY's of 6 Nov 1889; see p. 195.

stories illustrative of some phase of Irish life meaning the collection to be a kind of social history. I begin with *Castle Rack Rent* and give mainly tales ⟨of peasent life⟩ that contain some special kind of Irish humour or tragedy—*Molly the Tramp* is a very good tale but then it is above all things a tale and not also a little loop hole for looking at Irish life through. Molly is just a pathetic heroine of romance. She might have strayed over the sea from an English city.[1] The heroines of Carleton or Banim could only have been raised under Irish thatch. One might say the same in less degree of Griffen and Kickham but Kickam is at times, once or twice only & (merely in his peasent heroines I think), marred by having read Dickens, and Griffen most facile of all one feels is Irish on purpose rather than out the neccesity of his blood. He could have written like an English man had he chosen. But all these writers had a square built power no later Irishman or Irish woman has approached. Above all Carleton & Banim had it. They saw the whole of every thing they looked at, (Carleton & Banim I mean) the brutal with the tender, the coarse with the refined. In Griffen & Kickham the tide began to ebb. Kickham had other things to do and is not to be blamed in the matter. It has gone quite out now—our little tide. The writers who make Irish stories sail the sea of common English fiction. It pleases them to hoist Irish colours—and that is well. The Irish manner has gone out of them though. Like common English fiction they want too much to make pleasent tales— and that's not at all well. The old men tried to make one see life plainly but all written down in a kind of fiery shorthand that it might never be forgotten.

Miss Mulholonds little stories are very charming indeed (& one should not fight with cherry trees for not growing acorns)[2] A pleasent fire side feeling and a murmour of the kettle goes through them—a domesticity that is not especially Irish however. Certainly If I get her leave I will use one of her short tales and may quite reverse my feeling about her not giving us Irish life & Irish manner, like Carleton & Banim, when I have read one of the long novels which I shall do before criticising her in the Irish story book. I was

[1] Both of Rosa Mulholland's stories had appeared in the *Irish Monthly* in 1886: 'Bet's Match-making'—which tells how the self-effacing Bet in trying to further a friend's romance gets a husband for herself—was published in April, and 'Molly the Tramp'—an account of the moral and physical rehabilitation of a deprived slum-child by country air and country living—in August. WBY included neither in *RIT*.

Castle Rackrent (1800) by Maria Edgeworth (1767–1849) traces the decline and fall of the Rackrent family as seen through the sympathetic eyes of Thady, an old retainer. WBY, who reprinted the novel in its entirety in vol. I of *RIT* (27–139), described it (6–7) as 'one of the most inspired chronicles written in English. One finds no undue love for the buffoon, rich or poor, no trace of class feeling, unless, indeed, it be that the old peasant who tells the story is a little decorative. . . . She has made him supremely poetical, however, because in her love for him there was nothing of the half contemptuous affection that Croker and Lover felt for their personages.' He regarded Maria Edgeworth as 'the one serious novelist coming from the upper classes in Ireland, and the most finished and famous produced by any class there . . .'.

[2] For a similar fruity comparison concerning Allingham, a pear tree, and apples see p. 153.

not so much thinking of her as of one or two others in what is here said of later Irish novels in general. Probably I shall use *Bets Match Making* it is a charming story but then it is generalized life—such feeling, such incidents might have cropped up anywhere. Generalizing in all things, that is our big sin now—and virtue.

Did Scott send you my Carleton? If not let me know please.

I have yet to thank you for the book of poems "Remembrence". I wrote about them a short paragraph in my last Boston Pilot letter. There are lines & stanzas of a good deel of charm but all is too subjective and sad. She is so subjective that reading her poems is like looking through a window pane on which one has breathed. She also too seldom developes a single idia but instead stitches a number of different ones together. I have been looking for her book to pick out the pages I like especially but have mislaid it or lent it.[3]

It is very good of you to keep sending me the Monthly it constantly is full of most interesting things.

Yours very Truly
W B Yeats

ALS APH. Wade, 142–4.

To John O'Leary, [26 December 1889]

3 Blenheim Road | Bedford Park | Chiswick

Dear M^r O'Leary

Do you remember if *Father Connel* was among the Banims I returned? You have, I think you said, Kickhams *Salley Kavanagh* Could you lend it me to extract the "School Masters Story" or some such thing for the Putnham book.[1] It is getting on now to the time of winding up the matter. I

---

[3] Margaret Mary Ryan (1848–1932), author of *Songs of Remembrance* (see p. 174), was the sister of the Very Revd John Ryan D D, V G, who had died in 1887 and to whose memory the book is dedicated. The poems had appeared in the *Irish Monthly* from 1874 to 1889, at first over the writer's initials but then, as these were the same as the editor's, over the pseudonym of 'Alice Esmonde'. In his *Boston Pilot* article, 23 Nov 1889, WBY conceded (*LNI*, 88–9) that 'Miss Ryan can write very prettily sometimes' but found her 'too sad by a great deal. Most good poets have much sadness in them, but then they keep it more implicit than explicit. It comes in spite of them; they do not fondle it and pet it.'

[1] The eponymous hero of the Banims' *Father Connell* (see p. 170) is an idealistic Catholic priest who saves an orphan, Neddy Fennell, from a series of misfortunes including, in the finale, a false trial and the sentence of death.

Sally Cavanagh; or, The Untenanted Graves. A Tale of Tipperary, Kickham's first novel, deals with the evils of landlordism and emigration, which bring tragedy and death to Sally and most of her family. The story 'Why The Schoolmaster's Hair Grew Grey' begins as an interpolated tale in ch. XII but subsequently becomes a more integrated subplot on the anti-emigration theme. A young schoolmaster falls in love with one of his older pupils but is too shy to declare himself when poverty forces her to emigrate to America. There she falls into prostitution, but is rescued by the schoolmaster and the Sisters

promised them a list of contents by the 5ᵗʰ of Jan but will not get prefaces done yet a bit.

Please send me a postcard if you have Father Connel.

You mentioned some early works of Lefanus about Ireland. One you said was called the "Cock and Anchor" I think.[2] I do not find it in the Museum Catalogue. However plenty of Irish books are not in it.

So I hear that Rolleston is looking for a Proffesor ship in *Australia*. I am sorry to think we shall loose him. One looked forward to his gradually doing something in Ireland political or other—gradually drifting in to things.[3]

Coffey is over here as you know I dare say. I am going to breakfast with him tomorrow. I have not seen him yet. He was out here one day when I had gone to hunt up a publisher.

Sir Charles Gavan Duffy has not sent me those letters of Keegans he promised. I am thinking of writing about them and also about Mangan as I have a notion of beginning as soon as the stories are arranged for Putnham, the little history of "Irish Literature this Century". Rhys doubts not that Scott would publish it. I shall be systematically political or national anyway, through out the thing. Mangan will make a lecture to begin with. What is Sir Charles Gavan Duffey's address?[4]

The work at Blake goes slowly on. We found the other day a long mystical poem of his that had never been published or even read. Rossetti mentioned it merely but had not read a line or said where it was. It is about 2,000 lines about the longest poem he wrote. We go down every now and then, to a country house in Surrey to spend a day copying it out bit by bit. The owners of the poem & house are some very hospitable old brothers & sisters, who bring out for us port wine thirty years old, and talk theology. The poem was given to their father by Blake in MS.[5] When I am writing out, the oldest of

of Charity, and expires uttering earnest warnings to Irish girls to remain at home. WBY did not use this story in *RIT*, but chose instead 'The Pig-Driving Peelers', an episode from Kickham's novel *For the Old Land*.

  [2] Joseph Sheridan Le Fanu (1814–73), born in Dublin, was a barrister before turning to journalism and novel-writing. At its best his work is distinguished by his handling of suspense, intrigue and evil, often with a supernatural slant. His first novel, *The Cock and Anchor Being a Chronicle of Old Dublin City* (Dublin, 1845), was reprinted with alterations as *Morley Court* in 1873. Set in the early eighteenth century, it tells of a conspiracy to ruin a spendthrift young baronet and to compel his sister's marriage. Best-known among his 13 other novels are *The House by the Church-yard* (1863), *Uncle Silas* (1864), and *In a Glass Darkly* (1871). WBY did not publish anything by him in *RIT*.

  [3] Rolleston did not take up this appointment.

  [4] Gavan Duffy was living in Nice at this time, but was frequently in London and Dublin. He was later to make available to WBY some unpublished letters of the peasant poet John Keegan (1809–1849), together with information on Mangan (see p. 47). *Irish Literature of This Century* was never published; but see p. 179, n. 10.

  [5] The poem (actually more than 4,000 lines long) was *Vala, or The Four Zoas* (*c.* 1797), the MS of which was given by Blake to his friend and patron John Linnell (1792–1882); it was eventually included in vol. III of Ellis's and WBY's *Works of William Blake*. Linnell had built three houses at Redstone Wood, near Redhill, Surrey, in 1852 and these were occupied by his children's families. The old men

the old men sits beside me with a penknife in his hand to point my pencil when it grows blunt.

Yours very sincerely
W B Yeats

ALS Texas. Partly in Wade, 146–7.

To Katharine Tynan, [26 December 1889]

3 Blenheim Road | Chiswick | Bedford Park
Thursday.

My dear Katey

Could you get me the story or two you mentioned soon now, as I promised to give the publisher a list of contents by the 5ᵗʰ of January.

Father Russel sent me Miss Mulholonds "Molly the Tramp" and "Bets Match Making". I will try and use the last though neither comes exactly within the definition of my book being in no way distinctively Irish life, though happening in Ireland. However "Bets Match Making" is a very pretty tale.

Did I tell you that we have found a new long poem of Blakes. Rossetti mentioned its name no more. We are the only people who ever read it. It is two thousand lines long or so and belongs to three old men & their sisters who live away at Red Hill in Surrey.[1] Ellis & myself go from time to time and do a days copying out at it. The old men are very hospitable and bring out 30 year old port wine for us and when I am copying the oldest of the old men sits beside me with a penknife in his hand to point my pencil when it blunts. Their house is a great typical bare country house. It is full of Blake matters. The old men & their sisters are like "a family of pew openers" Ellis says. Blake is their church, at the same time they are no little troubled at the thought that may be he was heretical. I tried to convince them of his orthodoxy and found it hard to get the great mystic into their little thimble.

Yes my beard is off! and whether for good I dont know.[2] Some like it some not. Madame Blavatsky promised me a bad illness in three months

---

were his sons John (1821–1906), James Thomas (1823–1905), and William (1826–1906); all three were artists, as were their two sisters, Elizabeth Anne (1820–1903) and Sarah (1830–?1908). 'Mr Linnel', wrote SMY to Hone, 3 July 1939 (Texas), 'thought Willy looked delicate & used to give him a glass of his oldest & finest port, the older & finer the more like ink it was thought Willy.'

[1] See preceding letter.

[2] On 17 Nov 1889 SMY wrote to KT (Southern Illinois): 'I thought I would write & tell you that the poet has shaved off his beard & looks much better we all think—Jack got him to do it & when it was half off Willy nearly slaughtered him.'

through the loss of all the mesmeric force that collects in a beard—one has gone by. When she sees me, she professes to wonder at my being still on my legs. It makes a great change. I felt quite bewildered for a time at losing the symbol I knew myself by—I mean changing it so. I still feel some what like the sweep in the story whose face was washed in the night so that when he saw himself in the glass in the morning he said they had woke the wrong man.[3]

Do not leave me so long without a letter next time.

The Coffeys are over here. I am going to breakfast with them tomorrow.

So Rolleston is trying to get a professorship in Australia. He will be a loss in many ways I was always hoping he would drift into things—do some thing for Nationalism, political or literary, though indeed I fear the scholastic brand was to[o] deep in his heart. He is a loss anyway however.

Lilly has not been well just lately—she is taking a holiday for a few days now—going to stay with friends, the Gambles, until Monday and then perhaps, if not better, on, she & Lolly, to Brighton. To day she is at the Morris's spending the day.

Lilly & Lolly have had a lot of presents & cards—more than usual a good deel I think.

Jack is at Portsmuth He & a friend walked there. It took them three days. They com[e] back tomorrow. They are staying with some relations of the friends.[4]

Oscar Wilde mentioned his hearing from you about East & West and asked if it was a paper meant to improve people. I said not so he will probably write for it.[5]

There is a tintinabulation of tea things out side, bringing this to an end, but indeed I have written a good long letter, longer than yours are, wose luck.

Yours
W B Yeats

[*On back of envelope*]
I hear that a painter called Montofiore is making the subject of my East &

---

[3] Perhaps a misremembering of an incident in Kingsley's *The Water-Babies*, ch. 1.

[4] Of the sisters' projected stay in Brighton ECY wrote on 29 Dec 1889 to KT (Southern Illinois): 'I think it would be rather fun to go to a Boarding House but Lily doesn't much want to go as she will have to take extra holidays.' The Gambles were neighbours of the Yeatses in Bedford Park, who often helped SMY and ECY out with presents and clothing. In the same letter to KT ECY itemized their Christmas presents: 'Edie Wise sent us £3 between us wasn't that a jolly present & Mrs Gamble gave us 10/– each. Rose gave me a silver thimble Miss Veasey a Spanish fan, Lily a collection of short stories by Mrs Gaskell a pair of gloves from Grandmama & another pair from Mrs Geoghegan, one of those photographs on china of the lake in Sligo from an Aunt there & I think that's all & I think that is a pretty good list.'

Jack Yeats and his friend set off for Portsmouth on foot on 22 Dec 1889 and arrived there in the evening of Christmas Eve, returning to London by train on 28 Dec (Jack Yeats, 1889 diary, MBY).

[5] Oscar Wilde did not publish anything in *East and West*, of which only four more issues appeared.

West ballad the subject of his Academy picture.[6] He says it is the best subject he ever had.

WBY

ALS Huntington, with envelope addressed to Clondalkin, postmark 'CHISWICK DE 28 89'. McHugh, 106–7; Wade, 144–6.

To the Editor of Light, [*28 December 1889*]

3, Blenheim-road, | Bedford Park.

Sɪʀ,—A correspondent in your issue of the 21st inst. mentions the extremely hostile reception given to Colonel Olcott by various speakers in the Bedford Park Club, on the 7th inst. This was by no means the case.[1]

I live in the Park, and hardly a day goes by without bringing to me a word of someone extremely indignant with the speakers, or rather with two of them,[2] the others being neither more hostile nor friendly than one finds at any meeting for the spread of new notions—political, religious, or other.

W. B. Yᴇᴀᴛs.

Printed letter, *Light*, 28 December 1889 (619).

[6] No such painting by Montefiore (see p. 196) was exhibited at the RA.

[1] A controversy over the treatment of speakers at debates sponsored by the Bedford Park Club began on 2 Nov 1889 in the spiritualist weekly *Light*, when T. L. Henly (1826–1912) wrote to complain that he had been treated discourteously during his lecture on 'Spiritualism' on 19 Oct. The controversy was refuelled following the lecture to the club on 7 Dec by Col. Olcott, co-founder with HPB of the Theosophical Society (see p. 164), and Henly again wrote to *Light* on 21 Dec (608–9), comparing the reception of Olcott's lecture (on 'Theosophy and the Law of Life') with his own:

Member after member rose and said that he did not agree with what had fallen from the lecturer, whilst by way of clenching the argument, the gentleman who had invited Colonel Olcott down there, and was called upon to propose a vote of thanks 'for the very able lecture he had delivered', did so, using those very words, and then wound up by saying that it was complete humbug from beginning to end!

As well as this rejoinder by WBY, *Light* published a letter signed 'One of the Audience' which also argued that the response to Olcott had been much fairer than Henly suggested.

[2] Reports of Col. Olcott's lecture in such local papers as the *West London Observer* (11 Dec 1889), the *West Middlesex Standard* (14 Dec), and the *Richmond and Twickenham Times* (14 Dec) failed to name the two speakers, and their identity cannot now be established, although an anonymous correspondent in *Light* (14 Dec 1889, 603) describes them as '*poseurs*, assuming to themselves a position of leadership which they do not possess', and unrepresentative of Bedford Park. The chairman on this occasion was L. A. Atherley-Jones (see p. 180).

1890

To the Editor of The Nation, *3 January 1890*

3 Blenheim-road, Bedford Park, Chiswick,
London, January 3rd, 1890.

DEAR SIR—I have only just read your criticism of my "Stories from Carleton," in THE NATION of the 28th ult. I wonder does your critic know his Carleton well. I fear he scorned to read so "envenomed" a writer. He much preferred to cry "renegade," to take up the old calumny and pass it on.[1] Carleton came up to Dublin a young man, at the age when opinions change. What literature Ireland then had was Protestant; proselytism and letters, too, had just come together in most unnatural marriage. The tradition of the great Protestant orators of Ireland was still new. The young Northern peasant's mind was still unformed, and brilliancy, culture, enlightenment, all seemed to have made alliance against his old Faith. He changed his creed. There is not one fragment of evidence to prove he did so other than honestly, or that "he wrote for the market," as your critic puts it. For a few, a very few years, he was full of zeal for his new opinions—an ever-lessening zeal. As time went on, he crossed out zealous passage after passage from his stories, as their turn came to be reprinted—the more wrong-headed he never republished at all; and, by the time his powers had climaxed, found himself most fierce against proselytising of all kinds, Protestant kinds more than any. He showed by book after book that his heart was wholly with the Faith of his childhood. The "Irish Established Church" has only once been satirised since Swift by a man of genius; that man was William Carleton.[2]

---

[1] The anonymous reviewer of *Carleton* in the *Nation* of 28 Dec 1889 (4), while praising WBY's Introduction as 'a model of interpretative and sympathetic criticism', had gone on to attack Carleton's bias and bitterness after his apostasy. 'We thought we had passed the day', the review concluded, 'when his envenomed caricature would be accepted as portraiture. But it seems not. But till that day passes the slanderous Carleton should be kept by Irish critics in the literary pillory.'

[2] Although Carleton constantly revised his early stories and in general toned down the anti-Catholic

I have here beside me, gathered from the *Christian Examiner*, and bound into one volume the anti-Catholic tales of his childhood. I and not Carleton have gathered them together. Had he written for the market he would not have left them sleeping in the dusty pages of an old magazine, for they have power of a kind in plenty. They make, after all, but a slim volume; it does not weigh much in genius or avoirdupois. Besides, there are a few scattered passages in "Shane Fadh," a story of almost Chaucerian breadth and power, and in one or two others of "The Traits and Stories."[3] Into the other scale of the balance, Carleton threw all the works of his prime—the fierce advocacy of "M'Clutchy," the many impassioned scenes of entirely Catholic life of "The Black Prophet" and "Ahadara." From some years before the publication of "M'Clutchy," in 1846, until his death in 1870 book after book came from him in only too great profusion, and almost all contains some eulogy, defence, or tender description of the Faith of his childhood.[4] Yet your good critic has no word for him but "renegade;" no other mention of his genius than to call it "envenomed." Scotland left Burns in the Excise; the world has mocked her for it. The coming century would find it a strange thing to look back on, if we, many years after our great prose Burns had been rotting in his grave, and when all other reading folk had learned to honour him, if we in his own country should find nothing more for his memory than what your critic is pleased to call "the Literary Pillory." It would think us wholly given over to never-lifting night and ignorance. And yet Catholicism can well afford to be generous; no Catholic need show the bigotry of some poor sectary. Enough now of your critic. I feel wholly saddened to think that any countryman of Carleton's should make this letter needful at all.

There is no fear, however, of Carleton's name among our people. They are more generous than some who would teach them, and will not forget this one great peasant writer of their country, the man who remained ever a

---

element in them, the revisions were also made on stylistic and other grounds, and were not so consistent as WBY here suggests. His satire of the 'Irish Established Church' was *Valentine M'Clutchy* (see p. 174).

[3] For the *Christian Examiner* stories, see p. 197. WBY's personal copy of these stories seems now to have been lost. The reviewer had quoted from the story 'Shane Fadh's Wedding' (included in *Carleton*), to illustrate Carleton's anti-Catholicism.

[4] Catholic critics found nothing to fault in the treatment of religion in Carleton's *The Black Prophet: A Tale of Irish Famine* (Belfast, 1847), whose involved plot centres upon an unsolved murder and the love affair between the niece of the victim and the son of his supposed killer, worked out against the powerfully rendered background of the famine and typhus epidemic of 1817, which Carleton had witnessed at first hand. WBY praised the novel's 'sombre and passionate dialogue'; when he read any portion of it, he said (*Carleton*, xvii), he seemed 'to be looking out at the wild, torn storm-clouds that lie in heaps at sundown along the western seas of Ireland; all nature, and not merely man's nature, seems to pour out for me its inbred fatalism.' *The Emigrants of Ahadarra: A Tale of Irish Life* (1848), another of Carleton's novels to meet with Catholic approbation, is the story of a love affair continually threatened by the prospect of enforced emigration. WBY gets the dates both of the first edition of *Valentine M'Clutchy* (1845) and of Carleton's death (1869) wrong by a year. He may have been confused by the fact that Carleton was seventy when he died.

peasant, one of themselves, full of all their passion, all their feelings. Quite close to me, here in London, lives an old seamstress, very poor and pious, who remembers how he used to dine in her father's cabin—a peasant among peasants.[5] It is too late to cry "renegade" now, and fortunately the "literary pillory" is at no article-writer's command. It were much better work for Irish journalists to do what they can to get his great novels into print again. It is the fault of the Catholic publishers of Ireland that the "Black Prophet" and "Fardorougha the Miser"—making, together with Miss Edgeworth's "Castle Rackrent," our greatest fiction—should be out of print, while the early tales sown thinly with anti-Catholic passages and the Catholic, but feeble novels of his decadence, are for sale in countless bookshops. One can buy only at second-hand bookstalls the great works of his maturity wherein he shed the light of immortality on peasant and Catholic Ireland.—Yours, &c.,

W. B. YEATS.

Printed letter, *The Nation* (Dublin), 11 January 1890 (5). *UP* 1. 167–9.

To Katharine Tynan, 13 January [*1890*]

3 Blenheim Road | Bedford Park | Chiswick
13 Jan

My dear Katey

A great many thanks for the "Hibernian Magazine". I have not read more than the one story "a tepid bath" but as I have a few days longer than I thought to get ready the book will read further. "A tepid bath" is amusing but forgive me for not including it for it is not in any way illustrative of Irish life. Beside too I have plenty of humarous tales. Tragic matter foils me much more. "Hungrey Death" which Father Russel sent me will surely go in, it is very fine. "How I became a Zuave" will do also I think. Who is "Bridget"? I will have to write for leave to use it of course. "Tepid Bath" has a touch of the old "Handy Andy" stage Irish man—a creature half schemer half dunce with little truth to Nature about him and what truth there is, true only of the dependent class that grew up round a contemptuous and alien gentry.[1]

[5] Possibly a Mrs Watson who did washing and mending for the Yeatses and who lived near by.

[1] The anonymous story, 'A Tepid Bath', which had appeared in *Duffy's Hibernian Magazine*, September 1862, is told in the first person by Manus Reilly, a stage-Irishman gamekeeper who leads a supercilious English-educated guest of his master's into bogs and mires during a day's hunting. On their return, wet and cold, to the house the guest asks for a tepid bath. Manus, discovering from the local schoolmaster that tepid water 'is wather that is one half of it cowld and the other half of it hot', first douches the guest with four gallons of icy spring water and immediately afterwards with four gallons of

By the by have you seen my letter in the "Nation" last week on Carleton in reply to a review of "Stories from Carleton" that brought up his protestant period against him. At the foot of my letter they protest that they did not say anything against him as a whole but only against the anti catholic that was in him for a time. It is amusing to find printed after my letter a note from a Tipperary priest thanking them for their timely protest against this republication of Carleton's stories and wondering that I would edit such a book.[2] He at any rate read them as I did. O these bigots—fortunately their zeal is not equalled by their knowledge. I dare say I surprised some folk by reminding them of the numberless books full of the most ardent defence of the Catholic priesthood written by Carleton and by showing how very little their is of his anticatholic work & how early it was. I dare say though they are no bigots—people have so long passed on the calumny that unenquiring people might well come to beleive that all he wrote was bitterly sectarian.

Here is a little song written lately—one thing written this long while bar prose. It is supposed to be sung by a mother to her child—

> The angels are sinding
> A smile to your bed,
> They weary of tending
> The souls of the dead.
>
> Of tending the seven—
> The planets old brood:
> And God smiles in heaven
> To see you so good.
>
> My darling I kiss you
> With arms round my own,
> Ah how shall I miss you
> When heavy and grown.

scalding hot water. The unfortunate guest comes close to death as a consequence of these administrations, but on recovering learns to value the friendliness of Ireland and loses his Anglicized contempt for the country. For Handy Andy see p. 187, n. 4

The story was not reprinted in *RIT*, but WBY did include Rosa Mulholland's hitherto unpublished short story, 'The Hungry Death', a triangular love story set against a famine in Innisbofin in which Brigid Lavelle loses her betrothed through her pride but finally saves him and his new love from starvation at the cost of her own life. (The story was reprinted in the *Irish Monthly* in June and July 1914.) 'How I Became a Zouave',a recent magazine story by the anonymous 'Bridget', was not included in *RIT*.

[2] At the end of WBY's letter in the *Nation* on 11 Jan 1890 (see pp. 205–7) appeared a rejoinder by the editor: 'Mr Yeats's letter does not increase our respect for his powers as a critic; for he has misread our criticism, and totally misrepresents it. . . . Mr Yeats's twisting of our words is probably due to his own zeal in defence of Carleton. It is only another instance of how a man of genius may sometimes err in zeal.'

The last two lines are suggested by a gaelic song quoted in Griffen's "Collegians".[3]

I can write no more now. I have just had Russian Influnesa and it leaves one curiously week for a day or two[4] & I can by no means fix my mind further on this letter.

Yours Always
W B Yeats

16 January

I did not post the enclosed as I wanted to put in a new version of the small song and the influenza came on again at once after my making it, or rather influenza plus cold came. I am now much as I was when writing enclosed. Song in new version goes (I write it over the page, on second thoughts):—

A Cradle Song
The angels are bending
Above your white bed
They weary of tending
The souls of the dead;

And God smiles in heaven
To see you so good,
And the old planets seven
Grow sweet with His mood.

I kiss you and kiss you,
With arms round my own,
Ah how shall I miss you
My darling when grown.

A letter in the same issue, dated 30 Dec 1889 and signed 'A Tipperary P. P.', read in part:

As an Irishman and as a priest I cannot help thanking you for your outspoken, patriotic, and Catholic protest against the republication by an English popular publisher of the recent collection of Carleton's 'Stories'. They *are* stories in a sense which is not the best. It amazes me beyond measure that Mr Yeats could have been led to write . . . an 'introduction' to such a selection. . . . I cannot understand how any Irishman, priest or laic, with a particle of self-respect, could read its pages without contempt for the writer and disgust for his book.

[3] In ch. XXXII of *The Collegians* (see p. 187) Gerald Griffin gives, in phonetic spelling, the chorus of a Gaelic lullaby sung by an old nurse: 'Gilli beg le m'onum thu! / Gilli beg le m'chree! / Coth yani me von gilli beg, / 'N heur ve thu more a creena.' Griffin translates this in a footnote as 'My soul's little darling you are! / My heart's little darling! / What will I do without my little darling, / When you're grown up and old?' WBY's poem, 'A Cradle Song' (*VP*, 118), appeared, much revised (see below), in the *Scots Observer*, 19 Apr 1890.

[4] Russian influenza was sweeping through Europe and the United States at this period. *The Times* of 11 Jan 1890 reported that 'the epidemic at Chiswick still continues to prevail in that and the surrounding districts, and is of a very serious nature, one case having now, it is reported, ended fatally.'

Is not this better than the other? I write no more—writing this much with trouble.

[*On back of envelope*]
Could you get me a Nation for last week & current week there may be a letter I should answer?[5]—I can send you the money if you send them. I do not know if my letter came out last week or the week before—last week I think. If you find it was last week you need not get me that number. I hope this is not too much trouble but you will be in town I dare say and can so get it.

ALS Huntington, with envelope addressed to Clondalkin (postmark torn off); 16 January addition, *Middle Years*, 50. McHugh, 108–10, 141–2; Wade, 147–9.

To Katharine Tynan, 27 February [*1890*]

3 Blenheim Road | Bedford Park | Chiswick
Feb 27th

My dear Katey

I have been a long while without writing I fear. This Putnam book and some Blake copying has kept my thoughts busy and away from letter writing. When I let so long go by do be forgiving and write as I do when you are silent. But ah you are too law abiding and keep to the letter of the law and wait my answer.

Lilly is staying for a week at the Morris's but is here to night as we expect Edith Wise that was & her husband that is. They are passing through London on their honey moon.[1]

Lilly tells me that Lipman forged letters from Morris to himself and has been using them in New York. *The New York World* telegraphed to Morris to know if they were genuine. I dont understand that poor wretch Lipman, there was little real bad at the heart of him in the days we knew him. It must be a kind of mania—some queer thing awry in his immagination.[2]

Rolleston writes to me from Germany saying that he will settle in London

---

[5] The *Nation* printed no further letters or comments on *Carleton*.

[1] Edith Mary Wise (see p. 158, n. 1) was the only surviving child of JBY's favourite sister, Mary Letitia (see p. 158), and thus a cousin of the younger Yeatses. She had married Meredith Johnston, son of the late the Ven. Henry Johnston, sometime Archdeacon of Elphin, on 13 Feb 1890 at St. Stephen's Church, Dublin. In a letter to WBY of 12 Oct 1918 (MBY) JBY described Johnston as 'an extraordinary staunch and faithful man'.

[2] By 1889 WBY's colourful acquaintance R. I. Lipmann (see p. 120) had gone to America, settling first in Boston where he announced that he was Count Roman Ivanovitch de Lipmann Zubof, the son of a Russian nobleman. He was lionized by Boston society until the items of gossip he published in a New York society paper began to offend his select friends. On 22 Feb 1890 the *New York World* ran the first of four articles denouncing him as an impostor, and under the headlines 'Zubof Stands Unmasked—Not a Count, but a Convict; Not a Nobleman, but a Swindler', revealed something of his true history,

in a month or so and asking who it was reviewed him in the *Freeman* he thought I had done it. Do you know? No review pleased him so well— Feb 28 th

I had to break off last night on the arival of Edith Wise that was, now Mrs Meredith. The husband seems a good fellow. He is not handsome but is very pleasent looking.

To return to Rolleston. If you have the *Freeman* review by you I would like to see it as I have to review him for the *Scots Observer*.[3]

O'Leary writes that he also has some notion of coming to London. This Tipperary business seems to have crippled his income or else threatens to do so.[4]

My father is painting a large portrait of me for the Academy and using all my avalable time for sitting. He constantly reminds himself to do the sketch of me you asked for but finds himself—Academy time drawing near—too anxious I imagine to work, all sittings, on the portrait.[5]

Lolly has passed her Kindergarten examination all right, the first one, the next comes on in early summer—

There I have given all the news.

As for myself I am deep in Putnams job finishing the last two or three days work. Then comes an article on Nettleship's designs for "the Art Review"—great designs never published before—and later an article on Blake and his anti materialist art, for some where,[6] describing experiments lately made by me, Ellis, Mrs Besant Etc in clairvoyance I being the

including his prison record in Dublin, and the fact that he had forged letters of introduction from a number of famous Europeans, among them the Dean of Dublin University. William Morris, evidently another victim of this forgery, was probably the 'certain well-known poet Zubof had spoken of' who had, according to the *World* of 25 Feb, written to set the record straight. Lipmann remained remarkably cool in the face of the charges. In Boston, Chicago, and later in Philadelphia he published a number of novels set in the milieux he had tried to enter; when *Mrs Harry St. John*, 'a realistic novel of Boston fashionable life' by 'Robert Appleton', appeared in 1895 he was finally ostracized by its real-life prototypes. By December 1895 he was in New York, living in expensive hotels as a man of leisure and means. The following spring he proposed to Evelyn H. Peddie, a society beauty and heiress. She refused him, but in July 1896 Lipmann booked passage on the liner on which she was to sail to Europe. Arrested just as he was about to embark, for non-payment of his hotel bill, he hanged himself in his prison cell on the same day.

[3] The *Freeman's Journal* for 10 Jan 1890 had published a long unsigned review (3) praising Rolleston's Camelot Classics edition of the *Prose Writings of Thomas Davis* (1890), and observing that 'the glory of the achievement lies mainly with . . . the able editor of the volume.' No review of the book was published in the *Scots Observer*.

[4] A complicated political and social crisis developed in Tipperary in the autumn of 1889 when, as part of the agitation connected with the 'Plan of Campaign', the tenants of A. H. Smith-Barry, part of whose estate included the town of Tipperary, withheld their rents. Smith-Barry responded with wholesale evictions and the tenants established a substitute town, 'New Tipperary', outside his property. Since much of JO'L's income was derived from rents on property in old Tipperary, this agitation, which he vehemently opposed, had a disastrous effect upon his finances, as a result of which he was to move to London for some months in the second half of 1890.

[5] This portrait, if it was ever finished, was not exhibited at the Royal Academy.

[6] The short-lived *Art Review*, edited by the Scot, James Mavor, was published January–July 1890.

mesmerist; and experiments in which a needle suspended from a silk thread under a glass case has moved to & fro and round in answer to my will, and the will of one or two others who have tried, no one touching the glass; some experimets too of still stranger nature.[7] Probably if I decide to publish these things I shall get called all sorts of names—imposter liar and the rest for in this way does official science carry on its trade. But you do not care for magic & its fortunes and yet your church's enemy is also materialism. To prove the action of man's will, man's soul, outside his body would bring down the who[le] thing—crash—at least for all who beleived one but then who will beleive. Maybe my witnesses more prudent than I shall bid me remain silent.

What are you writing? I was greatly pleased to hear of your doing a life of some one, your prose is often so very good that it may be a quite notable book.[8]—Lady Wilde praised your prose style again to me yesterday. Have you heard Oscar's last good thing. He says that Sharps motto should be *Acutis decensus averni* (Sharp is the decent into Hell). The phrase as you know begins in the orthodox way *Facilis* (easy). By the by, have you gone on at all with your greek.[9]

March 4th

The Putnam book goes off, for certain to morrow thank goodness. The general introduction still remains however.

Is the story true that we have just heard that Miss Johnston is going to be married to Wright? We heard it was all settled.[10]

Lilly is home again from the Morrises she came last night.

WBY published nothing on Blake's art until 1896, when his three articles on Blake's designs for *The Divine Comedy* appeared in the *Savoy*.

[7] The experiments in clairvoyance of late January 1890 are recorded in WBY's journal, 'Occult Notes and Diary, Etc.', which runs from October 1889 to January 1890 (*Mem*, 281–2). He had been a member of the Esoteric Section of the Theosophical Society since December 1888, and in March 1890 was initiated into the magical society, the Order of the Golden Dawn (see Appendix).

[8] In 1891 KT published *A Nun her Friends and her Order; Being a Sketch of the Life of Mother Mary Xaviera Fallon Sometime Superior-General of the Institute of the Blessed Virgin in Ireland and its Dependencies*.

[9] For Wilde's *mot* (and better Latin), cf. Virgil, *Aeneid* VI. 126. KT's attempt to learn Greek had begun in the spring of 1889 and caused surprise and comment among her other correspondents such as Douglas Hyde and Fr. Russell. Her enthusiasm for Hellenic studies was perhaps not wholly unconnected with her friendship for Henry Albert Hinkson (1865–1919), a classical scholar at TCD, whom she met on 6 Sept 1888 and married five years later.

[10] Ada Catherine Johnston (1873–1948), younger sister of Charles Johnston and like him a theosophist and vegetarian, had become engaged to her brother's friend Claud Falls Wright (1867–1923), another of WBY's contemporaries at the High School, Harcourt Street. Wright had abandoned his medical studies for theosophy and became secretary of the Dublin Lodge when Charles Johnston left the city. The engagement was broken off in August 1890 and Wright moved to London to work directly for HPB. After her death he emigrated to America where he played a leading role in theosophical affairs and where he died. Ada Johnston returned to the family home at Ballykilbeg, Co. Down, later in the decade and in June 1904 was married there to Captain S. A. H. Brew. They emigrated to British Columbia, where she died at Summerland in 1948.

Todhunter has written a charming little Arcadian Play to be acted in Bedford Park. He read it out on Sunday evening. M rs Emery & Paget take chief parts.[11] Last time I wrote I sent you some little verses and you never said anything about them—did you like them?

Yours Always
W B Yeats

ALS Huntington, with envelope addressed to Clondalkin, postmark 'CHISWICK MR 4 90'. McHugh, 110–12; Wade, 149–51.

To W. H. Dircks,[1] *15 March* [*1890*]

3 Blenheim Road | Bedford Park | Chiswick
March 15

Dear Sir

My friend Edwin J Ellis and myself have made a special study of the mystical philosophy and poetry of William Blake and are preparing a complete edition of the "Prophetic Books" with we beleive a full exposition. We find however that there are many things in his drawings, letters & reported sayings that take a quite new complexion in the light of his philosophy. The wild words & writings that have made so many people call him mad have grown quite smooth and logical under this new light.[2]

We wish therefore to write a short life of him & I thought that perhaps such a book would suit Scotts "Great Writer Series". M r Rhys tells me that you are the best person to write to about it. Such a book would I beleive attract attention and have good sale, for up to this their has not been a single fragment of writing on Blake by anyone who had the needful knowledge of traditional mysticism to understand his "prophetic books" or even his smaller mystial poems or his more characteristic sayings and symbolical drawings. We have also at our command unpublished MSS of great value, including a long poem full as I beleive of some of the best poetry he has written.

It is important that such a life should be written now while the few remaining people who have Blake traditions still live. Gilchrist's life is

[11] Todhunter's *A Sicilian Idyll*, a pastoral verse play based on Theocritus, was to be performed later that spring with Florence Farr (Mrs Emery) and her brother-in-law H. M. Paget in the leading roles.

[1] William Henry Dircks (1857–1925) was born in Newcastle and attended the same school as Ernest Rhys, of whom he remained a close friend. After a period in a ship broker's office he had become reader and adviser for Walter Scott the publisher, and later held the same post with T. Fisher Unwin.

[2] Cf. the letter of late 1889 from Douglas Hyde to KT quoted at p. 193, n. 2, alluding to 'Blake (the madman and poet)'.

admirable on the purely artistic side but never having understood Blake the thinker, much in Blake the man, even as poet, remained unintelligoble to him.[3]

Yours sincerely
W B Yeats

W H Dircks Esq

ALS Yale.

To Charles Elkin Mathews, [? spring 1890][1]

[n. a.]

. . . I feel quite certain that we have found in William Blake one of the great mystics of the world, and that after reading our book no one at any rate will ever again say that he was mad unless they are also prepared to say as much for every other mystic who ever lived. As we go on working at him it becomes more and more clear that hardly any fragment of his poetry can be understood as he understood it, by any reader, until his system is also understood and that this book of ours should make people take him much more seriously. His lyrics even will seem more beautiful when they have taken their place in his general system. . . .

Extract from ALS (8 pp.) 8vo [undated], entirely relating to the production of a book on Blake. Sotheby's catalogue 15 November 1949, Item no. 422; sold to Maggs.

To Sir Charles Gavan Duffy, 17 March [1890]

3 Blenheim Road | Bedford Park | Chiswick
March 17

My Dear Sir Gavan Duffy
    When I met you with M^r O'Leary last year you very kindly offered me the use of some unpublished letters of Mangan's also of the peasent poet Keegan's. I am now thinking out a lecture on Mangan as a preliminary to writing a study of him for a projected little book on Irish literature that has

[3] The long poem was *Vala* (see p. 201). Neither WBY nor Ellis published a biography of Blake in the Walter Scott series. Alexander Gilchrist's 1863 *Life of Blake* (see p. 151) remained the standard biography for many years.

[1] See p. 191. The dating of this letter can only be conjectural unless the original comes to light, but from the extract quoted in the sale catalogue it seems to belong to the same period as the preceding letter. WBY may even have proposed to Mathews for the Bodley Head a short life of Blake along the lines of the one he had offered to Walter Scott, via W. H. Dircks (see above), for his Great Writer series.

been long in my mind.[1] I write to remind you of your kind promise in the matter of both men—Mangan & Keegan. I should have written before but up to this have had no time to turn to anything so unbusinesslike as lectures or essays on Irish poets. I am however free now for a bit. I sent off yesterday the MSS for a book of Selected Irish Fiction that has filled up all my days, this good while.

Yours very Truly
W B Yeats

ALS NLI. Wade, 151–2.

To James Mavor,[1] [mid-April 1890]

3 Blenheim Road | Bedford Park | Chiswick

Dear M\` Mavor.

Could you manage do you think to let me have a proof of "the gods", as you intend to have a proof taken in any case, even if not good enough to be printed it will be valuable to me as knowing the origonal I will be able to make allowance for its defects & I have always wished to have some kind of reproduction of them by me & besides it will help me in the description of them. If they cannot be printed I would suggest that you substitute a design that Nettleship showed me yesterday—a most finished & beautiful work more recent than most of the others & more perfect in a merely tecnical sence.[2] When will you be next in London? I would like—in case a substitution is to be made for "the Gods" which heaven forbid—to bring you to his studio to see the design I have mentioned & some others or I could send it you at once.

Yours sinely
W B Yeats

ALS Toronto.

[1] See p. 201. WBY hoped the Mangan letters would corroborate his version of the poet's love affair with Frances Stackpoole—subject of his 1891 article in *United Ireland* (see p. 47, n. 3)—since they apparently gave 'Mangan's own account of it'. WBY had lectured on Mangan to the Southwark Literary Club on 29 May 1889; there is no evidence of a further lecture.

[1] James Mavor (1854–1925), a political economist who was at this time editor of both the *Scottish Art Review*, published from Edinburgh 1889–90, and the *Art Review* (see p. 211), which was similar in format but published from London. In 1892 Mavor was appointed Professor of Political Economy in the University of Toronto and remained in Canada until his death. WBY visited him in Toronto during his North American tour of 1914.

[2] No reproduction of Nettleship's drawing, 'The Gods', is to be found among the Yeats papers (MBY) and presumably the original was too faded for a proof to be taken of it. The only drawing by

To Sir Charles Gavan Duffy, 18 April [1890]

3 Blenheim Road | Bedford Park | Chiswick | W
April 18th

My dear Sir Charles Gavan Duffy

Thank you very much for the Keegan letters. I will take great care of them & return them as soon as possible.[1] I shall try & find out who these Irish Exhibition Committee men are & write to them on the matter of Mangan's letters, unless you think Father Mehans friends are more likely to succeed than I.[2] I do not know anyone connected with the exhibition. I have not done more yet than glance at the Keegan papers but what I have seen promises well for their general interest.

Yours very sincerely
W B Yeats.

PS.

I have stamped this letter sufficiently at any rate & please forgive my forgetfulness about the last.[3]

ALS NLI. Wade, 152.

Nettleship in the archive is one entitled 'Madness' which may well be the substitute design that WBY mentions here. Although made in the summer of 1870, the design, which symbolizes a man near the summit of his career who has been struck down by madness, has a long commentary in the bottom margin in Nettleship's hand, dated 24 Apr 1890.

The *Art Review* ceased publication in the summer of 1890, before WBY's article on Nettleship's designs could be published.

[1] In an article for the *Boston Pilot*, written 12 Apr 1890, WBY reported (*LNI*, 110) that 'A bundle of about fifty letters written by the peasant poet, John Keegan, author of Caoch O'Leary, has just been placed in my hands. None have ever been published. They are full of gloomy interest, biographical and other. . . . I am always especially pleased to come across anything that throws light on the personal side of Irish history or literature in the way these Keegan letters do.' John Keegan (see p. 201), most popular of the Irish peasant poets, was the son of a small farmer; he was educated at a hedge school and wrote poems for a number of papers, including the *Nation*, the *Irish Penny Journal*, and the *Dublin University Magazine*. He eloped with and married a girl from an adjoining farm but the marriage was a disastrous failure. He died impoverished in the cholera epidemic of 1849.

[2] According to WBY's 1891 article (*UP* I. 196), Gavan Duffy had lent 'a dozen or more unpublished letters of Mangan's' to the Irish Exhibition, a trade fair held at Earls Court, London, in the autumn of 1888, 'but has never been able to recover them, owing to the scandalous neglect of the committee.'

Father Charles Patrick Meehan (1812–90) had been a supporter of the Young Irelanders, writing for the *Nation* under the pseudonym 'Clericus', and had known Gavan Duffy since early 1842. He had been a close friend of Mangan's and attended him on his deathbed. In 1884 he brought out a two-volume edition of the poems augmented with newly discovered songs. Fr. Meehan died on 14 Mar 1890, a few weeks before this letter was written. Neither his friends nor WBY were able to retrieve the letters.

[3] WBY had evidently forgotten that extra postage was necessary for letters going abroad—in this case to Nice.

To Katharine Tynan, [c. 18] May [1890]

3 Blenheim Road | Bedford Park | Chiswick
May

My dear Katey

The little poem you sent me is very preety—the language at once quaint & fervid a good combination not easy to get. Send a poem to the Art Review by all means. It is quite open for verse I think. I may be seeing the editor soon & will mention your name.[1] He is reproducing the Nettleship designs for my article & will I dare say see me about them on his next visit to London. My article must begin getting itself written this week. You should not have sent the poem to the Scots Observer it was too political—Irish exiles are out of their range I think. I am sending Henley a new ballad to day I think you will like it[2]—I wrote it for a literary club that Rhys Rolleston & myself have started at the old inn called the Cheshire chease. We meet once a week there & smoke & talk & hope to get all the yonger writers of verse in to it in time. It is called the "Rhymsters".[3] O Leary has been there the last two evenings. Those of us who are in funds dine there at seven & those of us that are not turn up later. Todhunter by the by—one of the Rhymster[s]—has written a beatiful pastoral play & had it acted here three times last week to over flowing audiences—I had done three articles on it one for the Nation one for Pilot—one for providence Journal.[4] So you see I am industrious four

---

[1] Nothing by KT appeared in the *Art Review*, which was soon to cease publication.

[2] KT's poem submitted to the *Scots Observer* was probably 'The Wild Geese', subtitled 'A Lament for the Irish Jacobites'—the 'Wild Geese' were eighteenth-century Irish exiles who sought military service on the Continent, usually in the armies of France or Austria. The poem appeared in the *Boston Pilot*, 17 May 1890, and was reprinted in *Ballads and Lyrics* (92–3). WBY's 'Father Gilligan', later entitled 'The Ballad of Father Gilligan' (*VP*, 132–4), appeared in the *Scots Observer* of 5 July 1890.

[3] In *Aut* (165) WBY recalls that he and Ernest Rhys between them founded, probably early in 1890, the Rhymers' Club, which for some years used to meet every night in an upper room with a sanded floor in an ancient eating-house in Fleet Street called the Cheshire Cheese. Lionel Johnson, Ernest Dowson, Victor Plarr, Ernest Radford, John Davidson, Richard Le Gallienne, T. W. Rolleston, Selwyn Image, Edwin Ellis, and John Todhunter came constantly for a time, Arthur Symons and Herbert Horne, less constantly, while William Watson joined but never came and Francis Thompson came once but never joined; and sometimes if we met in a private house, which we did occasionally, Oscar Wilde came. . . .We read our poems to one another and talked criticism and drank a little wine.

The date of the original inn, 'Ye Olde Cheshire Cheese', situated in Wine Office Court, off Fleet Street, is unknown, but the building WBY frequented, which is still standing, was rebuilt in 1667 after the Great Fire of London. It has been associated with literary figures since at least the Elizabethan period, including Ben Jonson, Dr Johnson, Goldsmith, and Dickens.

[4] Todhunter's *A Sicilian Idyll* was first performed at the Bedford Park Social Club on Monday, 5 May 1890, and repeated—'the one unmistakable success of his life,' WBY wrote (*Aut*, 120)—on the Wednesday and Friday of that week and on the Saturday of the following week. WBY's review for the *Nation* of 17 May 1890 was republished in *PSJ*, 8 June 1890 (12), while that for the *Boston Pilot* appeared

articles in eight day[s]—I did one on William Waston for the Provid. Journal.[5] Indeed as soon as I get Blake off my hands I may be able to do decenty from the money point of view & then I shall soon get away from London—a detestable cauldron of a place—. It is preety certain that Quaritch will publish our Blake book[6] we will get nothing for it—for the first edition anyway—but he will do it so very well, with such good paper & binding & so forth, that it will indirectly pay better than it would to get some small sum from an ordinary publisher for it. It will be in two volumes—the first containing the text of the prophetic books the second an interpretation of the philosophy contained in them. The book must rouse a good deal of interest among literer[y] people & what will please me better influence for good the mystical societies through out Europe. You will like his system of thought it is profoundly Christian—thogh wrapped up in a queer dress— & certainly amazingly poetical—It has done my own mind a great deel of good—in liberating me from fromulas & theories of several kinds. You will find it a difficult book—this Blake interpretation—but one that will open up for you I think as it has for me new kinds of poetic feeling & thought.

Have you thought at all about the "Miracle Play" I suggested to you? A play about the adoration of the magi say—you could do the bulk of the dialogue in the same metre as Joan of Arc & the rest in various lyrical measures.[7] You should attempt every now & then poems of some little length—they help one to think hard about one's verse & make one search for new kinds of feeling & keep one from falling into the merely pretty. A little play of the kind I suggest might be afterwards published in a little book by

on 14 June 1890 (*LNI*, 112–18; he had also mentioned the production on 17 May 1890 in the 'Celt in London' column he contributed irregularly to the *Pilot*). Although he was later to acknowledge that he had overestimated the importance of the play, at this time WBY was enthusiastic: 'acting, scenery and verse were all a perfect unity. It was like a dream' (*LNI*, 117).

[5] In 'A Scholar Poet' (*LNI*, 204–13), a review of William Watson's *Wordsworth's Grave and Other Poems* in *PSJ*, 15 June 1890, WBY found Watson accomplished rather than inspired, 'a fire that will not warm our hearths, but gives a thin flame, good to read by for a little, when wearied by some more potent influence.' Watson (1858–1935) was to take his revenge in a review of *The Countess Kathleen* in the *Illustrated London News*, 10 Sept 1892 (334), where he accused WBY of the opposite fault: artistic ambition without sufficient technical accomplishment.

[6] Bernard Quaritch (1819–99), the eventual publisher of *The Works of William Blake*, was born in Germany where he worked for booksellers in Nordhausen and Berlin. He came to London in 1842 and, after a short period in Paris, 1844–5, set up for himself as a bookseller in 1847, becoming a naturalized British subject in the same year. His excellent memory, stamina, and energy soon made him the outstanding book dealer of his generation. The first of his authoritative catalogues appeared in 1858 and in 1860 he moved his business to 15 Piccadilly where it remained for the rest of his life. He bought up all the major libraries on sale between 1874 and his death, specializing in incunabula, Shakespeariana, Bibles and fine manuscripts. In an article in the *Bookman*, July 1893, Edwin Ellis described him (111–12) as 'the actual head of the European book-trade . . . a pocket Hercules . . . He hates poetry—"I am an anti-poet!" he says of himself—but he is really a lost poet.'

[7] See p. 172, n. 5. KT's 'Joan of Arc', a monologue spoken by the saint on the eve of her execution (*Louise de la Vallière*, 25), was written in heroic couplets.

itself & become very popular, & might even perhaps be acted for some religious purpose somewhere.

I went to see the Meynells on Sunday week. They spoke of you of your being there again at some time. Any chance of its being this year?

I hear that O'Leary has really written a quantity of his "remincsecences" & Rolleston, who has read it, says it is very fine—full of irony & style.[8] Rolleston himself seems more genial that it was his wont to be. He is writting with ardour. At the present moment he is doing Todhunters Play for the "Academy".[9]

My father has two portraits to do down at Wimbledon for people called Wykins[10] I think & is getting on very well with them—they are the first portrait orders for some time. There is no other news that I can think of—I enclose the little ballad I spoke of. Tell me what you think of it. I send you verses before, by the way, & you said not a word of them. I fear I am in arrears with this letter. But forgive & do not avenge yourself with a long silence.

Yours always
W B Yeats

PS—

⟨On⟩ second thoughts I enclose an article I did on Todhunter play for Nation (it came last night) & will add the programe if I find it before post time.

Did I tell you that I am writing two articles for the Art Review on Nettleships designs. It will be illustrated plentifully. Who is it corrects your greek exercises?[11]

If I was over in Ireland I would ask you to collaberate together with me on that little miracle play I suggested to you on "the Adoration of the Magi". I have written so much in dramatic form that I could perhaps help by making a little prose sketch in dialogue to be turned into verse by you. Would collaboration make it hard for you to work or easy? If you think of being in London this year we could do it or perhaps I may get Blake done soon

---

[8] After his sister's death, a group of JO'L's friends formed a committee which issued a circular inviting subscriptions for the book of memoirs he had long contemplated. Their purpose was partly to spur him into writing but it was principally an attempt to help him in his financial straits. When the book, *Recollections of Fenians and Fenianism*, eventually appeared in 1896, WBY did not find it as fine as had Rolleston and in *Aut* (212) he describes it as 'unreadable, being dry, abstract, and confused; no picture had ever passed before his mind's eye'.

[9] Rolleston's notice of *A Sicilian Idyll* in the *Academy*, 17 May 1890 (344–5), commended Todhunter for having caught 'the true Theocritean spirit in this charming Pastoral' and praised in particular 'Mrs Emery, who acted the part of Amaryllis with a depth of poetic feeling which realised to perfection the intention of the character and the piece'.

[10] Probably the family of Arthur Wickens, who lived at 19 King's Road, Wimbledon, from 1884 to 1890.

[11] See p. 212, n. 9.

enough to go to Ireland before the winter has quite come. & see you on my way to Sligo.

Could you let me see your ballad on the Countess Kathleen O Shee story?[12]

ALS Texas. Partly in McHugh, 142; partly in Wade, 152–3.

To J. N. Dunn, [*26 May 1890*]

3 Blenheim Road | Bedford Park | Chiswick
Whit monday.

Dear M[r] Dunn

Do you owe me any thing for that little scrap of a poem "A cradle Song"? If so be that you do I would be glad of it now being a trifle short.[1]

Yours very truly
W B Yeats

ALS Tulane.

To Katharine Tynan, 30 May [*1890*]

3 Blenheim Road | Bedford Park | Chiswick
May 30th.

Dear Katey

I see by Irish Monthly that the 6[d] Poems & Ballad[s] of Young Ireland is out in brown paper & gilt (silver would surely have been the orthodox marking for brown paper covers?). Could you get Gill to send me a copy or two—say three—? I will try & get it noticed. I may get some sort of review in Pall Mall & Scots Observer as well as mention it myself in the Boston Pilot.[1]

---

[12] KT's poem 'The Charity of the Countess Kathleen' (*Ballads and Lyrics*, 45–50) recounts the legend WBY was using in his play *The Countess Kathleen*; a note to the poem (153) declares it to be 'an authentic folk-story of the West of Ireland, and . . . perhaps the only instance in legend of one who sold her soul for the Love of God'.

[1] See p. 209, n. 3. ECY recorded in her diary (MBY) for 28 May 1890 that WBY had received £1-1-0 from *Scots Observer*, presumably in response to this request.

[1] The *Irish Monthly* for June 1890 announced, 'price sixpence, with the name in gold on brown paper, which Philistines will consider aesthetically ugly, we welcome a second edition of "Poems and Ballads of Young Ireland" (Dublin: M. H. Gill & Son).' No review of the edition appeared in the *Pall Mall Gazette* or in the *Scots Observer*; WBY mentioned it in the *Boston Pilot*, but not until 11 Apr 1891, in the course of an article on Rose Kavanagh, when he described it (*LNI*, 121) as 'a little volume which has had a sale sufficient at any rate to warrant its present new and cheaper form'.

But please get me these review copies at once or I may be forestalled by some unfriendly or less friendly notice than I hope to secure.

By the by I thought you were to let us know—so that Todhunter & myself might put advertisements of our books at the end. I thought indeed that we were all to do so—dividing the extra expense. Perhaps it is not yet to[o] late to slip them in at the back of the cover if so I will tell Todhunter, and get him I doubt not to print a notice of his "Banshee"—with press opinions—at some local printers & send it. I will try & do the same. You have such things I dare say already. They would help the sale of the Ballad Book itself—as people would see by them when they turned over the leaves that we are folk who have "been praised by a heavy review" to quote a ballade by a neighbour of ours—it would influence reviewers likewise—[2]

I have to go work at Blake over at the Linnells at Chelsea[3]—they have a deel of Blake MS—& so wind up this note. Write soon to me.

Yours Always
W B Yeats

ALS Huntington, with envelope addressed to Clondalkin, postmark 'CHISWICK MY 30 90'. McHugh, 112–13; Wade, 153.

To Katharine Tynan, 1 July [*1890*]

3 Blenheim Road | Bedford Park | W.
July 1.

My dear Katey

I have been so long in writing because I hoped to send you some notes or perhaps an abstract of the little "Mystery Play" on the adoration of the Magi that I propose. I found however that I could not get on without knowing the Catholic tradition on the subject & so far I have not had time to look it up in some dictionary of legend at the Museum.[1]

I am working at Blake & such things. "The Art Review" has come to an end and so unhappily my article on Nettleships designs is useless. I shall get the editing of a book of reprints of lives of one or two such men as Fighting

---

[2] See p. 190. WBY had picked up this idea from Sparling, who had printed at the back of *Irish Minstrelsy* advertisements for the contributors' books. The 'ballade' is untraced.

[3] Although the family house of William Linnell, oldest of the three brothers (see p. 201), to whom Ellis and WBY dedicated *The Works of William Blake*, was at Hillsbrow, Redhill, in Surrey, he had a studio at The Avenue, 76 Fulham Road, Chelsea, and used to take a town house in Carlyle Square, Chelsea, for part of the London season. It was in the basement at Carlyle Square that WBY and Ellis worked on the Blake manuscripts, sometimes until the early hours of the morning.

[1] See p. 218. WBY's interest in the Magi may have stemmed from his introduction to the teachings of the Order of the Golden Dawn. His story, 'The Adoration of the Magi' (*Myth*, 308–15) appeared in 1897 and his poem, 'The Magi' (*VP*, 318), was published in 1914.

Fitzgerald I think.[2] These books do not really pay as well as articles but they help one to make up subjects that are afterwards of great use. I shall be writing some Blake articles at once now. We—Ellis & myself—intend posting one or two to Scribners.[3]

I have seen Miss Imogen Guiney several times. She was out here one Sunday. We all like her greatly. Some one here said she is just like one of the heroines in Howells novels.[4] I have gone to see her once or twice when going in to the Museum but have not seen her just lately for I have been doubly a prisoner through some work on Irish novelists for Putnam & a cough now taking its departure.

Lolly is getting ready for her kindergarten exam' now almost at hand.[5] Lilly goes to Sligo in August & Jack also. My mother is as usual that is better in actual health than she used to be but feable as to nervous power & memory. I dont know that there is much more news. Oh yes there is. Todhunter has written a new play – a prose & verse play on a subject mixed up with the discovery of the printing press. His "Sicilian Idyll" is being actied again tonight at St Georges Hall Holburn for the benefit of some charity. Mrs Andrew Hart bears all expenses. It will be published in an *edition de luxe* in Autumn, with frontespiece by Walter Crane—[6]

July 5th—

I have been in the museum much lately reading up the duellists & outlaws for this Unwin book—going through contemporary & chapbook records.

---

[2] Although WBY worked for some time on this projected selection of writings about Irish duellists and outlaws for T. Fisher Unwin's Adventure Series, and even drew up a proposed list of contents in 1893, the volume was never published. Some of WBY's views on the subject survive in an article, 'A Reckless Century. Irish Rakes and Duellists' (*UP* 1. 198–202), which appeared in *United Ireland*, 12 Sept 1891. George Robert Fitzgerald (*c.* 1748–86) was a famous duellist, hanged at Castlebar for killing an attorney.

[3] *Scribner's Magazine* (New York) published no articles on Blake by WBY or by Edwin Ellis.

[4] Louise Imogen Guiney (1861–1920), daughter of a Boston lawyer from Tipperary, published poems in a number of Boston papers, including the *Pilot*, during the 1880s. She paid a prolonged visit to England from May 1889 to February 1891, in the course of which she also travelled to France and, in March 1890, Ireland where she met KT. She returned to England in May 1895, and finally settled there in 1901, living in or near Oxford for the rest of her life. KT has a chapter on her in *Memories*. Miss Guiney published a number of books of verse as well as critical studies of Henry Vaughan and Lionel Johnson, and an edition of Mangan (see p. 47, n. 3). WBY was introduced to her by JO'L, who wrote about this time to Dora Sigerson (NLI) of his intention 'to bring young Yeats to see her and I suppose through him is the easiest way of my getting her to serve some Literary Society here.' In the summer of 1890 she was living in High Holborn, and from there wrote to KT on 20 July (Hinkson), 'Then there is your Willie Yeats, he and his, to whom I took at once.'

The American novelist William Dean Howells (1837–1920) created a number of heroines whose naturalness and sincerity contrasted favourably with their more conventional European counterparts.

[5] In fact ECY failed the examination for the Elementary Certificate of the National Froebel Union when she took it later this month. She managed to pass when she re-sat in July 1891 and went on successfully to take the two parts of the Higher Certificate in 1892 and 1893 respectively.

[6] Todhunter's play, *How Dreams Come True*, 'Specially written for the Conversazione of the Sette of Odd Volumes at the Grosvenor Gallery, July 17th, 1890', was based on a story told in Scott's *The Antiquary*, and dealt both with the love of Aldobrand, an apprentice printer, for Bertha, his master's daughter, and his development of an improved printing press in early sixteenth-century Nuremburg.

Whether the book comes off or no, they will serve me for articles at any rate.

Are you well on with the life of the nun you are doing. I hope they give you a fairly free hand in the matter & allow you to make her human not to[o] much of the white light of piety. Remember it is the stains of earth colour that make man differ from man & give interest to biography.

July 15th—

When I finished the above I had no stamp & then forgot it. A financial crisis of a moderately severe kind driving things out of my head—

The little poem you so much liked was in The Scots Observer a couple of weeks ago.[7] York Powell liked it greatly. I shall get to Ireland some time this year but when I do not know. The book of Duellists Etc & the Blake must first be finished—

Yours at all times
W B Yeats

Can you tell me what the Pilot gives you for a column or for an article of average length. They give me one pound for my Celt in London letter.[8] I am thinking of asking for more—I fixed a pound myself, I think, in the beginning. I dont want to write to Pilot on the matter until I know what their usual pay is.

ALS Huntington, with envelope addressed to Clondalkin, postmark 'LONDON W. JY 17 90'. McHugh, 113–15; Wade, 153–5.

To J. N. Dunn, 13 July [1890]

3 Blenheim Road | Bedford Park | Chiswick
July 13th

Dear Mr Dunn

Could you if quite convenient send me what ever is due for "Peter Gilligan".[1] I am afraid it is dreadfully irregular my bothering you this way

---

A Sicilian Idyll was performed on 1 and 2 July 1890 at St. George's Hall, Regent Street, in aid of the Popular Musical Union. The patroness of the performance was probably Lady Hart, widow of Sir Andrew Searle Hart (1811–90), mathematician and Vice-Provost of TCD, whose portrait JBY had painted. Elkin Mathews brought out a large-paper edition of the play, limited to 50 signed copies, with a frontispiece by Walter Crane, in the autumn of 1890.

[7] 'Father Gilligan' (see p. 217).

[8] Fourteen articles by WBY appeared under the heading 'The Celt in London' in the *Boston Pilot* between 3 Aug 1889 and 19 Nov 1892. The £1 payment was apparently per column since ECY's diary (MBY) lists sums varying between £1-3-od and £3 from this source. WBY seems to have asked for his raise since ECY records that he received £4 on 14 July 1890, double the sum for the previous month. KT's account book (Hinkson) shows that she got between £1-10-od and £3 for articles and £1 or £1-1-od for poems.

[1] i.e., 'Father Gilligan. [A Legend told by The People of Castleisland, Kerry]' (see p. 217), published the week before in the *Scots Observer*.

instead of waiting for the regular day if such there be, but my finances are generaly at ebb tide and tides of all sorts wait for no man.

I am sorry to have been unable to send any prose to the "Scots Observer" of late but have been very busy with some wretched bookmaking.[2]

Yours sincely
W B Yeats.

ALS Private.

To E. J. Ellis, [? 6 September 1890]

3 Blenheim Road | Bedford Park | Chiswick
Saturday Morning

My dear Ellis.

Yoark Powell is not in town. I should have let you know by return but I was out when your letter came & did not arrive in, until after post time. I write however first thing this morning & hope it my reach you in time to prevent your being on the look out for Powell.

The reason I have not attacked Jerusalem & Milton is that the Biblical part, so important in both books, is still a blank to me, I am pushing on with Boehmen & Swedenborg reading, in the hope to find it clear up.[1] I am anxious also to make my accounts of the books follow on each other with some kind of consecutiveness. For this reason I was working at the minor books first. I find I can never write other than consecutively. I meen I cannot write Chap 2 before Chap 1 or Chap 3 before Chap 2. I have by me

---

[2] The projected selection for Fisher Unwin's Adventure Series (see p. 222).

[1] The German mystic and shoemaker Jacob Boehme (1575–1624), also known as Behmen, was completely self-educated; he claimed direct divine inspiration and wrote more than 30 mystical books, beginning with *Aurora oder Morgenröte im Aufgang* in 1612 (published 1634) and ending with *Mysterium Magnum* in 1623. Blake apparently read Boehme in his youth—probably in the same edition as that possessed by WBY, the 4-vol. translation by John Sparrow with an unfinished commentary by the Revd William Law (1764–81)—and shows his influence particularly in *The First Book of Urizen* (1794). In a review of 1896 (UP I. 400), WBY claimed that Boehme 'first taught in the modern world the principles which Blake first expressed in the language of poetry; and of these the most important, and the one from which the others spring, is that the imagination is the means whereby we communicate with God.'

The Swedish scientist and mystic Emanuel Swedenborg (1688–1772), the son of a Lutheran bishop, from 1716 to 1746 produced an awesome number of publications on a wide variety of scientific subjects. In 1745 he had a vision and, believing he was called by God to devote himself to the exposition of the spiritual world, gave up his appointment at the Board of Mines. He spent the rest of his life writing his theological works, beginning with Part I of the *Arcana Caelestia* (1749) and ending with *True Christian Religion* (1771). Blake read many of these works when they were translated into English from the original Latin and they exerted a great influence on him, although he proclaimed that he had gone beyond Swedenborg in *The Marriage of Heaven and Hell* (c. 1790–3). In his 1914 essay, 'Swedenborg, Mediums, and the Desolate Places' (*Expl*, 30–70), WBY gives an account of some aspects of Swedenborg's thought and compares him with Blake.

for some time a careful scheme of my part of the work & will try to follow it. It will be as follows—

Chap. 1. The Mystical postulate
  „   2 The three persons. The three regions.
  „   3 The Four Zoas. The four Eliments
  „   4 The Four Atmosphere[s]. The States & Spaces.
  „   5 The types & correspondences of these things
Chap. 6. The Rotation of Zoas
  „   7. The Nine Months and the six days of creation
  „   8 Interpretation of large chart
  „   9 Blake & Genisis
             „   Apocylyps
  „   10 Blake & the Historical Books of the Bible
  „   11 Bake & ⟨Christ⟩ the crusifixion
  „   12 Blake & Boehmen
  „   13 Blake & Swedenborg
  „   14 Blake & the Alchemists.

[*Vertically in margin*]
⟨Note—I will probably compare Blakes doctrine all through with other mystic [*illegible*] mainly in reference [*illegible*] should⟩
And then the abstracts of prophetic books with a chart of the arrangement of periods Etc in most cases.

Some of the chapters mentioned above will be very short not more than a page perhaps as in Bishop Martensens book on Boehmen, while some may go to a number of pages.[2] The only chapters of the above that might perhaps be written out of their regular order (and I am not sure if they could) are the Biblical ones & I have not the knowledge for them yet. I am not however losing time in the matter of making it up. It would greatly help me if I had those Swedenborgs you have. Are they at Milson Road?[3] May I get them?

As to the matter of writing quite seperate accounts & putting our initials to them I do not think it matters provided we do not contradict each other but not to do so is all important. People would say "see the editors themselves cannot aggree—presently some one else will come along & find a third meaning & overturn both of them." I have already been told this—I mean the last part of it. The careless reviewer would seize with delight upon

[2] This scheme was considerably modified by the time of publication of *The Works of William Blake*. Bishop Hans Martensen's *Jacob Boehme: His Life and Teaching. Or Studies in Theosophy*, translated by T. Rhys Evans in 1885, is a handbook and guide to Boehme's teaching.
[3] In the early 1890s Ellis and his German-born wife, the former Mrs Edwards, née Philippa Becker (1858–*c.* 1935), whom he had married in 1882, were living at 40 Milson Road, Shepherd's Bush.

so good a joke as that two editors had worked for a year & a half on Blake & found he ment contradictory things. As it is many will beleive we have read our meanings into him. Let us work on seperately by all means (we can do none other nor should do other) but afterwards we must compare & bring our work into aggreement. It is a mere matter of saying more or less often that we see the same truth from different sides.

Let the question of signing our seperate parts stand over until they are written. The question is simply this—much that each of us writes is the result of discussions to which one contributed not more than the other. The matter however is unimportant *if* we do not contradict each other on any essential point. You felt as strongly as I did on this matter when I last saw you.[4]

Your short abstract of book of Los is admirable but difficult. You will have to difine carefully in your introduction to your part what you meen by "pliability" "up-within" "down within" "still division". These are tecnical terms as much as Blake's own & are rightly so but they need definition as you know I doubt not. Do not go too far with Los as interchangable by Time. In Boehmen & surely also in Blake Eternal Mind only takes on its aspect of Time in the third triad. Before that he is not Time but something of which Time is a type. He become[s] Time (as we know it) when Orc is chained. The first & second triads Boehmen says are the two interior worlds of good & evil, light & darkness, the third triad is the exterior world of the senses. That which is active spirit in the interior is Time in the exterior. The 3 triads are also in Boehme devided thus. Will, Mind, Senses Father son & holy ghost. Science in Boehme by the by is identical with Motion & with sense perception in general. Hence Blakes "Tent" that is Science.

It will be a great thing, perhaps a needful thing, for me to have your line by line comments by me when writing my abstracts. Any you send me will

---

[4] In a note dated 14 Nov 1899, inscribed in Lady Gregory's copy of *The Works of Blake* (Berg), WBY gives a fuller account of the methods of collaboration:

The book was written in this way. I wrote a life of Blake about as long as my life of him in 'The Muses Library Book', an account of the symbolic system as a whole, & a short interpretative argument of each prophetic book. Ellis expanded, or rather completely rewrote the life into its present form, he accepted with some additions & modifications the chapter on the symbolic system & expanded the short arguments to ten times their original length; & wrote a number of extra chapters. The actual interpretation of the philosophy, which is contained in both his book & mine was made out absolutely to geather. His mind was far more minute than mine, but less synthetic. I had a tendency to make generalisations on imperfect foundations, & he to remain content with detached discoveries. We worked about four years & our method was to collate every mention of a mythological personage, or symbol. Ellis compiled a concordance to aid us. . . . With the exception of the part called 'The Symbolic System' almost all of the actual writing is by Ellis.

See also *Bibl*, 217.

be gratefully received. I do not feel capable of doing my general account until the abstracts are done. They will not take long however.

Yours very siny
W B Yeats

My comparison of Blake Boehmen Alchemists Etc will not be confined to sepecial chapters but run through the general comment wherever it is useful as interpretation of Blakes meaning. The spicial chapters will be a more special, general, & final consideration of the relation in each case.

ALS Reading.

To Katharine Tynan, [7] *September* [1890]

3 Blenheim R ᵈ | Bedford Park | Chiswick. | W
September | Sunday.

My dear Katey

I have again delayed long in answering your letter. Blake and other matters have kept me busy & I put off writing from day to day. But do not think it is any forgetfulness brought on, as you put it, by "frivelous London life". London life, for one thing, has taken its "frivolity" to Brighton & elswere, this time of year, & all times I see but little of it. Nor if I did could it put you or Ireland or ought else much out of thought for I set small store by it & would gladly never look upon it again. I will if any chance makes it possible find my way to Dublin before the years end & avail myself of your invitation (it ought to have had quicker response from me) but some time now I am a prisoner. Blake keeps me to my desk. Quaritch has finally agreed to publish the book giving us by way of payment 13 large paper copies each—they will be worth at the smallest £3 a peice I suppose—We are to have reproductions of all the illustrations to the prophetic books—about 160 drawings in all—and charts & maps as many as we need. There will be two volumes one containing the mystical poems—one of these Vala, a poem of great length & beuty never having been printed or even read before—The other volume will contain our commentary.[1] The whole book will be in

---

[1] The Linnells' arrangement with the publisher was formalized on 22 Aug 1890 when Quaritch wrote to William Linnell (private): 'For the privilege of Mr Ellis being allowed to utilize the Blake materials in your possession, and under your surveillance, I agree to supply to you thirteen copies of Mr Ellis's work, on Large Paper, immediately after the completion of the work.' Linnell was to retain copyright in the work, and in a further letter of 27 Aug 1890 (private) Quaritch offered to 'give you two small paper copies for one Large Paper copy at any time'; the edition was to be 500 copies on small paper and 150 on large. Ellis meanwhile had agreed with Quaritch in August 1890 to 'write the work and to conduct it through the press without claiming an honorarium; to superintend the selections and reproductions of illustrations'; he was to receive in payment £100 and 30 copies of the large-paper edition (Quaritch

printers hands before Winter, I hope, & will be as far as illustrations & general size & get up are concerned the most important thing done as yet upon Blake. Our part will I beleive give to the world a great religeous visionary who has been hidden.

I am also editing or trying to edit a book of Irish Adventures for Unwin.[2] If my introduction pleases him I am to get twenty pounds if not five pounds. Whether it will please I do not know. I am to give in it "a vivid view of Irish life in the eighteenth century". And am quite new to historical writing as well as up to my ears in Blakean Mysticism with scarcely a moment for anything else. If all goes well I shall have this twenty pounds, & another from Putnam, for the book of Irish novlists, some time this winter, & so may manage to get some thing out of it for myself to take me to Ireland and on to Sligo for a while. I wish very much to finish, some where in peace, verse enough for another book & perhaps start a romance. I think now I have said all I need say of my own matters. I hope yours go on well—the nun & the rest. Always tell me of any poems you are doing. Our work after all is our true Soul & to know how that goes is the great thing.

Lilly & Lolly are back now—Lilly from Sligo—she stayed but a day in Dublin else she had gone to se[e] you—and Lolly from her seaside months tuition. Jack is still in Sligo he had some drawings in the *Daily Graphic* last Friday week but I have not seen them yet. He has been offered the illustrating of a book & will I conclude accept.[3]

Please forgive me if I write no more now. I am tired for some reason or other & therefore dispirited & have the wish to keep such ever away from what I write & so end this. Do not revenge my double delay by keeping me long out of an answer to this but write within a week or so.

Yours always
W B Yeats

ALS Huntington, with envelope addressed to Clondalkin, postmark 'LONDON W. SP [?] 12 90'. McHugh, 115–16; Wade, 155–7.

Archive and *The Book Collector*, Spring 1972, 92)—of which WBY, who was not named in the agreement, was presumably to receive a share.

    The edition as it finally appeared in 1893 was in three volumes, not two, the first containing a memoir and an account of Blake's symbolic system; the second largely concerned with interpretation and commentary; and the third containing Blake's text and illustrations.

    [2] See p. 222, n. 2.

    [3] Jack Yeats's illustrated letter about a race meeting at Drumcliffe was printed in the *Daily Graphic*, 29 Aug 1890. The book he had been offered to illustrate was presumably Ernest Rhys's *The Great Cockney Tragedy*, published in 1891 by T. Fisher Unwin.

To the Editor of The Academy, *2 October 1890*

London: Oct. 2, 1890.

The Rev. Percy Myles, in a review of Lady Wilde's *Ancient Cures, Charms, and Usages* (ACADEMY, Sept. 27), makes complimentary mention of my little compilation, *Fairy and Folk Tales of the Irish Peasantry*. He misunderstands, however, what I said about scientific folk-lorists in the Introduction. I do not want the fairy-tale gatherer to tell us "what he thinks he might have heard, or what he thinks his audience would like to hear."[1] But I deeply regret when I find that some folk-lorist is merely scientific, and lacks the needful subtle imaginative sympathy to tell his stories well. There are innumerable little turns of expression and quaint phrases that in the mouth of a peasant give half the meaning, and often the whole charm. The man of science is too often a person who has exchanged his soul for a formula; and when he captures a folk-tale, nothing remains with him for all his trouble but a wretched lifeless thing with the down rubbed off and a pin thrust through its once all-living body. I object to the "honest folk-lorist," not because his versions are accurate, but because they are inaccurate, or rather incomplete. What lover of Celtic lore has not been filled with a sacred rage when he came upon some exquisite story, dear to him from childhood, written out in newspaper English and called science? To me, the ideal folk-lorist is Mr. Douglas Hyde. A tale told by him is quite as accurate as any "scientific" person's rendering; but in dialect and so forth he is careful to give us the most quaint, or poetical, or humorous version he has heard. I am inclined to think also that some concentration and elaboration of dialect is justified, if only it does not touch the fundamentals of the story. It is but a fair equivalent for the gesture and voice of the peasant tale-teller. Mr. Hyde has, I believe, done this in his marvellous Teig O'Kane, with the result that we have a story more full of the characteristics of true Irish folk-lore than all the pages given to Ireland from time to time in the *Folk-lore Journal*.[2]

W. B. YEATS.

Printed letter, *The Academy*, 11 October 1890 (320). *UP 1*. 173–5.

[1] The Revd Percy Watkins Myles (1849–91), born in Co. Cork, had been a contemporary of Standish James O'Grady at school and at Trinity College, Dublin. He was Canon of St. Stephen's Church, Ealing, from 1884 to his death and wrote and reviewed extensively for the *Academy*. In his review of *Ancient Cures* he had criticized Lady Wilde for her extreme philo-Celticism and for her carelessness in omitting the 'authorities, local touches, chronological and topographical details' that would make it possible to distinguish genuine legend from modern invention. He censured this inaccuracy as a fault general among Irish folklorists and recalled that WBY in *FFT* ('a charming little book . . . from the purely literary point of view') had jibed at 'the honest folk-lorist who tells what he has actually heard, not what he thinks . . . his audience would like to hear'. Myles added that such procedures were likely to result in Irish folklore becoming 'a literary sham instead of a scientific reality'. This brought up once again a question of deep concern to WBY (see p. 145), who hastened to make his views clear.

[2] WBY continued to wage a vigorous campaign in these years on behalf of Hyde's methods (see p. 186

To Katharine Tynan, 6 October [*1890*]

3 Blenheim R^d | Bedford Park | Chiswick | W
Oct 6

My dear Katey

I got a list from Keegan Paul a little while ago of people who by oversight had not paid their subscriptions for Oisin. I find that A Tynan c/o Miss K Tynan Whitehal Etc is set down for 5/3. Forgive me bothering you but Keegan Paul is dunning for the amount due. O'Leary has written to some & I to the others. Please let the 5/3 be sent by your brother—your brother is it not?[1]—to Keegan Paul Trench Troubner & Co Paternoster Square London EC & not to me.

I have been photograped by Hollyer as Henley wanted one for some collection of his contributer photos he is making.[2] The proofs are except in one case—he gives four positions—not very good. I will send you one as soon as I get any. I suppose you heard that Ernest Rhys is engaged to Miss Little—the pretty one—Miss Grace Little.[3]

I have retouched my Story John Sherman & am trying to get it published. Edward Garnett, author of the Paradox Club, is going to read it & see if it will suit the publisher he reads for *ie* Fisher Unwin.[4]

---

and *passim*). (In fact, Myles had picked out Hyde as one of the three promising collectors of Irish folklore and hoped that his efforts would produce 'a *corpus* of genuine and unadulterated Irish folk-lore'.) Alfred Nutt wrote to the *Academy* on 18 Oct 1890 in response to WBY's criticism of the *Folk-Lore Journal*, which he edited, pointing out that it was hardly fair 'to compare the Transactions of a learned society, which are in duty bound to collect and print much that is fragmentary and of value only to experts, with a volume intended for the public at large'. He also recalled that one of the stories in *FFT* ['The Story of Conn-eda', see p. 79, n. 7] was in fact taken from the pages of his *Journal*.

[1] Andrew Tynan, KT's brother, had the same name as her father—hence WBY's question. He was the eldest of the twelve Tynan children.

[2] Frederick Hollyer, 9 Pembroke Square, Kensington, London, took WBY's photograph at this time. He also photographed JO'L.

[3] Grace Little (1865–1929), youngest daughter of Joseph Bennett Little (see p. 168), kept house for her uncle in Kilrush; she was visiting her two elder sisters in London when she met Ernest Rhys at a party at the Yeatses in the summer of 1890. Their engagement followed a holiday in Wales and they were married in Hampstead early in January 1891.

[4] Edward Garnett (1868–1937), a publisher's reader of genius who recognized and helped foster the talents of Joseph Conrad, W. H. Hudson, Ford Madox Ford, John Galsworthy, and D. H. Lawrence as well as WBY, was the son of the Keeper of Printed Books at the British Museum. He left school at sixteen and in 1888 began to work for the publisher T. Fisher Unwin (1848–1935), where he soon moved from tying up parcels to reading MSS. Unwin, who had started as a publisher in 1882 when he bought the firm of Marshal Japp & Co., and had subsequently moved to Paternoster Square, was a reserved man who had the knack of finding able and decisive lieutenants such as Garnett and later his nephew Stanley Unwin; but owing to his parsimoniousness and authoritarian business methods, he had difficulty in holding on to his staff.

Garnett stayed with Unwin until 1898 and thereafter read for Heinemanns, Duckworths, and Jonathan Cape. His novel, *The Paradox Club* (1888), is a love story interspersed with lectures given by members of the club in as paradoxical a manner as possible on topics of current interest.

M[r] O Leary showed me a letter in which you speak of publishing a new book next year[5] & of selecting the contents when I am with you. How glad I shall be to see you & go through the poems with you! I hope to get away in six weeks or so but am now a prisoner with perpetual Blake—Blake—Blake. Ellis I hear made a very brilliant speach on the subject at the "odd volumes" dinner last Friday. Quaritch our publisher brought him down & fired him off as it were.[6] It was intended for an advertisement I suppose. He exhibited a huge chart of mine representing Blakes symbolic scheme in a kind of gineological tree.

O'Leary has been staying with us for a few days. He left yesterday however. How I envy him going over to Ireland. London is always horrible to me. The fact that I can study some things I like here better than elsewhere is the only redeaming fact. The mere presence of more cultivated people too is a gain of course but nothing in the world can make amends for the loss of green field & mountain slope. & for the tranquil hours of ones own country side. When one gets tired & so into bad spirits it seems an especial misfortune to live here—it is like having so many years blotted out of life.

Write soon. You see I have not waited for your letter & so have especial claim on you in the matter of a speedy reply. When you write always tell me about your self and what you are doing or thinking about. It is not so much news I want as to feel your personality through the ink & paper. Think of me in this matter as most exacting—you cannot tell me enough about yourself.

Yours always.
W B Yeats

PS—

When I get over to Ireland I also will try & get a new book of poetry into shape that is to say I will finish up the play I showed you & write some more ballads & so forth. I shall also have to do then, or a little later, this Unwin Essay on Ireland in the last century for the book of Adventurers.

[5] KT's *Ballads and Lyrics*, which appeared in 1891.

[6] The *Year-Boke of the Odd Volumes*, No. 3, 1890–91 (1892), records that on 3 Oct 1890 'Mr Edwin J. Ellis made a remarkable and interesting speech in relation to a rare work exhibited by the librarian, namely, a coloured copy of Blake's "Jerusalem".' In a letter of 6 Oct 1890 to the Miss Linnells (Private), Ellis left his own account of the speech he gave, at Quaritch's invitation, to the 'genial company of book-lovers who call themselves the "Odd Volumes"'. Asked by the chairman to 'say a few words to the company about his contribution to the literary curiosities of the evening', Quaritch said he had

brought "Blake's Jerusalem, & that with the chairman's permission his friend here" (indicating me) "would explain it to the society." Then the chairman,—a noted traveller, & a genial gentlemanly man, not, perhaps, over curious in poetry,—called upon me by the name of "Mr Blake", to expound my own volume. In doing so I quite forgot, as I warmed to the work, his comic mistake, & presently found myself stating that "Jerusalem", was one of seven great poems, of which the sixth,—"Vala" was about to be published next season for the first time, having lain, an un-sorted manuscript, in the possession of the Linnell family for a hundred years. (It is less than that, but not much less). The expression of consternation on the face of the chairman was unique. He drew the inference that I must be about a hundred & twenty. I suppose I hardly looked it at the moment.

[*On flap of envelope*]
There was a well intentioned but absurdly patronizing review of "Oisin" in
the "Weekly Register" a week ago.⁷

ALS Huntington, with envelope addressed to Clondalkin, postmark 'CHISWICK OC 7 90'. McHugh,
116–18; Wade, 157–8.

To W. E. Henley, [*early*] November [*1890*]

3 Blenheim R ᵈ | Bedford Park | Chiswick
Nov

Dear M ʳ Henley
    I enclose two short poems for Scots Observer if suitable. "The Old
Pensioner" is an almost verbatim record of words used by an old Irish man.¹
    I will send the photograph you asked for a while since in a few days. I had
one taken for the purpose about a month ago² but for some reason or other
the copies have not turned up yet. Cloudy weather may explain it perhaps.
                                                            Yours very truly
                                                            W B Yeats.

ALS Wellesley. Wade, 158–9.

    ⁷ An anonymous review of *Oisin* in the *Weekly Register*, 27 Sept. 1890 (407–8), noted that 'Mr Yeats's
range is as yet limited, but lovely; he moves in a narrow circle, but it is an elfin-ring.'

    ¹ 'The Old Pensioner', later 'The Lamentation of the Old Pensioner' (*VP*, 131–2), was published in
the *Scots Observer*, 15 Nov 1890. WBY got the words from AE, who described his meeting with an old
veteran of the Crimean War while walking with John Hughes on a mountain road (*Dublin Magazine*,
January 1938, 11):

He stepped before me and began to speak. I remember every word: 'Over those hills I wandered forty
years ago. Nobody but myself knows what happened under the thorn tree forty years ago. The fret is on
me. The fret is on me. God speaking out of his darkness says I have and I have not. I possess the heavens.
I do not possess the world. Abroad if you meet an Irishman he will give you the bit and the sup. But if you
come back to your own country after being away forty years it is not the potato and bit of salt you get, but
only "who's that ould fella." The fret is on me. The fret is on me!'

AE continues: 'The appearance and voice and tone impressed themselves on me with unforgetable
poignancy. It was sorrow shaped by its intensity to be like a work of art. I did not write the song, but
Yeats to whom I told the story made out of it his first version of the Old Pensioner.' WBY mentions this
incident in *The Celtic Twilight* (23) and *Myth* (13 ff.).
    The other poem WBY sent was 'The Lake Isle of Innisfree' (see pp. 120–1), published on 13 Dec 1890,
by which time the periodical had changed its name to the *National Observer*.
    ² See preceding letter.

To John O'Leary, [c. 8] November [1890]

3 Blenheim R d | Bedford Park | Chiswick
Nov

Dear M r O'Leary.

I put off writing to you day after day in hope that the photographs would turn up & I could send you one. They came last night. The delay was caused by the cloudy weather in all liklihood. An other reasen why I did not write was that I hoped to be able to get near enough to a wind up of this Blake job to say when I could get to Dublin—However the "Weekly Review" has come to take three days out of every week & so prolong indefinately the length of the Blake writing especially as a bad influensa cold has lost me some time.[1] Ellis is away too. I could I dare say go over now & finish the book in Dublin but then I should have to return presently, to go through it all with Ellis. I may however at a later stage of the work go over. I am working at the paraphrases & chapters in the seperate books & when they are done may not wait here to do the general account but go to Dublin for the purpose. I can not say definately until I see Ellis. Meanwhile I am a prisoner.

Your letter has come since I wrote the foregoing sentences.

Many thanks for enclosure which I will send on at once to Keegan Paul Trench & Co.[2] I have been unable to send you the money you lent for things have been a little unfavourable to us lately. I have got at last the first proof sheets of that book for Putnam & so may have some soon but when I do not know [*10 words cancelled*].

Ellis's father old Alexander Ellis F.R.S. died a few days ago, suddenly while Ellis was at Brighton. I do not know if it makes any change in Ellis's affairs, I have not seen him.[3] The papers you sent us about Swift McNeil & Balfour were amusing & not cheerful in some ways. Firstly McNeil talked

---

[1] The first number of *The Weekly Review of Magazines, Books and Newspapers, and Index of Periodical Literature*, price 1d, appeared on 11 Oct 1890. Published by a Mr Fleming, the review's editor was John Davidson of the Rhymers' Club. Many of the other Rhymers, including WBY, seem to have contributed to it; ECY's diary (MBY) for 1 Nov 1890 records that WBY received £2-0-0 from the *Weekly Review*.

In a letter of 18 Nov 1890 to JO'L (NLI), JBY reported that 'Willie has been out of sorts lately—he overworks himself—or rather over fatigues himself seeing people upon various paradoxical subjects . . .'.

[2] See p. 230. JO'L was still collecting late subscriptions for *Oisin*.

[3] Alexander John Ellis FRS (1814–90), the philologist and mathematician, whom WBY described (*Aut*, 159) as 'perhaps the last man in England to run the circle of the sciences without superficiality', had died on 28 Oct 1890. JBY wrote later in the month (18 Nov 1890 to JO'L, NLI) that 'Edwin Ellis I hear has come in for £120 a year by his father's death.' WBY had first met Ellis *père* as a boy under circumstances which SMY described in a letter to Hone of 8 Apr 1942 (Texas): 'When Willy & I were about 9 & 8 he had us to lunch with him at his house in Kensington—just himself & a grown up lunch with a stately parlour maid to wait on us—he got us to talk quite an easy thing to do, he was making mental notes of our language & accent—Willy & I then spoke as spoke our greatest friends the old coach man & the young stable boy at our grandfathers in Sligo.'

possible sense rediculously in the wrong place & secondly that other
Nationalist McSweeny (or some such name) who opposed him was, when he
half apologised for having been in jail saying he *"probably deserved it for
breaking the law"*, something worse than rediculous. However, all roads lead
to Rome I suppose even those of McNeil & McSweeny. I meen that they are
Nationalists of a kind & intend right things.[4] I was at the Littles last night
with Rhys. He & Miss Grace Little will be married in January. He has taken
a cottage in South Wales.[5]

So I hear that Miss Johnston has started or has something to do with a
vegetarian resteraunt in Dublin. Do you know where it is? I hear also that
she has broken off her engagement to Wright.[6] Some Theosophical dispute,
or such thing, at bottom of it.

By the by I have had to resign from inner section of Theosophical society
because of my first article on Lucifer in Weekly Review. They wanted me to
promise to criticise them never again in same fashion. I refused because I
looked upon request as undue claim to control right of individual to think as
best pleased him. I may join them again later on. We are of course good
friends & allies—except in this matter & except that I told them they were
turning a good philosophy into a bad religeon. This latter remark has not

---

[4] Arthur Balfour (1848–1930), who was Chief Secretary for Ireland in the Conservative Government
and who had incurred great unpopularity for his coercive measures, made a lightning tour of Donegal in
the autumn of 1890, meeting local deputations and discussing long-term economic projects to help this
sorely distressed area. On 6 Nov (as the *Freeman's Journal* reported on the 7th [7]) he reached Dungloe,
close to the Farcarragh Estate where the landlord was carrying out wide-scale evictions. While Balfour
was addressing the Dungloe deputation (which included James Sweeney, a local shopkeeper), J. G. Swift
MacNeill (1849–1926), the MP for Donegal South, made an entrance and denounced Balfour for
hypocrisy in promising amelioration while his police were abetting evictions. Balfour chided MacNeill
for bringing up topics that were 'out of place' and threatened to withdraw, taking with him his plans for
economic development. Alarmed at this, Sweeney intervened with a speech of artless self-revelation:

He was vitally interested in the people, and he knew that this year the destitution would be very great. It
would be altogether out of the power of the merchants to supply the people unless the people get some
employment or the means of earning a living. There was £9,000 due to him from these people, of which
he did not expect to get one-third, and, therefore, he appealed to Mr. Balfour to help them in this
matter. . . . He felt as strongly as anyone could feel, as an extreme Nationalist and as one who had put in
fifteen days in jail, and quite possibly he deserved it for not fulfilling the law.

He went on to point out that MacNeill was not the MP for that part of Donegal and that he considered his
intrusion 'a bit of impertinence'. Having begged Balfour not to throw aside the practical schemes that
had been discussed, Sweeney then handed him an address denouncing him in violent language for his
policy of coercion. To make the farce complete he later called on Balfour to retract his 'hasty
observations' on Swift MacNeill but Balfour declined to see him.

[5] After their marriage in January 1891, the Rhyses went to live for a year and a half in a quarryman's
cottage at Gaenan Hir near Llangollen in Wales.

[6] The restaurant started by Ada Johnston and others may not yet have been open, for in an
unpublished letter to Carrie Rea, dated by Denson early 1891 (NLI), AE writes: 'Claud Wright is in
London working hard there for Theosophy. But two other members here have opened (or will rather, in a
week or so) a vegetarian restaurant. . . .' HPB had advocated vegetarianism and for a while it was the
vogue among the theosophists in Dublin. For the Johnston–Wright engagement, see p. 212.

been well taken by some of the feircer sort. Relations have been getting strained for about a year—on these points.[7]

How does the biography go on? I am very glad to hear about the poems.[8]

Yours very truly
W B Yeats

ALS Berg. Wade, 159–60.

To Katharine Tynan, [c. *18*] *November* [*1890*]

3 Blenheim Rᵈ | Bedford Park | Chiswick.
Nov

My dear Katey

I have put off writing to you day after day in hope of being able to come to some decission as to when I would be able to leave here for Dublin. I find however that I cannot yet say. Blake work still keeps me. I must leave a great portion of the book in a complete state even if I do some of it in Dublin. I must get over to Dublin or Sligo or somewhere soon however, for I am struggling with the difficulties of semi-colapse. I have some thing wrong with my heart but not of an important nature. The docter says that I have been wearing myself out & has directed me to live more deliberately & leasurely. By no means an easy thing for any one of my temprement. There is nothing serious wrong with me, I beleive, so be not alarmed. I am somewhat better than I was a few days ago as it is.

Ellis is working away at the reproductions of Blakes drawings. The book will contain a great number. It will be a very big book in two volumes—the second containing the reproductions of the "prophetic books" with their illustrations, the first, our account of the philosophy.

---

[7] Since no issues of the short-lived *Weekly Review* have come to light we cannot know precisely what WBY wrote, but from *Aut* (181–2) and *Mem* (24) it seems that he had criticized *Lucifer* and the London theosophists for their tendency towards abstraction and, perhaps, had advocated some psychic experiments. Called on to resign by an official of the Theosophical Society, he had retorted that 'by teaching an abstract system without experiment or evidence you are making your pupils dogmatic and you are taking them out of life. There is scarcely one of your pupils who does not need, more than all else to enrich his soul, the common relations of life. They do not marry and nothing is so bad for them as asceticism.' The lecture on 'Theosophy and Modern Culture' which he gave to the Blavatsky Lodge in August 1890, as part of a course of discussions on 'Theosophy in Relation to the Problems of Modern Life' which commenced on 10 July at the New Hall, Avenue Road, with Annie Besant in the chair, was apparently WBY's last public participation in the Society.

[8] JO'L's letters to KT (Texas) reveal that although he had been depressed by his progress on his memoirs in the early summer, the arrival of detailed notes from his friend and fellow Fenian Thomas Clarke Luby (1822–1901) had put him into better spirits by the autumn, and he was now getting on with the book. Meanwhile publication of Ellen O'Leary's *Lays of Country, Home and Friends* (see p. 127) was being organized in a rather leisurely manner by Dr George Sigerson and C. H. Oldham.

What are you doing in the matter of verse. I had a little poem in the Scots Observer the other day & they have another coming shortly. I have also done one that I meen to send to the English Illustrated. All three are Irish & I think fairly good.[1] How does the life of the nun go on? I expect it will be a very picturesque little book. I am sure you will make it so unless you are specially unfortunate in the life it describes. This is a miserably short & empty letter but I must go to work at Blake. Send me a good long letter though I do not deserve it for letting so long go by without answering your last.

Yours always
W B Yeats

ALS Huntington. McHugh, 118–19; Wade, 161.

To Ernest Rhys, [*19 November 1890*]

3 Blenheim R d | Bedford Park | Chiswick

My dear Rhys

Please forward the enclosed to Symonds.[1] I have lost his address. It is a reply to a note of his asking me to take him to M d m Blavatskys.

Sorry not to have seen you at Rhymsters. We had a mournfully small meeting—none but Davidson Green Johnston & myself & spent the time plotting articles for that Weekly Review.[2]

It is nearly certain, I find, that I shall go to Dublin in a couple of weeks or

---

[1] The two poems in the *Scots Observer* were 'The Old Pensioner' (15 Nov 1890) and 'The Lake Isle of Innisfree' (13 Dec 1890, after it became the *National Observer*); see p. 232. Nothing by WBY appeared in the *English Illustrated*. The next poem he published was 'In the Firelight' (see p. 140), which is not particularly 'Irish', in the *Leisure Hour* in February 1891, followed by 'A Man who Dreamed of Fairyland' (*VP*, 126–8; later retitled 'The Man who Dreamed of Faeryland'), in the *National Observer*, 7 Feb 1891.

[1] Arthur William Symons (1865–1945), poet and critic, a fellow member of the Rhymers' Club, had already produced a book of verse, *Days and Nights* (1889) and *An Introduction to the Study of Browning* (1886). He and WBY, to whom he dedicated his most famous book, *The Symbolist Movement in Literature* (1899), were to share rooms in the winter of 1895–6.

[2] The Scottish poet John Davidson (1857–1909) is best known for his *Fleet Street Eclogues* (1893, 1896). There was an antipathy between him and WBY which is recorded in *Aut* (316–18). George Arthur Greene (1853–1921), poet, translator, and editor, was educated at TCD and was Professor of English Literature at Alexandra College, Dublin, 1877–80. He was subsequently examiner to the Board of Intermediate Education and for long vice-chairman of the Irish Literary Society, London. He acted as unofficial secretary to the Rhymers' Club and edited and contributed to the Club's two anthologies of poetry. Charles Johnston, on sick leave from the Indian Civil Service, had returned to London to take up journalism. On 18 Nov 1890 JBY wrote to JO'L (NLI), 'The Weekly Review from what I hear means to be very energetic—I fancy C Johnston half literary man, half man of action, will make a good journalist. . . .' Despite their efforts the *Weekly Review* folded in early December, as Rhys recounts (*Letters from Limbo* [1936], 90).

so. I am slightly knocked up & feel anxious for change. Blake & the usual journalistic mill grinding have proved a somewhat trying combination.

Yours very truly
W B Yeats

ALS Delaware, with envelope addressed to 1 Mount Vernon, Hampstead, postmark 'LONDON W. NO 19 90'.

To John O'Leary, [c. *4 December 1890*]

3 Blenheim R^d | Bedford Park | Chiswick

My dear M^r O Leary

I send that photograph. I hope you will let me have one of yours if you have one to spare. This Parnell business is most exciting. Hope he will hold on, as it is he has driven up into dust & vacuum no end of insincerities.[1] The whole matter of Irish politics will be the better of it.

Yours very truly
W B Yeats

ALS NLI.

To Katharine Tynan, 4 December 1890

3 Blenheim R^d | Bedford Park | Chiswick.
Dec 4th | 1890

My dear Katey

I send you that long promised photograph. I shall expect your opinion of it quite soon. It is I think good.

My health is rather better but the docter has told my father to bid me take great care from which I judge that I shall be a trifle invalided these coming weeks at least. I find myself soon tired & other wise lacking my old initiative.

I see much of Johnston & his wife. He has been in all ways greatly

---

[1] In December 1889, Captain O'Shea filed suit for divorce from his wife, Katharine, citing Parnell as co-respondent. At the trial in November 1890 the divorce was granted. Although Parnell was re-elected leader of the Irish Party, it soon became clear that his continued leadership would cost the nationalists their Liberal support and, with it, any prospect of Home Rule. On 1 Dec a debate on the leadership question began in Committee Room 15 of the House of Commons, while on 3 Dec the Standing Committee of the Irish Hierarchy called upon Irish Catholics to reject Parnell as their leader. These debates and developments were followed avidly in the Irish and British press until, on 6 Dec, the majority of the Irish Party, 45 in all, led by Justin McCarthy, withdrew, leaving Parnell with 27 followers. The struggle continued with increasing acrimony in Ireland over the coming months.

improved by his Indian work.[1] He lives close to M^{dm} Blavatsky with whome he is on as good terms as he is on bad with her followers who say that he is conceited beyond undurance etc. I too have had a quarrel with the followers & withdrawn from all active work in the society. I wrote some articles they objected to about "Lucifer".[2] M^{dm} Blavatsky told me some months ago that the taking off of my beard would bring me disaster in matter of health through loss of "magnatism" of [*for* or] for some other excentric reasen of the same kind. So see now what you & my other friends have got upon your souls.

Yours very truly
W B Yeats

ALS Huntington. McHugh, 119; Wade, 161–2.

[1] Charles Johnston had served 18 months in India as Assistant Magistrate and Collector, first in the Murshidabad District and later at Cuttach (now part of Orissa), until June 1890 when, suffering from haemoptysis, he was granted extended home leave on medical grounds. In April 1892 he was permitted to retire from the Indian Civil Service for reasons of ill health.

[2] HPB would have been particularly sensitive to an attack on *Lucifer* at this time, as the magazine was in financial difficulties and she had to appeal, in the November issue of *Theosophical Siftings*, for subscriptions to keep it afloat.

1891

To Herbert Horne,[1] [19 January 1891]

3 Blenheim R[d] | Bedford Park | Chiswick

My dear Horne

I find that next Thursday week would suit the Rhymers very well for next meeting & that they would be very glad to accept your suggested invitation to 20 Fitzroy St.[2] I enclose a list of names. If Thursday does not suit you I have no doubt that any other day about the same date would serve them equally.[3]

Yrs
W B Yeats

[At top of letter]
Walter Crane was at our last meeting & read verse. Have you his address? I have not but could get it.[4]

ALS Penn State; recorded as addressed to 20 Fitzroy Street, postmark '19 JA 91'. *Yeats Studies* I. 203.

[1] See p. 57.
[2] Horne shared a house at 20 Fitzroy Street, Bloomsbury, with the poet and critic Lionel Pigot Johnson (1867–1902; see Appendix), the poet and artist Selwyn Image (1849–1930), and the architect Arthur Mackmurdo (1851–1942). Johnson had moved into the house on coming down from Oxford in July 1890; WBY describes visiting him there in *Aut* (304–5) and *Mem* (34–5).
[3] On 5 Feb 1891 Lionel Johnson wrote (BL) from 20 Fitzroy Street to Campbell Dodgson (1867–1948), a close friend from Winchester and Oxford, 'We entertained the other night eighteen minor poets of our acquaintance: from Oscar Wilde to Walter Crane, with Arthur Symons and Willie Yeats between. They all inflicted their poems on each other, and were inimitably tedious, except dear Oscar.'
[4] WBY met Walter Crane (1845–1915), the celebrated illustrator, painter, and designer, 'very constantly' at William Morris's house, and he came to the Yeatses' 'at homes'. At this period Crane had temporarily ceased to be president of the Arts and Crafts Society and was preparing for a big exhibition of his work at the Fine Art Society's Gallery. His address was Beaumont Lodge, Shepherd's Bush, London.

To Louise Imogen Guiney,[1] *21 January* [*1891*]

3 Blenheim R d | Bedford Park | Chiswick.

Jan 21.

My dear Miss Guiney

I have been hoping each day to get over to Hampstead to see you [&] find out when & where I am to bring the "Iron 'Os".[2] Blake work has however greatly thickened of late. I will however look you up next week. I hope you are not really going as soon as you say. I saw M r Day[3] a while since & he fixed the inauspicious moment for early February.

Yours very truly

W B Yeats

ALS Holy Cross.

To John O'Leary, 21 January [*1891*]

3 Blenheim R d | Bedford Park | Chiswick | W

Jan 21

My dear M r O Leary

My only excuse for not having written before is that I have been deeply entangled in Blake & so kept putting off. I had finished about ten days ago

[1] See p. 222.

[2] After a trip to France in the autumn of 1890, Louise Guiney and her mother returned to London in early December and took lodgings in Well Walk, Hampstead. This address apparently had more than its Keatsian associations to commend it, for, as she reported to F. H. Day, 8 Dec 1890 (LC): 'A. J. [Mrs Guiney] says this morning, with a grin of satisfaction: "Willie Yeats lives at the other end of the world now, doesn't he?" Poor pote!' Notwithstanding Mrs Guiney's satisfaction WBY did manage to make the journey, for on 31 Jan 1891 her daughter told Day (LC) that 'Willie' had been there 'from 7 until 5 minutes ago'. Whether or not WBY travelled from South Acton to Hampstead Heath via the 'iron horse'—the Broad Street railway line—is not recorded. ('Bring' for standard English 'take' is a common Irish usage.)

[3] The American Fred Holland Day (1864–1933), aesthete, bibliophile, spiritualist, publisher, and photographer, was a distant relative of Louise Guiney. He had met WBY on his second trip to England, in the summer of 1890, when WBY had taken him to meetings of the Rhymers' Club and discussed theosophy and spiritualism with him—evidently at some length, for on 22 Sept 1890 Miss Guiney wrote to him (LC): 'I had to roar at W. Yeats' long, long visit, and think that the tea must be of superior quality, and run in rivers. You poor old martyr!'

Day was an enthusiastic collector of Keatsiana, and after a visit to Oberammergau went in November 1890 to Madrid where he purchased 31 letters written by Fanny Brawne to Keats's sister, Fanny Keats y de Llanos, between 1820 and 1824. He stopped off briefly in London on his way back to America with his literary prize.

In later years Day became increasingly concerned with art photography, and in the late '90s gained notoriety for his depictions of the Crucifixion with himself posing as Christ. But his attempts to found a new school of American photography failed, and in 1917, after a series of disappointments and disasters, he took to his bed at his home in Norwood, Massachusetts, and remained there until his death.

almost the whole of the general account when I discovered a mistake unimportant intself but deeply woven into the method of expression & had to start several chapters afresh. I have until this week not been in town for a long time hence I have not yet sold your books but will do so in the next few days.[1] I have been working on in a kind of desperation putting off every thing not even writing a single verse or article of any kind. I have Miss O Learys book Todhunters "Sicilian Idyll" a book for "National Observor" (late "Scots") a volume of verse by Miss Wynn a play of Ibsens & O'Donnell's poems all waiting leasure for treatment.[2] The first mentioned will come first. The reason why I am afraid of leaving Blake for a time is that Ellis is in a hurry & if I leave it may do some of my chapters himself & do them awry. Providence has stopped off his terrible activity for the present with twelve lectures for The University Extension.[3] He may awake any moment however & attack my provinces with horse foot & artillery. The boundery mark between his & mine being a not over well defined bourne— ⟨except in my mind.⟩ I had to put up a notice against trespassers a couple of weeks ago. Ellis is magnificent within his limits but threantens to overflow them ⟨with his wonderful industry⟩ & beyond them he is useless through lack of mystical knowledge. It is just as well that he does perhaps as I am always tending to stop & consider & reconsider when I should be going ahead. I give up all hope of fixing a date for my Dublin visit until the printer has got the first half of this book. But for the mistake I spoke of—I should have fixed one perhaps. Enough of Blake & more than enough.

Todhunter I think will review Miss O' Learys poems. A copy should be sent to the Academy & one to him (for which he will send subscription). I fear I cannot do anything with "National Observer" in the matter as Henley I think looks after all the verse himself. If you send him a copy I will write to him about it but cannot foretell result. He is an unpersuadable kind of man. Have all the subscribers got their copies. A week or so ago M[rs] Hancock of 125 Queen's gate, Kensington[4] had not. I sent, her 2/6 & address, to Oldham (I beleive) a long while ago.

---

[1] The Tipperary agitation (see p. 211) having cut deeply into his income, JO'L was evidently raising money by selling off his books to London dealers through WBY.

[2] Three of the books mentioned here—Ellen O'Leary's *Lays of Country, Home and Friends*, Frances Wynne's *Whisper!* and John Francis O'Donnell's *Poems*—were reviewed by WBY in the *Boston Pilot*, 18 Apr 1891 (*LNI*, 124–30), but he did not notice Todhunter's play, *A Sicilian Idyll* (see p. 217), again until later in 1891 when it was revived at the Vaudeville Theatre. Though he published nothing on Ibsen until 1894 (see p. 167), WBY's mind was on the playwright at this time, for he mentions him in his review of Douglas Hyde's *Beside the Fire* (see n. 7 below).

[3] Edwin Ellis delivered a course of lectures on the history of Italian art for the University Extension in North Hackney during the Lent term of 1891.

[4] See p. 64.

Jan 22nd

In the last "Spectator" you sent, you ask me to forward it to Miss Tulloch but forgot to give her address—You ask me also to send her your "Byron". Do you mean the Academy article or the life of him by Roden Noel.[5] I will send the Irish books to morrow.

It seems as though Parnells chances had greatly improved these latter weeks. His last two speaches were wonderfully good. I wish I was over in Ireland to see & hear how things are going. The Hartlepool victory should help him by showing that his action has not injured the cause over here as much as people say. My father is bitterly opposed to Parnell on the ground chiefly now, of his attacks on his followers. To me, if all other reasens were absent, it would seem plain that a combination of priests with the "sullivan gang" is not likely to have on its side in political matters divine justice.[6] The whole business will do this good any way. The Liberals will have now to pass a good measure if any measure at all—at least so I read the matter.

Daily News this morning has a long article on Hydes book which I have not yet seen. I shall ask Scots Observer for it.[7]

Yours very sncely
W B Yeats.

[5] Jessie Tulloch (1845–1913), a close friend of the O'Learys, lived in Tipperary. The *Spectator* was full of comment on the Parnell crisis at this period. JO'L had reviewed Roden Noel's *Lord Byron*, a volume in Walter Scott's Great Writer series, in the *Academy*, 6 Sept 1890 (190–1), finding the book unnecessary though reasonably good, but criticizing its chaotic organisation and the 'occasionally incorrect and very often affected' style. An exchange of letters between Noel and JO'L followed in the next two numbers of the *Academy*.

[6] After the defeat of the Parnellite candidate at the Kilkenny North by-election on 22 Dec 1890, Parnell threw himself into vigorous campaigning throughout Ireland; two rousing speeches he made at Limerick on 10 and 11 Jan 1891 were widely reported in the Irish and British press. The Hartlepool by-election (declared on the day that this letter was written), which the Pro-Home Rule Liberal candidate won from the Unionists by 298 votes, was heartening, since in the previous English by-election, at Bassetlaw on 15 Dec 1890, the Conservatives had increased their majority.

JBY had been a supporter of Isaac Butt (see p. 163), whom Parnell had challenged for the leadership of the Irish Party in the late 1870s, and had consequently always been suspicious of Parnell. 'The Irish took to hatred when they deserted the statesman Isaac Butt for the politician Parnell,' he wrote in a letter of 20 Sept 1915; 'Parnell was not a great man' (*JBYL*, 210), The 'Sullivan gang'—T. D. Sullivan, A. M. Sullivan, Tim Healy, and John Barry, all related by marriage—were the most outspoken of Parnell's opponents. The Sullivan brothers controlled the *Nation*, which now allied itself with the Catholic hierarchy to denounce Parnell.

[7] On 22 Jan 1891 the *Daily News* made the Introduction to Douglas Hyde's *Beside the Fire* the occasion of a leader of 20 column inches. It quoted Hyde's view that the national schoolteachers, the priests, and Irish politicians had destroyed the Irish language and with it Irish culture. Like Hyde, the newspaper deplored the loss of cultivation and imagination that the disappearance of the language entailed, and pointed to the indifference of the Irish people about this loss as 'the moral Dr Hyde deduces from his popular tales, which he gives in English and Irish, and which are capital reading. We trust that his warning, though late, is not given in vain, and that a whole literature will not be allowed to die, or to become a fossil in the studies of the Dryasdusts.'

WBY reviewed *Beside the Fire*, under the heading 'Irish Folk Tales', for the *National Observer* (as the *Scots Observer* was now called) on 28 Feb 1891 (*UP* I. 186–90); the review was reprinted as 'The Four Winds of Desire' in *The Celtic Twilight*.

Am in much better health than I was—fortunately for Blake book. My heart troubles me now but seldom.

[*At top of first page*]

Called twice on Rev Mr Miles[8] but found no-one in once & found him away from home for his health the next time.

ALS Private. Wade, 162–4.

To J. N. Dunn, 25 January [1891]

3 Blenheim R^d | Bedford Park | Chiswick.
Jan 25th

Dear Mr Dunn

I have received Hydes book all right.[1] I return proof of poem.[2] You will find on looking the matter up that you owe me for two poems "the lake island" & "*the old pensioner*" which was sent with the "island" & *published on Nov 15*th.[3]

Yours vy truly
W B Yeats

ALS Texas.

To J. N. Dunn, [before 28 February 1891]

3 Blenheim R^d | Bedford Park | Chiswick

Dear Mr Dunn,

Many thanks for "Gypsy Sorcery"[1] which I shall set to work on as soon as I can get through a couple of articles that cry out for accomplishment. I will return "Beside the fire" as soon as I correct the proof of article. I may want the book for reference in the matter of gaelic word or some such matter.

The delay over "Beside the fire" review was caused by work on a big book on Blake which a friend & myself are getting ready for the press. It took

---

[8] The Revd Percy Watkins Myles (see p. 229).

[1] *Beside the Fire* (see preceding letter).
[2] 'A Man who Dreamed of Fairyland' (see p. 236).
[3] See p. 232. The underlinings were probably made by Dunn, not WBY.

[1] Charles Godfrey Leland's *Gypsy Sorcery and Fortune Telling* (1891), an account of gipsy charms, shamanism, superstitions and witchcraft, drawn mainly from eastern European gipsy lore, was reviewed anonymously by WBY in the *National Observer*, 18 Apr 1891 (568–9). WBY relished the folklore in the book but disputed Leland's scientific attempts to explain magic and prevision.

some time to pick off the mystical seaweeds even after I had emerged from the work itself—about three days of mental emptyness if I remember rightly.

Yours very truly
W B Yeats

ALS Bucknell.

To Katharine Tynan, 5 March [1891]

3 Blenheim R^d | Bedford Park | Chiswick
March 5

My dear Katey—

I am again greatly behind hand in this matter of letter writing. But do not think that you are out of my thoughts because I let the weeks go by without a letter. I am one of those unhappy people for whom between Act & Deed lies ever the terrible gulf of dreams. I sit down to write & go off into a brown study instead. At least if circumstance offer me the slightest excuse. My excuse these times has been that Blake still hangs in the ballance it always seems possible that a month, say, might finish it & yet now one thing now another brings delay. When I begin writing to you—I have so started several times—I stop & say "what shall I say about times & dates? " "when may I hope to be in Ireland?" & thereon I am down into the gulf, & the letter is put off until I have more exact information. Probably your London visit will come before my Irish one. One thing that delays us is that I no longer go to Edwin Ellis's house to work through the MSS with him but have to wait until we can meet here, or in the Museum, or at the publishers. Mrs Ellis got the curious delusion that I had some mesmeric powers over her that made her ill. The sight of me made her grow white with terror. She has now got over the delusion & wants me to go there again but I am afraid of its returning & so stay away.[1] She is so horribly histerical & has had her head turned by a too constant & wholly unthinking sense of the unseen universe & of its unknown powers.

Yesterday I got a paper with M^{iss} Kavanaghs death announced in it. It was a great shock to us all. Lolly had some knowledge of how very ill she was

---

[1] WBY's insistence that Ellis should have free time for the work on Blake led to difficulties with Ellis's 'half-mad foreign wife' (see p. 225, n. 3):

Sometimes I was turned out and weeks would pass and Ellis and I would have to meet at some Aerated Bread Shop near the British Museum. The longest expulsion followed a sudden conviction of his wife's that I had thrown a spell upon her—she had mistaken for the making of symbols a habit I have of beating time to some verse running in my head. And then I would be forgiven and fed with very rich cake covered with almond paste that neither pleased my palate nor suited my digestion. (*Mem*, 29–30)

but I had none. The last I heard was that she was better. I had had no expectation what ever that we would lose her so soon. Only the other day I reread her "St Michans Churchyard" & thought how charming it was.[2] Every thing she did was so like her self—it had the same quiet & gentle sincerity. It was so entirely untouched by the restless ambition that makes writers untrue to themselves. She was essentially it seems to me what people meen by the phrase "a beautiful soul". To you & me & all of us she is in every way a loss. Some of the pleasure of writing is gone in that we cannot send her anymore anything that we write. How our old circle is broken up— first Miss O Leary & now Miss Kavanagh. I think of sending some notice of her to the Pilot unless you wish to do so. I will write one tomorrow, & send it unless you tell me that you have intentions of so doing in which case my account can go elsewhere.[3] So please let me know at once. Miss Kavanaghs death is in itself much sadder than Miss O Learys. Miss O'Leary had had a full & not wholly short life while Miss Kavanagh dies with all her plans & projects uncompleted all her promise unfulfilled. I feel sure that we take up our half done labours in other lives & carry them to conclusion. If it were not so the best of lives were not worth living & the universe would have no order & purpose. I think you have some such thought in one of your poems.[4]

I think I shall be able to get "John Sherman" published. I am going next week to offer it to Hineman & if he does not take it I can I think get it taken by Fisher Unwin for his "Pseudonimous Library".[5] Edward Garnett Unwins reader is quite enthusiastic about it. If I can get "Sherman" & my play "The Countess Kathleen" together with "Blake" published this year I shall be well in evidence. The two volumes of collected "Irish Stories" I edited for Putnam are printed & may be published any day now. If Sherman gets printed I shall be greatly pleased. There is more of myself in it than in

---

[2] Rose Kavanagh died of consumption on 26 Feb 1891. In the *Boston Pilot* (see n. 3 below) WBY described her poem 'St. Michan's Churchyard' (published in *PBYI*; see p. 65) as one of her most finished pieces: 'Like most of the best Irish verse of recent years it is meditative and sympathetic, rather than stirring and energetic: the trumpet has given way to the viol and the flute. It is easy to be unjust to such poetry, but very hard to write it. It springs straight out of the nature from some well-spring of refinement and gentleness. It makes half the pathos of literary history.'

[3] WBY's article 'Rose Kavanagh' (*LNI*, 118–24) appeared in the *Boston Pilot*, 11 Apr 1891. KT contributed two poems about her to the *Irish Monthly*: 'Rose Kavanagh' (dated '2 March 1891') in April 1891, and 'To Rose in Heaven' (dated '15 April 1891') in the May issue (the latter reprinted in the *Boston Pilot*, 4 July 1891). Both poems were included in KT's *Ballads and Lyrics*.

[4] Cf the penultimate and last stanzas of 'In a Cathedral' as printed in the *Century Guild Hobby Horse* (see p. 149).

[5] William Heinemann (1863–1920) had joined the publishing firm of Trübner in 1879, but set up for himself in January 1890 at 21 Bedford Street, Strand. He had enjoyed a successful first year, his list including *The Bondman* by Hall Caine, *Hauntings* by Vernon Lee, and—the success of the season— Whistler's *The Gentle Art of Making Enemies*, and he was on the lookout for promising new authors. He also tried to refloat *East and West*, to which both KT and WBY had contributed (see p. 179, n. 9), but the new series ran for only two issues.

any thing I have done. I dont imagine it will please many people but some
few it may please with some kind of permiment pleasure. Except for the
wish to make a little money I have no desire to get that kind of passing regard
a book wins from the many. To please the folk of few books is ones great aim.
By being Irish I think one has a better chance of it—over here there is so
much to read & think about that the most a writer can usually hope for is that
kind of unprosperous prosperity that comes from writing books that lie amid
a half dozen of others on a drawing room table for a week.

You have not told me any thing about your life of a nun for a long time—
or indeed for that matter any thing about any thing. You have the bad habit
of keeping to the letter of the law in the matter of correspondence. Once
when you did not write to me for a great while—I wrote without waiting for
your letter. You however have a most unIrish love for law & order in this
matter.

Rhys is up in London again with his wife. We go to the Littles tonight to
meet them. He seems much rejoiced at the change in his prospects & grows
eloquent in person as before by letter over the general delightfulness of his
life in Wales.[6]

I hear Miss Mulholland is in London. I called on her last week but she
was out. The Meynells has expressed a wish to have her portrait in "Merry
England" and my father will make a sketch if we can get her to sit.[7]

When do you come to London. My own dislike for the place is certainly
not on the decrease. When Blake is done I shall go to Ireland & find my way
down to the West & stay there as long as possible. I have much to write &
much to think of—& can do it best down there.

Yours very truly
W B Yeats.

ALS Huntington, with envelope addressed to Clondalkin, postmark 'CHISWICK MR 6 91'.
McHugh, 120–2; Wade, 164–6.

Fisher Unwin's Pseudonym Library, in which *John Sherman and Dhoya*, by 'Ganconagh', appeared as
No. 10 in November 1891, was a cheap paperbound series which published work by 'Vernon Lee',
'Ralph Iron', 'Ouida', 'John Oliver Hobbes', and 'Lance Falconer'.

[6] In his autobiography, *Everyman Remembers* (1931), Rhys recalls this period: 'When one of its
children who has been living in exile crosses the Welsh border on returning to the *Hen Wlad* or Old
Country, it is as if some change of blood happens to him' (203).

[7] No portrait of Rosa Mulholland appeared in *Merry England*. JBY's only contribution to the
magazine at this time was a sketch of KT herself.

To Katharine Tynan, [late March 1891]

3 Blenheim R^d | Bedford Park | Chiswick | W.

My dear Katey

I enclose this with "Irish Tales". Please tell me what you think of the dedicatory lines to the Irish abroad.[1] I was very—very—sorry to hear that you were ill but hope that you are well now as I judge you to be from a review of Hydes book by you that O Leary sent me. A very good review better in some ways than my "National Review" one, & done I feel sure with much more ease & speed.[2] But please tell me whether you were seriously ill. This is but poor sympathy coming so late in the day but I kept waiting on for this book of Irish tales—due three weeks ago.

My "John Sherman" has at last been taken by Fisher Unwin for his Pseudonm Library. I am to get a royalty but not until it gets into its second thousand if it ever do so.

Blake "proofs" are coming in—2nd vol proofs—the MSS for the 1st vol is not quite finished. Printers will probably start at it next week—start at 1st pages before last are finished in MSS. The Illustrations look well in the proofs.

Did O'Leary show you a poem of mine in National Observer called "A man who dreamed of Fairy land"? Henley liked it very much & some friends here say it is my best that is to say Arthur Symonds and Edward Garnett do.

Yours very sincerely
W B Yeats

Your Cruikshank Sketch book if a genuine 1st edition—there was a reprint 10 years ago—is worth about 30/-.[3] I thought to see Quaritch about it months ago but have never done so—not having spoken to him since I lunched with him at the start of the bargain. Nothing has turned up to bring me to him & when something or other has sent me in to his shop he was not there.

ALS Huntington. McHugh, 122–3; Wade, 166–7.

[1] The poem printed as the dedication to *RIT* was subsequently entitled 'The Dedication to a Book of Stories selected from the Irish Novelists' (*VP*, 129–30); a much revised version appeared in the *Irish Statesman*, 8 Nov 1924, where WBY described it as 'a sheaf of wild oats'.

[2] KT reviewed Hyde's *Beside the Fire* in the Dublin *Evening Telegraph*, 20 Mar 1891; a further review by her appeared in *PSJ*, 30 June 1891. WBY's '*National Review*' is a slip for '*National Observer*'.

[3] George Cruikshank's four-part *Scraps and Sketches* was first published in London by the artist himself from 1828 to 1832. The value of KT's copy would have depended on the four parts being complete, and on whether it was in the plain, coloured, or large-paper India version. The book was reprinted twice in 1882.

To John O'Leary, [after 18 April 1891]

3 Blenheim R ᵈ | Bedford Park | Chiswick. | W

Dear Mʳ O Leary

The "proofs" of the Blake book are coming in slowly we are printing bit by bit—writing & printing going on at once. The illustrations look right well. I have reviewed "the Lays of Country Home & friends" for the Pilot & will try & do so for National Observer next week.[1] I am just now writing the preliminary memoir for the first volume of Blake—Ellis wants that at once.[2]

Could you send me a card with Ash Kings address that I may get Putnam to send him a review copy of "Irish Tales" also please tell me if Miss Gonne has returned to Dublin? I did not write to her because I wanted to get "Irish Tales" to give her a copy & do not like to chance sending it to that French address which by the by I could not read with any certainty.[3] Did you like the introduction to Irish Tales?

Putnam seems inclined to act on any suggestions as to Irish papers & Irish reviewers. Is Coffey noticing books anywhere? The book ought to make a good text for any-body who wants to do an article on Irish things in general—& Kings articles in Freeman are general enough God knows.[4] I shall have prospectus's of the Blake in a day or so & shall send you one or two. They give a specimen illustration that may interest you.[5] My story "John Sherman" has been taken by Unwin for the Pseudonim Series but dont tell any one the name of it as Unwin I beleive makes rather a point of the Pseudonimous nature of the books.[6]

How are you getting on with the Memoir?[7]

Yours very Snly
W B Yeats

ALS NLI. Wade, 167–8.

[1] See p. 241, n. 2, and p. 250, n. 4.

[2] Ellis had written the first memoir and sent it to WBY who added to it and considerably revised it. His version was, in turn, heavily revised by Ellis and only part of WBY's work survived intact in the final text, which was still being drafted in July 1891.

[3] Richard Ashe King was still living in Blackrock, Dublin (see p. 13). MG, who on 11 Jan 1890 had (unbeknownst to WBY) given birth to a son, George, by Lucien Millevoye, did not arrive in Dublin until July. She had just moved house in Paris from an apartment at 61 Avenue Wagram to a larger one in the Avenue de la Grande Armée.

[4] Although George Coffey did occasional reviews for the Dublin press, and had reviewed *Oisin* (see p. 144), he seems not to have noticed *RIT*. Richard Ashe King may have been responsible for a weekly series, 'In Bookland. Our Literary Letter', which began, over the pseudonym 'Fergus', in the Saturday issue of the *Freeman's Journal* on 21 Mar 1891. Each article began with discursive observations on Irish literature and the Irish character, followed by notices of a variety of books, but *RIT* was not reviewed there, nor in *Truth*, the London weekly of which Ashe King was literary editor (see p. 13, n. 3).

[5] No copy has been traced of Quaritch's prospectus for *The Works of William Blake*.

[6] Despite this warning to JO'L, WBY himself later went to some lengths to reveal his identity as the author of *John Sherman and Dhoya*.

[7] i.e., his *Recollections of Fenians and Fenianism*.

To Richard Le Gallienne,[1] *1 May* [*1891*]

3 Blenheim R ᵈ | Bedford Park | Chiswick
May 1ˢᵗ

Dear Mʳ Le Galleone

I met you once at Dʳ Todhunters as you will perhaps remember & have long known & admired your poetry & wished to renew ⟨my⟩ our slight acquaintanceship.

My sister & myself—my father & other sister are away—are "At Home" on Monday evening after 8 ᵒᶜ & would be very glad if you would come—not dress clothes. I expect Dʳ Todhunter & some other friends of yours.

Yours very truly
W B Yeats.

ALS Texas.

To [*? T. Wathen*] *Thompson,*[1] [*18 June 1891*]

3 Blenheim Road | Bedford Park.
Thursday

Dear Mr. Thompson: I enclose a ticket for two seats at the performance of Dr Todhunter's play tomorrow at the Vaudeville at 2.30.[2] It is well worth seeing . . .

Extract from ALS (1 p.), 8vo, John Wilson catalogue no. 3; since sold.

To John O'Leary, [*after 19 June 1891*]

3 Blenheim Road

Dear Mr. O'Leary,

I did not answer before because I knew I should have to write almost at once again if I took your hint about the postcard, as I want you to address the

---

[1] The poet, essayist, and later novelist Richard Thomas Le Gallienne (1866–1947), who had come to London from Liverpool in 1890, was subsequently a member of the Rhymers' Club. As reviewer for the *Star* and reader for Elkin Mathews and John Lane, who had published his first book at the Bodley Head (see p. 191), Le Gallienne was able to encourage many of the young writers of the period, of whom he gave an account in his *The Romantic '90s* (1925).

[1] Possibly T. Wathen Thompson, of 37 The Avenue, Bedford Park.

[2] Todhunter's *The Poison Flower*, a poetic drama based on Hawthorne's *Rappaccini's Daughter*, was produced, with his *Sicilian Idyll*, in matinée performances at the Vaudeville Theatre, 15–19 June 1891. WBY was helping to fill the theatre by distributing complimentary tickets.

enclosed to Rolleston whose Irish address I have mislaid.[1] I could not, however, write before to-day as I have been very busy. Todhunter has had a play on and I have had to review it twice and write only on chance of reviews being printed too;[2] to see it twice and lose time helping to hunt up people to fill empty places as well as writing hard at Blake. This last because I want to be in Ireland by the middle of July and must see a lot for the printers done before then. I am going to stay with Charles Johnston who will have Ballykilbeg to himself for a couple of weeks[3] and shall then endeavour to spend a week in Dublin if the Tynans will take me in. I can only get away for a very short time pending the completion of Blake and am afraid of facing Dublin distractions before I give a little while to country placidity. I see by your note that you hope to be in London. I hope your visit here will not coincide by any ill chance with mine to Dublin. I am rather in a difficulty about Miss O'Leary's poems. I find it almost impossible to review it for so ultra-Tory a paper as the *National Observer*; when I do an article I intend for *Providence Journal* I shall try again. In any case I shall again remind Todhunter about *Academy* (I did so remind him once but he has been busy with his plays); if he is not going to do it I can try and get it from Cotton and can write review either before leaving this three weeks hence or when in Ballykilbeg. . . . When I consented to Henley's suggestion that I should review it for him I had no idea how difficult it would be.[4] If I were a Tory it would be easy enough, or if I could descend to writing as a Tory who did not let his politics quite kill literary sympathies. A few saving clauses would make all well, but they are just what I cannot put in.

The article on Blake you sent me has proved most useful. When did it appear? . . . I cannot find where I put P.B. notice but will ransack my pockets and table for it, in a day or two.[5] *I promise.*

My novel has gone to press but does not come out until September. I have sent in with it, to be put in the same volume, a short tale of ancient Irish

---

[1] T. W. Rolleston had recently taken a house in London, at Spencer Hill, Wimbledon, but was probably spending the summer holidays in Ireland, at Glasshouse, Shinroane, nr. Roscrea, Co. Tipperary. WBY may have been sending him a copy of *RIT*, which Rolleston reviewed in the *Academy*, 10 Oct 1891 (306–7).

[2] See preceding letter. WBY reviewed Todhunter's *The Poison Flower* in *PSJ*, 26 July 1891, and in the *Boston Pilot*, 1 Aug 1891 (*LNI*, 213–22, 132–7). He further noticed it, with *A Sicilian Idyll*, in *United Ireland*, 11 July 1891 (*UP* I. 190–4).

[3] See p. 101, n. 21.

[4] Although Henley had in the event proved less than 'unpersuadable' (see p. 241), no review of *Lays of Country, Home and Friends* appeared in the *National Observer*, nor did WBY review the book for *PSJ*. J. S. Cotton was editor of the *Academy*, where Todhunter reviewed the book on 25 July 1891 (70), finding that the 'unpretending little volume' charmed 'by its absolute simplicity and absence of literary artifice'. It was 'racy of the soil' and demonstrated a 'stern reticence of feeling', though he occasionally wished that Miss O'Leary had 'studied the art of versification a little more closely'.

[5] The Blake article is unidentified. The 'P.B. notice' was probably WBY's *Boston Pilot* review of *Lays of Country, Home and Friends*, which had appeared on 18 Apr 1891 (see p. 241, n. 2).

legendary days and called the book *John Sherman and The Midnight Ride.* The second part of the title refers to second story.[6] My pseudonym is Ganconagh, the name of an Irish spirit. I am very glad to hear news about the progress of your book and the course of events in Tipperary.[7]

Yours very sincerely
W B Yeats

From a typed copy, reproduced in Wade, 168–9.

To John Lane,[1] [21 June 1891]

3 Blenheim Road | Bedford Park. | Chiswick | W

Dear M[r] Lane.

Le Galleone tells me that you are ready to have the Rhymers next Friday at 8[oc].[2] It will perhaps be better for me to send them the usual postcards to keep it in their memories. I will send them off, unless I hear from you to the contrary, on Tuesday morning.

Thanking you in the name of the Rhymers

I remain
Yours
W B Yeats

Please excuse postcard but it is Sunday & I have no stamps.

APS Westfield, addressed to 37 Southwick Street, Hyde Park, postmark 'CHISWICK JU 22 91'.

To John Lane, [23 June 1891]

[Chiswick]

I have written to the regular "Rhymers" who are now in London—Green, Radford, Symond, John Davidson, Le Galleone, Lionel Johnston,

[6] The title of 'The Midnight Ride' (or 'Rider') was later changed to *Dhoya.*

[7] See above, p. 211. The Tenants' Defence Association was finding New Tipperary to be financially disastrous and the whole project showed signs of collapsing; 'there has never been,' wrote JO'L in a letter to the *Freeman's Journal,* 26 June 1891 (2), 'in the whole history of Irish agitation, anything so reckless, ruthless and utterly ruinous as this Tipperary affair from beginning to end.'

[1] See p. 191. Along with his publishing activities, at first as partner with Elkin Mathews in the Bodley Head and later as sole proprietor of that imprint, Lane took a keen interest in contemporary art and literature. He founded the *Yellow Book* in 1894, becoming its art editor from vol. IV. When Lane and Mathews split up in 1894 there was some controversy in the Rhymers' Club over which publisher members should use.

[2] Lane's invitation to the Rhymers to meet at his house in Hyde Park may have been at the urging of Le Gallienne, reader at the Bodley Head, in order to plan the first *Book of the Rhymers' Club,* published by Lane and Mathews in February 1892.

E Garnet, Dowson, Todhunter & E Ellis but do not expect all will turn up.[1]
They seldom do.

Yours very truly
W B Yeats

APS Westfield, addressed to 37 Southwick street, Hyde Park, postmark 'CHISWICK JU 23 91'.

To Katharine Tynan, [late June 1891]

3 Blenheim Road | Bedford Park | Chiswick | W.
My dear Katey

I send you the Henley notes. I tell about all that I know but fear that but little of it will do for your purpose. Some of it would hardly do for the public press. I trust your discretion in the matter. The wild & reckless early life of the Stevenson Henley Circle for instance would hardly do for public press. I forgot, I see, to mention that Henley is a burly man with a beard & a restless way of sitting & moving—somewhat like W Morris in this & that one of his good points is his sympathy with young writers.[1]

Last week Todhunters play was acted. I saw it twice, helped hunt up people to fill vacant seats & reviewed it twice. I also wrote a very important essay called "The Necessity of Symbolism" for the Book on Blake & went through it with Ellis & made suggested alterations.[2] The visit to Ireland makes some hurry needed in order to leave the printers enough to go on with. This was the reason of my delay about the Henley notes. Take Oscar Wilde for another of your subjects. He is *actual* now because of his just published "Intentions" (a wonderful book) & his enlarged editon of "Dorian Grey". Describe the serious literary side of his life—his fairy tale book "A Happy Prince" & these last books & mention his poems slightly though not slightingly—Let Nettleship stand over until autumn when the book of designs will be out or until I can let you see "proofs" if such things come my way. It is not decided quite who will edit it but I may do so in all liklihood. His book on Browning should be known to you also.[3] "The

---

[1] See preceding postcard.

[1] KT was planning a series of articles on contemporary writers whose reputations were 'actual'. Her article on Henley, which borrowed much from WBY's notes, appeared in the New York *Sun* on 11 July 1891 and in the Dublin *Evening Telegraph* 8 Sept. She also wrote on Henley's friend James Barrie in the New York *Sun*, 15 July 1891, and the *Weekly Irish Times*, 8 Jan 1892. She seems not to have taken up WBY's suggestion in the following paragraph that she write about Wilde and Nettleship.

[2] 'The Necessity of Symbolism' became the opening section of 'The Symbolic System', the third part of vol. 1 of *The Works of William Blake* (235–45).

[3] Oscar Wilde's *Intentions* was published in London in May 1891 by Osgood, McIlvaine, and in October by Heinemann and Wolcott Balestier, of Leipzig, in their paperback English Library. *The*

Rhymers Club" will publish a book of verse almost at once. You might take it as a subject of one article. It will give you a chance of saying much about the younger writers—Le Galleone, A Symonds, ⟨ myself ⟩ & so forth.[4] I think Blake should justify you in giving me a notice ⟨ to myself ⟩—if it comes in time. In any case "John Sherman & the Midnight Rider by Ganconagh" will serve if you care for it. It comes out in September. The incognito will be pretty transparent because of a poem which is in both my book & in "The Midnight Rider".[5] You have not told me what you think of the introduction to Irish Tales. Please do so. Favourable or the reverse I want your opinion. Have you seen a pretty little book called "A Light Load" by "Dollie Radford"? It seems to me pleasent & is the work of the wife of one of our "Rhymers". I have heard several people praise "Whispers" by the by— "Light Load" & "Whispers" have the same kind of charm, & I hear them mentioned together. Mrs Radford gave me her book yesterday here is a stanza

> "The love within my heart for thee
>   Before the world was had its birth,
> It is the part God gives to me
>   Of the great wisdom of the earth"

Are they not fine? They have a largeness of thought & feeling above mere prettiness. It is the best stanza in the book I think but still there are other good things. All trifling more or less like "Whispers" but equally genuine and more thoughtful.[6] When does your new poem-book come? May I see the selection you have made for it when I get to Dublin. I hope you will be able to put me up for a few days on my way back from Johnston's. I am taking this chance of a short holiday as Blake seems stretching out beyond all

Picture of Dorian Gray, published by Ward, Lock in April 1891, had originally appeared in *Lippincott's Monthly Magazine* in July 1890; for the book version Wilde added a Preface and six chapters. *The Happy Prince* was published in 1888. WBY praised all three works in *United Ireland*, 26 Sept 1891 (*UP* 1. 202–5).

  At this time J. T. Nettleship was thinking of publishing a dozen of his pencil designs after the manner of Blake (see *The Artist and Journal of Home Culture*, XII, no. 140 [213]). The book did not appear and the drawings are now at the University of Reading. Nettleship's *Essays on Robert Browning's Poetry* (1868) had recently been incorporated in a book twice the length of the original, *Robert Browning: Essays and Thoughts* (1890).

  [4] *The Book of the Rhymers' Club* (see p. 251, n. 2), which KT was to review in the *Irish Daily Independent* on its publication the following year.

  [5] The poem 'Girl's Song' (see p. 144), which had been included in *Oisin*, appeared, untitled, in the second section of *Dhoya* ('The Midnight Rider').

  [6] Mrs Ernest (Dollie) Radford, née Maitland (b. 1858), wife of the secretary of the Rhymers' Club, produced several volumes of verse of which *A Light Load* (1891) was the first. The quatrain quoted is from the poem 'Out on the Moor' and also served as the epigraph of the volume (cf. WBY's 'Before the World was Made' [*VP*, 531–2]: 'I'd have him love the thing that was / Before the world was made'). In his review of *Whisper!* (see p. 241), WBY had found Frances Wynne's verses 'pretty, skilful and rather trivial'.

beleif & so making all waiting to get off after it is done useless. I am feeling the want of new scenes & old faces. I have not been out of London for longer than a few days at Oxford & two days with Edward Garnett in Surrey[7] since I came last from Ireland & feel my imagination rather over powered by continual London din. When Blake is done I shall get clear away however for a longer stay I hope. I must write more poetry & cannot do it here where everything puts ones nerves on edge. Perhaps my Ballikilbeg visit may help my imagination to work again. I want to get to Dublin not merely to see you & other good friends but to have some talk with knowledgable folk about my essay on Ireland in the Eighteenth Century for Unwins Adventure Series.[8] When will I get a copy of your life of the nun?[9] Please send me as soon as possible the full title for mention in the Pilot. They paid me for last two articles so I want to write for them again. You talk of *trying* to get me a copy. Now do manage it—I have surely earned it by never failing to let you have copies of my books & may beside be useful to you in the matter of reviews.

I like your Lynch man pretty well & my sisters like him very well. He has a vile philosophy & an unelastic though clever mind like Eltons whom you met here. He seems full of projects & has the advantage of being the first Irish man I have met who *has* a philosophy to be detested. I have done my duty by him & introduced him to some literary folk he wanted to meet, & shall try & see more of him, but find I judge people to a great extent by their attitude on certain great questions & that he is so far as I now see committed though less hopelessly than his prototype Elton to the side which is not mine. I shall however know when his book on the philosophy of criticism comes out.[10]

Yours Always
W B Yeats

ALS Huntington. McHugh, 123–6; Wade, 169–72.

[7] The Garnetts at this time had the use of a relative's cottage at Henhurst Cross, in Surrey.

[8] The essay became his 'A Reckless Century', published that September in *United Ireland* (see p. 222, n. 2).

[9] KT's *A Nun Her Friends and Her Order* (see p. 212, n. 8) was published by Kegan Paul, Trench Trübner at the end of June 1891.

[10] Arthur Alfred Lynch (1861–1934), born in Australia of an Irish father and Scottish mother, was a man of great versatility—civil and electrical engineer, physician, psychologist and surgeon, soldier, politician, and author of several books. He went to study in Berlin in the late 1880s and then moved to Paris and London. He fought on the Boer side in the South African war, and when he was returned as nationalist MP for Galway city, and arrived in England to take his seat in 1903, he was arrested on charges on high treason, but was later pardoned. He joined the British Army during the First World War, and was nationalist MP for West Clare until 1918. A man of strong opinions, he attacked prevailing literary taste in *Modern Authors: A Review and a Forecast* (1891); the 'vile philosophy' WBY opposed lay in Lynch's insistence (185) that 'it is science which holds the *formulae* of every step in the conditions of civilization'. Oliver Elton (1861–1945), scholar and critic, friend of JBY's and author of a 2-vol. study of Frederick York Powell (1906), published *The Augustan Ages* (1899) and three later volumes in a *Survey of English Literature*. He was Professor of English Literature at the University of Liverpool, 1900–25.

To Katharine Tynan, [early July 1891]

3 Blenheim Road | Bedford Park | Chiswick | W

My dear Katey

I see by "Irish Monthly" that your "A Nun—her friends & her order" is out. If you have not been able to keep me a copy get me a review copy at any rate. I can review it in the Pilot certainly & elsewhere probably. I can also if I care for it as I feel sure I will, get it reviewed probably in some of the papers over here—the Anti Jacobin & the Star I think very likely, & perhaps also in the Pall Mall & one or two others. To do so however I should have a copy as soon as you possibly can as I shall leave for Ireland in about ten days I expect & may have some difficulty in getting it read & in looking up friends about it if it comes late in the ten days. Owing to the Rhymers Club I have a certain amont of influence with reviewers. I can probably besides before mentioned papers get you a note in the "Speaker" at least & certainly can help you with the "Queen". "The Speaker" reviews are unfortunately very few & far beetween. The notes however are very much in the friendly hand of John Davidson. "The Academy" must also be looked up. If you like I can myself ask for it there. I must however read it first as it may be a very good book & yet a difficult one—if you have made it very catholic—to review for a churchless mystic like me. I meen that an ardent beleiver *might* be better for you as far as Academy is concerned. I think however that it is important that some one should ask for it or they may bunch it up with a lot of other books. I gather from "The Irish Monthly" that you have done your work in the very best spirit & look forward to reading it with excited expectation. Your first prose book is a momentous matter & may be the beginning of a new literary life for you.[1]

I am myself busy with new work. Fisher Unwin are going to reprint my articles on folklore etc from the National Observer with what aditional articles on Irish subjects I can get together this summer & Jack is to make twenty illustrations.[2] This is just the kind of thing I have been wishing for as it will enable me to write articles putting my best work into them without

---

[1] In 'Notes on New Books', the *Irish Monthly* of July 1891 (379–80) praised *A Nun* for its diligence, discretion, and literary skill, observing that it provided 'another of many instances that a poet's prose is the most perfect medium for the expression of thought.' The *Anti-Jacobin* published an anonymous notice of 'this pleasant book' on 8 Aug 1891 (673), but despite WBY's efforts it was not noticed by any of his fellow Rhymers in the journals for which they regularly reviewed—Le Gallienne for the *Star*, Rhys for *Pall Mall*, Davidson for the *Daily Chronicle* as well as the *Speaker*. The *Academy* gave the book to T. W. Rolleston who noticed it together with KT's *Ballads and Lyrics* in a long and favourable review, but not until 7 May 1892. In his own review in the *Boston Pilot*, 12 Sept 1891 (*LNI*, 141–2), WBY, while finding *A Nun* 'very picturesque and charming', admitted that he felt 'somewhat astray among those saints and holy people'.

[2] This book, which became *The Celtic Twilight*, did not appear until 1893 when it was published by Lawrence & Bullen, not by Fisher Unwin. It was not illustrated by Jack B. Yeats but did have a frontispiece by JBY.

feeling that they will be lost in mere ephemeral journalism. I have also expectations of getting "The Countess Kathleen" & some ballads & lyrics taken for the Cameo Series. The reader says he will take them if he likes the Countess as well as he does the rest of my poems. Dr Todhunter says "the Countess" is my best work so far & I dare say the reader will think the same.[3] I shall submit to him the 3 acts I have finished & do the rest in Ireland. I am also to edit a volume of Irish Fairy Tales for Children & in all liklihood a book of Irish Poems which will enable me to include you Rolleston & the rest of our little school of modern Irish poets.[4] I have likewise the Introduction to those wretched "Irish Adventures" waiting writing. "The Countess" however will be the first venture I think & may follow "John Sherman" almost immediately. So you see I shall be well represented this year even without the Magnum Opus which grows more & more intricate & I hope more & more profound every day. The mystics all over the world will have to acknowledge Ellis & myself among their authorities. We shall help good people "to make their souls" quite as much as any of your Irish Monthly writers[5] who seem, by the by, to be discovering, in the very kindest way however, the cloven hoof in my "Irish Tales". They kept dead silence over the Carleton & now awake to murmur—and yet I gave nothing but stories admitted by all men to be masterpeices of literature & literature alone was in my bond. The book has been very well received on the whole—much better received than anything of mine except the poems. The reviews have been longer than were given to the Fairy Tales—a much more elaborate & useful book—or as far as Ireland was concerned to "Oisin". There are still a number—"the Star", "the Pall Mall" & the "Academy"—which are a writing in friendly hands. "The Saturday Review" is the only hostile paper yet.[6] I am rather anxious about "Sherman". It is good I beleive but it will be

---

[3] Unwin's reader, Edward Garnett, did like the play and *The Countess Kathleen and Various Legends and Lyrics* was published in 1892 by Fisher Unwin as part of the Cameo Series.

[4] WBY's edition of *Irish Fairy Tales* appeared in Fisher Unwin's Children's Library in 1892 and contained two illustrations by Jack B. Yeats. The projected book of Irish poems was laid on one side until 1895 when it was published by Methuen as *A Book of Irish Verse*.

[5] The 'Magnum Opus': i.e., *The Works of William Blake*. 'To make my soul' is a common Irish idiom meaning to prepare spiritually for death; cf. 'Beggar to Beggar Cried' (*VP*, 299, 1. 4) and 'The Tower' (*VP*, 416, 1. 181).

[6] Besides attacking WBY's *RIT* (see p. 187, n. 4) for its 'mistaken notion of "representativeness"', the *Irish Monthly* of July 1891 (378–9) also criticised on religious grounds the inclusion of the story, 'Father Tom and the Pope', an 'obsolete squib' which, said the reviewer (undoubtedly Fr. Russell), should have been omitted since 'it concerns persons and subjects too dear to the hearts of most Irishmen to make its publication suitable anywhere else than in Old Ebony in its coarsest and most bigoted days.' 'Old Ebony' was a nickname for *Blackwoods Magazine* where the story, which tells how a country priest from Leitrim bests the Pope at drinking poteen, theological disputation and dog-Latin, first appeared. Unabashed by this censure, WBY continued to regard the tale highly and included it in his 1895 list of the Best Thirty Irish Books.

A scathing anonymous notice of *RIT* had appeared in the *Saturday Review*, 30 May 1891 (664–5): 'Mr W. B. Yeats writes himself down an American tourist insofar as Ireland is concerned and makes sad

a toss up how the reviewers take it—for if they look for the ordinary stuff of novels they will find nothing. Do what you can for it—for a success with stories would solve many problems for me & I write them easily.

I saw Miss Francis Wynn on Wednesday & asked her & her young man for Sunday evening.[7] Will get some people who know her book to meet her.

Yours

W B Yeats

[*Vertically at top of first page*]
This is a horribly bookish letter but I began it with your "Nun" & one book led to another.

Who wrote the charming article on Rose Kavanagh in current Irish Monthly it is signed O.K.?[8]

Write as soon as possible in the matter of "The Nun".

ALS Huntington. McHugh, 126–8; Wade, 172–4.

To Katharine Tynan, [*16 July 1891*]

3 Blenheim Road | Bedford Park | Chiswick | W.

My dear Katey

A great many thanks for your letter & for the book[1] which has just reached me. (It came yesterday—O'Leary has it until tonight.)

I am to do you for Miles at once, as the next volume is the volume of Ladies Poets. After my wish to see you this is the cause of my going to Whitehall on my way north. He told me the memoir would be to[o] late a month or three weeks hence.[2]

blunders in his subject too. . . . His style is mountainous even about mice.' T. W. Rolleston's lengthy and discriminating review in the *Academy*, 10 Oct 1891 (306–7), quarrelled with some of the selections and omissions in the book but was generally very favourable: 'The selection and editing of these tales could hardly have been put into better hands than those of Mr Yeats, whose acute and finely-written Introduction deserves to be read with close attention.' Despite WBY's hopes, neither the *Star* nor *Pall Mall* noticed the book.

[7] In a letter to Fr. Russell, dated 'Wednesday' from 17 Southampton Row, London (APH), and presumably referring to this meeting, Frances Wynne wrote: 'Willie Yeats I picked up today at the British Museum and trailed him off to tea. *Such* a figure. Hair a yard long and full of mysticism and magic.' Her young man was Henry Wynne (1861–1953), her cousin, to whom she became engaged in the spring of 1890 after getting to know him while she was helping an uncle in his deprived East End parish in the winter of 1889–90. They were married in Christmas week, 1891. Henry Wynne, son of the Revd. Frederick Richard Wynne, later Bishop of Killaloe, took holy orders in 1893 and was appointed to a curacy in Stepney Green, where, later in the same year, Frances Wynne died after childbirth.

[8] 'Uncle Remus', reminiscences of Rose Kavanagh by 'O.K.', appeared in the *Irish Monthly*, July 1891 (263–6). 'O.K.' is identified as the Revd Richard O'Kennedy by Fr. Matthew Russell in his *Rose Kavanagh and Her Verse* (Dublin, 1909). O'Kennedy was a parish priest in Co. Limerick.

[1] A copy of KT's *A Nun Her Friends and Her Order*, sent at WBY's request (see preceding letter).

[2] In the event, KT's poems were excluded for reasons of space from vol. VIII, *Robert Bridges and*

If you intend to have any people at your place on Sunday afternoon would you be so kind as to ask Russel.[3] I want to see him & talk of several matters.

Yours always affectionately

W B Yeats

I have only been able to read one chapter of your book but will get further with it before I see you.

ALS Huntington, with envelope addressed to Clondalkin, postmark 'CHISWICK JY 16 91'. McHugh, 128–9; Wade, 174–5.

To Katharine Tynan, [24 July 1891]

Ballykilbeg | Co Down[1]

My dear Katey

I arrived here yesterday & spent the evening letting up fire ballons & hunting them across country[2] & am to day writing the notice of Miss O'Leary for Miles.[3] I asked Charles Johnston did he remember a boy at Harcourt St called Hinckson.[4] He said he did and that he was a very nice fellow & had "the true instinct of the scholour". It is about the first instance in which I have heard him praise any Harcourt St boy.

Please tell me the date of your first book & also of Shamrocks. I did not bring either over with me unfortunately. Could you post me a copy of Shamrocks? I would return it & I fear I need it for this notice. Please tell me

Contemporary Poets (1893), of Alfred Henry Miles's 10-vol. anthology, *The Poets and the Poetry of the Century* (1891–7). She is mentioned (713) in an 'Ac Etiam' section in which WBY also appears, and which the editor concludes with an apology for having been 'compelled . . . to omit much that he had hoped to include, and to hold over all that is crowded out for a larger opportunity'. Poems by KT were however included in the second and enlarged edition of 1907, *The Poets and the Poetry of the Nineteenth Century*, in the volume entitled *Christina G. Rossetti to Katharine Tynan*, where they were accompanied by a biographical and critical note on her, signed 'Alfred H. Miles'.

[3] i.e. George William Russell (AE). WBY may have wanted to talk over the article, 'An Irish Visionary', which he was to publish on him later that year in the *National Observer*. Probably they also had theosophical matters to discuss before WBY's visit to Charles Johnston; and WBY perhaps wished to sound AE out about MG, whose reported ill-health was worrying him and whom he was to see again on 22 July.

[1] The home of the Johnston family; WBY had travelled to Co. Down via Dublin and Clondalkin, where he stayed with the Tynans at Whitehall.

[2] WBY recalled this visit (*Mem*, 45–6), when with Charles Johnston and his elder brother he 'made the fire balloons of tissue paper and then chased them over the countryside, our chase becoming longer and longer as our skill in manufacture improved'.

[3] WBY's introductory note to Ellen O'Leary's poem appeared in vol. VII (449–52) of A. H. Miles's *The Poets and the Poetry of the Century* (see preceding letter).

[4] KT must have told WBY of her engagement to Henry Hinkson (see p. 212, n. 9), whom she married in 1893; Hinkson had been at the High School in Harcourt Street 1878–82, and was a classmate of WBY's in Form 5, October 1881 to July 1882.

also the date of your first printed poem & where it appeared. Please say the nature of your first work was it Catholic or Irish or what. What writer first woke up your imagination. Was it Rossetti?[5] It would be a great convenience if you could post me both "Shamrocks" & "Louse De Vallière". It is a troublesome thing to ask but I need them & I would send them back the day after I sent the notice.

I left my razor strops behind me also my brush & comb & am rather a stray for lack of them. Could Dan find them & send them to me?[6]

Charles Johnston sends you his kind rembrances.

Yours always
W B Yeats

I saw the National Press review of the Nun in the train yesterday—most unjust. I suspect Taylor of being the author by the style. It touches a defect, but only a superfical one, & makes it appear typical of the whole. It will stir up your friends however. The poem he quotes with disoproval seemed to me particularly good. The National Press was probably glad enough to have an article attacking you in revenge for your fathers and your own Parnellism. The papers on your own side will be made all the more favourable by this attack.[7]

ALS Huntington, with envelope addressed to Clondalkin, postmark 'NEWRY JY 24 91'. McHugh, 129–30; Wade, 175–6.

[5] *Louise de la Vallière* was published in 1885; *Shamrocks* in 1887. Her first poem, 'Dreamland', appeared in *Young Ireland* in 1875, and another poem, 'August or June?', was published by the *Graphic* in 1877. For the influence of Rossetti see *25 Years* (70, 148). Even earlier influences were Longfellow and Adelaide Proctor.

[6] Dan was KT's younger brother, Daniel Joseph (1864–1924), who was later to settle in Liverpool.

[7] The *National Press* had been set up by Tim Healy as an anti-Parnellite alternative to the *Freeman's Journal*. WBY is being kind about the lengthy and very damaging review of *A Nun: Her Friends and Her Order* which appeared there on 23 July 1891 (6), under the title 'Eccentric Religious Biography'. The reviewer alleged that KT 'exhibits neither the sobriety of imagination with which such a theme should be handled, nor the staidness and gravity of thought and of language which such themes of their nature demand. She has, in fact, a "plentiful lack" of nearly all the qualifications requisite for the work she undertook, except enthusiasm; and the enthusiasm she possesses is too apt at times to degenerate into gush.' He went on to criticise KT's concentration on externals, over-use of superlatives and bad grammar, and closes by quoting a poem she had included:

> Lavender, grey-blue like her eyes,
> Southernwood that is sweet to press;
> Very wise are the butterflies,
> Brown bee knoweth his business.

The review is an exercise in sustained sarcasm, making WBY's guess that the author might have been John F. Taylor (see p. 73) a reasonable one. But KT observes (*25 Years*, 335), 'I was glad to learn in later years that the author was really a person who is now a Professor in the National University whom I remember as a pink-nosed boy lavishing complimentary epithets upon the young debaters in a Convent-School Debating Society of which I was President.' This was probably Robert Donovan (1852–1934), who had been on the *Nation* and now reviewed for the *National Press*. He became lecturer in English at

To Katharine Tynan, [late July 1891]

⟨3 Blenheim Road⟩ | Ballykilbeg | Co Down

My dear Katey

The poems arrived this morning & I have just finished the critical notice. "Shamrocks" has not however turned up yet & I cannot let Miles go to press with what you have sent, without "St Francis & the Birds",[1] so I shall only send him the critical notice this time & let the selection follow. I think you will like my notice of you. It is a success I think.

Could you send me that account the peasant woman gave of her vision of St Joseph? The "never starched in this world" thing. If you can give it me it will make the fortune of my introduction to the Fairy Tales.[2] I would like to get it at once because I shall be paid the moment the introduction is done & my sister wants some money.

The thing I asked you for was not a razor but a razor strop that is a thing for sharpening a razor on—Mine is a thing like a strap with a ring at each end like this

Dan will be able to find it.

I am doing a certain amount of writing—the notices of Miss O'Leary & Miss Wynne have gone in[3]—but much of my time is spent in helping to make fire ballons & in letting them off & in exploring old castles or in such like country pursuits. I have found no folklore nor heard of any to speak of and am in all ways living a good out-o-door life with little of the mind in it. I

the National University and in 1927 chairman of the Commission on Evil Literature and a member of the Censorship of Publications Board in 1932.

United Ireland did rally to KT's defence, on 19 Sept 1891, and criticized (1) the virulence of the *National Press* review: 'Miss Tynan is a Parnellite; but even that fact could not sufficiently explain to me why any Irishman should so very ungallantly and so very coarsely attack the most distinguished literary lady of our generation.'

[1] KT's poem 'St. Francis to the Birds' (see p. 20), a favourite of WBY's, was not among the poems included in the 1907 edition of Miles's anthology.

[2] KT evidently complied, for in his Introduction to *IFT*, WBY writes (5) of 'the pious Clondalkin laundress who told a friend of mine that she had seen a vision of St. Joseph, and that he had "a lovely shining hat upon him and a shirt-buzzom that was never starched in this world"'.

[3] WBY's notice of Frances Wynne and the selection of her poems suffered the same fate as those of KT (see p. 257). They were omitted as well from the 1907 edition of Miles's *Poets and the Poetry of the Nineteenth Century*, although the volume *Christina G. Rossetti to Katharine Tynan* contains a brief mention of Frances Wynne as author of *Whisper!* in an 'Ac Etiam' listing (476).

went into United Ireland office by the by before leaving Dublin & found them anxious for literary articles. Why dont you contribute?[4]

Yours always
W B Yeats

ALS Huntington. McHugh, 130; Wade, 176–7.

To John O'Leary, [? 4 August 1891]

54 Lower Mount St | Dublin.[1]
Tuesday

My dear M^r O'Leary,

Before I left London you were so good as to say that if I was in a fix for a pound or two when in Dublin you would lend it me. I am rather in a fix just this moment. I have enough for my own expenses but have just heard from my sister that she is going to Sligo a week earlier than I had thought & that she wants £2 I was to give her for her expenses. I had intended to send it out of some money I am to get from Fisher Unwin for my new book of Irish Fairy story but the MSS lies waiting for some stories that Douglas Hyde promises me[2] & I fear will not reach Unwin in time for the money to serve my sisters need. I can return the £2 next week together with what I already owe you. Could you send it me in time for me to send it to my sister this week as she starts for Sligo next Monday.

My father is doing well or about to do well. He has got a portrait of Mrs Conolly to do for which he will get £50 & after that another in Yourkshire for £40 & probably one of Miss Conolly.[3]

I had a good time in Co Down with Johnston & shall return there again next week in all liklihood. I came up yesterday for a week.

I have been down to United Ireland & was well received & find them

---

[4] KT contributed articles to *United Ireland* on Sarah Piatt's poetry (5 Sept 1891), on younger American poets (31 Oct 1891), and on Jane Barlow (13 Feb 1892), as well as her own poetry, which she had been publishing there since November 1882.

[1] 54 Lower Mount Street was a lodging house kept by a Mrs Deering.

[2] Hyde supplied WBY with only one tale for *IFT*, 'The Man Who Never Knew Fear', previously unpublished.

[3] JBY would have known the Connollys of Castletown House, Celbridge, Co. Kildare, because the Yeats estate was near by, at Thomastown. Sarah Elizabeth Connolly, née Shaw, had married Thomas Connolly in 1868; their daughter Catherine was born in 1871. However, the commission seems not to have materialized: on 22 Nov 1891 JBY wrote to JO'L: 'I have been hoping every day to hear that a portrait in Dublin for which I was to get £50 was ready for me but so far I have heard nothing' (NLI), and the Connolly heirs know of no portrait by JBY.

ready for articles. I have not yet seen Leamy but shall try to do so to day. I saw the sub-editor.[4]

> Yours very sincerely
> W B Yeats

Please excuse the soiled paper—it is studio paper & as such has a time honoured right to be soiled.

[*Vertically at top of first page*]
On second thoughts would you be so very good as to send the £2 direct to Lilly.

ALS NLI. Wade, 177–8.

To Katharine Tynan, [c. 22 August 1891]

> 54 Lower Mount | St.

My dear Katey.

I enclose £1 in solution of my debt & also 2/6 which please give to the servant. It suddenly occurs to me by the by that I owe you 1/– or so besides the £1 but as I have no postal order for that amount will have to let it wait until we meet. The Providence Journal money came to day.[1] I do beleive that I left that misarable strap for sharpening my razor on at your house again if so please send it. I wrote you a post card to this effect yesterday but do not think I posted it. Please send me also the MS of the Countess

---

[4] Edmund Leamy (1848–1904), whom WBY recalled (*Mem*, 57) as 'a pleasant, indolent man who had written a book of fairy stories', had helped Parnell to seize the *United Ireland* offices by force on 10 Dec 1890, after the split in the Irish Party, and was now the paper's editor. Born in Waterford, he qualified as a solicitor but abandoned the law for politics and literature, becoming nationalist MP for Waterford in 1880, for N. E. Cork in 1885, for South Sligo in 1887, and for Kildare in 1900. He published verse in a number of Irish journals; his *Irish Fairy Tales* appeared in 1890 and *The Fairy Minstrel of Glenmalure* in 1899; and his play, *Cupid in Kerry*, was produced posthumously in Dublin in 1906. Under his editorship *United Ireland* became the leading Parnellite organ until the setting up of the *Irish Independent*.

John McGrath (1864–1956), at this time the sub-editor, helped Leamy mould the literary side of the paper. Born in Portaferry, he contributed poems to *Young Ireland* in his youth and later served on the staff of the *Freeman's Journal*, but, after its defection to the anti-Parnellites, moved to *United Ireland*. On 10 Oct of this year he was to publish 'the famous article that accused the anti-Parnellites of the murder of Parnell' (*Mem*, 57) and the following spring helped WBY to set up the National Literary Society. Recalling this period in his article 'W. B. Yeats and Ireland', *Westminster Review*, July 1911 (3–4), McGrath wrote that he and Leamy had 'decided that "United Ireland" must be, not only the propagandist paper of Parnellism, but also a literary national organ after the style of the old *Nation* of Davis and Duffy', and that of all the writers they attracted to its pages the 'most interesting one to me . . . was Mr. Yeats, and not so much because of his contributions, as because, personally, he was something in the nature of an enigma. He looked the character—in a long yellow coat and sombrero hat—far more than he spoke it. But he did undoubtedly speak it also. He talked in the most amazing way about poetry. . . .'

[1] This was for WBY's final article for *PSJ*, the review of Todhunter's *The Poison Flower* which appeared on 26 July 1891 (see p. 249, n. 2).

Kathleen as I have some notion of going on with it.[2] I tried the experiments the Sigersons wanted on Monday evening with much success.[3] They will tell you about it if you care to ask. Please send me a post card to say when you get this as I have lost money in the post before now—

Yours Always
W B Yeats

"Mangan" out in United Ireland & viley misprinted.[4]
Jack comes to Dublin on Saturday.
[*On back of envelope*]
As I have registered this you need not acknowledge it.

ALS Huntington, with registered envelope addressed to Clondalkin; postmark torn off. McHugh, 130–1; Wade, 178.

To W. E. Henley, 4 September [*1891*]

3 Upper Ely Place | Dublin[1]
Sept 4th

Dear Mr. Henley,

I send you a book of sonnets by Rhys with drawings by my brother who is about 19 years old and means to take to illustrating. The drawings seem to me to have a very genuine tragic intensity that makes them something much

[2] 'I had Willie Yeats staying here since last Monday,' wrote KT to Fr. Matthew Russell on 17 Aug 1891 (APH). 'He is an extremely bothering visitor. He thinks all the rest of the world created to minister to him, and there is no rebuffing of him possible. I did nothing while he was here, nor should I if he was here a twelvemonth.'

[3] It may have been this or a similar occasion which KT describes in *Middle Years* (29), when WBY, having hypnotized a medium (probably Mrs Sigerson, with whom he conducted a number of psychic experiments) in Dr Sigerson's Clare Street study, set her to gaze into a 'magic crystal':

Dr Sigerson was standing by quietly, humorously observant. 'I see something golden.' 'Yes, yes, something golden—what is it like?' 'I cannot see clearly. There are golden letters of great size. There is a golden bar, and great jewels as big as a tea-tray, of the most glorious colour.' 'What else?' 'I see a gigantic figure. He extends great white arms above his head. He moves his arms this way and that way. He is between me and the golden letters. I cannot read them. The great jewels flash dazzlingly.'

At this point Willie's excitement was prodigious. But further developments were prevented by Dr Sigerson's remarking in his cool, dry voice: 'If you will come out of the magic crystal you will see that a man is cleaning the windows of the Medical Hall opposite. There is a brass bar below and gold lettering above. The sun is shining on the big coloured bottles. The man is in his shirt-sleeves. That is what you see in the crystal.'

[4] WBY's article, 'Clarence Mangan's Love Affair' (*UP* I. 194–8), appeared in *United Ireland*, 22 Aug 1891. 'Vilely misprinted' must refer to omissions since the text is free of errors except for the misprinting of 'marrying' for 'marring' in the opening sentence.

[1] WBY was to stay for short periods over the next two years at this address, which he described (*Aut*, 236) as 'The one house where nobody thought or talked politics . . . where a number of young men lived together, and, for want of a better name, were called Theosophists. Besides the resident members, other members dropped in and out during the day, and the reading-room was a place of much discussion about

more than caricatures—Perhaps you might, if you care for them, get some one to say a good word for them of some kind in the *National Observer*.[2]

Unwin will send you in a day or two a story of mine called *John Sherman*. There is a little thing bound up with it called *Dhoya* that may please you. There is a poem of mine that was in my book embedded in *Dhoya*,[3] so the pseudonymity—this thing comes out in the Pseudonym Library—is not very profoundly kept.

I send you by the same post with this an article on a curious Dublin visionary and a little poem.[4]

My visionary by the by showed me your 'God in the Garden' poem[5] and called it one of your best things. He is a reader of your verse and in all ways one of the few true students of poetry I know. I think with him about your 'God in a Garden.' Its verse has a fine ringing sound.

Yours very sincerely

W B Yeats

Please send proofs—if enclosed poem etc. suit you—to 3, Upper Ely Place, Dublin.

Text from Wade, 178–9.

philosophy and about the arts.' 3 Upper Ely Place was rented by Frederick Dick and from April 1891 became the headquarters of the Dublin Lodge of the Theosophical Society when 'five members and one associate'—Dick and his wife, D. N. Dunlop, G. W. Russell (AE), E. J. King, and H. M. Magee—had 'therein taken up their abode' (*Lucifer*, 15 May 1891). The Dublin Lodge moved to 13 Eustace Street in late 1896 or early 1897.

[2] *The Great Cockney Tragedy* by Ernest Rhys (see p. 228) had already been noted as one of the 'Books of the Week' in the *National Observer*, 29 Aug 1891. A further brief notice, mentioning that the book had been illustrated by Jack Yeats, appeared on 14 Nov. A more enthusiastic account of the illustrations appeared in *United Ireland*, 3 Dec 1891, and this too had no doubt been engineered by WBY.

[3] 'Girl's Song' (see p. 253).

[4] The article, on AE, was 'An Irish Visionary' (see p. 73), published in the *National Observer*, 3 Oct 1891. The little poem (*VP*, 115–16) had a long title: 'A Fairy Song / Sung by "the Good People" over the outlaw Michael Dwyer and his bride, who had escaped into the mountains'. Published 12 Sept 1891 in the *National Observer*, its title was later altered to 'A Faery Song / Sung by the people of Faery over Diarmuid and Grania, in their bridal sleep under a Cromlech'.

[5] Henley's poem, 'As like the Woman as you can', had been published anonymously in the *National Observer*, 18 July 1891. It was republished as no. IX of 'Rhymes and Rhythms' in his *The Song of the Sword and Other Verses* (1892). One of its refrains is 'God in the Garden . . .'.

To Susan Mary Yeats, [*11 October 1891*]

3 Upper Ely Place
Sunday

My dear Lilly

Please send me as soon as possible Allinghams Poems I want it to make selections from for Miles "Poets & Poetry".[1] I shall turn up in London in about ten days but may return here for a while after three weeks or so though this not at all likely.

I send you a copy of United Ireland with a poem of mine on Parnell written the day he died to be in time for the press that evening.[2] It has been a success.

The Funeral is just over. The people are breathing fire & slaughter. The wreathes have such inscriptions as "Murdered by the Priests" & a number of Wexford men were heard by man I know promising to remove a Bishop & seven priests before next sunday. Tommorow will bring them cooler heads I doubt not. Meanwhile Healy is in Paris & the people hunt for his gore in vain. Dillon & he are at feud & the feud is being fought out by the Freeman & National Press in diverse indirect fashions.[3]

Tell Jack I have no more fairy articles at present but will get some done soon.[4]

I have finished "the Countess Kathleen" & am doing stray lyrics & things.

Yours
W B Yeats

[*On back of envelope, in another hand*]
Dont let anybody see this letter

ALS MBY, with envelope addressed to Blenheim Road, postmark 'DUBLIN OC 12 91'. Subsequently decorated with drawings by the Yeats children. Wade, 179–80.

[1] WBY's selection of William Allingham's poems, with his introduction (*UP* I. 258–61), was included in Miles's *The Poets and the Poetry of the Century: Charles Kingsley to James Thompson* (1892).

[2] Parnell had died in Brighton on 6 Oct 1891 and his body was brought back to Dublin for burial on Sunday, 11 Oct. WBY's 'Mourn—And Then Onward!' (*VP*, 737–8) appeared in *United Ireland*, 10 Oct 1891, and was reprinted in the *Irish Weekly Independent*, 20 May 1893, but was not included in any of WBY's books.

[3] The quarrel between Healy and Dillon, Parnell's ablest lieutenants (see p. 13), who after his fall began to jockey for leadership of the anti-Parnellite majority in the Irish Party, was to drag on for many years. At this time it found its focus in the dispute between two newspapers. The *Freeman's Journal*, traditionally the nationalist daily paper, had only come over to the anti-Parnellites on 31 July 1891. While it had remained loyal to Parnell, Healy had set up the *National Press* (see p. 259), in the running of which he had neglected his law practice and income. After the defection of the *Freeman's Journal* from Parnell, Dillon insisted that the *National Press* should be absorbed into the older and more prestigious paper, but Healy was reluctant to give up a journal for which he had made such sacrifices and which gave him considerable political power. The two papers were not finally amalgamated until the summer of 1892, when the contest transferred itself to a dispute over control of the board of the *Freeman's Journal*.

[4] Jack Yeats was doing the illustrations for WBY's *IFT* (see p. 256).

To George Russell (AE), [? *1 November 1891*][1]

3 Blenheim Road | Bedford Park | Chiswick | W

Sunday—

My dear Russel

I forgot "Tireil" I wish you would send it me—also my "Fairy and Folk Tales of the Irish Peasantry" and Russeau's "Confessions" when ever you have read it. There is no hurry about Russeau, but "Tireil" & the other send soon—[2] I am very sorry to have to bother you about them.

I had a wonderfully smooth passage—the smoothest I ever remember, & arrived without any great fatigue but with no end of a bad cold—I am now getting on with Blake & hope to get the book done before long & myself back in Ireland. I have seen Miss Gonne several times & have I think found an alley in the cousin with whom she is staying. An accidental word of the cousins showed me that they had been discussing me together & reading my poems in the Vellum Book & yesterday the cousin gave me a hint to go to Paris next Spring when Miss Gonne did[3]—so you see I am pretty cheerful for the time until the next regement of black devils come. Tomorrow Miss Gonne is to be initiated into G D[4]—the next day she goes to Paris but I shall see her on her way through London a couple of weeks later—she promises to work at the Young Ireland League for me this winter.[5] Go & see her when she gets to Dublin & keep her from forgetting me & Occultism. Your vision about her has been curiously corroberated in all the main points by the Kaballistic seership of the Mathers helped out by Miss Gonnes own clairvoyance.[6] The story was worked out in great detail.

---

[1] This letter was clearly written before that of 9 Nov to JO'L (see below p. 269) and—as references to the journey suggest—shortly after WBY's return to England.

[2] WBY had written a commentary on *Tiriel* for *The Works of William Blake* although it was extensively altered by Ellis.

[3] MG's cousin, May Gonne (see p. 137, n. 2), trained as a nurse, and was at this time living with MG's sister, Mrs Pilcher, in Hans Place, London. The MS book, bound in vellum, containing his love poems had been WBY's gift to MG. In *Mem* (50) WBY recalled: 'I noticed that one evening when I paid her some compliment her face was deeply tinted. She returned to Paris, and her cousin, a young girl of like age, meeting me in the street, asked me "why I was not in Paris." I had no money.'

[4] On the evidence of Wade's dating of this letter, MG's initiation into the Order of the Golden Dawn is usually given as 16 Nov 1891, but if the letter was written a fortnight earlier (see note 1 above), her initiation must have taken place on 2 Nov. She took the initials PIAL ('Per Ignem Ad Lucem', Through Fire To Light), and writes in *SQ* (247–9) that WBY had persuaded her to seek initiation: 'I passed four initiations and learned a number of Hebrew words, but . . . I was oppressed by the drab appearance and mediocrity of my fellow-mystics.' She left the Order, not because of the dullness of the members but because she became convinced that it had connections with Freemasonry. WBY's recollections of the occasion (*Mem*, 49–50) are rather more romantic: 'We went to London and were initiated in the Hermetic Students, and I began to form plans of our lives devoted to mystic truth, and spoke to her of Nicholas Flamel and his wife, Pernella. In a propaganda, secret and seeking out only the most profound and subtle minds, that great beauty would be to others, as it was always to me, symbolic and mysterious.'

[5] For the founding of the Young Ireland League and WBY's subsequent involvement with it, see following letters.

[6] Both WBY and MG give accounts of these experiences. MG reports (*SQ*, 254) that she had told

Thursday

Since writing the above the initiation has taken place & Miss Gonne has started for Paris. I have been writing Blake all day or trying to do so which is quite as laborious & shall send off a good bulk of MSS to the printer this week. I am sending you a couple of books of Blakes of which I have other copies now—you have seen them but may like to own them.

Give my remembrences to Dick & Mrs Dick.[7]

Yours very truly
W B Yeats

I will write to Dick

ALS Indiana. Wade, 182–3 (dated 15 November 1891).

WBY about a 'beautiful dark woman . . . whom as a child, I had seen bending over my cot', and WBY and MacGregor Mathers concluded that she was MG's Ka: 'a part of my personality had survived death in a former incarnation.' At a subsequent seance Moina MacGregor (Mrs Mathers) invoked this 'grey lady' and gave 'an exact description of her. Willie couldn't see her. They said she had confessed to having killed a child and wrung her hands in sorrow and remorse. After this I began to think she must be evil and decided to get rid of her.' In WBY's account (*Mem*, 48–9) he, after a meeting with AE, summoned up an image of the 'grey lady' using symbols he had learned in the Golden Dawn, and

almost at once it became visible. I of course saw nothing beyond an uncertain impression on the mind, but Maud Gonne saw it almost as if palpably present. It told its story, taking up what was perhaps a later event of her dream of the desert. It was a past personality of hers, now seeking to be reunited with her. She had been priestess in a temple somewhere in Egypt and under the influence of a certain priest who was her lover gave false oracles for money, and because of this the personality of that life had split off from the soul and remained a half-living shadow.

These accounts, especially as they touch upon infanticide and a corrupting lover are not without psychological interest. Unknown to WBY, MG's son, George, had died on 31 Aug in Paris while she was in Dublin. To her maternal grief were added feelings of guilt at having been absent from the child at this critical moment.

Samuel Liddell Mathers (later S. L. MacGregor Mathers, 1854–1918; see Appendix) was one of the founders of the Order of the Golden Dawn, into which he introduced WBY in 1890. In June 1890 Mathers married Mina (later Moina) Bergson, (1865–1928), sister of the French philosopher, and that same year was appointed curator of the Horniman Museum at Forest Hill. He lost this post in 1891, moving the following year to Paris, where he set up another Golden Dawn temple. His attempts to retain control of the London temple from France were to cause trouble later in the decade.

[7] Frederick John Dick (1856–1927) and his first wife, Annie (d. 1904); 3 Upper Ely Place (see p. 263) had, as WBY recalled in *Aut* (236), been taken in the name of this 'engineer to the Board of Works, a black-bearded young man, with a passion for Manichaean philosophy, and all accepted him as host; and sometimes the conversation, especially when I was there, became too ghostly for the nerves of his young and delicate wife, and he would be made angry.' Dick joined the Dublin lodge of the Theosophical Society in 1888 and became its secretary after C. F. Wright moved to London in 1890. Before emigrating to the Theosophical Society headquarters at Point Loma, California, in 1905, he was a Government Inspector of Harbours.

To Father Matthew Russell, [early November 1891]

3 Blenheim Road | Bedford Park | Chiswick

My dear Father Russel

I send you a copy of my novel "John Sherman". If you will kindly review it & say that it is mine I shall be well pleased. People are given to thinking I can only write of the fantastical & wild & this book has to do so far as the long story is concerned with very ordinary persons & events—This is why I want it to be known as mine—the poem at page 187 is in my book of poems so the disguise is not very deep—[1] I shall probably write other stories but of a more dramatic & stirring kind if this goes at all well. Dowden quotes Sherman in the "Fortnightly" by the by.[2] He told me he likes the story that "it is full of beautiful things" and "very interesting" though not a strong and dramatic story in any way nor of course was it so intended. The American edition has been sold & success seems likely.[3]

Miss Tynan has just sent me the proofs of her new book.—[4] It will be a charming volume—& much the most artistic she has yet done.

Yours very truly
W B Yeats

[1] Fr. Russell in reviewing the novel in the 'Notes on New Books' section of the *Irish Monthly*, December 1891 (662–3), did as he was asked:

these pseudonymous authors have no objection to be known by their real names; and accordingly Ganconagh claims as his own a song already given to the world by Mr William B. Yeats. We are therefore justified in recognising our young Irish poet in this new character of storyteller. It is an additional surprise to find that this novel does not deal with anything wild or fantastical, but is a pleasant narrative treating of ordinary persons and events. . . . The descriptions both of scenery and character are full of quaint little touches of very subtle observation. The style is perhaps most remarkable for a dainty simplicity, lit up now and then by a striking thought and even a brilliant aphorism.

(Since Fr. Russell copied out two extracts from *John Sherman* on a blank sheet of this letter, it was probably of these aphorisms that he was thinking.)

In the novel John Sherman leaves his native Irish town of Ballah (Sligo) and his childhood friend, Mary Carton, to work in London. There he becomes engaged to a worldly and wealthy English girl, Margaret Leland, but soon realizing that she is not the wife for him, arranges a meeting between her and a pushing clergyman friend, the Revd William Howard. The two fall in love and Sherman, released from his engagement, hastens back to Ballah to ask Mary to marry him. See p. 155, n. 2.

[2] In 'The Interviewer Abroad', a long review of Jules Huret's *Enquête sur l'evolution littéraire* in the *Fortnightly Review*, November 1891 (719–33), Edward Dowden cites *John Sherman* in contrasting the shortened vistas of Parnassianism with 'that reaction towards idealism' of the Symbolists:

'He could think', writes a new story-teller in the 'Pseudonym Library', who masks under the name of an old Irish spirit, Ganconagh, 'he could think carefully and cleverly, and even with originality, but never in such a way as to make his thoughts an allusion to something deeper than themselves.' This is what the Parnassien poets could seldom attain to, and in admitting this we go far towards allowing the plea of their presumptive heirs.

[3] The book was published in New York by Cassell as part of their '"Unknown" Library'; it was entered for copyright at the Library of Congress on 2 Oct 1891 and two copies were received there on 10 Nov 1891.

[4] *Ballads and Lyrics.*

[*On verso of last page, in another hand*]
"Love is based on inequality, as friendship is on equality." "What have we in this life but a mouthful of air?"

ALS APH. Wade, 180.

To John O'Leary, [9 November 1891]

3 Blenheim Road | Bedford Park | Chiswick W
Monday.

Dear M^r O'Leary

A great many thanks for your post card. Mrs Miles has already sent me the book. It would not have mattered but for a notion I have of doing a poem on one of the stories to put into the book with the Countess Kathleen.[1] John Sherman comes out this week. I hear I am likely after all to get something for it. Garnett says £30 probably which will be very good indeed for a first story.[2] Blake goes slowly a head. Ellis took off a bundle of MSS for the printer last Friday. I am only too anxious to get it done that I may be back in Ireland. What did you decide—if any thing—at the Committee meeting? I want to know about this & about the political situation.[3] A copy of "United Ireland" will serve as an answer to the second question & a post card for the first when ever you feel inclined to send one. Lionel Johnston who is an Irish man talks of being in Ireland next spring & of lecturing if we like to the Young Ireland League or to our Dublin Social & Literary Club.[4] Rhys also

[1] The poem may have been 'The Death of Cuchullin' (*VP*, 105–11; later retitled 'Cuchulain's Fight with the Sea'), published in *United Ireland*, 11 June 1892; WBY notes in *The Countess Kathleen* that the poem is 'founded on a West of Ireland legend' given in Jeremiah Curtin's *Myths and Folk-Lore of Ireland* (1890). This volume, which WBY had mentioned with approval in the *National Observer*, 28 Feb 1891, would doubtless have been in the library of JO'L's acquaintance, the late Revd Percy Watkins Myles (see p. 229); Myles's widow, Ann Riley Myles, had 'shared his literary sympathies, and often helped him in his work' (obituary notice, *Academy*, 17 Oct 1891 [335]).

[2] See p. 247. Garnett's estimate of the royalties WBY would receive from *John Sherman and Dhoya* was based on the putative sale of the entire first printing, of 1644 copies in paper at 1s 6d and 356 in cloth at 2s (*Bibl*, 22).

[3] On 13 May 1891 the Literary Society of the National Club, Dublin, had decided to call for a convention of the various literary societies in Ireland with a view to amalgamating and strengthening them. The inaugural meeting of this convention, held in the Rotunda on 15 Sept 1891 with JO'L presiding, resolved to establish a 'Young Ireland League'. WBY, who seconded the resolution, wrote an article in *United Ireland*, 3 Oct 1891 (*UP* I. 206–8), setting out the League's aims, and since these involved a seven-point manifesto, much committee work remained to be done.

The political situation in Ireland was at a critical stage, any hopes that the Irish Party might reunite after the death of Parnell having been dashed by an uncompromising manifesto issued by his followers the day after his funeral. In the by-election for Cork City, Parnell's own seat, a bitter and acrimonious campaign ended in the defeat of the Parnellite candidate, John Redmond, on 6 Nov. The *Freeman's Journal*, now firmly anti-Parnellite, announced that with the Cork result 'faction dies and peace and unity revive', but the Parnellite *United Ireland* insisted that the fight would continue unabated.

[4] Lionel Pigot Johnson (see p. 239) was actually born at Broadstairs, Kent, but under the influence of

has intentions of turning up & would lecture but would sooner I imagine find some audience that would pay like the English & American audiences he is used to. He has a kind of Pan-Celtic enthusiasm which will spur him on to lecture under either condition however I think. He seems well content with his Welsh life & has a son. He was up here for a few days interviewing publishers etc. He is writing stories & is trying to get one of them taken with illustrations by my brother.[5] Rolleston I have not yet seen but expect him this evening—this being our monthly "at home". Lynch declares that "the Rhymers" are his "enemies". They have probably been reviewing him. I expect him also tonight & one or two of his "enemies".[6] We had a "Rhymers" meeting at Ellis's for Miss Gonne who has now departed for Paris where she stays for a week or ten days more, probably, & then returns here for a few days & so back to Dublin. Help her to help on the Young Ireland League for what she needs is some work of that kind in which she could lose herself & she is so far, enthusiastic about the League. Oldham who does not beleive in it will probably try to damp her ardour. She could help by getting people together at her rooms & persuading them to lecture. She could also help the Dublin Social & Literary Club greatly by the same kind of method.[7]

I have sent copies of Sherman for review to United Ireland & Irish Monthly & told them that they may say who wrote it if they like. I shall send

the Celtic revival and his recent conversion to Catholicism (he was received into the Church on 22 June 1891) managed to discover an Irish ancestry. 'He belonged', WBY recalled (*Aut*, 221), 'to a family that had, he told us, called itself Irish some generations back, and its English generations but enabled him to see as one single sacred tradition Irish nationality and Catholic religion.' Although WBY had ambitions to make Johnson the critic and theologian of the Irish literary revival, he later saw (*UP* 1. 382) that his best poems were written under influences 'which have no connection with Ireland'.

In the event, Johnson postponed his visit to Dublin until 1893; the following year, on 26 Apr 1894, he lectured to the National Literary Society on 'Poetry and Patriotism'. The Dublin Social and Literary Club was intended at this time to be the Dublin branch of the Young Ireland League, but in fact both organizations were superseded by the National Literary Society which WBY helped to found in 1892.

[5] Rhys's general shortage of money—perhaps accentuated by the birth of a son, Brian, on 4 Oct 1891—explains why WBY thought he would like to be paid for any lecture he gave. His visit to London in November 1891 resulted in some reviewing for the *Pall Mall Gazette*. Jack Yeats, having made drawings for *The Great Cockney Tragedy* (see p. 228), does not appear to have illustrated any more of Rhys's work.

[6] 'There are some people coming here this evening,' JBY wrote to JO'L on 9 Nov 1891 (NLI), 'Rolleston & Mrs R. among them—A. Lynch is asked & Mr Todhunter & Mrs, Tom Bonines [?] & Nashes & Stepniac & Mrs S—& Charles Johnson [*sic*] & Mrs Johnson'. Rolleston, now living in London, was to play an important part in setting up the Irish Literary Society, London, and WBY was clearly hoping to interest him in the Young Ireland League. The relationship between Arthur Lynch and the Rhymers was not good but none of them appear to have availed themselves of the opportunity of reviewing his *Modern Authors* (see p. 254), published in September 1891.

[7] MG was mourning the death of her 'adopted' son (see p. 248), and WBY was trying to find ways of occupying her mind. Although she did little for the Young Ireland League, she worked energetically for its successor, the National Literary Society. C. H. Oldham was a close friend of MG's and had helped introduce her into nationalist political circles in Dublin in 1888. He joined the National Literary Society, but was not particularly active in it.

a copy as soon as I get one to O'Donovan of the "National Press" & ask him for a notice.[8] If Ash King has not sent you his copy yet I will get you one. Please let me know by post card.

Yours always sincely

W B Yeats

Ellis is getting a volume of his poems with twenty or thirty drawings through the press.[9]

ALS NLI. Wade, 180–2.

To George Russell (AE), [20 November 1891]

3 Blenheim Road | Bedford Park | Chiswick. W

My dear Russel

Tell me about Miss Johnstons Resteraunt. Some one told me it had come to an end. I want to know as soon as possible because otherwise I should have one or two letters to write in connection with our attempt at a Social & Literary Club—letters to Ash King & Miss Johnston. I fear however that my news is correct. Tell me what you know of Miss Johnstons plans if she has any. I heard about the Veg from Ernest Rhys who heard of it from Miss Little.[1]

I am getting on with Blake—The Memoir, about 60 pages, is being printed & there is about as much more of the explanetory part ready to follow up with. "The Countess Kathleen" has not gone to Unwin yet for I am slowly correcting it & getting other verses ready to go with it. Henley has written to me about "Sherman & Dhoya". He likes them very much but likes Doya best. I hope he will review them.[2] ⟨ "The Book of the Rhymers Club" has been taken by a publisher & is to be [? out] by Xmas with a frontispeice by Ellis. ⟩ So much for my literary affairs.

I will write again more at length about the past incarnation story for now I write in haste merely seeking information about Miss Johnston & the Veg. Mrs Mathers who was the seer had not heard of your vision.[3] Hers was not

---

[8] A notice of *John Sherman and Dhoya*, identifying WBY as the author, appeared in *United Ireland*, 28 Nov 1891 (5). Although Robert Donovan (see p. 259, n. 7) was to be a founder member of the National Literary Society in the following year, the *National Press*—perhaps because of WBY's known Parnellism—appears not to have reviewed the book.

[9] *Fate in Arcadia* (see p. 55), to be published the following year.

[1] WBY seems to have been planning to use the restaurant (see p. 234) as a meeting place for the Social and Literary Society he wanted to establish in Dublin in connection with the Young Ireland League. Miss Emily C. Little, Ernest Rhys's sister-in-law (see p. 230), now lived at 6 Lower Fitzwilliam Street, Dublin.

[2] No review of *John Sherman and Dhoya* appeared in the *National Observer*.

[3] See p. 260.

absolutely identical in its details but curiously alike in total effect. She made Miss G— a priestess of a temple in Tyre & connected her with some one, whom, she said afterwards, resembled me, though she was not quite certain. This man lived in the desert & had much the same story as yours except that there was an episode apparently later than anything you arrived at in which he helped her to escape from the Temple. She afterwards went away by herself into the desert & died there. This was corrobirated by a dream continually recurring with Miss G— of journeying on & on in a desert.

Yours very siny
W B Yeats

ALS Indiana, with envelope addressed to 3 Upper Ely Place, postmark 'CHISWICK NO 20 91'. Wade, 183–4.

To John O'Leary [? *25 November 1891*]

3 Blenheim Road | Bedford Park | Chiswick—W
Wednesday

Dear M^r O'Leary

Could you lend me £1? I will return it to you as soon as any body pays me anything. I am owed various amounts by various people but my only regular & certain paymaster "the Providence Journal" has either not taken or has post poned my article sent last month. The late editor Williams is now doing most of the literary work himself—Hence the rest of us are elbowed out to some extent.[1] I can't trouble the "National Observer" until there proper pay day comes round as they rather resent one's doing so I think. They have asked me, by the by for stories like Dhoya if I can make them short enough to fit their pages. I doubt if it can be done but mean to try.[2] You need not return the copy of John Sherman which you have, as I have got a few more copies. Did Ash King like it? Henley praises it & it seems generally to be liked. If you meet Taylor ask him what he thought of it.[3]

Blake goes on slowly—A good big bundle of MSS has gone to the

[1] The last of WBY's articles in *PSJ* appeared on 26 July 1891 (see p. 262, n. 1). Alfred Williams retired as editor in 1891.

[2] WBY contributed a number of stories to the *National Observer*, beginning with 'The Devil's Book' (reprinted in *The Secret Rose* [1897] as 'The Book of the Great Dhoul and Hanrahan the Red'), 26 Nov 1892, and finishing with 'The Curse of O'Sullivan the Red upon Old Age' (reprinted in *The Secret Rose* as 'The Curse of Hanrahan the Red'), 29 Sept 1894.

[3] An unsigned review of *John Sherman and Dhoya* in the *Manchester Guardian*, 24 Nov 1891 (7), probably by John F. Taylor, reveals that he thought the book 'a good addition' to the Pseudonym Library. *John Sherman*, he found, 'savours in parts more of Boston than of Ballymacrasy. It is not, however, by any means purely imitative, and shows very considerable talent. . . . The story is nothing; the telling a good deal.' He thought *Dhoya* 'of the fairy order, and Crofton Crokerish'.

printer. I am bringing the MS of my new book of poems to Fisher Unwin today but do not think they will be out until next April as the man who is publishing "the Book of the Rhymers Club" wants to keep the copyright of the poems it contains until the end of March. Some of my best lyrics are to be in it so I must wait until April to reprint them.[4] What of The Young Ireland League? I wrote to Lavelle for information & got no answer. If you meet him please stir him up.[5] Miss Gonne will be in Dublin in 10 days or less—She returns to London from Paris in two or three days. The main reasen why I ask you for the loan of this £1 is that I do not want to be without the price of cabs Etc while she is here & I have promised to take her to one or two places. Some times post me a United Ireland as I never see an Irish paper here by any chance—

Yours Always
W B Yeats

[*Diagonally across top of first page*]
I have just heard from Lavelle about the League. They were waiting until things had settled down after Parnells death.

ALS NLI. Wade, 184–5.

To Katharine Tynan, [*2 December 1891*]

3 Blenheim Road | Bedford Park | Chiswick | W

My Katey—

The books I left with Dr Sigerson for you were Hyde's Beside the Fire The Kilkenny Journal[1] & one or two more whose names I do not remember. Of course I had nothing to do with the Menzoni & Brent Harte things. Did I tell you how fine I think the poems in your new book are? They are quite

---

[4] *The Book of the Rhymers' Club*, published by Elkin Mathews in February 1892, contained WBY's 'A Man who dreamed of Fairyland', 'Father Gilligan', 'Dedication of "Irish Tales"' (see p. 247), 'A Fairy Song', 'The Lake Isle of Innisfree', and 'An Epitaph' (*VP*, 123; subsequently retitled 'A Dream of Death'). In a copy of the book given to Lady Gregory (Emory), WBY wrote: 'This little book was put together at my suggestion. I suggested it because I wanted to have copies of Dowson's poems. He had read them to us at the Cheshire Cheese.' Ernest Dowson (1867–1900) had yet to publish the volume of *Poems* (1896) which made his name among the poets of the '90s.

[5] Letters had appeared in the press from Patrick Lavelle (b. 1866), of 11 Leahy's Terrace, Sandymount, Dublin, secretary of the National Club Literary Society, calling for the formation of a League of Young Ireland literary societies, and he announced the objects to the League at its inaugural meeting on 15 Sept 1891 (see p. 269). A native of Co. Tyrone, Lavelle had taken a BA in political economy and civil and constitutional law at the Royal University in 1890. He acted as secretary to the committee of the new organization until it was replaced by the National Literary Society in 1892.

[1] The *Kilkenny Journal* was an antiquarian magazine of some standing, which frequently published folklore.

your best work. The Apologia is exquitic—Rolleston likes it best of all your work.[2] There is a man here—a well known journalist Fox-Bourne by name—who has been wholly captivated by your "Nun".[3] I am very glad to hear that the book has sold so well. My own "Sherman" is doing well—I got my first £10 for it last Saturday & shall I hear get about £30 at any rate—Unwin is to bring out "The Countess Kathleen"—The Blake too is going a-head—But I am not very well these days & so take little joy out of this glimmering of ampler life & success. Never did the mountain of deeds seem so steep & my feet so poor at climbing. I have one of my fits of depression it will go by after a week or two. I imagine I have already written to you in the past from the deeps of more than one but as life goes on, they blacken. One knows at the worst of them however that the sun & the wind will together make the path merry again. I say all this to explain why I have not written before—I keep my black moods out of my letters by keeping my letters out of my black moods. I write now because I have your questions about the books to answer. Did you get a post card I sent you, asking for Miss Fagans address? I met her in an Omnibus & asked her to come & see us & then finding we would not be in that day wrote to you for her address that I might ask her for some other day. You did not send it & she came & found only my mother I beleive. I am going to write & ask her for next Monday however. Her address being I think "Alexandra Mansions".[4] My mother thinks it was that if it be not would you let me know—

"The Book of the Rhymers Club" has been taken by Elkin Mathews & will appear about Xmas. It is a very fine book & will give you material for an article or two. I enclose a page from the "proofs" of Edwin Ellis' book of poems "Fate in Arcadia". I think it is very pretty. It is not his best for it rather lacks music of which he has plenty at most times, but is good I think. I have a fancy for the last verse but one—[5]

Henley has asked me for things like Dhoya for "The National Observer" & writes praises of "John Sherman". When you review it you might perhaps, if you think it is so, say that Sherman is an Irish type. I have an

---

[2] KT's 'Apologia' (*Ballads and Lyrics*, vii) begins, 'Here in my book there will be found / No gleanings from a foreign ground: / The quiet thoughts of one whose feet / Have scarcely left her green retreat . . .'

[3] Henry Richard Fox-Bourne (1837–1909), social reformer and prolific author and journalist, was by this time secretary of the Aborigines Protection Society and was campaigning vigorously against the treatment of native peoples, especially in the Congo.

[4] Blanche Clara Fagan (b. 1869), 'a living rose', according to KT (*25 Years*, 283), was a sister of Charles Gregory Fagan (see p. 65). Their father, the Revd Henry Stuart Fagan (1827–90), was an enthusiastic supporter of Irish Home Rule. KT stayed with the family at Great Cressingham, Norfolk, on her visits to England in 1885 and 1889, and Blanche Fagan visited KT at Clondalkin in June 1887.

[5] In his review of Ellis's *Fate in Arcadia* (*UP* I. 234–7) in the *Bookman*, September 1892, WBY praised the poems which, despite their occasional obscurity, seemed 'to come out of a great depth of emotion which exists for itself alone'. The poem in question here cannot now be identified.

ambition to be taken as an Irish novelist not as an English or cosmepolitan one chosing Ireland as a background. I studied my characters in Ireland & described a typical Irish feeling in Sherman's devotion to Ballah. A West of Ireland feeling I might almost say for like that of Allingham for Ballyshannon it is local rather than national. Sherman belonged like Allingham to the small gentry who in the West at any rate love their native places without perhaps loving Ireland. They do not travell & are shut off from England by the whole breadth of Ireland with the result that they are forced to make their native town their world. I remember when we were children how intense our devotion was to all things in Sligo & still see in my mother the old feeling.[6] I claim for this & other reasons that Sherman is as much an Irish novel as anything by Banim or Griffen. Lady Wylde has written me an absurd & enthusiastic letter about it. She is queer enough to prefer it to my poems. The reviews are nearly all good so far.

Yours very siny
W B Yeats

ALS Huntington, with envelope addressed to Clondalkin, postmark 'CHISWICK DE 2 91'. McHugh, 131–3; Wade, 186–8.

[6] KT reviewed *John Sherman* anonymously in both the Dublin *Evening Telegraph*, 29 Dec 1891 (2), and in the *Irish Daily Independent* of 4 Jan 1892 (7). 'The interest of the story and the characters for us Irish', she wrote in the *Telegraph*,

is that both are Irish, and Mr. Yeats in creating 'John Sherman' has shown us a type Irish and pathetic which none of our other novelists has hit upon. Where in all the world but Ireland would you find John Sherman, whose world is in the things he has been born into, and has looked upon with round childish eyes, and the quieter eyes of youth and manhood! Your Irishman has indeed an untravelled heart, and to John Sherman even the dullness of Ballah is dear, because it is familiar and home-like . . . he is the bourgeois brother of the Irish peasant who clings to his bleak hillside as to a most precious inheritance, and is all his life a mixture of shrewdness and simplicity.

KT also went out of her way in the *Independent* review to stress that John Sherman was 'a distinctly Irish type'.

In *Aut* (31) WBY recalled that as a child in London 'I longed for a sod of earth from some field I knew, something of Sligo to hold in my hand . . . it was our mother . . . who kept alive that love. She would spend hours listening to stories or telling stories of the pilots and fishing-people of Rosses Point, or of her own Sligo girlhood, and it was always assumed between her and us that Sligo was more beautiful than other places.' Reviewing a 6-vol. collected edition of William Allingham's poems at this time, for *United Ireland*, 12 Dec 1891 (*UP* I. 208–12), WBY said that the poems 'enshrined that passionate devotion that so many Irishmen feel for the little town where they were born, and for the mountains they saw from the doors they passed through in childhood,' and that Allingham would be 'best loved by those who, like the present writer, have spent their childhood in some small Western seaboard town, and who remember how it was for years the centre of their world, and how its enclosing mountains and its quiet rivers became a portion of their life for ever.'

To John O'Leary, [c. 4 *December 1891*]

3 Blenheim Road | Bedford Park | Chiswick | W

Dear Mᵣ O'Leary

The day your postal orders came¹ a sum of £10 reached me as a first instalment for "John Sherman". I was not able to cash the checque until Monday & so used a fraction of your £1 for some short railway journeys I had to make upon Sunday. I had intended to return the £1 at once after Monday & so did not send acknowledgement & then I found so many small bills—house bills—crying out for payment that I was afraid I might not be able to manage it—Some days passed by in the same doubt—the orders which I enclose being all the time on my table awaiting posting. Only to day I found it was all right about the bills & that I will have plenty out of my £10 for all immediate need. I therefore send back the £1 with a very great many thanks. Miss Gonne is still in Paris. She wrote to me last week to say she was coming at once & would let me know when to expect her but as yet I have not heard anything definite. You misunderstood me about the cabs. She does not let me pay the whole fare but stipulated a good while ago that she should pay her own share. When I wrote to you I had however if I remember rightly just three halfpence & no hope of more for a month & had she come at once as I expected I should have been in a fix. Fisher Unwin has taken "the Countes Kathleen" & will publish it as the April volume of his "Cameo Series". I am to add lyrics & ballads at the end of the book. I have a vague chance of getting it acted but will write again when there is something definite.² "The United Irelands" Etc were very welcome. Again thanks and apologies.

Yours ever
W B Yeats

[*Diagonally across top of first page*]
Have you heard what Taylor thought of Sherman?

ALS NLI. Wade, 185–6.

¹ See p. 272.
² *The Countess Kathleen and Various Legends and Lyrics* was not in fact published until September 1892 in Unwin's monthly Cameo series. The play which gave the volume its title was not performed until the Irish Literary Theatre's production on 8 May 1899, but there was a reading to secure copyright in London in May 1892.

To Ernest Rhys, [*? 28 December 1891*]

3 Blenheim Road | Bedford Park | Chiswick. W

My dear Rhys—

I am unfortunately tied to my desk by Blake for some time to come or I should have been in Dublin now. I am glad to hear of your going over, I have written to Oldham sec of the Contemporary Club & asked him to invite you to a meeting of the club. It meets on Saturday evenings & will be an introduction to nationalistic people. You should go & see John O'Leary at 58 Mountjoy Square. He is always in between 1ᵒᶜ & 2ᵒᶜ & glad to see people. He can let you see some thing of nationalist Ireland.[1]

The Rhymers book is in the press but no proofs have come in as yet. Xmas work is the cause of delay I beleive. We have not had a meeting of late but will next week or the week after. My own work goes on somehow. Unwin has taken my Irish play & all the lyrics I have by me, for the Cameo Series & Blake is getting himself written—The play comes out early in April—I have a chance too of getting it acted.

I am busy just now in starting a London branch of The Young Ireland League & am expecting a batch of young Irishmen here this evening to consider project[2]—but am going on with things rather mechanically feeling bored to death by most things in life & out of it. Get these fits from the old serpent rather often but live through them anyhow. You have not told me what you are writing. I hope Dublin will use you well.

Yours very sincy

W B Yeats

ALS BL.

[1] Ernest Rhys and his wife, the former Grace Little, spent a week in Dublin at the end of 1891 with her brother, William Little, when Rhys made use of both WBY's introductions. In a letter to JO'L from 3 Victoria Terrace, Leeson Park, Dublin, dated 'Tuesday' (? 5 Jan 1892, NLI), Rhys wrote: 'Can you look in on us on Thursday evening, the 7th., about half-past six, in time for "high tea"? I am sorry not to have been able to reach Mountjoy Squ. during the hours you are to be found, having my work to detain me. . . . I had a very good time of it at the Contemporary Club on Saty., meeting Dr Sigerson, etc. there.'

The Rhyses were to have spent Christmas with Mrs Rhys's eccentric uncle, Roper Little, in Roscommon, but she was still too weak after the birth of her son (see p. 270) to make the further journey, thereby alienating her uncle.

[2] The first meeting to discuss an Irish Literary Society in London was held at WBY's house on 28 Dec 1891, and was attended by T. W. Rolleston, D. J. O'Donoghue, John Todhunter, W. P. Ryan, and J. G. O'Keeffe (late secretary of the Southwark Irish Literary Club). It was agreed that a central Irish Literary Society should be set up, holding regular lecture meetings and arranging for the publication and circulation of Irish books. There were numerous meetings in various places in London over the next few months before the Inaugural General Meeting was held at the Caledonian Hotel in May 1892.

To Katharine Tynan, [? 31 December 1891]

3 Blenheim Road | Bedford Park | Chiswick. W

My dear Katey

I have sent in a long review of your book to the Evening Herald. I sent it on Monday & am very sorry I was not able to send it before. I have been rather unwell this last fortneight & quite without the initiative needed for a start at any thing but my daily round of Blake chapters. The printer has about 170 pages in hands now & the rest will follow as fast as he can print it. All Xmas week I have been wretchedly headachy, & that kind of thing, & hope my headache has not got in to the review. It is enthusiastic at any rate. Will you not send me a copy of the book? I will review you again for the Pilot & perhaps some where else so I think I deserve a copy even if "old acquaintance sake" were not enough.[1] I am too hard up at present to buy a copy. I am busy getting up a London Irish Literary Society—to be a branch ultimately of Young Ireland League—we are asking Gavan Duffy to be President & are hoping to get Stopford Brook for one of the vice presidents & Rolleston promises to be another.[2] I have put your book down to be got for the library. I want you to review Dr Todhunters "Banshee" for the Evening Herald. He has published a 1/– edition, or rather a 1/– rebinding of his "remainders", with Seeley Bryers & Co & we must do all we can to sell it off. I will do it for United Ireland.[3] The Rhymers Book is in "proof" so you will soon be able to say a good word for us there I hope. Ernest Rhys is in Dublin. Do you know him? I am writing to give him a note of introduction to you.[4] His address is c/o Miss Little, 6 Lower Fitzwilliam St Dublin. He & his wife are both over. Did I tell you that my "Countess Kathleen" comes out in

---

[1] WBY's signed review of *Ballads and Lyrics*, 'Poems by Miss Tynan' (*UP* II. 511–14), appeared in the Dublin *Evening Herald*, 2 Jan 1892. In it he placed KT's work in an evolving tradition of Irish poetry, as well as seeing the book as a new stage in her own development, being 'well nigh in all things a thoroughly Irish book, springing straight from the Celtic mind, and pouring itself out in soft Celtic music. . . . in thus gaining nationality of style Miss Tynan has found herself and found the world about her.' He did not review the book for the *Boston Pilot*.

[2] As WBY hoped, Sir Charles Gavan Duffy became the first president of the Irish Literary Society, London. Stopford Brooke (see p. 53), a founder member of the Society, became one of its vice-presidents, and in March 1893 delivered its inaugural lecture on 'The Need and Use of Getting Irish Literature into the English Tongue'. Rolleston became the Society's secretary.

[3] KT did review the 1s edition of *The Banshee and Other Poems*, not for the *Evening Herald* but for the *Irish Daily Independent*, to which she began to contribute regular unsigned reviews, under the heading 'Our Reviewer's Table', in January 1892. In her notice (14 Jan 1892, 6) she stressed that the book was 'a cheap shilling edition' and hoped that it would 'find its way into whatever public or village libraries Ireland may possess' since it was 'Celtic of the Celtic, and in coming back to his motherland from Greece and the Greeks, Dr Todhunter has found himself.' WBY in his notice in *United Ireland*, 23 Jan 1892 (*UP* I. 215–18), praised Todhunter's poems on Irish themes but thought the inclusion of non-Irish ones a mistake, since they were 'full of poetic diction' unlike the 'primeval utterance' of the Irish poems.

[4] KT reviewed *The Book of the Rhymers' Club* in the *Independent* for 25 Feb 1892 (6–7), picking out WBY's poems for particular attention, and also mentioned Rhys's *The Great Cockney Tragedy* on 20 Jan 1892 (6).

Samuel Liddell MacGregor Mathers

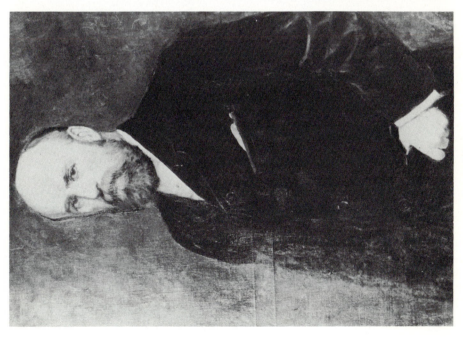

Edwin Ellis

Florence Farr

April & that the book of Fairy Tales I edited for Unwin is to appear soon. What a terribly bookish letter this is? But then the four walls of my study are my world just now. Do you see the National Observer? If you do, please tell me what you thought of my "Epitaph" & what you think, when you see it, of my next poem *Rosa Mundi*.[5] But I must wind up this now for when one is unwell there is only ink in one's veins & ink when one expects human nature is deadly dull & I must bore you with no more of it.

Yours Always
W B Yeats

ALS Huntington, with envelope addressed to Clondalkin, postmark 'LONDON W. DE [?]31 91'. McHugh, 133–4; Wade, 188–9.

[5] 'An Epitaph' (see p. 273, n. 4) had appeared in the *National Observer* on 12 Dec 1891; 'Rosa Mundi' (*VP*, 111–12; later entitled 'The Rose of the World') was published in the same paper on 2 Jan 1892.

1892

To John O'Leary, [c. 15 January 1892]

3 Blenheim Road | Bedford Park | Chiswick. W

Dear M^r O'Leary

Will you be so good as to help me out of a difficulty? There is still £2.3.10 owing to Keegan Paul on "Oisin" & they threaten me with lawyers. I want to take the remaining 100 copies out of their hand & get Fisher Unwin to sell them which he will do with ease—There is as it is, some slight sale & a steadily increasing one.[1] The new book will sell the rest of the copies. I want you to lend me £2.10.0 so that I can make the transfer at once.

Rolleston has told you I hear about our Literary Club. I am cheifly anxious about it because I have a plan for a new "Library of Ireland" which I have talked over with Garnett. He belives that if we could get 500 subscribers for books at 2/– to be published evry two months or so, through the Young Ireland League & its branches—of which the Irish Litery Club London will be one—that Unwin would take up such a library giving me a free hand and letting us couple an Irish publisher with him. He would trust to English sale to make it pay. We ought to get 500 subscribers with ease. If we got 800 hundred or so, we could do without Unwin at all. Each Branch of the Young Ireland League might take so many copies, & we could publish the Libry under its auspices.[2] Of course we cannot count on Unwin but there is a good chance.

I will get you some Occult catologues as soon as I get to town.[3] I have not

---

[1] Kegan Paul's accounts for December 1891 (KPA) show that he had failed to cover his publishing costs by the £2.3.10 WBY mentions, although no letter from him to WBY threatening to take legal action to recover these costs has survived. Annual sales of *Oisin* to non-subscribers had been: 1889, 35; 1890, 11; 1891, 29.

[2] The need for a series of inexpensive books dealing with Irish literature, history, and culture was stressed in the manifestos of both the Young Ireland League in Dublin and the proposed Irish Literary Society in London (see p. 277). Plans for a venture similar to the original 'Library of Ireland', published in the 1840s (see below, p. 298, n. 4), were to occupy WBY for most of 1892.

[3] Although JO'L was highly dubious of WBY's occult activities, his bibliophilia seems to have been stronger than his scepticism.

been very well lately & have been a little stay at home. The Blake is to be done by March at latest or by the end of February if possible & my poems will be out by April. Thank you very much for United Ireland I am always very glad to get it.

I was very sorry to hear that you have had the influenza.[4]

Yours Always
W B Yeats

ALS NLI. Wade, 198–9.

To John O'Leary, [c. 18 or 19 January 1892]

3 Blenheim Road | Bedford Park | Chiswick | London W

Dear M^r O Leary

Thank you very much for sending the money.[1] I would have acknowledge[d] it yesterday but I was away in town all day long & did not get home until late.

I will copy out the article you want the next time I am in the Museum which will be this week I think. There has turned up a new Blake MSS which will keep me out of town to day & perhaps tomorrow.[2] Our Irish Literary Society London promises well in all ways. We have an opening meeting very soon now[3] & it has done one good deed any way. It has stirred up Rolleston's Irish ardour again. I hear from Garnett that O'Grady is to do a book of Fin McCool stories for their "Children's Library". All such books seem to me to be clear gain for Irish feeling. My own "Irish Fairy Stories" will be out very soon now with two drawings by Jack.[4]

I am correcting the new book of poems for the press. The "Countess

---

[4] On 2 Jan 1892 the *Irish Times* had announced that JO'L was laid up with influenza.

[1] See preceding letter.

[2] WBY had discovered the MS of Blake's *An Island in the Moon* (1784–5), then in the possession of the Pre-Raphaelite painter and collector, Charles Fairfax Murray (1849–1919). A man of discriminating taste, Murray built up an exceptionally fine art collection, the main part of which is now in the Pierpont Morgan Library. In a letter of 31 January [1892] (Rylands), Ellis wrote to Murray: 'I have borrowed your Blake M.S. from Yeats. . . . I am very grateful for the loan, and the permission to use, which I have availed myself of more largely than you would suppose, having written out several pages of the droll conversation if all my extracts were to be pieced together. A sort of compressed account of the general drift of the thing from first to last comes between.' Extracts from the MS (now in the Fitzwilliam Museum, Cambridge) appear, somewhat inaccurately transcribed, in *The Works of William Blake* (1. 186–201).

[3] Ryan (56) reports that the formal decision to establish the Irish Literary Society of London was taken at a meeting held at the Clapham Reform Club on 13 Jan 1892. News of the projected Society was reaching the Dublin papers by mid-January.

[4] *Finn and his Companions* by Standish James O'Grady was published in October 1892 in Unwin's Children's Library—the same series in which *IFT* (see p. 256) appeared in May 1892.

Kathleen" takes 100 pages & there will be 30 or 40 pages of Lyrics & ballads.
It comes out early in April, about the same time as the Blake probably.
Fisher Unwin talks of reprinting Wolf Tones Memoirs with an introduction
by Rolleston & notes by Barry O'Brien. He first thought of Barry O'Brien
doing the whole thing but I got him to change his mind by talking it over
with Garnett.[5] He is going to bring out a series of Memoirs in which
Rolleston could I dare say get the doing of Wolf Tone. He is friendly to Irish
matters of all kinds.

Yours always
W B Yeats

ALS NLI. Wade, 199.

To D. J. O'Donoghue, [c. 19 January 1892]

3 Blenheim Road | Bedford Park | Chiswick. W.

My dear O'Donohue

I send the Blake prospectus—excuse its soiled condition. It is the only one
I have. If you are doing a note upon it for United Ireland you might say that
it will probably be published in April.[1] Say to[o] that my new book of poems
"The Countess Kathleen & other poems" will be out then in The Cameo
Series & contain a play, which is an attempt to write a national drama, of
about 100 pages, & 30 pages or so of lyrics & ballads (these all on Irish
subjects). About the same time I will have a collection of folk lore "Irish
Fairy Tales" in Unwins Children Series a volume suplementary to my
"Fairy & Folk Tales of the Irish peasentry". Will you mention the lecture in
the note.[2]

Yours very truly
W B Yeats

Mention my collaberators name in your note. He is an artist & is bringing out
his poems with illustrations by himself next month.[3] They are full of lovely
things, both poems & pictures. He is a member of the Rhymers Club.

[5] *The Autobiography of Theobald Wolfe Tone, 1763–1798*, edited by R. Barry O'Brien, was published
by Fisher Unwin in 1893; the introduction, not in the event by Rolleston but by Barry O'Brien, is dated
April 1893.

[1] *The Works of William Blake* was not to appear until February 1893.

[2] O'Donoghue did all that he was asked. *United Ireland* for 23 Jan 1892 published a full report (3) of
WBY's lecture on 'Nationality and Literature', delivered on 17 Jan 1892 to the Clapham branch of the
Irish National League of Great Britain. The same issue contained a paragraph from 'a London
correspondent' (5) mentioning that WBY and Ellis were 'shortly to publish their splendid edition of
Blake's poetic works in two volumes', and giving space to *The Countess Kathleen*, *IFT*, and even the
success of *John Sherman and Dhoya*.

[3] Ellis's *Fate in Arcadia*, not mentioned in the *United Ireland* paragraph.

In this scrawl of a letter you have probably enough information—& more than enough for your purpose—& I am in too great haste to write more.

ALS Texas.

To T. Fisher Unwin, [*31 January 1892*]

3 Blenheim Road | Bedford Park | Chiswick. W
Sunday

Dear Mr Unwin

I have between 90 & 100 copies (in sheets) of my book of poems "The Wanderings of Oisin" The edition was 500. I am taking these 90 copies from Keegan Paul & shall have them here in a few days. I want to know would you be so kind as to take them over & bind them & put a new title page.[1] My friend Edwin J Ellis has drawn & printed a charming frontispeice. He has a lithographic press & proposes to strike off a hundred copies [of] the frontispeice to be bound into the volume. The book might be advertised inside the cameo book "The Countess Kathleen" & would I doubt not sell off. The sale has been slow but latterly an increasing sale. Elkin Matthews had promised to take the book until he found that he was not going to get the publishing of "The Countess Kathleen". He then withdrew on the grounds that he could not make the book pay without the other to advertise it.[2] I have capital press notices from "The Saturday Review" "National Observer" "Academy" Etc.

Yours truly
B Yeats

ALS Texas. Dated by recipient '3.2.92'.

[1] See p. 280. Ninety-eight quires remained but before transferring them to Unwin WBY had 25 bound by Kegan Paul, to whom he paid the £2.3.10 outstanding on 4 Feb 1892. On 8 Feb, these 25 bound copies and 73 unbound quires were transferred to the author. Kegan Paul was left with 19 bound copies from unpaid subscriptions and by 22 Oct 1895 the sale of some of these had paid off a further £1.5.3. owing to him for additional binding, postage, and commission (KPA).

[2] In May 1892, Fisher Unwin published a second issue of *Oisin*, consisting presumably of the original 73 quires with a cancel title, a frontispiece by Edwin Ellis representing Niam, Oisin, and St. Patrick, and bound in green paper boards with parchment spine. Under the terms of their agreement (Berg) WBY bore the expense of inserting the cancel title-page and, if necessary, rebinding. No advertisement of *Oisin* appeared in *The Countess Kathleen* when it was published later that year. For WBY's attempt in 1889 to get Elkin Mathews to take unsold copies of *Oisin*, see p. 191.

To Ernest Rhys, [early February 1892]

3 Blenheim Road | Bedford Park | Chiswick. W

My dear Rhys

I return the poem. I like some of the stazas very much—especially the 6th & 7th of part one & the 1st of the third part also the last stanza of all. "From the ancient house of Hendra" is a genuine phrase of romance. I like the whole poem but not so well as others of yours I think. It is just a little perhaps too entirely a back-ground. It wants foreground—a central incident or some explanation why the house of Hendra should be more haunted than all others. At the same time it is very interesting.[1] I wish you would tell us even though it were but in a foot note who or what Hendra was. Its vagueness seems to me to take from the poems apparent antiquity & primeval quality & authenticity as a translation.[2] I dont know about the Welsh but the Irish bards any way, always were explicit rather than suggestive in dealing with the supernatural. I was coming from such & such a town & staid in the house of such & such a person when I saw such & such a spirit dressed in such & such a cloak—is their method. They surround the vague with the definite. They would, to use Blakes expression, always hide Wisdom "in a silver rod & Love in a golden bowl."[3]

I enclose the poem you asked for. Please give my best regards to Mrs Rhys—

Yours very sncy

W B Yeats

ALS BL.

[1] In Rhys's poem 'The House of Hendra', the Welsh bard Brechva sings of a Hallowmas vision he has had in the House of Hendra. The ghosts of the House performed a dance of death, and he was vouchsafed a glimpse of the bardic Heaven where he saw his own destined seat awaiting him. At the conclusion of his ballad, Brechva sets out once more for the House of Hendra to die joyful in the knowledge of his certain assumption into paradise.

When the poem was published in his *A London Rose and Other Rhymes* (1894) Rhys divided it into seven parts, but Part I consists of only four stanzas. The sixth and seventh stanzas of the poem occur in Part II. The 'phrase of romance' is from the last stanza of the poem:

> And all peace be yours and Brechva's
> Now, and fate
> In the ancient House of Hendra
> Yield him soon death's high estate!

Lionel Johnson, writing to Rhys 'probably in 1892' (*Letters from Limbo*, 102), also liked the poem: 'The House of Hendra is delightful,' he said; 'do more of this sort.'

[2] Rhys evidently took WBY's advice, for a note to the poem in *A London Rose* explains that 'Hendra' is the term used for an old or established habitation and that it forms part of the name of many old mansions in Wales. The title became 'The House of Hendrë' when the poem was again reprinted in Rhys's *Welsh Ballads and Other Poems* (1898).

[3] cf. Thel's Motto in Plate One of Blake's *The Book of Thel*: 'Does the Eagle know what is in the pit / Or wilt thou go ask the Mole, / Can Wisdom be put in a silver rod, / Or Love in a golden bowl?'

To John O'Leary, [after 17 February 1892]

3 Blenheim Road | Bedford Park | Chiswick | London. W
Dear M^r O'Leary

Miss Gonne returned to Paris last week. She was hear for about ten days & then went back to deliver a series of lectures which she prepared over here. She will be in London again in March on her way to Ireland where she hopes to be able to help in the work of the Young Ireland League. You will remember the plan for the starting of village libraries which was put forward at the convention. She will be able she thinks to get money in Paris to help on such a project as soon as it is properly under weigh.[1]

Our "Irish Literary Society" goes on well & promises to be larger than we expected. Our men are eager over the publication project.[2] What I suggest to do in the matter is this. Our London society will guarrantee a sale of (say) 200 copies at a 1/– each. 10 or 20 members or more can easily subscrible that ammount amongst them. Miss Gonne will get her French organization to take a certain number on the same understanding. There are now I think five literary societies in Dublin counting the new one at which Coffey spoke the other day. They might surely be got to take 40 or 50 copies a peice or (say) 300 amongst them.[3] Cork & Belfast & where ever else there are Young Ireland Societi[es] or branches of the Young Ireland League can be appealed to by circulers & other wise to take part. If we can get 800 or 900 copies subscribed we can start without chance of loss. Once under weigh with a couple of volumes or so the series would sell itself I beleive. Rolleston promises to do for the first volume a history of Fenianism of a popular nature & to fill it with sound national doctrine. I would myself do "a ballad chronicle of Ireland"—a Davis idia—selected from all the ballad writers & peice the poems to gether with short historical notes. For later volumes I

---

[1] MG had begun an energetic course of lectures in France, drawing attention to the wrongs done to Ireland, which WBY ensured got maximum coverage in the Irish nationalist press. The library scheme, for setting up reading rooms associated with country branches of the Young Ireland League, was later taken over by the National Literary Society and WBY and MG were active in promoting it in early 1893.

[2] 'There was naturally much talk,' as Ryan (58–9) recalled,

about a new Irish Library . . . at some of the initial gatherings. Certain necessary books were suggested, as well as the most capable men to write them. Several titles for the series were discussed, amongst them being 'The Shamrock Library', 'The National Library of Ireland', and 'The Red Branch Library'. Yeats believed that a good designation would be 'The Bell-branch Library' . . . under the influence of the growing enthusiasm, and with the prospect of improved means of distribution . . . hopeful results were expected.

[3] The Dublin societies of which WBY was thinking were probably the Leinster Literary Society, the Rathmines National League Literary Society, the Aran-Quay Literary Society, the National Club Literary Society, and the Ninety Club. The society which George Coffey chaired and addressed on 9 Feb 1892 was not a new literary society but the Central Branch of the Irish National League, a Parnellite political organization of some years' standing. Coffey's speech was reported both in the *Freeman's Journal*, 10 Feb 1892, and *United Ireland*, 13 Feb.

have been offered "the Ossianic Stories" by York Powell & Education in Ireland by Lionel Johnston. O'Grady would probably do a book also & I myself have a wish to write a manual of Irish literature in the present century.[4] Such a series should have I think three directors who would show the various parties that it was national & not party—You & Sigerson might make two of them. I should myself be editor & should have no Barry O'Brien or any one else except the directors associated with me to hamper my action (I am told that if Unwin took the series he would make this a condition for he knows me & not the others). Apropos of Barry O'Brien & the Wolf Tone.[5] I did not recommend Rolleston until I had found out from him that he knew the subject thoroughly. He told me he had worked at it exaustively & knew it quite as well as O'Brien. Irish literature has been far too much in the hands of the men of learning who cannot write. This is I think one of the reasons why so few people read Irish books. I wish you however would do the preface to the Wolf Tone instead of either Rolleston or O'Brien. By the by I helped to stop off another man of learning the other day who came trying to get a book from Unwin to do. The man of learning who has no literature is my natural enemy. I sometimes think he is the enemy of the human race. Did I tell you about the "Irish Saga Series" that Unwin is thinking of. Douglas Hyde who is now in London came with me to see Garnett the other day who thinks Unwin will take it up. It is to give standard translations by Hyde of the old Epic Tales & will consist of 8 or 9 volumes. Hyde is to send in a sheme for the first three or four in a couple of weeks. It will make the old stories accessible for the first time to every body.[6] It will I fear however make Unwin less inclined to start another Irish series at present—we can however surely get on with out him. I do not think any more than you do that we can work "The Young Ireland League Library" by subscription in the ordinary sense. But surely it can be done in the way I suggest i.e. by the Irish societies of all kinds guaranteeing a sale of so many copies among their members. 10 members if they subscribe 5/– a peice can guarantee 100 copies which should be sold by the sec of their society. As soon as I get to Dublin or before I propose to have printed a circular explaining the sheme. Our men here say that we should also have a pamphlet series giving reprints to some extent of famous speaches & selections from the works of forgotten or little read poets. If we do such a series Hyde would give us his translations from gaelic ballad writers to make

---

[4] Although Standish James O'Grady contributed *The Bog of Stars and other stories and sketches of Elizabethan Ireland* (1893) to the series, none of the other books mentioned here was in fact published in the New Irish Library. WBY had first thought of taking up Davis's idea of a ballad history of Ireland in 1889 (see p. 194).

[5] See p. 282.

[6] Douglas Hyde's diary for 17 Feb 1892 (Daly, 150) records that he 'went to lunch at a restaurant with Yeats and a man named Garnett, a pleasant young man who is a reader for Fisher Unwin. He urged me to make translations of Irish stories and [said] that he would publish them for me in four or six volumes.'

one pamphet of (say) 24 pages & would publish under our auspices *at his own expense* a pamphlet of his origonal ballads & Todhunter would do the same with his Irish poems—those already published & his unpublished Deirdre—if we would take them for the larger series. I mean he would pay all expenses.[7] I am not quite sure of the advisabily of this however. If you meet any of the Young Ireland League men I wish you would tell them of this project of publication. You might also I think try—if you approve of it—to enlist Coffeys good will & get him to talk over the others.

Fisher Unwin is taking over the 80 or 90 copies I have left of Oisin & is putting them into a handsomer binding with a frontispeice by Ellis. The Blake book is getting near the finish so you see my literary affairs are going not ill. I hardly think I shall get to Ireland until end of March.

Yours snly
W B Yeats

ALS Berg. Wade, 200–2 (dated '? *circa* January 1892').

To Katharine Tynan, 2 March 1892

3 Blenheim Road | Bedford Park | Chiswick. | London. W
March 2nd | 1892

My dear Katey

First to answer your questions about the collection of "Irish Love Songs" of which by the by I heard from Unwins reader with great satisfaction for no one could do it so well as you.[1] You should I think include a fair number from Davis. He is very Irish & I find he grows upon me partly because of his great sincerity. His "Plea for Love" is I think the best of all. You might also use "The Marriage" "Loves Longings" "The Boatman of Kinsale" & "Maire Bhan A Storr". You should I think get Sigerson or some one of that kind to give you phonetic equivalents the gaelic spelling he adopts is his own. "Eogan" for instance should be written as it is pronounced "Owen". Do not forget ⟨ among poetry other than Davis ⟩ to include "Kathleen O More" a

[7] The pamphlet series, including works published at their authors' expense, did not materialize. Todhunter's 'The Fate of the Sons of Usna', a re-telling of the Deirdre legend, was first published in his *Three Irish Bardic Tales* (1896).

[1] On 23 Jan 1892 KT had written to Fisher Unwin (Berg) saying she was 'very glad indeed to undertake your commission: no work could be pleasanter in the doing—and there is a large field for a book of Irish Love-Songs.' An undated reader's report (presumably by Edward Garnett; Berg) on her proposals for the book declares that 'Miss Tynan has made a careful & deliberate selection. The result is very pleasing, though it is a fact that Irish poetry naturalised into English is not generally of a very high order, & is small in amount.' *Irish Love-Songs*, selected by Katharine Tynan, was published by Unwin in December 1892 as a volume in the Cameo series.

marvellous lyric ⟨ usually ⟩ attributed to Reynolds. I think that "the girl of the fine flown hair" in Walshes "Irish Songs" is good to[o]. There was a little thing by Hyde in our ballad book "Have you been on the mountain & seen there my love" which might go in.[2] You might perhaps give from Oisin "to an Isle in the Water" and an "old song resung" for they are more obviously Irish than my recent attempts at love poetry of which I enclose one or two things. I could have been of much greater help to you a while ago but I have not been reading the Irish ballads very recently & so cannot advise you so well there. By the by would not "The Fairy Song" in the "Rhymers Book" do for your purpose It is extremely Irish & has been greatly liked—It is a love poem of a kind. You will be able to chose at any rate what you want of mine from Oisin, The R' book & the MS I send.[3]

But enough of this matter. Blake is getting through the press. About two thirds & that the most trouble some part is gone to press & most of it is already in proof. I am also correcting "The Countess Kathleen" for the press & getting ready a quantity of lyrics & ballads to go with it. It will be infinitely my best book. I have had rather a bad autumn with poor health & poorer spirits or I had made it better than it is. Health & spirits are I suppose mixed up in some queer way—not quite as the materialists say but in some fashion. I shall be back in Dublin again very soon now & look forward much to seeing you. I am always more at home in Dublin than any other where. My sisters send you greetings & ask when you will be in London as they enjoy your visits so greatly.

Yours always
W B Yeats

The following lyrics may perhaps help you to select something for your book. The first was written some months ago the second the other day.

When you are old.
When you are old and grey and full of sleep
And nodding by the fire, take down this book;
And slowly read and dream of the soft look
Your eyes had once, and of their shaddows deep;

---

[2] Despite WBY's suggestions, KT included in her anthology only two poems by Thomas Davis: 'The Boatman of Kinsale' and 'The Girl of Dunbwy'. She did use 'Kathleen O'More' by George Nugent Reynolds (*c.* 1770–1802), whom she described as a 'favourite song writer of the end of the last century', but not 'The Maid of the Fine Flowing Hair', from Edward Walsh's *Irish Popular Songs* (see p. 31). Douglas Hyde's poem from the Irish, 'Were You on the Mountain?' (which begins 'Oh, were you on the mountain, or saw you my love?'), was included.

KT had also asked Hyde for suggestions for the anthology. He replied (2 Feb 1892, Texas) recommending Mangan, Davis, and T. C. Irwin (1823–92), and offering her translations of Gaelic Irish love songs, with a note, if she wanted them.

[3] KT included both 'To an Isle in the Water' and 'An Old Song Resung' (better known as 'Down by the Salley Gardens'; see p. 97), but not 'A Fairy Song' (see p. 264), which had just appeared in *The Book of the Rhymers' Club*.

How many loved your moments of glad grace
  And loved your beauty with love false or true
  But one man loved the pilgrim soul in you,
And loved the sorrows of your changing face;

And bending down beside the glowing bars
  Murmur, a little sad, "from us fled Love;
  He paced upon the mountains far above
And hid his face amid a crowd of stars".

When you are sad.

When you are sad
  The mother of the stars weeps too
And all her starlight is with sorrow mad
  And tears of fire fall gently in the dew.

When you are sad
  The mother of the wind mourns too
And her old wind that no mirth ever had
  Wanders & wails before my heart most true.

When you are sad
  The mother of the wave sighs too
And her dim wave bids men be no more glad
  And then the whole world's trouble weep with you.

I dont know whether these poems may not be too literary for your purpose.[4] A book such as you are doing should be Irish before all else. People will go to English poetry for "literary poetry" but will look to a book like your collection for a new flavour as of fresh turned mould. Davis, Fergusson, Allingham Mangan & Moore should be your mainstay & every poem that shows English influence in any marked way should be rejected.[5] No poetry has a right to live merely because it is good. It must be *the best of its kind*. The best Irish poets are this & every writer of imagination who is true to him self absolutely, may be so. I forgot to say in my letter that I would if I were you include Lovers "Whistling Thief" & Walsh's "Mo Craobhin Cno" &

[4] Both these poems appeared in *The Countess Kathleen*; 'When You are Old' (*VP*, 120–1) appeared in subsequent collected editions but 'When you are Sad' (*VP*, 738) was not republished. KT included neither in her anthology.

[5] In her Preface to *Irish Love-Songs* (9) KT explained that she had 'sometimes rejected, but not always, because of an English influence, having the desire to make a book of Love-Songs of a new flavour, and literary in a fresh way.' Apart from Mangan's 'Dark Rosaleen', she believed her book 'will owe most to Edward Walsh and Samuel Ferguson, the two men who, above all others, knew how to transfuse the wild simplicity of the Irish songs into English, keeping their strange and lovely flavour as of wild bees' honey—sweet and unsophisticated.'

"Mairgréad ni Chealleadh" (quite love poem enough) also "A love ballad" by Mangan (it is in Gills 3ᵈ collection & is from the Irish).⁶

ALS Huntington, with envelope addressed to Clondalkin, postmark 'CHISWICK MR 3 92'. McHugh, 135–7; Wade, 203–6.

To John O'Leary, [mid-March 1892]

3 Blenheim Road | Bedford Park | Chiswick. W

Dear Mʳ O'Leary

Have you by any chance a copy of "Mitchells Apology of the British Government in Ireland" I particularly want to refer to it just at present.¹ Could you lend it me if you have it? I would send it back all safe.

There is a certain Mʳˢ Rowley who is a friend of Miss Gonnes & I think I may say of mine for I saw her several times when Miss Gonne was in London & liked her very much. She is Irish & anxious to help in any way she can in Ireland. Miss Gonne has filled her with the idea of trying to keep a kind of "salon" where conservatives & nationalists might meet & she has gone to Dublin & is now staying at 44 Stephens Green. If you come across her—she is anxious to see you & I promised to write to you about her—you might talk the matter over with her. She is kindly & well meaning & ardently Irish but has not a big intellect or anything of that kind.² She knows the Coffeys but does not seem I think to have quite hit it off with Mʳˢ Coffey whom she met in the old days before or just after her marrage. She knows the Parnells slightly.

About Rollestons proposed "History of Fenianism"—to which you

---

⁶ KT selected only Walsh's 'Mo Craoibhin Cno' of these poems. Mangan's 'Love Ballad' appears in his *Irish and Other Poems* (1886), published by M. H. Gill & Son in their O'Connell Press Popular Library series, price 3d.

¹ WBY begins his article, 'Maud Gonne', in the *Boston Pilot*, 30 July 1892 (*LNI*, 149), 'England has indeed, as Mitchel phrased it, gained the ear of the world, and knows right well how to tell foreign nations what tale of Ireland pleases her best.' This is the argument of Mitchel's *An Apology for the British Government in Ireland* (Dublin, 1860), which has an Advertisement dated from Paris and was written, Mitchel admitted, 'in a great part for the information of foreigners' (7). WBY evidently wished to draw a parallel between MG's agitation and that of Mitchel 30 years before, so placing her in a firm tradition of radical nationalism and those Irish nationalists who addressed themselves to continental audiences.

² In *Mem* (62) WBY speaks of Madam Rowley (he deletes the surname) as being present while MG underwent psychic experiments. On one occasion 'this friend, a pious woman, suddenly screamed in the middle of some vision [of] Maud Gonne's. She had found herself amid the fires of Hell and for days afterwards found all about the smell of sulphur—she said that her towels smelled of it in the morning. . . . She thought it a warning to herself because she had not joined the Catholic Church. She died a Catholic a few year later.' In Dublin in 1892, Mrs Rowley rented rooms at 44 Stephen's Green East and joined the National Literary Society later that year. She remained in Dublin for less than two years and by January 1894 was living in Paris, in the Avenue Bois de Boulogne.

object.[3] The way it presents to me is this. He can write better than most people & has an enthusiasm for the subject & could by going back to the newspapers of the time (as he is willing to do) & to the published books on the subject get easily enough information to make an inspiring book of 200 pages. If he does not do it now while there are people living who can correct his mistakes it will be done far more innacuratly by the historians of the future. It would be better too for it to be done by a man who can write so as to inspire people than by one who had perhaps more information but not the writing power. This is my feeling on the whole question of the projected series. Let them be done by good Irish men who can write & then they will be read. Rolleston is not the ⟨best man⟩ ideal historian of the subject but he has the right feeling & seems the best man ⟨possible⟩ we could get so far as I can see. He at any rate is trained in the art of making up a subject.

I hope to get to Dublin next month myself.

I have a copy of "The Book of the Rhymers Club" for you & will send it to morrow.

Yours truly
W B Yeats

[*Across top of first page*]
My poems are going to press first thing next week.

ALS NLI. Wade, 202–3.

To the Editor of The Academy, *16 March* [*1892*][1]

"Father Gilligan"

March 16th

Dear Sir

I thank your anonymous correspondent for giving me this oppertunity of explaining that "Tristrim St. Martins" ballad & my own have a common origin, although I never saw "He sent his angel" until some time after writing "Father Gilligan". The author of "Christ in London" himself told me the story on which both poems are founded as a curious piece of folklore given him by a friend. I wrote "Father Gilligan" at once; but knowing that "Tristram St Martin" himself intended a ballad on the subject, kept it back for some time in order to give him the ⟨courtesy⟩ advantage of prior

---

[3] See p. 286. JO'L, who was himself planning a history of the Fenian movement, had evidently objected to Rolleston writing such a book because he had not the required historical knowledge.

[1] This letter, a rejoinder to a communication from 'A Lover of Originality', published in the *Academy* on 12 Mar 1892, was printed by the editor the following Saturday. The autograph bears certain deletions and editorial emendations in another hand, reflected in the published version.

publication. When I did at last publish it, about two years ago in "The National Observer" I told him that I had done so and gave him the date of the paper;[2] & from that day to this he has never told me or any one else so far as I know that he considered himself illtreated. I have never claimed the story as mine, but both in "The National Observer" & in "The Book of the Rhymers' Club" have given full credit where it is due, namely to its inventors the peasentry of Castleisland, Kerry.[3] The passages quoted by your correspondent are almost word for word from the folktale as I heard it.

It may comfort "A lover of originality"[4] however to know that even if I had seen "Tristram St Martin's" ballad before writing mine and had never heard the story apart from the ballad I would none the less have considered myself perfectly justified in taking a legend that belonged to neither of us but to the Irish people. "Tristram St Martin" has done one ⟨tolerably⟩ intereseting ballad but I do not think he is so triumphantly successful in the present instance as to have made the story his until Time shall end. I am even inclined to say that he is but "illy blest" in having so ardent a champion ready to come forth with quotations that certainly do not show a very subtle sense of the peculiarities of Irish folk lore. On other subjects he is more at home & more worthy of quotation.

Yours sny\
W B Yeats

ALS Texas. Printed in *The Academy*, 19 March 1892 (280). Wade, 206–7.

[2] 'A Lover of Originality' had pointed out supposed similarities in Tristram St. Martin's poem 'He sent His Angel', published in 1890 in *The Christ in London and Other Poems*, and WBY's 'Father Gilligan' (see p. 217), first published in the *Scots Observer*, 5 July 1890, and recently reprinted in *The Book of the Rhymers' Club*. The *Academy*'s correspondent had compared, among others, the following lines from 'Father Gilligan',

> 'I have no rest, nor joy, nor peace,
> For people die and die:'
> And after cried he 'God forgive!
> My body spoke, not I!'

with St. Martin's

> 'More ill and dying! Shall one never rest?'
> He cried. 'There is no peace for sick and dead.
> Ah, who would choose a life so illy blest!
> What am I saying? Lord, what have I said?'

St. Martin's *The Christ in London* was published on 6 June 1890 by the Authors' Cooperative Publishing Co. Ltd., 22 St. Bride's Street. That WBY places inverted commas round 'Tristram St. Martin', and that there appear to be no other references to such a person, suggests that the name was a pseudonym. The 'Lover of Originality' was probably St. Martin himself, for he replied from Bristol on 26 March, giving the source for the legend and claiming copyright for his version.

[3] In both the *Scots Observer* and *The Book of the Rhymers' Club*, WBY had been careful to subtitle the poem 'A Legend told by the People of Castleisland, Kerry'.

[4] In the published version 'your correspondent' is substituted for ' "A lover of originality" '.

To Katharine Tynan, [12 April 1892]

[Chiswick]

United Ireland has asked me to fix the price of a long narrative poem—"The Death of Cuchullin"—about a column long which I have sent them.[1] They feel they say "a timidity" in doing so. You have done verse for them & can tell me what I should ask. let me know as soon as possible.

Yours truly
W B Yeats

Unwin praises your reviews of books in "The Independent" much.[2]

APS Huntington, addressed to Clondalkin, postmark 'CHISWICK AP 12 92'. Wade, 207.

To T. Fisher Unwin, [late April 1892]

3 Blenheim Road | Bedford Park | Chiswick. W

Dear Sir.

Please let me have 4 instead of the usual two copies of the "revise" of the enclosed proofs. I am making an attempt to get the play acted & require the extra proofs for the purpose—one for the manager, the other for the licenser of plays.[1] If I could have them at the earliest possible date, it would be an advantage as I have to go through certain preliminaries to secure acting rights before publication.

Your truly
W B Yeats

ALS Texas.

To T. Fisher Unwin, [?] 28 April [1892]

3 Blenheim Road | Bedford Park | Chiswick. W
April [?] 28

Dear Sir

I have a distinct remembrance of putting the proof of Motto into the package of proofs[1]—It must have fallen out—at any rate I cannot find it & I

---

[1] WBY's 'The Death of Cuchullin' (see p. 269), a poem of some 80 lines, was printed in *United Ireland*, 11 June 1892.

[2] For KT's reviews in the *Irish Daily Independent*, see p. 278, n. 3.

[1] Proofs of *The Countess Kathleen* were needed in order to arrange the copyright performance of the play given by WBY at the Athenaeum Theatre, Shepherd's Bush, on 6 May 1892.

[1] WBY printed one of his favourite quotations as a motto on the title-page of *The Countess Kathleen*: ' "He who tastes a crust of bread tastes all the stars and all the heavens"—Paracelsus ab Hohenheim.'

have searched high & low—I fear you will have to print another proof unless it be that it really is somewhere covered up amid those I have returned.

Yours truly
W B Yeats

ALS Texas.

To T. Fisher Unwin, 1 May [1892]

3 Blenheim Road | Bedford Park | Chiswick. W
May 1ˢᵗ

Dear Sir

Would you kindly get the clerk to find out what may be due to me for "John Shermon & Dhoya" & send me the amount some time this week.[1] I am going to Ireland, probably next Saturday, & find myself short of funds so please excuse my troubling you.

Yours truly
W B Yeats

ALS Texas.

To T. W. Rolleston,[1] [10 May 1892]

3 Blenheim Road | Bedford Park | Chiswick W
Tuesday

My dear Rolleston

I regret exceedingly that I shall be unable to be present at the first meeting of the Irish Literary Society.[2] I am going to Dublin to do my best to found there a society of like purpose and nature & shall have left London before the meeting. We cannot carry out our programe with full success—at least in the matter of Irish books—unless we persuade Ireland to take part with us. A society in Dublin could help our London organization to focuss

[1] As Garnett had predicted (see p. 269), *John Sherman and Dhoya* had sold well; it went into a second edition in 1891, and a third in 1892.

[1] See p. 13.

[2] After a number of pilot meetings held to plan the Irish Literary Society, London, the Inaugural General Meeting took place at the Caledonian Hotel, Adelphi, on 12 May 1892. Rolleston was then elected secretary, Major J. McGuinness, treasurer, and WBY, in his absence, to the committee of 14. Sir Charles Gavan Duffy had already been appointed president. WBY clearly intended this letter to be read out at the Meeting.

the scattered energies of lovers of Irish literature, & they & we together would be able to do much for the cause of Irish letters.[3]

Yours truly
W B Yeats

ALS Harvard.

To D. J. O'Donoghue, [c. 11 May 1892]

3 Blenheim Road | Bedford Park | Chiswick. W

My dear O'Donahue—

I enclose a notice of the copyright performance of "The Countess Kathleen" last Friday. Do you think you could make a note about it for "United Ireland"? Such a note would be of practical value as evidence of the date of performance should any dispute arise at any time over the copyright. I enclose a note about the play from the Star which may help out the note should it seem worth quoting.[1]

Perhaps you may find material for a note or two in the following. Standish O'Grady has contributed to Unwins "Childrens Library" a book of great vividness & picturesque power—I have read some of the proofs—called "Fin & his Companions". It endevours to reconstruct the age of Fin & Ossian from the legends & records and describes one after the other the most famous Fenian warriors.[2] Miss Gonne has, for the time being, closed her lecturing tour in France. She was so far successful in drawing attention to the Irish cause that 2000 articles were written about her speaches—or rather the articles had reached this number a considerable time ago.[3]

[3] WBY had decided to try again to found a central literary society in Dublin, as a basis from which to launch the new Library of Ireland he was planning and the travelling theatre company of which he and MG had talked since 1889. In *Mem* he recalls (51) that he first sent Rolleston himself to found the Dublin society, but that Rolleston had nearly become absorbed into a learned society: 'I had not set my thoughts on learned men and went to Dublin in a passion. The first man I sought out was a butter merchant . . . and a society, the National Literary Society . . . was planned out over a butter tub.'

[1] *United Ireland* reported on its front page, 14 May 1892, that 'Mr W. B. Yeats gave on Friday of last week at the Athenaeum, Shepherd's-bush, a copyright performance of his poetical play, "Countess Kathleen". The play will shortly be published by Fisher Unwin.' On 28 Apr 1892 'Logroller' (Richard Le Gallienne) had noticed *IFT* in the London *Star* (2), and gone on to puff the forthcoming *Countess Kathleen*, concentrating his remarks on the title play in which, he said, 'Mr Yeats will be seen to have solved that crux of the poetic drama — the necessary union of a lyrical intensity with vivid dramatic action.' *United Ireland* did not quote from this review.

[2] There was no mention of *Finn and his Companions* in *United Ireland* at this time, probably because a long and enthusiastic notice of O'Grady and his works (mentioning that he had signed a contract for *Finn*) had been printed only the week before, on 7 May 1892. A paragraph on 24 Sept 1892 noted that the book 'will be produced during the coming season', and it was reviewed at length on 24 Dec 1892.

[3] *United Ireland* waited until its issue of 2 July 1892—perhaps because it had already given considerable space to reports of MG's speeches, the latest as recent as 23 April—to note (1) that 'a few

And now to talk of other matters than newspapers "Notes"? I am off to Ireland, probably to morrow to try found a Dublin Irish Literary Society to work with our London one. Any names that occur to you of people likely to help would be useful. 3 Upper Ely Place will find me though I shall not be lodging there. I do not know where I shall stay until I get to Dublin.

Yours

W B Yeats

I see United Ireland notes O'Grady coming book in present number. If you cared to speak of it you might say that it was [*for* will] reconstruct the age of Fin in most masterly fashion.

ALS Texas.

To the Editor of United Ireland, *14 May 1892*

Sir—One windy night I saw a fisherman staggering, very drunk, about Howth Pier and shouting at somebody that he was no gentleman because he had not been educated at Trinity College, Dublin. Had he been an Englishman he would have made his definition of "gentleman" depend on money, and if he had been not only an Englishman, but a Cockney, on the excellence of the dinner he supposed his enemy to have eaten that day. My drunken fisherman had a profound respect for the things of the mind, and yet it is highly probable that he had never read a book in his life, and that even the newspapers were almost unknown to him. He is only too typical of Ireland. The people of Ireland respect letters and read nothing. They hold the words "poet" and "thinker" honourable, yet buy no books. They are proud of being a more imaginative people than the English, and yet compel their own imaginative writers to seek an audience across the sea. Surely there is some cause for all this and some remedy if we could but find it. I do not believe we are a nation of hypocrites.

Is not the cause mainly the great difficulty of bringing books, and the movements and "burning questions" of educated life, to the doors of a people who are scattered through small towns and villages, or sprinkled over solitary hillsides, and of doing so persistently enough to win a hearing amid the tumult of politics? The people have never learned to go to the book-shop, nor have they any brilliant literary journals and magazines to awaken their interest in thought and literature; nor would they read them if they

months ago the number of articles in French papers upon Miss Gonne and her work had reached 2,000, and since then the number has been altogether beyond counting . . .'. The lecture tour that began in January 1892 at the Cercle des Luxembourg took MG to Valenciennes, Arras, Rouen, Bordeaux, Cognac, Périgueux, and La Rochelle.

had. Yet surely some method of reaching them can be found. The *Nation* found a method, and "brought a new soul into Ireland,"[1] and to-day the need is almost greater. Ireland is between the upper and the nether millstone—between the influence of America and the influence of England, and which of the two is denationalising us most rapidly it is hard to say. Whether we have still to face a long period of struggle, or have come to the land of promise at last, we need all our central fire, all our nationality.

It was with the desire to do what we could to arrest this denationalisation that we founded the "Irish Literary Society, London," and not to do anything so absurd and impossible as to make London "the intellectual centre of Ireland,"[2] and it is with this desire in my mind that I now appeal to the four or five Dublin literary societies to do what they can to help us. The third object of our society, the first two being of purely local interest, is "to assist towards the publication in popular form of approved works on Irish subjects." We intend to do this by organising a circulation, "and not by incurring," to quote the prospectus again, "the liabilities of a publishing enterprise." We have, however, a definite scheme which will be put forward in good time, and are appealing to all the Irish literary societies in America to communicate with us in view of this scheme. Let the Dublin societies unite together in some fashion among themselves—the proposed constitution of "The Young Ireland League" a little altered will serve right well—[3] not of necessity sinking their separate individuality, and then put themselves into communication with the societies through the country.

---

[1] *The Nation*, the weekly newspaper founded by Charles Gavan Duffy, Thomas Davis, and John Blake Dillon (1816–66), first appeared on 15 Oct 1842 under Duffy's editorship and with the motto 'To create and foster public opinion, and make it racy of the soil.' It was an immediate success and continued far to outsell other Irish journals throughout the 1840s when, with contributions from Mitchel, Mangan, Carleton, and Lady Wilde, as well as the founders and many others, it brought a new cogency and vitality to the expression of Irish national aspirations. Primarily a vehicle for Young Ireland ideals, it resumed publication after the débâcle of 1848 and continued, although with diminished force and influence, until the fall of Parnell, when it adopted a violently anti-Parnellite line and finally amalgamated with the equally virulent *Irish Catholic* in 1891. Recalling the paper's early impact, A. M. Sullivan wrote in *New Ireland* (1877) I. 71: 'The effect was beyond all anticipation. The country seemed to awaken to a new life—"a soul had come into Erin."'

[2] This letter is WBY's contribution to a controversy, engineered by him and John McGrath, which had been running throughout the spring in the correspondence columns of *United Ireland* under the heading 'The Irish Intellectual Capital: Where Is It?'. The provocation for the debate was an article in the London *Daily Telegraph* on 7 Mar 1892 (4–5) which found it 'eminently fitting that, if an Irish Literary Society is to be formed, its seat should be in London and not in Dublin' on the grounds that 'so long as English is the language of Ireland, the literary and oratorical and characteristic genius of the country must of necessity gravitate towards the fountain-head and centre of the intellectual life of England.' McGrath took issue with this view in *United Ireland* on 12 Mar (4): 'We are very glad to see an Irish Literary Club started in London . . . But the very fact that such a club is being called into existence is liable to give rise to the impression that the centre of Irish intellectual life is London; and of such an impression we wish to disabuse the minds of all concerned.'

[3] For the societies in question, see p. 285; the constitution of the Young Ireland League had been proposed in September 1891 (see p. 269, n. 3).

When they have done so we and they will see what can be done to create and circulate a library of Irish books like the old "Library of Ireland," Duffy's ballads, "The Spirit of the Nation," Mitchel's "O'Neill," and all that noble series which spread themselves through Ireland by the help of the Repeal Reading Rooms;[4] and there seems to be no reason why the Young Ireland societies and literary societies of the day may not serve a like purpose. The periodical appearance of such books would give new interest to their debates, and new subjects for their lectures, and make them feel they were part of a great body of fellow-workers and not mere local debating clubs.

Eminent writers have offered their help. I have here before me a list of promised books on subjects ranging from Fenianism to the Education Question, from Oisin to Robert Emmet—and with a little energy and organisation we shall be able to circulate through Ireland a series of books which will be no mere echo of the literature of '48, but radiant from the living heart of the day.[5] Irish authors who have been compelled to make their pens the servants of a foreign literature, and foreign inspirations, will come gladly to our help, and in so doing they will themselves rise to greater status, for no man who deserts his own literature for another's can hope for the highest rank. The cradles of the greatest writers are rocked among the scenes they are to celebrate. Ireland has no lack of talent, but that talent is flung broadcast over the world, and turned to any rather than Irish purposes. Until it has been gathered together again and applied to the needs

[4] In 1845 Charles Gavan Duffy, influenced by an English publishing scheme of a similar kind, suggested that the Young Irelanders should bring out a series of shilling volumes of biography, poetry, and criticism to be called the 'Library of Ireland'. The paper-backed volumes were published by James Duffy at the rate of one a month and 22 volumes appeared in all; the venture was an immediate success and the volumes went into numerous editions throughout the rest of the century. *The Ballad Poetry of Ireland*, edited by Gavan Duffy, was vol. II in the series, the *The Life of Aodh O'Neill* by John Mitchel was vol. IV. The immensely popular and influential anthology, *The Spirit of the Nation* (see p. 174), compiled by Gavan Duffy from the ballads and poems contributed to the *Nation*, was not part of the Library of Ireland. It was originally issued in two parts in 1843 and 1844 and these, combined and expanded, became the standard edition of 1845, which went into more than 60 impressions.

A network of reading rooms was set up in the early 1840s by Daniel O'Connell's Repeal Association for the dissemination of political literature. In the *Nation* of 17 Sept and 5 Oct 1844, Thomas Davis suggested that the Repeal Association should widen the educational scope of these rooms 'by gifts of books, maps, etc., and thus a library, the centre of knowledge and nursery of useful and strong minds, will be made in that district.' The Repeal Reading Rooms were thus an attempt to compensate for the dearth of booksellers in rural Ireland; sporadic attempts to revive the idea, this time in connection with the Land League, were made in the early 1880s.

[5] Although acknowledging the considerable influence of the Young Irelander tradition in Irish literature, WBY found the writings of the Young Irelanders, whose movement broke up after the failure of their ill-planned insurrection at Ballingarry in July 1848, at once too didactic and too slipshod. As he wrote in his review of KT's *Ballads and Lyrics*, in the *Evening Herald* of 2 Jan 1892 (see p. 278):

In '48 they made songs and ballads from some passionate impulse of the moment. Often the same song would contain poetry of the most moving power, side by side with flaccid and commonplace lines. . . . We can reproduce now neither the merits nor defects of that poetry, in which all was done from sudden emotion, nothing from deliberate art. . . . Such periods cannot last.

of Ireland it will never do anything great in literature. "He who tastes a crust of bread," wrote Parocelsus at Hoenheim, "tastes all the stars and all the heavens,"[6] and he who studies the legends, and history, and life of his own countryside may find there all the themes of art and song. Let it be the work of the literary societies to teach to the writers on the one hand, and to the readers on the other, that there is no nationality without literature, no literature without nationality.[7] In the old days when Davis sang there was no need to teach it, for then Apollo struck his lyre with a pike-head, but now he has flung both pike-head and lyre into the sea.—Yours, &c.,

W B Yeats

London, May, 1892.

Printed letter, *United Ireland*, 14 May 1892 (1–2). *UP* I. 222–5.

To the Editor of the Daily Express *(Dublin), 2 June 1892*

SIR—The Irish people are proud to consider themselves a more imaginative people than the English and yet they read nothing but a few song books and a few second-rate books of stories. Many good judges believe that the fault is not so much in the Irish people as in the great difficulty of circulating books in a nation where there are no recognised organs of literary opinion, and where the people are scattered here and there far from book shops and the "burning questions" and "literary cult" of educated life. In the Young Ireland days books, like Duffy's "Ballad poetry of Ireland," circulated in thousands. They did this by the double instrumentality of the *Nation* newspaper and the Repeal Reading Rooms.[1] Is it not possible to find a like mean to do a like work for Ireland to day? A number of Irishmen in Ireland and England, and elsewhere, are asking this question, and propose to make the attempt to circulate a new "Library of Ireland" through the existing literary societies, and by establishing new bodies for the purpose. They propose also to aid the educational influence of the library by well organized lectures and discussions upon notable figures in Irish history, and notable epochs in the national life, and on the problems and difficulties of to day. These books and lectures will be national but not political in any narrow sense of the word. They will endeavour to make the patriotism of the people who read them both deeper and more enlightened, and will set before them the national and legendary heroes as they present themselves to the

---

[6] Cf. p. 293, n. 1.
[7] WBY quoted this adage of JO'L's on numerous occasions at this time; cf. *LNI*, 103–4.

[1] See preceding letter.

minds of scholars and thinkers. Whether that project be or be not carried out successfully, depends upon the circulation we can organize. As a first step, we are endeavouring to form a strong "National Literary Society" in Dublin which will put itself into communication with the literary societies throughout Ireland. Support is coming in from all sides, and members are joining rapidly. To make our objects more generally understood, we intend to hold a meeting at the Rotunda on June 9th. This meeting will be in no sense a meeting of the National Literary Society, which, properly speaking, does not yet exist, but a meeting to explain our aims and purposes to the members of the half [dozen] Dublin literary societies, and to sympathisers generally.[2] The meeting will be addressed by Ashe King, Count Plunkett, Dr Sigerson, Miss Maud Gonne, myself, and others.[3] Mr Kelly, 1 Pembroke terrace, Dundrum, will be happy to send tickets and circulars to anyone that sympathises with our objects.—Yours truly,

W B Yeats

Printed letter, *Daily Express* (Dublin), 2 June 1892 (6).

To T. Fisher Unwin, [*July 1892*]

53 Mount Joy Square[1] | Dublin.

Dear Sir—

I return proofs of "Countess Kathleen". In sending "revises" please note my change of address. There being sent on from my old address makes a

[2] A first meeting, to discuss the setting up of a National Literary Society, had been held at the Wicklow Hotel on 24 May 1892, soon after WBY's arrival in Dublin. At a meeting on 31 May of the provisional committee it was decided to hold a public meeting on 9 June. At this meeting, which duly took place in the Small Concert Room of the Rotunda, with Dr Sigerson in the chair, WBY's resolution 'that it was desirable to found a National Literary Society' was passed with acclamation. In his speech to that motion he elaborated on the points made in this letter, insisting upon the need for a new Library of Ireland which would (as *United Ireland* on 18 June 1892 [2] reported the speech)

be National in the widest sense of the word, for he believed that it was only possible to reach the people by seizing upon the National sentiment and by enlisting it in their service. The National heroes and the great epochs of the National struggle would supply the main theme for the books they contemplated. The speaker then . . . said that it should be the object of the writers of Ireland to make the National feeling noble and enlightened, and to teach the people that the public welfare was of more moment than the welfare of any class or individual. He appealed to the young men of Ireland to keep the watch-fire of Irish Nationality burning, for it was a sacred charge which they had received from leaders and patriots of other days.

[3] Besides those mentioned by WBY, there were also speeches from Sigerson, J. T. Kelly, Robert Donovan, Fr. Thomas Finlay, and JO'L. A letter from Sir Charles Gavan Duffy was read, congratulating them on the foundation of the Society and indicating his willingness to take the chair at the Inaugural Meeting.

[1] 53 Mountjoy Square, on the north side of Dublin, was occupied by the Carew family, distant cousins of JO'L. Both WBY and JO'L lodged there from time to time.

considerable delay. The proof of title page is blotty but that is I suppose merely temporary.

Yours truly
W B Yeats

ALS Texas.

To John O'Leary, [mid-July 1892]

53 Mountjoy Square

Dear M^r O'Leary

I wrote to Mathers but find that he is as I feared in Paris. He has written me a long letter going into the question of organization. I would send it on to you but he has mixed up with it some occult matters which are of course private. He would be glade to meet any one who came from us, & would go carefully into the whole question. If you know any one in Paris or going to Paris they might see him. His address is S L MacGregor Mathers. 121 Boulevard St Michel. Paris.[1] He will hardly be in London for some time. He is strong for a[n] immediate commencement on the ground of the length of time such things take. I am writing to him an explanation of my own position in the matter ⟨2½ *lines cancelled*⟩ and the reasons I see for some delay. My own occult art (though I cannot expect you to accept its evidences) has again & again for a longish time now been telling me of many curious coming events & as some have come true (all that have had time) I rather expect the others to follow suit & the time for his plan among the rest.

The Literary Society goes on well. We have got leave to hold our committee meetings in the "Mansion House".[2] Miss Gonne who is back here since Sunday has secured ⟨Ledwidge⟩ Ludwic to sing at her concert. He is coming over on purpose.[3] She did not speak for Morton. She offered to go down for two days & he said she should go for ten days & that two would be worse than useless & that his whole chance of election depended on her. She replied that she had work to do in Dublin & could not. He then wrote

---

[1] After his move to Paris, Mathers (see p. 266) took the additional name MacGregor, claimed succession to the Jacobite title of Comte de Glenstrae, and often appeared in full Highland dress. He considered himself an expert in two fields: ritual magic and military training, and it is possible the 'organization' mentioned here had some bearing on the latter; see *Aut* 415.

[2] The Society held meetings in the Mansion House by permission of the Lord Mayor, the Rt. Hon. Joseph Michael Meade (1839–1900) until December 1892, and thereafter at 4 College Green.

[3] 'Ludwig' was the stage name of William Ledwidge (b. 1848), a professional singer of 94 Cromwell Avenue, Highgate Hill, London, who performed widely in Britain and America. A baritone with an extensive repertory, he excelled in Irish ballads and gave frequent concerts in Dublin, often on behalf of nationalist causes; the *Weekly Freeman*, 20 Oct 1888, found his singing 'all that the most enthusiastic lover of national music could wish'.

that if he was not returned he hoped he might never see her again. He must have quite lost his head over this election.[4]

When am I to do that "Causerie" for the Speaker? I have waited to hear from Barry O'Brien but have not done so.[5]

Ellis is out of town in a House Boat at Henley-on-Thames.

Yours very siry
W B Yeats

ALS NLI. Wade, 208–9.

To John O'Leary, [week ending 23 July 1892][1]

53 Mountjoy Square | Dublin—

Dear M^r O'Leary

We have postponed our concert until after the inagural meeting which will I beleive take place in the second week in August at the Ancient Concert Rooms. We hope by that time to have the program of our Autumn session arranged so that we can distribute it at the meeting. The concert which will probably take place in Horse Show week will be an item. We will have our permament reading room taken too I hope by the opening of our session. We have had to postpone the concert through delays about Ludwic & other things of the kind.[2] Next Monday—the 25—we have a general meeting of *the members* to adopt rules & nominate the officers.[3] We intend to start a "contemporary" of our own as soon as we have our reading room. This is I beleive all the news concerning society.

As to my suggestion about Mathers. In suggesting to you that if any

---

[4] E. J. C. Morton (1856–1902), a barrister and University lecturer in Astronomy, was a founder and the secretary of the Home Rule Union. A Liberal of advanced ideas, he contested the seat for Devonport for the first time in the General Election of 1892. Though he was a suitor of MG's and had asked her to marry him, she does not seem to have been so crucial to his campaign as he supposed, for he won the seat in July 1892 and retained it until his death.

[5] The *Speaker*, on whose editorial staff R. Barry O'Brien was, published in each number a longer than average article, called a *causerie*, on general literary themes. WBY did not contribute to this series until August 1893; see below, p. 360.

[1] This letter is tipped into John Quinn's copy of *The Countess Kathleen* (1892); the book also has the bookplate of W. T. H. Howe.

[2] The projected concert seems not to have taken place, either in Horse Show Week at the beginning of August, or later.

[3] In a letter dated 18 July 1892, published in *United Ireland* on 23 July (3), J. T. Kelly had announced that 'a general meeting of the members will be held at 8 p.m. on Monday, July 25 at Costigan's Hotel, 38 Upper O'Connell Street, for the purpose of adopting rules for the government of the society and of nominating the officers and members of the council for the ensuing year.' John Tarpey Kelly (1864–99), born at Clanmacnoise and educated at Blackrock College, had moved to London in 1882, where he was an active secretary to the Southwark Irish Literary Club, before returning to Ireland in 1892 to become a founder member of the National Literary Society. He contributed ballads and poems under various pseudonyms to a number of Irish periodicals.

advanced nationalist was going to Paris he should see Mathers I was acting to some extent on the advice of Quinn to whom I showed Mathers letter—he gave me leave to show it. Quinn held the matter of some possible importance. Mathers is a specialist & might have given useful advice to any one who thinks as you do. "He might be useful" was your own phrase.[4] Now as to Magic. It is surely absurd to hold me "week" or otherwise because I chose to persist in a study which I decided deliberately four or five years ago to make next to my poetry the most important pursuit of my life. Whether it be, or be not, bad for my health can only be decided by one who knows what magic is & not at all by any amateur. The probable explanation however of your somewhat testy post card is that you were out at Bedford Park & heard my father discoursing about my magical pursuits out of the immense depths of his ignorance as to everything that I am doing & thinking. If I had not made magic my constant study I could not have written a single word of my Blake book nor would "The Countess Kathleen" have ever come to exist. The mystical life is the centre of all that I do & all that I think & all that I write. It holds to my work the same relation that the philosophy of Godwin held to the work of Shelley[5] & I have all-ways considered my self a voice of what I beleive to be a greater renaisance—the revolt of the soul against the intellect—now begining in the world. By all this I have however probably called down upon my self another reproving postcard which shall be like to the other in all things. It is my own fault I dare say for I sometimes forget that the word "magic" which sounds so familiar to my ears has a very outlandish sound to other ears.

Miss Gonne has given up her rooms in Paris—Which meens I imagine that she intends to live more constantly in Ireland & devote her self to the work here. She is now with her sister, 25 Hans Place, but returns next week I beleive. When do you return? Duffy comes over I beleive in a week or two.[6]

I have Armstrongs collected works—nine volumes—to review for Bookman & have given them a preliminary notice mainly hostile in this weeks United Ireland also like treatment to Larminie.[7]

[4] See preceding letter. Since none of the correspondence between WBY and Mathers has so far come to light, it is uncertain what is at issue here, but since JO'L, as a Fenian, was suspicious of Parliamentary agitation, it is possible that there was some thought of bringing Mathers into association with the Irish Republican Brotherhood. Joseph Patrick Quinn (1863–?1915), the 'young Mayo doctor' (*Mem*, 71) whose Dublin lodgings WBY was to share later in the '90s, had been acting secretary of the Land League in 1881, and was imprisoned in Kilmainham Gaol in October of that year. An admirer of Michael Davitt, he continued to work for the land movement and the Irish National League throughout the 1880s. He later took up medicine, and had a hand in the founding of the National Literary Society.

[5] At this time, under the influence of Edward Dowden, WBY seems to have thought that Shelley's poetry owed more to Godwin's *Political Justice* (1793) than he was later to allow. See *E&I*, 65–7.

[6] MG used the Hans Place house of her sister Kathleen, now Mrs Pilcher, as a base when she was in London. JO'L was back in Dublin by 8 Aug 1892, and Gavan Duffy arrived before 30 July.

[7] Reviewing the *Collected Works* (1892) of George Francis Savage-Armstrong (1845–1906), Professor

Does Barry O'Brien want that "causerie"? he was to write to me & has not.

Hyde has settled with Unwin about his translation of gaelic Sagas, & got very good terms.[8]

I am writing this post to Duffy.

Yours very sincely
W B Yeats

ALS Berg. Wade, 210–11.

To Sir Charles Gavan Duffy, [week ending 23 July 1892][1]

our Dublin society. About [a] fortnight or three weeks later we hope to be ready for our inaugural meeting. Perhaps you will be in Dublin then & will be so kind as to take the chair. The young men wish greatly that you would.

J T Kelly will I beleive also write to you.

Yours very truly
W B Yeats.

PS.
⟨Since coming over here it has become plain that it would⟩
It seems to Mᵣ O'Leary & myself that it would be a good step towards insuring circulation to fix as soon as possible upon the first 3 volumes of the

of History and English Literature at Queen's College, Cork, in *United Ireland*, 23 July 1892 (*UP* I. 229), WBY said that Armstrong had 'cut himself off from the life of the nation in which his days are passed, and has suffered the inevitable penalty'; he found only one of the nine volumes to have lasting value. He contributed a further and longer review of Armstrong's work under the title 'Noetry and Poetry' (*UP* I. 237–9) to the *Bookman*, September 1892. The *Bookman* review drew blood, for on 7 Sept 1892 an aggrieved Savage-Armstrong wrote to D. J. O'Donoghue (UCD):

I didn't imagine that any person of brains & education is likely to be influenced by Willy Yeats's opinion on any subject, and a literary paper in which he figures as a critic of poetry can, I should think, have very little weight with men of ability & learning. . . . if a young man's conscience will not permit him to speak well of the writings of his father's old friend and one who has been not unkind to himself, his instincts as a gentleman might at least withhold him from criticizing them in the public prints. . . . One looks for nobler qualities in a young man who aspires to be a poet.

In his notice of *Fand* (Dublin, 1892), by William Larminie (1849–1900)—also in *United Ireland* of 23 July 1892 (*UP* I. 229–30)—WBY, while finding Larminie Irish enough, thought that he might 'do better when he has either abandoned or perfected the experimental rhythmic metres he has invented'. Larminie went on to collect and translate a volume of *West Irish Folktales and Romances* (1893) which WBY praised in a review in the *Bookman*, June 1894 (*UP* I. 326–8).

[8] See p. 286. Although Hyde records in his diary for 30 Mar 1892 that he was 'making a list of the Irish stories for Garnett', Fisher Unwin did not publish any Gaelic sagas by Hyde until *The Three Sorrows of Storytelling*, which appeared in 1895.

[1] Only the last three pages (the last two numbered 10 and 11) survive of this letter, apparently the one referred to in the preceding letter. In view of their subsequent falling out over the scheme for a new Library of Ireland (see below, p. 329), it may even be that Gavan Duffy destroyed the earlier pages, in which WBY had apparently set out fully his own ideas for the Library.

proposed library. M^r O'Leary & myself think that a good first volume would be a life of Wolf Tone by T W Rolleston who has long wished to do such a book & would I doubt not do it gladly for the Library. M^r O'Leary has written to him on the subject but has not yet heard. M^r O'Leary thinks that my "ballad chronicle" would make a good second volume. For the Third volume he suggests that Lady Wilde be asked to take up again the book on Sarsfield that had been projected for her.[2] We of course wish to know if you think this a good selection or if you have anything to say in opposition or in modification.

ALS (fragment) NLI. Wade, 212.

To John O'Leary, [week ending 23 July 1892]

53 Mountjoy Square | Dublin

Dear M^r O Leary

The meeting on Monday is not our inagural meeting but the general meeting of members to nominate President, Vice Presidents Committee etc & to adopt the rules. You will I beleive be elected president while Father Finlay, Dr Sigerson, Count Plunkett, Ash King Father Denis Murphy,[1] Douglas Hyde & Gavan Duffy will be put for forward for election as Vice Presidents. There is I admit a certain difficulty in putting up Gavan Duffy as one of several vice presidents but it is inevitable. He is coming over in his own words "to consult with our committee" & he can only do this properly by being on that Committee. We could hardly put him on in any other way than as a Vice President.[2] Finlay & Donovan are afraid of your presidency & so we put on as you see a fair number of Federationists.[3]

---

[2] For the first two proposals, see p. 285–6; JO'L seems in the interim to have been won over to Rolleston as an authority on Wolfe Tone. Lady Wilde's life of Sarsfield had been planned as one of the volumes in the original Library of Ireland. In the event, Todhunter took up the biography of Sarsfield.

[1] The Revd Denis Murphy, SJ (1833–96), born in Newmarket, Co. Cork, taught at Clongowes Wood College and University College, Dublin. One of the leading Irish historians of his generation, he published a study of *Cromwell in Ireland* (1883), edited O'Clery's *Life of Hugh Roe O'Donnell* (1893), and at his death had just completed his major work, *Our Martyrs*. He edited the *Journal of the Kildare Archaeological Society*, was a vice-president of the Royal Society of Antiquaries of Ireland, and became a member of the Royal Irish Academy.

[2] According to the Minute Book of the National Literary Society, the provisional committee did not elect an official council until 18 Aug 1892, and then its membership differed somewhat from that suggested here. Douglas Hyde was president, D. J. Coffey (1864–1945) honorary treasurer, and the vice-presidents were Dr Sigerson, WBY, Ashe King, Count Plunkett, KT, MG, and Fr. Finlay. There was in addition a council composed of 20 members including JO'L. Though not elected to a vice-presidency, Gavan Duffy—as WBY seems to have forgotten—had already been co-opted as a member of the provisional committee on 21 June. Coffey, a doctor, became the first president of University College, Dublin, 1908–40.

[3] The Revd Thomas A. Finlay, S J (1848–1940), Rector of Belvedere College 1882–7 and later

The Inagural meeting will be in the second week in August probably and at the Ancient Concert Rooms. Sigerson agrees to give the address—[4]

I think this is all the news I have. Let me know if you know what Rollestons vews are as to the book scheme. I have not heard from him.

Yours very truly

W B Yeats

ALS NLI. Wade, 212–13.

To T. Fisher Unwin, [*late July 1892*]

53 Mountjoy Square | Dublin.

Dear Sir

I return the proof of the frontispeice of The Countess Kathleen with inscription.[1]

Yours truly

W B Yeats.

I am sorry that there is no way of making visable the fact that the drawing is by J T Nettleship. Would the words "drawn by J T Nettleship" be too much out of place underneath?[2] In any case it might be well to mention that the frontispeice is by him in any anouncements that may be made.

ALS Texas.

To the Editor of United Ireland, *30 July 1892*

Sɪʀ—Mr Rolleston, unless, indeed, it be a slip of the reporters, stated at the inaugural meeting of the Irish Literary Society, London, last Saturday,

Professor of Political Economy at the Royal University and at University College, Dublin, 1909–30, helped Fr. Matthew Russell establish the *Irish Monthly* and was founder-editor of the *Lyceum* (1887–94). He supported Sir Horace Plunkett (1854–1932) and the co-operative movement, becoming a member of the first committee of the Irish Agricultural Organization Society founded by Plunkett in 1894 and editorial chairman of the *Irish Homestead*. Like the journalist Robert Donovan (see p. 259, n. 7), he was an anti-Parnellite, or 'Federationist'—to use the term of abuse applied by the Parnellites to their opponents, whom they accused of seeking a federal solution to the Home Rule question.

[4] Dr Sigerson delivered the address on 'Irish Literature: Its Origin, Environment, and Influence' at the Society's Inaugural Meeting, which took place on 16 Aug 1892 under the presidency of Sir Charles Gavan Duffy, at the Antient Concert Rooms, Great Brunswick Street (now Pearse Street).

[1] The frontispiece depicts Cuchullin fighting the waves. In March 1904 WBY wrote in a presentation copy to John Quinn (*Bibl*, 25), 'Nettleship who made this rather disappointing picture might have been a great imaginative artist. Browning once in a fit of enthusiasm said a design of his of "God creating Evil" was "the most sublime conception of ancient or modern art".'

[2] The words 'Frontispiece by J. T. Nettleship' appear on page 4 of the book.

that his society hoped to have branches in "England, Ireland, America, and the Colonies."[1] I find that this statement has caused a certain amount of dissatisfaction among the members of the National Literary Society, as they wish it to be kept perfectly plain that their society is wholly distinct from the London one. I am sure that Mr Rolleston, under the circumstances, will forgive my saying that the centre of Irish literary activity can only be had in Ireland, and that whatever body may undertake the starting of "branches" in Ireland, the London Society is, of necessity, incapacitated from doing so.[2] When at the close of last autumn I proposed the foundation of the "Irish Literary Society, London," it was with the direct object of federating it with a central body in Ireland,[3] and it was neither my fault nor the fault of the provisional committee that circumstances made the intention of no avail.—Yours very truly,

W B Yeats

53 Mountjoy-square, Dublin.

Printed letter, *United Ireland*, 30 July 1892 (4). *UP* 1. 230–1.

[1] At the inaugural meeting of the Irish Literary Society, London, at Oak Tree House, Hampstead, on 23 July 1892, T. W. Rolleston, opening the proceedings, had sketched out the aims of the Society and 'enlarged upon the benefits' (as the *Irish Daily Independent* (5) reported, 25 July) 'which the society, with all its branches all over England, Ireland, America, and the colonies might do in making known Irish literature to the people of our race and amongst those by whom they were surrounded.'

[2] As WBY makes clear, he was not alone in the dissatisfaction which these remarks aroused. A leading article in the same (30 July) issue of *United Ireland* (5) rebuked Rolleston for demanding

a position for the London Society which we are fully justified in saying neither the Irish National Literary Society, whose headquarters are in Dublin, nor any resident Irish men or women who take any interest in these matters, will concede to it. . . . To make London the headquarters of the new literary endeavour would be to abandon the first essential principle of such a movement, to give away our whole position at the start, and to prepare the way for a dismal failure. We have had quite enough London centralization without making London the centre of an attempt one of whose great objects will be to break down the system.

[3] WBY's insistence that he himself was the originator of the Irish Literary Society in London was not mere egotism. An eye-witness report by 'Mac' of the Hampstead meeting, which also appeared in *United Ireland* on 30 July, credited Rolleston with being the moving spirit behind the London society, but the editor of *United Ireland* went to the trouble of correcting this error in a brief note on the same page (5).

Rolleston replied to WBY's and the paper's criticisms in a letter published on 6 Aug 1892 (4), saying that he had been misreported and warning against internal dissension in the literary movement. 'You are perfectly right,' he continued, 'in correcting your London correspondent as to the quarter in which the idea of the London society originated. I first heard of it from Mr Yeats, and I suppose Mr Yeats got it in some measure from the old Southwark Irish Club. In its complete form, and with all its various features, it certainly cannot be put down to any single mind.'

To Edward Garnett, [early August 1892]

53 Mountjoy Square | Dublin

My dear Garnett

I am more busy than ever over this "National Literary Society". It is growing under our hands into what promises to be a work of very great importance. We are endevouring to found reading rooms in connection with federated societies through the country & propose to supply them with small collections of books—worth not more than £5 or £6 pounds—as *neucleuses* of lending libraries & to send them lecturers from time to time. This is Miss Gonne's special part of the work & she proposes to lecture through the country in its aid.[1] I send you Duffy speach which will explain the other part of the work—the book publication—which we expect to help considerably by turning these reading rooms into centres of distrebution.[2] We are having two meetings in the next two weeks—the first a small gathering of representative people to launch the publishing company, the second a large public one to open in due order our session of lectures etc.[3]

When will "The Countess Kathleen" be out. It would be an advantage if it came soon as the reviews, here in Ireland, would help the society, & the sale would in its turn be helped probably by the coming meetings at which my name will of necessity be rather prominent. They are dreadfully dilatery it seems to me over it. Even if the publication is delayed for any reasen surely it is bound by this & I could have some advanced copies for friends.

Ellis has just published his book of poems "Fate in Arcadia". It seems to me a very marvellous book. If you come across it read "The Hermit Answered" "The Outcast" "The Maids Confession" & "Himself " though

[1] The Minute Book of the National Literary Society reveals that on 14 June 1892 'a sub-committee consisting of Count Plunkett, and Messrs Coyne, Quinn, O'Leary and Yeats' was appointed 'to consult with Miss Gonne as to the best means of promoting her scheme of Reading Rooms and Libraries.' William P. Coyne (1867–1904), a native of Tipperary, was called to the Irish Bar in 1895, and later held the Chair of Political Economy and Jurisprudence at the Royal University, Dublin. He was a frequent contributor in the 1890s to the *Freeman's Journal* and the Dublin *Daily Express*.

[2] Gavan Duffy had outlined his proposals for a new Library of Ireland in the course of his speech at the inaugural meeting of the Irish Literary Society, London (see p. 306), in Hampstead, London, on 23 July 1892. His speech was widely reported in the Irish press and especially in *United Ireland*, 30 July. At this point Gavan Duffy was thinking of a limited liability company to publish the books, which, he suggested, might be distributed by means of canvassers at home and abroad and through the agents of popular Dublin journals.

[3] The first of these meetings, held on 8 Aug 1892 in the Oak Room of the Mansion House in Dublin, discussed the revival of Irish literature and the foundation of a publishing company to circulate Irish books. The Lord Mayor was in the chair and speakers included WBY, Gavan Duffy, JO'L, Rolleston, Ashe King, and J. F. Taylor. The second meeting, on 16 Aug, was the Inaugural Meeting of the Society (see p. 306).

indeed all have I think some beauty of their own. They seem to me too to have much that is profound in them & in their strange mysticism.[4]

Yours always

W B Yeats

I wonder will destiny ever drive you in the direction of Dublin.

ALS Texas. Wade (dated '[? June or July 1892]'), 207–8.

To T. Fisher Unwin, [23 August 1892]

53 Mountjoy Square | Dublin

Dear M[r] Unwin

There are I beleive a few pounds still due to me as royalties for "John Sherman" at least so I heard when I received the £10 for the American edition.[1] It would be very convenient if you could send them to me now.

If you would send a copy of "the Countess Kathleen" to J F Taylor 4 Ely Place Dublin he will review it in the Manchester Guardian.[2] I suppose it will be out soon now & that my free copies will reach me almost at once. It will be well considered over here at any rate

Yours very sinry

W B Yeats

ALS Texas. Dated by recipient '24.8.92'.

To T. Fisher Unwin, [c. 2 or 3 September 1892]

3 Upper Ely Place | Dublin

Dear M[r] Unwin

If you care to send me O'Gradys "Finn & his Companions" which I see is out I will review it for either United Ireland or some Irish American paper.[1]

You were so kind as to send me copies of the reviews of "Irish Fairy

[4] When WBY reviewed *Fate in Arcadia* in the *Bookman*, September 1892 (see p. 274), he picked out for particular praise the poems he mentions here, and quoted at length from 'Himself' and 'Outcast'.

[1] Published by Cassell in November 1891; see p. 268.
[2] Although the *Manchester Guardian* noticed most of WBY's books, there appears to have been no review of *The Countess Kathleen*; this may have been because of the quarrel soon to erupt between WBY and J. F. Taylor over the New Irish Library (see below, p. 312 ff).

[1] Fisher Unwin or one of his clerks later noted on this letter that O'Grady's book (see p. 295) had been 'sent to 53 Mountjoy Sq. Dublin on publication'. WBY noticed the book in the *Boston Pilot*, 19 Nov 1892 (*LNI*, 158), as giving 'the most vivid pictures of the Ossianic age I ever hope to see. Caoilte, having survived to the time of St. Patrick by enchantment, describes to the saint the life of the Fenians, and tells numbers of the old tales out of the bardic poems in English both powerful and beautiful.'

Stories" & I would be very much obliged if you could let me see the notices of "The Countess Kathleen" as there have been several which I have heard of but not seen & must have been others which I have neither heard of nor seen.[2]

I suppose it is too early to know how the book is doing.

Yours very truly

W B Yeats

ALS Texas.

To the Editor of The Freeman's Journal and National Press, *6 September 1892*

It is now almost certain that "The National Publishing Company" will get the £3,000 it has asked for.[1] The question is now, not will it be able to publish at all, but will it publish the right books on the right subjects, and if it does so, will it be able to put them into the hands of a sufficient number of Irish readers? Whether it does or does not succeed in doing these things must largely depend on whether or no it keeps itself in touch with the young men of Ireland whom it wishes to influence, with those who represent them, and with the various organisations which they have formed or are forming through the country.

It would be easy for men of position and of literary knowledge to publish an excellent series of books which would be quite unfitted for the Ireland of to-day, and it should be the business of the shareholders of this company to guard against this danger. No one man, however profound his knowledge of the Ireland of forty years ago, however eminent be his name, should have all the power thrust upon him. Ireland is a complex nation and has many needs and many interests, and no man, above all no man who has lived long out of Ireland, can hold the threads of all these needs and interests within his

---

[2] The first London review of *The Countess Kathleen* appeared in *The Times* on 25 Aug 1892. Further reviews appeared in the *Daily Chronicle* and the *Star* on 1 Sept (sent on to WBY by his father on the same day); there were other notices on 2 and 3 Sept.

[1] On his arrival in Dublin in late July, Gavan Duffy had proposed (see p. 308) a loose-knit limited liability company, the Irish National Publishing Company, with a capital not exceeding £5,000, made up of £1 shares, to issue the projected new Library of Ireland. When it became evident that this would not work, he arranged with Edmund Downey (see p. 11) to set up in London a 'National Publishing Company' which would eventually have a capital of £10,000, with Downey himself contributing £1,000 provided he was made managing director, at a salary of £300 per annum, and with Duffy as chairman. At a meeting of the publishing company on 29 Aug 1892, in the Oak Room of the Mansion House, J. F. Taylor announced that subscriptions had already reached £700 and Duffy, who was in the chair, said that he had no doubt they would get the money they wanted.

Drawing of W. B. Yeats, *c.*1894, by J. B. Yeats

W. B. Yeats in the mid 1890s

hands. Sir Charles Gavan Duffy has asked to be made editor-in-chief of the proposed new "library of Ireland," that we may guarantee the freedom of the books from any sectarian or sectional colour, but zeal for a great name and a great career should not induce the shareholders to press upon an old man, somewhat weary, as he has told us, of this world and its cares,[2] a greater burden of responsibility and power than he has felt compelled in the interest of the company to ask for. Sir Gavan Duffy has expressed his willingness to work with an editorial committee situated in Dublin,[3] and this committee should be constituted as soon as possible, that the writers may be chosen and set to work, for good books cannot be written in a day. The instructions should mainly rest with this committee, for it should know best its generation and what that generation needs and is capable of. It is probable that only a small proportion of the books published in such a "library" will be spontaneously offered, at least during the first few months. Writers will have to be sought out and started writing on the subjects they are most fitted for. Sir Gavan Duffy himself found out John Mitchel in this way, and set him to write the life of Hugh O'Neill, and at this moment there may be men as obscure as Mitchel was when the editor of *The Nation* chanced upon him,[4] who could do as picturesque and moving histories and biographies.

A somewhat considerable experience of the editing of cheap books—I have edited five, some of which were sold in thousands—[5] and of the editors and writers of such books and of the methods used by the editors of the various "libraries" and "series" they appear in, has convinced me that it would mean certain failure were the shareholders to persuade Sir Charles Gavan Duffy, living as he is forced to do out of Ireland, to become sole editor. A committee, say, of five should be formed, and this committee should be selected from men like Mr. Richard Ashe King, Dr. Douglas

[2] At his fractious first meeting with the provisional committee of the National Literary Society on 30 July (as *United Ireland* reported, 6 Aug 1892, 1), 'When the business in which he was engaged was finished,' the seventy-six-year-old Duffy 'turned to Dr Sigerson [in the chair] . . . and said he would like to get away, as he was "an old and weary man".'

[3] At the meeting on 29 Aug, Gavan Duffy had suggested (*United Ireland*, 3 Sept 1892, 2) that on a board of seven directors, 'three should be men of known commercial capacity, and three of recognised literary ability, with a chairman to preside over their meetings. He himself would have charge of the work of selecting the books to be published, which, he could promise, would be of such a character as to be free from any matter which would add to the causes of distraction already existing in the country.' Duffy had already outlined this position in an interview in the Dublin *Evening Telegraph* of 9 Aug 1892 (4).

[4] A letter to the *Freeman's Journal* of 8 Sept 1892, signed 'Historicus', pointed out that it was Thomas Davis, not Gavan Duffy, who had asked John Mitchel to write *The Life of Aodh O'Neill* (see p. 298), but Duffy had been the first to discover Mitchel and, in any case, WBY probably wished to introduce the name here in order to remind his readers of the 1847 quarrel between Mitchel and Duffy, of which WBY was to make polemical use in later stages of the controversy.

[5] Only four such books edited by WBY had thus far appeared: *Fairy and Folk Tales* (1888), *Stories from Carleton* (1889), *Representative Irish Tales* (1891), and *Irish Fairy Tales* (1892). WBY had evidently included in his calculation the edition of the lives of 'Irish Adventurers and Raperees' which he was finishing off but which was never published.

Hyde, Dr. Sigerson, Mr. Robert Donovan, Count Plunkett, Mr. Magrath,[6] Mr. George Coffey, whose archæological knowledge would be of the first importance, and Mr. John O'Leary, whose unequalled familiarity with the Irish literature of the past would help greatly if the question of reprints arose. A "library" so edited would be truly national, and would command the confidence of all sections and parties of the Irish race. We have now a great opportunity, and we must tread warily, for it may not occur again. If we fail now to interest the people of Ireland in intellectual matters by giving them books of the kind they seek for,[7] if we fail to enlist the sympathy of the young men who will have the building up of the Ireland of to-morrow, we may throw back the intellectual development of this country for years.

W B Yeats

Printed letter, *Freeman's Journal*, 6 September 1892 (6). *UP* 1.239-42.

To the Editor of The Freeman's Journal and National Press,[1] *7 September 1892*

September 7th.

Dear Sir—I find by this morning's *Freeman* that you consider "that the shareholders of the proposed Irish Publishing Company do not take to Mr. Yeats's proposal of a committee to assist Sir Charles Gavan Duffy in his task as editor." You forget, at any rate, one very distinguished shareholder— I refer to Sir Charles Gavan Duffy himself—who explained to a representative of the *Evening Telegraph* some few weeks ago that he would gladly accept such assistance,[2] nor did he express any alarm less "the new company should be used as a propagandist machine for sectional ideas and principles." He evidently considered that his position as "editor-in chief" would be ample

---

[6] i.e. John McGrath of *United Ireland*; see p. 262, n. 4.

[7] The disagreement between WBY and Gavan Duffy as to the nature of the new Library of Ireland had come out clearly at the meeting on 8 Aug to discuss the scheme (see p. 308). Duffy had said then (as *United Ireland* reported, 13 Aug 1892, 3) that 'The training of books was the best training a young man could get, and if they formed a library they should publish books of a practical character. . . . Formerly the people were stimulated with poetry, but the condition of the country was now too serious for madrigals.' At the same meeting, WBY argued that the books 'must not appeal to special interest . . . but to such interests as were universal—heroism, the love of true manhood, and so on.'

[1] After long and difficult negotiations (see p. 265), Tim Healy had agreed to amalgamate his anti-Parnellite *National Press* with the *Freeman's Journal* which had defected from Parnell in July 1891, and for a short period both names appeared on the paper's masthead.

[2] Gavan Duffy, interviewed in the Dublin *Evening Telegraph* on 9 Aug 1892 (see p. 311) and asked whether he objected to a literary committee in Dublin taking an initiative in the selection of books for the new Library of Ireland, replied: 'Not at all, such a committee if it were chosen by a vote of the shareholders or appointed by the directors might perform a very useful function. . . . You cannot have too many men's minds engaged in the project if their single desire be to help it, and if young men they will necessarily know more of the wants and wishes of their generation than older ones.'

guarantee of the innocuous nature of the books. The rest of your leader deals with matters of opinion rather than matters of fact, and needs no comment from me, except that free discussion of the question must of necessity do good and help the right opinion to prevail. I am sorry to see by the tone of Mr. Taylor's letter that the discussion is less welcome to him than to me, and I very genuinely regret, for the sake of his own reputation, that he should have felt impelled to write such a letter—a letter which certainly calls for no further answer than that I have met several shareholders who assure me that he had no mandate from them.[3] I have tried in vain to understand what bearing his extraordinary last paragraph has upon the question at issue,[4] or why he has dragged such matters into a discussion which I, at any rate, have carried on with courtesy and good temper.—Yours sincerely,

W B Yeats

Printed letter, *Freeman's Journal and National Press*, 8 September 1892 (5). *UP* 1. 242–3.

To the Editor of The Freeman's Journal and National Press, *9 September 1892*

September 9th.

DEAR SIR—I am beset by two difficulties in answering Mr. Taylor. I can neither descend to the weapons which he has thought it compatible with his

---

[3] An editorial in the *Freeman's Journal* of 7 Sept 1892 (4) had endorsed J. F. Taylor's view, expressed in a letter on the following page, that the shareholders were opposed to the proposals WBY had made in his letter of 6 Sept. 'We are not surprised,' it commented; 'divided responsibilities are always bad; but in this case they would be fatal.' The paper went on to pick out the 'one danger to be guarded against':

and Sir Charles Gavan Duffy is a safeguard; the danger is lest the new company should be used as a propagandist machine for sectional ideas and principles in conflict with the sentiment of the people. Such a danger lurks in Mr. Yeats's proposal. "Assisting" Sir Charles Gavan Duffy is the polite [word] for superseding him, and the supercession would lead to the withdrawal of a good deal of the support upon which as long as toleration and respect is shown all round and the debates of party kept clear of, the new company may count.

[4] Taylor's letter concluded:

the shareholders see in Sir Charles an effective guarantee that the company will be worked on broad principles, and not in the interest of any coterie however "precious".

It is not an edifying spectacle to see A reviewing B, and B in turn reviewing A, and both going into raptures of admiration. Such things have happened, even in modern times. A poet, not of the Della Cruscan school, has commemorated such things in moving verse—

> You'll praise and I'll praise,
>   We'll both praise together, O!
> What jolly fun we'll have
>   Praising one another, O!

It will be gratifying to Mr. Yeats to know that Sir Charles, as editor, will be able to restrain such "log rolling", and to work the enterprise in an earnest and honest way.

dignity to make use of, nor can I enter like him into the discussion of what was said and done at committee meetings and private conferences. In order to make the fabric of personalities and insinuations which he has built up crumble, it is only necessary for me to say that I have taken no single step in this matter of the company except after consultation with my friends and fellow-workers, and that my whole endeavour has been to arrange a compromise between those who object altogether to the predominance of Sir Charles Gavan Duffy and those who wish to make that predominance absolute.[1] But now enough of Mr. Taylor. I will answer him no more.

You ask in your Thursday's issue for an assurance that I and my friends are not seeking to make the company the mouthpiece of party.[2] I give that assurance most heartily, and I am glad to add that the question I raised had been solved in the way I suggested, Sir Charles Gavan Duffy having consented to act with a committee which will consult with him and offer advice without in any way overriding his decisions.[3]—Yours sincerely,

W B Yeats

Printed letter, *Freeman's Journal and National Press*, 10 September 1892 (6). *UP* 1. 243–4.

[1] In a further letter to the *Freeman's Journal*, published on 9 Sept 1892 (6), Taylor tried to show that WBY, although claiming to speak for a number of interested parties, was in fact carrying on a personal and perverse campaign against Duffy's editorship of the proposed New Irish Library. He did this partly by citing private meetings, insisting 'that the scheme set out by Mr. Yeats was discussed and debated to death before ever any public appeal was made for support, and that we went before the public on the clear understanding that Sir Charles was to be solely responsible for the editorial work,' and partly by a direct attack upon WBY, arguing that Duffy, 'a man of large and varied experience both of men and things', was 'willing to be useful if our "young men" would only kindly allow him to serve Ireland, and, although admittedly they cannot do his work, they set themselves to thwart, obstruct, retard, and wreck all that he undertakes. When I say "they" I mean "he", as I know of no "young man" except Mr. Yeats who has not warmly welcomed Sir Charles's project.' Taylor went on to insinuate that WBY, driven by 'febrile vanity', was acting treacherously and maintained that if any man of genius were to arise in Ireland he would prefer to deal with Duffy than 'the freaks of any coterie of select and kindred spirits'.

[2] Presumably a reference to the *Freeman*'s editorial of Wednesday (not Thursday), 7 Sept 1892; see p. 313, n. 3.

[3] This apparently happy conclusion to the dispute rested in fact upon a misapprehension. WBY and JO'L had misinterpreted a sentence of T. W. Rolleston's which JO'L quoted in a letter printed in the *Freeman's Journal* immediately above this one by WBY: 'I received a letter from London this morning, telling me that Sir Gavan Duffy "will have no objection to make to the formation of any editorial committee in Dublin, it being understood that this committee will have no power except to advise and suggest".' Rolleston was quick to deny that this was his intended meaning and, writing to the *Freeman's Journal* on 12 Sept (letter published 14 Sept [5]) set the record straight:

Mr. O'Leary, without naming the writer, quotes a sentence from a recent letter of mine to him, which was certainly not written for publication, and which, if I recollect aright, he has not transcribed correctly. . . . I am pretty sure I did not say "any" editorial committee. . . . I have spoken to Sir Charles Duffy on the subject and he says . . . that since the controversy began he never made any communication (as one would infer from the letters of Mr. O'Leary and Mr. Yeats) of his willingness to act with a committee. Several weeks before the controversy he told a representative of the *Evening Telegraph* [see p. 312] that he had not the slightest objection to a committee, not self-selected, but chosen by the directors or shareholders, who might make any suggestions they thought fit to him—suggestions

To the Editor of United Ireland, *10 September 1892*

"DEAR SIR—Two or three of the reviews of my 'Countess Kathleen' have misread my rhyming claim to be considered 'one with Davis, Mangan, Ferguson,' and one of them has based on this misconception a reproof for my supposed lack of modesty.[1] I did not in the least intend the lines to claim equality of eminence, nor does the context bear out such a reading, but only community in the treatment of Irish subjects after an Irish fashion. I send this letter to you as the matter concerns my Nationalist readers,[2] if it concerns anybody at all, and but little the readers of the papers that made the comment.—Yours very truly,

                                                   "W B Yeats"

Printed letter, *United Ireland*, 10 September 1892 (1). Wade, 213.

which he would take into careful consideration. But if his name was to be associated with the project in any manner he would require to have the same control over this library as he had over the Library of Ireland—a control which would enable him to protect the books from becoming imbecile, extravagant, or partisan.

[1] In lines 17–22 of his poem, 'Apologia addressed to Ireland in the coming days' (subsequently revised and entitled 'To Ireland in the Coming Times', *VP*, 137–9), WBY wrote:

> Nor may I less be counted one
> With Davis, Mangan, Ferguson,
> Because to him who ponders well
> My rhymes more than their rhyming tell
> Of the dim wisdoms old and deep,
> That God gives unto man in sleep.

An unsigned review of *The Countess Kathleen* which appeared in the *Sunday Sun*, 28 Aug 1892 (3), had concluded with a 'word in this young poet's ear. He is young, and modesty will the better become him. Is it not rather soon for him to rate himself—and somewhat queer to do so himself—as "one with Davis Mangan and Ferguson," names, we believe, rated amongst the highest in Ireland.' The review was identified by *United Ireland* as the work of Justin Huntly McCarthy (1861–1936).

[2] Justin Huntly McCarthy was the son of Justin McCarthy, leader of the anti-Parnellite party, and had been the last of the Irish MPs to desert Parnell; T. P. O'Connor (1848–1929), the editor and proprietor of the *Sunday Sun* had been a supporter of Parnell but had turned against him—facts which account for the partisan edge in WBY's letter, addressed to the leading Parnellite journal. The editor of *United Ireland*, who had a paragraph on the same page attacking O'Connor for his sycophantic attitude towards the British royal family, prefaced WBY's letter with a supporting note and went on to quote from his covering letter about the New Irish Library, identical with that sent to the *Freeman's Journal* on 6 Sept 1892 (see pp. 310–2).

To T. Fisher Unwin, [mid-September 1892]

⟨53 Mountjoy Square⟩
11 Waltham Terrace | Blackrock[1] | Co Dublin

Dear Sir.

Is the large paper edition of "The Countess Kathleen" out yet?[2] I put my name down for a copy (over & above any copy I may be entitled to). Could you let me know when it comes out?

Yours sincerly
W B Yeats

My address will be as above until Saturday. I then return to 53 Mountjoy Square.

ALS Texas.

To J. T. Kelly, [16 September 1892]

Blackrock Office
4–27 P.M.

TO J. T. Kelly   Secretaries office   General Post office   DUBLIN.
Tell McCall to see eyre Trenches Remedy Depot about rooms not agent[1] important

Yeats

Telegram Private. Post Office stamp 'SE 16 92'. *Hill's Guide to Blackrock* (Blackrock, 1976), 2.

¹ WBY was staying with Richard Ashe King at Blackrock.
² At about the same time as the main, 500-copy, edition of *The Countess Kathleen and Various Legends and Lyrics* was published, in September 1892, an edition of 30 copies was issued in Japan vellum boards.

¹ The National Literary Society at a meeting on 15 Sept 1892 had decided to take rooms in South Frederick Street, next door to the Nassau Hotel, for one year at a rent not exceeding £40, and the poet P. J. McCall (see p. 22) was apparently negotiating for them. The residence of J. R. Eyre (see p. 136), another member of the Society, at 37 South Frederick Street was a few doors away from Trench's Remedies Depot Ltd. ('Trench's Remedy for Epileptic Fits promises Immediate Relief and Permanent Cure'), of which he may have been manager. The proprietor of the Remedies Depot, J. Townsend Trench, was also a house and land agent with an office round the corner at 14 Molesworth Street. The South Frederick Street rooms were not in the end taken.

To the Editor of United Ireland, *24 September 1892*

Sɪʀ—Would you kindly publish the enclosed circular,[1] which I am issuing in connection with the Libraries Scheme of the Literary Society.—Yours truly,

W B Yeats.

"Dᴇᴀʀ Sɪʀ—In the small towns of Ireland are few bookshops and few books. Here and there are literary societies, some of which have started reading-rooms where in most cases there is nothing to read except the newspapers, and in the few cases where there is every book has been read three or four times over. The National Literary Society hopes to remedy all this and set up small lending libraries wherever a reading-room already exists, or wherever a local committee is willing to start one.[2] The number of cheap series of standard books have made it possible to buy for four or five pounds a fairly representative collection of books of both Irish and general literature. The society proposes to organise lectures in connection with the scheme and to send lecturers at stated intervals to every local society which is ready to work with it in the way described and to begin at once to carry out its programme. A sufficient amount of money has been subscribed to enable it to make a beginning; but much more is needed if the work is to be carried out on any considerable scale. Small donations, either in books or money, can be sent to the Hon Treasurer of the Library Committee, Count Plunket, 25 Upper Fitzwilliam-street, Dublin; or to myself, at 2 Russell-street, Dublin.[3]—I remain, yours sincerely,

W B Yᴇᴀᴛꜱ, Hon Sec."

Printed letter, *United Ireland*, 24 September 1892 (4). *UP* ɪ. 244–5.

[1] This letter with is enclosure was also published in the *Tuam Herald* of 8 Oct 1892, in the *Dublin Figaro* of 15 Oct, and may have been reprinted by other periodicals and provincial newspapers.

[2] At a meeting on 15 Sept 1892, the Committee of the National Literary Society had set up a Libraries Subcommittee 'for the establishment of Libraries through the country.' There were seven members: MG, Mary Hayden, JO'L, WBY, W. P. Coyne, J. P. Quinn, and J. F. Taylor.

[3] At a meeting on 22 Sept 1892, WBY was made Hon. Sec. of the Libraries Subcommittee and Count Plunkett co-opted as Treasurer. 2 Russell Street was the family home of Samuel Charles Bell (b. 1868), who coached candidates for the Civil Service examinations and was a founder member of the National Literary Society.

To Thomas Stuart,[1] [*c. 3 October 1892*]

c/o George Pollexfen | Thorn Hill | Sligo

Dear Mr Stuart

You must have thought it rude of me not to have replied before but I have been very busy & so let your letter & many another wait a while. You must not think however that this means any lack of appreciation of your kindness in sending me so many good wishes & in writing so many pleasant things about me in the Figero. Though the copies you sent me must have gone astray in the post for I never received them, I had seen your notes about the Harcourt St School & myself & Foster & so on—& my "bloody nosed beetle" of which I have a very vague memory.[2] I remember your name very well & will I have no doubt remember your personality also, as soon as a meeting bring it to memory. It floats dimnly before me & may at any time take visible shape. I shall be back in town early in November or the end of

---

[1] Thomas Patrick Stuart (b. 1867) was born at Landhead, Co. Antrim. His parents subsequently moved to Dublin, where he enrolled at the Dublin High School in February 1880 and left in the summer of 1883. From October 1882 to July 1883 he was a classmate of WBY's in Form 5 but, as in the case of H. A. Hinkson (see p. 258), WBY's memory for schoolfellows seems to have been short. Stuart wrote verse at school and contributed an elegy on Queen Victoria, 'Lacrimae Britanniarum', to Forshaw's anthology *In Memoriam* (1901). He wrote occasionally for the *Pall Mall Budget*, *Sketch*, and *Fun*.

[2] Seven paragraphs, recalling WBY's career in the fifth form at the Dublin High School, appeared on 24 Sept 1892 in the *Dublin Figaro* (501–2; subsequently recast into a more barbed anonymous article in *T.P.'s Weekly*, 7 June 1912), a Unionist magazine given over to society gossip. To Stuart it seemed

but yesterday that we were all working away in the fifth form classroom at our curds [*sic*] and quadratics under the watchful eye of the severe and autocratic, but greatly popular, Mr. T. W. Foster, M.A., familiarly known amongst enlightened fifth as 'Tommy'. Yeats would have a portable chess-board on his knee under the desk, wholly absorbed with some companion in a protracted tournament (he always had a handsome ivory set of chessmen, I remember them well). 'Tommy' ever vigilant, spying the converging heads, would suddenly sing out 'Yeats and Smith bring up your work.' Then would there be collisions of collapsing knights and bishops amongst the meaner pawns. Then would there be hurryings of hands from board to pocket, and pocket to board. Then would there be lengthened faces, and whispered but despairing appeals to industrious neighbours of 'give us a few quadratics.' After that the deluge.

Thomas William Foster (?1849–98) as a scholar of Trinity College, Dublin, won a Gold Medal in Mathematics. He was senior mathematics master of the Dublin High School from 1871 to 1890, when he became headmaster of the Royal Academy, Belfast. As well as teaching WBY mathematics, he was his fifth-form classmaster from autumn 1881 to December 1883. 'Smith' is an invention of Stuart's; there was no boy of that name at the High School with WBY.

In another *Figaro* paragraph, Stuart recalled that WBY

was continually in a state of anxiety and unrest consequent on the number of live specimens imprisoned in match-boxes, etc., which were always concealed about his person, brought to school for exchange or comparison. One day the blow fell. An insect escaped from its box and ran along the floor, Yeats, excited, after it, upsetting everything in his path, we, ignorant and cruel young ruffians, endeavouring to stamp on it as it ran. At last the owner, fearful of our efforts and unable to prevent us, cried imploringly to the angry and perplexed master—'Oh, stop them! stop them! It's my bloody-nosed beetle' . . . I can see all still. The frantic biologist disordered as to his hair running along by the hot-water pipes calling in agony to the gods and the fifth form to spare his bloody-nosed beetle.

present month & shall hope to meet you then—3 Upper Ely Place always finds me sooner or later.

Yes I have just published a book called "The Countess Kathleen & various Legends & Lyrics" ("Cameo series" T Fisher Unwin).

You mentioned Charley Johnston in your notes but did not seem to have heard that he is back from India, teaching Sanskrit—He has just published a sanskrit grammer & won praise from Max Muller. I had a letter from him a couple of days ago from Hampstead where he lives now—[3]

Yours truly

W B Yeats

I have very vivid memories of that chessboard & the hot water it used to get me into.

ALS Southern Illinois.

To J. F. Fuller,[1] [mid-October 1892]

C/o George Pollexfen | Thorn Hill | Sligo—

Dear Sir

I did not reply to your letter before as I waited to read the novel.[2] I have read a good deel of it but a sudden presure of work has made my progress slower than I intended—I will however write again when I have finished it. I should have thanked you at once for it had I thought I should have had to delay so long.

I am delighted with the gayiety & dash of what I have read & with the character drawing. I hope I may have the pleasure of making your

---

[3] Stuart in his *Figaro* paragraphs had also remembered Charlie Johnston, whom he described as 'a judge away in India', as a friend of WBY's. *Useful Sanskrit Nouns and Verbs in English Letters*, compiled by Charles Johnston (1892), was an introduction to Sanskrit grammar and gave simple declensions and conjugations transliterated into English. The Sanskrit scholar Friedrich Max Müller (1823–1900) was Professor of Comparative Philology at Oxford. Johnston was giving tuition in Sanskrit to candidates for the Indian Civil Service examination. The information on him provided here by WBY was incorporated by Stuart in a further article in the *Figaro*, 8 Oct 1892 (534).

[1] An architect by profession, who designed many churches and country houses in Ireland, James Franklin Fuller (1835–1924) was a novelist (sometimes under the pseudonym 'Ignotus') and genealogist in his spare time.

[2] Fuller had sent WBY his novel, *The Chronicles of Westerley* (1892), which had originally appeared serially in *Blackwood's Magazine*, April 1891 to February 1892. A sequel to his *Culmshire Folk* (1873) and *John Orlebar, Clk.* (1878), the novel narrates in a breezy style the romantic attachments of the 201st regiment (Do or Dies) whose departure from Westerley-on-Sea for foreign service causes a number of entanglements. The one Irish character, the 'irrepressible' 2nd Lt. Fitzmaurice Bateman, owes rather more to Charles Lever than to the Celtic Twilight.

acquantance when I return to Dublin.[3] I am staying with a friend of military tendencies & am urging him to set to work on your book.[4]

Yours truly
W B Yeats

ALS Private.

To Richard Le Gallienne, [c. 15 October 1892]

c/o George Pollexfen | Thorne Hill. | Sligo.
My dear L'Galleone

My father has just sent me a Daily Chronicle with the review of your poems in it. Who is the entirely absurd being who wrote that review. I think it was the same man who noticed my book in an even more offencive fashion. The quotations he makes from you are beautiful—especialy the second.[1] I asked the Bookman to send me your book but they had already sent it out.

I have long wanted to thank you for your magnificent notice of "The Countess Kathleen". You gave me the best lift I have yet had—with this or any book. The ordinary poetry reading folk I imagine are more influenced by

---

[3] A native of Kerry, Fuller had a house at Kenmare but lived most of the year in Dublin. His private residence there was 5 Sydenham Road, Dundrum, and he had offices at 179 Great Brunswick Street.

[4] WBY's uncle George Pollexfen, who kept 'among his workmen a discipline that had about it something of a regiment or a ship . . . ' (*Aut*, 71). In a letter to WBY, 20 July 1919 (MBY), JBY asked: 'Do you remember George and his regrets that he was not an army officer? Whenever he met an officer he would seek his acquaintance. The attraction was merely the pomp, the magnificent orderliness of war. He ought to have ended his days as an old Major. . . .'

[1] The anonymous reviewer of Le Gallienne's *English Poems* (1892) in the *Daily Chronicle* for 11 Oct 1892 (3), probably John Davidson, pointed out that Le Gallienne was 'a young writer of much promise, who happily unites critical capacity with a genuine sense and feeling for poetry', but criticized him for over-sweetness: 'Mr. Le Gallienne's Muse is a too persistently kissing, embracing, and cuddling Muse. A more entirely blissful young poet we never met—a poet with his mouth chock-full of nectar and ambrosia.' The reviewer quoted from the poems 'Never-Ever' and 'The Decadent to his Soul'; the 'especialy' beautiful quotation is from 'All Sung', beginning, 'What shall I sing when all is sung, / And every tale is told . . . ', and ending with the quatrain:

> Why should I strive through weary moons
> To make my music true?
> Only the dead men knew the tunes
> The live world dances to.

Davidson was probably also the author, as JBY and WBY supposed, of the anonymous notice of *The Countess Kathleen* in the *Daily Chronicle*, 1 Sept 1892 (3). It gave an ironic and critical account of the title play, finding that the 'morality is excellent, but as an artistic achievement the drama has much to lack . . . there are no lines which go straight home and linger in the memory.' The reviewer found the themes of the other poems 'romanceful and poetic enough, but the execution is halting and undistinguished. . . . The verses have not enough beauty of diction or true lyrical quality to make up for their want of any other attraction.'

the Star than by the Academy even. Its praise is rarer. You & Johnson have been of great help to me.[2] Last night I had a rather interesting magical adventure. I went to a great fairy locality—a cave by the Rosses sands—with an Uncle & a cousin who is believed by the neighbours & herself to have narrowly escaped capture by that dim kingdom once. I made a magical circle & invoked the fairys. My uncle—a hard headed man of about 47—heard presently voices like those of boys shouting & distant music but saw nothing. My cousin however saw a bright light & multitudes of little forms clad in crimson as well as hearing the music & the[n] the far voices. Once their was a great sound as of little people cheering & stamping with their feet away in the heart of the rock. The queen of the troop came then—I could see her—& held a long conversation with us & finally wrote in the sand "be careful & do not seek to know too much about us". She told us before she wrote this however a great deal about the economy of the dim kingdom. One troop of the creatures carried quicken berries in their hands. My cousin saw them very plainly.

I tell you this because I have used my symbols with you so that you will understand that such things are possible.[3] I am on the look out for a copy of your poems. I am too desperately hard up to buy one but will probably borrow a copy from Miss Tynan when I get to Dublin again. I will then write to you about them

Yours sny
W B Yeats

ALS Yale.

[2] JBY had sent the *Daily Chronicle*'s notice of *The Countess Kathleen* to WBY along with Le Gallienne's laudatory notice, also on 1 Sept, in the *Star* (2)—'the poison and the antidote'—on the day they appeared (*JBYL*, 53). Le Gallienne devoted most of his space to the play, which, he said, showed an increase of control and economy over WBY's earlier poetry: 'All its elemental qualities, its Irish glamor, its deep mysticism, its dreamlike imagination, its sheer beauty, are preserved, but they are now controlled as well.' He praised in particular the scene where the peasants come to barter away their souls, and that in which the spirits of earth and water carry off the Countess's treasure: the 'wizardry' of the latter scene, he said, 'in which horde after horde the demons thus invoke their various powers, fairly sets one's hair on end. I can imagine nothing, in its way, finer.' Lionel Johnson's enthusiastic review of *The Countess Kathleen*, in the *Academy*, 1 Oct 1892 (278), is reprinted in *W. B. Yeats: The Critical Heritage*, ed. A. Norman Jeffares (1977), 78–82.

[3] WBY published an account of this invocation, under the title 'Regina, Regina Pigmeorum, Veni', in *The Celtic Twilight*. He made a number of magical experiments with his uncle, George Pollexfen (now in fact aged fifty-three); the cousin was Lucy Middleton, whom WBY described in a letter to Lady Gregory (25 May 1930, MBY) as 'the only witch in the family'. In his sympathetic notice of *IFT* in the *Star* (see p. 295), Le Gallienne had mentioned WBY's assurance 'that the fairies are still literally believed in by the Irish peasantry at the present time' and described WBY's chats with old Biddy Hart, 'who, while he sits by her turf fire eating griddle cake, tells him of "her friends the fairies who inhabit the green, thorn-covered hill up there behind the house".'

To John O'Leary, [16 October 1892]

c/o George Pollexfen | Thornhill, Sligo
Sunday

Dear M^r O'Leary

Thank you very much for Miss Gonnes note which I return.[1] I had however heard from herself. She has indeed been better in the matter of letters & written at greater length & in a more cordial spirit than she has done for a long time. I had a long letter yesterday & another the day before. She is to be in Dublin on the 1st of November & was to leave Royat for Paris yesterday (15th). She is very eager about the work & asks many questions. I have heard from Quin about the society. I have almost finished my introduction to the volume of "Irish Adventurers". I really think this is well nigh all the news I have barring various incantations & invokations of the fairies at their secret spots, but these things are hardly in your line.

I think that Leamy ought to be asked for a lecture by our Society. The thing of his in the "Independent" seems very right in spirit though somewhat flimsy in substance so far as report goes.[2] You will have heard of my grandmothers death—I send paper with funeral in it—[3] my grandfather is dying too—

Yours truly
W B Yeats

ALS NLI. Wade, 213–14.

[1] This is probably MG's note to JO'L dated '4 October' (NLI):

I had hoped to be in Dublin for the anniversary of the 6th [the anniversary of Parnell's death] but the Doctor would not hear of [it] . . . so I sent a wreath. . . . I hope to be in Dublin by the end of the month. I am writing to all my friends for books for the libraries. Thank you so much for sending me the papers which contained the correspondence on the subject of the Literary Society. It seems a pity that the somewhat too personal discussion was raised so early as it gives our enemies a chance of saying "As usual" . . .

JO'L had presumably sent her the exchanges of letters in the *Freeman's Journal* from 6 Sept onward (see pp. 310–4). Although the note is dated from Paris, MG was probably writing from Royat, the watering place in the Puy-de-Dôme where she spent much of the month of October.

[2] Edmund Leamy's lecture, 'Our Irish National Literary Revival', delivered to the Literary Society at 113 Capel Street, Dublin, on 13 Oct 1892, was reported in the *Irish Daily Independent* on the following day. There was, Leamy said, 'in the Irish mind of the day an uprising intellectual life struggling for expression in a literature native and to the manner born'. He urged that this literature should be grounded in the ancient Celtic stories and praised Ferguson, Standish O'Grady, and Eugene O'Curry (1796–1862) for their work to this end. (O'Curry, a leading authority on Irish manuscript material, was best known for his *Lectures on the Manuscript Materials of Ancient Irish History* [Dublin, 1860] and *On the Manners and Customs of the Ancient Irish*, 3 vols. [1873].) Leamy insisted that those founding the New Irish Library would have to discover the best means of bringing books into the homes of the people, 'as that would be essential for the success of the movement', and called upon his audience to give every assistance to the men who were 'endeavouring to work up a literary movement'.

[3] Elizabeth Pollexfen died on 2 Oct 1892; her death and funeral were reported in the *Sligo Champion*, 8 Oct 1892.

To Edward Garnett, [c. *17 October 1892*]

c/o George Pollexfen | Thorn Hill | Sligo | Ireland

My dear Garnett.

I shall finish my introduction to the "Irish Adventurers" tomorrow & post it to you. I hope the thing will do. It is I think fresh & has a little novel information in it. I want you to let me know whether I can include "Freeney the Robber" or does Whibbly still intend to use him.[1]

Why have you not sung out. I was very triumphantly successful in an invocation of the Fairies at a noted location of theirs two days ago.[2] My uncle & cousin both got into the trance the first very slightly & the second very deeply & all kinds of strange music & voices were heard & all sorts of queer figures seen. You I think have seen the symbols worked & so may under stand the methods.

Please let me know about the "adventurers" introduction as soon as possible as I shall be in suspence until I hear.

How does the "Imaged World" thrive. Please let me know before any book of yours comes out as I am now reviewing on the Bookman & may be able to be of use.[3]

Yours truly
W B Yeats

ALS Texas. Wade, 214.

[1] Charles Whibley's *A Book of Scoundrels*, published by Heinemann in 1897 (most of the chapters having already appeared in periodicals), includes nothing on the highwayman James Freney (see below, p. 354), and a chapter on him remained in the contents of WBY's proposed volume until at least 1893. Born in Kent and educated at Jesus College, Cambridge, Whibley (1859–1930) was one of the young men who with WBY congregated around W. E. Henley; he was working at this time for Cassell & Co. and writing for the *National Observer*. In 1894 he joined the *Pall Mall Gazette* and was sent to Paris where he met Whistler, Mallarmé, and Verlaine and married Whistler's sister-in-law. In later years he contributed to the *Spectator* and to the *Daily Mail* and was much admired by T. S. Eliot; his series entitled 'Musings without Method' ran in *Blackwood's Magazine* for 30 years.

[2] See p. 321.

[3] WBY began reviewing for the *Bookman* in July 1892, and by the time of his last notice, in July 1899, had contributed more than 50 reviews, as well as poems and stories, to the magazine. When Garnett's *An Imaged World: Poems in Prose* eventually appeared, in 1894, it received a bad notice in the *Bookman* of August 1894, but this is unlikely to have been by WBY. His review was probably the anonymous one published in the *Speaker*, 8 Sept 1894 (*UP* I. 341–3).

To John O'Leary, [c. *25 October 1892*]

c/o George Pollexfen | Thorn Hill | Sligo

Dear M^r O'Leary

I return on Monday & want to know if Mrs Carew can put me up at any rate for a time at Clontarf?[1] Please let me know—I hope that she can at any rate let me go there until I look round & get other lodgings.

Miss Gonne is to be in Dublin on November 1st. Such were at any rate her last plans. She is at present in London on her way or else is just leaving Paris for there. She is full of schemes for the Tenants & for the libraries.[2]

I have finished the Adventurer introduction but have not yet heard from Garnett anent it. Very good notice of my book in the "Saturday" & wildly laudatory one in "Irish Society".[3]

Yours ever
W B Yeats

ALS (black-bordered paper) NLI.

To the Editor of The Bookman,[1] [*November 1892*]

The one great difficulty that besets all speculation as to who should be Laureate is that for one cause or another the only men who have clear right to the position are the last to whom it is likely to be offered, or by whom it would be accepted if it were. Mr. Swinburne has hardly so entirely thrust underground his old convictions, or so utterly forgotten his lines about "a linnet chirping on the wrist of kings" to take an office directly from the Court; nor would Mr. William Morris be ready to exchange lectures at

[1] JO'L himself lodged with his cousin, Mrs Carew, at Lonsdale House, St Lawrence Road, Clontarf; see p. 336.

[2] MG's departure from Paris was again to be postponed, partly because she was lecturing in France on behalf of evicted tenants in Ireland.

[3] A friendly notice of *The Countess Kathleen* appeared in the *Saturday Review*, 22 Oct 1892 (484–5). The review in *Irish Society*, 22 Oct 1892 (1008–9), was indeed 'wildly laudatory'. 'There can be no doubt,' wrote the reviewer, Louis H. Victory, 'that, as an Irish poet of abnormal powers, Mr Yeats stands alone today . . . something of a seer it is . . . given to him to see and to understand things that other men may not see and understand. . . . I have no hesitation in saying that Mr. Yeats's poems will live and will find innumerable commentators and would-be interpreters, as long as the world lasts.'

[1] Alfred Lord Tennyson, the Poet Laureate, had died on 6 Oct 1892 and there was much discussion in the press as to who would succeed him. In the November issue of the *Bookman* the editor announced that he had written 'to four distinguished poets asking whether, in their opinion, the laureateship should be continued, and if so, on whom it should be conferred'. The four resulting letters were published in the same issue, under the heading, 'The Question of the Laureateship', the third being signed 'R.B.' (?Robert Bridges) and the others unsigned. WBY revealed his authorship of the second letter in his letter to JO'L which follows.

Kelmscott House for songs about royal marriages, no matter how large a hogshead of sherry were made over to him in the bargain.[2] When the conditions attaching to a post intended for the chief poet of an age are such as to render it impossible to the only two men fitted for it alike by genius and the acclaim of the best public of their day, surely the time has come when these conditions should be mended. If they be not mended, for the ending of any so venerable and honourable a thing as the Laureateship should be out of all question, we shall see the supreme artist who is gone succeeded by some unreadable mediocrity or fluent monger of platitudes, his throat still hoarse from self-advertisement. All the public officers, from the Prime Minister downwards, were once Court officials, but now they are responsible to the nation and to the nation alone. Surely it is time to transform the Laureateship also, and to expect no Laureate in return for his pension and his sherry to do other than celebrate, if he be so minded, for the muses make but indifferent drudges, matters of national importance, great battles if he hold them to be waged in a just cause, the deaths of famous men of thought and action, and the ever-coming never-come light of that ideal peace and freedom whereto all nations are stumbling in the darkness. In the old days the imagination of the world would have fared but ill without its kings and nobles, for in those times, when few could read and pictures were many a mile between, they kept before men's minds a more refined and ample ideal of life than was possible to the small chief in his rush-strewn tower or to the carle in his poor cottage. By a phantasmagoria of royalties and nobilities the soul of the world displayed itself, and whatever there was in the matter of court poet or court pageantry helped it to draw them away from their narrow circle of eating and sleeping, and getting and begetting. It showed them life under the best conditions, and king or queen, baron or duke, became to them a type of the glory of the world. Thus, at any rate do I, with my perhaps too literary eyes, read history, and turn all into a kind of theatre where the proud walk clad in cloth of gold, and display their passionate hearts, that the groundlings may feel their souls wax the greater. But now no man can say that life displays itself under the best conditions in royalties and nobilities, for refinement and ample life have gone out into the highways and byways, and the Laureate should go after them, and be their master of the revels.

Surely most of us, whatever be our politics, feel that 'The Idylls of the King' are marred a little by the dedications to the Prince Consort and to the Queen,[3] and not necessarily because either was unworthy of exceeding praise, but because neither represents to us a fuller and more beautiful kind

---

[2] The lines quoted are from stanza 32 of Swinburne's 'Mater Triumphalis', and should read: 'And chirp of linnets on the wrists of kings'. A butt of 'the best Canary Wyne' had been part of the traditional stipend for the Poet Laureate until 1790, when Henry Pye commuted it into cash.

[3] Tennyson dedicated the *Idylls of the King* to the Prince Consort, whom he styled 'Albert the Good':

of life than is possible to any mere subject, and because the attempt to make them do so, even though so mighty a poet made it, has a little lessened the significance of the great imaginative types of Arthur and Guinevere, and cast round the greatest romantic poem of the century a ring of absurdity. We can only just tolerate Spenser's comparison of the Queen of the Fairies to Queen Elizabeth,[4] for even then all such comparisons were growing obsolete, whereas we can hardly forgive at all this injury which the Court poet of our day has done to the laurelled poet of the people. Were not this alone sufficient reason, even if all others were lacking, for nationalizing the laureateship? Once do this in some conspicuous fashion, and the post will become the greatest honour any country could confer upon a man of letters, and neither Mr. Swinburne or Mr. Morris will find reasons to refuse it. Either would make a worthy successor to Wordsworth and Tennyson, Morris the worthier of the two, perhaps, for he is still producing work scarce a whit less moving than were the songs and stories of his youth, while Mr. Swinburne has been these many days, if we consider his verse alone, too careful of the sound, too careless of the sense.

This letter of mine has gone into matters far removed from literary criticism and is more than a little discursive, but I know not when a man has so good right to be discursive and have his say according to his whim as when he is suggesting something which has not the slightest chance of being done. Besides, if I had not talked somewhat of things in general I should have had to discuss the claims of all kinds of perfectly absurd people, and even to take seriously him of whom it has been said that he calls himself "of Penbryn," to be distinguished from his namesake of Parnassus.[5]

Printed letter, *The Bookman*, November 1892 (53). Wade, 218–20.

> These to His Memory—since he held them dear,
> Perchance as finding there unconsciously
> Some image of himself—I dedicate,
> I dedicate, I consecrate with tears—
> These Idylls.
>   And indeed He seems to me
> Scarce other than my king's ideal knight . . .

Later in the dedication he exhorts Queen Victoria to endure Albert's loss stoically.

   [4] Elizabeth I is associated with Gloriana, Queen of the Faeries, throughout Spenser's *Faerie Queene* and he prefaces each of the six books with a dedication to her.

   [5] Lewis Morris (1833–1907), an educationalist and poet, whose volumes of verse went into numerous editions in the late nineteenth century, lived at Penbryn House, Carmarthen, Wales. WBY's tilt at him is not so adventitious as it may now appear, for, although Morris did not become Laureate, he was a strong contender; he had already received the Jubilee Medal from the Queen for Odes on the Jubilee and on the foundation of the Imperial Institute—the latter written on request, owing to the illness of the Laureate—and his name was mentioned frequently in the press at this time as a likely successor to Tennyson. His *Collected Poems* were published in a 1-vol. popular edition in 1890, and he was knighted in 1895.

To John O'Leary, [c. 5 *November 1892*]

Thorn Hill | Sligo.

Dear M^r O'Leary

Miss Gonne has returned to Paris to carry out her "Tweed" schemes & to give a few lectures. She promises to return by the 12th or 14th & says she has got a great many books for the libraries.[1] I have remained here not because I heard this but because my grand father had a sudden change for the worse yesterday week & was not expected to live more than a few days.[2] My uncle did not wish me to return just then. I had ment to go on Monday morning but have staid on. Quinn promised me news of the literary society but has not written so that I know not what is being done but expect that it must be time to begin the lecture session in due course so that I should not remain much longer.[3] I am anxious however to get a story written & another article done so as to get a certain amount of money due to me. I will telegraph when I am starting. Unwin writes to say that Countess Kathleen is selling "very fairly well" but gives no particulars. "It is always difficult" he writes "to sell a book of poems" but mine is having "a very friendly reception". I imagine that there will be a steady sale write [*for* right] on.

You did not see last "Bookman" did you? the second of the four letters on the Laurreatte ship was mine.[4] I review Tennysons "Death of Œnone" for next number. Also I hope, O Grady "Fin & his Companions". I have done a couple of poems & a story for the "National Observer" also article for "United Ireland" & for "Chicago Citizen".[5] The "Adventurer Volume"

---

[1] On 5 Nov 1892 *United Ireland*, perhaps prompted by WBY, reported (1) that 'Miss Maud Gonne has left Royat, where she has been staying for some time past for the benefit of her health. She is at present spending a few days in Paris before returning to Ireland.' A further paragraph in the same newspaper on 12 Nov reported (5) that MG had addressed a large meeting at Arras, 'the first of a series she is to speak at in France', on behalf of evicted tenants in Ireland and had sent the proceeds of a collection taken there to the Bishop of Raphoe for their benefit. The 'Tweed' scheme was an attempt to encourage the export and distribution of Irish tweeds on the Continent.

[2] William Pollexfen had gone into a decline after the death of his wife (see p. 322); he died on 12 Nov 1892.

[3] JO'L replied on 8 Nov 1892 (MBY), telling WBY, 'I should not stir, if I were you, till she [MG] were here. I know you can't be kept away then. . . . We arranged at last meeting of Com. of Lit. Soc. for a lecture a month, from end of Nov. beginning with Hyde, and taking you in, when and where the Sec. to find out from you, and we have names which will take us on till June, and can of course interput a man here and there if want to.' A series of seven public lectures, by Douglas Hyde, George Coffey, Fr. T. A. Finlay, Standish James O'Grady, Richard Ashe King, Count Plunkett, and WBY, were given in Dublin in the following months under the auspices of the National Literary Society; the inaugural lecture, by Hyde, took place on 25 Nov 1892 (see below, p. 341).

[4] See preceding letter. JO'L replied on 8 Nov (MBY) that he 'didn't see that Bookman'.

[5] WBY's review of Tennyson's *The Death of Oenone, Akbar's Dream, and Other Poems* (1892) appeared in the *Bookman*, December 1892 (*UP* I. 251–4); he does not seem to have reviewed *Finn and his Companions* for the *Bookman*, though he mentioned it (see p. 309) in his 19 Nov 1892 letter to the *Boston Pilot*. The only poem of WBY's to appear in the *National Observer* at this time was 'The Rose in my Heart' (reprinted as 'Aedh tells of the Rose in his Heart'; *VP*, 142–3), published 12 Nov 1892; the story

will I fear be delayed for a short time as they are going to bring out a re-issue of the series.[6] I am writing to Garnett to let me know the date of publication.

Yours always

W B Yeats

[*At top of first page*]

a post card about literary society would be a god send.

ALS (black-bordered paper) Berg. Wade, 220–1.

To Edward Garnett,[1] [*early November 1892*]

[*First pages missing*]

Miss Gonne has raised a certain amount of books & money for the purpose & a good many people have promised me books. We will start three libraries as soon as Miss Gonne returns from Paris which she does on the 12th or 14th & make these libraries & the societies the centre of our work for the winter.[2] We shall have a course of lectures in Dublin touching on the main men in Irish History & literature[3] & will send the best of our lecturers to the three country branches from time to time. The papers have taken us up warmly & we may have a very considerable literary movement if only our work this winter is followed as we expect by the publication of a series of Irish books. If Duffy sheme were to break through we have an offer from an Irish publisher[4] who wants however a guarrantee from us of a sale of 1000 copies of each shilling book. We can easily arrange this guarrantee among our own members in

'The Devil's Book' (see p. 272) was published there on 26 Nov. The article for *United Ireland* may have been his 'Hopes and Fears for Irish Literature' (*UP* I. 247–50), which had appeared there on 15 Oct 1892; no article by him seems to have been published in the *Chicago Citizen*.

  [6] Unwin's Adventure Series comprised 19 volumes, most of which were published in the early 1890s. Very few titles were added after 1893, which perhaps explains why WBY's volume failed to appear. Although a few of the titles were reprinted, there was no general re-issue.

  [1] A loose page from a letter evidently sent just before WBY learnt full particulars of the negotiations for the New Irish Library now being carried on independently with Unwin by Gavan Duffy and T. W. Rolleston.

  [2] The three libraries eventually started were at Loughrea, New Ross, and Listowel, but the effort to gather books for these and other local reading rooms went on throughout 1893.

  [3] See previous letter.

  [4] George Bryers (*c.* 1849–1908), publisher and printer, a partner in Sealy, Bryers & Walker, of 86 Middle Abbey Street, Dublin—the firm through which WBY's first book, *Mosada*, had been published—had offered to take on publication of the New Irish Library if the efforts to form a National Publishing Company (see p. 310) failed.

Dublin & the country societies which are putting themselves into communication with us. ⟨*5 lines cancelled*⟩

I am yours ever

W B Yeats

Best regards to Mrs Garnett.[5]

ALS (fragment) Texas.

To Edward Garnett, [*c. 9 November 1892*]

c/o George Pollexfen | Thorn Hill | Sligo | Ireland.

My dear Garnett

I hear that Rolleston & Duffy have been trying to negociate with Unwin for a series of national books. A difficulty arose some time ago between Duffy & all the most important members of the committee of the national literary society Dublin who consider themselves unfairly treated by Duffy. In any case it is rather unfair of him—if the rumour be true—to try to continue negociations which you will remember I began last spring, without consulting me, as he only heard of these negociations and of Unwins views on the subject of Irish books from me. I wrote him a letter upon the whole matter when I began my work in Ireland. The same holds good for Rolleston. Can you let me know what has really occured.[1] We have had for some time an offer from a[n] Irish publisher who is ready to publish a series of books for us—for the National literary society Dublin—on condition that we guarrantee a sale of 1000 shilling copies. Perhaps Unwin would make ultimately some arrangement whereby the Dublin publisher & himself could work together as an Irish name upon the books is important.[2] Do not make

---

[5] Constance Garnett, née Black (1861–1946), whom Garnett married in 1889, was to translate nearly every Russian novel of note into English.

[1] In *Aut* (226–8) WBY recorded that following the abandonment of the National Publishing Company scheme (see p. 310), 'the always benevolent friend [i.e. T. W. Rolleston] to whom I had explained in confidence, when asking his support, my arrangements with my publisher, went to Gavan Duffy and suggested that they should together offer Mr Fisher Unwin a series of Irish books, and Mr Fisher Unwin and his reader accepted the series under the belief that it was my project that they accepted.' Rolleston made the proposal in a letter to Gavan Duffy (who had returned to Nice on 1 Oct) shortly after the collapse of the joint stock company. Duffy replied on 25 Oct 1892 (NLI) thanking him 'very much for suggesting the alternative of Fisher Unwin', accepting the plan and adding, wisely but, as subsequent letters show, unavailingly, that 'Silence would be prudent till we have something finally settled.' Rolleston consequently wrote to Garnett on 29 Oct 1892 (Berg) asking him to recommend Unwin to take over the publishing scheme and setting out four conditions, one of which was that Gavan Duffy should have absolute control over the enterprise. JO'L, learning of the negotiations from Barry O'Brien in London, wrote to WBY on 12 Nov 1892 (MBY) protesting that Gavan Duffy, in presenting the scheme to Fisher Unwin, was 'making use of knowledge got from us'. WBY's letter to Duffy 'upon the whole matter' was presumably that of the week ending 23 July 1892 (see pp. 304–5).

[2] See previous letter. The imprint of Sealy, Bryers & Walker did in fact appear on the volumes of the New Irish Library, as co-publishers with Unwin.

any arrangement for giving the editorship to Duffy for there is the strongest possible fealing here against the series being edited from Nice. Duffy is also much too old & much too long out of Ireland to be a good editor.[3] Count Plunket, Douglas Hyde or my self would be the right people to chose from. At any rate as I practicaly planed & started this whole Irish literary movement I do not think that any thing should be done behind my back. The National Literary Society here promises to be quite strong enough to make the success of a series of books but it certainly will not put its shoulders to the wheel to back up a series of Duffys for he has enraged ever[y] member by some complex series of false moves. If I can make arrangements such as will be required for the circulation of books among the literary Societies & Young Ireland Societies in the country I think that I should be consulted about the editor ship. It is a question that needs very careful consideration. I hope you will let me know about the whole matter for I am quite in the dark about it.

I should also say that many of the books proposed by Duffy for his Irish series were books which I got promised for the series I explained to you. I was quite ready to let the "company" have them but now the "company" appears to be abandoned I do not think that I should let Duffy & Rolleston— who is entirely under the influence of D at present—go with my sheme to Unwin as if all came out of Duffys head. Or rather with my sheme mingled with his own ever changing plans and not consult me about the proceeding to the very slightest extent.

Do what you can to help me in this matter & beleive me that I see in it no personal issue but one important for the literary movement here in Ireland. Remember that Duffy is so unpopular here in Ireland—for old reasons[4] which I need not go into—that we were only able to partially suppres[s] a disturbance got up against him at our inagural meeting & that we have more than once kept the papers from attacking him.

Yours tr

W B Yeats

O'Leary feals even more than I do on these points & has [*continued in purple pencil*] been urging me for some time to write a protest to Rolleston against his general conduct in connection with the company. He has to day forwarded me a letter from a well known Irish man in London saying among much else "the real truth is if Rolleston is not careful in working with M[r] Duffy we shall be all at cross purposes" and complaining of Duffy's attempts to "boss", as he puts it, the whole sheme.[5] It is this letter which now is inducing me to write to you.

ALS Texas.

[3] Because he suffered from chronic bronchitis, Gavan Duffy settled in Nice on his return from Australia. He had been out of Ireland, apart from short visits, since October 1855.

[4] A reference to Gavan Duffy's 1847 quarrel with John Mitchel (see p. 311, n. 4).

[5] In his note of 8 Nov 1892 (MBY; see p. 327, n.3), JO'L urged WBY to write to Rolleston

To John O'Leary, [c. *9 November 1892*]

c/o George Pollexfen | Thorn Hill | Sligo

Dear M^r O'Leary

I have written a letter to Garnett asking for information about Duffys & Rollestons negociations & putting our case in such a way as will I think stop all such treacherous dealing.[1] Duffy & Rolleston only heard of Unwins views on the question of a national series from me & knew quite well that it was I who had interested him in the matter it was therefore treacherous to go & try to continue negociations which I had begun without consulting me. I cannot understand why Rolleston cannot see this. I will not I think write to Rolleston until I have Garnetts reply.[2] I suggest to Garnett that Bryers & Unwin might perhaps share the ⟨matter⟩ the risk between them. I have however put the case very strongly against any dealing what ever with Duffy. This last action of his & R's simply means war & I think now that they have chosen ⟨a London publishing house⟩ Unwin's house for a battle ground we rout them with ease, especially as Unwin makes all depend on the Irish organization. I am inclined to think that I should go to London in December or January & try & arrange the matter. Bryers (supposing Unwin does not join in) asks to have 1000 copies sale guaranteed. Barry O'Brien & myself could get the Council of the London Society—(no matter what Rolleston did)—to guarrantee about 300 I beleive. The Dublin Society could do at least as well. The other four hundred should be easily managed among some of the other societies. As soon as I return to Dublin I shall draw up a definite proposal for series of books submit this to you & to Count Plunkett & after modification send it to Unwin & ask him to agree upon certain guarrantees to publish such a series uniting his name with Bryers & appointing myself Plunkett or Hyde editors. One advantage such a series will have over a series published by a *definitely national* publishing company is that O'Grady will write for us without fear of the Express in his heart.[3]

Yours truly
W B Yeats

reprimanding him for his conduct, 'but needn't tell him (tis one of your faults that you often tell what not authorized to do) where got the information. Indeed should have written R. long ago, as urged you to do.' The letter he forwarded was probably from Barry O'Brien, now playing a leading role in the Irish Literary Society, London, of which he was to be chairman and eventually president.

[1] See preceding letter.

[2] Although JO'L had recently written (see above) urging WBY to write to Rolleston, in his reply to this letter (12 Nov 1892, MBY) he approved of WBY's delay in doing so: 'Your action right, far as I can see. Negociation with U. does seem making use of knowledge got from us without our consent. Can you at all make out R? Should lose no time in writing him when have heard from G. May have to go to London, but have enough to think of that when get here.'

[3] Standish O'Grady was at this time a sub-editor on the Conservative and Unionist Dublin *Daily Express*, and it would have been difficult for him to contribute to a publishing scheme that appeared to be organized on nationalist party lines.

I am for some reason or other not over well—the doctor says that I should rest from thought to some extent & that is not over easy as I have rather too much time for it down here. I am however getting plenty of writing done & setting my purse in order I hope though payment will not come in just yet. And I am doing this without I think writing too much. I am a deal better than I was.

[*Continued in purple pencil*]

Are you sure I did not return you Miss Gonnes letter. I seem to remember doing so. The more I think over that Duffy & R business the worse it looks. When I hear from Garnett I shall probably write to Unwin himself. Our point of view is clear—all depends on our organization & we will not work for a sheme ruled by Duffy. I think we had better try how the ground lies with Unwin before putting R on his guard by remonstrating with him.

ALS (black-bordered paper) NLI. Wade (dated '? late October 1892'), 216–17.

To Susan Mary Yeats, [*15 November 1892*]

Thorn Hill | Sligo

My dear Lilly

I am afraid that Grandpapas death will make Mamma worse. Please let me know how she is every now & then. Grandpapa died quite painlessly. He said "George fetch your mother" (thinking that Uncle George was there—there was no one but Aunt Elizabeth & Mrs Harte or Miss Parke—not sure which) and then after a pause held out his hands saying "ah there she is" & with that died. They thought at first he was asleep. I am writing this while waiting for the funeral.[1]

I return to Dublin sometime before the 21st for that is the date of the first lecture of the session of the National Literary Society.[2] I shall then be busy for a bit founding two or three country branches & after that shall have to go to London I fear in order to check mate Gavan Duffy & Rolleston who are working in a way neither I nor O Leary can understand. The company seems to have been abandoned which brings to the front an offer we have received from an Irish publisher. We will probably issue according a series

---

[1] The funeral of William Pollexfen, who died on 12 Nov 1892 aged eighty-one, took place on 15 Nov. The death of her father badly affected WBY's aunt, Elizabeth Pollexfen Orr (see p. 48), who on her return to England suffered a temporary mental breakdown. The families of Mrs Harte and Miss Parke were friends and neighbours of the Pollexfens in Sligo whom the Yeats children visited when staying with their grandparents.

[2] In fact, Douglas Hyde's inaugural lecture for the National Literary Society was delivered on 25, not 21, Nov 1892.

of books next spring or summer which either I or Count Plunkett or both
will edit.

Your affectionate brother
W B Yeats.

ALS (black-bordered paper) MBY.

To T. Fisher Unwin, 16 November 1892

c/o George Pollexfen | Thorn Hill | Sligo
Nov 16 1892.

Dear Mr Unwin

I hear from a letter written by a prominent member of the London Irish
Literary Society & forwarded to me by Mr John O'Leary that Mr Rolleston
has opened negociations with you for the publication of a series of Irish
books.[1] I firmly beleive that such a series will be a great success if backed by
the enthusiasm of the young men over here & by the help of our Irish
writers. I think however that it is only fair for me to tell you that
Mr Rolleston has acted a little hastily in submitting to you a scheme the
details of which are quite unknown to us here. We hold strong views about
the proposed books & about the choice of the writers[2] Etc & would naturally
like to have a voice in drawing up what ever scheme be submitted to you for
acceptance, rejection, or modification. I am writing this post to
Mr Rolleston & suggest to you to postpone finally settling matters until I
have had time to submit Mr Rolleston's proposal—which I have asked him
for—to a committee of our best men here Count Plunket, Douglas Hyde,
John O'Leary, Richard Ashe King[3] Etc. I propose then, if it prove
necessary, to go to London & see a corresponding committee of the best men
of the "Irish Society London". There has been considerable friction
between Sir Gavan Duffy & our men & I am afraid, if some such method of
bringing them all into line be not adopted, that Count Plunkett will
conclude negociations which he began two months ago with an Irish
publisher & our movement may split up on lines which the press will soon
turn into one of Parnellite Dublin, & the Parnellite young men in the
country parts, against what they will call "West British" & "Whiggish"
Duffy & Rolleston. The most ardent of the youn[g] men are Parnellites &

---

[1] An undated draft version of this letter (MBY) begins slightly differently: 'Mr John O'Leary has sent
me a letter written to him by a prominent member of the Irish Literary Society London from which I
learn that Mr Rolleston', etc. The 'prominent member' was evidently Barry O'Brien (see p. 329).

[2] The draft version reads: 'We hold strong views about the question of these proposed books and their
writers . . .'.

[3] Ashe King's name does not appear in the draft version.

would be ready enough to raise such a cry against Duffy who is unpopular for Michellite reasons[4] (his reasonable but not very readable defence never having made itself heard against the magnificent rhetoric of the "Jail Journal").[5] It should however be perfectly easy to get the series accepted as a great National work but to do this it must be backed by our organizations, our lecturers & by the press over here. I propose to return to Dublin on Sunday & shall call a committee for the next day.

Yours very truly
W B Yeats

[*In pencil, vertically at top of first page*]
No copy of "Finn" has come[6] though I wrote to Dublin. "Bookman" has sent me a copy however.

ALS (black-bordered paper) Texas. Wade (who prints a draft of this letter, from a typed copy), 221–2.

[4] In December 1847 the Irish Confederation—formed the year before when John Mitchel (see p. 17), Gavan Duffy, and other Young Irelanders seceded from Daniel O'Connell's Repeal Association—split over whether the organization should, as Duffy believed, try to combine all classes in Ireland into a united front against England, using legal methods, or, as Mitchel wished, disregard the upper classes and appeal to the peasants and small farmers, using physical force against English rule if necessary. Mitchel's policies were defeated and he left the Confederation to set up the *United Irishman*, which urged complete Irish separation from England. Seven years later, after his escape from Australia to which he had been transported on charges of sedition, Mitchel attacked Duffy's personality and politics in his *Jail Journal*. Duffy replied in an open 'Letter to John Mitchel' and a sharp controversy between the two men was carried on in the *Nation* of April and May 1854. Duffy's 'reasonable but not very readable defence' appears in vol. II of his *Young Ireland* (1880), 208–9.

In *Aut* (225–6), WBY recalls how this ancient quarrel strengthened his own hand in dealing with Duffy:

No argument of mine was intelligible to him, and I would have been powerless, but that fifty years ago he had made an enemy, and though the enemy was long dead, the enemy's school remained. He had attacked, why or with what result I do not remember, the only Young Ireland politician who had music and personality, though rancorous and devil-possessed. At some public meeting of ours, where he spoke amid great applause, in smooth, Gladstonian periods, of his proposed Irish publishing firm, one heard faint hostile murmurs, and at last a voice cried, 'Remember Newry', and a voice answered, 'There is a grave there!' and a part of the audience sang, 'Here's to John Mitchel that is gone, boys, gone; Here's to the friends that are gone'. The meeting over, a group of us, indignant that the meeting we had called for his welcome should have contained those malcontents, gathered about him to apologize. He had written a pamphlet, he explained: he would give us copies. We would see that he was in the right, how badly Mitchel had behaved. But in Ireland personality, if it be but harsh and hard, has lovers, and some of us, I think, may have gone home muttering, 'How dare he be in the right if Mitchel is in the wrong?'

The incident apparently took place at Gavan Duffy's meeting on 30 July 1892 with the provisional committee of the National Literary Society (see p. 311).

[5] A cancelled passage at this point in the draft version reads: 'Any such rival project would probably be disastrous for both proposed series & for the whole movement. At any rate it is clearly much better to have one series & not two.'

[6] See p. 309, n. 1.

To Edward Garnett, [*16 November 1892*]

Thorn Hill | Sligo.

My dear Garnett

I have written to Unwin on the matter[1]—do not be alarmed for I wrote in quite dispassionate mood & cursed no man. I have also written to Rolleston & cursed him & Gavan Duffy as cur[t]ly as but as vigorously (can you understand the combination) as I can. I have asked that his proposal to Unwin be submitted to a special committee in Dublin & then with its modifications be submitted to a special committee in London & that the two organizations abide by the result.[2] I have merely written to Unwin to tell him that some consideration of Rollestons proposal is necessary on our part if we are to throw our selves into the thing with vigour & stave off a rival library to yours which an Irish publisher offered to bring out two months ago. O'Leary & others are ready to press on this Dublin library & write to me about it. I asked Unwin not to sign the agreement until he has heard from us. I have done this not because I doubt that your good offices are all sufficient but because I want Duffy & Rolleston to feel my hand in the matter in as direct a way as possible & so stave off future trouble. They have so far ingnored us here in every way in their power—making use of us however as a spring board when needful.

Please send me the heads of Rollestons proposal.

Yours vy truly
W B Yeats

I go to Dublin on Sunday. Will then consult a committee & if need be cross over to London as soon as I have its recommendations. Thank you for good offices in the matter of the "Adventurers" volume. Ellis writes to me that Blake will hardly be out of the binders hands much before exmas. It has gone to 3 vols.

ALS Texas. Wade, 222–3.

[1] See preceding letter.
[2] The letter to Rolleston has not survived but obviously had its effect, for in a letter of 18 Nov 1892 to WBY (*LWBY* 1.9) Garnett wrote, 'I can see that the letter he told me you had written him has wounded him & that he would[be] glad to be friends.' Garnett went on to ask 'what's the use of you writing to Rolleston saying they have stolen your ideas, your plan of publishing & all the rest?' On 17 Nov, presumably the day he received WBY's letter, Rolleston wrote to Unwin (Berg): 'I've just written a letter to Mr. Garnett, intended for transmission to Yeats, which I think ought to make a reconciliation easy if they are prepared to meet us halfway.'

To John O'Leary, [c 16 November 1892]

Thorn Hill | Sligo.

Dear M^r O'Leary

I have received the enclosed from Garnett & have written both to Garnett, Rolleston & Fisher Unwin.[1] I have asked Unwin to wait until I have submitted the Rolleston proposal to a special committee of the Dublin Society. This committee should meet I think on Monday (I will return Sunday). I may then have to cross to London & get a special committee there. The thing to be secured is a simple matter enough so far as statement go—Duffy must not have all the power. We must be firm about this. I would go to Dublin to day but I have three articles to finish for "Bookman".[2]

Let us draw up a series of books, propose editors or editions, propose that Bryers have his name on the cover with Unwins & then get Barry O Brien to consider these proposals & let he & I submit them to a London special committee. If we do not get a substantial part of them agreed to our course is clear—first put our own sheme before Unwin & if he rejects it go on with Bryers.

It might be well if you were to get Barry O'Brien to move in the matter among the members of the London society or if you found out at any rate whether or not he would approve of my suggestion of a settlement of the difficulty. There is no need for us to regard Duffy at all in this matter.

Yours v truly
W B Yeats

ALS (black-bordered paper) NLI.

To T. Fisher Unwin, [? 21 November 1892]

7 Howth Terrace | St Lawrence Road | Clontarf[1] | Dublin

Dear Mr Unwin

Thank you very much for the £5 [and] for your information about the sale of my books. Thank you also for "the Phantom from the East" & "Finn &

[1] See preceding letters, pp. 333–5, and n. 2, p. 335. In his reply of 17 Nov 1892 (MBY) JO'L said he thought Garnett's letter (now lost) valuable and sensible: 'Can't say I approve of your writing R. save to demand an explanation, and you have *no* authority to make proposition to him you have done.'

[2] These were probably his forthcoming reviews of Tennyson's *The Death of Oenone* (see p. 327, n. 5) and of *The Vision of MacConglinne*, and possibly the article on *Finn and his Companions* (see p. 327) which failed to appear.

[1] WBY was lodging with Mrs Carew (see p. 324) at Lonsdale House.

his Companions" which have reached me after some delay and for your promise of the "pseudonym" volumes which I look forward to with great interest.[2]

I should have replied to your letter before but it has been chasing me from place to place & only found me last night.

Yours very sinry
W B Yeats

ALS Texas.

To Edward Dowden,[1] [*? 27 November 1892*]

Lonsdale House | St Lawrence Road | Clontarf.
Sunday.

My dear Prof Dowden

Keegan Paul has forwarded me a letter from a man in cambridge asking leave to set a rhyme of mine out of 'the Wanderings of Oisin' to music.[2] Keegan Paul advises me to charge 'the usual fee £2.2.' Is it usual to ask 'the usual fee'? I dont want to do anything mean & know no body to ask except yourself. Please drop me a postcard & forgive my troubling you.

Yours ever
W B Yeats

ALS Southern Illinois.

[2] See WBY's requests in earlier letters, pp. 309, 334. *A Phantom from the East*, by Pierre Loti (trans. J. E. Gordon), was published by Unwin in November 1892 as part of the Independent Novel series. More volumes appeared that autumn in the Pseudonym series, of which Unwin may have sent WBY *Through the Red Litten Windows*, by Theodore Herz-Garten.

[1] See p. 8, n. 4.

[2] The Cambridge composer was probably the Dublin-born Charles Villiers Stanford (1852–1924), who in 1893 published *Thirty Irish Songs* 'with words by A. P. Graves'; the latter's *Irish Song Book* of 1894 (see below, p. 383) was to include WBY's 'Down by the Sally Gardens' (entitled 'An Old Song Resung' in *Oisin*)—perhaps the poem referred to here. Organist of Trinity College, Cambridge, and conductor of the Cambridge University Musical Society 1872–93 as well as of the Bach Choir and the Leeds Philharmonic Society, Stanford, who was knighted in 1902, had a life-long interest in Irish music. He served on the committee of the Irish Folk Song Society and, under the auspices of the Irish Literary Society, London, edited the Petrie Collection of Irish music. In December 1892 he was living at 10 Harvey Road, Cambridge. Regrettably, Stanford did not in the end set any of WBY's poems.

To the Editor of United Ireland, *17 December 1892*

DEAR SIR—I agree with every word you said last week about Dr. Hyde's lecture, and, like many another, am deeply grateful to you for your reprint of it in the current number. Without going as far as some enthusiastic members of Dr. Hyde's audience, whom I heard call it the most important utterance of its kind since '48, I will say that it seems to me the best possible augury for the success of the movement we are trying to create. Its learning, its profound sincerity, its passionate conviction, are all pledges that the President of the National Literary Society, at any rate, will go the whole journey with us, come foul or fair weather.[1] At the same time there was a good deal in Dr. Hyde's lecture which would have depressed me had I agreed with it. He seemed to base the bulk of his hopes for the "de-Anglicising" of Ireland upon the revival, or, at any rate, the preservation, of the Gaelic language, and at the same time to pronounce it "impossible to find either men or money" to carry out the one scheme he held capable of doing this. Alas, I fear he spoke the truth, and that the Gaelic language will soon be no more heard, except here and there in remote villages, and on the wind-beaten shores of Connaught.

Is there, then, no hope for the de-Anglicising of our people? Can we not build up a national tradition, a national literature, which shall be none the less Irish in spirit from being English in language? Can we not keep the continuity of the nation's life, not by trying to do what Dr. Hyde has practically pronounced impossible, but by translating or retelling in English, which shall have an indefinable Irish quality of rythm and style, all that is best of the ancient literature? Can we not write and persuade others to write histories and romances of the great Gaelic men of the past, from the son of Nessa to Owen Roe, until there has been made a golden bridge between the old and the new?[2]

[1] The theme of Douglas Hyde's presidential address on 'The Necessity for De-Anglicising Ireland', delivered to the National Literary Society on 25 Nov 1892, was that the Irish while struggling for political independence from England had been slavishly aping her culturally and socially and had abandoned their own traditions. Because of racial differences the Irish could not fully assimilate English ways and were stuck in a shabby halfway house between two cultures. The only hope for national dignity was a return to Gaeldom and this would be largely effected through reviving the Irish language and also through restoring Irish personal and place names, music, games, and clothes. The lecture, which Hyde delivered on numerous other occasions over the next few years, was immensely influential and in part led to the formation of the Gaelic League in the following year. *United Ireland* had published a slightly shortened version of the lecture on 10 Dec 1892, and oh 3 Dec the editor had commented (1) that: 'It was one of the best, and what is better, one of the most practical lectures on a National topic I have heard for a long time.'

Hyde's listener's 'since '48' was a reference to the Young Ireland Movement, which had come to an end with the abortive insurrection of 1848.

[2] Although Hyde made an approving, if passing, reference to Anglo-Irish literature at the end of his address, the whole tenor of his argument was that an Irish national literature in English was an impossibility and it was this that worried WBY.

America, with no past to speak of, a mere *parvenu* among the nations, is creating a national literature which in its most characteristic products differs almost as much from English literature as does the literature of France. Walt Whitman, Thoreau, Bret Harte, and Cable,[3] to name no more, are very American, and yet America was once an English colony. It should be more easy for us, who have in us that wild Celtic blood, the most un-English of all things under heaven, to make such a literature. If we fail it shall not be because we lack the materials, but because we lack the power to use them. But we are not failing. Mr. Hyde, Lady Wilde in her recent books, and Mr. Curtin, and the editor of the just-published "Vision of M'Comaile," are setting before us a table spread with strange Gaelic fruits,[4] from which an ever-growing band of makers of song and story shall draw food for their souls. Nor do we lack creative artists either. Has not Miss Tynan given us her "Legends and Lyrics," Miss Barlow her "Irish Idylls," Miss Lawless her "Grania," and Mr. O'Grady his wonderful and incomparable "Fin and his Companions," within the last year or two?[5] Let us make these books and the books of our older writers known among the people and we will do more to de-Anglicise Ireland than by longing to recall the Gaelic tongue and the snows of yester year. Let us by all means prevent the decay of that tongue

Conchubar, the son of Nessa, who succeeded to the kingship of Ulster after the abdication of Fergus, is a leading figure in the Ulster Cycle of Irish bardic tales, and appears as a cunning statesman in WBY's plays, *On Baile's Strand* (1903) and *Deirdre* (1907). Owen Roe O'Neill (1590–1649), having served in the Spanish army, returned to Ireland in 1642 to take command of the Ulster Rebellion. He won a series of brilliant victories against the English, but because of disagreement with other rebel commanders failed to press home his advantages; his death in 1649 deprived Ireland of the only commander capable of withstanding Oliver Cromwell.

[3] The American novelist George Washington Cable (1844–1925), born in New Orleans, based much of his fiction on the Creoles, the French-speaking natives of Louisiana.

[4] Jeremiah Curtin (1835–1906), Irish-American anthropologist, folklorist, and linguist, had published *Myths and Folk-Lore of Ireland* (see p. 269, n. 1) in 1890, and went on to compile *Hero-Tales of Ireland* (1894) and *Tales of the Fairies and of the Ghost World* (1895). He also collected North American Indian folklore and translated novels from Polish and Russian. '"M'Comaile"' is probably a compositor's misreading for *The Vision of MacConglinne* (1892), which WBY reviewed (*UP* I. 261–3) for the *Bookman*, February 1893. The *Vision*, a twelfth-century aisling, was edited by the Hamburg-born Celtic scholar Kuno Meyer (1858–1919), from 1895 Professor of Teutonic Languages at Liverpool University, who in 1903 helped found the School of Irish Learning in Dublin. In it, the itinerant story-teller MacConglinne, sentenced to death for satirizing a bishop and monks, has a vision which helps him cure the King of Munster of an evil spirit and win his case against the monks. WBY used a significantly altered version of the plot for his 1894 story, 'A Crucifixion' (included in *The Secret Rose*, under the title 'The Crucifixion of the Outcast'). The image here of the spread table is taken from the *Vision*.

[5] Jane Barlow (1857–1917), daughter of the Vice-Provost of TCD, a writer of popular poems and sketches of Irish life, in 1892 published *Bog-Land Studies* and *Irish Idylls*, the latter a collection of sentimental stories set in the small and isolated village of Lisconnel. The poet and novelist Emily Lawless (1845–1913), eldest daughter of Lord Cloncurry, came to know the people of western Ireland through staying with her mother's family in Galway. Her first novel, *Hurrish* (1886), about Land League activities in Co. Clare, was a great success in England. By 1895 WBY had come to feel that in *Grania* (1892), a romance set against the harsh conditions of the Aran Islands, her imperfect sympathy with the Celtic nature had 'made her . . . magnify a peasant type which exists here and there in Ireland, and mainly in the extreme west, into a type of the whole nation . . .' (*UP* I. 369).

where we can, and preserve it always among us as a learned language to be a fountain of nationality in our midst, but do not let us base upon it our hopes of nationhood. When we remember the majesty of Cuchullin and the beauty of sorrowing Deirdre we should not forget that it is that majesty and that beauty which are immortal, and not the perishing tongue that first told of them.—Yours, &c.,

W B Yeats

Printed letter, *United Ireland*, 17 December 1892 (1). *UP* 1. 254–6.

1893

[Chiswick] [1]

My dear "Scotia" [2]

I am trying to arrange the following set of lectures for you & am writing to all the places except Omagh which Plunkett undertakes & Cork for which a certain John O'Mahony [3] will be responsible. The[re] will I think be no difficulty as we have been already applied to by all the places mentioned. At Cork between 20 & 27 th of January, at Westport (Co Mayo) between 27 th & 2 nd Feb at Castlerea (Roscommon) between 4 th & 8 th of Feb, Lougrea between 12 th & 15 th Feb. There is a meeting in Dublin on 17 th February at which we hope you will speak & report progress. You will then go to New Ross & lecture between 20 th Feb & Feb 25 & then go on to Listowel & [4]

[*Unsigned*]

AD (fragment) MBY.

[1] Although undated and without an address, this fragmentary draft was apparently written in London, where WBY had returned in December 1892 to consult Fisher Unwin and the appropriate committee of the Irish Literary Society about Gavan Duffy's pre-emptive scheme for the New Irish Library (see p. 335).

[2] The name used by WBY for MG in the '90s; he also referred to her by her Golden Dawn initials, PIAL ('*Per Ignem Ad Lucem*'; see p. 266), and later by the name 'Maura'.

[3] John O'Mahony (d. 1904), a member of the National Literary Society, was a native of Cork, now living in Dublin and writing for the *Weekly Independent*. He went on to become a successful barrister, of whom JBY was to write (letter of 7 Aug 1903 to WBY [MBY]), 'John O'Mahony has more friends than anyone I ever heard of.' In 1895 O'Mahony married KT's younger sister, Nora; KT has a sympathetic portrait of him in *Middle Years* (161–77).

[4] On 12 Jan 1983 the council of the National Literary Society resolved 'that a deputation, consisting of Miss Maud Gonne, Dr Sigerson, Count Plunkett. . . . be authorised to hold a meeting in Cork in the interests of the Society' (Minute Book); but the *Cork Examiner* of 24 Jan 1893, reporting on the meeting held there the day before, noted that 'Miss Maud Gonne was unable to leave Paris owing to illness.' MG apparently lectured later in February at Loughrea and New Ross, but was unable to be present at the other meetings planned, most of which appear to have been cancelled.

To T. Fisher Unwin, [early January 1893]

3 Blenheim Road | Bedford Park | Chiswick. W

Dear Mr Unwin

You asked me some time ago to let you know from time to time how our movement in Ireland was going on. I do so now the more readily as I have some hope that you may be able to help us in one matter.

We have arranged for a course of lectures in Dublin (of which I enclose list) as well as lectures of a less public kind and other kindred entertainments, in the rooms of our society (4 College Green, Dublin).[1] What is however of much greater importance is that we are federating a number of provincial societies and starting new ones where there are none, & arranging lectures in connection with these. We have a scheme for giving small lending libraries of standard and other books to federated societies. We intend to give about 4 or 5 pounds worth of books in each case. We ourselves choose *not more* than half these books & allow the local body to chose the rest from our lists.[2] Our first experimental libraries are to be at New Ross & Listowel in both of which places are strong societies with good reading rooms & no books. In connection with this sheme we are giving the following series of lectures— half the profits to go to local society half to library fund in each case. Between 20 & 26 of Jan at *Cork* (seven local societies to be represented some of which will probably federate).[3] Between 26 of Jan & 1 of February *Ballinasloe* (society will I beleive federate). Between 1st & 3rd of Feb at *Westport* (new branch of our society). Between 4th & 8th of Feb at Castlerea (Federated

---

[1] In December 1892 the National Literary Society had taken two apartments at 4 College Green, in the centre of Dublin, at an annual rent of £20. In addition to its series of public lectures (see p. 327) given at the Leinster Lecture Hall in Molesworth Street, the Society held weekly meetings in its own rooms, interspersed with lectures, discussions, and musical entertainments. On 26 Jan 1893 WBY gave a reading from *The Countess Kathleen* at a social meeting of the Society and papers were read by members of the Society at roughly fortnightly intervals from 23 Mar to 15 June 1893.

[2] A set of 12 rules in MG's hand entitled 'A Scheme for working the Libraries', together with a draft of some of the rules in WBY's hand, is in NLI.

[3] On 23 Jan 1893 Douglas Hyde recorded in his diary (Daly, 160):

I went to Cork with Yeats on the 9.15. . . . Count Plunkett and O'Mahony were there before us. We went to the Victoria Hotel where we had dinner and I had two good glasses of punch. Then we went to the meeting organised to promote the National Literary Society. Denny Lane was in the chair and made the first speech, reading from a script. I then spoke, and I was in top form. Yeats spoke after me, and Count Plunkett after him. There were about 150 people present, including representatives of every literary society in Cork.

Commenting on these proceedings in its leader of 24 Jan (4–5), the *Cork Daily Herald*, which maintained a strong line in local patriotism, noted: 'Mr Yeats asserted that our people read nothing. This may be true of certain classes; but we can assure Mr Yeats that a Society exists in Cork City from which we could select forty members, any one of whom could compile an essay on any period of Irish history.' Denny Lane (1818–95), former Young Irelander and now the Grand Old Man of Cork letters, was a successful businessman and president of the Cork Literary and Scientific Society.

society) between 12th & 15th Feb at *Loughrea* (Federated branch). Between 20th & 25th at *New Ross* (Federated branch). Between ⟨27 Feb & 3⟩ on the 3rd of March at Listowel (Federated branch). After that lectures will be given at Omagh & Belfast certainly & probably also at Waterford, Limerick Rostrevor & Skibereen in all which places are either friends of the society or societies anxious for lectures.

The [?] lectures will deel with the programs of our society & with the need for it. Count Plunket & Miss Gonne & myself will all speak at Cork other not yet decided upon will speak at Belfast, the smaller places will be addressed by Miss Gonne only.[4]

Now what I want you to do for us is to give us some books for the libraries. You must have plenty on your shelves that would serve us & be no loss to you. Any donation of the kind will of course be acknowledged in all the Irish papers & would prove a good advertisement especially in view of the proposed series of Irish books.

Yours very truly
W B Yeats

ALS MBY.

To John O'Leary, [? week of 9 January 1893]

3 Blenheim Road | Bedford Park | Chiswick | London W.
Dear M^r O'Leary

I did not write before for there was nothing definite to say. Barry O Brien at first was strong for the proposal which he told you of. It was however obvious that Gavan Duffy would refuse it at the same time our position is strong for Unwin refuses to go into the scheme at all unless we are all agreed. At the Committee last Saturday the following proposal was agreed to by those present though a vote was not taken. That Sir Gavan Duffy be editor in chief with two sub-editors—T W Rolleston & Douglas Hyde (to represent us & have his name on all books) & and this the most important point that the London Society elect a committee of three to draw up list of books, the Dublin Society to do the same.[1] These lists to be thrown into one each

---

[4] See preceding letter.

[1] O'Brien had evidently proposed that both the London and Dublin Societies should elect editorial committees to advise on the choice of books for the New Irish Library—the course subsequently agreed upon by the London committee at its Saturday meeting, probably on 7 Jan 1893. At a meeting of the Dublin Society on 12 Jan 1893, attention was drawn 'to the fact of an offer having been made by Messrs Fisher Unwin & Co. to issue a series of National Books on the condition that the series should receive the support of the two societies in Dublin and London. Sir Chas. G. Duffy to be chief editor. Two editors one from London the other from the Dublin Society' (Minute Book). But the question of a three-man subcommittee was not raised at that meeting.

perhaps giving way in smaller matters so that the final list represent both &
yet be not too long. This final list to be sent to Gavan Duffy for his approval.
If he agree to it or to the greater portion all will be well. If not we should have
to do without him.[2]

Duffy has accepted the Hyde proposal but has not yet been informed
about the second one nor perhaps need be until the list is made. We should I
think merely formally agree to the list of books I brought over (to the bulk of
which Rolleston says Duffy makes no objection). The Society should
appoint you, Plunkett & myself as committee. This will bring us all into
harmony & establish our right to a voice in the matter.

The London Society will circularize all its members in the matter of the
review & beleives that it can sell 200 at least.[3]

I am editing a volume of Blakes lyrics for "The Muses Library" & shall
get £25 pounds for it.

The Blake book will be ready some time next week I beleive.[4]

Yours ever
W B Yeats

ALS NLI. Wade, 226–7.

To John O'Leary, [? week of 16 January 1893]

3 Blenheim Road | Chiswick | London W

Dear M^r O'Leary

Could you not get the Committee elected next Thursday? Make plain to
Sigerson or to any one who opposes from his side that Rolleston does not

---

[2] In the event WBY could not persuade the London Society to adopt this hard line. In a letter of
20 Jan [1893] (Private) Rolleston told Hyde that 'it would be undesirable for many reasons to have the
Societies putting forward authoritative lists of books . . . Therefore we mean as far as our own Society is
concerned to make the function of the Literary Committee purely *advisory* and in no way *dictatorial.*' He
reiterated these points in a formal letter of 26 Jan (Private) to be read to the Dublin Committee and
emphasized 'Sir C Duffy's determination—expressed be it remembered, from the very beginning—to be
sole editor-in-chief'.

[3] Plans were in hand for a literary review to be produced jointly by the London and Dublin Societies
but when the *Irish Home Reading Magazine* finally appeared, for two issues in May and October 1894, it
was published under the auspices of the Irish Literary Society, London, alone.

[4] WBY's edition of *The Poems of William Blake* appeared in Lawrence & Bullen's series, The Muses'
Library, later in 1893. The first copies of the 3 vol. *Works of William Blake*, over which WBY and Edwin
J. Ellis had laboured since 1889, were not in fact ready until the last week of January, when Quaritch
wrote to William Linnell (25 Jan 1893 [Private]): 'It is only the small paper issue of Blake's Works 3
vols 8vo which has been delivered yet by the binder, and the circulation of even these has been delayed
owing to a slip of Errata Mr Ellis had to add.' A fortnight later the large-paper copies had still not been

oppose this scheme at all, & that it will make peace & that Unwin refuses to go on with the project unless we support him & support meens influence over the series or must be made to mean this. The London Society has chosen a committee of six or seven. This is I think too large. The committee should be elected next Thursday so that both committees can get to work at once.[1] Douglas Hyde consents to be assistant editor. I would not have taken the post as people would have been liable to accuse me of having fought for my own hand.[2]

The company is definitely dead. They found that a capital of 3000 shares would not be enough to keep the necessary staff of manager clerks Etc going. They then started the project of a General publishing company with 10,000 shares and were getting support when Duffy withdrew because it suddenly struck him that he could only control the Irish series & not the whole publishing work. "He would not be responsible for what he could not control" Etc. The old cry in a more absurd form![3]

I have written to Plunkett about the proposed committee & told him that

delivered, 'one of the plates having been lost; it is now being reprinted' (Quaritch to Linnell, 8 Feb 1893 [Private]).

[1] So strong were suspicions on both pro- and anti-Duffy sides of the National Literary Society that JO'L failed to get agreement on the three-man subcommittee WBY had recommended (see preceding letter). Discussions of the proposal became extremely acrimonious, and a meeting, not on the following Thursday but on Friday, 27 Jan 1893, at which WBY was present, broke up after a violent row. At a subsequent meeting on 2 Feb JO'L moved that a committee of six should be appointed to advise on the projected series of books and that the six should be Sigerson, Ashe King, Count Plunkett, WBY, McGrath, and himself. Such a committee would have had a majority in favour of WBY's views, but the proposal was overturned when an amendment 'That the committee appointed consist of the entire council' was carried by 7 votes to 4. This substantial enlargement would have rendered the committee all but ineffectual, and on 27 Feb a proposal by Sigerson was carried with only JO'L dissenting, 'That the Council of the Irish National Literary Society approves of the arrangement by which Sir Charles Gavan Duffy is editor and Mr Rolleston and Dr Hyde sub-editors of a series of Irish books:—That so long as this arrangement is maintained this council will loyally and cordially promote the circulation of the series.' WBY supported his motion, for he had called at the meeting.

[2] WBY's Dublin friends had evidently urged his claims to be one of the Assistant Editors for, replying on 23 Jan [Private] to a letter from Hyde, Rolleston had told him that 'Yeats editorship wd be absolutely out of the question owing to the line he took in his letters to the Freeman (see pp. 310–14). Sir C. D. could not possibly be expected after that to let Y be his representative in Dublin. And I think Y fully perceives this. He has been most sensible and disinterested throughout.—Moreover I think that for such a post one must possess more scholarship (of the Dryasdust kind if you like) than Y does.'

[3] Edmund Downey, who was to have been managing director of the National Publishing Company (see p. 310), with Gavan Duffy as chairman, had perhaps frightened Duffy by suggesting (3 Oct 1892, NLI) that they should publish other profit-making books 'which though they would not be objectionable to Irish readers, would be of a less patriotic and ennobling character than the books which Sir Charles indicated in his address to the Irish Literary Society at Hampstead.' WBY gives a somewhat different account of these events in *Aut* (226–8): 'Suddenly, when the company seemed all but established, and a scheme had been thought out which gave some representation on its governing board to contemporary Irish writers, Gavan Duffy produced a letter from Archbishop Walsh [William Joseph Walsh (1841–1921), the Catholic Archbishop of Dublin, who in 1899 was to attack the first performance of *The Countess Cathleen*], and threw the project up. The letter had warned him that after his death the company would fall under a dangerous influence.'

all here are anxious to have the committees in working order by next Saturday.[4]

Yours veyry truly

W B Yeats

ALS NLI. Wade (dated '[? late autumn, 1892]'), 226.

To Richard Le Gallienne, [? 21 January 1893]

Lonsdale House | St. Lawrence Road | Clontarf | Dublin.

Saturday

My dear Le Galleone

Your letter reached me this morning. I have as you see returned to Dublin for the present. I wish it were not so for I would greatly like to dine with you at the Omar Khayyam Club.[1]

I have been reading your poems & like especially the Franscesca poem.[2] I have not yet had the book long enough to read it right through. A number of the things seems to me to have a fine songlike rapture in them, a true lyrical enthusiasm, marking them out from the bulk of our new verse. I will write more upon them when I have read more. I left the book in London by mischance but expect it after me in a box that is on its way.

Yrs ever

W B Yeats

ALS (black-bordered paper) NYU.

[4] Presumably the date, 21 Jan 1893, of the next London Society committee meeting.

[1] WBY had returned to Dublin shortly before 21 Jan 1893, to be present at meetings of and on behalf of the National Literary Society (see pp. 342). The Omar Khayyám Club, founded at Pagani's Restaurant, London, 13 Oct 1892 by Clement Shorter, Frederic Hudson, and George Whale, had a literary and artistic membership of 59 (commemorating 1859, the year in which FitzGerald published his translation of the *Rubaiyát*), including Andrew Lang, William Sharp ('Fiona Macleod'), Sir Arthur Conan Doyle, Edmund Gosse, Justin McCarthy, and Augustine Birrell. The club held three dinners yearly, two in London, usually at Frascati's Restaurant in Oxford Street, and one at a country inn or hotel. Le Gallienne had invited WBY to the second dinner of the club, which was held at the Florence Restaurant, London, 27 Jan 1893.

[2] The first poem in Le Gallienne's *English Poems* (1892; see p. 320) is a retelling of the story of Paolo and Francesca in Spenserian stanzas.

To Edward Garnett, [late January 1893]

Lonsdale House | St Lawrence Road | Clontarf | Dublin—
My dear Garnett

A friend of mine who has I think considerable literary promise has sent you in some verse for an opinion as to its publication prospects.[1] He to pay I beleive £20 to the expenses. He asks me to ask you to let him know as soon as may be as he [has] some new plan for publishing it in his head I think—

I would like to give him a note of introduction to you. He is a young Irishman of fine ambition. Let me know what you think of his work.

Yours ever
W B Yeats

ALS (black-bordered paper) Texas.

To Charles Fairfax Murray,[1] [early February 1893]

Lonsdale House | St Lawrence Road | Clontarf | Dublin
Dear Mr Murray

I am editing for 'Lawrence & Bullen' an edition of Blakes lyrical poems & would like to include three of the lyrics from 'The Island of the Moon' which you kindly permitted Mr Ellis & myself to print in the big book for Quaritch. The three are the one beginning 'Phoebe dressed like beauty's queen' 'Leave o leave me to my sorrow', and 'This city & this country has brought forth many mayors'.

I will of course make all due acknowledgement & thanks.[2]

Yours sny
W B Yeats

ALS (black-bordered paper) Texas.

[1] Probably Charles Alexandre Weekes (1867–1946), who had attended the Erasmus Smith High School in Dublin at the same time as WBY. A friend of Charles Johnston and George Russell (AE), Weekes was associated with the Dublin Theosophists, although he never formally joined them. His first book of poems, *Reflections and Refractions*, was published by Fisher Unwin in May 1893, and later reviewed by WBY; but Weekes made efforts to withdraw it from circulation almost immediately on publication. (KT, asked to supply a title for the volume, remembered [*25 Years*, 244] that 'I suggested, in Charlie Johnston's private ear, "Mr. Weekes, His Squeaks"; but my confidence was not kept.')

Weekes moved to England in 1893, but returned to Dublin the following year to set up the publishing house of Whaley, mainly to publish AE's first book of poems, *Homeward, Songs by the Way* (1894), which was dedicated 'To C. W., truest friend'. Weekes stopped publishing in 1896 and lived the remainder of his life in London. A second book of poems, *About Women*, appeared in Dublin in 1907.

[1] See p. 281, n. 2.
[2] WBY's *The Poems of William Blake* includes the three lyrics, retitled respectively as 'The Pilgrim' (95), 'A Song of Sorrow' (102), and 'Old English Hospitality' (135), with the promised acknowledgement to Fairfax Murray. He found *An Island in the Moon* 'clumsy and slovenly satire', but justified the inclusion of some of the lyrics 'not to be found elsewhere'.

To F. H. Day,[1] *[after 8 February 1893]*

Lonsdale House | St Lawrence Road | Clontarf | Dublin.
My dear Day

I should long since have answered your letter but alas it vanished almost at once after its arrival. I went round to Todhunter & asked your question of him—if you remember it after so long a time—& found him unwilling to sell the picture but very ready to let you get it photographed. I quite forget about the picture but you doubtless remember.[2]

Blake is just out & have written to my sister to send you a copy. Send the money to me & not to Quaritch. He is only paying me in copies so that I am right glad to sell one. I am told he is selling the copies at £3.3 net.[3] I asked him what would be the price of the Chaucer. He does not yet know but says *not more* than £20 & maybe less.[4]

If you see Miss Guiney tell her that I will write & thank her for her little book soon but am waiting its arrival in London where I forgot it.[5]

I am busy with all kinds of things here in Ireland—mainly with a National Literary Society which is doing good work I think.

Thank you very much for that beautiful specimen page of the new Mag'

---

[1] See p. 240.

[2] Over a year before, on 5 Feb 1892, Day, an enthusiastic collector of Keatsiana (see p. 240, n. 2), had written to WBY (Norwood) asking him if he could persuade Todhunter to sell him a drawing of the Knight in 'La Belle Dame sans Merci' which was in his collection. The drawing, by Todhunter's friend, the Scots painter George Wilson (1848–90), was one that Day had recently seen reproduced in a magazine. If Todhunter was unwilling to sell the original, Day hoped that he might at least 'permit it to be photographed at my expense'.

[3] In his letter of 5 Feb 1892 Day had written: 'We are all very impatient over here for the Blake several notices of which Quaritch has already sent me. Of course you understand you have an order from me for a copy of the book when it arrives. I say *you* because you will undoubtedly make something more out of these that go from your hand than Quaritch's.' Copies of the large-paper edition of *The Works of William Blake* (see p. 344, n. 4) had apparently now reached Blenheim Road; the work was not officially on sale until March.

[4] The Kelmscott Press edition of *The Works of Geoffrey Chaucer*, edited by F. S. Ellis, with 87 woodcut illustrations designed by Sir Edward Burne-Jones, was the most elaborate example of William Morris's attempt to revive the art of printing; it eventually appeared in an edition of 425 copies on paper at £20 and 13 on vellum at 120 gns. Although not published until June 1896, it had been planned since June 1891, and was first announced in December 1892, when no price was given. Quaritch, with other leading booksellers, acted as agents for the Press; by December 1894 the paper copies had been fully subscribed. WBY was given a copy of the edition as a present from his friends on his fortieth birthday and described it (letter of 29 June 1901 to John Quinn, NYPL) as 'the most beautiful of all printed books'. Day, who had met Morris in the summer of 1890, when Morris apparently invited him to go into partnership with him in the Kelmscott venture, bought a copy of the *Chaucer* by subscription, and also owned one of seven vellum copies of *The Poems of John Keats*, also edited by F. S. Ellis (1894), one of the most sought-after of the smaller Kelmscott Press books.

[5] Probably *Monsieur Henri: a Footnote to French History* (New York, 1892), a biographical sketch of Henri Rochejaquelein, a leader of the anti-republican rising in the Vendée, 1793–5, following the French Revolution. Miss Guiney had 50 signed copies of the volume, a favourite among her own books, specially bound in Chollen plaid, Rochejaquelein's colour.

you sent me a good while ago. I never saw so beautiful a cover.[6]

Yours ever
W B Yeats

ALS (black-bordered paper) Texas.

To Edward Garnett, [c. 12 February 1893]

Lonsdale House | St Lawrence Road | Clontarf | Dublin.

Private

My dear Garnett

I write partly on my own motion & partly on the motion of M[r] John O Leary. I think we ought to try & come to some arrangement about the book scheme.[1] I am satisfied that it is a matter of vital importance to secure the help of the National Literary society. If this society could establish libraries & federate branches through out Ireland the scheme would be made a success. The books could be taken round by our lecturers—Ashe King who is just about to start to lecture at Loughrea or Hyde who will go to Westport in a few weeks could do much in this way[2]—& sold at the lecture as the Fabian Society people do. We could get our agents in provincial towns to push them also. In fact there are many ways in which the Society could help the project. But the Irish Society must be considered & consulted if it is to help. To put the matter into practical form I would suggest that an agreement between Fisher Unwin on the one hand & Sir Gavan Duffy & Douglas Hyde (who is to be sub-editor)[3] on the other should be prepared & that the agreement should contain a clause binding Sir Charles Duffy & Douglas Hyde to secure the co-operation of the Irish & the London Society in promoting the sale of the books. A clause of this kind will bring Duffy & the

---

[6] The *Mahogany Tree*. Day had written in his letter of 5 Feb 1892; 'I am in no way connected with the "M.T." excepting as the designer of a cover and occasionally supplying a book note when copy fails them. I asked that it be sent to you before I knew aught of its character and now I am half sorry for foisting on you a thing so amateurish.' No copy of this ephemeral publication survives.

[1] This letter is a last-ditch attempt to prevent Duffy's complete appropriation of the publishing scheme. WBY's hopes that the London and Dublin societies would formally block Duffy's sole editorship had been disappointed and he is now reduced to arguing about the quality rather than the fact of their support for the New Irish Library.

[2] See p. 341–3. The *Galway Vindicator* of 25 Jan 1893 announced that MG would 'deliver a lecture in St Patrick's Hall, Loughrea, on Tuesday evening, February 14th' under the auspices of the National Literary Society. Ashe King may have accompanied her on this occasion. Since Hyde spent a good deal of the following weeks in England, it is probable that his lecture at Westport was delayed until later in the spring.

[3] Hyde's appointment, with T. W. Rolleston, as assistant editor of the New Irish Library was not officially ratified by the Council of the National Literary Society until 27 Feb, but negotiations on the matter had been in progress since early January (see p. 343).

two societies into line. I would further suggest that a draft of the proposed agreement be sent to John O'Leary for his perusal[4]. It is not merely a question of getting the societies to do nothing against the scheme but of getting their *active* & enthusiastic support & of keeping it when got.

Yours very sincerely
W B Yeats

[*On a separate sheet*]

PS.

M^r O Leary asks me to say that the need for this arrangement comes largely from the fact that Rolleston—perhaps against his will—will other wise be completely ruled by Duffy. Duffy though very ready to bow to force will bow to no advice not backed by force. Such is at anyrate M^r O'Leary beleif & he should know him.[5] Of course there will be no opposition to the series. We all want books. But the lack of enthusiasm for the series may prevent its being properly pushed here. M^r O'Leary has immense influence & it were well to get his support & not merely his tolerance. I thought the proposed committee might serve all purposes but have been met by the statement that it has no means of enforcing its decissions. The result is that M^r O'Leary's supporters here do not take enough interest in the proposed arrangement to come down & vote for it. Hence though the society *nominally* is quite content with Hydes editorship it is *really* quite the other way. What ever be the result of this letter or of arrangements generally I shall do all I can ⟨personally⟩ to push the series but should feel more certain of success if we had ⟨positive power⟩ positive influence.

This is of course private but if you want any definite expression of

---

[4] No such clause was included in Unwin's contract with Duffy, although he did apparently ask for a formal pledge of support from both societies.

[5] In his role of honest broker, Garnett had been urging WBY to make a private arrangement with Rolleston so as to keep effective control of the book scheme. As early as 18 Nov 1892 (*LWBY* 1, 6–8) he wrote: 'If you & he would join hands . . . you would find that you & he are practically of the same mind about the books & that *your own ideas would be carried through*'. The real power could remain with WBY and Rolleston: 'Dont let loose the dogs of war against a Duffy Dictatorship when it could be turned into a Duffy Figureheadship'. He also warned that 'formal Committees on both sides will only embroil matters more'. It turned out, however, that Rolleston was more firmly committed to Duffy than Garnett had supposed, and on 25 Nov 1892 wrote to Unwin (Berg):

As to affairs in Dublin I believe, though I have written in a friendly tone to Yeats & received friendly answers, that there is no possibility of a rapprochement between him & Sir C. Duffy. He has taken his line, he has chosen to make himself the leader of a small clique of what are called 'advanced' men in Dublin who object to Sir C. Duffy on the score of his old quarrel with John Mitchel, & I think he cannot so far retrace his steps as to make it possible for Sir C. Duffy to work with him unless he is prepared to break with this clique altogether, which he certainly will not do.

He could also assure Unwin that there was no possibility of a rival Irish book scheme, nor of the National Literary Society doing 'anything which wd have the effect of driving out many of its prominent members, like Dr Sigerson & Fr Finlay, who are "Duffyite" '. In these and other letters there is nothing to suggest that Rolleston was being 'completely ruled' by Duffy or that he was doing anything but expressing his own considered opinion.

opinion, either for Unwin or for the committee of Irish literary society you can get it by writing to Mr John O Leary. He is at Lonsdale House, St Lawrence Road, Clontarf Dublin.

Though this is private I leave you to act upon your own judgement as to the use you make of its contents.

ALS (P.S. on black-bordered paper) Texas. Wade, 223–4.

To Edward Garnett, [?16 February 1893]

Lonsdale House | St Lawrence Road | Clontarf | Dublin.
Thursday.

Private.

My dear Garnett

I telegraphed to you to day because I heard from London that Unwin was getting alarmed about the book project.[1] Under these circumstances we must be very cautious. We want books—books under good conditions if possible—but books at any rate. My own pathway in the matter is particularly difficult. If in trying to carry out the proposed compromise I had been too Duffyite I would not have got the section who have opposed him to have anything to do with the arrangement. I have therefore emphasized the influence the society will have through Hyde as much as possible & there by drawn down the thunders of Duffys two supporters[2] & I fear that some rumour of said thunders may have got to ⟨London⟩ Unwin.

I beleive that if Unwin were to put the clause which I suggest into the agreement[3] it would bring us all into line. The section here who have opposed the absolute predominance of Sir Gavan Duffy would become enthusiastic or sufficiently so to carry every thing we want & to work up a public, while the two thick & thin supporters of Duffy would have to come into line with us. M^r O'Leary would have a real influence over the scheme then & his name would ballance the "federationist" name of Duffy[4] & all would become smooth.

At the same time do as you think fit about letter. Find out Unwins state of mind before using it. It might be the way out of the difficulty. Duffy could

[1] WBY's telegram has not survived. News of Unwin's 'alarm' (no doubt caused, as WBY suggests, by reports of the rows in the National Literary Society) probably reached WBY through Barry O'Brien.

[2] 'Dr Sigerson and J. F. Taylor sided with Gavan Duffy against me', wrote WBY in *Mem* (64), 'and the movement was soon divided, the young men on the whole taking my side'. Relations were at their most strained during the Council meeting held on 27 Jan (see above p. 345, n. 1) when, as Hyde recalled (Daly, 154), 'There was a terrible row between Taylor and Yeats, between O'Leary and Sigerson. We broke up at about 11. I never saw anything like it, but I escaped without a blow, thank God'.

[3] See preceding letter.

[4] See p. 305; Gavan Duffy had been one of the first federalists in Australia.

guarrantee the support of the London Society & Hyde of the Irish. In this way Unwins interests would be safe-guarded.

Please send me word as to Unwin's point of view & as to what he has heard from Dublin. I may be able to give some information of a useful kind.

Yours ever
W B Yeats

If it be needful to say who the suggestion about the "clause" comes from M^r O'Leary says that his name may be mentioned. My name must on no account be mentioned to any one.[5]

ALS (black-bordered paper) Texas. Wade, 225.

To E. J. Ellis, [after 16 February 1893]

c/o George Pollexfen | Thorn Hill | Sligo

My dear Edwin

Why dont you sing out. I have found the answer to the question anent the rhyme in the MS book, but wait to hear how you are getting on with the 'Songs of Innocence'[1]—alas my job is at stand still for the present—& how the Blake book has sold. Did you see Le Galleones notice in Star?[2]

I am projecting an Irish Magazine & would like to have the publishing of that Irish Poem of yours—the Scancan thing.

I am not to be editor but shall have charge of the poetry & considerable influence over the rest of the paper. I meen to try & make it the organ of what the journalist's delight to call 'the New' this or that. In this case it will be the new poetry and the new mysticism, so far as the Catholicism of the propriotor permits.[3] I fear we shall have no money to pay contributors at the outset but you will appear in good company—Stopford Brooke, Rolleston & so on.

---

[5] See p. 350, n. 4. Rolleston had written to Hyde on 26 Jan 1893 (Private): 'Mr O'Leary knows well that one of our friends in the new literary movement, Yeats to wit, has given great and – although there was an element of misunderstanding in the matter – not unjust cause of offence to Sir C. D. He knows well also that Sir C. D.'s view of Yeats's literary gift is quite the reverse of appreciative.'

[1] Although WBY in *The Poems of William Blake* thanks Ellis for lending him his copy of 'the MS book' (Blake's Notebook, formerly known as 'the Rossetti MS') used for their 3-vol. edition, and for 'kindly reading the proofs of my introduction', it is evident from what follows that Ellis was reading the proofs of the text as well. The 'rhyme in the MS book' is unidentified.

[2] In his 'Books and Bookmen' column in the *Star* of 4 Feb 1893 (2), 'Logroller' (Richard Le Gallienne) commented on *The Works of William Blake*, 'Messrs Ellis and Yeats have, as the reader knows, claimed to have discovered the thread to the labyrinth. What that thread is we must enquire again.' A longer review appeared on 25 Mar and was reprinted in his *Retrospective Reviews* (1896), I. 245–51.

[3] Ellis's verse play *Sancan the Bard* (1894) did not appear in what eventually became the *Irish Home Reading Magazine* (see p. 344). The Catholic 'proprietor' in question was at this stage, as for the projected New Irish Library, George Bryers of Sealey, Bryers & Walker, see p. 328, n. 4.

By the by do you know? that when I came to read for the first time your amendations to 'Edward III' I was surprised at their number. I half sympathize with Bullen. They are quite in their place in a big book for the library like our 'Works of William Blake' which being so expensive would come into no ones hands who had not already some other & literal Blake. In a 5/– edition however they would leed to a feeling of unrest in the readers mind (he having probably no other Blake). In any case Bullen's objection that the reviewers would be scandalized held good.[4] The reason I was so disgusted at your bringing them direct to him was that I had already corrected the printed version (I sent in the amended text from the big book to save time) restoring the original version & had intended (knowing the kind of man Bullen was) to forward your proof sheet which I was expecting every day & my own with it, & to say that I wanted Bullen to decide himself upon the matter and that I thought there was no half way house possible between your very much amended text & Blake's irregular one & that he should take one or the other. If ever I get any more proofs from Bullen or get any further with this book I will send you a proof of what I say about the text. I think you will see that it is fair & justefies the text in the small book without being unjust to the text in big book.[5] I incline myself, to the irregular text on the ground that the 'tincture' to quote the Lavater notes 'has entered into' the errors & made them 'phisiognomic'. On this ground I was always as you know afraid of the emendations. I feel least doubt about the 'Sampson'.[6]

My best regards to Mrs Ellis.

Yrs ever
W B Yeats

ALS (black-bordered paper) Reading.

<hr>

[4] The notes to the text of *Edward III* in vol. III of *The Works of William Blake* state that 'most of Dante Gabriel Rossetti's emendations as used by Gilchrist are adopted.' As this letter suggests, the texts in WBY's popular edition of the *Poems* revert to Blake's original versions. This was partly at the urging of Arthur Henry Bullen (1857–1920), Elizabethan scholar and one of WBY's principal publishers in the 1890s. Born in London, the son of George Bullen (d. 1894) who came from Cork and later became Keeper of Printed Books at the British Museum, A. H. Bullen edited a great number of Elizabethan writers. In 1891 he set up a publishing firm in Henrietta Street, Covent Garden, with Harold Lawrence, a man of wide cultural interests and secretary of the Medici Society. Their partnership ended in 1900 and in 1901 Bullen joined with Frank Sidgwick, later of the firm of Sidgwick and Jackson. In 1904 the two of them founded the Shakespeare Head Press at Stratford upon Avon, which was to publish WBY's *Collected Works* in 1908, as well as a number of his plays. Besides the book on Blake, WBY also published *The Celtic Twilight* (1893) and *The Secret Rose* (1897) with Lawrence & Bullen.

[5] While not commenting directly on his and Ellis's text in the 'big book', WBY in his notes to the *Poems* (235) argues that Rossetti's emendations to Blake's *Poetical Sketches*, while made with admirable judgment, leave the text as irregular as he found it. 'There seems', WBY continues, 'no logical position between leaving the poems as they are, with all their slips of rhythm, and making alterations of a very sweeping nature, which would be out of place in a working text like the present. The present editor has accordingly simply reprinted Blake's own text. . . .'

[6] In his annotation on No. 532 of Lavater's *Aphorisms on Man*, Blake distinguishes between the

To Edward Garnett, [after 16 February 1893]

c/o George Pollexfen | Thorn Hill | Sligo | Ireland

My dear Garnett

I sent you from Dublin part of the contents of 'The Adventure volume'. You have some where a list of the total contents. It was some what as follows—

Introduction.
1 Fighting Fitzgerald
2 Tiger Roche
3 ——Maguire (British Museum)
4 Freeney the Robber
5 Rogues & Rapperies
6 Michael Dwyer.
Notes—

I have sent you no 1 not 2 no 4 not 5—3 & 6 will have to be got at Museum I fear—at least 3 will. 6 I could get probably.[1]

substantive exuberance of genius or character and accidentally acquired extravagance: 'for how can Substance and Accident be predicated of the same Essence? I cannot concieve [*sic*]. But substance gives tincture to the accident, and makes it physiognomic.'

WBY omitted 'Samson', the prose poem which concludes Blake's *Poetical Sketches*, from his popular edition, choosing only to quote from it, in the notes (237), Samson's direction to Delilah beginning, 'Go on, fair traitress; do thy guileful work . . .'. In doing so WBY follows Blake's prose original, so that 'in no case has fresh characterization, fresh poetry, fresh cadence, or any intrusion of qualities other than Blake's own, been attempted' (179). W. M. Rossetti in the Aldine edition had broken the prose up into irregular blank verse, and Ellis, in vol. 1 of the *Works*, had gone a stage further and so edited the verse as to make it regular.

[1] For the later abandoned 'Irish Adventurers' volume, and 'Fighting' Fitzgerald, see pp. 221–2. 'Tiger' Roche, born in Dublin in 1729, the son of a gentleman, earned his soubriquet in America fighting in the French and Indian wars: wrongfully accused of theft and dismissed the service, his retort was to tear the throat of one of his accusers with his bare teeth, observing afterwards that it was 'the sweetest morsel he ever tasted'. Some years later, in 1775, he was tried at the Old Bailey for the murder of a fellow passenger on the way out to India but was subsequently acquitted. Bryan Maguire was the 'huge, whiskered bully' described by WBY in his article 'A Reckless Century' (see p. 222), who harassed the citizens of Dublin by 'standing at a narrow crossing and daring the passerby to jostle him'; his skill as a marksman was 'so great that he always rang his bell with a bullet and could snuff a candle held in his wife's hand with a pistol shot'. James Freney became the leader of a gang of highwaymen and housebreakers who terrorized Kilkenny and the surrounding country for years, before Freney secured a free pardon by betraying the last of them to the authorities. Given a place in the Revenue Service, he wrote an autobiography which attained great popularity and made him a local celebrity. Michael Dwyer (1771–1815) was a United Irishman who after the defeat of 1798 took to the Wicklow hills as leader of a band of insurgents. A price of £1,000 was put on his head and he had a number of hairbreadth escapes. He was ready to join Emmet's rebellion of 1803, but never received the signal to rise and later surrendered voluntarily to the authorities. He was transported to Botany Bay and eventually became High Constable of Sydney. The original version of WBY's 'A Fairy Song' (see p. 264) and KT's poem 'The Grave of Michael Dwyer' (see p. 66) both refer to him.

How do you prosper with Blake for I hear the Speaker has sent it to you—[2]

> Yours ever
> W B Yeats

ALS Texas. Wade, 227–8.

To Lionel Johnson,[1] [after 16 February 1893]

Thornhill

My dear Johnson, Some friends and myself are interested in [a] projected Irish Magazine which is intended to be the organ of our literary movement. It is to cost 6d a month and the first number is to appear if possible on May 21st (June number).[2] Will you give us some contribution, verse or prose? You need not do so at once but let us have your name to put in our list of contributions. We want to get a strong list as it is the only way of getting advertisements.

Thank you very much for your review of Blake in *Westminster* (my sister says it was yours) it was the best yet in every way. The mention of occult societies and the like came very much from our resolve not to hide our debt to the men who have been fighting the battle. It is so easy to earn a little credit for a kind of academical mysticism which ignores or even sneers at the true students. It was for this reason and from no wish to claim secret knowledge that we put in the book the hints you objected to.[3] My own position is that an idealism or spiritualism which denies magic, and evil spirits even, and sneers at magicians and even mediums, (the few honest ones) is an academical

---

[2] An unsigned review, 'Two Mystics on Blake', in the *Speaker*, 15 Apr 1893 (429–30), although complimenting the editors of *The Works of William Blake* on their industry, expressed reservations about the nature of their achievement. While they had 'undoubtedly rendered much of hitherto obscure poetry intelligible', and had 'demonstrated that Blake's tedious allegories are often based fundamentally on deep conceptions', they shirked, said the reviewer, 'discussing the genesis of certain Blakeian ideas for the very good reason that by doing so they would infallibly destroy the sanctity of the Great Myth.'

[1] See p. 269, n. 4.

[2] WBY was overoptimistic: on 29 Apr 1893 the *Irish Weekly Independent* reported that plans for the new magazine were 'as yet very much in the air', and a list of contributors seems not to have been announced until the autumn. When the *Irish Home Reading Magazine* was finally published, in 1894 (see p. 344), Johnson was one of the editors.

[3] An unsigned review, 'A Guide to Blake', in the *Westminster Gazette*, 16 Feb 1893 (3), pronounced the Ellis–Yeats edition 'the best service yet done to Blake' but complained that while 'Rosicrucians, and Kabbalists, and Hermetical Brothers may have the very truth, the pearl of price. . . . mysterious airs and alusive hints are not the way to win anyone over to anything; and if some readers should pronounce much of this book to be humbug and charlatanry, or delusion and lunacy, they would be wrong indeed, but not without excuse for their mistake.' A more substantial review of the edition, signed by Johnson, was published in the *Academy*, 26 Aug 1893 (163–5), and reprinted in a collection of his essays, *Post Liminium* (1911).

imposture. Your Church has in this matter been far more thorough than the Protestant. It has never denied *Ars Magica* though it has denounced it.

Yours ever

W B Yeats

Text from Wade (from a typed copy), 228.

To Edward Dowden, [*24 February 1893*]

Lonsdale House | St Lawrence Road | Clontarf | Dublin.[1]

My dear Mr Dowden

If you happen to know any body who wants a copy of the Blake, either large or small paper, please tell them that I have some copies & would be glad if they will buy from me as these copies are the only payment that wretch Quaritch has given us.[2] The green of the small paper has been improved and is now a very tolerable gray green.[3]

Yrs ever

W B Yeats

ALS (black-bordered paper), Private, with envelope addressed to 1 Appian Way, postmark 'DUBLIN FE 24 93'.

To Ernest Rhys, 2 June [*1893*]

3 Blenheim Road | Bedford Park | Chiswick. W

June 2

My dear Rhys

I am very anxious to get over to see you & may manage to do so on Sunday but I am not quite sure yet. If I do not I will write & ask you to suggest an evening.[1] I am deep in folk lore trying to get a book called 'the Celtic Twilight' off the stocks & into the water. It is partly reprints from National Observer articles.[2] Many best regards to Mrs Rhys—

Yours v truly

W B Yeats.

ALS Private.

[1] WBY had apparently returned to Dublin from Sligo, after a brief stay with his uncle at Thorn Hill, to attend the meeting of the Council of the National Literary Society on 27 Feb 1893 (see p. 349, n. 3).
[2] Quaritch's Publications Book (Quaritch) records that he had paid Ellis the agreed £100 (see p. 227, n. 1) on 28 Dec 1892.
[3] The colour of the binding cloth of the small-paper *Works of William Blake* was a light green.

[1] Rhys was now living in Hunts' Cottage in the Vale of Health, Hampstead.
[2] *The Celtic Twilight* (see p. 255) was published by Lawrence & Bullen in December 1893.

To Constance Gore-Booth,[1] *[21 June 1893]*

3 Blenheim Road | Bedford Park | Chiswick. W
Wednesday.

My dear Miss Gore Booth

Yes I can come on Friday & will with great pleasure. I find I have missed the post & hope my late reply may not inconvenience you—alas I have no better excuse than a long days tramp from library to publisher & publisher to library during which I kept reminding myself to write & then forgetting to do so.

Yours sincerely
W B Yeats

ALS Harvard, with envelope addressed to 35 Bryanston Square W., postmark 'CHISWICK JU 22 93'.

To Count Plunkett,[1] *21 June 1893*

3 Blenheim Road | Bedford Park | Chiswick. W

My dear Plunkett

The Council of the National Literary Society has passed a resolution asking for a report of the proceedings of the Library Committee. I have written the enclosed which please read to them, adding at the same time financial statement. It is better for you to be there to represent the library committee even apart from the financial side of the thing.[2]

---

[1] Constance Georgina Gore-Booth (1868–1927) was born and raised at Lissadell House near Sligo but had recently moved to London, where she was staying with friends in Bryanston Square, to begin art classes at the Slade under Alphonse Legros. In 1898 she went to Paris to continue her studies and there met Count Casimir Markiewicz, a Polish artist, whom she married in 1900. They returned to Dublin, where she became actively involved in Sinn Fein politics. She was sentenced to death for her part in the Easter Rising of 1916, but reprieved—events recorded in WBY's poem, 'On a Political Prisoner' (*VP*, 397)—and was later a member of the first Dail Eireann and a Cabinet minister. WBY's elegy for her and her sister, Eva Gore-Booth, 'In Memory of Eva Gore-Booth and Con Markiewicz' (*VP*, 475–6), was written shortly after her death.

[1] See p. 80.
[2] Plunkett, the treasurer of the Libraries subcommittee of the National Literary Society, read WBY's report to a meeting of the Society on 29 June 1893. It met with disapproval: a motion by P. J. McCall, seconded by W. O'L. Curtis, and carried, requested Plunkett 'to convey to the Libraries Sub-Committee the dissatisfaction of the Society regarding the manner in which the meetings of the Sub-Committee have been conducted, the want of system in its arrangements, the apparent absence of minute book, or report of its proceedings.' 'The trouble', wrote WBY in *Aut* (229–30), 'came from half a dozen obscure young men, who having nothing to do attended every meeting and were able to overturn a project that seemed my only bridge to other projects, including a travelling theatre. . . . I returned to find a great box of books appropriated for some Dublin purpose and the whole scheme abandoned.' However, it appears that 100 volumes in all were sent to the Loughrea Literary Society, 100 to the New Ross Commercial Club, and 100 to the Listowel Young Ireland Society. At the end of 1893, 50 books were sent to the Arklow Commercial Club, and other grants were made to societies in Ballygarret and Westport.

I am up to my ears in getting a new book out—'The Keltic Twilight' by name.

Yours ever
W B Yeats

[*Enclosure*]
Report of Hon Sec of Library Committee—

June 21 1893.

The Library committee of the National Literary Society has held a large number of meeting during the winter & spring. It received application for books from several county societies & chose Loughrea, New Ross & Listowel. It decided to send about £4 or £5 worth of books to each place. Each society was to receive 100 books, 50 to be chosen by committee & 50 chosen by the local body from a list supplied by us. We sent to Loughrea & Newross two sets, containing fifty books each—25 Irish 25 general literature—& packed & left another 50 ready for Listowel as soon as that society federated with us. In connection with the scheme Miss Maud Gonne lectured at Loughrea & New Ross & would have lectured at Listowel also had she not been unavoidably prevented. She also reported upon the condition of the two societies she visited & told us that their reading rooms were in good condition & their membership good. I am unable to give the list of books selected by us as my absense from Dublin has removed it out of reach. The further list, that from which the country societies are to select their further 50 books cannot be completed at once as it will contain the names of books given to us as well as of books bought by us & it is desirable to wait a little in order to have it as large as possible.

W B Yeats
Hon. Sec

ALS and enclosure, NLI, with envelope addressed to 'Count Plunkett, 25 Upper Fitzwilliam St, Dublin', postmark 'CHISWICK JU 21 93'.

To F. L. Gardner,[1] [*10 July 1893*]

[Chiswick]

My dear Gardiner
Yes I will lecture on 'The Nature of beauty'.[2]

Yours
W B Yeats

APS Albany, addressed to '—Gardiner Esq, 25 Barrowgate Road', postmark 'CHISWICK JY 10 93'.

To John O'Leary, *13 July* [*1893*]

3 Blenheim Road | Bedford Park | Chiswick, W
July 13th

My dear M^r O'Leary
I was unable to go to Gower St to day.[1] I have asked Johnson for Sunday &
Elkin Mathews is coming & bringing a man named Bruce who is writing a
book on the Irish rebellions & very anxious to meet you.[2] So do not fail to
come. I did not send the books because I heard you were coming over.

Yr ever
W B Yeats

Bruce is a Unionist.

ALS NLI.

[1] Frederick Leigh Gardner (1857–1929), a stockbroker, had joined the Theosophical Society on HPB's first visit to London in 1884, and by January 1890 was Hon. Sec. of the Blavatsky Lodge of the Society. In November 1893 he applied to join the Golden Dawn and was initiated into the Order in March 1894. Gardner had lived at 37 Barrowgate Road, Chiswick, in the early 1890s and his mother was still living there in 1892–3, while he himself had removed to 14 Marlborough Road, Gunnersbury.
[2] WBY lectured on 17 July 1893 to the Chiswick Lodge of the Theosophical Society at a public meeting held at 37 Barrowgate Road. His subject was 'The Nature of Art and Poetry in Relation to Mysticism'. In its account of the occasion the *West London Observer*, 22 July 1893 (6), identified him as 'Mr W. B. Yeates (the well known author of Wm. Blake's work [sic], "The Mystic")'. WBY began by showing the way in which mystics work, and then illustrated 'the divorce between morality and mystic perfection' with 'an instance of a mystic artist known to him, who was an habitual drunkard and associated with very low surroundings', yet able to produce 'mystic pictures of a very high order'. The true nature of the imagination was to be found in 'the doctrine of *Mahat* or the universal mind'; and having 'thrashed his question out very ably in detail', WBY closed 'by showing the effect of coloured glasses in Italy upon lunatics, in some cases effecting cures, and in others rendering great relief.'

[1] JO'L was presumably lodging as usual near his friend Dr Ryan (see p. 184, n. 5) in Gower Street.
[2] This may have been JO'L's first encounter with Lionel Johnson. The Unionist Bruce was possibly Robert T. Hamilton Bruce (1846–99), part proprietor of the *National Observer* and friend of W. E. Henley, who lived in Edinburgh but was frequently in London. Neither he, nor anyone else named Bruce, published a book on Irish rebellions.

To D. J. O'Donoghue, [*? July 1893*]

THE IRISH LITERARY SOCIETY | LONDON | BLOOMSBURY

MANSION | HART ST. | W.C.[1]

My dear O'Donahue

Lady Wylde has written to me to say that she resigns her membership of the society as she is unable to attend meetings etc. but that as she does not wish to be forgotten altogether by us she sends her 'Social Studies' for the library.[2] Please tell the proper person about her resignation & thank her for the book.

Yours ever
W B Yeats

ALS Amherst.

To R. Barry O'Brien,[1] [*early August 1893*]

3 Blenheim Road | Bedford Park | Chiswick. W—

Dear M^r O'Brien

I enclose 'the middle' upon 'The Ghost Word' which you asked for & which I promised in time for next number in case you require it so soon.[2] I should of course get proofs of both this & the other article—[3]

Yours very truly
W B Yeats

I have read every one of the 400 & over pages & am therefore on this occassion a conscientious reviewer—

ALS NLI.

[1] The Irish Literary Society, London, occupied rooms in Bloomsbury Mansion until 24 Oct 1894, when it moved to Adelphi Terrace, to provide its members with easier access to the railway stations.
[2] Lady Wilde was now largely confined by ill health to her home in Oakley Street, London. Her *Social Studies*, published in June 1893, is a collection of 15 essays and stories on a variety of topics including women's emancipation, Irish leaders and martyrs, an enquiry into the possibility of life on other planets, and a plea for emigration to Australia.

[1] See p. 44.
[2] WBY's 'middle', 'The Message of the Folk-Lorist', a review of T. F. Thistelton Dyer's *The Ghost World* (1893) (*UP* I. 283–8), was printed in the *Speaker* of 19 Aug 1893 under the standing heading 'A Literary Causerie'; see p. 302. A MS version of the article is in MBY, and a corrected galley proof in NLI; not all the corrections to this proof were made in the printed version.
[3] 'Two Minor Lyrists' (*UP* I. 288–91), an unsigned review of *Verses by the Way* by James Dryden Hosken and *The Questions at the Well* by Fenil Haig (an early pseudonym of Ford Madox Ford) (both 1893), appeared in the *Speaker* of 26 Aug 1893. Of Ford's first book of poetry WBY remarked that it was 'one of the few new books of promise which come to a reviewer in a season; nor is the promise the less evident because one does not quite know what it promises.'

To J. S. Cotton,[1] *[late September 1893]*

56 North Circular Road | Dublin.[2]

Dear Mr Cotton—

There is a book of poems by a young Dublin man 'Reflections & Refractions by Charles Weekes'.[3] May I review it for you?

Yours very sincerely
W B Yeats

ALS NLI.

To Frederick Langbridge,[1] *[late September 1893]*

56 North Circular Road | Dublin

Dear Mr Langbridge

I have wired title of my story. The story itself I hope to send to morrow. I have finished it but want to make a few corrections. Meanwhile I have broken my glasses & until they are mended can only write a few lines. I think my story would be just the kind of thing for my brother to illustrate. It is founded on a wild folktale.[2] I will write & ask my father as soon as my glasses come.[3]

Yours truly
W B Yeats

ALS Private.

[1] James Sutherland Cotton (1847–1918), editor of the *Academy* 1881–96, was a barrister by training. An expert on Indian history and statistics, he contributed to the *DNB*, *Chambers's Encyclopaedia*, and the *Encyclopaedia Britannica*. Chesterton described him (Dudley Barker, *G. K. Chesterton* [1973], 68) as 'a little bristly, bohemian man, as fidgetty as a kitten, who runs round the table while he talks to you'.

[2] WBY had returned to Dublin in mid-September with Lionel Johnson, to plan the founding of a national magazine. They were sharing lodgings with WBY's friend Quinn (see p. 303) in the house of a Miss E. Walsh, on the corner of Florinda Place near the Mater Misericordia Hospital where Quinn was a medical student.

[3] See p. 347.

[1] The Revd Frederick Langbridge (1849–1922), poet, novelist, and playwright, was born in Birmingham, educated at Oxford, and ordained in 1877. In 1883 he became rector of St. John's and Canon of St. Munchin's, St. Mary's Cathedral, Limerick, a living he retained until his death. At this time he had already published four books of verse, as well as children's stories, and was contributing prose and verse to a large number of periodicals. His ambition to found an Irish literary magazine was to result, in December 1893, in the publication of *The Old Country*, which although advertised as a Christmas Annual, was intended to be the first of a monthly series.

[2] The story WBY contributed to *The Old Country* (158–64) was 'Michael Clancy, The Great Dhoul, and Death', which he described as 'Founded upon a legend I heard down in Sligo.' The story was illustrated by Jack Yeats.

[3] Evidently Langbridge had asked WBY to enquire whether his father would illustrate the story, 'Mrs Wynniatt's Skeleton', by 'Dick Donovan' (pseudonym of Joyce Emmerson Muddock), in *The Old Country*; JYB agreed.

To George Bryers,[1] *26 September* [*1893*]

56 North Circular Road | Dublin
Sept 26th

Dear Mr Bryers

Would you please prepare for me estimates of the probable cost of a
Monthly Mag upon the three following scales 2000 copies of 56 pages of the
size of the University Review; 2000 copies of 40 pages of the size of the Cork
Archeological Journal; 2000 copies of 64 pages of the size of the Irish
Monthly.[2] If you can have these estimates ready for me by 12 on Thursday
I will call with Mr Johnson & discuss the matter with you. We have seen
Mr Bell & have reasen to know that he is willing to let his scheme give way to
ours & in a few days we will know definitely about our financial position.[3]

Yours ever
W B Yeats

ALS Private.

To Katharine Tynan Hinkson,[1] [*c. 27 September 1893*]

56 North Circular Road | Dublin

⟨ My dear Miss Tynan ⟩
My dear Mrs Hinkson,

Unless it be too late please cross out the mention of 'The Secret Rose' in
the 'Sketch' interview. Its a little too soon. As you have written on me for the
'Bookman' what will be, I imagine, a signed article do you not think it would
be well to leave the Sketch thing unsigned the blackguards over here of the
Taylor type are ever crying out about what they call log-rolling.[2] Johnson

---

[1] See p. 328, n. 4.

[2] The size of *DUR* had been $5\frac{1}{2} \times 8\frac{3}{4}$ ins.; that of the *Journal of the Cork Historical and Archaeological
Society*, $6\frac{3}{4} \times 9\frac{7}{8}$ ins.; and that of the *Irish Monthly*, $5\frac{1}{2} \times 8\frac{1}{8}$ ins.

[3] S. C. Bell, of the National Literary Society (see p. 317), had evidently had plans of his own for an
Irish literary magazine. This and other obstacles were seemingly overcome, for on 28 Sept 1893 the
following announcement appeared in the London *Daily Chronicle*: 'The Irish Review—a new Irish
monthly is announced to appear in Dublin in October. No editor is named, but the list of contributors is
attractive—Stopford Brooke, John O'Leary, Katherine [*sic*] Tynan, T. W. Rolstone [*sic*], Douglas
Hyde, R. Ashe King, John Todhunter, W. B. Yeats, Standish O'Grady, Lionel Johnson, Barry O'Brien,
and John McGrath.' See pp. 344, n. 3, 355.

[1] KT had married H. A. Hinkson in London on 4 May 1893 and was now living in Ealing.

[2] The reference to *The Secret Rose* (not published until 1897) was, however, retained in KT's
interview with him, printed in the *Sketch*, 29 Nov 1893 (256); WBY speaks there of two volumes about to
appear, one *The Celtic Twilight*, while 'The other is to be called "The Secret Rose", and is to be a
collection of weird stories of the Middle Ages in Ireland; some of them have appeared in the *National
Observer*.' The interview was printed over the initials 'K.T.', even though her biographical article on

(Lionel) is over here with me & we are busy drawing up scheme for National Mag

Yours ever
W B Yeats

ALS Harvard.

To J. S. Cotton, 6 October [1893]

56 North Circular Road | Dublin
Friday—Oct 6.

Dear Mr Cotton

I enclose the review of "Refractions & Reflections" which I promised some time ago.[1]

Yours truly
W B Yeats

ALS NYU.

To Laurence Housman, 10 October [1893]

56 North Circular Road | Dublin.
Oct 10

My dear Housman

Your letter found me over here some while ago & I have been intending to answer it from day to day. I felt myself in a difficulty about your book.[1] I certainly thought it highly probable that your book was out of your hands

---

WBY in the *Bookman*, October 1893 (13–14), had been signed 'Katharine Tynan'. For the accusation of 'log-rolling' by WBY and his friends in John F. Taylor's letter to the *Freeman's Journal* of 7 Sept 1892, see p. 313, n. 4.

[1] See p. 361. The review (*UP* 1. 302–5) was published in the *Academy*, 4 Nov 1893. WBY found the book 'as interesting as it is rugged and obscure' and praised Weekes for his originality, daring and promise.

[1] Housman's letter (now lost) had obviously protested against WBY's unfavourable review of his *Selections from the Writings of William Blake* (1893) in the *Bookman*, August 1893 (*UP* 1. 280–3). WBY had used Housman's book as an occasion to attack the whole nineteenth-century tradition of editing Blake and the habit of scorning the Prophetic Books. He had to some extent mitigated the particularity of his criticisms by explaining that he regarded Housman as a representative figure and by suggesting that the greater blame lay with the publisher of the book, Kegan Paul:

But what excuse can be offered for a publisher, for I do Mr Housman the credit of supposing that publishers' reasons prevailed over the dictates of scholarship, who, months after the correct text has been printed in 'The Works of William Blake' (B. Quaritch), re-issues the old doctored text not only without a word of explanation or excuse, but without a single sentence to warn the reader that this is not Blake's own text?

before my book & Ellis' got into them but I did not know whether you had or
had not passed the appendix or initial note stage & felt also that I had no
right to say that I knew you were at work at your proofs before my book
came out & that I therefore threw all the blame upon your publishers for not
giving you a chance of retouching even at some little expense. I felt that I
had no right to bring any private matter into my review. I did however as
you will remember cast the blame, as far as I could, on to the broad
shoulders of Keegan Paul. I suggest[ed] if I remember rightly that
"publishers reasens" prevailed over scholourship. My whole desire was to
expose the old Blake text & to protest against the non-mystical way of taking
the prophetic books. I should have very much prefered to have attacked
some other editors work but you were the only new Blake in the field. I think
by the by that you did say that "The Island of the Moon" was never before
printed but I have not your book at hand to refer to. You can look it up
yourself. Lionel Johnson who is with me thinks you said so.[2] A way out of the
difficulty would perhaps have been an initial note however you were but the
outpost of the enemies army. I of course agree with you that the form of
much of the prophetic writing is bad I only plead that the substance should
not therefore be despised. I do not however agree with you about the metre
which seems to me to be when at its best as in "Thell" & parts of "The
daughters of Albion" & "Vala" quite perfectly adapted to his purpose &
very musical. In the explanatory portions it is often very bad but then his
blank verse & even his lyric verse are so on occasion & yet neither blank verse
nor rhyme is to blame.[3] Of course you have a perfectly clear right to take Blake
as a writer of "belle lettres" only you should make this compatable with a
respectful attitude towards his mysticism also.[4] Mysticism has been in the
past & probably ever will be one of the great powers of the world & it is bad
scholourship to pretend the contrary. You may argue against it but you
should no more treat it with disrespect than a perfectly cultivated writer
would treat (say) The Catholic Church or the Church of Luther no matter

[2] In his Introduction Housman speaks (xxx) of 'a manuscript entitled, "An Island in the Moon," now
in the possession of Mr. C. Fairfax Murray' and gives the impression that he has been the first editor of
Blake to discover and print extracts from this work. In fact Ellis and WBY had already provided a
description of the MS, cited its provenance, and quoted copious extracts from it with a full commentary
in vol I of *The Works of William Blake* (186–201). See p. 347.

[3] WBY had not discussed metrics in his review, although in his Introduction (xxviii–xxix) Housman
attacks Blake's defence of the metres in *Jerusalem* as a 'peculiarly harassing instance' of 'mental bad
manners' since

it binds every faithful editor to reprint his prophetic writings in the bad metrical form he claims for them,
and not as the poetical prose they really are. All that can be said therefore on behalf of the fine passages
from the 'Daughters of Albion' and the 'Milton,' included in these selections, is that only when read with
disregard to the divisions of metre can their exceeding beauty be heard.

[4] Housman had quoted from 'An Island in the Moon', as he explains in his Introduction (xxx–xxxi),
to show the variety of Blake's verse and to illustrate 'the spirit of banter' in 'this amusing trifle.'

how much he disliked them. Did you ever read Garth Wilkinson's attack upon the prophetic books in the introduction to the first type-printed edition of "The Songs of Innocence & Experience"? One can make no complaint against its tone. It is very hostile but quite respectful.[5]

By the by I have been asked to ask you if you would care to do some slight work—sketches for an Irish Magazine.[6] I am however ashamed wellnigh to tell you the terms. I quote the letter of the editor & but forward them at his request. They would improve if the venture prospered.

"Per 'Idea'   page   £1.0.0
  „   „   ½ „   10.0
Minimum   5.0."

It is a new venture & therefore timid.

Yours ever
W B Yeats

ALS Bryn Mawr.

To Frederick Langbridge, 12 October [1893]

56 North Circular Road | Dublin—
Oct 12

Dear Mr Langbridge

My brother will draw for you at the rates you name on the understanding that the amount increase if the venture prosper[1] & that the lowest sum paid

[5] John James Garth Wilkinson (1812–99), a leading Swedenborgian and homeopathic doctor, edited a number of Blake's early poems. His edition of *Songs of Innocence and of Experience*, which considerably amended Blake's text, was published in 1839. As a Swedenborgian Wilkinson had no difficulty in accepting the visionary nature of Blake's inspiration, but felt that in trying to go beyond Christianity and in too readily rejecting the reasoning faculty Blake, like Shelley, had fallen into 'Ego-theism', a radical solipsism whereby both imagined (xix) 'that they could chop and change the universe, even to the confounding of Life with Death, to suit their own creative fancies.' Wilkinson's hostility to the prophetic writings arises not from a facile dismissal of their obscurity but from his appalled awe at their daemonic power:

Of the worst aspect of Blake's genius it is painful to speak. In his 'Prophecies of America,' his 'Visions of the Daughters of Albion,' and a host of unpublished drawings, earth-born might has banished the heavenlier elements of Art, and exists combined with all that is monstrous and diabolical. In the domain of Terror he here entered, the characteristic of his genius is fearful Reality. (xviii)

[6] See p. 361 and the following letter.

[1] Langbridge's hope that *The Old Country* would continue as a monthly publication is clear from a paragraph in *United Ireland*, 4 Nov 1893 (1): 'Those not in "the know", of course, will imagine that *The Old Country* is a Christmas Annual merely, but, if I am rightly informed, the December issue, if successful, will be succeeded by *Old Countrys* every month.' The prospectus of the new magazine, which *United Ireland* also printed, read in part:

The Old Country consists of 200 royal octavo pages, well printed, on good paper, and profusely illustrated

be 5/−. He says that there is really no difference in the trouble which a very slight & slightly less slight sketch costs. I suppose he means that the thought required is about the same and that the execution being not very laborious in either case the thought is well nigh the whole of the trouble.

I enclose a couple of Stories which Miss Vynne has sent me for your approval. 'The Grave of Queen Clair' struck me when I read it some months ago to be a vigerus interesting Irish story. It has not much style or a great deal of local colour but is I beleive well worked out. The other which I have only just read is a kind of fairytale & is fairly good.[2]

Miss Vynnes most characteristic work is modern, witty & realistic & I hardly know whether you will care for the things I send. All I can say is that I read them myself with eager interest.

Yours very try

W B Yeats

I would suggest that you get C H Oldham to do an article on "the Contemporary Club" & get it illustrated by a lot of sketches which belong to it of various notable members & guests. These sketches were made by my father & include sketches of William Morris, Stead, T W Russell, John O Leary the Fenian, Etc.[3] Such an article would be a most interesting record

by the best and newest processes. Eschewing politics and theology, and all controversial matters, we have tried to make its pages light and bright, pure and wholesome. We hope that our readers will enjoy many hearty laughs—laughs of which it may be said: "There is not a heartache in a hogshead of them." Not that serious interest will be lacking. There is the story with a grip; the song that reaches the heart. The harmless necessary ghost unobtrusively keeps his tryst, and other seasonable 'creeps' are not lacking. . . . The Bill of Fare will, we venture to believe, tempt the very coyest shilling out of its owner's pocket.

The list of contributors included WBY and KT, along with Langbridge himself, Edwin Hamilton, Edmund Downey, Samuel K. Cowan, W. G. Wills, Mary H. Tennyson, Mrs Henniker, Edward Dowden, and 'Dick Donovan'. The Christmas number was also to include unpublished poems by Lord Byron and Thomas Moore, and illustrations by Walter Osborne, W. C. Mills, JBY, and others.

  [2] Nora Vynne (1869–1914), novelist, short-story writer, and champion of women's rights, began to publish articles and stories in the *Speaker*, the *Star*, the *Sketch*, the *Pall Mall Budget*, and elsewhere in the early 1890s; her first collection, *The Blind Artist's Pictures*, was published in 1893. Her story, 'The Grace of Queen Clare', appeared in *The Old Country* with illustrations by W. F. Osborne (193–9), and was subsequently reprinted in *Honey of Aloes* (1894). Set in Ireland in early times, the story tells of the generosity of a suitor of the Queen's, the bard Kanaghan, in releasing her from her promise to marry him when he perceives that she loves another. The other story, not published in *The Old Country*, was probably 'One of the Queen's Sons', about the healing of a crippled prince through the agency of a magic philtre. It was later included in *Honey of Aloes*.

  [3] For C. H. Oldham and the Contemporary Club, see p. 127 and Appendix. JBY made a number of sketches (now in the National Gallery of Ireland) of members of the Club and their visitors in the mid-'80s. William Thomas Stead (1849–1912), the innovatory journalist and social reformer, whom JBY had sketched on his visit to Ireland in 1886, had been editor of the *Pall Mall Gazette* and was now editing and publishing the *Review of Reviews*. Thomas Wallace Russell (1841–1920), a member of the Contemporary Club, was Liberal Unionist MP for South Tyrone 1886–1900, Under-Secretary of the Local Government Board from 1895, and was active in the Irish temperance movement. After 1900 he was converted to support for Home Rule, and served as vice-president of the Department of Agriculture and Technical Instruction, 1907–18.

of the personal & social side of politics in this country for the last 8 years & should interest people quite apart from their political beleifs & offend no one.

ALS Texas.

To F. J. Bigger,[1] [*? week of 13 November 1893*]

56 North Circular Road | Dublin

Dear Sir

I was very sorry not to have seen you while in Dublin & would have done so had I not been laid up Thursday Friday & the bulk of Saturday with a feverish cold which I nursed & nurse that I may have some voice next Tuesday.[2] Yes the 2 o'clock train on Tuesday will suit me right well. Many thanks for your kind offer to "dedicate" Wednesday to my whims. I shall be indeed glad to see something of your North Country or North Country people.

Yours very truly
W B Yeats

Francis Joseph Bigger Esq

ALS Texas.

To Ernest Radford,[1] [*late November 1893*]

56 North Circular Road, Dublin

My dear Radford,

Thank you very much for your note. The misprint is, I believe, set right in the selections which I have done for the Muses Library at least I think so—The book should be out in a few days.

The part of the big Blake which gave the Songs of Innocence and

---

[1] Francis Joseph Bigger (1863–1926), a Belfast solicitor, although better known as a historian and antiquarian, was editor of the *Ulster Journal of Archaeology* 1894–1914, and published a number of books on Irish culture and antiquities. He was active in the restoration of ancient buildings and stone crosses and became a member of the RIA and a Fellow of the Royal Society of Antiquaries of Ireland.

[2] On Tuesday, 21 Nov 1893, WBY lectured on 'Irish Fairy Lore' to the Belfast Naturalists' Field Club in the Museum, College Square North, Belfast. The lecture was reported the next day in the *Irish News and Belfast Morning News* (8).

[1] Ernest Radford (1857–1919), sometime secretary of the Rhymers' Club and one of its founder members, was the author of two volumes of poems, *Measured Steps* (1884) and *Chambers Twain* (1890), as well as *Translations from Heine and Others* (1882). In 1895 he published another book of verse, *Old and New*.

Experience was not facsimile but a very hasty reprint made at the last moment to satisfy a desire of Quaritch to have the book complete. The original idea was merely to have reproduced the prophetic books in facsimile with an interpretation. The book contains most possible misprints and among them I have no doubt the one you complain of.[2] My little book in the Muses Library is however I think letter perfect (and yet one never knows).

Yours ever

W B Yeats.

ALS Private (text from a MS copy). *Yeats Studies* 1. 204.

To Susan Mary Yeats, [*after 2 December 1893*]

56 North Circular Road | Dublin.

My dear Lilly

Miss Pursur was at the contemporary club last night & asked me if I had seen a note in the Daily Express to the effect that "Mr Yeats the artist" was seriously ill & ordered to the South of France. She had heard from you recently & so of course had I, so neither of us were particularly alarmed. Irish papers are never notable for accuracy. Still you might as well send me word that all is well.[1]

I send you a *UI* with a letter from the editor of the "Artist" and a short report of my Belfast lecture.[2]

Hyde is in Dublin with his wife. She is very rich an Austrian Countess & fairly good looking.[3]

[2] Since, as WBY confesses, there were many misprints in the Ellis–Yeats *Works of William Blake*, it has not been possible to trace the one pointed out by Radford—apparently in either the *Songs of Innocence* or the *Songs of Experience*, printed in vol. III of the edition. WBY's edition of *The Poems of William Blake* was published at the end of November 1893.

[1] There appears to have been no such note in the Dublin *Daily Express*; but the *Irish Times*, 23 Nov 1893 (5) announced that 'Mr. Edmund Yates is in ill-health' and had been 'ordered to the South of France for four months by his medical advisers'. Edmund Yates (1831–94) was a journalist and popular novelist.

[2] *United Ireland* for 2 Dec 1893 carried (3) a report of WBY's Belfast lecture (see p. 367) and, on its front page, a letter dated 26 Nov 1893 from the editor of *The Artist*. The correspondence arose out of an article on WBY by 'T.G.W.' (Theodore Wratislaw), which had appeared in *The Artist* on 1 Oct 1893 (297–8) and which ran in part: 'To regenerate Irish literature, says Mr Yeats, is his chief aim; but to do this, he must remember that it is necessary to make it acceptable to aliens . . . and in this he has not yet succeeded.' This had prompted a rejoinder from *United Ireland*, which in its issue of 11 November maintained that WBY's 'Celticism' was not exclusive. The 26 November letter from the editor of *The Artist* concluded: 'Will you not agree with us then that the rare and beautiful muse of Mr Yeats should not be shut up in Celtic interests, but that his service to Ireland would be found in treating general issues with Celtic "style and natural magic".'

[3] Douglas Hyde married Fräulein Lucy Kurtz, not an 'Austrian Countess' but the daughter of a German manufacturing chemist and art collector, in Liverpool on 10 Oct 1893. After a honeymoon on

I have a sort of dim notion of going to Sligo to write some lyrics & idle a bit by taking long walks. For I am fealing rather fagged out after a rather severe cold in the midst of which I had to go North to lecture. But am kept here for a while by the Nat Lit Society which is struggling with its lecture list.

Yrs affy

W B Yeats

There is a book called "Irish Folk Lore" by "Lageniensis"[4]—It has a green cover is in or was in the study. I want it rather badly. Could you send it?

ALS MBY.

To the Editor of United Ireland, *23 December 1893*

DEAR SIR—The writer of the leading article called "A Candid Critic," admits that he was not present at the lecture which Mr. King gave last week under the auspices of the National Literary Society. This has been a double misfortune, for it has made him miss one of the most brilliant lectures I have ever heard, and be very unjust to Mr. King. Mr. King did not say that politics laid waste the Irish intellect, but only that partisan politics laid it waste. He went so far indeed as to affirm that everything which has been won for Ireland has been won by politics.[1] It is, of course, difficult to say where the politics of the partisan end and the politics of the patriot begin, but the line of division is thus, and the politician who does not find it brawls his way into chaos. It seems to my eyes, at any rate, that politics become partisan when the great principles of the national demand are made less visible than

the Continent, they returned to Dublin on 17 November before going on to Hyde's home at Frenchpark, Co. Roscommon, on 3 December.

   [4] See p. 81.

   [1] In a lecture entitled 'The Celt: the Silenced Sister' given to the National Literary Society on 8 Dec 1893, Richard Ashe King argued that a preoccupation with politics and political rhetoric had seriously impaired Irish literature and Irish genius, so that, by comparison with English writers, the Celt seemed 'silent'. *United Ireland*'s leader of 16 Dec, entitled 'A Candid Critic' (5), took issue with King on several points but in particular with his remark that politics had not only laid 'waste the Irish intellect but kept it waste—it absolutely and diabolically kept it waste.' It offered as counter-examples Thomas Moore, the Young Irelanders, and the poets associated with the Land League, pointing out that each had been inspired by political interests. Besides WBY, Ashe King himself wrote on 23 Dec to set the record straight: 'I took special pains,' he said, 'to distinguish between the patriotic politics which, through O'Connell, emancipated the Irish intellect, and the partisan politics which absorbs what intellect it does not drive away.'

   The memory of this controversy remained with WBY and in 1925, when he dedicated *Early Poems and Stories* to Ashe King, he remembered (*VP*, 854) his lecture as 'a denunciation of rhetoric, and of Irish rhetoric most of all; and that it was a most vigorous and merry lecture and roused the anger of the newspapers.'

what are held to be the failings of opponents; and how perfectly this kind of thing ruins the sense of proportion upon which literature is built up, can be discovered by anyone who will read "Valentine M'Clutchy." Carleton was a man of genius, but the habit of dividing men into sheep and goats for the purposes of partisan politics made havoc of what might have been a great novel.[2] Carleton was so bedevilled by partisan vehemence that he forgot to remember how men ally themselves with any and every cause for the best of motives. He forgot that the Crusader, if he have anything of nobility, must be prepared to find many a fool and self-seeker among his allies, and many a wise and just person among his opponents. I think I may add that newspapers become partisan when they give columns to some heated and trivial gentleman who is explaining that his opponent, Mr. John Redmond, Mr. John Dillon, or Colonel Saunderson, as the case may be, is immensely deceitful and desperately wicked;[3] while they can spare but a few lines at the utmost for a lecture upon some of the momentous problems in the life of a nation by one of the most eloquent and thoughtful of our men of letters. Nor can they repel the charge by pleading that the people hunger and thirst for the words of the most trivial of Town Councillors and most heated of M P's, and feel indifferent to the serious and careful thought of the man of letters, for it was they who fed the gaping mouths with the east wind until they had destroyed all taste for better food. UNITED IRELAND has, however, always done what it could, and kept up the good fight bravely.

"I Olkyrn" wrote you a very beautiful letter, and her slight mis-understanding of my own speech would never have led me to break silence if I had not been forced to do so by your article upon Mr. King.[4] I did not say

---

[2] For *Valentine M'Clutchy* (1845), William Carleton's most national and anti-Protestant book, see p. 174.

[3] WBY picks out three leaders of opposed political groupings in Ireland at that time: John Edward Redmond (1856–1918) was MP for New Ross and leader of the Parnellite faction of the Irish Party, now bitterly opposed to the anti-Parnellites. Although the ex-Parnellite John Dillon (see pp. 13, 265) was not to replace Justin McCarthy at the head of the anti-Parnellites until 1896, he was clearly one of the most powerful forces in that faction. Col. Edward James Saunderson (1837–1906), a wealthy landowner, was leader of the Ulster Unionists and an important member of the Ulster Loyalist Anti-Repeal Union. It was he who had invited Lord Randolph Churchill to Belfast in 1886—a visit that did much to harden Unionist determination to oppose Home Rule by force if necessary.

[4] 'I. [Iris] Olkyrn' was the pseudonym of Alice Milligan (1866–1953) who, although a Northern Irish Presbyterian, had espoused the nationalist cause and who in 1896 was to co-found and edit the nationalist magazine *Shan Van Vocht*. Her letter, printed on the front page of *United Ireland*, 16 Dec 1893, is of interest for its bearing on WBY's later poem, 'The Grey Rock' (*VP*, 270–6). It dealt with the question of whether 'men of culture and taste, for the sake of developing Irish literature,' should 'leave the noisy field of political warfare, and attempt to develop their art in some quiet paradise apart . . .' 'I. Olkyrn' thought that WBY had, wrongly, opted out of the political arena, for in replying to Ashe King's lecture he told of a Hindu who had sought perfection in art and found immortality. Recalling an episode in the Gaelic account of the battle of Clontarf in which Dunlaing rejected immortal fairy life to face up to his political and military responsibilities with his friend Murrough, she contrasted this with WBY's Hindu: 'Here we have in the persons of Murrough and Dunlaing, heroism and culture entering the fray side by

the man of letters should keep out of politics, but I remember the examples of Hugo, and Milton, and Dante but only that he should, no matter how strong be his political interests, endeavour to become a master of his craft, and be ever careful to keep rhetoric, or the tendency to think of his audience rather than of the Perfect and the True, out of his writing. It is, however, a pleasure to be misunderstood when the misunderstanding helps to draw out so beautiful a letter.—Yours very truly,

W B Yeats.

Printed letter, *United Ireland*, 23 December 1893 (5). *UP* I. 305–7.

To the Editor of United Ireland, *30 December 1893*

DEAR SIR—In my letter last week I dealt with Mr. King's attack upon partisan politics,[1] but have still a few words to say about his no less vigorous condemnation of our national devotion to oratory. Mr. King has found an ally in Mr. Standish O'Grady, the first Irish man, I believe, who has tried to write Irish history which shall be no mere chronicle of bills and battles, or arid analysis of party dialectics. Mr. O'Grady, having told how the Irish gentry were bribed and wheedled into passing the Act of Union, continues as follows:—"I believe myself that they were stupefied by too much oratory. For the last quarter of a century they had yielded themselves up to the intoxicating delight of fine speaking. This was the age of Grattan, Flood, Hussey Burgh, and other famous rhetoricians, who charmed their ears and darkened their understandings with tropes and figures of ridiculous sublimity, so unlike the plain and honest speaking of Swift and Berkley. Oratory, like pride, comes before a fall, an assertion which universal history bears out."[2]

side. This is as it should be. Irish literature cannot be developed in any hedged-in peaceful place, whilst a conflict is raging around. It must be in the thick of the fight, and if brought apart from it and commanded to declare spiritual gospels to an awaiting world, the silence will come at last. . . .' In re-treating this incident for 'The Grey Rock' in the changed political climate of 1912–13, WBY reverses the moral drawn by Miss Milligan, suggesting that Dunlaing made the wrong choice in deserting the goddess and muse Aoife for worldly praise.

  [1] See preceding letter.

  [2] The quotation is taken verbatim from Standish James O'Grady's *The Story of Ireland* (181–2), which had been published earlier in the month. Henry Grattan (1746–1820) was one of the greatest orators of his day and a member first of the Irish Parliament (1775–97) and, after the Act of Union, of the English Parliament (1805–20). Henry Flood (1732–91), lawyer, statesman, and orator, was largely responsible for the organization of a powerful opposition to the English party in the Irish Parliament; his reputation as an orator derived from his powers of reasoning and invective, qualities displayed to the full after he quarrelled with Gratton. Walter Hussey Burgh (1742–83), a distinguished statesman, lawyer, and outstanding orator, worked closely with Gratton in the Irish Parliament on several important issues,

Now, I have not sufficient knowledge of the period and of its oratory to know whether Mr. O'Grady speaks correctly or not, and I am certainly no more inclined to agree with his view than with Mr. King's description of oratory as a "mountebank art."[3] But I do feel, upon the other hand, that historians like Mr. O'Grady do not make statements like this without weighty reasons. I believe that the reason in this case is, that Mr. O'Grady, like Mr. King, has seen that though fondness for oratory is inevitable and necessary in a country like Ireland, it is none the less a danger and a cause of many evils, and that he has allowed his fears for the present to colour his impressions of the past.

It is of the very nature of oratory that the orator should make his hearers feel he is convinced of what he is saying, and, therefore, he is for ever tempted to assume, for the sake of effect, a show of sincerity and vehement conviction, or, what is worse, to become really sincere and vehemently convinced about things of which he has no adequate knowledge. In the world God made are none but probabilities, and, as the Persian poet sings, a hair divides the false and true; but too often there are none but certainties in the world of the orator.[4] If once a nation is thoroughly stupefied by oratory of this kind, she loses all sense of proportion, all sense of reality, for has she not discovered that her orators can convince themselves and her of anything at a few minutes' notice, and bring both, by the pleasant pathway of a few similes, a few vehement gestures, to that certainty which the scholar attains after years of research, and the philosopher after a lifetime of thought? Once set her upon that pathway and she will come to the fall Mr. O'Grady speaks of, for she will find no high and remote thing anywhere, nothing worth making herself really uncomfortable about. Convictions will be cheap and common in her world, and if a few be damaged or battered for a price, behold there are plenty of others to be had for the asking. We are a nation of orators, and must suffer the defects of our quality with a good grace; but we would soon go headlong into unreality were there not men like Mr King and Mr O'Grady ever ready to raise the red flag before us.[5] Has not oratory

notably the repeal of legislation restricting Irish trade. He was said on occasion to have excelled even Grattan as a speaker.

[3] This was one of the remarks in Ashe King's 8 Dec lecture (see preceding letter) that had upset the leader writer of *United Ireland* on 16 Dec, for 'as the Celts are an oratorical race we must conclude, that in Mr. King's opinion, there is a great deal of the mountebank in your genuine Celt.'

[4] See *The Rubáiyát of Omar Khayyám*, trans. Edward FitzGerald (1859), stanza 50. After the turn of the century, WBY was to distinguish more carefully between 'oratory' and 'rhetoric' as legitimate and illegitimate uses of the arts of language. At this time, and smarting under the attacks of orators like J. F. Taylor (see p. 313), he is less precise about the difference.

[5] WBY's 'nation of orators' seems to combine *United Ireland*'s 'the Celts are an oratorical race' (see n. 3 above) and the observation that Oscar Wilde had made to him, 'we are a nation of brilliant failures, but we are the greatest talkers since the Greeks' (*Aut*, 135). The red flag is a reference to a recent Act of Parliament whereby automobiles had to be preceded by a man carrying a red flag to warn pedestrians and other traffic.

played the devil with us of late in public life, for have we not seen a number of our politicians affirm with every mark of passionate sincerity that Mr Parnell was the only possible leader, and then a few hours after, with equal passion, that he was the one leader quite impossible? Do not our newspapers, with their daily tide of written oratory, make us cry out, "O God, if this be sincerity, give us a little insincerity, a little of the self-possession, of the self-mastery that go to a conscious lie." Is not our social life ruined by the oratorical person? Whether his subject be the sins of the Parnellites or the anti-Parnellites, protection, the liquor laws, literature, or philosophy, all worthy and kindly converse dies when he enters a room. We all know his vehement intolerance—for how can he be tolerant whose world contains none but certainties?—his exaggerated opinions—for how can he be moderate who must always have a profound conviction?—his scorn of delicate half lights and quiet beauty—for how can he who is ever affirming and declaring understand that the gentle shall inherit the earth?

But what is the remedy for all this? Must we give up oratory? Surely no! But let us respect the orator, not because he makes an effect, but because he tells a new, forgotten, or seasonable truth, and, above all, let us war upon the idea that the expedient is justifiable in public life. I have heard even Parnellites say that Mr. Healy was justified from the point of view of his party, because his underbred and untruthful articles and speeches helped more than anything else to bring about the change which took place in Irish opinion.[6] And, above all, let us attack the cause of these evils, and educate our people by philosophy and literature, for these teach there is a truth and a beauty which, not being made by hands, are above all expediencies, above all nations; and first, as a small help towards this education, let us cease to clamour and call out "West-Briton!" Whenever a lecturer talks of our national dangers and weaknesses, do not let us be blind to what is true in his criticism because of some passing over-emphasis, some chance exaggeration of phrase.—Yours very truly,

W B Yeats.

P.S.—While thanking you for your kind review of "The Celtic Twilight," I take this opportunity of saying it is not "founded upon fact," as your review says, but, with the exception of one or two changes of name and place, literally true. Your reviewer doubts the existence of "sorcery" in Ireland. He should read a series of letters from a Dublin glass-stainer given in Dr. Adam Clark's memoirs. He will find there far more "sensation" than anything in my work. They refer to events which came under the eyes of the

---

[6] Timothy Healy (see pp. 13, 265) was one of the bitterest and most effective of Parnell's opponents after the split.

glass-stainer, of whose good faith Dr. Clark, a celebrated theologian, as you will remember, appears to have had no doubt whatever.[7]

Printed letter, *United Ireland*, 30 December 1893 (1). *UP* 1. 307–10.

[7] John McGrath, in a lengthy review in *United Ireland*, 23 Dec 1893 (5), had remarked that, notwithstanding WBY's assertion that the stories in *The Celtic Twilight* were 'more or less founded on fact', it was 'sometimes hard to know whether or not one should treat Mr. Yeats seriously. . . . The story of "The Sorcerers"—to adopt an expression I once heard used by a County Down fisherman—rather "hits me on the mouth".' None of the various volumes of biography or memoirs of the Revd Adam Clarke (*c.* 1762–1832), the famous Wesleyan preacher, theological writer, and biblical commentator, to which WBY could have had access yields any trace of letters from the Dublin glass-stainer he mentions here.

1894

To Mrs Chan-Toon,[1] 8 January 1894

ALS, with envelope, listed in Dobell's catalogue, December 1925, Item 391.

To Frederick Langbridge, 21 January [1894]

3 Blenheim Road | Bedford Park | Chiswick | London | W
Jan 21

My dear Langbridge

I have written to W T Coyne who usually does the literary leaders in the Freeman & asked him to say what he can for the magazine. I am not however very hopeful of the result of an appeal of this kind. Even Stead has failed utterly I hear to get the money he asked ⟨in much the same way⟩.[1] I beleive however the money can be got other wise. I went yesterday evening & saw Edward Downey (late of Ward & Downey) & urged upon him that now was the ⟨psychological⟩ fit moment if he wished to do anything for Irish publishing (I knew he had been prepared to put £1000 in Duffy proposed

---

[1] Mrs Mabel Chan Toon, née Cosgrave (b. 1872), had married a nephew of the King of Burma. In 1925 she was accused for forging *For Love of the King*, a 'Burmese Masque', which she alleged was by Oscar Wilde. In January 1926 she was imprisoned for theft under the name of Mrs Wodehouse Pearse. Thereafter she posed variously as Princess Chan Toon and Princess Arakan, and claimed that she had been Wilde's fiancée and Eamon de Valera's secretary. Since she attempted to sell forged letters from Wilde in 1926, this letter to WBY, advertised by Dobells but otherwise untraced, may have been spurious.

[1] No appeal on behalf of *The Old Country* (see p. 361) appeared in the *Freeman's Journal*, and WBY's letter to W. P. Coyne (see p. 308) has not survived. W. T. Stead (see p. 366) had made an abortive attempt in the summer of 1893 to launch *Borderland*, a 'Quarterly Review and Index of the Periodical Literature Relating to the Occult World'. From the prospectus (advertised in the *Irish Theosophist*, 15 June 1893) it appears that Stead hoped the magazine might become 'a veritable College of the Occult Sciences'. The annual subscription was to have been 10s, but the first number, due to appear on 1 July 1893, seems not to have been published.

company) & found that he was inclined to go into such a venture, that he had in fact almost decided upon making the attempt him self when he heard of your venture. He is not hopeful of the success of a magazine but beleives entirely in the chance that lies before an Irish publishing house. If he went into such a thing he would require I think to have the London part of the business in his hands. It is however absolutely necessary that he should have an opportunity of consulting with either you or Bryers & he suggests that one or other might perhaps be able to come over to London. I urged upon him that it would not do to bring either so far unless he intended business & he said he did. Could not you & Bryers raise enough money to run the magazine part of the project & Downey raise money for the publishing? Perhaps they cannot be seperated in this way ⟨but each would help out other I think⟩ but at any rate it seems to me that there ought to be a conference between you & Downey or Briers & Downey.

I think it is very possible that when I return to Dublin I may be able to get £200 or so there but am not sure. I can do nothing by letter. I beleive your prospects will be greatly improved in every way if you join Downey with yourself & Bryers. I imagine he can get money over & above what he him self has & he is trusted by Irish men here.[2]

The Fairy article will need a few slight alterations. I gave it as a lecture & wrote it for that & I must take the tone of the lecture out of it.[3] I must give a couple of days to it. I dont want to give the time until I hear it is quite due. As soon as you have ways & means settled ⟨2 *lines cancelled*⟩ I will send it. My play keeps me busy for three days still. Give me as long as you can & then let me know & you will have the article at once. It would illustrate well by the by.

Yours ever
W B Yeats

You have E Downeys address of course as he wrote for you so I do not send it.[4]

ALS Private. Shotaro Oshima, *W. B. Yeats and Japan* (Tokyo, 1965), 16–17.

[2] Nothing came of this hoped-for collaboration between Langbridge, Downey, and George Bryers of Sealey, Bryers & Walker over a monthly *Old Country*. For Edmund Downey's role in the General Publishing Company (later the National Publishing Company) proposed in 1892 by Gavan Duffy, see p. 310, n. 1.
[3] Presumably the lecture on 'Irish Fairy Lore' which WBY had given in Belfast on 21 Nov 1893 (see p. 367). Excerpts from this lecture were published in the *Annual Reports and Proceedings* of the Belfast Naturalists' Field Club, ser. II, vol. IV (1894), 46–8.
[4] Downey had contributed a humorous short story, 'An Italian from Cork', to the 1893 Christmas Annual, *The Old Country* (see p. 366, n. 1). He was living at this time at Munster House, Lucien Road, Tooting Common, London SW.

To John O'Leary, 5 [February 1894]

3 Blenheim Road | Bedford Park | Chiswick- | London. W

Jan 5th[1]

Dear M^r O'Leary

The cause of the delay about the money is this. I owed last summer about £14 but while over here had as much money as I required for my expenses & some pounds over with which I paid a portion of my debts—a number of small sums which I was afraid of forgetting—& set aside £4 or £5 as well to lessen the remainder. The day before I started for Ireland there was a sudden crisis here at home, which swept away £4. When I got back to Ireland my income went down at once for various reasens. I had not expected this & I never have had more than a few shillings over my expenses which few shillings went in small driblets into my only extravagence, a few picture frames an[d] the like. But including this I do not think I have ever spent more than 25/- a week. Now that I am back here I shall have money again but at the present moment have little more than my fare to Paris where I am to stay with some friends for ten days or so. I do not look upon this as an extravagence however as I must live somewhere. I always contribute here of course. I have for about two months now done work which cannot bring in a penny for a month or two. I have been writing a play ever since I came over, for instance, which is to be produced in March & am now merely going to Paris, until the time comes for the rehersals.[2] I thought to pay you something at Xmas when I got £10 as the second instalment for the Celtic Twilight but found that my landlady absorbed too much of it & with the exception of a couple of pounds from the "Bookman" I have had nothing since.[3] Mean while I have plenty of comissions for work if I can only do it & can I think promise the £7.10 or the bulk of it before the end of March—or at any rate the bulk of it.

Please burn this letter.

Mrs Rowley's address is

11 Rue Traklin

Avenue du Bord du Boulugne

This last work does not look very legible but it is a copy of the word

---

[1] Evidently a mistake for 5 February; see subsequent letters of about this time.

[2] WBY's one-act play, *The Land of Heart's Desire*, was to be produced in March 1894 by Florence Farr (Mrs Emery) at the Avenue Theatre, as a curtain-raiser with Todhunter's *The Comedy of Sighs*.

[3] Fisher Unwin had published *The Celtic Twilight* in December 1893, while WBY was still in Dublin, lodging at 56 North Circular Road. Two of his poems had appeared in the *Bookman* at the end of 1893: 'The Stolen Bride' (*VP*, 143–5; reprinted as 'The Host of the Air') in November and 'Wisdom and Dreams' (*VP*, 743) in December; a review of E. J. Ellis's long poem *Seen in Three Days* (1893) appeared in the February 1894 *Bookman* (*UP* 1. 317–20).

as written by Miss Gonne who is also in Paris. I have the address also in Mrs Rowley writing but there it is absolutely illegible.[4]

Yours truly
W B Yeats

⟨PS No 2—
Grein of the "Independent Literary Society"[5] or some such⟩

[*Diagonally across top of first page*]
I thought I had given you "the Celtic Twilight" but finding I had not went to Lawrence & Bullen to get you a [copy] & found both out of town. You shall have one immediately.

ALS Berg. Partly in Wade (dated 5 January 1894), 228–9.

To John O'Leary, 7 February [1894]

3 Blenheim Road | Bedford Park | Chiswick | London W
Feb 7th

Dear M^r O'Leary

An egg I had thought the reverse of ripe hatched last night unexpectedly, hence I send £1 to the lessening of the debt.[1] If the hatching of the next were a little more certain I would send a few shilling more but cannot as things are. The effort to get my play finished has tired me out & now that it is done & gone to the typewritter for the actors I shall rest till rehersals begin. I am going to Paris to night to say [*for* stay] with the Mathers at 1 Avenue Duquesne & am taking introductions to Verlaine & Melermè, other

---

[4] The Paris address of Mrs Rowley (see p. 290) appears to have been Rue Traktir, Avenue du Bois de Boulogne (16e).

[5] J. T. Grein (1862–1935) was born in Amsterdam and although set to work in a bank spent his free time in visiting and writing about the theatre. He moved to London in 1885 and quickly involved himself in the English stage. Already an admirer of Ibsen, he witnessed the beginnings of Antoine's Théâtre Libre during an extended business trip to Paris in 1886–7 and in 1889 he proposed a similar experiment in England. On 13 Mar 1891 the Independent Theatre Society's first production, Ibsen's *Ghosts*, provoked bitter hostility, but the club continued to produce plays, including those by Shaw, George Moore, and Todhunter, throughout the early 1890s. WBY, who may have heard of Grein from Shaw or Todhunter, would have been interested in his theatrical schemes, and later saw the Irish Literary Theatre as part of the same dramatic reaction against the commercial theatre, albeit with different aesthetic goals. Because of business commitments, Grein took a less active role in the Independent Theatre after March 1895, although he retained a life-long interest in the drama and theatrical projects.

[1] See preceding letter.

introductions I have refused,[2] for just now I want a quiet dream with the holy Kabala for bible & naught else, for I am tired—tired.

I send you a Celtic Twilight.

Yours ever

W B Yeats

ALS Berg. Wade, 229–30.

To J. P. Quinn,[1] 9 February [1894]

1 Avenue Duqesne[2] | Paris.

Feb 9th

My dear Quin

Weekes has written to me in an almost heart broken fashion about his Homer. Would you kindly post it to him at 5 Churchill Villas. Sandymount.[3]

I am as you will see by the address in Paris. I am resting after completing my Irish drama & waiting for the rehersals to begin when I must return. My little play has turned out one of my best things. I got here yesterday morning. I have not yet seen Miss Gonne who is ill but will probably tomorrow. ⟨I have not liked to call without hearing.⟩[4] I am staying with the Mathers—my occult friends & have introductions to a good many French men of letters but as I am anxious to rest after the work on the play shall use two or three of these. I expect to see Mrs Rowley tonight.

Yr ever

W B Yeats

ALS MBY.

[2] For MacGregor Mathers and his wife, see p. 266.

[1] See p. 303.

[2] The Paris flat of MacGregor Mathers and his wife described by WBY (*Mem*, 73–4); Mathers had an income from a member of the Golden Dawn, Miss Annie E. F. Horniman (1860–1937), which provided for 'some frater or soror, as we are called staying with him'.

[3] Evidently a book belonging to Charles Weekes (see p. 347, n. 1), borrowed by WBY and left behind at 56 North Circular Road, Dublin.

[4] WBY's delicacy was not misplaced since, although he did not know it, MG was two-months pregnant. She was to give birth to a daughter, Iseult, on 6 Aug.

To D. J. O'Donoghue, 13 February [*1894*][1]

1 Avenue Duquesne | Paris
13 Feb

My dear O Donoghue

I give on the next page a little scrap of verse which is all I can remember away from my MS. It means much the same as "the Man who dreamed of Fairy Land". The wind is the vague idealisms & impossible hopes which blow in upon us to the ruin of near & common & substantial ambitions—some such explination had better be given by who ever reads it. It is out of my little play "The Land of Hearts Desire" which will be performed in March.[2]

Yours ever
W B Yeats

The Wind blows out of the Gates of the Day,
The wind blows over the lonely of heart,
And the lonely of heart is withered away;
But the fairies dance in a place apart,
Shaking their milk white feet in a ring,
Tossing their milk white arms in the air,
For they hear the wind laugh, & murmur & sing
Of a land where even the old are fair,
And even the wise are merry of tongue;
But I heard a reed of Cooluny say
When the wind has laughed & murmured & sung
The lonely of heart must wither away.

ALS Berg.

[1] This letter is tipped into Elizabeth Houghton's copy of *The Land of Heart's Desire*; the book also has W. T. H. Howe's bookplate.
[2] The poem appears with some alterations as the fairy's song (*VPI*, 194–5) in *The Land of Heart's Desire*. It is probable that O'Donoghue had asked WBY for some new verse of his to be recited at a social gathering of the Irish Literary Society, London.

To Stéphane Mallarmé,[1] [24 February 1894]

1 Avenue Duquesne | Champ de Mars
Saturday.

Dear Sir

Mr Paul Verlaine knowing my great wish to meet you has told me to mention his name as an introduction.[2] I am leaving Paris for London on Monday or Tuesday & will therefore call upon Sunday afternoon about 4 or 4.30 on the chance of finding you.[3] I may mention that Mr Henley is a friend of mine & that I ⟨like your self⟩ am a contributor to the National Observer.

Yours sincerely
W B Yeats.

Do not trouble to write as I will take my chance of finding you.

ALS Doucet. *TLS*, 26 November 1954 (759); Stéphane Mallarmé, *Correspondance*, vol. VI, ed. H. Mondor and L. J. Austin (Paris, 1981), 223.

[1] Stéphane Mallarmé (1842–98), the French poet and leader of the Symbolist movement, first became known for his translation of Edgar Allan Poe's 'The Raven' (1875). This was followed by his own *L'Après-midi d'un faune* (1876), *Poésies* (1877), *Vers et prose* (1893), and a prose work, *Divagations* (1897). A schoolmaster for many years, he taught English at first in the provinces and later in Paris *lycées*; he was to retire later in this year to Valvins, near Fontainebleau, where he died. Reading Roger Fry's translation of Mallarmé in early May 1937, WBY wrote to Dorothy Wellesley (Private), 'I find it exciting as it shows me the road I & others of my time went for certain furlongs. It is not the way I go now but one of the legitimate roads. . . . He escapes from history you & I are in history the history of the mind.'

[2] The French poet Paul Verlaine (1844–96) had started writing in the early 1860s under the influence of the Parnassians and Baudelaire. His brief, intense but troubled friendship with Rimbaud, which began in 1871, his estrangement from his wife, his imprisonment and reconversion to Catholicism gave emotional depth to the musical and impressionistic style that he had already begun to create and resulted in his two major collections of poetry, *Romances sans Paroles* (1874) and *Sagesse* (1881). WBY called on Verlaine during this visit to Paris 'in a little room at the top of a tenement house in the Rue St Jacques, sitting in an easy chair, with his bad leg swaddled in many bandages'; finding him 'a great temperament, the servant of a great daimon', he recorded his memories of 'Verlaine in 1894' in the *Savoy*, April 1896 (*UP* I. 397–9), later revising his account in *Aut* (341–2).

[3] Mallarmé's literary 'evenings' in the Rue de Rome were famous among those *au fait* with contemporary poetry. WBY, however, did not succeed in meeting him, for Mallarmé had just set out for England, where he was to deliver a series of lectures organized by JBY's friend Frederick York Powell. Mallarmé's daughter, Geneviève, reported WBY's note and visit in a letter to her father of 26 Feb 1894: 'Il en est venue une autre [lettre], d'un espèce d'Anglais, qui est arrivé hier après-midi, voulant te voir et ne sachant pas un mot de francais. Maman a mimé ton voyage et il a enfin saisi, puis s'est retiré.' (Mallarmé *Correspondance*, III. 235). The French classes at Morris's (see p. 64) had evidently left much to be desired.

To Frederick Langbridge, 3 March [*1894*]

3 Blenheim Road | Bedford Park | Chiswick. W
March 3rd

My dear Langbridge.

I returned from Paris a couple of days ago & saw Johnson upon the earliest available date (last night). I was unable to return before as I was waiting for a dramatic performance which was three times postponed & which I am to write about.[1]

Johnson says that he would put his name to the circular but only on the condition that you put him in possession of the exact condition of affairs, as he would not like to connect his name—except of course in the minor capacity of proposed contributor—with an attempt which came to nothing. He would want to know exactly how you stand financially etc. Mrs Hinkson would put her name provided doing so implies no responsibility.[2] I have for the moment mislaid your last letter to me. You suggested I remember my going to some London publishing houses to see if they would take up the venture. Do you meen, take it up as agents, as part proprietors or as whole proprietors? If you have a certain amount of capital could you not perhaps begin with a quarterly? You would of course lose More's story however by this I suppose. Downey might perhaps share this minor risk.[3]

Yrs ever
W B Yeats.

You might perhaps write direct to Johnson about his difficulty. He is at 20 Fitzroy St.[4]

ALS Texas.

[1] On 26 Feb 1894 WBY, with MG, attended one of the two performances at the Théâtre de la Gaîté in Paris of the poetic drama *Axël*, by the Symbolist writer Philippe-Auguste Villiers de l'Isle-Adam (1838–89). This performance, coming at a time when WBY was preparing for the first production of one of his own poetical plays, had a profound effect upon him; in the preface to H. P. R. Finberg's translation of *Axël* (1925), dated 20 Sept 1924, he recalled how Villiers's symbols 'became a part of me, and for years to come dominated my imagination. . . . I was in the midst of one of those artistic movements that have the intensity of religious revivals in Wales and are such a temptation to the artist in his solitude.' His enthusiastic review of the play, 'A Symbolic Drama in Paris' (*UP* I. 322–5), appeared in the *Bookman*, April 1894.

[2] KT had contributed a 13-stanza poem, 'November Eve', to Langbridge's 1893 Christmas Annual, *The Old Country* (see p. 365).

[3] Langbridge had apparently been promised a story by George Moore for his projected monthly. For Downey's possible help in financing the magazine, see pp. 375–6.

[4] See p. 239, n. 2.

To A. P. Graves,[1] *11 March* [*1894*]

3 Blenheim Road | Bedford Park | Chiswick. W
March 11th

Dear Mr Graves

I send the poems I promised. You have I think "the Countess Kathleen" so I take none from it.[2]

Yrs ever
W B Yeats

ALS Private.

To John O'Leary, [*28 March 1894*]

THE IRISH LITERARY SOCIETY | LONDON | BLOOMSBURY
MANSION | HART ST. | W.C.

Dear M^r O'Leary

My play comes on tomorrow[1] & I am over head & ears in work at rehersals Etc. But for this I should have written before or at more length now.

You will have since you wrote heard more I doubt not of the quarterly. The proposed list of contents—as it at present stands—was made out by Johnson & myself a couple of weeks ago & sent to Barry O Brien.[2] It is, I think, good but will I have no doubt be greatly modified in practice.

I shall cross over with Johnson when he goes to lecture unless these plays keep me. Should we have a success & I am not very hopeful I shall put on another & longer play—also Irish—I mean if Miss Farr find that she can

---

[1] Alfred Perceval Graves (1846–1931), born in Dublin, is best remembered for his ballad 'Father O'Flynn' (1889); for many years an inspector of schools in the London borough of Southwark, Graves edited a number of anthologies as well as publishing several volumes of his own verse. The title of his autobiography, *To Return to All That* (1930), echoes that of his more famous son Robert Graves, *Goodbye to All That*, first published in 1929.

[2] Graves had evidently asked WBY to contribute to his anthology, *The Irish Song Book with Original Irish Airs*, published later this year by Fisher Unwin as part of the New Irish Library. He included WBY's 'Down by the Salley Gardens' as no. 39 (p. 55).

[1] The first night of *The Land of Heart's Desire* at the Avenue Theatre was 29 Mar 1894.

[2] On 10 Mar 1894 R. Barry O'Brien had announced to George Sigerson (NLI) that 'The Irish Literary Society have resolved to start a Quarterly Review; and the work of floating it has devolved on Lionel Johnson, Perceval Graves, W. B. Yeats, Edward Garnett, & myself.' The *Irish Home Reading Magazine* (see pp. 344, n. 3) was to make its first appearance in May 1894, with Johnson and Eleanor Hull as co-editors.

keep the theatre open.³ She is desirous of doing my next play as it is a wild mystical thing carefully arranged to be an insult to the regular theatre goer who is hated by both of us. All the plays she is arranging for are studied insults. Next year she might go to Dublin as all her playrights by a curious chance are Irish.⁴

Mrs Rowleys address is

18 Rue Teckler
Bois de Boulogne

if I remember aright.⁵

Yours ever
W B Yeats

[*Across top of first page*]
Your letter to Independent & the Ryan interview very good.⁶

ALS NLI.

To Ernest Rhys, [*c. 12 April 1894*]

3 Blenheim Road | Bedford Park

My dear Rhys

Yes Sunday with great pleasure. My little play goes on again with Shaw but goes off with Todhunter for the present on Monday.¹ I enclose orders

---

³ The season of new plays mounted by Florence Farr (see p. 165) at the Avenue Theatre with the financial backing of Annie Horniman (see p. 379), who was later to perform a similar role in the founding of the Abbey Theatre, Dublin, continued until 7 July 1894. WBY's own play ran until mid-May. Thus he did not accompany Lionel Johnson to Dublin when Johnson went to lecture to the National Literary Society on 'Poetry and Patriotism' (see p. 270, n. 4), at the Leinster Lecture Hall on 26 Apr 1894.

⁴ *The Shadowy Waters*, which gave WBY a good deal of trouble in its composition, was not performed until 4 Jan 1904, when the Irish National Theatre Society produced it in Dublin. Nor did Florence Farr go to Dublin in 1895.

⁵ Cf. pp. 377–8.

⁶ In a letter, dated 15 Mar, published under the heading 'What we mean by Home Rule' in the *Irish Daily Independent*, 16 Mar 1894, JO'L took issue with John Redmond over the meaning of the term, maintaining that 'in so far as any measure falls short of Colonial Home Rule or Repeal of the Union, it will be but a mere temporary settlement of the Irish question.' The *Independent* of 26 Mar carried an interview with Dr Mark Ryan (see p. 184, n. 5), chairman of the Parnellite Irish National League of Great Britain, in which he denounced the anti-Parnellite faction of the Irish Party for their failure to force the Liberals to bring in a full-blooded Home Rule Bill. Like JO'L, Ryan insisted that Home Rule must mean an 'Irish Parliament based on the Colonial system'; both were clearly afraid that the Home Rule movement was being fobbed off with half-way measures such as the Local Government Bill.

¹ *The Land of Heart's Desire* ran with Todhunter's *The Comedy of Sighs* from 29 Mar to 14 Apr 1894, after which the Avenue Theatre closed for rehearsals of George Bernard Shaw's *Arms and the Man*. The Shaw play opened on 21 Apr, with *The Land of Heart's Desire* continuing as curtain-raiser until 12 May. WBY gives an account of these productions in *Aut* (280–3).

for Saturday in case you should care to see the plays again & have friends who would care to. They go very well now & are well received.[2]

Yrs ever
W B Yeats

This elegent paper is not mine & therefore please excuse it.[3]

ALS BL.

To John O'Leary, [*15 April 1894*]

3 Blenheim Road | Bedford Park | Chiswick. W

Dear M^r O'Leary

I have been unable to write for the last three weeks as I have been in the hands of the occulist & without glasses[1]—or I should have written before this. For a couple of years it has been getting more & more difficult for me to do any steady reading as my eyes begin to get uncomfortable in a few minutes. I find now that I am to never read more than a quarter of an hour at a time. I have then to stop & rest for a few minutes—the same in a less degree applies to writing. I have 'conical cornea' in the left eye and 'stigmatism' in the right. The left eye is now practically useless. At the same time I should get on all right with care. I suppose I shall have to very much dropp reviewing & take to stories entirely which will be better artistically at any rate. The immediate result of all this on top of my work at the theatre has meant very little money. I had hoped to send you some before this. I got last night a bill from Mrs Carew the existence of which I had absolutely forgotten. I shall however I think be able to pay it this week as the Speaker owes me some pounds.[2]

---

[2] This had not been the case on the first night when, as WBY recalls in *Aut* (281), 'For two hours and a half, pit and gallery drowned the voices of the players with boos and jeers. . . .' *The Times* on 30 Mar 1894 (10), remarking on the 'running commentary of titters' which had greeted Todhunter's play, noted that it 'had the misfortune to be preceded by a small piece on an Irish theme, which invited the banter of the house, a measure of the author's eccentricity being afforded by the strange line on the programme:— "The characters are supposed to speak in Gaelic." ' WBY put the audience's hostile reaction down to 'outraged convention', but D. J. O'Donoghue, recalling the incident in the *Irish Independent*, 9 Mar 1908, suggests more plausibly that the trouble arose because the Avenue Theatre had hitherto played mainly pantomime; its normal clientele, deceived by the titles of Todhunter's and WBY's plays, felt themselves cheated of their expected entertainment.

[3] The notepaper is a delicate shade of lavender.

[1] WBY's visit to the oculist seems to have been precipitated by an untimely accident; in recalling the 1894 production of *The Land of Heart's Desire*, SMY wrote to Hone, 3 July 1939 (Texas), that 'Poor Willy lost his glasses down a grating in the Strand the day of the first performance & so saw it as in a dimming mist.'

[2] For Mrs Carew, WBY's landlady at Clontarf in 1892–3, see p. 324. The *Speaker* had published two items by WBY in previous months: 'An Impression' in October 1893 and 'Our Lady of the Hills' in November 1893, both reprinted in *The Celtic Twilight*.

Enough however of such mere bothers.

Todhunters play 'The Comedy of Sighs' was taken off last night.

My little play 'The Land of Hearts Desire' is however considered a fair success & is to be put on again with the play by Shaw which goes on next week. It is being printed by Unwin & will be sold in the Theatre with the programes.[3] The whole venture has had to face the most amazing denunciations from the old type of critics. They have however been so abusive that a reaction has set in which has brought a rather cultivated public to the theatre. The takings at the door rose steadily but not rapidly enough to make it safe to hold on with Todhunters play which was really a brillient peice of work.[4] If Shaw's play does well a new play of mine will be put on—a much more ambitious play than anything I have yet done. It will give you some notion of the row that is going on when I tell you that 'chuckers out' have been hired for the first night of Shaw. They are to be distributed over the theatre & are to put out all people who make a row.[5] The whole venture will be history any way for it is the first contest between the old commercial school of theatrical folk & the new artistic school.

Yrs ever

W B Yeats

ALS NLI. Wade, 230–1.

[3] *The Land of Heart's Desire* was published by Fisher Unwin in April 1894, at 1s.

[4] WBY did not hold to this opinion, and in *Aut* (280) he described Todhunter's play as 'a rambling story told with a little paradoxical wit'. For the critics' reaction, see preceding letter.

[5] There is no confirmation of this statement either in Shaw's letters or in the reviews of *Arms and the Man* when it opened on 21 Apr.

To [*Victor Plarr*][1], *10 May* [*1894*]

3 Blenheim Road | Bedford Park | Chiswick. W
May 10th

Dear Sir

In reply to your circular of the 8th instant I send the enclosed account of my life for 'Men & Women of Our Time'[2] & remain

Yrs very sincely
W B Yeats

To 'The Editor of Men & Women of the Time'

ALS.Philadelphia.

[1] Victor Gustave Plarr (1863–1929), the original of 'Monsieur Verog' in Ezra Pound's poem, *Hugh Selwyn Mauberley*, was at this time Librarian of King's College, London. He published two volumes of verse, *In the Dorian Mood* (1896) and a brief epic based on Nordic myth, *The Tragedy of Asgard* (1905); his reminiscences of Ernest Dowson appeared in 1914. In 1897 he became Librarian to the Royal College of Surgeons, a post which he held until his death.

In 1895 and 1899 Plarr edited *Men and Women of the Time*, a compendium in which WBY's name was included for the first time in the 14th edn., published in late April 1895.

[2] Plarr announced in the introduction to the 14th edn. that he had sent out 'hundreds of courteously-worded requests for information' in 1894. Although WBY's enclosure with this letter does not survive, it was presumably very close to, if not identical with, the paragraph that was printed about him in the 1895 *Men and Women of the Time* (918–19) and gives an insight into the way he wanted to present himself to the public at this period:

YEATS, W. B., Irish poet, was born on June 13, 1865, at Sandymount, Dublin, and is the son of J. B. Yeats, portrait painter and illustrator. He spent the greatest portion of his childhood in Sligo with his grandparents, but joined his father and mother in London when about nine years old, and then for some years attended the Godolphin School, Hammersmith, as a day scholar, spending his holidays usually in the West of Ireland. When he was fifteen he removed with his parents to Dublin, and there attended the Erasmus Smith School in Harcourt Street. When about nineteen he began studying art at the Royal Dublin Society, but soon gave up this for literature, contributing articles and poems to the *Dublin University Review*, and other Irish periodicals. In 1888 [*sic*] he moved to London, and in 1889 published his first book of verse, "The Wanderings of Oisin" (Kegan Paul, Trench & Co.), and his first book of prose, "Fairy and Folk Tales" (Walter Scott). The latter is a compilation from the Irish Folk-Lorists, with notes based on Mr. Yeats's own investigations in the West of Ireland. He has since published "Stories from Carleton" (Walter Scott, 1890), a compilation; "Irish Tales" (Putnam's, 1891), a compilation; "John Sherman and Dhoya" (T. Fisher Unwin's *Pseudonym Library*, 1891), two stories about the West of Ireland; "The Countess Kathleen and Various Legends and Lyrics" (T. Fisher Unwin, 1892); "The Celtic Twilight" (Laurence & Bullen, 1893), a volume of essays mainly about Irish fairy lore; "The Poems of William Blake" (Laurence & Bullen), a compilation; "The Land of Hearts Desire," a one-act play in verse, acted at the Avenue Theatre, London, for the six weeks beginning March 29, 1894; and, together with Mr. Edwin J. Ellis, "The Works of William Blake" (B. Quaritch, 1893), a book in three volumes, the first of which [*sic*] gives for the first time a complete collection of Blake's writing, and the other two an analysis and exposition of the philosophy of his so-called prophetic works. Mr. Yeats has also been a frequent contributor to the *National Observer* and the *Bookman*, and has published poems in the two books of the "Rhymer's Club."

To Louise Imogen Guiney,[1] *11 [May 1894]*

3 Blenheim Road | Bedford Park | Chiswick. | London. W

March[2] 11th

My dear Miss Guiney

I send you a little book of mine which may amuse you—a play acted at the Avenue Theatre—with tolerable success—it is just finishing a run of about six weeks—& a book of essays.[3] Nothing but an overwhelming habit of procrastination has prevented me writing to you long ago to thank you for the beautiful article you wrote about the Countess Kathleen. It has introduced me for the first time to those lovely lines of Nash's begining

'Brightness falls from the air'

than which there is nothing upon this earth more wonderful.[4]

I am busy with a new play 'The Shadowy Waters' which shall be acted this Autumn if all goes well. The 'Avenue' has taken it.[5]

I hope you are prospering with your work—getting more charming little bits of history, French or other wise,[6] or new vigerous and touching lyrics on to the stocks & off them into the wide seas.

Yours ever

W B Yeats

ALS Holy Cross.

To T. Fisher Unwin, 18 May [1894]

3 Blenheim Road | Bedford Park. | W.

May 18th.

Dear M[r] Unwin

I enclose the agreement about the 'Land of Hearts Desire' signed also a receipt which I thought I had sent long ago.

M[rs] Emery ('Miss Florence Far') has asked me to remind you about

---

[1] See p. 222, n. 4.

[2] A mistake for 'May'; this letter could not have been written in March.

[3] i.e. *The Land of Heart's Desire* and *The Celtic Twilight.*

[4] Miss Guiney's review of *The Countess Kathleen,* titled 'Enter William Butler Yeats', appeared in the New York *Independent,* 28 Dec 1893 (4). She introduced WBY to her American readers as 'a genius, and unlike anybody; robed with fantasies', and described the title play as having 'the essence of literary perfection in every line and phrase'. Observing that WBY 'finds used meters and plain words serviceable and draws rich results from simplest elements', she discovered in this 'something of the sheer miracle of our early English' and quoted Thomas Nashe's famous lines from 'In Time of Pestilence' (which were to become one of WBY's favourite quotations) in support of this.

[5] See p. 384, n. 4.

[6] For her *Monsieur Henri,* see p. 348, n. 5.

returning to her the original Beardsley drawing from which you took the cover of my play.[1]

Yours sincerely
W B Yeats

Thank you very much for the invitation to meet the book sellers. I sent acceptance to you at Cliffords Inn Hall which was I suppose the correct procedure.[2]

ALS Texas.

To Richard Le Gallienne, 28 May [1894]

3 Blenheim Road | Bedford Park | Chiswick. W
May 28th.

My dear Le Gallienne

I have heard with the deepest sympathy of your great sorrow[1] & for some days the desire to write & tell you so has competed in my mind with the fear that you might not think [me] sufficiently intimate a friend & find my words intrusive. When we are in the presence of death there is nothing to be said except what has been said from the beginning of the world; our new philosophies, our new sureties leave us & we have nothing but the old faith that the dead are happier than the living & that they are always some where near us.

Bleive me yours with utmost sympathy
W B Yeats.

ALS Texas.

[1] The design by Aubrey Beardsley (1872–98) for the Avenue Theatre poster was reproduced on the left-hand half of both the cover and the title-page of the first (1894) edn. of *The Land of Heart's Desire* (see *Bibl*, 29).

[2] On 20 May 1894 Fisher Unwin held a reception in the old Hall of Clifford's Inn 'to meet the booksellers of London', on the occasion of the opening of an exhibition of pictures of Himalayan scenery by Arthur David McCormick (1860–1943), artist with Sir Martin Conway's expedition to the Karakorams, 1892–3. Unwin, who was himself a keen mountaineer, published Conway's *Climbing and Exploration in the Karakoram-Himalayas*, with 300 illustrations by McCormick, on 16 May. Besides a large number of booksellers, many artists and literary figures attended the reception, among them Aubrey Beardsley, Walter Sickert, and Samuel Butler. Clifford's Inn, one of the Inns of Court situated close to Chancery Lane, was demolished in 1935.

[1] Le Gallienne's first wife, Eliza Mildred, née Lee (1867–94), died of typhoid fever on 21 May 1894. They had been married in October 1891.

To Thomas Hutchinson,[1] *26 June* [*1894*]

3 Blenheim Road | Bedford Park | Chiswick. W

June 26th—

Dear Sir

I have long had it in my mind to write & thank you for your pleasent verses[2] but one thing or another has put it out of my head. Accept my best thanks

And beleive me yours

very truly

W B Yeats

ALS Manchester.

[1] Thomas Hutchinson (1856–1938), headmaster of Pegswood Voluntary Board School, Northumberland, for more than 40 years, was the author of *An Essay on the Life and Genius of Robert Burns* (1887), *Ballades and Other Rhymes of a Country Bookworm* (1888), *Jolts and Jingles: A Book of Poems for Young People* (1889), and *Fireside Flittings: A Book of Homely Essays* (1890).

[2] This letter is pasted into a copy of *The Wanderings of Oisin*; on the flyleaf of the book are Hutchinson's 'pleasant verses' addressed to WBY on his twenty-ninth birthday:

> To W. B. Yeats: 13/6/94.
> Although your land out-does ours
>   In all things in which there scare is,
> In its ruins and round towers,
>   In its phantoms and its fairies,
> And, perchance, because so doing
>   Has been deemed by ours a dire land,—
> We our misdeeds now are ruing,
>   And our hearts go out to Ireland.
>
> And how better could we show it
>   Than by making this a mirth-day,
> And dispatching to her Poet
>   Joyous greetings on his birthday?
> Sir, your health! and inspiration
>   To your Muse for fifty years yet!
> May she win the Irish nation
>   Myriad smiles and myriad tears yet.
>   T.H.

In August 1901 WBY wrote again to Hutchinson (Kansas) to thank him for a letter in praise of *The Countess Cathleen*; on 28 May 1901 he had described him to Lady Gregory (MBY) as 'the man who used to write to me on my birthday &, if I remember rightly he sent me a birthday ode.'

To John O'Leary, 26 June [*1894*]

3 Blenheim Rd | Bedford Park | Chiswick. W
June 26th.

Dear M^r O'Leary

I fear I never sent you a copy of my play. I now do so. The edition is quite exausted. An edition has been arranged for in America & Unwin is considering the wisdom of a new edition here.[1] George Russell has as I dare say you know published a little book of verse which is exceeding wonderful. I think we will be able to organize a reception for it. It is about the best peice of poetical work done by any Irish man this good while back. It is the kind of book which inevitably lives down big histories & long novels & the like. It is full of sweetness & subtelty & may well prove to have three or four immortal pages.[2] I send you 'The Second Book of the Rhymers Club' in which everybody is tolerably good except the Trinity College men, Rolleston, Hillier, Todhunter & Greene who are intollerably bad as was to be expected—Todhunter is of course skillful enough with more matter of fact themes & quite admits the dreadful burden of the T C D tradition—& some are exceeding good notably, Plar, Dowson, Johnson & Le Galliene.[3]

I should have gone to Dublin before this even though it were but to return in the autumn for the performance of my new play but for sheer impecuniosity which I am about to clear off to some extent by an Irish Anthology which is nearly finished. ⟨Do you remember getting from me a little green paper covered book called I think 'Irish Ballad Poetry' & containing work by Kickham, & De Veres 'Bard Ethell'? If you have it by you I wish you could send it me as it would save me a very great deal of trouble. I have tried to buy a copy but neither Gils or Duffy's agent here

---

[1] The first American edition of *The Land of Heart's Desire* was published in Chicago by Stone and Kimball in 1894. The next English printing of the play was in *Poems* (1895).

[2] AE's *Homeward, Songs by the Way* was published in Dublin in June 1894. WBY reviewed it for the *Bookman*, August 1894 (*UP* 1. 336–9) and gave it a further notice in his article 'Dublin Mystics' (*UP* 1. 357–8) in the *Bookman*, May 1895.

[3] *The Second Book of the Rhymers' Club*, to which WBY contributed six poems, was published by Elkin Mathews and John Lane in June 1894. WBY's disparagement of TCD is part of a sustained attack he made on the College during the 1890s. In an article, 'Dublin Scholasticism and Trinity College' (*UP* 1. 231–4), which appeared in *United Ireland*, 30 July 1892, he had written that

Trinity College with the help of the schoolmasters keeps the mind of Ireland for scholasticism with its accompanying weight of mediocrity. All noble life, all noble thought, depends primarily upon enthusiasm, and Trinity College, in abject fear of the National enthusiasm which is at her gates, has shut itself off from every kind of ardour, from every kind of fiery and exultant life. She has gone over body and soul to scholasticism, and scholasticism is but an aspect of the great god, Dagon of the Philistines.

Of the TCD men named, T. W. Rolleston contributed four poems to the anthology, and the poet, novelist, and translator Arthur Cecil Hillier (b. 1858), six; Todhunter contributed six poems, and George Arthur Greene (see p. 236) six.

knows anything of it. It cost 6ᵈ when I bought it.⟩ [*Written across cancelled passage*] I find I was mistaken. The book has just turned up.⁴ I have written a severe article on 'The New Irish Library' which will appear in the August Bookman. An inevitable reorganization of the schemes is at hand & therefore it seemed better to speak out. I beleive that my article will only make patent the latent convictions of all the people here.⁵ Surely the world has not seen a more absurd 'popular series' than this one, & the sale has very properly fallen steadily.

I have no information about the Library Committee or the Nat Lit Society itself though I have written twice for it—the last time to Kelly.⁶

Dora Sigerson is here & she & Miss Piatt came with me to see Bernard Shaws play at the Avenue & were I think well pleased—⁷

Any news of your book. I saw a passing allusion to its approaching publication, in the Pall Mall or Westminster.⁸

Yours ever
W B Yeats

ALS Berg. Wade, 231–3.

⁴ The book was *Street Ballads, Popular Poetry, and Household Songs of Ireland*, collected and arranged by 'Duncathail' (the pseudonym of Ralph Varian), published in Dublin in 1865. Varian (*c.* 1820–*c.* 1886), a native of Cork, was a brother of Mrs. Hester Sigerson. His collection included de Vere's 'The Bard Ethell', and Kickham's poems 'Patrick Sheehan' and 'The Irish Peasant Girl', all three of which WBY reprinted in *BIV*, published by Methuen in March 1895. The Dublin publishers and booksellers M. H. Gill & Co. and James Duffy both had agents in London at this time.

⁵ In the *Bookman* for August 1894, under the title 'Some Irish National Books' (*UP* I. 332–5), WBY reviewed three books, among them the two latest volumes in the New Irish Library series. He attacked both these: *The New Spirit of the Nation*, edited by Martin MacDermott, for its mediocrity and staleness, and *A Parish Providence* by E. M. Lynch, an adaptation of Balzac's *Le Médecin de campagne*, for its crushingly didactic purpose. Extending his criticism to the whole series, he laid the blame for its lack of success on the general editor: 'The truth of the matter is that Sir Charles Gavan Duffy has let that old delusion, didacticism, get the better of his judgement . . . and has given us a library which, however pleasing it be to "the daughter of science, the gift of the god," is, if we except Mr O'Grady's stories [*The Bog of Stars*], little but a cause of blaspheming to mere mortals. . . . '

⁶ i.e. J. T. Kelly (see p. 302, n. 3).

⁷ The only daughter of J. J. Piatt (see p. 41) had been a particular friend of both the Sigerson girls and was now, presumably, staying with them, since her parents had returned to America in 1893.

⁸ 'Literary Notes', in the *Pall Mall Gazette* of 23 June 1894, contained two paragraphs on the unsatisfactory quality and quantity of the New Irish Library (see n. 5 above), concluding: 'By the way, Mr John O'Leary's memoirs will be shortly published, and his views on the Young Ireland period and personages will be very different from those of Sir Charles Duffy.' In fact, *Recollections of Fenians and Fenianism* (see p. 219) did not appear until 1896.

To Constance Gore-Booth, 28 June [*1894*]¹

3 Blenheim Road | Bedford Park | Chiswick. W.

June 28th

My dear Miss Gore Booth

I went to see Mrs Mathers yesterday to ask her if she would tell your fortune & Miss Gyle's² & fared much better in the matter than I expected without faring very well. She at first refused absolutely on the ground that she had ceased to tell them at all except when she was certain that her doing so would do good, but after a moments thought said that if either you or Miss Gyles thought you were at a great crisis ⟨in your lives⟩ of any kind & would promise to consider carefully any advice she gave, she would devine on the matter. She would however only tell the fortune of the one whose affairs were at this crisis. If there fore you write to me that one of you feels it *of great importance* ⟨to be told about the future⟩ I will write & tell Mrs Mathers and she will arrange a meeting before she returns to Paris which will be in a week. She is, despite her youth, a very advanced Kabalist & always busy & very little of the world so you must grant to her these exacting conditions.³ She has really had to adopt this attitude because if she did not she would be always doing things for people & never getting on with her own work. Of course even the most expert will at times make mistakes but she is usually wonderfully accurate, marvellously intuitive, so that if you do decide to consult her you will probably hear truth. Though she will only tell for one you must both come to see her as she is charming.

Yrs snly

W B Yeats

⟨She thought it would be⟩

ALS Northwestern.

¹ WBY seems to have been meeting Constance Gore-Booth in the summer of 1894, for he inscribed a copy of *The Land of Heart's Desire* to her on 18 July 1894.

² Althea Gyles (1867–1949), a symbolist painter whom WBY describes anonymously in *Aut* (237–8), was born in Co. Waterford. Like Constance Gore-Booth, she came from a well-connected Ascendancy family, but quarrelled with her father over her decision to study art and lived in poverty at first in Dublin, where she studied at the Art School with WBY, and later, in the early 1890s, in London. There she attended Pedders and, from 1893, the Slade School, at which Con Gore-Booth was also a student. She was later to design the covers of WBY's *The Secret Rose, Poems* (1899), and *The Wind among the Reeds*.

³ Like Althea Gyles and Con Gore-Booth, Moina Mathers, née Bergson, had been an art student at the Slade, before she met MacGregor Mathers (see p. 266) and in March 1888 became one of the first members of the Order of the Golden Dawn. WBY had met her through Mathers early in 1890, and it was at her studio that he was initiated into the Golden Dawn. The Matherses had probably come to London in May for the annual Corpus Christi ceremony of the Order, and were staying at 52 Oakley Street, headquarters of the R. R. & A. C. (Rubidae Rosae & Aureae Crucis), a section of the Golden Dawn.

To Mrs William Allingham,[1] *20 July* [*1894*]

⟨Bloomsbury Mansion | Hart St. | W. C.⟩[2]
3 Blenheim Road | Bedford Park | Chiswick. W
July 20th.

My dear Madam

I am compiling an anthology of Irish lyric poets & desire to give M[r] Allinghams work not only in my introduction but in the body of the book the importance due to its exquisite genius. I hope therefore for your leave to quote 'The fairies' 'Farewell to Ballyshannon' 'Twilight Voices' & 'The Abbot of Innisfallen' & 'The Lover & the Bird'.[3]

I remain yours sincerely
W B Yeats

ALS Illinois.

To John O'Leary, [*? late July 1894*]

3 Blenheim Road | Bedford Park | Chiswick | London. W
Dear M[r] O'Leary

Please send on 'proofs.' You said you were sending them so I did not write about them.[1]

I fear there is but little news of any kind—unless one talk about the

---

[1] Helen Allingham, née Paterson (1848–1926), was educated at the Royal Academy Schools and then worked as a black and white artist for the *Graphic* and *Cornhill*. Best known as a water-colour painter of rural scenes and for her studies of children, she exhibited at the Royal Academy and was at first an Associate and in 1890 a Member of the Royal Watercolour Society. Ruskin wrote admiringly of her work in *The Art of England* (1883). She married the poet William Allingham (see p. 70) in August 1874.

[2] The address of the Irish Literary Society, London.

[3] WBY's changing attitudes to the poetry of Allingham are a paradigm of the development of his aesthetic in the '90s. In 1888 (*LNI*, 163–74; see p. 104) he thought that Allingham's 'want of sympathy with the national life and history has limited his vision, has driven away from his poetry much beauty and power—has thinned his blood.' Now, in an effort to provide an alternative literary tradition to the popular but rhetorical Young Irelanders, he began to extol Allingham for the depth and sincerity of his work, remarking in the introduction to *BIV* (xx), 'He is the poet of the melancholy peasantry of the West, and, as years go on . . . will take his place among those minor immortals who have put their souls into little songs to humble the proud.' On 7 Dec 1904, he told Mrs Allingham (Illinois), 'I have the greatest possible admiration for Mr Allingham's poetry. I am sometimes inclined to believe that he was my own master in Irish verse, starting me in the way I have gone whether for good or evil.'

Mrs Allingham granted the permission sought, for she noted at the top of WBY's letter, 'Yes if keep to *Collected Edins* & send me proofs for correction.' WBY included in *BIV* all the poems mentioned here, together with 'Four Ducks on a Pond'. (The correct title of 'Farewell to Ballyshannon' is 'The Winding Banks of Erne; or, The Emigrant's Adieu to Ballyshanny'.)

[1] Possibly the proofs of his article for the August 1894 *Bookman*, 'Some Irish National Books' (see p. 392, n. 5).

weather which is horrible like a furnace.[2] My 'Sullivan the Red' stories have roused York Powell into great enthusiasm.[3]

I am going in to Elkin Matthews one of these days to arrange for a volume of Irish essays cheefly to be feirce mockery of most Irish men & things except the men & things who are simple poor & imaginative & not I fear too many.[4]

Yours ever
W B Yeats

Lilly Lolly & Jack are all now away.

ALS NLI. Wade (dated '[? autumn 1894]'), 235.

To F. H. Day, [before 6 August 1894]

3 Blenheim Road | Bedford Park | Chiswick. W

My dear Day—

Yes—I shall come with much pleasure. I suppose about 4 on Monday sixth.

I enjoyed Keats meeting very much & thought your short address admirable.[1]

Yours ever
W B Yeats

ALS Boston.

[2] In the week of 23 July 1894 *The Times* recorded afternoon temperatures in London in the upper 70s F., noting on the 28th that *maxima* temperatures exceeding 75° F. had been recorded the previous day 'over the inland parts of England'. After a thunderstorm on Sunday, 29 July, the London temperature fell; but it rose again on Tuesday, 31 July, to 77° F., and the atmosphere was 'close, unsettled, the barometer falling slowly'.

[3] Two of WBY's stories about O'Sullivan the Red (rechristened 'Red Hanrahan' in later publications) had appeared in the *National Observer* on 26 Nov and 24 Dec 1892 and a further two were to appear in the same magazine on 4 Aug and 29 Sept 1894 (see p. 272).

[4] This project, perhaps prompted by WBY's anger at the outcome of his controversy with Gavan Duffy over the New Irish Library, was never realized.

[1] On 16 July 1894, 1,000 people attended the unveiling in Hampstead Church of a memorial bust of Keats, for which Day and Louise Imogen Guiney had been collecting funds for some two years. Day made the presentation of the bust, a copy of Anne Whitney's head of the poet, at the ceremony, and Edmund Gosse gave the acceptance speech. The invitations to the occasion were printed at the Kelmscott Press.

To Olivia Shakespear,[1] *6 August* [*1894*]

3 Blenheim Road | Bedford Park | Chiswick. W

August 6th

My dear M[rs] Shakespear,

I have been wanting to make another suggestion about 'Beautys Hour'; and as you are getting near the end make it now instead of waiting until I see you in Setember. I think Gerald wants a slight touch more of definition. A few lines early in the book would do all needed. You find he developes into rather a plastic person; and this is the best thing for the plot, but you should show that this is caracterization & not a limitation of knowledge. Might he not be one of those vigerous fair haired, boating, or cricket playing young men, who are very positive, & what is called manly, in external activities & energies & wholly passive & plastic in emotional & intellectual things? I met just such a man last winter. I had suspected before that those robust masks hid often and often a great emotional passivity and plasticity but this man startled me. He was of the type of those who face the cannons mouth without a tremour, but kill themselves rather than face life without some girl with pink cheeks, whose character they have never understood, whose soul they have never perceived, & whom they would have forgotten in a couple of months. Such people are very lovable for both their weakness & their strength appear pathetic; and your clever heroine might well love him. She would see how strong & courageous he was in the external things, where a woman was weak, & would feal instinctively how much in need of protection & care in those deeper things where she was strong.[2] This criticism occured to me soon after I left you & I longed to ask you to read me all the Gerald bits

---

[1] Olivia Shakespear, née Tucker (1863–1938; see Appendix), a cousin of Lionel Johnson, appears in *Aut* and *Mem* under the pseudonym 'Diana Vernon' (heroine of Scott's *Rob Roy*). She had married a solicitor, Henry Hope Shakespear, in 1885 and published several novels, the first, *Love on a Mortal Lease*, in May 1894.

[2] OS's novella *Beauty's Hour* appeared in the *Savoy* in August and September 1896, but was not published in book form. It is the story of the plain but intelligent Mary Gower, who on her father's death becomes secretary to Lady Harman, and falls in love with the athletic but emotionally wooden Gerald, son of her employer. He is in turn attracted by the beautiful Bella Sturgis. Mary finds herself transformed one evening into a perfect beauty, and though the transformation fades at sunrise, in her night-time persona thereafter she arouses Gerald's passion. But the dual role is increasingly difficult to sustain, and she is warned by her father's friend Dr Trefusis that the nightly transformation is the work of the Devil. She therefore bids farewell to beauty and, commending Gerald to Bella Sturgis, goes to keep house for Dr Trefusis.

OS took WBY's advice about Gerald. Early in the novella Mary says of him:

as with many finely bred, finely tempered Englishmen, sport was a passion; more, a religion. He put into his hunting, his shooting, his cricket, all the ardour, all the sincerity that are necessary to achievement: I respected this in him, even while it moved me to a kind of pity; for I felt instinctively that though he might have skill and courage to overcome physical difficulties or danger, he was totally unfitted to cope with the more subtle side of life; and would be helpless in the face of an emotional difficulty.

again before you started but did not do so because I knew you would be busy your last afternoons in London. I only bother you with it now that you may have it while you are writing, instead of its pursuing you through I know not what travellers vicesitudes.

I think you have chosen wisely in making Dr Trefusis read the mystics rather than the purely magical books I suggested. 'The Morning Redness' by Jacob Boehmen is a great book beautifully named, which might do, & 'The Obscure Night of the Soul' by St John of the Cross is among the most perfectly named things in the world.[3]

I will perhaps write to you again about your kind letter for I have much to say and I want this to reach you this evening & so must end now. I saw Mrs Emery yesterday & found that she had been very delighted with you.

That you like my stories is a very great pleasure & the best of pleasures.

Yours always sincerely and gratefully
W B Yeats

The books have just come: many thanks. I am sorry you took so much trouble.

ALS MBY. Wade, 233–4 (with P.S. belonging to a later letter).

To the Editor of United Ireland, 1 September 1894

"DEAR SIR—It is no manner of use our deceiving ourselves about the sale of the 'Patriot Parliament.' It is perfectly well known that the first volume of any much-talked of series is certain of a large sale, quite independent of its merits, and the ten or fifteen thousand sold is not exceptional. The question is whether it did or did not help the other volumes, and I have reason to know that numbers of the peasantry refused to buy 'The Bog of Stars' because of the dulness of its predecessor.[1] Believing, as I do, that literature is

---

[3] In trying to account for Mary Gower's transformation, Dr Trefusis, although a confirmed scientist and 'the ardent advocate of materialism', is finally obliged to turn to mystical and magic books, though not those recommended here by WBY. We are told that he reads the *Magia Naturalis* of Johannes Faust, and Cornelius Agrippa and 'strange volumes; full of odd, symbolical drawings, and with wonderful titles, such as: "The Golden Tripod": "The Glory of the World, or the Gate of Paradise": "The All-Wise Doorkeeper." ' 'The Morning Redness'—*Morgan Röte im Aufgang* (1612)—was the major work of the German shoemaker mystic, Jacob Boehme (see p. 224).

[1] *The Patriot Parliament of 1689* by Thomas Davis, edited with an introduction by Sir Charles Gavan Duffy, had been published in 1893 as the first volume in the New Irish Library. The book, an apologia for the Parliament held in Dublin by the deposed James II, is overcrammed with fact and detail and a large part of it taken up with an arid listing of the Acts passed by the Parliament. In his *Bookman* review, 'Some Irish National Books', of August 1894 (see p. 392), WBY had described it as 'an historical tractate which, if modified a little, had done well among the transactions of a learned society, but it bored beyond

almost the most profound influence that ever comes into a nation, I recognise with deep regret, and not a little anger, that the 'New Irish Library' is so far the most serious difficulty in the way of our movement, and that it drives from us those very educated classes we desire to enlist, and supplies our opponents with what looks like evidence of our lack of any fine education, of any admirable precision and balance of mind, of the very qualities which make literature possible. Perhaps honest criticism, with as little of the 'great day for Ireland' ritual as may be, can yet save the series from ebbing out in a tide of irrelevant dulness, and keep the best opportunity there has been these many decades from being squandered by pamphleteer and amateur. We require books by competent men of letters upon subjects of living national interest, romances by writers of acknowledged power, anthologies selected from men like De Vere, and Allingham, and Fergusson, and impartial picturesque lives of Emmet, Wolfe Tone, Mitchel, and perhaps O'Connell,[2] and, if they are not to be obtained, let us bow our heads in silence and talk no more of a literary renaissance, for we can, at least, cease to be imposters.

If you re-read my remarks in the *Bookman* upon 'The Patriot Parliament' you will find that instead of criticising its historical merits I assumed them and called it a good book for the proceedings of a learned society. I made no other criticism than that it was 'dull,' whereas, you prefer the words 'not brilliant' or 'particularly readable'. I accept your amendations with pleasure, and we are at one again.—Yours sincerely,

W B Yeats."

Printed letter, *United Ireland*, 1 September 1894 (1). *UP* 1. 339–40.

measure the unfortunate persons who bought some thousands of copies in a few days, persuaded by the energy of the two societies [i.e. the National Literary Society and the Irish Literary Society, London], and deluded by the names of Sir Charles Gavan Duffy and Thomas Davis upon the cover.' Commenting in *United Ireland*, 18 Aug 1894, on WBY's review, John McGrath agreed with WBY's general condemnation of the New Irish Library but defended *The Patriot Parliament* and noted that it had 'a bigger sale than any Irish book of our time'. This letter is WBY's reply to McGrath, who prefaced it with the explanation that 'Mr. W. B. Yeats sends me the following with reference to some paragraphs which appeared in this column a fortnight ago on the New Irish Library.'

Standish O'Grady's *The Bog of Stars* (see p. 286, n. 4) was published in 1893 as the second volume of the New Irish Library.

[2] WBY's selection of Emmet, Tone, and Mitchel, and his hesitation about the constitutionalist O'Connell (1775–1847), signal his identification with the radical nationalist tradition. The name of Mitchel may have been included partly to embarrass Gavan Duffy (see p. 334). Robert Emmet (1778–1803) led an abortive Irish rebellion in July 1803, fled, and was eventually hanged for high treason. Theobald Wolfe Tone (1763–98), one of the leaders of the 1798 rebellion, was captured and condemned for treason; refused a soldier's death, he committed suicide in his prison cell. For R. Barry O'Brien's edition of Tone's *Autobiography* (1893), see p. 282.

To Alice Milligan,[1] *23 September* [*1894*]

3 Blenheim Road | Bedford Park | Chiswick. W
Sept 23rd

My dear Miss Milligan

I did not send 'Kathleen Ny Hoolihan' because—alas—I have sent my only copy to my publisher. I will send you a copy as soon as I can. It is part of a story which is part of a book called 'The Secret Rose' & I send to Lawrence & Bullen each fragment as I complete it. I fear it would dissapoint you for it is rather a dramatic utterance than a personal expression. I have often noticed that Irish men who have no personal dignity or nobility will yet have a true & devoted love for their country & I have made a story to describe this & put the song into it.[2] My experience of Ireland, during the last three years, has changed my views very greatly, & now I feel that the work of an Irish man of letters must be not so much to awaken or quicken or preserve the national idea among the mass of the people but to convert the educated classes to it on the one hand to the best of his ability, & on the other—& this is the more important—to fight for moderation, dignity, & the rights of the intellect among his fellow nationalists. Ireland is terribly demoralized in all things—in her scholourship, in her criticism, in her politics, in her social life. She will never be greatly better until she govern herself but she will be greatly worse unless there arise protesting spirits. I am doing what I can by writing my books with laborious care & studied moderation of style; & by criticism when ever the chance offers; but I have not the temprement that can have much effect outside a few more or less subtle spirits who need no phisician. I write this partly because your last letter to 'United Ireland' reminds me that you are a very effective prose writer & if ever the sacred anger decend upon you will do good work.[3]

I return your poems, & only extreme amount of work keeps me from writing much more about them. I go to Ireland this week & shall meet you probably & criticise at length. I hope you will find all needful leisure for your

---

[1] See p. 370, n. 4.

[2] The lyric later titled 'Red Hanrahan's Song about Ireland' (see p. 4, n. 10) was included in WBY's story 'Kathleen-Ny-Hoolihan', published in the *National Observer*, 4 Aug 1894, and reprinted (under the title 'Kathleen the Daughter of Hoolihan and Hanrahan the Red') in *The Secret Rose*.

[3] On 15 Sept 1894 *United Ireland* (2) had published a letter from Alice Milligan over her pseudonym 'I. Olkyrn', suggesting that practical steps ought to be taken to stimulate an Irish reading public; the National Literary Society, she said, should appoint a corresponding member in each district to monitor local literary and cultural activities and to provide a quarterly report that 'would give us material from which to judge of the intellectual condition of the people. We would see where progress was being made, where local effort was to be stimulated, where total inanition called for action on the part of the society.'

work in Donegal. If you were to get & read—you read French?—
Joubainville's 'Mythologie Irelandais' it would be of great help.[4]

[*no signature*]

AL Texas.

To Richard Le Gallienne, 4 October [1894]

3 Blenheim Road | Bedford Park | Chiswick. W
Oct 4th.

My dear Le Gallienne

I have long been intending to write to you about your 'Prose Fancies' but
I am a slow reader, no matter how greatly I like a book, & read a page now &
a page agen; and desperately procrastinate into the bargain. I have however
read your book much & often & found it always fruitful, always full of an
abundance like that of nature. I think that a 'spring morning' ⟨the first
thing⟩ that I read weeks & weeks ago & 'fractional humanity' which I have
but recently discovered are the most moving & beautiful. The book shall
stand beside your 'religeon' on my shelf in Dublin watching for opportu-
nites to make forays & salleys among the youths & girls who make up our
new Ireland & will I doubt not take many captives. Your exposition of one of
Blakes doctrines in 'Fractional Humanity' strikes me greatly especially in
that it is so much better than my own.[1] I wish however that you would do
another 'Book bills' for neither this last nor yet the Religeon have I think put
down such deep roots.[2] The greater weight of subject helped you there I
think to escape some [of] that over abundance which makes your river at
times a little over spread the bank just as mine in its too great meagreness

---

[4] The work of Henri d'Arbois de Jubainville (1827–1910), Professor of Celtic Languages and
Literature at the Collège de France, was to exert an influence on the Irish Revival, partly through
J. M. Synge, who attended his lectures in Paris after 1898. WBY cannot have known d'Arbois de
Jubainville's *Le Cycle mythologique irlandais* . . . (see p. 104) well in French; a translation, by Richard I.
Best (1872–1959), later director of the National Library of Ireland, appeared in 1903.

[1] 'A Spring Morning', the first essay in Le Gallienne's collection of *Prose Fancies*, published in June
1894, is a generalized poetic impression, which begins: 'Spring puts the old pipe to his lips and blows a
note or two. At the sound, little thrills pass across the wintry meadows. . . .' In 'Fractional Humanity',
the fourth essay, which deals with the fragmentation of life, Le Gallienne writes (33):

. . . the mystic would describe it as dividing ourselves more and more from God, the primeval unity in
which alone is blessedness. Blake in one of his prophetic books sings man's 'fall into Division and his
resurrection into Unity'. And when we look about us and consider but the common use of words, how do
we find the mystic's apparently wild fancy illustrated in every section of our commonplace lives.

[2] Le Gallienne's *The Religion of a Literary Man* was published in 1893. His *The Book-Bills of
Narcissus: An Account Rendered* (1891) is a whimsical fictionalized treatment of a writer's life and of the
world of books.

runs half dry too often & shows the rocks & half ⟨dead tree or⟩ buried ⟨tree trunks debris⟩ wreckage at the bottom. This last book in its felicity, its ease, its rapidity is a thing to be glad of surely but I wish such skill were at the service of one ⟨growing⟩ careful & masterful conception and not of the flying fancies of journalism but in complaining thus I do but rail upon Providence who has ordained that he who does not write 'middles' shall be short of his dinner.

I have long wanted to apologise to you for introducing to the Rhymers Club that exceedingly unnecessary countryman of mine, Arthur Lynch & of there by giving him the chance of writing certain absurd things which you may have seen in a book called 'Our Poets'. I wrote him a short but sufficiently severe letter about the breach of good manners he was guilty of in describing a private gathering. He is a dissapointed, tongue tied fellow half or whole mad with vanity & deserves no worse than pity.[3]

I return to Ireland in a few days but shall hope to see you when I return for I have much to say anent your 'Religeon of a Literary Man' & its relation to religeon in general.

Beleive me Yours ever
W B Yeats.

ALS Texas.

To T. Fisher Unwin, 11 October [1894]

56 North Circular Road | Dublin.[1]
Oct 11th.

Dear Mr Unwin

I write to continue & recapitulate our conversation of Tuesday. I want to get out early next spring a new & corrected edition of the poems which have

---

[3] *Our Poets!*, a volume of verse and prose by Arthur Alfred Lynch (see p. 254), published in July 1894, was a satirical survey of the contemporary literary scene and included (11) the poem 'Le Gallienne': 'But thus we creep to ignominious fame, / And popinjays usurp the place of men; / As witness, you've already guessed the name, / That sugar-coated prig, Le Gallienne.' In a short essay, 'Cliques, Coteries, and Critics', in the same book Lynch recalls being introduced by WBY to the Rhymers' Club, going on (48–9) to give an account of one of its meetings and making much of the mediocrity, vanity, and silliness of the members: 'Now it so happened that nearly every man in the room was not only a poet, but a critic, nay they were a ring of critics, bent on "booming" and "log-rolling" each other's productions, and of course correspondingly truculent in stamping out others'—as, he complained, they had done to his own *Modern Authors* (but see p. 270). Elsewhere Lynch paid WBY the back-handed compliment of describing him (58) as having 'in one sense, "more in him" than any of the other Irish writers, even in the volatility, or elasticity, with which he presses on through the quagmires of his affectations, perversities, and shallow theories'.

[1] WBY had returned, probably on 10 Oct, to the same lodgings he had occupied in Dublin at the end of 1893.

already appeared of mine. I got a good offer for them on Monday[2] but as our relations have always been friendly & pleasant I would just as soon go on with you if we can come to terms. I am very anxious to get out the volume in such a way that I can make all my future books of verse resemble it in size & printing & the special advantage of the offer I got on Monday was that it would enable me to satisfy my whim to the utmost. If you care to take the volume, I would therefore ask first that it be of a certain height & breadth, second that it be printed by either Clarke or Constable, third that I be consulted about an artist to do the title page—good 'decorative' men are fairly plentiful just now & fairly cheap—I have a liking for one or two. As to the contents—It should contain the long poem 'The Wanderings of Oisin' 'The Countess Kathleen' (in which the copyright period of two years mentioned in agreement has just expired) & 'The Land of Hearts Desire' (The copyright period on which expires next spring) & the best lyrics from the 'Oisin' volume as well as from 'The Countess Kathleen' one. And last I would ask you for a royalty from the first copy & that the agreement should be for a term of years as before. These conditions are the same in every particular with those offered to me on Monday.[3] I want to get the matter settled as soon as possible as I am off to the West in a few days & wish to be able, free of all business matters, to devote the next two months to the revision of my poems.

Yours sincerely
W B Yeats

ALS Texas.

To T. Fisher Unwin, 19 October [1894]

56 North Circular Road | Dublin
Oct 19th

Dear Mr Unwin

You may be right about the advisability of including the new drama in the proposed volume but this is not possible as I have promised it to Matthews. Matthews is a friend & a neighbour & I was glad to give him the book as he

---

[2] The offer was made by Elkin Mathews, who was to publish *The Wind Among the Reeds* in 1899, and who in 1889 had thought of taking over the unsold copies of *Oisin* (see p. 191).

[3] All these conditions were met when Unwin published *Poems* (1895) the following October (not in the early spring, as WBY had hoped). The crown octavo volume was printed by T. & A. Constable, Printers to her Majesty at the Edinburgh University Press, who later printed *The Shadowy Waters* (1900) for Hodder and Stoughton. (The first of WBY's books to be printed by R. & R. Clark Ltd. of Edinburgh was *Reveries over Childhood and Youth*, in 1916.) The artist eventually chosen by WBY to design the title-page was Herbert Granville Fell. The contents of the volume were as WBY describes them.

thought it would help him in the present crisis of his affairs.[1] Besides he has a special public I would be glad to get at. When I promised him the book I had no immediate thought of a reprint of the other poems. As things are my prose & verse is so scattered between Lawrence & Bullen—who have some prose—you & Matthews that a collected edition is far off.[2] I can but keep the way clear for it & have accordingly made such arrangements with both Matthews & Lawrence & Bullen that I can bring my books together with little trouble when the time come. I must ask you to make a like arrangement & to draw up such an agreement as to make the book return to me *unconditionally at the end of a term of years.* I partly insist on this because if ever a first rate publishing house arise in Ireland I must needs publish in part with them. Partly in answer to your last & partly to summarise my first letter I ask the following conditions.[3]

(1) That the book be yours *for 4 years* & then return to me.

(2) that my royalty for this period be *12½% from the first copy* insted of 10% for the first 500 as you suggest & 12½% for the next 1000 & so on.

(3) that I choose the paper (not necessarily handmade) & the artist to make title page & cover orniment; that I select the size of the page Etc. that the book be printed with either Constable or Clarke.

(4) that I receive ⟨twelve⟩ six free copies.

Yours very sinly
W B Yeats

from next Tuesday my address will be

c/o George Pollexfen
Thorn Hill
Sligo

Copeland & Day might take the American rights.[4] I have no objection to make as you suggest a different arrangement for America than the proposed royalty one.

ALS Texas.

[1] Elkin Mathews had quarrelled with his partner, John Lane (see p. 251), as a result of which he left the Bodley Head to set up a publishing firm under his own name. He did not in the end publish *The Shadowy Waters*; it first appeared in print in 1900 in the *North American Review*, and was later issued in book form by Hodder & Stoughton.

[2] WBY's *Collected Works in Verse and Prose* did not appear until 1908, when it was published in 8 vols. by the Shakespeare Head Press, in which A. H. Bullen was a partner (see p. 353). At this time only Lawrence & Bullen, who had brought out *The Celtic Twilight* in 1893 and were to publish *The Secret Rose*, held any rights in WBY's prose.

[3] Cf. preceding letter. Several unsigned drafts of the present letter (MBY and Anne Yeats) contain some variations in wording.

[4] F. H. Day had recently gone into partnership with Herbert Copeland (d. 1929) to launch a Boston publishing venture under their joint names. The firm imitated William Morris's Kelmscott Press (see p. 348, n. 4) in many of its designs and was influenced in its publishing policy by the Bodley Head, from which it imported a number of titles. Copeland & Day did publish the American edition of WBY's *Poems* in 1895.

To Robert Louis Stevenson,[1] 24 October [1894]

C/o George Pollexfen | Thorn Hill | Sligo | Ireland.
Oct 24th.

Dear Sir

I need hardly tell you that your praise of 'The Lake Isle of Innisfree' has given me great pleasure.[2] After all it is the liking or disliking of one's fellow craftsmen, especially of those who have attained the perfect expression one does but grope for, which urges one to work on—else were it best to dream ones dreams in silence.

My grandfather a very passionate old retired sailor—quite the reverse of literary—read 'Treasure Iseland' upon his death-bed with infinite satis-faction. It is well nigh the only book I ever heard of him reading. I wonder at the voice, which while delighting studious & cloistered spirits, can yet hush into admiration such as he, much as I wonder at that voice which stilled the waves of old.

I shall ask my publisher to send you a copy of my next book 'The ⟨Celtic Twilight⟩ Shadowy Waters' but you need not acknowledge it. I shall send it but as a mark of thankfulness for your kind words.[3]

Yours sinsly
W B Yeats

ALS Yale.

[1] Robert Louis Stevenson (1850–1894), novelist, poet, and essayist and author of *Treasure Island, Kidnapped, The Master of Ballantrae*, and numerous other stories; for health reasons, he had settled at Apia in Samoa in 1890.

[2] Stevenson had written to WBY on 14 Apr 1894 to tell him that he had been deeply moved as a boy by Swinburne's poems and later by Meredith's *Love in the Valley* and that it might 'interest you to hear that I have a third time fallen in slavery: this is to your poem called the *Lake Isle of Innisfree*. It is so quaint and airy, simple, artful, and eloquent to the heart—but I seek words in vain. Enough that "always night and day I hear lake water lapping with low sounds on the shore," and am, yours gratefully, Robert Louis Stevenson.' (*The Letters of Robert Louis Stevenson*, ed. S. Colvin [1911], IV. 254–5) Since Stevenson died suddenly of a brain haemorrhage on 3 Dec 1894, he cannot have read this reply from WBY.

[3] Word of the Stevenson letter had circulated in Dublin, for John McGrath, in a note in *United Ireland*, 1 Sept 1894 (1), wrote:

By-the-way, I hear Mr. Yeats is working on a new Irish poem, which he expects to publish before Christmas. One of Mr. Yeats's latest admirers is Mr. Robert Louis Stevenson, the celebrated novelist, who has just written him from his far-away home in Samoa to say that his poetry has taken him "captive". This is a remarkable tribute from such a critic. Mr. Stevenson was taken captive by Swinburne when a boy, and ten years ago by the verses of George Meredith. Our Irish bard, you see, is climbing up into high company.

To F. H. Day, 27 October [1894]

c/o George Pollexfen | Thorn Hill | Sligo | Ireland.
Oct 27th

My dear Day

Many thanks for 'The Knight Errant' & for the little book 'Vagabondia' which I have not yet had time to do more than glance at but which seems strong athletic open-air verse touched here & there with a more brooding spirit.[1] I hope to have a good read at it one of these days. Just now & for the last few days I have been buried in a mountain of correspondence the accumulation of months & when it is level with the plain shall set to work putting my new poem 'The Shadowy Waters' in final shape. Yes Mathews is to publish it as well as a prospective book of lyrics.[2] I am at present waiting a final statement from Unwin as to whether he will agree to my terms for a reprint of all the things he has of mine *ie* 'The Countess Kathleen', 'Oisin', 'The Land of Hearts Desire' & certain lyrics.[3] He will I think agree as his last letter conceeded nearly everything—if he refuse Mathews will take them. In any case all my future books will be published in a uniform shape.

Have you seen Johnsons book on Hardy? It is very stately & fine.[4]

Please give my best remembrances to Miss Guiney if you see her. I hope she has got her own Goblin book & my promised 'Celtic Twilight' by this. I asked my father to get Lawrence & Bullen to send the first with the second.[5]

Yrs ever
W B Yeats

ALS Southern Illinois, with envelope addressed to 69 Cornhill, Boston, postmark 'SLIGO OC 27 94'.

[1] Although The Knight Errant, a quarterly 'Magazine of Appreciation' and 'Review of the Liberal Arts' published in Boston from spring 1892, had ceased publication in January 1893, Day had presumably sent WBY one of the remaining copies. The joint production of Ralph Adams Cram, the designer Bertram Goodhue, Francis Watts Lee, Day himself and his partner Herbert Copeland, the magazine was intended as an American counterpart of Herbert Horne's *The Hobby Horse*. The medieval knight depicted on its cover represented, as the first issue explained, 'men against an epoch' in which 'one by one . . . the beautiful things have disappeared'. This, it went on, 'is the condition that demands the new chivalry.'

Songs from Vagabondia, by the American poets William Bliss Carman and Richard Hovey, was published jointly in 1894 by Copeland & Day in Boston and Elkin Mathews and John Lane in London. The breezy, hedonistic tone of the *Songs*,—set by the first poem, 'Vagabondia': 'Off with the fetters / That chafe and restrain! / Off with the chain! . . . Midnights of revel, / And noondays of song! / Is it so wrong? / Go to the Devil!'—earned the volume great popularity in America where it became something of a cult book.

[2] This was to become *The Wind Among the Reeds*, published by Mathews but not until April 1899.

[3] See pp. 401–3.

[4] Lionel Johnson's *The Art of Thomas Hardy*, published by Elkin Mathews and John Lane earlier in this month.

[5] See p. 388. The 'Goblin book' was probably Louise Guiney's *Brownies and Bogles* (Boston, 1888), a compilation of 12 fairy stories for children. She may have loaned a copy to WBY during her visit to England but now wanted it back as the work had gone out of print in 1890 and was never reissued.

To William Linnell,[1] *28 October* [*1894*]

C/o George Pollexfen | Thorn Hill. | Sligo. | Ireland
Oct 28th

Dear M[r] Linnell

I think I once heard you say that you hoped someday to see the whole set of the Dante designs published. A while ago I mentioned the designs to M[r] J M Dent the publisher & he expressed a great desire to see you with a view to their possible publication.

I promised to see you & arrange an interview, if possible, so that you might hear what he had to say but I was too busy before I left London & so must trust to a letter. Dent will probably call at your studio; & you will I hope think this a sufficient introduction. He is a most excellent publisher, as you no doubt know, and can certainly be trusted to bring out any designs entrusted to him in the most artistic way, & a very pleasant personage into the bargain. Whether you accede to the request of the publisher or not, I am sure you will be pleased with the man.[2]

Yrs vry sincely
W B Yeats

Please remember me to your daughters.[3]

PS. I feel that the getting Blake as adequately before the world as possible in this age of artistic materialism is something of a sacred charge. One never knows what mind he may awaken, what imagination he may quicken.

ALS Fitzwilliam.

[1] See pp. 202, 221.

[2] Joseph Mallaby Dent (1849–1926) had begun business as a book-binder in 1872 but turned to publishing in 1888; his firm specialized in cheap and popular series such as the Temple Shakespeare, Temple Classics, and Everyman's Library. In 1894–5 he commissioned JBY to illustrate a complete edition of Defoe's novels.

Blake executed his 102 designs and 7 engravings for Dante's *Divine Comedy* from 1824 to 1827 on a commission from John Linnell who permitted WBY to reproduce 10 of them with his three articles, 'William Blake and His Illustrations to the Divine Comedy', published in the *Savoy*, July–Sept 1896 (*E & I*, 116–45). Although Dent remained interested in publishing the whole series for some years, he did not do so and in March 1918 they were bought at auction by the National Art Collection, which issued the 102 designs as *Illustrations to the Divine Comedy of Dante by Wiliam Blake* in 1922. WBY bought a copy of the book, writing to his wife on 25 Nov 1922 (MBY): 'I am being very extravagant. I am giving £10 for the reproductions of Blakes 105 [*sic*] Dante designs. It is a great treasure. . . .'

[3] William Linnell had two daughters, Katharine Anna (b. 1865), and Isabelle (b. 1869). WBY inscribed a copy of *Oisin* on 30 Mar 1890 to Katharine Anna, and gave her a copy of *The Celtic Twilight* on her marriage in 1894 to Thomas Nelson Maclean.

SOME OF THE FOLK IN "THE LAND OF HEART'S DESIRE"

From Photographs by Messrs. Hills and Saunders, Sloane Street, S.W.

MAIRE BRUIN (MISS WINIFRED FRASER).

"A little queer old woman, cloaked in green,
came to buy a porringer of milk."

A FAIRY CHILD (MISS DOROTHY PAGET).

"Oh, what a nice, smooth floor to dance upon!"

I can lead you, newly married bride,
Where nobody gets old and crafty and wise,
Where nobody gets old and godly and grave

"Come away!
I hear my brothers bidding us away!"

Scenes from *The Land of Heart's Desire*, from *The Sketch*, 25 April 1894

Constance and Eva Gore-Booth

To T. Fisher Unwin, 5 November [1894]

C/o George Pollexfen | Thorn Hill | Sligo | Ireland
Nov 5th

Dear M[r] Unwin

I return the agreement[1] which is quite satisfactory.

I cannot prepare the MS just at present but will get to it very shortly.

No I was not thinking of Beardsley. The fact is I do not want to decide for the moment as I am waiting to find out more about a Belgian artist. Should he prove impracticable, I have an English artist in my mind who would I think commend himself to you.[2]

However there is no use our going into these points just yet.

Yrs snry
W B Yeats

ALS Texas.

To J. B. Yeats, 5 November [1894]

C/o George Pollexfen | Thorn Hill | Sligo | Ireland
Nov 5th.

My dear Papa—

I am doing nothing except the play 'The Shadowy Waters' which will I think be good. It is however giving me a devil of a job. More than anything I have done for years. In my struggle to keep it concrete I fear I shall so over load it with legendary detail that it will be unfit for any theatrical purpose— at least as such are carried out at present.

George has been away at Leapardtown where Dunmorgan ran second, & is in good spirits.[1] He has just come back—with a racing man with him, under whose tecnical conversation, I groan.

[1] For *Poems* (1895); see pp. 401–3.

[2] Beardsley had probably been mentioned by Unwin because his poster design had been used on the cover and title-page for *The Land of Heart's Desire* (see p. 389). In 1896, Beardsley was to have done six pictures for a projected edition of *The Shadowy Waters*, but he finished only one and died before he could do the rest. The Belgian artist was probably Fernand Khnopff (1858–1921) who had exhibited with the British Society of Pastellists at the Hanover Gallery in 1890 and at the New Gallery and Grafton Gallery in 1893. A friend of Burne-Jones, Hunt, and Watts, Khnopff had illustrated poems by Christina Rossetti in 1891. In his article 'English Work at *La Libre Esthetique*', *The Studio*, April 1894, Khnopff referred to the charming work of Lane and Mathews. The English artist was probably H. Granville Fell, whose work WBY had seen for the first time in the autumn of 1894.

[1] George Pollexfen's horse Dunmorgan, ridden by P. Hegarty, finished second by half a length, at odds of 7 to 1 against, in the Milltown Nursery Handicap at the Leopardstown race course near Dublin on 2 Nov 1894. The 'racing man' may have been J. James, the horse's trainer.

Many thanks to that Westminster. I am in many ways glad the Judge row has broken out, as I have disliked & suspected the man for years. I am writing for the papers containing the other articles—I have known the facts ⟨myself⟩ for twelve months or so. The paper seems to have got them pretty correctly—at least as Judges opponets hold them to be.[2]

I want you to send me a copy of 'the Fortneightly' which is lying about somewhere with Johnsons article on Pater; also Miss Vynnes book 'Honey & Alloes' which I forgot.[3]

Yrs affly

W B Yeats

Unwin has accepted my terms finally & will bring out 'Countess Kathleen' 'Land of Hearts Desire' 'Oisin' & the lyrics which he has as soon as I find time to correct them.

ALS MBY. Wade, 236–7.

To the Editor of United Ireland, *10 November 1894*

"Sligo, Nov 10.

"DEAR SIR—In a notice of Mr. M'Call's wholly interesting and partly charming little book, you mention 'that Americans did not mind the London critics,' and point the moral with the statement that 'an adamantine indifference to the judgment' of every public but the public of Ireland is 'the only honourable position for an Irish book to take up.'[1] I am afraid that the history of America is hardly upon your side, for Walt Whitman, the most National of her poets, was so neglected and persecuted that he had, perhaps,

---

[2] William Quan Judge (1851–96) was born in Ireland but taken to America as a boy. He later worked as a clerk in the New York law office of the brother of Col. H. S. Olcott (see p. 164), and with the latter and HPB helped to found the Theosophical Society. After the death of HPB in 1891 Judge challenged Annie Besant's leadership of the Society by producing a series of 'messages' allegedly from the mysterious Tibetan masters or 'mahatmas' which he alleged had been communicated by astral means, and which insisted that Judge's plans for the Society were the right ones. The row that broke out in the Society over the authenticity of these communications (in which Col. Olcott sided with Annie Besant) became public when F. Edmund Garrett published a series of articles in the *Westminster Gazette* between 29 Oct and 8 Nov 1894 under the heading 'Isis Very Much Unveiled. The Truth about the Great Mahatma Hoax'. The articles, which accused Judge of fraud, stirred up a vigorous controversy, and in its issues of 8 and 10 Dec 1894 the paper published a reply from Judge in which he refused to face an inquiry of any kind, claiming that the 'messages from the masters had not ceased'. As a result of this dispute the American Theosophists in 1895 declared themselves a separate organization, with Judge as their permanent president. AE and the Dublin Lodge of the Society, differing with WBY, continued to support Judge until his death.

[3] Lionel Johnson's 'The Work of Mr Pater' appeared in the *Fortnightly*, 1 Sept 1894. For *Honey of Aloes and Other Stories*, by Nora Vynne, see p. 366.

[1] John McGrath had made these remarks in a review of P. J.M'Call's *Irish Nóiníns* (Daisies) (Dublin, 1894), in *United Ireland*, 10 Nov 1894 (1).

fallen silent but for the admiration and help of a little group of Irish and English artists and men of letters;[2] while countless feeble persons reproduced in crude verse amid wild American applause the fashions of other countries and the sentimentalities of their own. The truth is that the public of America was, and the public of Ireland is, uneducated and idle, and it was often necessary for an original American writer, and it is often necessary for an original Irish writer, to appeal first, not to his countrymen, but to that small group of men of imagination and scholarship which is scattered through many lands and many cities, and to trust to his own influence and the influence of his fellow-workers to build up in the fullness of time a cultivated public in the land where he lives and works. The true ambition is to make criticism as international, and literature as National, as possible. A contrary ambition would, in Ireland, be peculiarly evil, for it could but get the opinions of our daily papers above the opinions of great scholars, and make a vacant and uninstructed public the masters of the men of intellect.

"I write this letter because your notes seem to me to represent a common opinion and one which can only postpone the day when writers, whom you admire not less than I—Miss Barlow, Miss Lawless, Dr Hyde, and Mr O'Grady—whose memorable 'Coming of Cuchullin' lies upon my table—and others[3], shall have as much influence in purely intellectual matters as, say, members of Parliament, Town Councillors, and other illustrious but not very literary personages.—Yours sincerely,

"A STUDENT OF IRISH LITERATURE"[4]

Printed letter, *United Ireland*, 24 November 1894 (1). Wade, 238–9.

To *John O'Leary, 10 November* [*1894*]

C/o George Pollexfen | Thornhill | Sligo.
Nov 10th.

Dear M^r O'Leary

A great many thanks for the newspapers (where by the by did you clip the little fragment of Lang's article from?).[1] I am working at my new poem 'The

---

[2] See p. 9.

[3] For Jane Barlow and Emily Lawless, see p. 339. WBY's 'log-rolling' on behalf of Standish O'Grady's *The Coming of Cuchulain* (1894) had the desired result, for the novel was given a lengthy review in *United Ireland* on 24 Nov 1894.

[4] In a note replying to WBY's letter, printed on 24 Nov 1894, McGrath commented on the signature: 'he should have signed himself "A Maker of Irish Literature," for such he really is.'

[1] JO'L had evidently sent WBY a cutting of Andrew Lang's enthusiastic review of *The Celtic Twilight*, which had appeared in the *Illustrated London News* on 23 Dec 1893 (802). Lang had described

Shadowy Waters' & when this is done & dispatched to Elkin Matthew begin correcting my other poems for a collective edition with Unwin. I was very glad to get out of Dublin for Dublin & London between them had tired me out, or I should have run down to see you one morning before leaving. I however made my stay as short as I was able & every hour was full—a great many of them with running the erratic O'M to earth.[2]

I have just sent off a letter arguing with McGrath for his remarks *apropos* of McCall about the iniquity of writing for an English audience—the upshot of it is that as long as the Irish public knows nothing of literature, Irish writers must be content to write for countries that know nothing of Ireland. I wonder will McGrath publish my letter.[3]

I have got some more Folklore but have no time to use it yet, & have got some books to review but no time to review them till this play is done. O'Grady's Cuchullin is a wonderful thing & the best thing he has done.[4] Miss Lawless's last book should be good by 'Independent' review. I hear that Hinkson is editing for Matthew a book of verse by T C D men.[5]

I heard from Hyde who was much pleased with the result of the meeting at the Irish Lit in London.[6] Talks of running down here.

Yrs ever
W B Yeats

ALS McGill. Wade, 237–8.

WBY as 'a Celtic Charles Lamb' and affirmed that 'for a pleasant, pathetic, charming view of Irish people and Irish manners, no modern writer is to be matched with Mr. Yeats.' WBY would also have been interested in Lang's observation that it was 'an astonishing thing that, with all the poetry of the popular Irish imagination, the country has had no great literary poet.' KT described JO'L's private press-cutting agency in *25 Years* (197): 'John O'Leary was always snipping bits out of papers and magazines which he thought would interest his young friends, and sending them on to us. Like many people of high moral rectitude he disregarded post-office rules, and used to send whole sheaves of clippings enclosed inside newspapers.'

  [2] Probably John O'Mahony, who had accompanied WBY and Hyde on their trip to Cork in January 1893 (see p. 341).

  [3] See preceding letter.

  [4] WBY was to give O'Grady's *The Coming of Cuchulain*, published in November 1894, an enthusiastic review (*UP* I. 350–1) in the *Bookman*, February 1895.

  [5] An extensive unsigned review in the *Irish Daily Independent* of 5 Nov 1894 (6) described Emily Lawless's *Maelcho: A Sixteenth Century Narrative*, published in October 1894, as 'a splendid and even ennobling tragedy; unlike the corroding grime and gloom that go with the record of the travail of other nations.' WBY's passing disparagement—in a review (*UP* I. 384) in the *Bookman*, October 1895—of H. A. Hinkson's edition of *Dublin Verses: By Members of Trinity College*, published by Mathews in April 1895, was to cause a coolness between WBY and the Hinksons.

  [6] Douglas Hyde inaugurated the 1894–5 session of the Irish Literary Society, London, on 31 Oct 1894, with a lecture on 'The Last Three Centuries of Gaelic Literature' at the Society of Arts, John Street, Adelphi. The lecture was enthusiastically received and the *Freeman's Journal* of 1 Nov carried a lengthy report of the proceedings.

To T. Fisher Unwin, 23 November [1894]

C/o George Pollexfen | Thorn Hill | Sligo | Ireland
Nov 23rd

Dear Mr Unwin

I was away from here when your last letter arrived or I had replied at once. I have asked my people in London to send you a photo of me—please return it after reproduction as I think it is probably the only one they have which is any way presentable.

I cannot do you a poem I fear, as I write very slowly & correct still more slowly & so could never be done in time. I enclose however the title & contents ⟨list etc⟩ of my book. One of your clerks can probably put it into the form required for your annual. Perhaps however you want a full list of contents & if so I dare say I can make out a fairly accurate one but until I begin rewriting some of my more faulty things I do not know with certainty how much I will include from the earlier volume. ⟨I think you had best leave it indefinite as in the enclosed paragraph.⟩

Yrs sinly
W B Yeats

On second thoughts I enclose a full list of probable contents which you can use or not as you think fit.[1]
I am afraid the enclosed paragraph is not what you want but I cannot think of anything better.[2]

---

[1] The list apparently enclosed with this letter is substantially what was published in *Poems* (1895) although the order was considerably changed and many of the titles were altered. 'When you are sad' and 'Girl's Song' were not included, but two lyrics from *The Countess Kathleen*, 'A Dream of a Blessed Spirit' (*VP*, 124–5) and 'Who Goes with Fergus?' (*VP*, 125–6), appeared as separate poems.

[2] Fisher Unwin had written asking WBY to contribute to his publicity annual, *Good Reading About Many Books Mostly By Their Authors*. Although the paragraph WBY enclosed has not survived, an announcement of his forthcoming book in the 1894–5 edition read:

UNDER THE MOON

Old writers were of opinion that the moon governed by her influence peasants, sailors, fishermen, and all obscure persons; and as the symbols of Mr. Yeats's poetry are taken almost wholly from the traditions and manners of the Connaught peasantry, he has selected the title "Under the Moon" for his forthcoming book. It will contain "The Wanderings of Oisin" and "The Countess Kathleen," corrected and partly rewritten, the best of the lyrics originally bound up with them, and also the more recent "Land of Heart's Desire"—in fact, all that he cares to preserve from his already published volumes. Mr. Yeats has written of the beautiful and singular legends of Ireland, not from any archæological or provincial ambition, but with the desire of moulding the universal substance of poetry into new shapes, and of interpreting, to the best of his power, the spirit of Ireland to itself.

The paragraph was not signed by the author himself, as were the other contributions, and it is probable that a copywriter in Unwin's office put it into final shape, as suggested here by WBY. On the title (later abandoned), cf. *Expl*, 25: 'all that is under the moon thirsts to escape out of bounds, to lose itself in some unbounded tidal stream . . . '.

[*Enclosure*]

            1 Under the Moon
Introductory verses
The Wanderings of Oisin
The Land of Hearts Desire
The Countess Kathleen
To the Rose upon the Rood of Time
Fergus and the Druid
The Rose of the World
The Rose of Peace
The Death of Cuchullin
The White Birds
Father Gilligan
Father O'Hart
When you are old
The Sorrow of Love
The Stollen Child
The Lamentation of the Old Fisherman
The Lamentation of the Old Pensioner
Down by the Salley Gardens
To an isle in the Water
King Goll
The Ballad of Moll Magee
The Ballad of the Foxhunter
A Faery Song
The Pity of Love
The Lake Isle of Innisfree
A Cradle Song
The Man who Dreamed of Faeryland
Dedication of 'Irish Tales'
When you are sad
The two trees
The Rose of Battle
An Epitaph
Apologia addressed to Ireland in the coming days

Crossways
Introductory verses
Kanva the Indian on God
Jealousey
Indian Song
Ephemera

The Falling of the Leaves
Sorrow
The Sad Shepherd
Song of the Last Arcadian
Girl's Song.

ALS (with enclosure) Texas.

To Susan Mary Yeats, 23 November [1894]

Thorn Hill | Sligo
Nov 23rd

My dear Lily

Unwin wants to put a photo of me in some sort of annual he is getting out & writes to me for one. I have none by me & so must ask you to send him that Holyer one[1] at once—I have asked him to return it.

I have been staying at Lisadell for a couple of days and have enjoyed myself greatly. They are delightful people. I am to lecture to the parishioners of their clergyman a Rev Mr Lefanu—some relation of the great man of that name—on Irish fairy lore.[2] All the while I was at Lisadell I was busy telling stories—old Irish stories—first to one then another & then telling them over again to the sick Miss Gore upstairs.[3] Miss Eva Gore Booth shows some promise as a writer of verse. Her work is very formless as yet but it is full of telling little phrases.[4] Lisadell is an exceedingly

[1] See preceding letter. The photograph reproduced in Unwin's annual was not by Hollyer (see p. 230) but by Elliot & Fry of London.

[2] The Revd Fletcher Sheridan Le Fanu (1860–1939) served 1885–99 as incumbent of Lissadell, home of the Gore-Booth family, a few miles north of Sligo town. The son of William Le Fanu, Commissioner of Public Works and author of *Seventy Years of Irish Life* (1893), he was a nephew of the novelist Joseph Sheridan Le Fanu. After service with the Cameronians he entered the Church, being ordained a priest in 1885, the same year as he married Jane Hore. In 1899 he became rector of St. John's, Sandymount, Dublin, where he remained until his retirement in 1930. On 29 Sept 1900 he was to officiate at the marriage of Constance Gore-Booth and Count Casimir Markiewicz at St. Marylebone Parish Church, London.

[3] Augusta Elizabeth Gore-Booth (d. 1906); the only surviving unmarried daughter of the 4th baronet, was in her fifties at this time.

[4] Eva Selena Gore-Booth (1870–1926), the third child and second daughter of Sir Henry Gore-Booth, the 5th baronet, had just returned to Ireland after extensive travels with her father in the West Indies and America. In 1897 she moved to Manchester and took up the struggle for women's rights and the work of organizing trades unions. In a letter to her of 26 Dec 1898 (Harvard), WBY praised her first book, *Poems* (1898), as a work of 'poetic feeling . . . and great promise'. She published verse widely in Irish and British periodicals and six further books of poetry appeared in the new century.
    During this visit WBY found himself in close sympathy with Eva,

whose delicate, gazelle-like beauty reflected a mind . . . subtle and distinguished. Eva was for a couple of happy weeks my close friend, and I told her all of my unhappiness in love; indeed so close at once that I

impressive house inside with a great sitting room as high as a church & all things in good taste—much more pleasant than the Conmelleys which was full of eighteenth century curiosities & otherwise uncomfortable to the mind & memory. But outside it is grey square & bare yet set amid delightful grounds.⁵ They talk of my going there again to interview some old man who is beleived to have much folk lore.

The new play has had [? to wait] for several things this week but to day I take it up again. It will be my best I think.

Uncle George has made about £60 by a bet on Dunmorgan who won at Newmarket yesterday. It does not seem to have greatly raised his spirits however; as his rheumatism is still rather bad & Kate threatening—as she does periodically—to leave him.⁶ She is divided between apparent desire to go & intense jealousy of the woman she quite erroniously beleives selected to succeed her.

Yrs affecly
W B Yeats

ALS MBY, with envelope addressed to Blenheim Road, postmark 'MIDLAND DAY NO 24 94'. Wade, 239–40.

To Olivia Shakespear, 28 November 1894

C/o George Pollexfen | Thorn Hill | Sligo | Ireland
Nov 28th 94

My dear Mʳˢ Shakespear

Your little novel is delightful. It does not try so difficult a thing, it is not so complex & subtle as 'Love on a Mortal Lease' but within its narrower limits it is both wise & moving. Your heroine—your Mʳˢ Brandon—is a delightful person & Felicia only less so.¹ My uncle has also read the book with great

nearly said to her, as William Blake said to Catherine Boucher, 'You pity me, there[fore] I love you.' 'But no,' I thought, 'this house would never accept so penniless a suitor,' and, besides, I was still deeply in love with that other and had but just written 'All Things Uncomely and Broken'. I threw the Tarot, and when the Fool came up, which means that nothing at all would happen, I turned my mind away.
(*Mem*, 78–9)

⁵ Lissadell, celebrated by WBY in his poem, 'In Memory of Eva Gore-Booth and Con Markiewicz', is a house in the neo-classical style, designed by Francis Goodwin and built 1832–4. In being invited to such a house WBY had, as he explains in *Mem* (77), broken out of his class: 'No matter how rich we grew, no matter how many thousands a year our mills or our ships brought in, we could never be "county", nor indeed had we any desire to be so. We would meet on grand juries those people in the great houses . . . and we would speak no malicious gossip and knew ourselves respected in turn, but the long-settled habit of Irish life set up a wall.' For the Connollys of Castletown, Co. Kildare, see p. 261.

⁶ It was, in fact, at Manchester that Dunmorgan (see p. 407) won the Ordsall Nursery Handicap on 23 Nov 1894. The horse (ridden by G. Barrett) made all the running on a five-furlong course and won by a length and a half at odds of 10 to 1. George Pollexfen's discontented housekeeper Kate was standing in for Mary Battle who 'was again ill and away' (*Mem*, 85).

¹ In OS's novel, *The Journey of High Honour*, published in November 1894, Elizabeth Jordan, a champion of women's rights, marries Stephen Branden, who is burdened with a sense of failure. Chilled

satisfaction. What fault I would find I have already found with 'Love on a Mortal Lease'. First of all you do not know man kind anything like as well as woman kind—I wonder how you would fare were you to pick out some eccentric man, either from among those you know, or from literary history, from the Villiers De Lisle Adams & Verlainnes, & set him to make love to your next heroine? If you could make your men salient, marked, dominant you would at once treble the solidity of your work. As yet your heroes are not only a little shadowy in characterization, but too passive, too much driven hither & thither by destiny. They are refined, destinguished, sympathetic not because you have given them this for their character but because your own character & ideals are mirrored in them.[2] And even in quite obvious things—things which you have certainly imagined for them—you leave them too indefinite. I had a clear unchanging vision of your heroines at once but I found that both the men kept taking the appearance of various pictures friends & the like. After a bit Brandon settled down despite my best endevours into the likeness—the perfectly irrelevant likeness—of a distracted husband in one of Orchardsons pictures; while Christopher, as soon as I had discovered his aproximate age, put on the form of a certain ungainly, long-suffering & freckled publishers reader.[3] You will remember that this is an old complaint of mine. You *think* the events sometimes when you should *see* them & make your
[*End of letter missing*]
PS.
    I have just found your letter. I think Lionels book very wonderful & agree

by his wife's spiritual and moral superiority, Branden turns to her great friend, Felicia Noble, who reciprocates his love. When Christopher Jordan, Elizabeth's cousin, proposes to her, Felicia decides to accept him; but Elizabeth, glimpsing her embracing Branden, understands her motives and dissuades her. Instead Felicia goes to Germany to study music, and Branden makes an extended tour abroad but promises to return to Elizabeth.
    Elizabeth's development exemplifies the epigraph to the book, taken from Sidney's *Arcadia*: 'The journey of high honour lies not in plain ways.' At the beginning of the novel she is described (10–11) as 'touched deeply with the modern spirit . . . but untouched as yet by the sense of failure, of irony'. The gradual awareness of her husband's alienation and the shock of his relationship with Felicia teaches her (149) that 'happiness is dependent on the life of the soul; the soul's vitality depends on its growth, and growth often means pain; therefore our happiness may have its root in pain.' Beautiful, generous, and forgiving, Elizabeth by the end of the book has apparently won back her husband's affections.
    [2] In her next book, *The False Laurel* (1896), OS did draw an eccentric, but it is a woman, the half-genius, half-insane Daria West. Daria's husband, Jonathan, is once again 'refined, distinguished, sympathetic' and the other man in her life, Hall Ravenscroft, although more devious, is hardly 'eccentric . . . salient, marked, dominant'. Her fourth novel, *Rupert Armstrong* (1898), does, however, attempt a more penetrating treatment of the masculine and artistic temperament.
    [3] Sir William Quiller Orchardson RA (1832–1910) became well known for his depictions of dramatic situations particularly in upper-class domestic life; WBY may have had in mind, for Stephen Branden, the husband in one of Orchardson's better-known paintings such as *Mariage de Convenance—After* (1886) or *The First Cloud* (1887). OS's character Christopher Jordan has a 'humorous, half cynical turn of mind' as he waits patiently if vainly for Felicia, agreeing to marry her even though she tells him that she loves another. The 'freckled publishers reader' of whom WBY was reminded was the tall and ungainly—and freckled—Edward Garnett.

with you about caring more for his theories about literature in general than those about Hardy in particular.[4] However his summing up of the scenic qualities of Hardy in the chapter 'Wessex' & elsewhere is very stately. I feel however that there is something wrong about praising Hardy in a style so much better than his own. I wish he had written instead of Dante or Milton.

I hope you have not been seriously ill & will soon be able to work again as vigerously as of old. I am glad that not writing makes you miserable—heartless though the remark be—for that insures me the pleasure of many another 'Journey of High Honour'.

ALS MBY. Partly in Wade, 240–1.

To the Editor of United Ireland, *1 December 1894*

"DEAR SIR—I know perfectly what Emerson wrote about the 'wit and wisdom' of the 'The Leaves of Grass', but cannot see how his praise alters the fact that while Mr. W. M. Rossetti was bringing out an English selection from Whitman's poems, and Mr. Ruskin and George Elliot celebrating their power and beauty, the American public was hounding their author from a Government post because of their supposed immorality, or that when in his old age all Europe had learned to honour his name the leading magazines of his country were still not ashamed to refuse his contributions.[1] Whitman appealed, like every great and earnest mind, not to the ignorant many, either English or American, but to that audience, 'fit though few,' which is greater than any nation, for it is made up of chosen persons from all, and through the mouths of George Elliot, Ruskin, and Emerson it did him honour and crowned him among the immortals.

"However, I expect that we are merely quarrelling about words, for I agree

---

[4] *The Art of Thomas Hardy*, by Lionel Johnson, was published in October 1894.

[1] In publishing WBY's letter of 10 Nov 1894, signed 'A Student of Irish Literature' (see pp. 408–9), in *United Ireland* of 24 Nov, John McGrath commented (1) that he

traverses my reference to America by referring to Whitman. He is evidently not aware that the first real word of encouragement that came to Whitman when he published his "Leaves of Grass" was from his countryman Emerson. "I find it," wrote the philosopher to him, "the most extraordinary piece of wit and wisdom that America has yet contributed." Nor was it for a year afterwards, and only by an accident, that they knew of the book in England, when William Bell Scott fell across some copies and sent one to William Michael Rossetti.

Emerson's letter had been written on 21 July 1855. W. M. Rossetti's edition of *Poems by Walt Whitman* appeared in 1868, while the widely quoted letter to H. J. Bathgate, in which Ruskin extolled the 'deadly' truth of Whitman and Emerson, was dated 29 June 1880. George Eliot had quoted extracts from sections 6 and 32 of *A Song of Myself* as part of an unsigned review, 'Art and Belles Lettres', in the *Westminster Review*, April 1856.

with you that if we are ever to have an Irish reading public we must have an Irish criticism to tell it what to read and what to avoid. I do not, however, think that it is brought any nearer by bidding Irish writers develop 'an adamantine indifference to the judgment of every public but the public of Ireland' as 'the only honourable position' to take up.[2] It is not a matter in any sense for the authors, but for the journalists, editors, and newspaper owners of Ireland. If good criticism be written in Irish newspapers it will carry its due weight with authors and public alike; but so long as Irish critics are forced to criticise Irish books in English papers you will have no criticism in Ireland that any man will listen to. One or two of our papers are doing a little, a very little, but in the main the amateur is supreme, and the few articles that show knowledge, and that far rarer thing, judgment, are lost and unnoticed amid an empty ritual of convention and prejudice.—Yours sincerely,

"A STUDENT OF IRISH LITERATURE"

Printed letter, *United Ireland*, 1 December 1894 (1). Wade, 241–2.

To T. Fisher Unwin, 7 December [1894]

⟨3 Blenheim Ro⟩
Thorn Hill | Sligo | Ireland
Dec 7th

Dear Mr Unwin

I return you the proof of the note.[1] It was sent on yesterday from my London address. I hardly knew the kind of thing you wanted, and was rather loth to interview myself. I am working at the MSS every day now.

I have not yet thanked you for Mr Chessens novel[2] but will do so when I have found time to finish it. I can but read a chapter now & then & so far as I have gone find it decideldy interesting.

Yrs sincely
W B Yeats

ALS Texas.

   [2] In recommending P. J. M'Call's *Irish Nóiníns* (see p. 408), 'J. M'G.' had written in *United Ireland*, 10 Nov 1894, 'You feel instinctively on reading it that it has gone out into the world ready to stand or fall by the judgment of Irish people, and equally ready, if necessary, to maintain an adamantine indifference to the judgment of all the rest of the world.'

   [1] See p. 411.
   [2] *Name This Child* by Wilfred Hugh Chesson (1870–1953) was published in 2 vols by Unwin in November 1894. A mannered *bildungsroman* which stylistically owes much to Meredith, it tells how a sensitive child named Narcissus grows into morbid manhood but is saved by the sacrifice of a godfather and the love of a good woman called Dulsworth. Chesson was employed by Unwin and in March 1901 was to marry the poetess Nora Hopper.

To Susan Mary Yeats, 16 December [*1894*]

Thorn Hill | Sligo
Dec. 16.th

My dear Lilly

I have just returned from Lissadell where I have been staying first with the Gore Booths & afterwards at the Parsonage. I lectured in the School House on Fairy lore chiefly to an audience of Orangemen.[1] It was a novel experience. I found that the comic tales delighted them but that the poetry of fairy lore was quite lost on them. They held it Catholic superstititon I suppose. However I had fortunately chosen nothing but humourous tales. The children were I beleive greatly excited. Mr Jones of Roughley said afterwards that now there should be another lecture to put my lecture 'on a sound religeous basis' for he feared it may have sent away many of the audience with the idea that the fairies really existed. Mr Jones was christened by our great grandfather.[2] I got a good lot of folk lore at Lissadell for the Gore Booths brought me to see an old tenant who poured out quantities of tales. Folk lore was a new experience to them. They had not thought it existed. They have now got all my books—including a large paper copy of 'The Countess Kathleen'. They are a very pleasent, kindly, inflamable family. Ever ready to take up new ideas & new things. The eldest son is 'theoretically' a homeruler & practically some kind of a humanitarian, much troubled by the responsibily of his wealth & almost painfully conscientious. He & the clergyman—Lefanu—are full of schemes. He is not however particularly clever & has not, I imagine, much will. He was on a ranch in America & picked up his ideas there.[3] The strongest willed of them, is I think old Miss Gore who is an invalede & is mostly invisable but is always more or less behind the scenes like an iron claw. She is very much of a Tory & cares for nothing but horses. Sir Henry Gore Booth thinks of nothing but the north pole, where his first officer to his great satisfaction has recently lost him self & thereby made an expedition to rescue him desirable.[4]

---

[1] See p. 413.

[2] Charles Gore Jones (*c.* 1821–1912) lived at Raughley Lodge, Ballinfull, Carney, Co. Sligo. The Revd John Yeats (1774–1846), rector of Drumcliffe 1805–46, may have christened him, but he evidently neglected to enter his birth in the parish register. Jones married in 1855 but outlived his wife and later moved to Dublin where he died.

[3] Josslyn Augustus Richard Gore-Booth (1869–1944) succeeded as 6th baronet on his father's death in 1900. He had spent two years after leaving school studying agronomy and livestock management in the USA and Canada, where he became convinced that co-operation was the only way forward for Irish farmers. On his return to Ireland, he made a number of agricultural experiments at Lissadell in an attempt to improve production. He was a warm supporter of Horace Plunkett's Irish Agricultural Organization Society, and in June 1895 was to help set up the Drumcliffe Dairy Society, the first of several co-operative creameries in the Sligo district; the following year he assisted with the first Sligo conference of the IAOS. In 1902 he set up and ran the Sligo Manufacturing Society, a co-operative shirt-making venture.

[4] Sir Henry William Gore-Booth (1843–1900), 5th baronet, made his first polar expedition in 1879,

You ask about 'Under the Moon'.[5] I have got fairly good terms. A royalty from the first copy & recovery of the copyright after a term of years, also the right to decide all questions of binding printing etc. I am correcting 'Oisin' & find it a job. I intend to make additions to the Countess Kathleen.

Your horoscopes struck me as very good—yours less so than the others—Lolly's was particularly good. Jack's was good too.[6]

Yrs affec
W B Yeats

[*On back of envelope*]
I am always glad to see papers

ALS MBY, with envelope addressed to Blenheim Road, postmark 'SLIGO DE 17 94'. Wade, 242–3.

To Susan Mary Yeats, 26 December [*1894*]

Thorn Hill | Sligo
Dec 26th

My dear Lilly

A great many thanks for the handkerchief & please convey my thanks to Lolly for the other. I am sorry to have sent you nothing, but I possess nothing but a 2/– peice & a half penny—borrowed—& will be no wealthier until Methuen chooses to publish 'A Book of Irish Verse'.[1] I have been doing next to no articles for all my time has been taken up with the new poem & the revision of the old ones. I am half through the revision of 'The Wanderings of Oisin', now 'The Wanderings of Ussheen'.[2] I do the new poems always before dinner & work at the old one after, & am getting on

travelling as far north as 70° 24' with Capt. A. H. Markham in the Norwegian schooner *Isbjörn*, making studies of ice drifts in the Barents and Kara Seas. Thereafter he went on a number of other Arctic explorations in his own yacht, *Kara* (named in memory of his first expedition), and he held a master's certificate. Something of his fascination with the polar regions appears in a chapter he contributed on 'Whaling' to John Bickerdyke's *Sea Fishing* (1895): 'The Arctic seems to have an extraordinary and incomprehensible attraction for some people. . . . Indeed, writing this chapter brings back vividly to [the author's] imagination the pleasant days he has spent in the ice and on the fishing grounds, until he longs once more to hear the old cry "A fell!" and seems drawn by some magnetic power towards the north.'

The identity of Sir Henry's first officer (perhaps on the *Kara*) and particulars of his rescue, if one was attempted, are untraced.

[5] See p. 411, n. 2. The book eventually appeared as *Poems* (1895).

[6] George Pollexfen, whom WBY had been introducing to cabbalistic magic at this time (see *Mem*, 75–6, and *Aut*), had found that he had a talent for casting horoscopes. On this occasion, however, he had had the horoscopes of the younger Yeatses cast by an astrologer in England—possibly Walter Gorn Old, who wrote under the name of 'Sepharial', and had contributed articles on astrology to *Lucifer* in the early 1890s.

[1] Methuen published *BIV* in March 1895.

[2] Although the name became 'Usheen' in *Poems* (1895), it was restored to 'Oisin' for the 1899 revised edition of that volume, and remained so until the 1912 revision, when 'Usheen' again prevailed temporarily.

very slowly. Matthews has sent me proofs of Johnsons book of verse. It is exceeding stately & impressive & will make a stir. It is however monotinous & will scarce be ever popular. He has sent me also proofs of a charming little book by Selwen Image.³ I have just finished reading "The Prisoner of Zenda". It is a book, certainly not to be laid down till one has got through it; but infinitely below Stevenson, from whom Hope has evidently learned all he knows—at least in romance. The characters are puppets—very witty & gallant puppets, but puppets all the same.⁴ I am very bookish at present, being busy, so you must excuse no better letter than this. Mʳˢ Shakespere— Johnson's cousin—has sent me her last novel a most subtle delicate kind of book.⁵

Is there a book called 'The Heroick Enthusiasts' lying about belonging to York Powell.⁶ I cannot remember if I took it to Dublin. If I did not you might send to me.

Yr affely
W B Yeats

ALS MBY. Wade, 243–4.

To Charles Elkin Mathews, 30 December [1894]

C/o George Pollexfen | Thorn Hill | Sligo.
Dec 30th

My dear Mʳ Matthews

A great many thanks for Johnson's & Images poems. They are both delightfull books & must I think succeed. There are verses, as fine as any man of this generation has written, in Johnson's, & Image is at times near as good. I like both books infinitely better than 'Vagabondia' which was too American, too noisy, too full of mere ingenuities of phrase to be any way delightful to me. I shall get both books if possible from the Bookman.¹ They have sincerity, simplicity & music & of these are the best always.

---

³ Mathews published both Lionel Johnson's *Poems* and Selwyn Image's *Poems and Carols* in 1895. Image (see p. 239, n. 2), for several years a curate, gave up the Church to become a full-time artist, and was especially well known for his stained-glass designs. From 1910 to 1916 he was Slade Professor of Fine Art at Oxford University.

⁴ *The Prisoner of Zenda* by Anthony Hope had been published in Bristol in April 1894.

⁵ *The Journey of High Honour*; see pp. 414–5.

⁶ Giordano Bruno's *The Heroic Enthusiasts (Gli Eroici Furori)*, trans. L. Williams (1887–9), consists of 10 dialogues which comment upon and amplify a series of interspersed poems on the theme of the soul's struggle towards purification and freedom. This was the first English translation of the book and volume I (1887) had been warmly reviewed by WBY's friend Charles Johnston in *Lucifer*, 15 Oct 1888. York Powell was a keen advocate of the Italian philosopher Bruno (1548–1600) and had apparently already lent the book to Oliver Elton.

¹ See preceding letter. WBY did not review either Johnson's or Image's 1895 book, although he was to

'The Shadowy Waters' is going on very slowly despite the fact that I am working at it every day for some hours. I worked at it till a little while ago all day long, but am now working in the afternoons at the revision of the other poems for Unwin. They may possibly be ready first & if well received should help, I would think, 'The Shadowy Waters'. I may have the play ready for you in a month but may not be ready quite so soon, as I must give a few days to a story for Henley.[2]

Yours ever
W B Yeats

ALS Leeds.

review Johnson's later volume, *Ireland, with Other Poems* (1897), in the *Bookman*, February 1898. (*UP II.* 88–91). For *Songs from Vagabondia*, see p. 405.

   [2] W. E. Henley had ceased with the issue of 31 Mar 1894 to be editor of the *National Observer*. In December 1894 he took over the editorship of the *New Review*, which he revitalized and continued to edit until December 1897. WBY's story 'Wisdom' appeared in the *New Review* in September 1895; it was reprinted as 'The Wisdom of the King' in *The Secret Rose*.

1895

To Susan Mary Yeats, 6 January [1895]

Thorn Hill | Sligo
Jan 6th

My dear Lilly

I have asked Uncle George if the astrologer—who does not live in London—could have known anything about Lolly; & he says certainly not, & that, he only sent the date of Lolly's birth & not her name. The same with the others. I asked him about my horoscope but he seems disinclined to deliver it up or send it & sugessts that you, or papa, send my birth date, or anybody elses you chose, to the address, which he has put on the sheet of paper, enclosing at the same time 6/–. The astrologer whose name he gives is not the same he got mine told by before, but Uncle George beleives him good.[1] I dont suppose you are likely to do as he says, however he seems desirous that I should send you the address.

---

[1] See p. 419; the address written out by George Pollexfen has not survived. A horoscope of WBY—cast, it seems, by a different astrologer remained in his uncle's keeping at least until December 1901, when it was copied out (copy now at MBY) by SMY:

Worked out in 1894.
Copy of Horoscope of W. B. Yeats
Planets
Saturn—significator moon in ascendent Mercury trine to ascendent Saturn & hershel both trine to the moon, Jupiter sextile to moon.
Personal appearance
Dry cold lean body medium height slender build, dark swarthy complexion, black hair dark eyes, black eyebrows meeting in centre curving over brow & sloping down at outer ends. This nose inclined to bend down over lips, nostrils closed chin long & rather large underjaw somewhat projecting, holds head slightly forward or stooping.
Matters of mind etc
Native profound in imagination reserved patient melancholy, in arguing or disputing grave & austere in manner a composed manner, tender, lover of all honest sciences & a searcher into & delighter in strange studies & novelties. Inclined to flit about & shift his habitation, rather timorous loving peace & to live free from cares of life but delighting in society— ☽ in ♒ gives fondness for science & astrology & a good linguist—also being born near midnight will be very imaginative subject to see vision & dream dreams & to be a beleiver in the unseen world— ☽ in ascendent also gives travelling & success in old age is

Please send me any Pall Mall or 'Westminster' you may have which reviews Wilde's play.[2]

No I have not seen Miss Hoppers book but will buy it as soon as I have any money. I am at present writing a story for Henley for 'The New Review' & must then do a poem for 'Saturday Review' which has written and asked me.[3]

I have not seen Mrs Hinksons review of Miss Hopper but have heard of it. A man here—Fizgerald—mentioned it & supposed I was the writer of it.[4]

We have had some excellent storms here, accompanied by hail, rain & lightining.

Yr ever
W B Yeats

ALS MBY, with envelope addressed to Blenheim Road, postmark 'SLIGO JA 7 95'.

foreshadowed by ⊙ in 4th house. ☿ in 3rd also makes for frequent journeyings while some say it signifies mathematical aptitude. Ultimate success in life fortune through Literature.
Science or commerce—
I take it that his success in life & fortune will be considerably affected probably in a good direction by the affect upon his mind & imagination & the influence of his feelings towards women. The two planets nearest the moon may personify two who may so influence his life, the first tall light brown hair good looking fond of animals, honorable generous, brave, subject to no reason, ready to hazard herself in all perils, slighting all things in comparison to victory. The second a very Venus like person, tall graceful slender fair hair agreeable musical & winning but also fond of ruling—but as ♂ is the planet in 7th house nearest the cusp it shows disagreements & quarrels & this together with the ☽ in △ with ♄ is against marriage so he may marry neither of these. The planet most friendly to the ☽ being ♄ I would not say but that there might ultimately be a third person of a Saturnine type.
The ☽ in axt by aspected favourably by the △ of ♄ & the △ of the ⊙ etc.
So well placed I should judge the native to be gifted with an imagination of a most brilliant & glorious kind as aspected by the sun also of a very spiritual & solemn order.
♃ being in ♊ he will always be loved & helped in his best aspirations by attached & admiring friends.

Copied by Lily Yeats
Dec 6th 1901. Sligo

[2] Oscar Wilde's *An Ideal Husband* had opened at the Haymarket Theatre on 3 Jan 1895. Both the *Pall Mall Gazette* and the *Westminster Gazette* carried unsigned, mainly unfavourable, reviews on 4 Jan.

[3] The story was 'Wisdom' (see p. 421). The poem, 'The Twilight of Forgiveness' (reprinted as 'Michael Robartes asks Forgiveness because of his Many Moods'; *VP*, 162–3) did not appear in the *Saturday Review* until 2 Nov 1895.

[4] An unsigned review, almost certainly by KT, of Nora Hopper's *Ballads in Prose* (1894) had appeared in the *Irish Daily Independent*, 26 Dec 1894. Nora Hopper (1871–1906), later the wife of W. H. Chesson (see p. 417), was born in Exeter, England, into a military family of Irish and Welsh stock. She spent a considerable time studying folklore and allied topics at the British Museum, and then worked as a free-lance journalist on a number of English and Irish newspapers and periodicals. Her second book, *Under Quicken Boughs*, was published in 1896. WBY's Sligo acquaintance Fitzgerald has not been identified.

To Katharine Tynan Hinkson, 15 January [*1895*]

Thorn Hill | Sligo | Ireland
Jan 15th

My dear Mrs Hinkson

I have asked Ellis to send you his 'Scancan the Bard'. It is a poem on an Irish story out of Lady Wilde & is a bit of 'The Celtic Revival' which may interest you. Ellis is a pure Celt a Welshman but has no Irish blood I am sorry to say. Say if you can a good word for him.¹ I hear you have Miss Hopper's book.² I have not seen it yet & would be greatly obliged if you would lend it me—posting it here. You shall have it back safely. I would buy it but I am even poorer than usual. I am working very hard—every moment indeed of the day—correcting my poems for a new edition & writing a new one 'The Shadowy Waters' which will I hope be my strongest as it certainly will be my strangeist thing. I am looking out for your miracle plays which should be your masterpeice.³

By the by I wish you or some one else would do a general article in some monthly, either on the recent literature of Ireland, or on its more popular past, the recent Irish stories—Miss Barlows & Miss Lawlesses & O'Grady's books & such books as 'The Real Charlotte'—I have not read this but Henley praised it greatly to me—& send copies—the editor would do this if you asked him—to all the important Irish papers. The article might contrast the recent work with the earlier.⁴ My own idea is that our verse is better than the old but that our prose—except in essays like bits of Hydes Love Songs— is far behind Carleton & Lover & Croker at their best. Miss Barlow, Miss Lawless have more lyrical fealing & belong therefore to a higher type but they have not the central fire of the old people, (I feel the same about my

---

¹ Edwin Ellis's play, *Sancan the Bard* (see p. 352), published by Ward & Downey in December 1894, was based on the story of 'Seanchan the Bard and the King of the Cats', in vol. II of Lady Wilde's *Ancient Legends, Mystic Charms and Superstitions of Ireland* (see p. 71). Ellis had been quick off the mark in sending KT a copy of his play for her unsigned notice had already appeared in the *Irish Daily Independent*, 11 Jan 1895 (6): The 'little Celtic play rendered with Celtic grace and imaginativeness . . . often reminds us of W. B. Yeats . . . of Tennyson . . . Mr Ellis has got rid of the obscurity that spoilt his last volume of poems, and this little book is extremely clear and sweet. The simplicity and the purity are alike Celtic.' In 1904 WBY was to borrow 'some ideas' from *Sancan the Bard* for his own play *The King's Threshold*.

² *Ballads in Prose*; see preceding letter.

³ KT's *Miracle Plays* were not published until the autumn of 1895.

⁴ Finally, WBY was to take his own advice and produced a series of four articles on 'Irish National Literature' in the *Bookman*, July–October 1895. In the second, (*UP* I. 366–73) he dealt with 'Contemporary Prose Writers—Mr O'Grady, Miss Lawless, Miss Barlow, Miss Hopper, and the Folk-Lorists'. The first of the articles (*UP* I. 359–64) discussed earlier Irish writing 'From Callanan to Carleton', but he did not make as much of the contrast between that and recent work as is suggested here. *The Real Charlotte*, by Edith Somerville (1858–1949) and Martin Ross (pseudonym of Violet Florence Martin, 1865–1915), published in 3 vols. in 1894, he mentioned as describing 'with unexampled grimness our middle-class life'.

youthful 'John Sherman' it also is languid). They are the bottom boys of a head class, while Carleton & Lover & Croker & Lever were the head boys of a lower class.[5] The only person who while belonging to the head class has the central fire of the old people is O'Grady. Everything he does is a new creation, a new miracle.

Yrs ev
W B Yeats

ALS Harvard, with envelope addressed to Mount Avenue, Ealing, postmark torn.

To Katharine Tynan Hinkson, 20 January [1895]

C/o George Pollexfen | Thorn Hill | Sligo
Jan 20th

My dear Mrs Hinkson

Many thanks for the book. You are certainly very badly plagerized in 'the lay brother' which amazes me. The only way I can account for it is that the author has, by some freke of fancy, elected to consider you as a 'document' an authority, & to use you much as I have used the Middle Irish 'Oisin & Patrick' poems in 'The Wanderings of Oisin'. She has done this with me. For instance she quotes as a legendary authority a purely fanciful line out of 'The Man who dreamed of faeryland'. She must have taken your Iona poem as a versification, perhaps a translation of some Gaelic original & never perceived the resemblance of her manner to the manner of yours.[1] I feel less inclined to be severe than you, for she seems to have great artistic fealing, & very considerable imagination. Besides she has paid us 'the sincerest form of flattery'. I am greatly delighted with her evident use of my two folklore

[5] Charles James Lever (1806–72) was born in Dublin, the son of an English builder, and practised medicine for a decade, latterly in Brussels, before making a success with his novels *Harry Lorrequer* (1839) and *Charles O'Malley* (1841). In 1842 he took up the editorship of the *Dublin University Magazine*, where his early work had appeared, but, wearying of attacks from both the Young Irelanders and the Unionists, he resigned in 1845 and again went to live abroad. Later he held minor diplomatic posts in Italy, and in 1867 Lord Derby promoted him to the Consulship at Trieste with the words, 'Here is £600-a-year for doing nothing; and you, Lever, are the very man to do it.' Of great personal charm and with genuine creative and comic gifts, Lever suffered from a temperamental indolence and a constant need for money which led him to write too much too quickly. This, together with his Ascendancy associations and flair for stage-Irish caricature, rendered his work suspect to a later generation of Irish critics and in *RIT* (II, 209) WBY observed, 'It will be a long time before the world tires altogether of his gay, witty, reckless personages, though it is gradually learning that they are not typical Irish men and women.'

[1] In Nora Hopper's 'Lament of the Lay Brother', as in KT's 'In Iona' (published in *Ballads and Lyrics*, 148–9), a lay brother laments St. Columba's banishment of cattle from the holy island of Iona. In her unsigned review of *Ballads in Prose* in the *Irish Independent* (see p. 423), KT had compared the first stanzas of the two poems, referring to her own, discreetly, as by 'an elder writer'. The reference to WBY's poem is in the Glossary to *Ballads in Prose*, where it is explained that the quicken tree, or mountain ash, 'is sacred to the Gentle People, and in the Isle of the Blessed the happy dead dwell under "woven roofs of quicken boughs" as W. B. Yeats has exquisitely described in "A Man that Dreamed of Fairyland".'

Anthologies for I compiled them, that they might influence Irish literature & help lift it out of rhetoric. I like the simplicity of her style too. 'The Fairy Fiddler' & 'Una of the West' & 'The Silk of the Kine' among the verses are delightful & 'Daluan' 'The Gifts of Aodh & Una' (this has a wonderful scene in a temple) & 'The Four Kings' among the prose. Her great lack is solidity & lucidity.[2] However she is a fine ⟨recruit to⟩ new coming in our little ⟨regiment⟩ group & can only help to foster a taste for our Celtic wares. She has unfortunately copied the title of my new book, 'The Wind Among the Reeds', which has been mentioned under its name in several places, & made a poem out of it, & put a verse of it on her title page, which is exceedingly anoying but may be chance.[3]

However there is no getting over the fact that she is an artist of very considerable destinction & artists are few in Irish literature. Her next book will probably be quite her own. I wish this one had come in good time for my Anthology.[4] She may have done all the iniquitiles in the new gate Calendar but she can write & that, in a writer, is the main matter.

Yrs snly
W B Yeats

I shall keep the book yet a while.

ALS Harvard, with envelope addressed to Mount Avenue, Ealing, postmark 'SLIGO JA 21 95'.

To Susan Mary Yeats, 20 January [*1895*]

Thorn Hill | Sligo
Jan 20th

My dear Lilly

I have read Miss Hopper & like her. I wrote to Mrs Hinkson for the book. The only inexplicable plagiarism is I think 'The lay brother' which she should have seen is lifted body & bones from Mrs Hinkson. The rest are the plagiarisms of inexperienced enthusiasm I think. She has take[n] us as documents, just as if we had written hundreds of years ago. There is an

[2] In the story 'The Gifts of Aodh and Una', Aodh sacrifices his human attributes and Una her life to the ancient gods of Ireland to deliver the people of Brefny from plague; WBY was to quote at length from the temple scene when he wrote about Nora Hopper's work in the second of his *Bookman* articles on Irish literature (see p. 424), in August 1895. But in that article and another of 1898, he was critical, as here, of her lack of 'solidity & lucidity', finding (*UP* I. 370) here and there 'too much of filmy vagueness, as in visions in the wizard's glass, before the mystical sweeper has swept the clouds away with his broom'.

[3] Her four-stanza quatrain poem 'The Wind Among the Reeds' appears on page 79 of *Ballads in Prose*. The final stanza of the poem is also printed on the page opposite the title-page of the book. WBY's collection with that title (see p. 402, n. 2) was not to appear until 1899.

[4] Although no poems by Nora Hopper appeared in the 1895 edition of *BIV*, WBY included two in 1900, 'The Fairy Fiddler' from *Ballads in Prose* and 'The Dark Man' from *Under Quicken Boughs*.

amusing note in which she takes a wholly fanciful line out of 'A man who dreamed of faery land' as a mythological authority. She has great artistic gifts, great gift for style but is as yet lacking in solidity & clearness. I like best 'Deluan' 'The Gift of Aodh & Una' & 'The Four Kings' which are wonderful. I am looking out for a place to review her in.[1] 'The Irish Literary Movement' is flourishing. A lecture on Sir Samuel Ferguson which was read at the *Irish Lit Society London* by Roden Noel, was read in Dublin the other day by Miss Hickey, with the Archbishop in the Chair & Dowden, Sir William Stokes, Prof Mahaffey, Judge Fitzgibbon, The Master of the Rolls & Prof Ingram all to make speaches about it;[2] & the best of the joke is that it was described by one of the speakers as a lecture written for, and delivered to, an English Audience—not one word was said about the Irish Lit Society & Prof Dowden expressed scorn for the Irish Lit movement & Irish Lit generally for which he has been catching it from all the Dublin papers— even the Irish Times which had a leader on him. He has written a rather feable protest.[3]

---

[1] See preceding letter. Though WBY did not review Nora Hopper's *Ballads in Prose*, he described it in August 1895, in the second of his *Bookman* articles on Irish literature (see p. 424), as having 'the beauty of a dim twilight' and praised it 'with hardly a reservation'. He discussed the book again, together with her 1896 volume, *Under Quicken Boughs*, in an article, 'The Poems and Stories of Miss Nora Hopper' (*UP* II. 124–8), in the Dublin *Daily Express*, 24 Sept 1898.

[2] Roden Noel's lecture on 'The Poetry of Sir Samuel Ferguson' was read by Emily H. Hickey (see p. 173) at the Leinster Lecture Hall on 14 Jan 1895. Noel had given the lecture himself to the Irish Literary Society, London, in May 1894, but had died later in the same month. Born in 1834, Roden Berkeley Wriothesley Noel was the youngest son of the 1st Earl of Gainsborough but considered himself Irish through the influence of his mother, a daughter of the Earl of Roden. He published a number of books of verse and a life of Byron (see p. 242), to whom he was distantly related; his *Selected Poems*, edited by Percy Addleshaw, appeared in 1897.

Of the other notables present or speaking at the Dublin reading of the lecture, William Conyngham, 4th Baron Plunket (1828–97), formerly Bishop of Meath, and Protestant Archbishop of Dublin from 1884, had been a long-standing friend of Ferguson. Sir William Stokes (1839–1900) Professor at the Royal College of Surgeons of Ireland and appointed Surgeon-in-ordinary to Queen Victoria in Ireland in 1892, was the younger brother of Ferguson's great friend and colleague, Whitley Stokes (1830–1909), and attended Ferguson during his last illness in 1886. Sir John Pentland Mahaffy (1839–1919), Professor of Ancient History at TCD, a prominent Dublin wit and personality for over half a century who published widely on Greek history and literature as well as on Irish history, education, and Egyptian papyri, had been a friend and neighbour of Ferguson's. His signed obituary of the poet in the *Athenaeum*, 14 Aug 1886 (205), although it mentioned Ferguson's association with the Young Ireland movement, went out of its way to stress his loyalty, and had on that account been censured both by WBY (*UP* I. 89) and *United Ireland*, 11 Sept 1886 (5). Gerald Fitzgibbon (1837–1909), successively Solicitor-General of Ireland, Lord Justice of Appeal, and a Privy Counsellor, was also active in educational matters, and at this time a Commissioner of National Education. Andrew Marshall Porter (1837–1919) was Master of the Rolls in Ireland 1883–1906. John Kells Ingram (1823–1907), poet, scholar, and economist, was Professor of Oratory and later of Greek at TCD. A friend of Ferguson's and a fellow member of the Royal Irish Academy, in 1843 he had written one of the most popular nationalist poems, 'Who fears to speak of Ninety-eight?'

[3] In commenting on Ferguson's poetry after the lecture, Dowden was reported as saying (*Daily Express*, 15 Jan 1895) that he did not take the enthusiastic view of Irish poetry of some of the other speakers, finding in it in general an undue tendency to rhetoric, sentimentality, and a deficiency of technique. Although Ferguson was free of these literary vices, he was not popular because he belonged to

428 SLIGO: JANUARY 1895 *Aet. 29*

Uncle George has had an astrological triumph. Some friend sent him the birth date of a child & asked him for a horoscope. He made one but wrote— he did not even know the childs name by the by or whether it was a boy or a girl—that it was no use judging it, as the child, if it had not died at birth, could not out live infancy, & that death would probably be caused by fits.

He showed me the answer the other day. The friend had sent the birth date as a test. The child had died of fits ten or eleven days after birth. He showed me the figure before sending it, & I remarked, that the mental planets were so afflicted, that if it lived it would have something wrong with its brain. Unfortunately he did not put this in the judgement. The doctor said had the child lived it would have been an idiot. He has done one or two others & they have all been excellent.

I have had to put 'the Shadowy Waters' aside for the present & the poem for the 'Saturday Review,' & am trying to get the revision of the Countess Kathleen done & some more stories.[4]

I have been to the Cockrans to lunch[5] but otherwise have been only out of

an age of faith and was writing in an age of doubt: 'They could not expect people who were asking questions about the existence of God to interest themselves in Cuculain.'

The *Irish Times* of 15 Jan 1895 gave two columns (6) to a report of the lecture on Ferguson and in an editorial in the same issue (4–5), censured Dowden for his attitude towards Irish poetry:

Professor DOWDEN would have been honester if he had declared that he did not believe in the existence of Irish poetry at all. Its defect is "a tendency towards rhetoric," a somewhat obscure phrase which can only be accounted for on the supposition that it belongs to the "higher criticism." Whatever truly touches the heart of humanity, various as sources of inspiration may be, *is* poetry, and the mere schoolman, who is the worst of all critics because the least broadminded, cannot make it out to be otherwise, nor is his small standard of comparison the most accurate or just. According to Professor DOWDEN, Sir SAMUEL FERGUSON's misfortune was that of his birth in "an age of faith." If he had lived a little later and made verses on Anarchists and labour leaders, and such noble spirits of the improving time, he would have done better, and best of all John Bull would have bought his books. . . .

In replying to these criticisms on the following day, Dowden maintained that he had been misreported in saying that Ferguson's 'misfortune was that of his birth in "an age of faith" ', and reminded the *Irish Times* that some years before he had asserted that there was 'more of the Homeric—the highest epic— spirit in Samuel Ferguson's "Conary" than in all that Tennyson has written'. An immediate rejoinder by the editor admitted the misquotation but refused to 'suffer Professor Dowden to escape from his condemnation of the spirit of Irish poetry on the ground of a technical misunderstanding. . . . To his general estimate of Irish poetry we have taken exception as belonging to a school of artificial criticism' (*Irish Times*, 16 Jan 1895 [6]).

   [4] For the poem for the *Saturday Review*, see p. 423. The stories, intended eventually for publication in *The Secret Rose*, included 'Wisdom' (later 'The Wisdom of the King'; see p. 421) and 'St. Patrick and the Pedants' (reprinted as 'The Old Men of the Twilight'), which appeared in the *Weekly Sun Literary Supplement*, 1 Dec 1895.
   [5] William Cochrane (1823–1907) was the borough engineer in Sligo and had been responsible for building the Sligo waterworks. In *Aut* (284–5) WBY recalled dining at this time

with Cochrane of the Glen, as he was called, to distinguish him from others of that name, an able old man. He had a relation, a poor mad girl, who shared our meals, and at whom I shuddered. She would take a flower from the vase in front of her and push it along the tablecloth towards any male guest who sat near. The old man himself had strange opinions, born not from any mental eccentricity, but from the solitude of his life; and a freedom from all prejudices that were not of his own discovery. 'The world is getting

the house for my constitutionals with Uncle George. I am reading French & getting on with my work fairly well.

Yrs affely\
W B Yeats

ALS MBY. Wade, 244–6.

To T. Fisher Unwin, [*21 January 1895*]

Thorn Hill | Sligo | Ireland.

Dear Mr Unwin.

I am very anxious for my book to come out this spring & am pushing on with the revision as rapidly as I can. I shall be through in a month. I suppose that will be soon enough.

I was sorry not to have been able to send you something more of the kind you wanted, than the few lines I gave you for your catalogue,[1] but the fact is if it got out that I interviewed myself, or anything of the sort, some one or other of the excellent people, I have vexed over the Gavan Duffy dispute, would have remembered it to me this side the water—& remembered it for ever.

I have mislaid your note but I beleive you asked me for the full title of my book. '*Under the Moon: poems mainly legendary* by W B Yeats' occurs to me as sufficient. If you want, when advertising it, to give any press opinion— Langs in the Fortnightly would be a good one, however this is your province & not mine. If you dislike the title let me know & I may find a better.[2]

Yours sincely\
W B Yeats

ALS Texas. Dated by recipient '23/1/95'.

more manly,' he would say, 'it has begun to drink port again', or 'Ireland is going to become prosperous. Divorced couples now choose Ireland for a retreat, just as before Scotland became prosperous they began to go there. There are a divorced wife and her lover living at the other side of the mountain'.

    Cochrane lived at Glen Lodge, Cullinamore.

  [1] See pp. 411, 417.

  [2] *Under the Moon* (see p. 411) was for long the projected title of the volume published in October 1895, eventually called simply *Poems*. For Andrew Lang's notice in the *Illustrated London News* (not the *Fortnightly*), see p. 409.

To the Editor of the Daily Express *(Dublin)*[1], *26 January 1895*

Sir—Prof Dowden says that Irish literature has many faults,[2] and this is indeed obvious; nor could it well be otherwise in a young literature, an experimental literature, a literature preoccupied with hitherto unworked material, and compelled to seek an audience for the most part among the poor and the ignorant. The only question at issue is whether we can best check these faults by carefully sifting out and expounding what is excellent, as Mr Stopford Brooke, Mr Rolleston, Dr Hyde, Mr Ashe King, Mr Alfred Perceval Graves, Mr Lionel Johnson, and the other leaders of "the Irish literary movement" are endeavouring to do;[3] or by talking, like Professor Dowden, occasional vague generalities about rhetoric and sentimentality and bad technique. It does not seem to me a question for us whether this literature be important or unimportant, but only whether it be new or not new. If it be new no man living can measure its importance, or say what sails may be filled by it in the future, not merely in Ireland but out of Ireland. And I think that the man who cannot find a distinct character in Callanan's "Outlaw of Loch Lene," in Walsh's "Mairgreod Ni Chealleadu," in Davis' "Marriage" and "Plea for Love," in Mangan's "Ode to The Maguire" and "Woman of Three Cows," in Doheney's "A Cushla Gal ma Chree," in Allingham's "Winding Banks of Erin," in Ferguson's "Conary," in de Vere's "Wedding of the Clans," and in countless other poems, which are neither rhetorical nor sentimental, nor of flaccid technique, must be either prejudiced or a little lacking in artistic sensitiveness.[4] I am sure that if

---

[1] The Dublin *Daily Express*, founded in 1851 and edited at this time by G. V. Patton (d. 1898), was the most firmly Unionist and Protestant of the Dublin papers, but had been losing circulation and influence to the more moderately Unionist *Irish Times*. In 1898 the paper was bought by James Henry Dalziel (1868–1935), MP for Kirkcaldy 1892–1921, a Liberal of advanced views and the proprietor of *Reynolds's News*, who put up the money for Horace Plunkett (see p. 306), Unionist MP for Dublin 1892–1900, to operate it. The paper was edited thereafter by T. P. Gill, under whom its literary pages flourished, until late 1899 when it was sold to Lord Ardilaun.

[2] The controversy over Dowden's remarks on Irish literature at the 14 Jan lecture on Ferguson had spread to the *Daily Express* when the *Irish Times* (see p. 427) refused to publish a letter from T. W. Rolleston critical of Dowden's stand; Rolleston thereupon sent it to the *Express*, which printed it on 21 Jan 1895. The letter argued that Dowden misjudged Ferguson's importance because Dowden's critical canons were English, not Irish, and claimed that Ferguson was still loved and revered in Ireland. Dowden replied in the *Express* of 22 Jan with a passage extracted from the introduction to his forthcoming *New Studies in Literature* designed to show that he was not against Irish literature as such, but that he opposed an Irish literature of false rhetoric, defective craftsmanship, and shrill and flabby patriotism. A rejoinder from Rolleston on the following day pointed out that the writers of the Irish Literary Revival were strongest in their condemnation of the faults that Dowden mentioned, and that there were already writers in Ireland who cared for craftsmanship. WBY joined in the controversy with the present letter.

[3] These were not only all Irish men of letters but also held office in the National Literary Society, Dublin, or the Irish Literary Society, London and had lectured to one or both of the Societies.

[4] All the poems listed, with the exception of Ferguson's 'Conary' (which was too long for quotation),

Professor Dowden does not perceive this distinct character it can only be because he has given the subject too little attention; and if he does perceive it I ask him does he think he has quite done his duty by this new creative impulse. It is not possible to separate out Ferguson and say that he alone has it, for the men I have named have each written something as distinguished, as pathetic, as characteristic as any of his poems. They fall short of his epic aim and of his sustained excellence, but at times excel him in delicacy and in mastery over what Blake has called "minute appropriate words."[5] Professor Dowden has been for years our representative critic, and during that time he has done little for the reputation of Ferguson, whom he admires, and nothing for the reputation of these others, whom Ferguson admired. Our "movement," on the other hand, has only existed three or four years, and during that time it has denounced rhetoric with more passionate vehemence than he has ever done. It has exposed sentimentality and flaccid technique with more effect than has been possible to his imperfect knowledge of Irish literature, but, at the same time, it has persuaded Irish men and women to read what is excellent in past and present Irish literature, and it has added to that literature books of folk-lore, books of history, books of fiction, and books of verse, which, whatever be their faults, are yet the expression of the same dominant mood, the same creative impulse which inspired Ferguson and the poets I have named. Nor is it a self-conscious endeavour to make a literature, but the spontaneous expression of an impulse which has been gathering power for decades, and which makes itself heard in the lull of our political tumults. I have not seen any mention in the reports of the Hon Roden Noel's lecture of the fact that it was originally delivered before the Irish Literary Society, London, and is therefore itself a specimen of our work.—Yours truly,

W B Yeats

Printed letter, *Daily Express* (Dublin), 26 January 1895 (5). *UP* I. 347–8.

were included in WBY's anthology *BIV*. Michael Doheny (1805–63), a Young Irelander and a barrister, fled to the USA after the failure of the 1848 insurrection and helped to found the Fenian Brotherhood there.

    [5] Cf. Blake, 'Public Address': 'Ideas cannot be Given but in their minutely Appropriate Words . . . ' (Notebook, p. 62). WBY used the same quotation in the introduction to *BIV* (xix), dated 5 Aug 1894, where he says that Ferguson 'is frequently dull, for he often lacked the "minutely appropriate words" necessary to embody those fine changes of feeling which enthral the attention . . . .'.

To Nora Hopper,[1] *27 January* [*1895*]

C/o George Pollexfen | Thorn Hill | Sligo | Ireland
Jan 27th

Dear Madam.

Our Irish literature is yet so small, & what work of sublety & style it possesses is so inconsiderable, that I cannot resist the pleasure of writing to tell you of the great pleasure your exquizite book has given me. It is the most finished, the most distinguished volume we have had out of Ireland this decade. It has given me great pleasure to find by stray words & sentences that my own little collections of Irish folk lore have been of use to you. I put them to gether, for no other purpose what ever than to help what I beleive to be a growing school of legendary literature, to fling off the rhetoric of '48' & put on the humility & wisdom of the ancient world. I say this because I am told that one of the Dublin papers, while admitting your literary power, has said something about your 'copying' or 'plagiarising' from some thing of mine; & I want you therefore to know how much I admire your book.[2] I shall take every oppertunity—as soon as I get to London or Dublin—to introduce your book to Irish journalists & readers. Though our people do not yet read very much, they love greatly what they read & the few among them who are students make their books part of their lives & not mere playthings as so many ⟨more copious readers do⟩ in England do. I like best of all 'Daluan' & 'The Gifts of Aodh & Una'—the scene in the temple is among the most imaginative things I have ever read—& 'The Four Kings' & 'Aonan-na-Righ' among the prose; among the verse 'The Fairy Fiddler' 'The Silk of the Kine' & 'Una of the West'. These have all that strange mystery, that sense of a meloncholy in which their is no gloom, a sadness as of morning twilight which I find in the legends of the west.

Yours sincly
W B Yeats

ALS Texas.

[1] See p. 423.

[2] An unsigned review of *Ballads in Prose* in the Dublin *Daily Express*, 11 Jan 1895 (6), commented that 'The rhymes are fascinating in their melody, and an undercurrent of sadness is felt in them all. We fancy we must have seen some of them before.' The reviewer then goes on to quote 'A Connaught Lament': 'I will arise and go hence to the West;/And dig me a grave where the hill-winds call . . .'

To Lionel Johnson, 27 January [*1895*][1]

Thornhill, | Sligo
27 January

Have you seen or heard of the controversy anent Dowden and his views in *The Daily Express?* Dowden at Sir Samuel Ferguson lectures the other day—one old lecture new by Miss Hickey—made an attack on the Irish literary movement—with such 'malice' and evident 'intent to injure' says O'Grady in a note to me today. The amiable Rolleston has complimented him on his tour and Rolleston replied and in the *Express* wrote a vigorous defence of Irish poetry; Dowden replied by sending to the Dublin papers an extract from the preface to a new book of his in which he says by implication that we go about raving of 'Brian Boru' and 'plastered with Shamrock'. Rolleston sent a rejoinder and then was followed by Larminie and myself and on Monday the *Express* will contain a letter of O'Grady's.[2] I hear too that *The Times'* correspondent will give a little to the controversy in his own paper on Monday or Tuesday.[3] Dowden thinks we praise every kind of Irish work 'whether good or bad', and Rolleston has alluded in reply to a 'scattering exposure of bad technique recently delivered in a lecture at the 'National Literary' (Your lecture).[4] I have urged Methuen to publish my anthology at once as a shot in the battle, but don't know if he will or not.[5] I wish some of the London men would write. How is the Society getting on? Has Nutt's lecture come off?[6] Am busy with a revision of my poems for a collected edition and have rewritten *The Countess Kathleen.* . . .

A. N. Jeffares, *W. B. Yeats, Man and Poet* (1962), 97 (fragment).

[1] The original of this letter, formerly in the possession of Mr Adrian Earle, is untraced. The transcription as it stands is evidently corrupt, as in the reading 'new' for what must have been 'read' in line 3.

[2] What Dowden actually wrote in the introduction to *New Studies in Literature*, and in his letter in the *Daily Express* of 22 Jan 1895 (see p. 430), was: 'Let an Irish prose writer show that he can be patient, exact, just, enlightened, and he will have done better service for Ireland, whether he treats of Irish themes or not, than if he wore shamrocks in all his buttonholes and had his mouth for ever filled with the glories of Brian the Brave.' WBY is here quoting the version given in T. W. Rolleston's letter in the *Express* on 23 Jan (see p. 430). William Larminie's letter was published in the *Express* on 26 Jan, along with WBY's (see pp. 430–1). O'Grady's letter appeared on 28 Jan (see below, p. 435, n. 1).

[3] There were no further reports of the controversy with Dowden either in *The Times* of London or the *Irish Times*.

[4] i.e. the lecture on 'Poetry and Patriotism' delivered by Johnson to the National Literary Society on 26 Apr 1894; see p. 384, n. 3.

[5] *BIV* did not appear until March 1895.

[6] The lecture given by Alfred Nutt (see p. 95) in December to the Irish Literary Society, London, dealt with the 'ideas of the Irish Elysium, which have filtered down through Irish folk-lore' (*New Ireland Review*, January 1895, 736).

To T. Fisher Unwin, 27 January [*1895*]

C/o George Pollexfen | Thorn Hill | Sligo
Jan 27th

Dear Mr Unwin

I did not write to you about the designer before becuase I was ballanced beetween two names. I now however suggest Charles Shannon—of 'Rickets & Shannon' fame—& if there be no objection to him & he undertake the job (his address is I imagine, 'the Vale', Chelsea) I will write to him & tell him what I want.[1] I think that the designer of the cover should be consulted about the cloth—as a design usually requires a particular texture & colour to look its best. I would suggest, that the designer be asked to make the book as much a work of art as he can, and (after you have put what ever be a needful limit of expense & I have given a firm command that it be not green & have no shamrocks, & that it be one or two other things) he be left very free. If he prefer to simply furnish a design & leave colour & texture to us I shall ask for a smooth texture & a dark colour.[2]

(2) I should like to see specemins of paper.

(3) Yes Constable by all means. (4) I shall send you a sheet of paper folded to the size of page in a couple of days. I like no headlines, the number of the page to be at the bottom, & single commas for quotation marks, & fairly large type but must leave type & the like to you & the printer, as I have no books here to consult & compare.

(5) I want a title page & cover decoration—not a frontespeice.[3]

(6) Will send list of contents in a few days. The book had better be called simply 'Poems: by W B Yeats' as 'Collected Poems' is a title which would be soon, I hope, made obsolete by my new books of verse.[4]

(7) The book will contain about as much matter as 240 pages of a Cameo volume but will not count to so many as the pages will be larger.[5]

Yours sincerely
W B Yeats

ALS Texas.

[1] Charles Hazlewood Shannon RA (1863–1937), WBY's first choice as designer for *Poems* (1895) (see pp. 403, 407), was responsible either singly or with Charles De Sousy Ricketts (1866–1931) for the design and decoration of many of Oscar Wilde's books, and they had worked together for the Bodley Head. They co-edited *The Dial*, 1889–97, one of the most striking of Aesthetic journals, and at this time shared a house in The Vale, Chelsea.

[2] *Poems* (1895) was issued in light brown cloth with gold lettering and designs (though not by Shannon) on the front and back covers as well as on the spine. WBY's prohibition on shamrocks was respected: the design features an angel and a dragon.

[3] The book was printed by T. and A. Constable in a format measuring $7\frac{1}{2} \times 5$ in. (crown octavo). WBY's stipulations (4) and (5) were complied with.

[4] Fisher Unwin had apparently objected to the title *Under the Moon* (see p. 429), preferring to call the volume *Collected Poems*.

[5] The book comprised pp. xii, 288.

To the Editor of the Daily Express *(Dublin)*, *30 January 1895*

SIR—Professor Dowden has told us how much he loves sobriety and accuracy, and I readily admit that his criticism is usually an example of both, but am afraid that the introduction to his forthcoming book will have little of either virtue. He now admits that a large portion, at any rate, of its heated rhetoric was written more than eleven years ago, and yet he is about to republish it as a criticism of a movement which did not then exist, and which has done its utmost to check the very vices he condemns.[1] Nor is it possible to congratulate him upon the urbanity and justice of the last sentence but one of his curious letter—for in no part of the world is it considered self-advertisement, or shrinking from criticism, to reply to an attack upon a public movement, especially when that attack is markedly heated, and—Professor Dowden must forgive my saying so— interpenetrated with inaccuracy through the very conditions under which it was written—[2] Yours sincerely,

W B Yeats.

Sligo, January 30.

Printed letter, *Daily Express* (Dublin), 31 January 1895 (4).

To J. B. Yeats, [c. *1 February 1895*]

Thorn Hill | Sligo | Ireland

My dear Papa.

Did you see O'Grady letter about Dowden in the express? If not let me know & I will send it. He wrote two, & I have only one, but the one I have is the best.[1] I shall probably send the 'Express' a letter next week on 'The best thirty Irish books'—O'Grady has spoken to them about it—& am only

[1] In a letter in the *Daily Express* on 28 Jan 1895 (4), Standish James O'Grady had alleged that the introduction to Dowden's forthcoming *New Studies in Literature*, of which an extract was published in his letter on 22 Jan (see p. 430), had been written many years before for the *Fortnightly Review*; at the time Dowden had been stung into attacking the Irish school because WBY had censured him in *DUR* for neglecting Ferguson. Dowden, replying to O'Grady in the *Express* on 29 Jan (4), maintained that the passage in question had been written, not in reply to WBY's article ('The Poetry of Sir Samuel Ferguson', *DUR*, November 1886), which he had not noticed, but as a speech given at the College Historical Society (the TCD debating society) on 14 Nov 1883—before WBY had written about him. 'Perhaps', he concluded, 'my plea for sobriety and accuracy is not even now out of date.'

[2] The penultimate sentence of Dowden's 29 Jan letter ran: 'The faults of my own writings . . . I readily admit; yet one merit I claim—I have never advertised myself, and I have never shrunk from being criticised.'

[1] The letter of 29 Jan, see above; a much shorter letter by O'Grady appeared in the issue of 29 Jan and a further one on 2 Feb.

waiting for some books which I want to mention in it to begin it. The contraversy has I think done good. Dowden has certainly got the worst of it. I am still busy with the correction of my poems for Unwin. I have rewritten the first two parts of ⟨Usheen⟩ 'Oisin' &, I am convinced, enormously improved it; & completey altered the end of 'The Countess Kathleen'.

I wrote to Miss Hopper to say how much I admired her little book & have got a letter from her, in which she talks of my things & says my praise has pleased her more than any review etc. I thought 'Daluan' & 'The Gifts of Aodh & Una' very wonderful things. Sigerson writes to me to say that her verse is an exact imitation of my own & of Mrs Hinkson's. Curiously enough I can see the resemblance to Mrs Hinkson, & in one place to Hyde, but not to my self.² I suppose however one cannot recognise ones own manner. I do see however that she has taken a good many names & allusions from my folklore books, & that two or three of her plots are suggested by my things. She tells me that she has never set foot in Ireland & I should say by her hand writing, which is more commercial than anything else, that she must be in an office or have been in one.³

I am rather desperate about my work. I have worked very hard & got on very slowly. 'The Shadowy Waters' is but half done & this correction of the old work drags on. I read a little French every day & am improving.

Yrs affecly
W B Yeats

ALS MBY.

To T. Fisher Unwin, 6 February [*1895*]

Thorn Hill | Sligo
Feb 6th

Dear Mr Unwin

let the book be Crown Octavo.¹ I enclose a list of contents. ⟨Do ask your [?] people to wait until you have the whole.⟩² I am copying out the corrected version of the poems as rapidly as I can & you will receive it next week.

Yrs snly
W B Yeats

ALS Texas.

² Cf. pp. 425–6, 432.
³ Nora Hopper's handwriting, unlike WBY's, is large, round, and legible, but there is no evidence that she worked in an office.

¹ This was the size (7½x5 ins.) of the book as published; see p. 434.
² The list of contents has not survived; it was presumably a later and revised version of that sent on 23 Nov 1894 (see pp. 411–3).

To the Editor of the Daily Express *(Dublin)*, *7 February 1895*

SIR,—A very amusing proof of the unfounded nature of one of Professor Dowden's charges against the Irish literary movement has just reached me. At the very time Professor Dowden was sending to the Press an introduction, saying that we indulged in indiscriminate praise of all things Irish, and went about "plastered with shamrocks and raving of Brian Boru," a certain periodical was giving the hospitality of its pages to a long anonymous letter making a directly contrary charge. The writer of the letter accused some of the members of the Irish Literary Society of discouraging "worthy workers in the field," of endeavouring to substitute the pursuit of what he called "high art" for the old, easy-going days when every patriotic writer was as good as his neighbour, and even of making allegations against the literary merits of the Young Ireland Party. His feelings about one member, who had been rather active in criticism, so completely overpowered him that he could only say this member's walk was ungainly, his personal habits objectionable, and his face dirty, but then he said these things with an exuberant eloquence which I cannot even try to rival.[1] I will not advertise this periodical by naming it, but I shall be delighted to send Professor Dowden my own copy, though it is one of my most precious possessions, and with a little industry I can find him, I dare say, much more of the same kind in other periodicals. If proof were required of the extent to which Dublin is dominated by scholastic—perhaps I should say school room—ideals, Mr Colles gives that proof by finding it "ludicrous" that a young writer like myself should make "an earnest protest" against some of the opinions and methods of an older and better known man of letters.[2] Has Mr Colles forgotten that every literary

---

[1] For Dowden's introduction, cited in the *Daily Express* of 22 Jan 1895, see p. 433. The anonymous letter, signed 'O.X.' and entitled 'Kleinbier, The Poet: A Literary Portrait', had appeared in the *New Ireland Review*, February 1895 (803–7). It purported to give a 'visionary appreciation' of a poet called William Blütiger Kleinbier, the son of a washerwoman who walked affectedly, borrowed small sums of money without repaying them, and despised conventional cleanliness. He and his followers were said to gibe 'at worthy workers in the field of Irish literature' and to make 'absurd and confused allegations against the literary merits of the Young Ireland party.' The concluding part of the letter deals with Kleinbier's quarrel with 'Sir Cavan Toughy' who although given a figurehead role in a publishing scheme 'asserted himself unduly; insisted upon the publication of useful booklets and discountenanced our High Art. Kleinbier was likely to be the chief sufferer by such extinguishing tactics in as much as he could not afford to publish at his own expense. . . .' The letter was a response to a long article on WBY, taking an anti-O'Duffy line, in the series 'From a Modern Irish Portrait Gallery' which had appeared over the initials 'O.Z.' (W. P. Ryan) in the *New Ireland Review*, December 1894 (647–59).

[2] A letter from Ramsay Colles (see p. 128) supporting Dowden's position was published in the *Daily Express*, 4 Feb 1895 (5). Referring to arguments put forward in O'Grady's letters (see p. 435), Colles wrote: 'To cite the authority of Mr Yeats, and write of his "serious protest" addressed to one of Professor Dowden's position in the world of letters, is to have no sense of proportion, and that Mr Yeats, whose achievements no one more heartily applauds than I, should accept such a role is extremely ludicrous.'

revolution the world has seen has been made because of the readiness of the young to revolt against what Walt Whitman has called "the endless audacity of elected persons?"[3]—Yours sincerely,

W B Yeates [*sic*]

Printed letter, *Daily Express* (Dublin), 7 February 1895 (5). *UP* I. 348–9.

To T. Fisher Unwin, 8 February [*1895*]

C/o George Pollexfen J P | Thorn Hill | Sligo
Feb 8th

Dear Mr Unwin

I shall probably be contributing a letter to 'The Daily Express' next week on 'The best thirty Irish books'. I wrote to Standish O'Grady, who is on the staff, about it & he has replied that it will almost certainly be agreed to, but the matter is not quite decided. We want to start a new contraversy, in continuation of a present one on 'Prof Dowden & Irish Literature'. I see by the papers that Hydes 'History of Early Gaelic Literature' will be out next week. If you can send me an *early* copy I will put it in the list of the 30 books or give it a favourable notice in my comment on the list. If I wait to get it through the Sligo shops it will be too late—besides a review deserves a copy. If you could send me a copy of 'The Irish Song Book' by Graves, which I have not seen, I will bring it in either in the list or in the comment.[1]

Yrs sncly
W B Yeats

ALS Texas.

---

[3] Cf. Whitman, 'Song of the Broad-Axe', line 121: 'Where the populace rise at once against the never-ending audacity of elected persons.' To quote Whitman against one of his foremost European champions (see p. 9, n. 5) was a nicely calculated stroke.

[1] Pinned to this letter is a note in another hand: 'We are sending Mr Yeats, per Book-post, in one parcel, Rough sets of sheets of "Story of Early Gaelic Literature" & "Three Sorrows of Story-telling," also a paper copy of "Irish Song-book." ' WBY did include Hyde's *The Story of Early Gaelic Literature* (1895) in his *Daily Express* list of the best thirty Irish books, though when he came to review it in the *Bookman*, June 1895, he found it (*UP* I. 358–9) 'too full of exposition and appeal . . . and too full of crowded facts to touch the imagination'. Hyde's *Three Sorrows of Story-telling and Ballads of St. Columkille* (1895) was not mentioned in the *Daily Express*, and *The Irish Song Book*, edited by Alfred Perceval Graves (see p. 383), described as being 'compiled more for the music than for the verse', was not listed among the best thirty.

Olivia Shakespear

W. B. Yeats with T. W. Rolleston's children in 1894

Fountain Court, The Temple, where Yeats took rooms with Arthur Symons in the autumn of 1895

To T. Fisher Unwin, 16 February [*1895*]

Thorn Hill | Sligo. | Ireland
Feb 16th

Dear Mr Unwin

My letter containing the size of book & the list of contents must have crossed yours as I wrote it a considerable time ago.[1] The sample of paper & the specemin of printing are both all that could be desired. I would be glad if you would see Shannon. I want him to do a decorative title page & to design a cover & to have a say in the choice of the substance & colour of the binding as the effect of his design will be to some extent dependent on this. If he undertake the job I propose to send him a copy of 'The Land of Hearts Desire' & to ask him to try & get the fealing of that poem into his design if possible. At the same time I wish to leave him fairly free. You might perhaps tell him—as it will show him the side of his genius I most admire—that I have chosen him because of my great admiration for a drawing of an old man with a lantern among sheep in the 'Dial', a drawing which seemed to me to perfectly express the union of simplicity & refinement which I hope some day to get into my own work.[2] If however he undertake the job I will write in forwarding the book.

I am getting on gradually with the revision—like most things it takes a little longer than I expected. If it would hasten things I could let you have the first 70 or 80 pages at once & the remainder very soon after. The entry in your 'Announcements' is quite correct except that it might be better to say 'with title page & binding designed by Charles Shannon' instead of simply 'frontespeice' which implies, I think, a slightly different thing. I look upon a frontespeice, as an external & extrinsic decoration, which I would be very glad of, but only if I had also my decorative title page, which I look upon as making an essential part of the book more beautiful. The book should have rough edges.

Many thanks for 'Song book' & proofs of Hyde's book. I have given both a good mention.[3]

Yours sncly
W B Yeats

ALS Texas.

[1] See pp. 436, 411–3.
[2] 'Shepherd in a Mist', drawn on the stone and bitten by Charles Shannon (see p. 434), appeared in the *Dial*, no. 2, 1892, facing page 8.
[3] See preceding letter.

To the Editor of the Daily Express *(Dublin),* 27 *February 1895*

S<small>IR</small>—During our recent controversy with Professor Dowden certain of my neighbours here in the West of Ireland asked me what Irish books they should read. As I have no doubt others elsewhere have asked a like question, I send you a list of thirty books, hoping Mr O'Grady, Mr Rolleston, Mr Ashe King, or some other Irish literary man will fill up the gaps.[1] I have excluded every book in which there is strong political feeling, that I may displease no man needlessly, and included only books of imagination or books that seem to me necessary to the understanding of the imagination of Ireland, that may please myself and the general reader. By this means I may have got nearer to what the next century will care for than had I enumerated substantial volumes "that no gentleman's library should be without." For it is possible that people, both in and out of Ireland, will be singing—

"'Tis my grief that Patrick Loughlin is not Earl of Irrul still,
And that Brian Duff no longer rules as lord upon the hill;
And that Colonel Hugh O'Grady should be lying cold and low,
And I sailing, sailing swiftly from the county of Mayo."[2]

when the excellent books of criticism, scholarship, and history that we teach in our schools and colleges, and celebrate in our daily papers, shall have gone to Fiddler's green. For the best argumentative and learned book is like a mechanical invention and when it ceases to contain the newest improvements becomes, like most things, not worth an old song. Here then is my list, and I will promise you that there is no book in it, "that raves of Brian Boru" half as much as Burns did of Bruce and Wallace, or has an "intellectual brogue" more "accentuated" than the Scottish characteristics in Scott and Stevenson.[3]

[1] The drawing up of lists of best books on various subjects had been a pastime of the British and Irish press in the 1880s. In reviving the custom, WBY was probably influenced by a series on 'The Best Hundred Irish Books' which ran in the *Freeman's Journal* in 1886 and was published as a separate pamphlet in Dublin the same year. T. W. Rolleston and D. J. O'Donoghue were among those joining the controversy in the *Daily Express* in the weeks following WBY's letter.

[2] A verse from 'The County of Mayo', translated by George Fox (?1809–after 1848) from the Irish of Thomas Lavelle. The poem was included in WBY's *BIV*.

[3] An allusion to Dowden's letter of 22 Jan 1895 (see p. 433). In this same 27 Feb issue of the *Daily Express*, an editorial leader commented (4): 'We publish an interesting letter today from Mr W. B. Yeats, in which he gives his personal views in reference to the best thirty Irish books. . . . There is no reason why the merits or the demerits of Irish literature cannot be discussed with calmness and with candour. . . . This subject will be discussed this evening at a meeting of the College Historical Society, at which Professor Dowden will preside.'

NOVELS AND ROMANCES.

1. Castle Rackrent: by Miss Edgeworth.
2. Father Tom and the Pope: by Sir Samuel Ferguson (In "Tales from Blackwood").
3. Fardarougha, the Miser: by William Carleton (out of print).
4. The Black Prophet: by William Carleton (out of print).
5. Traits and Stories of the Irish Peasantry: by William Carleton.
6. The Nolans: by John Banim (out of print).
7. John Doe: by John Banim (bound up with "Crohore").
8. The Collegians: by Gerald Griffin.
9. Barney O'Reirdan: by Samuel Lover (In "Legends and Stories of the Irish Peasantry").
10. Essex in Ireland: by Miss Lawless.
11. Charles O'Malley: by Charles Lever.
12. The Bog of Stars: by Standish O'Grady (New Irish Library).
13. Ballads in Prose: by Miss Hopper.

FOLK LORE AND BARDIC TALES.

14. History of Ireland—Heroic Period: by Standish O'Grady (out of print).
15. The Coming of Cuchullin: by Standish O'Grady.
16. Fin and his Companions: by Standish O'Grady.
17. Old Celtic Romances: by P W Joyce.
18. Silva Gadelica: by Standish Hayes O'Grady.
19. Beside the Fire: by Douglas Hyde.
20. Teig O'Kane: by Douglas Hyde (In "Fairy and Folk Tales of the Irish Peasantry").
21. History of Early Gaelic Literature: by Douglas Hyde (New Irish Library).
22. Mythologie Irlandaise: by Darbois Joubainville.

HISTORY.

23. The Story of Ireland: by Standish O'Grady.
24. Red Hugh's Captivity: by Standish O'Grady (out of print).
25. A Short History of Ireland: by P W Joyce.

POETRY.

26. Irish Poems: by William Allingham.
27. Conary: by Sir Samuel Ferguson (In "Poems").
28. Lays of the Western Gael: by Sir Samuel Ferguson.
29. Love Songs of Connact: by Douglas Hyde (second edition in the press).
30. Ballads and Lyrics: by Mrs Hinkson.

"The Nolans" and "Fardarougha the Miser" and "The Bog of Stars" are probably the most memorable among the tragic, "Castle Rack-rent" among the half tragic half humorous, and "The Traits and Stories", "Charles O'Malley," "Father Tom and the Pope,"[4] and "Barney O'Reirdan" among the humorous tales. I do not think modern fiction has any more strange, passionate and melancholy creation than the old miser Fardarougha, or anything more haunting than the description of the household of the spendthrift squireen in the opening chapters of "The Nolans," or the account a little further on of the "spoiled priest" taking the door from its hinges to lay upon it the body of his mistress and of the old men bringing him their charity. These books can only have been prevented from taking their place as great literature because the literary tradition of Ireland was, when Carleton and Banim wrote, so undeveloped that a novelist, no matter how great his genius, found no fit convention ready to his hands, and no exacting public to forbid him to commingle noisy melodrama with his revelations. England can afford to forget these books, but we cannot, for with all their imperfections they contain the most memorable records yet made of Irish habits and passions. "Charles O'Malley," "Father Tom and the Pope," "Barney O'Reirdan" and "The Traits and Stories" are also in a sense true records, but need no recommendation, for the public has always given a gracious welcome to every book which amuses it and does not bid it take Ireland seriously, while "Castle Rackrent," which it has begun to forget, is still, and will be for generations to come, a classic among the wise. I have included, though with much doubt, "Essex in Ireland," because despite its lack of intensity, it helps one, when read together with the passionate and dramatic "Bog of Stars," to imagine Elizabethan Ireland, and certainly does contain one memorable scene in which the multitudes slain in the Irish war rise up complaining;[5] and I have regretfully excluded Miss Barlow's "Irish Idylls" because despite her genius for recording the externals of Irish peasant life, I do not feel that she has got deep into the heart of things. I, indeed, feel always that both Miss Lawless and Miss Barlow differ as yet from the greater Irish novelists in being only able to observe Irish character from without and not to create it from within. They have, perhaps, bowed to the fallacy of our time, which says that the fountain of art is observation, whereas it is almost wholly experience. The creations of a great writer are little more than the moods and passions of his own heart, given surnames and Christian names, and sent to walk the earth. "Ballads in Prose" is, on the

---

[4] See p. 256. WBY had discovered his error in ascribing this in *RIT* (II. 92) to William Maginn.
[5] *With Essex in Ireland, being-extracts from a diary kept in Ireland during the year 1599 by Mr. Henry Harvey* . . . , edited by the Hon. Emily Lawless (1890), is a fictional account of Essex's disastrous Irish campaign written in the literary equivalent of mock-Tudor, supposedly by his secretary. While billeted in the monastry at Asheaton (135–48) Essex and his men see a ghostly procession of the people of the district 'an hundred and thirty thousand—men, women, and children of all degrees—slain or died of famine' during the Elizabethan wars.

other hand, an absolute creation, an enchanting tender little book full of style and wild melancholy. It contains also many simple and artful verses about gods and fairies, which will probably outlive estimable histories and copious criticisms that the proud may be humbled.

The most memorable books in the section Folk Lore and Bardic Tales are Mr O'Grady's "History of Ireland: heroic period," and his "Coming of Cuchullin," and his "Fin and His Companions." But as he, like the men who cast into their present shape the Icelandic Sagas, retells the old tales in his own way, he should be read together with "The History of Early Gaelic Literature," and if possible, with the "Silva Gadelica."[6] However, it will not be to these indispensable and learned books that the imagination will return again and again, but to his description in "The Coming of Cuchullin" of Cuchullin hunting the iron-horned enchanted deer in his battle fury, or to that chapter in the "History" where he stands dying against the pillar stone, the others [*for* otters] drinking his blood at his feet; or to the account in "Fin and his Companions" of the seven old men receiving Fin upon the mountain top and putting the seven pieces of the lark upon his platter, and saying one to another, when he weeps because of their poverty, "The young have sorrows that the old know nothing of." Lady Wilde's "Ancient Legends" is the most imaginative collection of Irish folk-lore, but should be read with Dr Hyde's more accurate and scholarly "Beside the Fire." Lady Wilde tells her stories in the ordinary language of literature, but Dr Hyde, with a truer instinct, is so careful to catch the manner of the peasant story-tellers that, on the rare occasions when he fails to take down the exact words, he writes out the story in Gaelic, and then translates it into English. If the reader have a special liking for folk-lore, he can pass on to Mr Larminie's copious collection or to Mr Curtin's two books, or to the various books and articles of the late Patrick Kennedy. I have added one book of a foreign writer, "Mythologie Irlandaise" for it is scarcely possible to understand Irish bardic and folk lore at all without its vivid and precise account of the ancient Pagan mythology of Ireland and of the descent of the mischievous fairies and spirits from the ancient gods of darkness and decay, and of the descent of the beautiful and kindly people of the raths and thorn trees from the gods of light and life.

Mr O'Grady's "Story of Ireland" and his "Red Hugh" are the only purely artistic and unforensic Irish histories we have, but as they are limited, like every work of art, by the temperament of their writer, and show all

---

[6] Standish James O'Grady's *History of Ireland: Heroic Period* was published in 2 vols. (1878, 1880); the 2-vol. *Silva Gadelica* (1892) is a collection of tales from Ancient Irish manuscripts, with notes and a translation by Standish Hayes O'Grady (1832–1915). The latter, a cousin of Standish James, qualified as a civil engineer and worked for some years in the USA before becoming interested in Irish antiquities and Old Irish manuscripts. A catalogue of Irish manuscripts in the British Museum on which he worked, and which had been started by Eugene O'Curry, was finally completed by Robin Flower in 1926.

events in a kind of blazing torchlight, they should be read with Dr Joyce's careful and impartial and colourless volume.[7]

A reader new to Irish poetry had best begin with Allingham's "Irish Poems" and Dr Hyde's "Love Songs of Connoct", for in them is the blossom of all that is most winning in Irish character; and pass on to the epic measures of "Conary" and "The Lays of the Western Gael;" nor should he neglect "Ballads and Legends," for Mrs Hinkson has given a distinguished expression to much that is most characteristic in Irish catholicism. The greater portion of Irish poetry is, however, made up of stray ballads and lyrics by Mangan, Davis, Doheney, Casey,[8] Callanan, Walsh, Reynolds, Moore, Fox, and others among the dead, and by Mr Aubrey De Vere, Mr Johnson, Mr Rolleston, Dr Todhunter, and "AE," among the living; and of these there is no excellent anthology. Unless the reader will accept a forthcoming anthology of my own, he must in most cases search for the best Irish verse through old ballad books, and be content to find one or two good poems to a volume. There are, however, a few books other than ballad books, such as Mangan's Poems (the little threepenny edition), De Vere's "Innisfael," and "AE's" "Songs by the Way"—this a very notable book, but not specially Irish in subject—and two ballad books, Sir Gavan Duffy's "National Poetry" and Mrs Hinkson's "Irish Love Songs," which do not lose the needle in the haystack. "The Irish Song Book" (New Irish Library) also contains some good verses, but, as it was compiled more for the music than for the verse, it excludes much of the best and includes much which, though very singable, has little of the rapture and precision of good poetry.

Many of the best books in my list can only be got at the second-hand book shops, while in some cases poorer books by the same writers are constantly reprinted. The truth is that chance has hitherto decided the success or failure of Irish books; for one half Ireland has received everything Irish with undiscriminating praise, and the other half with undiscriminating indifference. We have founded the National Literary Society and the Irish Literary Society, London, to check the one and the other vice, and to find an audience for whatever is excellent in the new or the old literature of Ireland. Political passion has made literary opinion in Ireland artificial, and, despite

---

[7] Standish James O'Grady's *Red Hugh's Captivity: A Picture of Ireland, Social and Political, in the Reign of Queen Elizabeth* (1889) centres around the young Gaelic chieftain Red Hugh O'Donnell. P. W. Joyce's *Short History of Ireland* (1893), an account of Irish history 'From the Earliest Times to 1608', follows, as the author explained, 'the plan of weaving the history round important events and leading personages'.

[8] John Keegan Casey (1846–70), born near Mullingar, the son of a peasant farmer, contributed poems and sketches to the *Nation, Irishman*, and *Irish People*, and published *A Wreath of Shamrocks* (1866) and *The Rising of the Moon* (1869), for which he is best remembered. He joined the Fenian movement and was imprisoned in 1867 for his involvement in the rising. Describing Casey as 'a clerk in a flour-mill', in *BIV* (xx–xxi) WBY associates his verse with that of Kickham and Ellen O'Leary, finding it 'at times very excellent', lacking the oratorical vehemence of Young Ireland, and 'plaintive and idyllic'.

one of your correspondents, we are not to blame if our remedy seem artificial also. Our justification is the steadily increasing sale of Irish books, and the steadily increasing intelligence of Irish criticism.—Yours truly,

W B Yeats

Printed letter, *Daily Express* (Dublin), 27 February 1895 (5). Wade, 246–51.

To Katharine Tynan Hinkson, [c. *2 March 1895*]

Thorn Hill | Sligo | Ireland
Oct 30th[1]

My dear Mrs Hinkson

I send you an 'Express'. I wish you would write a few words & get your husband to do the same. It is the best chance we have had yet of getting some Irish criticism into the Dublin scholastic mind. The value of the last contraversy was proved by the debate in The College Historical. The resolution that 'the Irish literary revival is worthy of support' was carried in a large meeting with eight dissentients. I think you admire O'Grady as much as I do. If so back me up in my praise of him.[2] I want to run him against Dowden with the unionists. As yet the letters about my list have been unimportant but Monday will probably bring a letter from O'Grady or Rolleston.

Many thanks for 'Maelcho' which came to[o] late for my letter but not too late for me to greatly enjoy it. It is hardly so artistic as 'Essex' but shows far higher powers.[3]

Yrs ev
W B Yeats

You will get 'A Book of Irish Verse' in a few days.

ALS Harvard.

[1] Evidently a misdating for what WBY took to be 30 February; see subsequent letter.

[2] Neither KT nor her husband, Henry Hinkson, appear to have taken part in the controversy set off by WBY's letter in the 27 Feb *Daily Express.*

[3] *Maelcho: A Sixteenth-Century Narrative* by the Hon. Emily Lawless had been published in 2 vols. in October 1894; a further edition appeared in June 1895. WBY included it in a list of the best Irish books (*UP* I. 386) in the *Bookman* in October 1895. In the second of his *Bookman* articles on Irish literature, August 1895 (see p. 424), he found Miss Lawless 'in imperfect sympathy with the Celtic nature'; she portrayed stereotyped Irish and English characters in her novels, he said, except when she described visions and visionaries as 'in the madness of Maelcho and in his last days in the cavern with the monks. There is a kind of greatness in these things, and if she can cast off a habit of mind which would compress a complex, incalculable, indecipherable nation into the mould of a theory invented by political journalists and forensic historians, she should have in her the makings of a great book, full of an arid and half spectral intensity.'

To John O'Leary, [c. 2 March 1895]

Thorn Hill | Sligo
Feb 30th[1]

My dear M[r] O'Leary

I enclose a cutting ⟨from⟩ a review from 'New Ireland Review' which quotes a passage evidently about the Contemporary Club, yourself, & a some body made up of Taylor & Oldham.[2] I send also a ⟨copy⟩ copies of Wednesdays 'Express' with letters by myself & a M[r] Haniman on 'The Best Thirty Irish Books'.[3] I wish you would write. It seems to me an excellent oppertunity for getting a little information about Irish books into the heads of Dublin Unionists. The good effects of the Dowden contraversy is shown by the debate & vote at the College Historical.[4] I have written to a long list of persons, even to Stopford Brooke among the rest, asking them to contribute, in the hopes of a long discussion like that in the Freeman on the best hundred. I have asked Barry O Brien to slang my frivolity.[5]

[1] Presumably an error for 2 March.

[2] The cutting from the *New Ireland Review*, March 1895 (63), was an unsigned review of *After the Manner of Men: a novel of today*, by Robert Appleton (Boston, 1894). 'Artistic haunts in London and national and social spheres in Dublin in 1887 are the main scenes of its interest,' said the reviewer, 'and the blend of art, Bohemianism, and Irish politics is curious, to say the least.' He quotes, from the author's 'pictures of a Dublin club and its notables', his composite portrait of J. F. Taylor and C. H. Oldham: 'That is a young barrister—a coming man, as he has been reputed to be these ten years, but who hasn't come yet. . . . He is remarkable for his prodigious memory and versatile knowledge. He remembers everything, only he frequently forgets himself.' And this, 'more kindly', of a JO'L-like figure: 'He is another famous man—more famous for his sufferings than his achievements. 'Tis such martyrs, after all, that make heroes of us all! Some years ago he was one of the leaders of the physical force party, and he has expiated his guilt of daring by years of imprisonment. Well, he is at liberty now, as little inclined to compromise as he was twenty years ago.' The reviewer, in praising the energy and interest of 'what the sympathetic, though not well-informed Yankee, has to say about our capital', appears to have been unaware as was WBY that 'Robert Appleton' was yet another alias of the protean Roman I. Lipmann, sometime Count Zubof (see pp. 120, 210), who knew Dublin—as it knew him—all too well.

[3] See preceding letter. On the following day, Thursday, 28 Feb 1895, the *Daily Express* printed a letter (5) from D. F. Hannigan, of 27 Lower Mount Street, giving his own 'Best Thirty Irish Books'. Hannigan had already written on 5 Feb in support of Dowden against O'Grady's strictures (see p. 435), and he now attacked WBY's selection of Irish books as 'a new experiment in "log-rolling"' since seven out of the thirty books were by O'Grady, in Hannigan's view a bad and biased historian whose books were 'artistically unfinished and in other respects fragmentary and bald'. Denis Francis Hannigan (b. 1855) had been educated at Queen's College, Cork, and contributed poems-to his native Waterford papers and stories to the *Shamrock, Irish Fireside*, and the *Weekly Freeman*. He became a journalist in Dublin and translated three of Flaubert's novels (his version of *L'Éducation sentimentale* was James Joyce's favourite book). In 1899 he moved to London and later emigrated to the United States.

[4] In a debate at the Trinity College Historical Society, on 27 Feb 1895, the motion 'That the movement for the revival of Irish literature deserves our support' was carried by a large majority. Dowden, who was in the chair, speaking after the vote, said that he was pleased the motion had been passed; everyone had the good of Irish literature at heart. But (according to an account in the *Express* on 28 Feb, 5) he 'depreciated the spirit of exclusiveness which seemed to be a characteristic of the new movement'. Nor did he think that the best Irish books were necessarily those which treated of Irish literature.

[5] For the *Freeman's Journal* discussion of 1886, see p. 440, n. 1. Neither Stopford Brooke nor Barry O'Brien took part in the *Daily Express* controversy.

I have had the influenza but am better & almost through the rewriting of my things for the collected edition. 'A Book of Irish Verse' will be out in a few days.

 Many thanks for papers.

Yrs ev
W B Yeats

I sent Mrs Carew a small instalment of my debt.

ALS NLI. Wade, 251.

To Susan Mary Yeats, 3 March [1895]

Thorn Hill | Sligo
March 3rd

My dear Lilly

 I am always [*for* almost] through with the correction of my things for Unwins republication of them. Tell papa that the *Countess Kathleen* is radically different at the end & the *Wanderings of Usheen* at the beginning & middle.[1] I am beginning to think of getting on into Roscommon to Duglas Hyde but may think & no more for a bit. I shall go from that to Dublin & be there a few days then go to London. I started a new contraversy in 'The Express' last Wednesday with a long letter—a collumn & a half—on 'the best thirty Irish books' & would send you a copy but I have none, all having gone to various people I want to contribute. The Dowden contraversy has had for one of its results a well attended debate in College Historical Society which passed almost unanimously the resolution 'that the Irish Literary revival is worthy of support.' Dowden was in the chair & had some more dabs at us.

 George has got the influenza is in bed very bad with it at present. I had it lightly last week—was in bed a part of two or three days with it.

 We had great skating here—the river up to the lake being frozen as far as the windmill. The Miss Gore Booths were there & made coffey on the shore.

Yrs affly
W B Yeats

Am beginning to think about writing to Jack as I here he said something in a letter to George about joining the Irish Lit Society.[2]

ALS MBY, with envelope addressed to Blenheim Road, Irish postmark torn off. Wade, 252.

[1] WBY had recast *The Countess Kathleen* from five scenes into four acts for *Poems* (1895). The ending, in contrast to the rather languid pageant of the first version, was now far more dramatic, with devils and angels fighting for the soul of the Countess amid lightning and thunder and visionary light. In revising 'The Wanderings of Oisin', WBY had cut away much in language and imagery that was merely decorative.

[2] There is no evidence that Jack Yeats was ever a member of the Irish Literary Society, London.

To the Editor of the Daily Express (Dublin), 8 March 1895

SIR—I should have replied before to my critics but for my difficulty in finding out what the most important of them—Professor Dowden—did or did not say. The reports of his speech at "The Historical" which I found in the morning papers were too meagre to reply to. A friend has, however, just sent me Saturday's *Herald* with a full and manifestly fair exposition of his argument.[1] He began by accusing us of telling people "to boycott English literature," and built up much elaborate and irrelevant eloquence upon this absurd charge, and then, becoming for a moment the serious critic we are accustomed to, gave an admirable definition of an Irish national literature, and after making some comments on my list, which showed, I cannot but think, less than his old scrupulous accuracy, passed on to expound a list of his own. He said that a national Irish literature "must be based on the old Celtic legends, must come from the Celtic people of the country, must have the basis and inspiration of race and racial tradition, and must not and cannot be divorced from the philosophy and influences of the Catholic religion." With the obvious corrections, which Prof Dowden will at once accept, this Ireland is not wholly, Celtic any more than England is wholly Saxon, or wholly Catholic any more than England is wholly Protestant, I agree with this definition, and affirm that it covers every book upon my list. Are not "Beside the Fire," "The Coming of Cuchullin," and "Fin and his Companions" "based on the old Celtic literature and legends?" Are not "the ballads and lyrics" of Mrs Hinkson "full of the philosophy and influence and inspiration of the Catholic religion?" Are not "Fardarougha the Miser," "The Nolans," and "Castle Rackrent" informed with the inspiration of our "racial tradition?" On the other hand, does his definition cover a single one of the books selected from Ussher and Swift and Berkeley, which he desired us to consider our national literature?[2] He named none but admirable books, certainly, but "Gulliver's Travels" and "Tristram Shandy" will be substitutes for the books I have named only when the books of Hume are considered Scotch literature in the same sense as the books of Burns and Barrie, or when the writings of Welshmen like Mr George Meredith and Mr William Morris are thought as full of the spirit of Wales as the triads of

---

[1] The *Evening Herald* of 2 Mar 1895 (4) gave, as WBY says, a far longer and more detailed account of the 27 Feb debate at the College Historical Society (see p. 446) than the *Daily Express* or the other morning papers.

[2] Dowden's choice as reported in the *Herald* was: 'Ussher, Swift (Gulliver's Travels), Berkeley, Steele, Farquhar (The Beaux' Stratagem), Sterne (Tristram Shandy), Sheridan (Plays), Burke (American War), Goldsmith (Vicar of Wakefield), and Lecky (Irish Volumes of History of England in the Eighteenth Century).'

Taliesin. Professor Dowden must have been dreaming, or very eloquent, which comes to much the same thing, or he would never have included in the same speech so admirable a definition, so irrelevant a list. He also stated that all Mr Yates' books had been produced during the present century, and founded upon this supposed fact some argument which the reporter appears to have forgotten. If he referred to the print and paper, or even to the editor's comment and the like, he was accurate; but if he referred, as I think he must, to the contents, inaccurate, for "Beside the Fire," "The Love Songs of Connaught," and the "Silva Gadelica," a collection of many books under our [*for* one] ample cover, are translations of stories and verses all older than this century and some of great antiquity. I could, as Professor Dowden must have known, have added indefinately to these translations, but translations are seldom satisfactory literature. By insisting on the modernness of the works I named, he wished I suppose, to show that Irish literature grew from a shallow soil, and yet it is obvious that the literature of a country which has recently changed its language must be very modern. I have now, I think, dealt with every argument of Professor Dowden's which was quoted in the Press, and I have done so, because it is important to show that "our acknowledged authority" brings to a merely Irish literary matter something less than that careful logic, that scrupulousness accuracy, that sympathetic understanding, which he brings to an English literary question; in fact that he is no authority at all when he speaks of Irish verse or Irish legend, but a partisan ready to seize upon any argument which promises a momentary victory.[3] He has indeed made that fatal mistake which critics who have more knowledge than impulse are ever prone to, he has set himself upon the side of academic tradition in that eternal war which it wages on the creative spirit.

Others object to my giving six books of Mr Standish O'Grady's, and would have me set Haverty's "History of Ireland," Lefanu's novels, or Griffin's verses in their place.[4] I could do no other than give Mr O'Grady the lion's share, because his books have affected one more powerfully than those of any other Irish writer, and I know of no other criticism than a candid impressionism. I believe them to be ideal books of their kind, books

---

[3] The *Daily Express* of 9 Mar 1895 (5) published Dowden's riposte:

Sir—Mr Yeats tilts against a windmill. The account of what I said before the College Historical Society furnished to the *Herald* came not, as Mr Yeats has stated, from a reporter, but from an auditor, who mentions that he wrote from recollection without notes. He misstated my attempt to characterise a literature truly national, and forgot the most essential part of my argument.—Your obedient servant, Edward Dowden

[4] D. F. Hannigan in the *Express* of 28 Feb 1895 (see p. 446) had raised this objection. Martin Haverty (1809–87), historian and librarian, was best known for his frequently reprinted *The History of Ireland, Ancient and Modern* (1860).

of genius, but even if they were not, they would still contain more of ancient legend and circumstance than any other.—Yours, &c,

W B Yeats.

Printed letter, *Daily Express* (Dublin), 8 March 1895 (7). *UP* 1. 351–3.

To Katharine Tynan Hinkson, [12 March 1895]

Thorn Hill | Sligo

My dear Mrs Hinkson

I have just discovered a terrible mistake in 'A Book of Irish Verse'. Several verses are left out of your 'Children of Lir' & I can only ask you not to be too hard on me. I got that wretch Sousie Orr to copy the poem out & also some of Allinghams things & evidently forgot to compare your poem with the original. It is certainly a serious injury to you for the 'Children of Lir' is almost your most beautiful thing but it is even more serious to myself for I will be thought to have mutilated the poem intentionally. Rolleston went over my proofs for me but had not your book, I think, to compare it with then. If I had the money I would cancell the edition rather than let this blunder stand but as things are I can only hope for a second edition. I read the poem over & over in proof & always with a sense of dissapointment which I could not understand. Only last night, just before I went to bed, the exquisite line 'Peace said Fionuala that was long ago' flashed on my mind & I re-read the poem looking for it in vain. Of course Sousie's carelessness is no excuse as I should not have forgotten to go over her copy.[1] I included no verses of my own in the book, because I have left out or criticised unfavourably in the introduction so many well known Irish poets & did not want to appear to prefer my own work. I hope you were not displeased with my slight mention of you in the Express letter but I was afraid of the charge of 'log rolling' which would have taken the significance away from my placing of you among the few poets in my list.[2] Your poems in 'A Book of Irish Verse', despite the mistake, seem to me by far the finest things in all the latter part of the book. I wish I were as certain of the immortality of anything I have or will write as I am of the immortality of 'Sheep & Lambs'. Now that Christina Rossettie is dead you have no woman rival.[3] You Fergusson & Allingham are I think the Irish poets who have done the largest quantity of

---

[1] There was a 2nd edn. of *BIV* in 1900, in which the missing portion of KT's text was restored, including the line ' "Peace," saith Finnuola, "that was long ago." ' Susan Marcia Agnes Pollexfen Orr (c. 1877–1960) was the daughter of WBY's aunt Elizabeth Pollexfen Orr.

[2] See pp. 441, 444.

[3] WBY included five poems by KT, including 'Sheep and Lambs', in the 1st edn. of *BIV*, but one of them, 'In Iona', was omitted in the 1900 edition. Christina Rossetti had died on 29 Dec 1894.

fine work. ⟨*4 lines cancelled.*⟩ Mangan & De Vere have each done three or four wonderful things but have in them no copious stream of beauty. The others Walsh Callanan Hyde etc are merely men who prolong delightfully the inspiration of the gaelic poets they have no fountain of song in themselves no streaming beauty.

I have been busy correcting my own things getting ready a collected edition containing all I like in the 'Oisin' & 'Kathleen' volumes & putting them together with 'The Land of Hearts Desire'. I have rewritten almost every thing from the 'Oisin' book & large quantities of the play of 'The Countess Kathleen'. It has been a frightful business but is now practicaly finished.

Yours ever
W B Yeats

I hope you will not think my introduction to 'A Book of Irish Verse' unpleasantly faultfinding[4] but I felt my criticism would carry no weight unless I seperated myself from the old gush & folly. I want people to accept my praise of Irish books as something better than mere national vanity.

Yrs ever
W B Yeats

ALS Harvard. *Yale Review*, Winter 1940, 313–14; McHugh, 143; partly in Wade, 252–3.

To John O'Leary, 12 March 1895

Thorn Hill | Sligo.
March 12th 1895

Dear Mr O'Leary

I send you 'A Book of Irish Verse'. Please let me know what you think of it. Did you see my letter in 'Express'.[1] The College Historical debate & vote shows that we are doing some good there.

Yours ever
W B Yeats

ALS NLI.

[4] In the introduction to *BIV* WBY wrote (xxiii–xxiv) that KT had 'published four books of poems, two being very admirable. . . . She has no revery, no speculation, but a Franciscan tenderness for weak instinctive things,—old gardeners, old fishermen, birds in the leaves, birds tossed upon the waters.'

[1] See preceding letter.

To Mary Cottenham Yeats,[1] [c. 15 March 1895]

Thorn Hill | Sligo
March

My dear Cottie

Uncle George has asked me to answer your letter for him, as he is to[o] ill to write. He was vaccinated about three weeks ago & has been in bed ever since with a doctor coming twice a day & trying to persuade him it is influenza. The doctors got up a smallpox scare & have reaped a noble harvest for they have vaccinated every man woman & child in the county. The smallpox has passed away, (if it was ever here & there are them that say it was but measles) but the vaccination remains.[2]

I hope the shamrock which I send will be in time. The frost has killed, or at any rate driven out of sight, almost all of it. I looked to day my self & got the stable hand to look yesterday but could find none. However just now, too late for the mail, a boy I had captured earlier in the day, came with a bunch.

Please give my thanks to Jack for the ciggarette holder. It has helped many a cigarrette to resolve it self into verses. As soon as Uncle George is better I shall return to London. He will I am afraid be some time before he will be himself again. As soon as he is quite able to consider things, he will be urged to go away for change & if he consent he & I will probably go to London together. 〈But just at present it would never do to add vacillation to his other ailments. [*1 line indecipherable.*]〉

Yours ever
W B Yeats

A great many thanks for your invitation to the boat & the cushions & the dreams.[3]

ALS Anne Yeats.

To the Editor of United Ireland, 16 March 1895

DEAR SIR—I perfectly agree with you about the unwisdom of including an unpublished book in a list of "The Best Thirty Irish Books." The fact is

[1] Mary Cottenham Yeats, née White (1868–1947), was married to Jack Yeats on 23 Aug 1894 in Gunnersbury, London. At this time they were living at The Chestnuts, Eastworth, Chertsey, Surrey.

[2] An outbreak of smallpox in Dublin at the beginning of the year had reached Sligo by late February and the *Sligo Champion* reported on 23 Feb 1895: 'A good deal of uneasiness is experienced at the outbreak of small pox in this town and in the Primrose Grange School, where four cases of a mild nature have occurred, from the contagion having been communicated by a student who returned from a visit to Dublin.' Suspected cases were put into isolation and meanwhile the paper advised that 'a sure preventative—one within the reach of all—is that of re-vaccination'.

[3] Chertsey is close to the river Thames and Cottie had evidently invited WBY to stay with them and to take leisurely excursions on the river. He was to visit them on 14 Sept of this year.

that I saw "advanced sheets" of Dr Hyde's "Story of Early Gaelic Literature" some little time ago, and when writing my letter to the *Express* was deceived by a paragraph in the papers into the belief that it was already out.[1] The historical section of my list is, as you say, rather meagre, but is less eccentric when read with the explanatory comment. Had I not avowedly excluded all books of strong political feeling, and all books which are neither works of imagination, or books of research, helping one to understand the imaginations of Ireland, it would probably have been as follows—

Lecky's "History of Ireland in the Eighteenth Century."

O'Grady's "Red Hugh" and "Story of Ireland."

Joyce's "Short History of Ireland."

Bagwell's "Ireland Under the Tudors."

Mitchel's "Jail Journal."

Wolfe Tone's "Autobiography."[2]

You make no comment on the poetic section, but will permit me to say that I omit some of the best of our poets merely because the editions of their poems are too uncritical to rank among our best books. I trouble you with this letter because I would rather be held possessed by any fiend, even by "Modo" or "Mahu," than by "the foul fiend Flibbertigibbert."[3]—Yours truly,

W B Yeats.

Printed letter, *United Ireland*, 16 March 1895 (3). *UP* I. 355–6.

[1] In its issue of 9 Mar 1895, *United Ireland* reprinted the list of 'The Best Thirty Irish Books' from WBY's letter in the *Daily Express* of 27 Feb, with an editorial comment (4):

It will at once be seen that here there is nothing conventional. But surely Mr Yeats is not wise to include so many new works. Very few of us have yet read Miss Hopper's volume, and it is not judicious to make Irish classics out of books which the Irish public have not had time to judge; much less is it judicious to make a new Irish classic of a book which is not yet published—this being the present condition, so far as we know, of Dr Hyde's "History of Early Gaelic Literature".

Hyde's book (see p. 438) was not published until late March 1895.

[2] *A History of Ireland in the Eighteenth Century* (1892), taken from a 12-vol. *History of England* by the historian and Liberal-Unionist politician William Edward Hartpole Lecky (1838–1903), was said to have converted everyone who read it to Home Rule except its author.

O'Grady's *Red Hugh's Captivity* (see pp. 443–4) had been criticized by nationalists for its defence of the Elizabethan conquest of Ireland and for its praise of Sir John Perrot, the Elizabethan Viceroy. His (in O'Grady's own words) 'unconventional and loosely-flowing' *Story of Ireland* from the coming of the Milesians to Parnell is written from an Anglo-Irish imperialist point of view. Both books approach history through biography, which helps to mitigate their political bias.

The nationalist P. W. Joyce writes in the Preface to his *History of Ireland* (iv), 'I have, I hope, written soberly and moderately, avoiding exaggeration and bitterness, and showing fair play all round. A writer may accomplish all this while sympathising heartily, as I do, with Ireland and her people.' Richard Bagwell (1840–1918) on the other hand was an active speaker and writer in the Unionist cause; his detailed if somewhat pedestrian *Ireland Under the Tudors*, 3 vols. (1885–90), argues that English rule in Ireland suffered from a want of firmness caused by the chronic impecuniousness of the Crown.

[3] Cf. *King Lear*, IV. i: 'five fiends have been in poor Tom at once . . . Mahu of stealing; Modo, of murder; and Flibbertigibbet of mopping and mowing, who since possesses chambermaids and waiting women . . .'

To Katharine Tynan Hinkson, 25 March [*1895*]

Thorn Hill | Sligo
March 25th

My dear M ͬ ˢ Hinkson

I should have written before to thank you for your review—a most
admirable one—of 'A Book of Irish Verse'[1] had I not been busy getting the
last touches put to my collected volume of verse. I have just tied up the
package & am free again for the moment. You should be rather glad than
other wise at attacks like the 'Figero' one.[2] They always mark the period
when a reputation is becoming fixed & admitted. At first a writer is the
enthusiasm of a few. He is not yet important enough to be attacked. Then
comes the day when the pioneer spirits ⟨*5 lines cancelled*⟩ think his fame
assured & perhaps a little slacken in their advocasy; and the yet unconvinced
many begin to carp & abuse. Do you remember how Kipling got at that stage
& stayed in it for a few months some years ago? Your next book of verse will
probably reach the general public—the public who are not professed
readers of verse—& after that you will be abused no more for the journalist
must respect his paymasters. I wish you could get your best things all under
one cover. Why not follow The Miracle plays with a not too large volume—a
book of lyrics gets scrappy if too big—selected from all your old books.
Keegan Paul, (as he has given you no money—without which there is I
understand no bargain—or even if he had) could not object to your picking
out the nine or ten best things from 'Legends & Lyrics'. You could add
enough from other books & from new work to make a volume of sufficient

---

[1] In a long unsigned notice of *BIV* in the *Irish Independent*, 19 Mar 1895 (4), KT drew attention to the
controversial nature of WBY's selection, questioned a number of his choices, and stressed the polemical
aspects of his introduction 'which, if not in itself disputatious, will be a battle-ground for many disputes'.
She thought WBY had brought to his task 'a fresh mind and taste . . . uncoloured by old prejudices' and
urged that the book should 'be in all town libraries, and in village libraries, if any such exist.'

[2] On 16 Mar 1895, the *Irish* (formerly the *Dublin*) *Figaro* carried a satirical attack (168–70) on KT for
her supposed snobbery and self-advertisement as exhibited in an article she had published in the *Young
Woman* of March 1895 on 'The Women of Ireland': 'Such is the title of a paper contributed by this
"divine daughter of song"—Yeates [*sic*], of course, is the divine son—to a journal called *The Young
Woman*. With the paper she was good enough to contribute a photograph of her gifted self, draped and
barbered à la ancient Greek model, only that Greek models rarely wear *pinces nez*.' WBY also came in for
abuse: 'The hog-wash anent mystic braided ebon locks on the pale marble brow of a gentleman named
Yeats does not flow as freely, though I sometimes hear it dribble down some of the various channels,
which it appears are always to be found available in London as conduits for stuff of the kind.' The attack
continued with a parody of WBY's 27 Feb list of the 'Best Thirty Irish Books', concluding with a Poetry
section: '26. Miss Tynan about Dr Hyde. By K. Tynan. 27. Standish O'Grady about Miss Tynan. By
Standish O'Grady. 28. Miss Tynan About Yeats. By K. Tynan. 29. Yeats about Miss Tynan. By Yeats.
30. My Wife's Aunt about them All. By my Wife's Aunt.' The *Figaro* attack was signed by Sydney Brooks
(1872–1937), a journalist shortly to leave for America where he lived 1896–1900; he wrote two books
about Ireland and became editor of the *Saturday Review* in 1921. In the *Figaro* of 23 Mar 1895 Brooks
again referred to KT's 'rubbishy contribution' to the *Young Woman*.

size. Could you not perhaps get the miracle plays & this selected book made uniform?[3]

I beleive that in about a year or perhaps two years we will find that Irish Unionists will begin to read Irish things greedily. I have been amazed at the interest the people here have taken in anything I have told them & in the Expres[s] controversy. The vote at the College Historical must mean something to[o]. I wrote that combative introduction to 'A Book of Irish Verse' partly with a view of this type of reader. The great thing I thought was to convince them that we were critics & writers before all else & not heady & undiscriminating enthusiasts. Every new Irish writer will increase the public for evry other Irish writer. Your copy of Miss Hopper is at this moment crusading at Lady Gore Booths & the whole family have taken to Irish things. They are now busy with O'Grady & were a little while ago on the hunt for folk-lore among their tenants. 'Maelcho', despite my promise to return it at once, has only just returned from another Unionist house hold where it has carried on a not less effective evangel. They have got from me 'The Coming of Cuchullin'. A copy of Russell is also on the wander & one of the Gore Booths has taken to your section of 'A Book of Irish Verse', and has asked many questions about you.[4] These people are much better educated than our people & have a better instinct for excellence. It is very curious how the dying out of party fealing has nationalized the more thoughtful Unionists. Parnellism has greatly help[ed] also, & the expectation of Balfours threatened emmense local Goverment scheme.[5] However this is to[o] big a subject to get into at the end of my second sheet.

Very glad to hear you are doing me for the 'Speaker'.[6]

I had for a moment forgotten 'In a Garden'.[7] Do please send it me. I wish very much to see it.

Yrs ev
W B Yeats

ALS Harvard, with envelope addressed to Mount Avenue, Ealing, postmark torn off. *Yale Review*, Winter 1940, 314–15; McHugh, 144–5; partly in Wade, 253–4.

[3] A substantial selection of KT's verse, *Poems*, appeared in 1901, and in 1907 the Cuala Press published *Twenty-One Poems* by her, selected by WBY. Her *Collected Poems* was published in 1930.

[4] For Miss Lawless's *Maelcho*, see p. 445. WBY had reviewed Standish James O'Grady's *The Coming of Cuchulain* in the *Bookman* in February (see p. 410). For AE's (George Russell's) *Homeward, Songs by the Way*, see p. 391. The Gore-Booth interested by KT's poems in *BIV* was probably Eva.

[5] Gerald William Balfour (1853–1945), Chief Secretary for Ireland in the Conservative Cabinet, had begun preparations for a sweeping Local Government Act which, when it became law in 1898, radically shifted the balance of power in Irish local politics away from the Ascendancy to the nationalists.

[6] No book by WBY was reviewed in the *Speaker* in 1895, a year in which KT was much occupied with pregnancy and the birth of a child (see below, p. 471, n. 3). The *Speaker's* notice of his *Poems* (1895) on 4 Jan 1896 may have been by her.

[7] KT's long poem, 'In a Garden' (*Shamrocks*, 138–47), tells of the restoration of Eden through Christ's suffering, and of how the memory of Eden was kept alive in the wailing of the wind among the

To T. Fisher Unwin, 27 March [*1895*]

Thorn Hill | Sligo | Ireland
March 27th

Dear Mr Unwin

I send you at last the MS of my book of poems. A light but sufficient attack of Influenza & some other small matters have delayed me to this.

You will I suppose now push on the printing at once & let Shannon—if he undertake the job—have proofs that he may choose a theme or at any rate the right fealing for his decoration. I have exausted both my copies of 'The Land of Hearts Desire' on the printer & cannot come on another & so cannot carry out my promise to send him a copy to work from.

Yours sncly
W B Yeats

Please let me know as soon as possible if Shannon consents as I will write to him about what I want.
PS.

I have never yet thanked you for Mr Will Fosters very charming poems. I have been so busy this winter revising these poems for you & doing a new one that I have dropped out of reviewing otherwise I would gladly say a word for him. He is rather too much under the shadow of Wordsworth & one or two others, but if he could only shake himself free has charm enough to win a position.[1]

ALS Texas.

To T. Fisher Unwin, 29 March [*1895*]

Thorn Hill | Sligo | Ireland
March 29th.

Dear Mr Unwin

Copeland & Day have written to ask me to suggest to you that you offer them the American rights to my forthcoming book. I have mislaid their letter & so may forget a name or two, but they said certainly that they had already the American rights of books by Watson, Francis Thompson, John Davidson & Richard Le Gallienne & that they wished to get books by all the

reeds. WBY may have been reminded of it by its prefiguring of the title of his own *The Wind Among the Reeds*, or by the publication of a rather inferior poem by KT, 'The Gardener', in the *New Review*, February 1895.

[1] *The Legend of Lohengrin* by Will Foster was published by Unwin in February 1895. Foster was also the author of *The Fallen City* (Edinburgh and London, 1892), and of two later volumes, *Poems* (1903) and *Isabelle* (1920).

new generation of poets.[1] I know they beleive in my work & so should be ready to push it. This is of course entirely your province but if they are making a speciality of the kind they should be worth considering. They asked me to write because, they say, you might not other wise let them know in time, that you did not do so before, or something of that kind.[2]

They appear to be under the impression that it is a new book, but as they ask after my 'collected edition', will not, I beleive, raise any objection on finding that it is not. Day told me, when he was in England, that he would gladly have had the American rights of 'The Countess Kathleen'.

Yrs sncly
W B Yeats.

ALS Texas.

To Katharine Tynan Hinkson, 7 April [1895]

Thorn Hill | Sligo
April 7th

My dear Mrs Hinkson

A great many thanks for Le Galliennes article. I wonder who has been anoying him, or what he has got into his head, to make him suppose that Irish enthusiasts 'despise English Literature'. There are several things in the article that convince me he has reviewed the book not from itself but from some recent plunge into Irish work.[1]

I forgot to say in last letter that my beleif that 'Conary' is the best of all

---

[1] The Boston publishing firm of Copeland & Day (see p. 403) were at this time the American publishers of all the poets WBY names, and also of Pater and Wilde as well as Lionel Johnson, Stephen Crane, Bliss Carman, Richard Hovey, and numerous other young American, British, and Canadian poets.

[2] Copeland & Day imported copies of Unwin's edition of *Poems* (1895), adding their own imprint on the spine and later, for a second issue, on the title-page (*Bibl*, 35).

[1] This was probably the unsigned review of four Irish books, WBY's *A Book of Irish Songs* [*sic*], A. P. Graves's *Irish Song Book*, Standish O'Grady's *The Coming of Cuculain*, and Jeremiah Curtin's *Hero Tales of Ireland*, which appeared in the *Athenaeum*, 6 Apr 1895 (434–5). The reviewer devotes the bulk of the article to WBY's anthology and praises the editor for his rigorous critical standards and his attempts to correct the prevalent Irish error of giving

that uncritical and unmeasured praise of everything Irish that has done so much to create in Ireland an admiration for verse of native manufacture, no matter of what quality. Not so long ago an Irishman of position gravely asserted at a meeting of the Irish Literary Society in London that England owed all her literature to Irishmen, and that there was neither humour nor poetry in the Anglo-Saxon race. And so universally were green glasses worn on this occasion that this extraordinary assertion was received with enthusiasm by an audience which included a good three fourths of the literary Irishmen resident in London. . . .

Although 'a Saxon', the writer shows an informed knowledge of Irish poetry and poets.

Irish poems (you disagree with it in the 'Independent') is also the beleif of De Vere. I saw his opinion quoted, I think, in O Hagan's little booklet on Fergusson. Dont confuse 'Conary' with 'Congal' which is intolerable except in bits.[2]

My new book is in the press. All the old things are re-written. I wonder how they will receive it in Ireland. Patronize it I expect & give it faint praise & yet I feel it is good, that whether the coming generations in England accept me or reject me, the coming generations in Ireland cannot but value what I have done. I am writing at the end of the day & when I am tired, this endless war with Irish stupidity gets upon my nerves. Either you or I could have more prosperous lives probably if we left Ireland alone, & went our own way on the high seas—certainly we could have more peacable lives. However if the sun shine in the morning I shall be full of delight of battle & ready to draw my bow against the dragon.

Yr ev
W B Yeats

ALS Harvard, with envelope addressed to Mount Avenue, Ealing, postmark torn off. Partly in *Yale Review*, Winter 1940, 316; McHugh, 145; Wade, 254–5.

To Charles Elkin Mathews, 7 April [1895]

Thorn Hill | Sligo
April 7th

Dear Mr Matthews

A great many thanks for Miss May Probyns Poems. It is a delightful book in every way. The poems are delightful & your sisters designs on title page & cover are worthy of the poems. They have just that quiet richness which the book requires.[1] I am not sure that the non religious poems in the book move

---

[2] In *BIV* (xix) WBY had written that Ferguson's 'Vengeance of the Welshmen of Tirawley' was 'the best Irish ballad', and his 'Conary' 'the best Irish poem of any kind'. KT, in her *Irish Independent* review of *BIV* (see p. 454), while acceding to the former judgement, had found the latter claim 'extravagant'. WBY had noted as early as October 1886 that De Vere thought 'Conary' 'the best Irish poem' (*UP* I. 86). De Vere's opinion is not quoted in John O'Hagan's *The Poetry of Sir Samuel Ferguson* (1887), but in his own *Essays, Chiefly Literary and Ethical* (1889) De Vere wrote that 'It would be difficult to find, amid our recent literature, a poem which at once aimed as high as "Conary" and as adequately fulfils its aim . . . this work belongs to the "great" style of poetry.' 'Conary' is a long blank-verse poem based on the Old Irish bardic tale of 'The Destruction of Ua Derga's Hostel' (Togail Bruidne Ui Derga); 'Congal' is an epic in five books drawing on the Irish bardic romances 'The Battle of Moyra' (Cath Muighe Rath) and 'The Banquet of Dunangay' (Fleadh Duinna n-Gedh), and is in rhymed iambic heptameters.

[1] *Pansies*, a volume of poems by May Probyn (see p. 67), was reviewed by KT in the *Irish Independent*, 19 Apr 1895. Published by Mathews in March 1895, the book has a pleasing design of pansies embossed on the front and back covers; the title-page also has a design of flowers with intertwined stems in the manner of William Morris. The designs were by Mathews's sister Minnie (1858–1941), an illustrator and painter who exhibited at the Royal Academy in 1886 and 1887.

me much but the religious poems are profoundly imaginative. They have not the thrift, the careful casting away of all that is not essential, which goes to really immortal verse, but they move me always, and even their faults are the faults easiest to forgive. There are things in them which startle one like old folk songs—such things as the last verse of 'Holy communion for the sick'.[2] If only she could shed off some of her birds & flowers & get her moods into absolutely simple rhymes she might live down some great reputation, & even as it is may send some of her baggage into the future. This is the first I have seen of her work & I am grateful to you for the sight.

I wonder some essayist does not make a small book of criticism of the schools & movements of our new generation. What an interesting essay could be made upon this Catholic school?

Johnson has sent me his book & it grows on me more & more. Its austerity & monotony—both really necessary parts of his method—make me more or less anxious about the criticisms. I wrote to you about it before, I beleive, & so say nothing now.[3]

Yrs snly
W B Yeats

ALS Reading.

To Olivia Shakespear, 7 April [1895]

Thorn Hill | Sligo
April 7th

My dear M[rs] Shakespeare,

Alas I am still here in the West & cannot get away for the next three weeks or so. I had to lay the play aside[1] & revise my already published poems for a one volume re-issue & after three months work completed the revision last week. The earlier things & much of the Countess Kathleen are completely rewritten. I am now trying to do some wild Irish stories which shall be not mere phantasies but the signatures—to use a medieval term—of things invisable & ideal.[2] I should greatly like to have a talk with you about

---

[2] The last stanza of the poem 'Holy Communion for the Sick' (*Pansies*, 54) is:

> Oh, Victim, helpless borne here in the Host,
> I will entreat Thy Mother with that most
> Pure heart of love to make amends to Thee
> For all thou lackest whilst thou art with me.

[3] See p. 420.

[1] i.e. *The Shadowy Waters*.

[2] These stories were eventually to be published in *The Secret Rose*.

Maeterlinck. His play about the blind people & the dead priest in the snow is delightful. I feel about his things generally however that they differ from really great work in lacking that ceaseless revery about life which we call wisdom. In all the old dramatists, Greek & English, one feels that they are all the time thinking wonderful, & rather mournful things, about their pupets & every now & then they utter their thoughts in a sudden line or embody them in some unforseen action. I said to Verlaine, when I saw him last year, 'Does not Maeterlinck touch the nerves sometimes when he should touch the heart?' 'Ah yes' said Verlaine 'he is a dear good fellow, and my very good friend, but a little bit of a mountebank'. This touching the nerves alone, seems to me to come from the lack of revery.[3] He is however of immense value as a force helping people to understand a more ideal drama.

What have you found beyond the monk? You might possibly find a sepulchre but as you have begun with a religious porter at the gate have more probably kept to religious symbols. The symbol is a complex one so that I cannot define its influence shortly.[4]

Yrs snly
W B Yeats

Lionels poems are delightful & curiously distinguished but they would need a letter to them selves & I want you to get this by Friday & so must to the post.

ALS MBY. Wade, 255–6.

To T. Fisher Unwin, 7 April [1895]

Thorn Hill | Sligo | Ireland.
April 7th

Dear Mr Unwin

Refuse Miles by all means. I merely gave my provisional consent because it is usual to do so & because I have been a maker of anthologies myself.[1] As a general rule I get no pleasure but rather the reverse from seeing my work in

---

[3] In an 1897 review of *L'Aglavaine et Sélysette* by Maurice Maeterlinck (1862–1949), the Belgian dramatist and poet, WBY wrote (*UP* II. 52–4) that 'the serious fault of his best plays, even of "Les Aveugles" and "L'Intruse", is that they have not the crowning glory of great plays, that continual revery about destiny that is, as it were, the perfect raiment of beautiful emotions.' He had probably read *Les Aveugles* (1890) in its 1892 English translation, *The Sightless*, by Lawrence Alma Tadema. WBY quoted Verlaine's comments on Maeterlinck in his article 'Verlaine in 1894' which appeared in the *Savoy*, April 1896.

[4] OS had apparently had a vision, which WBY was to analyse further in a subsequent letter; see below, p. 463.

[1] Presumably Alfred H. Miles had asked to include some of WBY's poems in a forthcoming volume of his anthology, *The Poets and the Poetry of the Century* (see p. 257).

anthologies. Up to a certain point ⟨it⟩ they helps a writer but there is a point, rather difficult to fix, at which they cease to do so.

As to the American rights question. Certainly Stone & Kimball have the first claim. In any case the matter is outside my province. I merely passed on to you Copeland & Day's request & what I could remember of their argument. The piracy of the poster is certainly a good reason against them— taking it is an indication of their business habits.[2]

Yr sny
W B Yeats

ALS Texas.

To Constance Gore-Booth, 8 April [1895]

Thorn Hill | Sligo
April 8th

My dear Miss Gore Booth

I have looked out those Autographs. I find I have the following

> W E Henley's
> Richard Le Galliennes
> John O Learys
> Miss Hopper's
> Aubrey De Vere's
> Mrs Hinksons (Miss Tynan)
> Standish O Grady's
> George Russell's ('AE')
> Mrs Allingham's (Helen Patterson the artist)
> Douglas Hyde's (this in Gaelic)[1]

I am afraid these are of very unequal value but I dare say you will find some among them which you may care to keep. I have been so much out of things these last months that I have been unable to get better but I dare say when I go to London I can come on some more.

---

[2] The Chicago publishers Stone & Kimball had brought out the first American edition of *The Land of Heart's Desire* (1894), and could thus be considered to have an option on WBY's next book. If Copeland & Day (see pp. 456–7) had made unauthorized use of the Beardsley poster for the Avenue Theatre production of the play (later used on the cover and title-page of the book; see pp. 388–9), the 'piracy' is untraced.

[1] Seven of these autographs (all torn from correspondence) are still with the original letter: those of Hopper, Le Gallienne, JO'L, KT, O'Grady, Mrs Allingham, and Hyde. With O'Leary's autograph WBY has inadvertently torn a part of the characteristically forthright letter to which it was appended: '. . . seems to be working like a galley slave, but more (I fear) to her profit than her fame. She's certainly no critic, and I'm strongly of opinion that neither are you, save within very narrow limits, but then she's also a horrible word-monger which you mostly are not, at least now, for you were bad enough in that first book you edited. As ever, JO'L.'

I hear you were rather bruised at the hunt the other day. I hope the rumour is wholly untrue. Sligo is always full of rumours & the slightest one about its wild huntswoman naturally & properly echoes from mountain to mountain.[2]

Yr sncly
W B Yeats

ALS (with enclosures) Harvard.

To T. Fisher Unwin, 10 April [1895]

Thorn Hill | Sligo.
April 10th

Dear Mr Unwin.

I have written for the address of the other man I had in my mind & will let you know the moment I hear it. He is a man called —— Fell who had two or three drawings at Dents exhibition which struck me more than anything else in the place.[1]

I prefer his work in some ways even to Shannon & long vacilated between the two men. I have never seen any of Mr Jacksons work & though I think the design to Olive Shreineres 'Dream', by the other artist you name, a very fine striking thing—I have always admired it—I am not quite sure if it would do my type of work; & I have seen no other work by him.[2]

Yr snly
W B Yeats

I was for some years an Art student myself & am therefore opinionated & probably crotchety over this question of design.

ALS Texas.

[2] If Sligo's 'wild huntswoman' came to grief at a hunt, no account of the incident reached the local papers at this time.

[1] Charles Shannon evidently being unable to undertake the design for *Poems* (1895), the job was given to Herbert Granville Fell (1872–1951), whose work WBY had first seen at an exhibition of black and white drawings and bookbinding organized by J. M. Dent at the Royal Institute of Painters in Water Colours in September and October 1894. Fell, who first exhibited at the Royal Academy in 1891, later became art editor of the *Ladies' Field* and the *Strand Magazine*, and editor and then art critic of the *Queen*.

In the event, WBY disliked Fell's design for his book, and in John Quinn's vellum copy (NYPL) wrote: 'The man who made this cover made a beautiful design, which I saw at an exhibition, but after I saw it Dent had spoilt him, with all kinds of odd jobs & when he did this the spirit had gone out of him. I hate this expressionless angel of his. W B Yeats, 1904.' (*Bibl*, 34–5)

[2] The reference is probably to Frederick Hamilton Jackson RBA (1848–1923), painter, illustrator, and designer. The artist who provided a striking front-cover design for Olive Schreiner's collection of occasional parables, *Dreams*, published by Unwin in 1891, is unidentified; the design, carried out in gold and blue against a grey ground, shows a large multi-rayed sun suspended over the face of a sundial.

To Olivia Shakespear, 12 April [1895]

Thorn Hill | Sligo.
April 12th

My dear Mrs Shakespeare

The vision is correct in one thing & the rest is merely the opening of a vision. I do not tell you what is right, or the exact nature of the symbol you have used, because I will make the vision complete it self when I see you, & it is best that it do all the explaining. You had better not try to go on with the vision yourself. You are probably very sensitive to these 'astral forces'—to give them the old name—& once one gets to hetrogenous symbols—the ploughed field, the smoke, the little figures Etc—one gets into dangerous ground. Every ⟨symbol has sep⟩ influence has a shadow, as it were, an unballanced—the unballanced is the Kabalistic definition of evil—dublicate of itself. There are means of driving away an influence the moment one finds it to be unballanced, or unpleasant in any way but I cannot give you these means. You may be seeing these things very faintly—merely as phantasies— but you can never tell when they may become vivid & masterful, so had best try & see no more for the present.

I am delighted at your liking 'the Two Trees'.[1] It is a favourite of mine & you & one other person are the only people who have said they liked it. The other person, by the by, is a Miss Eva Gore Booth, daughter of Lady Gore Booth of Lisadell, Sligo. She has some literary talent, & much literary ambition & has met no literary people. I have told her about you & if the chance arise, ⟨have promised to⟩ would like you to meet her. I am always ransacking Ireland for people to set writing at Irish things. She does not know that she is the last victim—but is deep in some books of Irish legends I sent her—& may take fire. She needs however like all Irish literary people a proper respect for craftsmanship & that she must get in England.

I shall look forward to your new novel with great curiosity & interest. I think you have done exactly right in taking a saliant character.[2] You have an inaleanable delicy and subtelty of treatment. You need never seek for the half-tints, but must strive for the blacks & whites. I wish you would do the same with your men. In a letter some time ago you said I complained that you wrote too exclusively of love. I did not mean to. I meant that the parts of

---

[1] WBY's poem 'The Two Trees' (*VP*, 134–6) had first appeared in *The Countess Kathleen*.

[2] In OS's next novel, *The False Laurel*, published in June 1896 (see p. 415, n. 2), the 'saliant' character was the heroine, Daria West, a gifted writer caught 'between the difference that means madness, and the difference that means genius' (179). After the failure of her marriage she has a great public success with a play, but eventually, living alone in London and fearing madness, commits suicide. She is described by one of the other characters in the novel as 'positively poisonous. . . . he was conscious of something in her which was cold, and yet passionate, that repelled him: passion of the heart, he felt she would never know; and passion of the intellect was a dangerous quantity' (81).

your books which were not about love were not carefully studied enough, were not saliant enough. I no more complain of your writing of love, than I would complain of a portrait painter keeping to portraits. I would complain however if his backgrounds were too slightly imagined for the scheme of his art. ⟨It is years however since⟩ I have never come upon any new work so full of a kind of tremulous delicasy, so full of a kind of fragile beauty as these books of yours however.

I have not re-written 'Innisfree' or 'the two trees'. The things I have re-written are 'The Wanderings of Oisin' & all the lyrics practically which I care to preserve out of the same volume; and the end & beginning of 'The Countess Cathleen'.

Lionel scoffs at the monk & his like,[3] because in his heart of hearts, he beleives in them & holds them to be powers of the air & of darkness.

Yrs srly
W B Yeats

ALS MBY; with envelope addressed to Porchester Square, London, and redirected to Hollydale, Keston, Kent;[4] postmark 'SLIGO AP 13 95'. Wade, 256–7.

To T. Fisher Unwin, 12 April [*1895*]

RATRA. | FRENCHPARK. | CO. ROSCOMMON.[1]
April 12th

Dear Mr Unwin

The full name & address of the artist I mentioned to you[2] is

H Granville Fell Esq
34 Cathcart Road
S W

If he will undertake the work please let me know and I will write to him.

Yrs sry
W B Yeats

My address is as above for the next week.

ALS Texas.

[3] See p. 460.
[4] See p. 467.

[1] WBY way staying with Douglas Hyde at Frenchpark and was, according to *Mem* (54), 'the only man from Dublin who had ever stayed in his house.' It was during this visit—on 16 May—that WBY discovered Castle Rock in Lough Key, which he later hoped to make the centre of an Irish mystical Order (*Aut*, 253–5).
[2] See p. 462.

To T. Fisher Unwin, 22 April [1895]

RATRA. | FRENCHPARK. | CO. ROSCOMMON.

April 22nd

Dear Mr Unwin

I have not yet written to Mr Fell[1] because I want to send him a proof of certain parts of the book to give him the right inspiration. If however the delay of waiting for proofs will be too great please let me know & I will do as best I can to make him understand what I want by letter alone. My address will be as above until I let you know to the contrary

Yr srly

W B Yeats

ALS Texas.

To Mrs Fletcher Sheridan Le Fanu,[1] 3 May [1895]

Thorn Hill | Sligo.

May 3rd

My dear M^{rs} Le fanu,

I have long intended to send you 'The Irish Song Book' thinking it might be of use to you for some of your parish concerts or the like.[2] And to day I was looking over my books, as a preliminary to starting for Dublin & London to-morrow, & came on a bound up set of proofs of Lionel Johnsons poems[3] & as it may perhaps interest you, send it you with the song book. Johnson is about the most stately & learned of the new generation of poets.

Yours sncly

W B Yeats

ALS Texas.

To Edward Dowden, 19 May [1895]

3, Blenheim Road | Bedford Park | Chiswick. W

May 19th

My dear Prof Dowden,

I went to try & see Wilde today & to tell him how much I sympathised with him in his trouble. He had left Oakley Street but they told me this

---

[1] See preceding letter.

[1] Jane Le Fanu (1851–1926), daughter of Walter Hore, of Baggnalstown, Co. Carlow, married the Revd Fletcher Sheridan Le Fanu, vicar of Lissadell (see p. 413), in November 1885.

[2] *The Irish Song Book*, edited by Alfred Perceval Graves (see p. 438).

[3] See p. 459. Johnson had now presented WBY with a published copy of the book.

much about his movements. A yact & a very large sum of money was placed at his disposal & all settled for his flight but he refused to go. He says he will stand it out & face the worst & no matter how it turns out work on. He will not go down, they said, or drink, or take poison". I mentioned how I had found some of our Dublin literary men sympathetic to him & my words were received with most pathetic gratitude & I promised to tell them ⟨ what I have just told your hour when ⟩ about his plans.[1] I write to suggest that you either write direct to him, some sympathetic words, Morris has already written, or write some answer to this which I can get shown to him.[2]

> Yours sinly
> W B Yeats

Oscar Wildes address is
  146 Oakley St
  Chelsea

ALS Southern Illinois.

To T. Fisher Unwin, 2 July [1895]

> 3 Blenheim Road | Bedford Park | Chiswick | W
> July 2nd

My dear Mr Unwin

Please tell your clerk that I am not still at Sligo. I got a letter this morning telling me to hurry about my proofs[1] but as it was sent first to Sligo it was not remarkably effective.

I sent back the proofs yesterday & have marked all except a very few pages 'for Press'. These few pages should not add appreciably to the expense & will not add at all to the necessary delay as it is would have in any case to see a second revise of the preface.

> Yrs sinly
> W B Yeats

ALS Texas.

[1] Oscar Wilde had lost his libel case against the Marquess of Queensberry and his own trial on charges of indecency, arising out of this, was to begin on 20 May 1895. He had stayed a few days with his mother and brother William at 146 Oakley Street, before his friends Ernest and Ada Leverson, of 2 Courtfield Gardens, took him in. WBY's visit to Oakley Street is described in *Mem* (79–80), *Aut* (287–9), and by Hesketh Pearson in *The Life of Oscar Wilde* (1946), 306.
[2] Morris's letter has not survived, and Dowden apparently declined to write, for, as WBY recalls (*Aut*, 287), 'I asked various Irish writers for letters of sympathy, and I was refused by none but Edward Dowden, who gave me what I considered an irrelevant excuse—his dislike for everything that Wilde had written.'

[1] Of *Poems* (1895).

To Charles Elkin Mathews, 6 July [*1895*]

3 Blenheim Road | Bedford Park | Chiswick. W
July 6th

Dear Mr Matthews.

The books Mr Sharp asks about are as yet so incomplete that it is difficult to say what shape they will finally take. Much of them especially of the 'Shadowy Waters' is indeed written but I find that things alter enormously in getting finished. 'The Shadowy Waters' is a play of the days before the coming of christianity into Ireland, & is transacted on board a war galley. It will contain some lyrics & has more of intensity than my old things I beleive. 'The Wind Among the Reeds' is a book of short lyrics Irish & personal.¹ Mr Sharp may perhaps care to know, as he is so good as to intend to write about my work, that 'Poems' (T Fisher Unwin) which will be out early in Autumn will contain 'The Wanderings of Oisin' entirely rewritten, 'The Countess Kathleen' expandened & altered in many ways, 'The Land of Hearts Desire' unchanged & the best of my already published lyrics; also that 'The Secret Rose' (Lawrence & Bullen) which will follow it fairly rapidly, will be a tolerably portly volume of Irish stories many of them reprinted from the National Observer & certainly my best prose book.

Please thank Mr Sharp for me & beleive me

Yrs snly
W B Yeats

ALS Reading.

To Olivia Shakespear, 11 July [*1895*]

3 Blenheim Road | Bedford Park | Chiswick. W
July 11th

My dear Mrs Shakespear

I have heard from Mrs Fox¹ about Tuesday & replied that I shall be delighted to go. She however leaves it to us to fix the train, & to let her know,

---

¹ William Sharp ('Fiona Macleod', see p. 24) was writing the introduction and notes to *Lyra Celtica, an Anthology of Representative Celtic Poetry* (Edinburgh, 1896), being edited by his wife, Elizabeth A. Sharp. He mentions WBY in his introduction (xliv–xlvii) and, in a note saying that *The Shadowy Waters* and *The Wind Among the Reeds* are imminent, comments (399) that WBY 'is one of the two or three absolutely poetic personalities in literature at the present moment; and in outlook, and, above all, in atmosphere, stands foremost in the younger generation'.

¹ Elizabeth Valentine Fox, née Ogilvy (1861–1931), was a close friend of OS, who dedicated *Rupert Armstrong* (1898) to her; she married Thomas Hamilton Fox in 1889 and lived at Hollydale, Keston, Beckenham, Kent, 13½ miles south-east of central London. She perhaps acted as 'sponsor' during the

that she may meet it. Any train would suit me so please decide for both of us & tell me your decission.

The end of my story seems to me the end of all mere hunger for possession, even for the possession of the ideal, but not the end of affection, of pity, & of the love which is built more upon pity than upon admiration— the pity one feels for all temporal things the moment that one loves them. It is the end of that warp of the clay which even the noblest must, & perhaps should, weave into the woof of their spirits. The face of the monkey, with its whimsical, mourful withered, mocking pretence of wisdom has always seemed to me the symbol of the end of the glory & the triumph of the world, of all the life of desire & hope—and the dead monkey of all these things done with forever, of the time when even desire, the shadow of the quest of the ideal, has passed away & the merely human soul dies.[2] But the love that is half pity is of eternity.

Yours very sincerely
W B Yeats

ALS Private, with envelope addressed to Porchester Square, London; postmark 'CHISWICK. JY 11 95'.

To T. Fisher Unwin, 12 July [*1895*]

3 Blenheim Road | Bedford Park | Chiswick W
July 12th

Dear M[r] Unwin

I enclose receipt for the money for which many thanks.

M[rs] Sharpe has written for leave to include 'The Lake Isle of Innisfree' 'The White Birds' and three other short poems, from my forth coming book, in an anthology of Celtic poetry called 'Lyra Celtica'.[1] Celtic poetry is so

early period of OS's attachment to WBY for, as he recalled (*Mem*, 86): 'We decided to consult each a woman friend that we might be kept to these resolutions [of waiting to become lovers], as sponsors of our adventure, and for nearly a year met in railway carriages and at picture galleries and occasionally at her house.'

[2] Probably a reference to the end of 'The Eaters of Precious Stones' (*The Celtic Twilight*, 169–71), in which WBY recalls imagining in a waking dream

an immense pit of blackness, round which went a circular parapet, and on this parapet sat innumerable apes eating precious stones out of the palms of their hands. The stones glittered green and crimson, and the apes devoured them with an insatiable hunger. I knew that I saw the Celtic Hell, and my own Hell, the Hell of the artist, and that all who sought after beautiful and wonderful things with too avid a thirst, lost peace and form and became shapeless and common: . . . I saw on another occasion a quantity of demons of all kinds of shapes—fish-like, serpent-like, ape-like, and dog-like—sitting about a black pit such as that in my own Hell, and looking at a moon-like reflection of the Heavens which shone up from the depths of the pit.

[1] Three poems by WBY were included in *Lyra Celtica* (see p. 467), published in March 1896: 'They

much my business that I can hardly refuse her leave to include something. Unless you object I will therefore write her permission.

There are still a very few pages of proofs—the preface in chief—which I am waiting a revise of.[2] I marked all the rest 'for press' & fear I forgot to mention these exceptions when talking to you the other day. I suppose they will arrive in due course.

Yrs sry
W B Yeats

ALS Texas. Dated by recipient '15/7/95'.

Mrs William Sharp,[1] *12 July* [*1895*]

3 Blenheim Road | Bedford Park | Chiswick. W
July 12th

My dear Mrs Sharpe

Your letter has found me after wandering in Ireland. Mr Unwin has a share in my copyrights, so far as I understand the matter which is but dimly, & I have written to ask him whether he objects to your quoting the poems you name;[2] so far as I am concerned you are welcome to them. I will let you know what he says as soon as I have heard.

I shall look forward very much to 'Lyra Celtica'.

Yr sny
W B Yeats

Do you know Miss Hoppers verse? She is very Celtic.[3]

ALS NLS.

went forth to the Battle, but they always fell' (*VP*, 113–15; afterwards 'The Rose of Battle'), 'The White Birds' (*VP*, 121–2), and 'The Lake of Innisfree' (*sic*) (*VP*, 117).

   [2] See p. 466. The preface of *Poems* (1895) as published retains the date 'Sligo, March 24th, 1895'.

   [1] Elizabeth Amelia Sharp (1856–1932) married William Sharp ('Fiona Macleod') in 1884. She translated selections from Heine, including his *Italian Travel Sketches* (1892), and edited several anthologies of poetry, among which were *Songs and Poems of the Sea* (1888) and *Women Poets of the Victorian Era* (1890). In 1910 she published a memoir of William Sharp and edited his *Collected Writings*, 7 vols. (1909–11).

   [2] See preceding letter.

   [3] Three poems by Nora Hopper, 'The Dark Man', 'April in Ireland', 'The Wind Among the Reeds', appear in the 'Irish (Modern and Contemporary)' section of *Lyra Celtica*.

To Louise Imogen Guiney, 17 July [*1895*]

3 Blenheim Road | Bedford Park | Chiswick. | W
July 17th

My dear Miss Guiney

I wrote to say that I will drop in on you, on Thursday evening; but it occurs to me that I put the wrong number on the letter; and therefore write again to make sure.[1] I shall turn up about 8 o'clock unless I hear that you would prefer some other hour.

I have just met Mrs Moore[2] who was delighted to hear of your being in London.

Yrs sincerely
W B Yeats

ALS Holy Cross.

To Katharine Tynan Hinkson, 31 July [*1895*]

3 Blenheim Road | Bedford Park | Chiswick. W
July 31st

My dear Mrs Hinkson,

I have asked the 'Bookman' people to send you the August number which contains my article on contemporary Irish prose writers; & I enclose herewith a copy from 'United Ireland' of my first article the one on the writers of the past.[1] The next will be on 'cemporary Irish poetry' and deal with your work very largely perhaps mainly (this depends whether I decide to re-do De Vere or, as is more likely, content myself with the mention I have given him in the first article. Only the accident of his long life makes him a contemporary & I should not think of doing him again, were not my first mention of him so slight).[2]

---

[1] Louise Guiney had reached London on 10 July—having made her way across country from Liverpool, where she arrived on 26 May 1895, via Chester, Wales, Devon, and Dorset—and had taken lodgings at 28 Gower Street.

[2] Mrs Moore, an old Irishwoman, a native of Dublin, lived near the Yeatses in Bedford Park and became a friend of theirs early in 1889. She was a well-travelled woman, whom ECY described (diary, MBY) as 'such a clever old Lady, reads everything & talks well'.

[1] For WBY's four articles on Irish literature in the *Bookman*, July–October 1895, see p. 424. The first article was reprinted both in *United Ireland*, 13 July 1895, and the *Daily Express*, 5 July. A leader in the *Freeman's Journal*, 5 Aug 1895 (4), was devoted to the article on prose writers; although the writer found WBY's 'characterizations of Miss Lawless and Miss Barlow . . . felicitous', he complained that Standish James O'Grady and Nora Hopper had been overpraised.

[2] KT was one of eight poets mentioned by WBY in his September *Bookman* article on 'Contemporary Irish Poets' (*UP* I. 375–82), but her poetical work, like that of Hyde and AE, was discussed at greater

I should be glad of some notice in the 'Independent' & it had best come before my criticism of your work.[3] These Bookman articles are my only way of getting at the Irish public. The first was copied by the 'Express' as well as by 'United Ireland'.

The cover of my book with Unwin has caused quite a flutter of aproval among his clerks but I have not yet seen it. Fells design I have seen & that is very admirable. I have chosen for the substance a curious dove-grey.[4] I wonder when your miracle plays come out? ⟨Not I fear⟩[5]

Yours snly
W B Yeats

ALS Huntington. McHugh, 138; Wade, 257–8.

To Standish James O'Grady,[1] 31 August [1895]

5 Blenheim Road | Bedford Park | Chiswick. W
August 31st

My dear M^r O'Grady,

I got the N O & read the story & like it, though I do not think it among the best of your things. I think you have not quite realized the picture enough in detail. The blind old man, the last conquered king, is a great oppertunity for a kind of shadow of doom & I wish you had described him with as much of emotion as you describe, in the 'Story of Ireland', the 'ghost' seen by the new landlord at his tenants hearth.[2] The fact is your very excellence, in this little

length than the others. Aubrey de Vere's longevity did earn him a further mention, but he was found to be 'seldom master of the inevitable words in the inevitable order' and his works to be 'but slightly related to the Irish lyrical movement of to-day . . .'

[3] No notice of the *Bookman* articles appeared in the *Irish Daily Independent*, since KT had more important matters to occupy her: on 17 Aug 1895 she gave birth to her second son (the first had been stillborn). But as SMY recorded in her diary (MBY) 'the poor child is so weakly that there is no likely hood of it living.' On 14 Sept she reported: 'Willy has seen the Hinkson baby says it looks as if it came out of a match box.' The little boy died shortly after this and the Hinksons, in need of recuperation, set out for a six-week stay in Ireland.

[4] The colour of the binding cloth of *Poems* (1895) was closer to a pale brown (see p. 434) than a dove grey. Fell's design (see p. 462, n. 1) more closely resembled St. George and the Dragon than an angel and a serpent.

[5] In his September *Bookman* article, WBY anticipated (*UP* 1. 380) that KT's *Miracle Plays* (published by John Lane in November 1895) would be 'her best and her most popular book . . . for her best inspiration has ever come from Catholic belief, and to give an excellent expression to the ancient symbols is to be for a delight and a comfort to many ardent and dutiful spirits.' He gave a copy of the book to SMY as his 1895 Christmas present.

[1] See p. 126, n. 6 and Appendix.

[2] O'Grady's story ' 'Ware the Spring' an account of the deposition and blinding in 1133 of the King of Tir-Cullen, by Dermot MacMurrough, King of Leinster, appeared in the *National Observer*, 31 Aug 1895. In *The Story of Ireland*, O'Grady tells how a 'new squire'—a Protestant given Catholic lands after William III's victory at the Boyne—encounters the ghost of the Jacobite whose lands he has appropriated.

tale, is your enemy for it awakes the imagination & makes it exacting I imagine that we differ more about the meaning of the word 'National' than about the historical facts of Irish wars. I should perhaps in my Bookman article have used the phrase 'the armed hand of race' instead of 'the armed hand of nationality'. I find it hard, knowing how jelous one country is of another, even to day, when people travel so much, to beleive that the Irish had no racial hatred (no matter how completely they lacked a racial policy *i.e.* nationality) for invaders who spoke a different tongue & had different customs & interests. Then too, one cannot forget a lot of gaelic poems like 'the battle song for the clans of Wicklow' (translated by Ferguson). It is not possible that while the racial unity of England expressed itself in a method of goverment, the racial unity of Ireland expressed it self in things like the bardic order & in popular instincts & prejudices. That while the English nobles therefore expressed English racial purpose at its best, the Irish nobles, warped by their little princedoms & their precarious dynasties were more for themselves & less for Ireland, than the bards, & harpers & the masses of the people? You of course know & I do not. You speak from particular knowledge, I from general principles merely.[3]

I saw Henley a couple of weeks ago. He taked about a Perrot chapter you had sent him which he seemed about to take, after he had got you to change one or two things. I am afraid I did you an ill turn unwittingly. I began talking of Cuchullin—the part yet to come. 'I wont have Perrot then' said Henley 'that is the thing for me'. I hope he has been better than his word & taken Perrot which he thought of great interest & only quarrelled with over some matters of detail. But in any chase it would be a great thing to get 'Cuchullin' into the Review, or into any review, or finished anywhere, for the story from the laying on of the spell till the death, as you tell it in the 'history', is not less than any epic tale in the world.[4]

I wonder if 'Hodder & Staughton' (they publish 'the Bookman') would

---

[3] In his *Bookman* article of August 1895 (see p. 424), WBY, after praising O'Grady's work, went on to say (*UP* I. 369): 'I disagree with his conclusions too constantly, and see the armed hand of nationality in too many places where he but sees the clash of ancient with modern institutions, to believe that he has written altogether the true history of Ireland. . . . ' O'Grady had presumably written to point out that the concept of 'nationality' was a relatively modern one. WBY was to take up the discussion again in his August 1897 review of O'Grady's *The Flight of the Eagle* (*UP* II. 48–9). The poem, 'O'Byrne's Bard to the Clans of Wicklow', appeared in Ferguson's *Lays of the Western Gael* (1865).

[4] Sir John Perrot (?1527–92), Viceroy of Ireland, had been a leading figure in O'Grady's historical narrative about Red Hugh O'Donnell, *Red Hugh's Captivity* (see pp. 443–4), which he was now engaged in expanding and recasting into a more popular novelistic form. It appeared in 1897 as *The Flight of the Eagle*, with a first chapter entitled 'Sir John Perrott'. O'Grady had also written extensively of Cuchulain (whose name he habitually mispelt and mispronounced 'Cuculain') in his *History of Ireland*; in the 1890s he decided to use this material for a series of novels, the first of which, *The Coming of Cuculain*, was published in 1894. The two remaining volumes were not published until much later: *In the Gates of the North* in 1910 and *The Triumph and Passing of Cuculain* in 1920. Nothing of O'Grady's on Perrot or on Cuchulain appeared in the *National Observer* or in the *New Review*.

be good people for 'Red Hugh'. Dr Nicoll is there reader & my notice of you in 'Bookman' article may have prepared his mind as he edits 'the Bookman'.[5] I saw Dent the other day & praised your historical work but he seemed bent on getting the projected new 'Romance'. In fact I have a notion that his reader misled by the vividness of your history thought Red Hugh was a romance a little loaded with historical detail. I charged him with this & his answers were rather uncertain. The ordinary man doest think any book is history unless it be dry as the remainder biscuit.[6]

'The Chain of Gold' has just come: for which many thanks.[7]

Yrs ev
W B Yeats

Henley had read 'Fin & his companions' at a sitting & seemed to want the like for his review. Why not give him 'the Battle at the Ford' and then the last adventures & the Death?[8]

ALS Kansas.

To Sarah Purser,[1] 1 September [1895]

3 Blenheim Road | Bedford Park | Chiswick. W
Sept 1st

My dear Miss Pursur,

I have been an unconscioble time about writing to thank you for your charming embroidered book cover & can only ask you to excuse me because—well, on general principles.

---

[5] *The Flight of the Eagle* was published not by Hodder & Stoughton but by Lawrence & Bullen, in 1897. William Robertson Nicoll (1851–1923), clergyman and man of letters, had turned to journalism when forced by ill health to resign his living as a minister of the Free Church; he was editor of the *British Weekly* and of the *Bookman* from its inception in 1891. He was knighted in 1909. (Of Nicoll, WBY told Rhys [*Wales England Wed* (1940), 154]: 'When you look at his fine brow frontways he is like an old Scottish divine. But when you look at him sideways, as he sits rubbing his hands together, he looks like some mean little Scottish tradesman.')

[6] J. M. Dent & Co. published O'Grady's *In the Wake of King James* in 1896.

[7] In an unsigned review in the *Bookman*, November 1895, WBY gave (*UP* II. 515) an enthusiastic but basically accurate synopsis of the plot of O'Grady's boys' adventure story, *The Chain of Gold* (1895):

a history of two boys who go out fishing, and are hurled, boat and all, into the mouth of a cave far above the sea level, by one of the best storms raised in modern fiction, and there keep body and soul together by contrivances as excellent as any of Crusoe's, and encounter the phantom of an ancient Irish hermit, or else endure a strange delirium from hardship and thirst—for we are left in doubt—and return at last to common things and safety.

[8] The 'Fightings at the Ford' is a chapter in O'Grady's *In the Gates of the North*; Cuchulain's last adventures and death make up the substance of *The Triumph and Passing*.

[1] See p. 74.

The book cover is at this moment helping to civilize a novel all about North of Ireland presbeterians & succeeding as well as could be expected under the circumstances.[2] It shall have a better & easier task presently.

I have heard of you in the letters of that imp out of 'The Land of Hearts Desire', (letters M[rs] Paget has shown me), & which are so very life like, that I am almost convinced of the real existence of the imp.[3] This is a sign of the return of the age of faith.

Yours sincly

W B Yeats

ALS NLI. Wade (dated '[? 1894]'), 235–6.

To Ernest Rhys, 8 September [*1895*]

3 Blenheim Road | Bedford Park | Chiswick. W

Sept 8th

My dear Rhys

are you back yet from Holy Island?[1] If so may I come over to see you on Thursday evening. I want to have a word about my fathers drawings.[2]

Yours snly

W B Yeats.

ALS Kansas.

[2] Probably *A Maid of the Manse* (1895), the latest novel by Mrs Erminda Esler (1853–1924), whom WBY mentions in the *Bookman* in August 1895 (*UP* I. 371) as a novelist of Presbyterian life. It is a romantic story set among Presbyterian clergymen in Co. Donegal.

[3] The imp in the play is 'A Faery Child', played at the first performances by Dorothy Paget (1885–1974), a girl of just ten. WBY later recalled (*Aut*, 280) that Florence Farr had asked him to write a one-act play in which Dorothy, her niece, 'might make her first stage appearance, and I, with my Irish Theatre in mind, wrote *The Land of Heart's Desire*, in some discomfort when the child was theme, for I knew nothing of children. . . . ' 'That imp' had started a three-month theatrical tour in August 1895, and had evidently met Sarah Purser while acting in Dublin.

[1] Rhys and his family had evidently spent the summer holiday of 1895 on Lindisfarne, or Holy Island, off the Northumberland coast.

[2] In 1894 JBY had been commissioned by Rhys's employer, J. M. Dent, to illustrate the 16 vols. of *Romances and Narratives by Daniel Defoe*, edited by George A. Aiken. By August 1895 he had begun work on the illustrations for *Roxana* but in mid-month his progress was interrupted by an illness which was to continue throughout the autumn. WBY presumably wished to tell Rhys the reason for the delay over the drawings and to ask him to intercede with Dent, but it seems that he had not yet returned from Lindisfarne, for SMY records in her diary (MBY) that she had to call on Dent in the week ending 12 Oct 1895 to explain the situation. The unsympathetic Dent insisted that the drawings must be done whether the artist was ill or not and on 13 Oct Paget 'like a good angel' offered to help JBY.

To T. Fisher Unwin, 3 November [*1895*]

C/o Arthur Symons | Fountain Court | Temple.[1]

Nov 3rd.

Dear M[r] Unwin,

I have been so busy that I have only just found time to find & tare out the articles on Irish Literature which I want you to publish in a pamphlet under the title 'What to Read in Irish Literature'. When I have restored certain quotations, cut out by the Bookman people for lack of space, & written half a dozen pages or so of introduction on the relation of Irish literature to general literature & culture & to contemporary movents there should be material enough for a decent shillings worth.[2]

Yrs snly

W B Yeats.

ALS Texas. Wade, 258.

[1] On 4 Oct 1895 SMY in Sligo heard from ECY that 'WB has taken a room says he can live on 10/– a week, let him try.' (diary, MBY). SMY on her return to Blenheim Road recorded in her diary for 13 Oct: 'Willy came full of his new start—very good thing, I think.' The room was part of a set rented by Arthur Symons in the Middle Temple and sub-let since late 1893 to Henry Havelock Ellis (1859–1939), who describes the arrangement in *My Life* (1940), 284–5:

Fountain Court, with the two little rooms which I rented from Symons until he gave up the chambers on his marriage in 1901, was for my purposes absolutely ideal. The chambers consisted of four rooms at the top of the building, two overlooking the Court and occupied by Symons, two of smaller size overlooking Essex Street which were mine. A narrow passage joined Symons's rooms to mine, but there were two separate doors on to the landing (double doors, so that when we wished it was possible for each of us separately to "sport the oak" and exclude importunate callers) and each of us with his visitors was completely shut off and independent of the other, while yet we were in close touch whenever we so desired. It was part of the arrangement that Symons should be free to put anyone else in my rooms when I was away in Cornwall; I do not recall that he ever made use of this freedom except during one season for W. B. Yeats the poet, and again to instal Verlaine during his brief visit to London.

Symons was replacing the now frequently inebriated Lionel Johnson as WBY's closest friend, 'and my thoughts gained in richness and in clearness from his sympathy, nor shall I ever know how much my practice and my theory owe to the passages that he read me from Catullus and from Verlaine and Mallarmé' (*Aut*, 319–20). Nevertheless WBY's move was primarily dictated by his desire to further his relationship with OS, whose lover he was shortly to become. He remained at Fountain Court until the beginning of March 1896 and recalled with affection (*Aut*, 322) the 'chambers in the Temple that opened through a little passage into those of Arthur Symons. If anybody rang at either door, one or other would look through a window in the connecting passage, and report. We would then decide whether one or both should receive the visitor, whether his door or mine should be opened, or whether both doors were to remain closed. I have never liked London, but London seemed less disagreeable when one could walk in quiet, empty places after dark, and upon a Sunday morning sit upon the margin of a fountain almost as alone as if in the country.'

[2] WBY evidently hoped to publish in a more permanent form his four *Bookman* articles on 'Irish National Literature' (see p. 424). The book, which never appeared, would have marked a further stage in his attempt to make Irish writers and critics more self-critical and self-aware, and was perhaps intended to supercede JO'L's influential Davisite pamphlet, *What Irishmen Should Know* (Dublin, [1886]).

To Edmund Gosse,[1] [*23 November 1895*]

Fountain Court, | Temple.
Saturday.

Dear M[r] Gosse, I have been so busy of late working against time at a wretched story which has in the end refused to acheive it self that I have postponed everything including my answer to your kind letter about my book.[2] Besides I have had a better reasen M[r] Heineman's reissue of 'King Erik' has been looking at me from the bookshelf opposite my seat, for the last few weeks, & I have waited for the leisure to discover if some bits that facinated me when a boy would or would not have faded by this. The scene that gave me the most pleasure was scene ii of Act IV & I find the old charm there & elsewhere. For quite a time the learned princess sitting among the tropical flowers haunted me; & one line used constantly to run in my head

> The knowledge of strange worlds has been a thirst
> Unslaked

as the center of the scene. I remember even; in a way I then had; trying to symbolise the impression of the scene, & writing some lines of bad verse about a dead lizard covered with the pollen of flowers.[3]

Thanking you again for your kind letter I remain

Yours sncly
W B Yeats.

ALS BL. Dated by recipient '25/11/95'. Wade, 258–9.

[1] Edmund William Gosse (1849–1928), critic (see p. 92, n. 9), minor poet and author of the celebrated autobiography *Father and Son* (1907), was emerging as an important figure in the British literary establishment. Although he started his working life at the British Museum and later became a translator at the Board of Trade and, finally, the librarian of the House of Lords, he managed to write prolifically on English and European literature, acquiring a particular reputation as an authority on the Scandinavian writers. Apart from some coolness in the early 1920s he remained a good, if not close, friend of WBY's, helping him, among other things, to raise money for the Abbey Theatre and to secure a Civil List Pension. Although WBY had described him in 1886 as 'an admirable, but altogether trivial, English poet' (*UP* I. 92), he later praised him (*UP* II. 40) for helping to bring about the reaction against Victorian rhetoric in poetry by his 'delight in the most condensed of lyric forms.' Gosse was knighted in 1925.
[2] The 'wretched' story was presumably one of those intended for *The Secret Rose*. Gosse had written on 17 Oct 1895 (*LWBY* I, 13) to thank WBY for sending him *Poems* (1895): 'I have no words too strong (& yet I am not fond of flinging words about) to say how I delight in these penetrating, poignant lyrics of yours. You are indeed, what one dares so seldom say, a poet. . . .' That he liked the poems was fortunate, since on 4 Nov (BL) Lionel Johnson, in his role as 'purveyor-in-ordinary of Willie Yeats to Edmund Gosse', sent him yet another copy of 'this perfected book'.
[3] Gosse's *King Erik*, a five-act tragedy in blank verse first published by Chatto & Windus in 1876, was reissued by Heinemann in 1893 with an introductory essay by Theodore Watts[-Dunton]. In Scene ii of Act IV King Erik of Denmark, on a pilgrimage to the Holy Land, arrives with his Queen in Constantinople. They are welcomed in a garden of the palace by the Emperor's daughter, Anna Comnena, who astonishes them by conversing in fluent Danish. She explains that she has learnt it from

To Florence Farr,[1] [*after 19 December 1895*]

Fountain Court

My dear S S D D,[2] Has the magical armageddon begun at last? I notice that the *Freeman's Journal*, the only Irish paper I have seen, has an article from its London correspondent announcing inevitable war and backing it up with excellent argument from the character of Cleveland.[3] The war would fulfil the prophets and especially a prophetic vision I had long ago with the Mathers's, and so far be for the glory of God, but what a dusk of the nations it would be! for surely it would drag in half the world.[4] What have your divinations said or have they said anything? When will you be in town next? Could you come and see me on Monday and have tea and perhaps divine for armageddon?

Yours ever
W B Yeats

Text from Wade, 259–60.

the wives of her father's Danish mercenaries, and that 'all my days/The knowledge of strange worlds has been a thirst/Unslaked within my nature.' The scene (137–9), which was presumably WBY's first introduction to Byzantium, contrasts the languorous sophistication of Constantinople with the rude vigour of the Danes. Princess Anna, who has affinities with a number of WBY's early heroines, is beautiful and sagacious but world-weary and burdened with the sense of mortality. The tone of the scene is set by a series of *carpe diem* lyrics sung by her servant, Eros, and WBY's symbolic poem about the lizard may have been inspired by one of these (135):

> So crowned and chapleted with flowers,
>   I pray you be not proud;
> For after brief and summer hours
>   Comes autumn with a shroud;—
> Though fragrant as a flower you lie,
> You and your garland, bye and bye,
> Will fade and wither up and die!

[1] See p. 165, n. 7.

[2] i.e. 'Sapientia Sapienti Dono Data', Florence Farr's initials in the Order of the Golden Dawn.

[3] The *Freeman's Journal* on 18 Dec 1895 and subsequent days carried news reports and editorials on the possibility of war between Great Britain and the United States over the disputed boundary between Venezuela and British Guiana. President Grover Cleveland had invoked the Monroe Doctrine in a message to Congress on 17 Dec. The *Freeman's Journal* commented in its editorial of 19 Dec (4): 'even if we accept the not improbable view that the character of his language was dictated by political contingencies in the States, [President Cleveland] has everything to gain by adhering to the interpretation of the Monroe Doctrine, and its relevancy to the actual crisis in Venezuela, which he has so categorically stated.' Although greatly excited by the prospect of a war, the paper nowhere announced it as 'inevitable'.

[4] WBY seems to have been reading the recently published English edition of Max Nordau's *Degeneration* (2): 'In our days there have arisen in more highly-developed minds vague qualms of a Dusk of the Nations, in which all suns and all stars are gradually waning, and mankind with all its institutions and creations is perishing in the midst of a dying world.'

On this occasion, however, the threat of Armageddon was withdrawn by the 1897 Treaty of Washington, and on 3 Oct 1899 the principal British claims were upheld.

To Mrs Edmund Gosse, [*22 December 1895*]

Fountain Court | Temple
Sunday.

My dear Mrs Gosse, I accept your kind invitation for New Years eve with great pleasure; & hope you will excuse my long delay about answering.[1] Symons has just come in & asks me to say that he can get out of his previous engagement & will be delighted to come:

Yours sinclly
W B Yeats

ALS Cambridge, with envelope addressed to 29 Delamere Terrace, Westbourne Square, W., postmark 'BEDFORD ST DE 24 95'.

To an unidentified correspondent, [*? late 1895 or early 1896*]

Fountain Court | Temple.
Wednesday.

Dear Sir, What time would suit you best to call? I can be in either on Saturday or Monday evening at about 8 o clock or some other day if you would prefer. I am always glad to meet any friends of Mr Day's.[1]

Yours sincerely,
W B Yeats

PS.

I am at the top of Fountain Court. The top flat. My name is on the door on a visiting card.

ALS Southern Illinois.

[1] Edmund Gosse and his wife Ellen (Nellie), née Epps (1850–1929), were married in 1875. They lived in Paddington, overlooking the Grand Union Canal. Mrs Gosse was apparently just as enthusiastic about WBY's poetry as her husband, who in his letter of 17 Oct (see p. 476, n. 2) had added the P.S.: 'I am now going to read "The Rose" aloud to my wife & my daughter: but they know most of it.'

[1] F. H. Day, whose firm, Copeland & Day, had just brought out WBY's *Poems* (1895) in the USA.

BIOGRAPHICAL AND HISTORICAL
APPENDIX

BEDFORD PARK, where WBY lived from 1879 to 1881 and from 1888 to 1895, was a new departure in town planning, a garden suburb first envisaged by the property speculator Jonathan T. Carr in 1875. Carr, who was in touch through his brother with the Aesthetic Movement, wished to create on the estate of Bedford House, near Chiswick in south-west London, a development that would have the atmosphere of a country village and yet 'artistic and sanitary advantages superior to those to be found in any other suburb of London'. The first houses, finished in the autumn of 1876, were by Ernest Godwin and the firm of Coe and Robinson; subsequently many of the designs were executed by Norman Shaw in the 'Queen Anne' style, while others were the work of E. J. May and Maurice B. Adams. The prevailing taste in interior design was that of William Morris. Just as there was a good deal more variety in the architecture than contemporary commentators noticed, so was there a greater heterogeneity among the Park's inhabitants, with business men, professionals and retired military officers, as well as artists and writers, taking houses there. Nevertheless, the suburb was popularly regarded as entirely the product of the Aesthetic Movement, and in fact it probably did boast more artists and writers per acre than any other comparable area in London. The communal spirit was enhanced by the building of a Clubhouse in 1879; it was here that WBY first saw Todhunter's *A Sicilian Idyll*, put on by the Amateur Dramatic Club. There was also the Calumet, an informal debating club to which JBY belonged, a music society, and frequent conversaziones and fancy-dress balls. WBY's intense dislike of London sounds throughout his early letters, but he found that the Park 'had some village characters and helped us to feel not wholly lost in the metropolis'.

HELENA PETROVNA BLAVATSKY (1831–91), founder of the Theosophic Movement, was born in Ekaterinoslav in Southern Russia, the daughter of Colonel Peter von Hahn. At eighteen she married the middle-aged Nikifor V. Blavatsky, Vice-Governor of the Province of Yerivan, but deserted him after only a few months and always alleged that the marriage had never been consummated. For the next twenty-five years she travelled widely, in 1851 meeting in London her Master 'Moyra', an 'Initiate' of Rajput birth who told her of the religious work in store for her. She made many attempts to enter Tibet, apparently succeeding in 1855 (or 1864, depending on which version one accepts) and there supposedly underwent occult training. Ordered by her Master in 1873 to go to New York, she joined Colonel Henry Steel Olcott and William Quan Judge in founding the Theosophical Society (q.v.) in September 1875. She began at once to write *Isis Unveiled* (1877) in order to provide an exposition of theosophical thought. A brief bigamous marriage to M. C. Betanally ended in May 1878, and in December she and Olcott sailed for India. In 1880 they both took Buddhist vows, and in May 1882 bought the estate at Adyar that became the headquarters of the Theosophical Society. Two years later came her servants' allegations that HPB had forged psychic phenomena, and Richard Hodgson's report on behalf of the Society for Psychical Research, which summed her up as 'one of the most accomplished, ingenious, and interesting impostors in history'. With her health undermined, in 1885 HPB resigned as Corresponding Secretary of the Theosophical Society and returned to Europe.

After a period of ill-health and neglect on the Continent she arrived in London in May 1887 and moved in with Mabel Collins in Upper Norwood. It was here that WBY first visited her, finding her 'an old woman in a plain loose dark dress: a sort of old Irish peasant woman with an air of humour and audacious power,' but with only three followers left. After an uneasy beginning he became a regular visitor. In September 1887 she launched a monthly magazine, *Lucifer*; later in the autumn she moved to Holland Park, where her growing band of disciples had leased and furnished larger premises and where she formally established the Blavatsky Lodge of the Society. In 1888 she published *The Secret Doctrine* and set up the Esoteric Section of the Society, which WBY joined in December. In 1890 she moved to 18 Avenue Road, where, in a purpose-built meeting hall, she proclaimed her Lodge the centre of the TS in Europe. Shortly after this, WBY's criticism of the Society and his unapproved psychical experiments led to his expulsion, rather to his regret.

WBY's attitude to HPB was always ambivalent. 'I have no theories about her,' he wrote to JO'L (q.v.). 'She is simply a note of interrogation.' Having read Hodgson's report he 'awaited with impatience the explanation that never came', but responded to the vividness of her personality, so conspicuously lacking in her pallid followers: 'A great passionate nature, a sort of female Dr Johnson . . . she seemed impatient of the formalism and the shrill abstract idealism of those about her.' She died in May 1891, and was cremated at Woking. WBY recalled her as 'vast and shapeless of body, and perpetually rolling cigarettes—humorous and unfanatic', and said that in her company he had escaped 'from the restlessness of my own mind'.

THE CONTEMPORARY CLUB began in 1885 with informal Saturday-night gatherings in C. H. Oldham's rooms in Trinity College, Dublin. It was at these meetings that the editorial policy of the *Dublin University Review*, which first published WBY, was discussed, and WBY attended a number of them, together with John Walker, the printer of the magazine, Rolleston (q.v.), its editor, Gregg, Hyde (q.v.), Crook, and Lipmann. In November of that year the Club was officially constituted and took rooms at 116 Grafton Street. Oldham chose the name 'Contemporary' because the members needed to have nothing in common apart from being alive at the same time. He was a Protestant Home-Ruler and wished to provide a forum for all shades of Irish opinion on the political, literary, and social questions of the day. Since he wanted to create a relaxed, informal atmosphere, where any view might be debated, the Club was forbidden by its rules from taking public action. Membership was at first limited to fifty, but later raised to seventy five; women were not admitted in its early years, although 'Ladies' Nights' eventually became a regular feature. Although the Club continued into the 1940s, its most vigorous period was the decade after its inauguration when, apart from regular members such as JO'L (q.v.), Davitt, J. F. Taylor, Sigerson, Coffey and T. W. Russell, it numbered among its guests William Morris, T. W. Stead, and Mohini Chatterji. Both JBY and WBY attended regularly from 1885 until their return to London in 1887, and JBY did a series of sketches of the members and visitors.

WBY, who continued to call in at the Club well into the next century, said that he joined it as a means of acquiring self-possession, recalling that 'harsh argument which had gone out of fashion in England was still the manner of our conversation, and at this club Unionist and Nationalist could interrupt one another and insult one another without the formal and traditional restraint of public speech'. Hyde records many meetings with him there, and on 11 December 1886 speaks of WBY's brilliant exposition of his ideas on drama, while on another memorable occasion JO'L announced to the assembled members that 'young Yeats is the only person in the room who will ever be reckoned a genius'.

EDWARD DOWDEN (1843–1913) the son of a Cork linen draper, became the most distinguished Irish literary critic and scholar of his generation. As a student at Trinity College, Dublin, he overlapped with JBY (q.v.), who was already a friend of his elder brother John (later Bishop of Edinburgh). After a distinguished undergraduate career, Dowden was elected to the Chair of English at Trinity in 1867, only four years after graduating, and he also held the Chair of Oratory from the same date. In 1866 he married Mary Clerke, some ten years his senior: the marriage was not a success, but in 1867 he met in his classes at Alexandra College (a women's college associated with Trinity) Elizabeth Dickinson West, with whom he enjoyed an intellectual and emotional relationship and whom he married in 1895, three years after the death of Mary. Dowden had ambitions to be a poet but remained at his academic post for the security it provided, ignoring JBY's frequent appeals to come to London. His scholarly repuation was established by his book, *Shakspere: His Mind and Art* (1875) and further consolidated with the publication of *Studies in Literature* (1878), *Life of Shelley* (1886), and shorter biographies of Southey, Browning, and Montaigne. Urbane, cool, ironic, and sceptical, Dowden often distressed JBY by his caution and fastidiousness, without ever forfeiting his friendship. He lent JBY considerable sums of money without hope of repayment, and commissioned pictures from him.

With WBY the situation was different; after an initial period of admiration and respect in the mid-1880s, he began to see Dowden as representative of all that he disliked in the Victorian frame of mind, particularly in its West British, Anglo-Irish manifestation. Dowden shocked WBY by confessing shortly before the publication of his biography of Shelley that he had lost interest in its subject; but it was his attitude towards Irish literature that most offended WBY, one of whose earliest published essays contains an attack on Dowden for not having done more to establish the reputation of Sir Samuel Ferguson as a poet. Dowden compounded his sin by disparaging the Irish literary movement in the *Fortnightly Review* in 1889, and by similar comments at the Trinity College Historical Society in 1895. WBY also alleges that he, alone of the Irish men of letters approached, refused to write a letter of sympathy to Oscar Wilde during his trial.

At the outset of WBY's career Dowden had been circumspect in his judgement, writing to John Todhunter (q.v.) that 'Willie Yeats . . . hangs in the balance between genius and (to speak rudely) fool. I shall rejoice if it be the first. But it remains doubtful.' When WBY showed him poems he was, however, 'wise in his encouragement, never overpraising and never unsympathetic', and he wrote enthusiastically on the publication of *The Wanderings of Oisin*. Nevertheless, WBY began to find something patronizing in his commendations. When he came to write *Reveries over Childhood and Youth* in 1916, therefore, WBY portrayed Dowden as the conventional and 'unreal' foil to JO'L (q.v.). He had come to believe with JBY (although he expressed it more pointedly than his father would have done) that Dowden's irony stemmed from timidity, his graciousness from evasion, and that he had surrendered passionate life to provincial orthodoxy.

SIR CHARLES GAVAN DUFFY (1816–1903) was born in Monaghan, the youngest of six children of a Catholic shopkeeper. His nationalist sentiments were first aroused by local Protestant bigotry, and as a youth he began to write for the *Northern Herald*, edited by the United Irishman, Charles Hamilton Teeling. In 1836 he went to Dublin to train as a journalist on the *Morning Register*, the organ of O'Connell's Catholic Association, and from 1839 to 1842 successfully edited the newly founded *Belfast Vindicator*, a bi-weekly also sympathetic to O'Connell's movement. While in Belfast, Duffy married Emily MacLaughlin, the daughter of a local businessman and the first of three wives. During a vist to Dublin in 1842 John Blake Dillon introduced him to Thomas Davis, then emerging as the leader of the Young Irelanders, and the three men founded the *Nation*, a weekly paper to support Repeal and 'create and foster public opinion in Ireland and make it racy of the soil'. The paper first appeared on 15 October 1842 and, with its combination of news, literary criticism, poetry, and political comment, was a spectacular success. Although Davis was its main inspiration, Duffy was the proprietor and his journalistic experience was crucial to its management. As a consequence of these activities he was imprisoned with O'Connell for a few months in 1842; in the following year came the double blow of the sudden deaths of his wife and of his hero Davis.

Duffy now ran the *Nation* single-handed and also organized and edited the 'Library of Ireland' (see The New Irish Library). With his increasing involvement in Young Ireland politics, he handed over the management of the *Nation* to John Mitchel, an outspoken Presbyterian Nationalist from Ulster. As the full horror of the Great Famine unfolded, and under the influence of James Fintan Lalor, the agrarian radical, Mitchel's leading articles grew inflammatory and in 1846 involved Duffy in a trial for seditious libel. This helped to widen a split, already apparent, between the Young Irelanders and the more cautious O'Connell, and in January 1847 the former seceded from the Repeal Association to establish the Irish Confederation. The revolutions of 1848 in Europe persuaded the Government to suppress the Confederation, and in July Duffy was the first of its members to be arrested: the Young Irelanders responded with a forlorn uprising at Ballingarry in Tipperary but this was easily quelled and the insurgents transported. Duffy was tried for treason-felony in February 1849 and again in April but, in spite of attempts by the authorities to pack the juries at both trials, he was finally acquitted.

In 1849 Duffy refounded the *Nation*. Appalled by the effects of the Famine and disabused of any hope in an armed struggle, he became an MP, and now attempted to work for national regeneration through constitutional organizations. His growing despair at the spiritless state of Ireland was aggravated by ill-health and by attacks on him by John Mitchel, now in New York and publishing *Jail Journal* serially there. In 1855 he sold the *Nation* and emigrated to Melbourne, Australia, where, however, he soon found himself once again involved in politics. Elected to the State Parliament of Victoria, he was later appointed Minister for Public Works and, in 1871, Prime Minister—although his ministry fell the following year. He was knighted in 1873 and in 1876 became Speaker of the Parliament of Victoria, a post he held until 1888 when he returned permanently to Europe, settling in Nice because of his bronchial condition. He now devoted himself to writing his memoirs and a biography of Thomas Davis, making frequent visits to Ireland and Britain, and contributing letters and articles on Irish politics to newspapers and periodicals.

Duffy was a man of unprepossessing appearance, who knew himself to be impatient and peremptory: 'How little tranquillity in my life and though I believe I was right on each occasion, how much rashness and want of temper so many controversies argue.' His controversy with WBY over the New Irish Library exasperated him: he had returned to Ireland as a distinguished statesman to finish a work begun in his patriotic youth only to find himself opposed by a young man whose poetry he disliked, whose literary ideas he could not fathom, and whose politics (Duffy had taken the anti-Parnellite side) he mistrusted. For WBY, he came to represent the philistine aspects of the emergent Catholic middle class. Duffy won the battle for the New Irish Library but his victory was pyrrhic: the series of books was not a success and he had to endure much criticism and sniping from the Irish press. Later, WBY was to look back with amused tolerance upon a quarrel in which he had believed he 'stood with Plato and Socrates', and it was he who in 1899 moved the vote of appreciation on Duffy's retirement from the Presidency of the Irish Literary Society, London (q.v.).

Duffy died in Nice in February 1903, and, true to the end to his literary ideals, recited a Young Ireland poem as he lay dying. His body was brought back to Ireland and buried at Glasnevin.

EDWIN JOHN ELLIS (1848–1916) was the son of the Victorian polymath, Alexander Ellis. He met JBY (q.v.) at Heatherley's Art School in 1868 and the two men soon became close friends; they shared a studio for a time and Ellis joined 'The Brotherhood'. JBY admired his vitality and outspokenness, but these struck others as ill-mannered brashness and Susan Yeats found his frequent visits trying. In 1870 he went to Italy where he married, but his wife died after a year, and he returned to London in the autumn of 1872. Later in the decade he was once more in Italy, settling near Perugia. In 1882 he married a German widow, Phillipa Edwards, née Keller, and in the late 1880s brought her to London. Here he picked up his friendship with JBY and began a new one with WBY, in whose poetry he took a sympathetic interest. Early in 1889 the two of them decided to collaborate on a commentary on Blake's poems; although not without its difficulties, this was a success and the three-volume *Works of William Blake* was published by Quaritch in 1893. Meanwhile Ellis's illustrated book of poetry, *Fate in Arcadia*, had appeared in 1892, to be followed by a further volume, *Seen in Three Days* in 1893. WBY reviewed both books, and dedicated the revised version of 'The Wanderings of Oisin' in *Poems* (1895) to Ellis. Ellis's play, *Sancan the Bard*, which influenced WBY's *The King's Threshold*, was published in 1895. Shortly after this the Ellises moved to Paris; they remained there until 1901 when they returned to London and took a house in Bedford Park (q.v.). They seem to have lived in various parts of London and the home counties over the next few years before moving in 1905 to Darmstadt in Germany, near Mrs Ellis's family home. Here Ellis continued to work on Blake, publishing a two-volume *Poetical Works of William Blake* in 1906 and a biography, *The Real Blake*, in 1907. In 1911 he suffered his first stroke and moved to Seeheim. Following a second attack in the summer of 1913 he was taken temporarily to Folkstone, where WBY visited him in late August, finding him paralysed and unable to speak, but capable of understanding others. He returned as a permanent invalid to Germany, where he died in November 1916.

WBY said he owed to Ellis, 'who was very sane and yet I think always on the border of insanity, certain doctrines about the Divine Vision and the nature of God which have protected me for the search for living experience, and owe to him perhaps my mastery of verse'. Ellis's painting seemed to WBY to derive too obviously from a late Victorian conventionality, but he admired some of his poems as well as his facility in verse. It was Ellis who first taught WBY 'that I might find perfect self-expression in the management of a cadence'. WBY was also impressed by Ellis's psychic gifts and his ability to express subtle and profound philosophical intuitions in abstract or symbolic form.

FLORENCE FARR (1860–1917) was the daughter of the statistician, William Farr. Having failed to become a schoolteacher, she decided to go on the stage, and in December 1884, on a theatrical tour, she married a young actor, Edward Emery. The marriage was not a success; in 1888 Emery was persuaded to emigrate to America and they divorced in 1894. WBY was greatly impressed by her performance as Amaryllis in the Bedford Park (q.v.) production of Todhunter's *A Sicilian Idyll*, in May 1890. They met and became friends, although there is no evidence of an affair between them. In the early 1890s she had a close relationship with Shaw, under whose guidance she acted in a number of plays, including Ibsen's *Rosmersholm* and an unsuccessful revival of *A Sicilian Idyll* at the Vaudeville Theatre. Although a gifted actress, she lacked the application and motivation to make the most of her powers—failings that were to annoy Shaw increasingly, especially after her undistinguished performance in the Independent Theatre's production of his *Widowers' Houses* (1892). In February and March 1894 the Avenue Theatre was taken in her name (although Annie Horniman put the money up) and there she acted in the first public production of a play by WBY, *The Land of Heart's Desire*, as well as in pieces by Todhunter (q.v.) and Shaw. Her novel, *The Dancing Faun*, was published that summer.

Her main interest in the 1890s was less the theatre than the Golden Dawn (q.v.). She joined the Order in 1890 and in 1895 became Praemonstratrix of the London Temple, but after the expulsion of Mathers (q.v.) her inefficiency and heterodoxy in forming special 'groups', brought her into conflict with Annie Horniman and WBY, and she left to join the Theosophical Society (q.v.) in 1902. WBY appointed her general manager for the first season of the Irish Literary Theatre in 1899; she quarrelled with George Moore, but helped to direct rehearsals and played Aleel in the first production of *The Countess Cathleen*. During the first decade of the new century she frequently accompanied WBY in his experiments of speaking verse to the psaltery. She acted in a number of plays at the Court Theatre at this time, and in January 1905 produced a masque of her own, *The Mystery of Time*, at the Albert Hall. In July she acted the part of Dectora in the Theosophical Society's production of WBY's *The Shadowy Waters*.

After a short recital tour in the USA in 1907, she began to contribute articles on the 'new woman' question to the *New Age* and drama criticism to the *Mint*. In 1908 she toured in Pinero's *The Thunderbolt* with Mrs Pat Campbell, and continued to give her own recitals from time to time. In September 1912 she suddenly left for Ceylon, where she became the principal of a girls' school, took up vegetarianism, and immersed herself in Tamil culture. Late in 1916 she was diagnosed as having cancer of the breast, and she died in Colombo in April 1917.

From the first time he saw her act WBY recognized that Florence Farr had 'qualities no contemporary professional practice could have increased', and as he got to know her better realized that these qualities grew out of the gifts of, 'a tranquil beauty . . . an incomparable sense of rhythm and a beautiful voice'; but, he adds, 'there was scarce another gift that she did not value above those three'. She sacrificed her talents in an attempt to be witty, paradoxical, and learned, so that WBY 'formed with her an enduring friendship that was an enduring exasperation'.

THE ORDER OF THE GOLDEN DAWN, which WBY joined on 7 March 1890, was a society dedicated to the study of Rosicrucianism and ritual magic. Officially, it originated with the translation by William Wynn Westcott of five mystical rituals from an apparently ancient cypher manuscript, discovered in 1884 by the Revd A. F. A. Woodford. The manuscript also contained the name and address of a Fraulein Sprengel, apparently an important German Rosicrucian, who, after some correspondence, authorized Westcott to establish an English section of the German occult order of 'Die Goldene Dammerung'. Westcott invited MacGregor Mathers (q.v.) to amplify the five rituals, and with Dr D. R. Woodman, a fellow Freemason and occultist, they founded on 1 March 1888 the Isis–Urania Temple of the Hermetic Order of the Golden Dawn.

Although Westcott traced the Order back through Father Rosenkreuz to ancient religious beliefs, Ellic Howe has argued persuasively that the cypher manuscript was in fact of recent date, that Fraulein Sprengel was an invention of Westcott's, and that the Golden Dawn rituals were an accomplished synthesis of higher and pseudo-Masonic rites with Ancient Egyptian and Cabbalistic texts. Westcott and Mathers divided the Society into three ascending orders. The First began at the Neophite ($0° = 0°$) grade and progressed to Philosophus ($4° = 7°$); while the Second Order (which soon became the most significant section) had three grades, Adeptus Minor ($5° = 6°$), Adeptus Major ($6° = 5°$), and Adeptus Exemptus ($7° = 4°$). The Third Order also had three grades, leading to the highest, Ipsissimus ($10° = 1°$), but the Hidden Chiefs who had attained these exalted ranks were thought not to live on the earthly plane.

Other Temples were subsequently established in Bradford, Edinburgh, and (briefly) Weston-super-Mare, but the London group was the most vigorous. Membership, which was respectably middle class, drew heavily upon Masonic lodges and the Theosophical Society (q.v.), and included Annie Horniman, Florence Farr (q.v.), George Pollexfen, John Todhunter (q.v.), and, for a short time, MG (q.v.) and Constance, the wife of Oscar Wilde. The rituals, which have now been published by Israel Regardie, made light their central symbol; initiates were required to take an oath of submission and to study, among other topics, alchemical and astrological symbolism, the Hebrew alphabet, the ten Sephiroth and twenty-two Paths of the Cabbalistic Tree of Life, and the tarot trumps.

By 1891 a number of the members had advanced through the grades of the First Order, and Mathers began to prepare rituals for the Second Order. In so doing, he transformed the society from a scholarly occult club into an organization for the study and practice of magic. He made the transition from the First to the Second Order, (now known as the R. R. et A. C.) more difficult by instituting a special Portal examination, and those who passed this were enjoined to keep their new status secret. To preserve this secrecy, the Second Order had by early 1892 moved to separate premises, first at Thavies Inn, and from August 1892 at Clipstone Street, where an elaborate ceremonial Vault, based upon the description of Father Rosenkreuz's tomb, was constructed and decorated. It was in this Vault that WBY underwent the rites for the Portal and $5° = 6°$ grades on 20 and 21 January 1893; as a full member of the Second Order (which by that autumn had thirty-six members) he could now learn the use of magical instruments, talismans, invocation, conjuration, and scrying on the astral plane.

Mathers had moved to Paris in 1892, but attempted to enforce an increasingly dictatorial rule over the London Temple, demanding written statements of submission from the Adepts, and expelling Annie Horniman from the Order shortly after she had cut off her financial help to him. In March 1897 Westcott resigned from his many offices in the society after his employers had been apprised of his membership (probably through the duplicity of Mathers). After this, Florence Farr took charge of the Isis–Urania Temple, and with Mathers's approval weakened its organizational structure by dispensing with examinations and by permitting the formation of secret 'groups'. In February 1900, Mathers in a further attempt to bolster his authority, announced that he was the only member of the English Order to have been in touch with the Secret Chiefs, and that the letters between Fraulein Sprengel and Westcott, upon which the validity of the English society rested, were forgeries. The London magicians at once instituted an enquiry into these allegations, against Mathers's express orders. Refusing to attend a meeting of the Second Order to explain his claims, he sent Aleister Crowley to seize the Vault by force, an initiative that was finally foiled by WBY's determined opposition. On 21 April 1900 Mathers was expelled from the Isis–Urania Temple; a new constitution was framed, and WBY appointed Imperator of the Outer (i.e. First) Order and Instructor in mystical philosophy to the Second. Annie Horniman, lately re-admitted to the society, and now Scribe, at once denounced the irregularities that had flourished during Florence Farr's leadership, especially the conduct of the special 'groups'. The quarrel came to a head at a contentious meeting in February 1901, when Miss Horniman and WBY, her single supporter, were outvoted. In an attempt to convince the Adepti of the need to respect rules and authority, WBY issued four open letters and an essay, 'Is the Order of R. R. & A. C. to remain a Magical Order?', but his views did not prevail and thereafter he ceased to play a significant role in the society's affairs.

Further trouble arose in the autumn of 1901 when a Mr and Mrs Horos, who had failed in an attempt to insinuate themselves into the society, but who had managed to get hold of a set of rituals, were tried for the rape of a young girl at a spurious 'Golden Dawn' initiation ceremony. The rituals were read out in court and the case attracted so much adverse publicity that the Golden Dawn had to change its name to the Hermetic Society of the Morgenrothe. A revised constitution put the Second Order under a Triumvirate of new Chiefs, but this could not prevent a further split in 1903 when Dr R. W. Felkin seceded with a majority of the members to form the Amoun Temple of the Stella Matutina. WBY chose to go with Felkin and continued with his occult studies: on 10 January 1912 he was admitted as a Theocritus Adeptus Minor, and in October 1914 took the $6° = 5°$ grade. By then George Hyde-Lees was also a member, and both continued in the society after their marriage in 1917. In 1916 Felkin emigrated to New Zeland; in his absence the Stella Matutina, racked with dissension and radical doubts as to the authenticity of its origins, went into decline and finally disintegrated in 1923. WBY's membership probably lapsed in 1921, when he hoped to put his followers into Rudolph Steiner's 'motherly care', and in his *Autobiographies* he recalls that he left 'amid quarrels caused by men, otherwise worthy, who claimed a Rosicrucian sanction for their fantasies'.

Shorn of its more exotic and ludicrous aspects, WBY's membership of the Golden Dawn was a sustained attempt to explore questions about the relationship of the noumenal to the phenomenal world that were central to his philosophical quest and to his identity as a late Romantic poet. His essay on 'Magic', written in 1901, sums up many of the answers he found there. As well as this philosophical grounding, the rites also offered him a symbolic language that he supposed was sanctioned by ancient usage. From them he took his most important image of the 1890s, the Rose, and *The Wind among the Reeds* and *The Secret Rose* in particular are permeated with symbols and figures that he had encountered in his occult studies. In his elaborate proposals for the Castle of Heroes he was clearly planning an Irish version of the Order, a sort of 'Green Dawn'. The doubts about the antiquity of the rituals and their sanction, which came to the surface in 1900, helped to alter the direction of his poetry, but he, unlike Florence Farr and Annie Horniman, remained in the Society and was, by the time he resigned, its most senior member.

MAUD GONNE (1866–1953) was born in Tongham, Surrey, the daughter of Thomas Gonne, a London-born Captain in the British Army. In 1869 Captain Gonne's regiment moved to Ireland and MG spent her childhood there. Her mother died in 1871, and in 1878, after two years back in England, her father was posted overseas. Until his return in 1881, MG and her sister Kathleen (1868–1918) were brought up by a nurse and various governesses in England and France. In 1882 the now Colonel Gonne was once more sent to Ireland and MG acted as his hostess in Dublin until his death in November 1886. While staying in France she had fallen in love with Lucien Millevoye, a lawyer, journalist, and fervent Boulangist politician, and in 1888, after settling in Paris, she became his mistress. Partly through Millevoye's anti-British influence and partly because of her experience of evictions in Ireland, she decided to devote herself to the movement for Irish independence, casting herself in the role of an Irish Joan of Arc. She returned to Dublin in the autumn of 1888 but her flamboyance and extremism aroused the suspicion of the Irish Party. A meeting with C. H. Oldham put her in touch with JO'L (q.v.), and, although he never took her nationalism seriously, she made him 'her Irish philosopher and friend'.

In January 1889 Ellen O'Leary gave her an introduction to the Yeatses; WBY came immediately under her spell and 'the troubling of my life began'. The rest of the family were less beguiled, JBY (q.v.) in particular being chilled by her easy endorsement of violence. WBY himself sensed in her a potentially destructive conflict between violence and pity, which he dramatized in the play inspired by their meeting, *The Countess Kathleen*. For her part she admired the young poet but had no intention of marrying him.

Within a few months of meeting WBY she was to conceive a child by Millevoye. Her son George was born in Paris in January 1890. That summer she made her first political speech, at a by-election in England, and joined the campaign for the release of Fenian prisoners held in British gaols. In July 1891 she returned to Ireland, where WBY found her wasted and unhappy. Overcome with pity for her he proposed marriage but was refused, and shortly afterwards she was suddenly recalled to Paris, ostensibly on political matters, but in reality because her son had been stricken with meningitis. The child died on 29 July, leaving MG prostrate with grief. She crossed over to Ireland in October in the boat carrying Parnell's body for burial and people assumed that her deep mourning was an over-theatrical tribute to the lost Irish leader.

In the pain of loss, WBY's psychical beliefs and notions of reincarnation suggested by AE (q.v.) took on a greater significance for her. She later told WBY that he had 'saved her from despair', and he perceived that she had come to 'have need of me, as it seemed, and I had no doubt that need would become love'. In November 1891 they went to London together and WBY initiated her into the Golden Dawn (q.v.), forming 'plans of our lives devoted to mystic truth.' MG returned to France where WBY was too poor to follow and where, partly for distraction, she undertook in the spring of 1892 a crowded lecture tour on behalf of the Irish cause. In July she was back in Dublin to help found the National Literary Society (q.v.), and early in 1893 she collaborated with WBY in his work as its Libraries Sub-Committee secretary. Later that spring, however, they had a bitter quarrel over J. F. Taylor; a few days after this, MG was taken seriously ill and the doctor forbade WBY to visit her. She was carried back to Paris to recuperate and her Irish nurse circulated the story in Dublin that she had had an abortion, WBY being her lover.

Recalling in Paris what AE had told her of reincarnation she once more conceived by Millevoye—apparently in the memorial chapel to her dead son—and was with child (although he did not realize it) when WBY saw her during his visit to MacGregor Mathers (q.v.) in February 1894. Her second child, Iseult, was born on 6 August. Although living mainly in Paris, MG made frequent visits to London and Dublin on behalf of the Irish prisoners. Millevoye became editor of *La Patrie* in 1896 and opened its columns to her Irish propaganda. In January 1897 WBY helped her found L'Association Irlandaise, a Parisian branch of the Young Ireland League; he contributed articles to *L'Irlande Libre* which she started in May; and in July she involved him in the Jubilee riots in Dublin. Her first visit to the USA, in November 1897, was not a success, several leading Irish Americans being suspicious of her motives.

Her deteriorating relationship with Millevoye brought her closer to WBY and together they helped organize the centenary celebrations to mark the 1798 rebellion. Although she had left the Golden Dawn because she thought it had Masonic connections, she worked with WBY on the Celtic Mysteries, magical rites to be established in the Castle of Heroes on Lough Key. In December 1898 a vivid dream convinced her that they had contracted a 'spiritual marriage' and she kissed him for the first time. Later she told him the full story of her life, including her affair with Millevoye and the birth of her children; on 8 December he wrote in anguish to Lady Gregory: 'Today & yesterday I have gone through a crisis that has left me worn out. MG is here & I understand everything now.'

The outbreak of the Boer War in 1899 gave MG another vent for her political energies and she was active in the pro-Boer Transvaal Committee. In the late summer of 1900 her affair with Millevoye ended irrevocably: he had taken up with a new mistress. That November, however, she met Major John MacBride, who had led the Irish Brigade on the side of the Boers, and in February 1901 she joined him on a lecturing tour of the USA.

In April 1902 she acted the title role in WBY's *Cathleen ni Houlihan* with the Fays' company and later in the year took a house in Dublin. She had seen a good deal of MacBride in Paris (he was unable to return to Ireland under pain of arrest for treason) and accepted his proposal of marriage. Through his persuasion she joined the Catholic Church in February 1903, and the wedding took place on 21 February. WBY was devastated. The marriage, however, began to founder even before the honeymoon was over. By May 1903 MG was in London and telling WBY of her unhappiness, confessing that she had 'married in a sudden impulse of anger'. She spent a good deal of the year in England and Ireland, drawing public attention by her protest against the King's visit to Ireland in the summer, and by her resignation from the National Theatre Company in November over the production of Synge's *In the Shadow of the Glen*. On 26 January 1904 a son, Sean Seagan, was born in Paris, but just over a year later she sued MacBride for a divorce. The suit charged MacBride with drunkeness, violence, and a sexual assault upon MG's half-sister, allegations which he denied. The case was heard in the summer and on 9 August 1905 MG was granted a legal separation, with custody of the child.

The divorce gave rise to much gossip. Although WBY, Lady Gregory, and John Quinn took MG's part, Dublin sympathized with MacBride, and in 1906 MG was hissed at a performance in the Abbey and an attempt was made to blackball her at the Arts Club. For these reasons, and also because, under Irish law, MacBride (who had now been allowed to return home) could have regained the custody of his son, she spent more time in France, passing the winters in Paris and the summer at Vierville on the Normandy coast. WBY visited her in Paris in May and December 1908, and in the late spring and early summer of 1909 she saw a great deal of him in London; there is reason to believe that at this time the two became lovers. In 1910 she began to visit Dublin again and WBY was now a regular summer visitor to Vierville. In 1914 she helped him investigate a reported miracle at Mirabeau, and on the outbreak of the war volunteered to nurse wounded French soldiers. John MacBride, one of the leaders of the Easter Rising, was executed in 1916 and when WBY went to Normandy in late June he once again asked MG to marry him and was once again refused. He lingered in Vierville, however, finding his interest in Iseult growing; in August he proposed to her, in vain. A further proposal the following summer was also unsuccessful, although he remained in France to help the family with their removal to Ireland via England.

On arrival in England, MG was forbidden by the authorities to proceed to Ireland and she took a flat in Chelsea. In February 1918 she reached Dublin in disguise but was arrested in May on suspicion of being party to a pro-German plot and imprisoned in England. Released on medical grounds in November (largely through WBY's efforts), she once again entered Ireland illegally, arriving unexpectedly at 76 St. Stephen's Green, the house which she had let to WBY. Mrs Yeats, now in her seventh month of pregnancy, was seriously ill with pneumonia and WBY, fearing that police raids or other probable disturbances would be dangerous for her and the unborn child, refused MG access. This resulted in a violent quarrel and a breach in their friendship. In late July 1920, however, she appealed to WBY to come to Ireland to help the family during a difficult period in Iseult's marriage to Francis Stuart, and he played the role of honest broker with wry success.

During the struggle for Irish independence in the early 1920s MG's house became a centre for the IRA. In the Civil War which followed the Anglo-Irish Treaty of December 1921 the family took the Republican side; Sean MacBride was interned by the Free State authorities and MG became active in the Women's Prisoners' Defence League. On 12 November 1922 her house was raided by Free State soldiers and many of her papers, including letters from WBY, destroyed. She was imprisoned in January 1923 but released after a hunger strike. Alienated from WBY because he had agreed to serve as a Free State senator, she occupied an increasingly marginal place in Irish politics as the Republicans were gradually worn down over the 1920s. The election of de Valera in 1932 did not have the political results that she had anticipated, and before long she was opposing him as she had the Cosgrave Government. In 1936 she stood unsuccessfully as a candidate for her son's new party, the Cumann Poblachta na hEireann, and her memoirs, *A Servant of the Queen*, appeared in 1938. During the thirties she resumed her friendship with WBY. In 1947 her son's party took office as part of the coalition government which declared Ireland a Republic and withdrew from the British Commonwealth. MG planned a second volume of her reminiscences, but died in Dublin on 27 April 1953 before completing it.

MG fascinated WBY but also perplexed him throughout his life. Overwhelmed at their first meeting by her beauty and energy, he had at the same time detected in her 'something declamatory, Latin in a bad sense, and perhaps even unscrupulous'. Impressed with a Faustian story she told him of her youth—she thought she had bartered her soul for freedom from family constraints— he saw her character in manichean terms with two troops of spirits fighting for control of her mind, and resolved to lead her from destructive restlessness to peace and self-fulfilment. At moments of emotional and physical exhaustion she would let her guard drop and show him the generosity, vulnerability, and gentleness which he took to be the true centre of her personality. The relationship continually oscillated: at moments when her political or emotional life was under strain she would turn to him and find comfort in his unwavering devotion. At other times, when she was fired by some political scheme or emotional certainty, he found a hardness and obduracy in her. At an early stage he had perceived the fundamental difference between them: 'We were seeking different things: she, some memorable action for final consecration of her youth, and I, after all, but to discover and communicate a state of being.'

WILLIAM ERNEST HENLEY (1849–1903) was born in Gloucester, the eldest son of an unsuccessful bookseller, and attended the local grammar school; his education was interrupted by serious illness, which led in 1865 to the amputation of his left leg. Two years later he went to London to work as a free-lance journalist, but in 1872 moved to Margate in an attempt to arrest a tubercular infection of his right foot. When this failed he travelled by sea to Edinburgh where from 1873 to 1875 he put himself under the care of Joseph Lister in the Royal Infirmary—an initiative that probably saved his life. During his long recuperation Henley taught himself French and Italian, began his verse sequence 'In Hospital', and met his future wife, Anna Boyle. In January 1874 Leslie Stephen brought Robert Louis Stevenson to visit him and the two men became firm friends. After his discharge from hospital in April 1875, Henley remained in Edinburgh, writing for the *Cornhill Magazine* and the *Encyclopaedia Britannica*, but in 1876 he returned to England to take up the editorship of the weekly *London*. Although the magazine was never a financial success, it provided enough security, by April 1878, to enable him to marry. After it ceased publication in 1879 Henley returned to free-lance journalism and collaborated with Stevenson on a series of plays; and from late 1881 until 1886 he found more regular employment as editor of the *Magazine of Art*.

Henley met WBY in 1888, an eventful year: in March he had a serious quarrel wth Stevenson (now *en route* for Samoa); in June his first volume of poetry, *A Book of Verses*, was published; in September his only child, Margaret, was born; and in December he was asked to take over the editorship of the *Scots Observer*. As a consequence of this appointment the Henleys moved to Edinburgh early in 1889 and remained in Scotland until June 1892. In November 1890 the magazine's name was changed to the *National Observer* in an attempt to widen the readership. Until late 1888 Henley's politics had been generally conservative, but his friendship with Rudyard Kipling and with Walter Blaikie, a proprietor of the *National Observer*, converted him into an Imperialist and an active supporter of the Conservative Party, as his subsequent periodicals forcefully demonstrate. His book of poems, *The Song of the Sword*, published in April 1892, shows the influence of Kipling.

Early in 1894 he was desolated when his daughter died of cerebral meningitis; in April of the same year the loss-making *National Observer* changed hands and he was encouraged to resign by the new management, although by December he had been asked to take over the *New Review*. An attempt to have him elected Professor of English at Edinburgh University failed and in December 1897 he gave up his editorship of the *New Review*, partly because of ill-health. A Civil List pension eased his last years of chronic illness. Sixteen months before his death he gave great offence by publishing an outspoken article on his estranged and late friend, Stevenson.

Although his magazines never achieved financial success, Henley was ac-knowledged as an editor of genius. His ebullient energy, uncompromising vision, and eye for literary talent gave his publications a distinctive quality. WBY recalled him as an awesome but human figure who 'alarmed me and impressed me exactly as he did those others who were called Henley's young men', and accounts for the affection he commanded: 'he made us feel always our importance, and no man among us could do good work, or show the promise of it, and lack his praise.' He was disconcerted by Henley's habit of rewriting his verse, but later said that writing stories under his editorial eye was 'my first discipline in creative prose'. For his part, Henley recognized WBY's gifts, and gave *The Wanderings of Oisin* an enthusiastic review.

It was the force of Henley's personality that most attracted WBY. His poetry he disliked mainly on technical grounds and he found his prose 'violent and laboured', yet he was always ready 'to test myself and all I did by the man's sincere vision'. Part of that vision WBY could share for, like him, Henley repudiated the Victorian idea of progress; no less congenial were his 'aristocratic attitudes, his hatred of the crowd and of that logical realism which is but popular oratory . . . frozen and solidified.' Yet he seemed to possess a force that could never find appropriate expression; WBY felt that the drama of Henley's life was inadequate to the passion of his character: he appeared 'like a great actor with a bad part'.

DOUGLAS HYDE (1860–1949) spent his early childhood in Co. Sligo, but from the age of seven lived at Frenchpark, Co. Roscommon, where his father was the Church of Ireland rector. Although the Irish language was fast disappearing from the area, he managed to pick it up from the local people, and in 1879 joined the Society for the Preservation of the Irish Language and later the Gaelic Union. He enrolled as an undergraduate at Trinity College, Dublin, in 1880, taking up residence in 1882 and going on to a brilliant academic career. Under the pseudonym An Craoibhin Aoibhinn (The Pleasant Little Branch) he had already begun to contribute poems in Irish, often outspokenly nationalist in sentiment, to the *Irishman* and the *Shamrock*, and in 1885 he became associated with the *Dublin University Review*. He met JO'L (q.v.), Standish James O'Grady (q.v.), and WBY in that year, and, although he sometimes found WBY's abundant conversation tiresome, the two met frequently to discuss literature and folklore. Hyde had joined the Dublin Young Ireland Society in 1884, and was a member of the Contemporary Club (q.v.) from its inception in November 1885. Undecided about taking holy orders, he embarked upon an LL.D. which he obtained in 1887. His first book, of folklore, *Leabhar Sgeulaigheachta*, appeared in 1889, although he had already contributed verse to *Poems and Ballads of Young Ireland*. In 1890 he published *Beside the Fire*, described by WBY as 'the one quite perfect book of Irish folklore', and in September went for a year to teach modern languages at the University of New Brunswick. After his return to Europe he helped found the National Literary Society in Dublin (q.v.), to which in November 1892 he delivered his influential address, 'The Necessity of De-Anglicising Ireland'—a lecture that WBY thought began a new epoch in Ireland. At WBY's instigation, Hyde became, with T. W. Rolleston (q.v.) a sub-editor of the New Irish Library (q.v.) after the acrimonious disputes over this project in the autumn and winter of 1892. In July of the following year he helped establish the Gaelic League, the aim of which was 'to keep that language alive among the people', and in August he was elected its president. Having been a Parnellite since the 1880s, he now eschewed politics entirely, because they might divide the campaign to restore the Irish language. In October he married Lucy Kurtz, with whom he seems to have been perfectly happy, although WBY regarded her as 'a dragon'.

The Gaelic League enjoyed a popularity that surpassed the founders' hopes, and this involved Hyde increasingly in administration and organization—much to the chagrin of WBY who thought that he should be producing more books like *The Love Songs of Connacht* (1893). Although he did publish more bilingual editions of Irish verse and folklore, as well as histories of Gaelic literature, he devoted much of his time to propaganda work for the League, speaking at its now numerous branches, and presiding at the annual Ard Feis (general meeting) and Oireachtas (cultural festival). In 1899 he led the fight to make Irish a subject for intermediate education, succeeding despite determined opposition from the Irish academic establishment. He also wrote several short plays in Irish for the National Theatre. From 1905 to 1906 he lectured with huge success in the USA, raising over £11,000 for the League. On his return to Ireland he orchestrated a campaign to make Irish a compulsory matriculation subject at the newly established National University, and this policy was adopted by a narrow vote of the governing body in 1909. From 1908 to 1932 he held the post of Professor of Modern Irish at the National University, and he served on the Senate of the University from 1909 to 1919.

Hyde had tried to keep the Gaelic League free from political affiliation, but after the formation of the Irish Volunteers it became clear that the more radical nationalists were gaining an ascendency in the organization, and at the Ard Feis of 1915 he resigned the presidency. He withdrew from public life and, although co-opted as a Free State senator in 1925, spoke only twice and did not seek a further term of office. In the early 1930s he was chairman of the Folklore Institute, retiring to Frenchpark in 1935. He re-emerged unexpectedly into official life from 1938 to 1944 when he was appointed, as compromise candidate, to the newly created post of President of Ireland.

An Anglo-Irish squire by birth and disposition, Hyde stumped the country on behalf of the language, mingling with those who differed radically from him in class, politics, and attitudes. He seems to have protected himself by a mixture of apparent non-involvement—criticized by some as equivocation—and general *bonhomie*: George Moore describes him as 'vociferously enthusiastic . . . the one manner for everybody'.

At the outset of their careers Hyde was a compelling example to WBY for, although from a similar background, he had managed to immerse himself in the culture and language of the people—so much so that on their first meeting WBY set him down as an authentic peasant. WBY, preoccupied by the need for an audience and a style, responded at once to Hyde's gifts as a folklorist and to his verse and prose 'written in the beautiful English of Connacht, which is Gaelic in idiom and Tudor in vocabulary': he 'began to test my poetical inventions by translating them into like speech'. But this was not the tongue that interested Hyde; he was more concerned in trying to preserve the Irish language itself, and curtailed his own literary work to devote his energies to accomplishing this. WBY thought that Hyde had thereby betrayed his greatest gifts, and 'beaten into prose / That noble blade the Muses buckled on'. But Hyde himself had never wanted to be known as a writer in English and had from the very beginning regretted the need to make any translations at all from his Irish texts.

THE IRISH LITERARY SOCIETY, LONDON grew out of the Southwark Irish Literary Club, founded in 1883 with the purpose of keeping the London Irish of that district in touch with Irish culture. By the late 1880s the Club, which had in its day attracted such lecturers as Douglas Hyde (q.v.), T. D. Sullivan, WBY, John Todhunter (q.v.), KT (q.v.), Charles Gavan Duffy (q.v.), and Oscar Wilde, was in decline. In late 1891, however, WBY returned to England determined to set up a branch of the Young Ireland League and to this end decided to resuscitate the Southwark Club under its new name. At a pilot meeting of the new organization, held in his house on 28 December 1891, he introduced the more energetic members of the old Club to T. W. Rolleston (q.v.) whose superior social and administrative skills had soon enrolled 'every London-Irish author and journalist' in the Society.

An inaugural General Meeting took place in May 1892. By this time WBY was back in Dublin to found a National Literary Society (q.v.) there, and, in deference to its sister organization, the London Society postponed its opening lecture until March 1893, when Stopford Brooke spoke on 'The Need and Use of Getting Irish Literature into the English Tongue'. By then Duffy had been elected its first president, Rolleston appointed secretary, and WBY and Todhunter were on the committee. As well as arranging lecture programmes, the Society took an active part in the New Irish Library (q.v.), and had started Irish classes even before the foundation of the Gaelic League (which, after 1893, shared its rooms). In an effort to remedy the lack of Irish periodicals it launched *The Irish Home Reading Magazine* (1894), edited by Lionel Johnson (q.v.) and Eleanor Hull, and, later in the decade, the longer-running *Irish Literary Society Gazette*, which gave news of the members and reports of lectures. The Society also sponsored more specialized cultural initiatives, such as the Irish Text Society, which issued scholarly editions of important Gaelic works, and the Irish Folk Song Society, which published Irish airs with expert commentaries. It was under the auspices of the Society that Sir Charles Stanford edited the Petrie Collection of Irish music; and WBY first unveiled his plans for an Irish Literary Theatre in a lecture to it. The first London productions by the Irish National Theatre Company, the success of which did much to establish its reputation in Ireland, were organized by the Society. Although WBY resigned in March 1901 over the blackballing of George Moore, he was soon reinstated as an honorary member. Thereafter he remained in the Society (which is still in existence) and attended its functions from time to time until the end of his life.

LIONEL PIGOT JOHNSON (1867–1902) was born in Kent, the third son of an army officer, but lived for some time in Wales, which became the setting for a number of his poems. He had an outstanding academic career at Winchester College and in 1886 went up to New College, Oxford, as a Classics Scholar. There he read widely in English as well as classical literature and came under the influence of Walter Pater. After graduating he went to live with Herbert Horne, Selwyn Image, and Arthur Mackmurdo, at 20 Fitzroy Street, London, where he had often stayed as an undergraduate. He began to contribute reviews and articles to a number of London periodicals and newspapers, sleeping most of the day and working through the night. In June 1891 he was received into the Catholic Church, to which he had been drawn by his asceticism and love of mysticism, tradition, and ritual. Under the influence of WBY and the Rhymers Club (q.v.), Johnson began to discover Irish antecedents, and in the autumn of 1893 visited Dublin, where he met many of those involved in the literary revival. His book, *The Art of Thomas Hardy*, appeared in 1894, followed by *Poems* in 1895 and *Ireland with other Poems* in 1897. He collaborated with Eleanor Hull in editing the *Irish Home Reading Magazine* in 1894 and initially played a vigorous part in the Irish Literary Society (q.v.) in London; as the nineties progressed, however, his health and effectiveness were steadily eroded by heavy drinking. He moved to Gray's Inn in 1895, where he lived alone, and made a final trip to Ireland in the spring of 1898. On 29 September 1902 he fell while attempting to sit in a chair at a public house in Fleet Street and fractured his skull; the official post-mortem reported that he had died of a ruptured blood vessel.

WBY and Johnson first met sometime after the publication of *The Wanderings of Oisin*, probably in the spring or summer of 1889. Johnson later told John McGrath that when he first read that volume, ignorant of the author, he had said to himself 'here is a new Shelley and a new Keats!' He never lost his admiration for WBY's poetry. WBY visited him regularly, and they also met at gatherings of the Rhymers' Club and, later, at the Irish Literary Society. In the spring of 1894 Johnson helped to arrange meetings between his cousin, Olivia Shakespear (q.v.), and WBY.

The friendship of Johnson, erudite, cultured, and elegant in mind and body, was of importance to WBY, who in the early 1890s often felt himself to be under-educated, gauche, and provincial. He was for a few years WBY's closest London friend, and introduced him to the ideas of Pater and to theories of impersonality in poetry that were to influence *The Wind Among the Reeds*. WBY and his circle saw Johnson as 'our critic, and above all our theologian', and WBY's persona, Owen Aherne, is partly modelled on him. The discovery in 1895 that Johnson was drinking greatly disturbed WBY and 'altered my general view of the world'.

In alerting him to the importance of style and craftsmanship in writing, as well as by putting him in touch with the aesthetic movement, Johnson influenced WBY's poetic development. Yet WBY felt that Johnson had applied 'in too literary a form the philosophy of Pater' and had exchanged the necessary accidents and confusions of Nature for the exquisiteness of bookish impressions. He encouraged Johnson to take a practical interest in Irish affairs, but did not succeed, as he had hoped, in providing him with a literary focus; his Irish poems fall into a rhetoric that WBY managed to avoid. At its best, as WBY notes, Johnson's poetry 'conveys an emotion of joy, of intellectual clearness, of hard energy', qualities which are seen at their most impressive in his non-Irish poems.

SAMUEL LIDDELL MATHERS (1854–1918) later Macgregor Mathers, 'Comte de Glenstrae', was born into humble circumstances in London. His father died when he was a child and he was brought up by his widowed mother, mainly in Bournemouth. He became a Freemason in 1877, and later joined the Societas Rosicruciana in Anglia, a Rosicrucian Society made up of Master Masons with an interest in occultism, where he met Dr William Wynn Westcott and Dr W. R. Woodman. After the death of his mother in 1885 he moved to London, and lived in considerable poverty, studying esoteric and mystical texts in the British Museum. In London he got to know Madame Blavatsky (q.v.) and Anna Kingsford, whose ideas on esoteric Christianity and the advancement of women he found sympathetic. Mathers was also interested in military matters; he had joined the First Hants Infantry Volunteers, and his first book was *Practical Instruction in Infantry Campaigning Exercise* (1884). In 1885 he published *The Fall of Granada: A Poem in Six Duans*, but his first significant contribution to occult studies was *The Kabbalah Unveiled* in 1887; the following year he issued a work on the occult significance of the tarot cards, and in 1889 a translation of *The Key of Solomon the King: Clavicula Salomonis*.

In October 1887 Westcott invited him to join the Golden Dawn (q.v.). With Westcott and Woodman, Mathers became one of the three Chiefs of the Order in England and it was he who composed its elaborate rituals, drawing heavily upon his knowledge of Freemasonry and Ancient Egyptian religions. WBY first encountered him at the British Museum, describing him as 'a man of thirty-six, or thirty-seven, in a brown velveteen coat, with a gaunt resolute face, and an athletic body, who seemed . . . a figure of romance', and on 7 March 1890 Mathers initiated him into the Golden Dawn in the studio of Moina Bergson, (sister of the philosopher, Henry Bergson), whom Mathers was to marry in June of the same year. Mathers, who had a stronger personality than Westcott or Woodman, began to stamp his authority on the society and in 1891 undertook to reorganize its influential Second Order, by introducing new rituals and orientating it towards the practice of magic.

Mathers was living off Annie Horniman's benefactions, and she also found him a post as curator of the Horniman Museum in south London. He lost this job in 1891, and in May 1892 he and his wife moved to Paris. There he took to using the title 'Comte de Glenstrae', supposedly conferred upon an ancestor by Louis XV, adopted highland dress, and was so vigorous in the cause of Scottish nationalism that WBY attempted to put him in touch with Irish nationalists of advanced views. In January 1894 Mathers set up a Golden Dawn Temple, the Ahathoor, in Paris. He was drinking heavily and WBY thought him 'under some great strain' when he visited him that spring. The Matherses were still receiving regular payments from Annie Horniman, but she, increasingly concerned at his extravagance and neglect of occult matters in favour of Jacobite politics, cut off the allowance in the summer of 1896. Mathers responded by expelling her from the Golden Dawn, and refused to reinstate her even though a petition was organized on her behalf.

Throughout the nineties Mathers became more involved in his Parisian work, and especially in the Rite of Isis, of which he and his wife gave public performances in 1899. He ran the London Temple through Florence Farr, but his dictatorial attitudes caused unrest among the English initiates. His suspicion that they were plotting against him led him to try to discredit Westcott by revealing that he had forged the correspondence with Fraulein Sprengel. When this redounded upon him, he despatched Aleister Crowley to seize the Vault of the Adepti by force. This Crowley achieved—wearing a black mask and full highland rig—but a counter-movement, led by WBY, regained the premises, and Mathers was formally expelled from the London Society on 21 April 1900.

The Ahathoor Temple continued to function for a time in Paris and a breakaway London group, to which Westcott belonged, remained loyal to Mathers, as did the Golden Dawn Temples in Bradford and Edinburgh. But Crowley, whose faith was shaken, turned against him, and he sank into penury and obscurity. During the First World War, according to WBY, he turned his house into a recruiting office and raised volunteers for the French Foreign Legion. He died in Paris just after the end of hostilities.

WBY, like others who knew him, thought Mathers an accomplished magician; he conducted many psychical experiments with him, and describes him in his unfinished novel, *The Speckled Bird*, under the name 'Maclagan'. His importance to WBY was to give a practical dimension to the ideas on symbolism he was deriving from Blake and Shelley, and to convince him that 'images well up before the mind's eye from a deeper source than conscious or sub-conscious memory'. This helped to confirm WBY's belief in the *anima mundi*, a concept that influenced much of his thinking on art and philosophy. From the first he realized that Mathers was the governing mind in the Golden Dawn, and thought that behind his imperious manner he was 'gentle, and perhaps even a little timid'. He saw it as Mathers's tragedy that he was never prepared to confront both aspects of his nature. He regarded him as an extreme example of the Faustian element in Romanticism: being 'an unscholarly, though learned man, he was bound to express the fundamental antithesis in the most crude form, and being arrogant, to prevent as far as possible that alternation between the two natures which is, it may be, necessary to sanity'. As Mathers became authoritarian and erratic a quarrel was inevitable—especially as WBY was one of the few in the Order with a personality strong enough to stand up to him. Although there was no reconciliation, WBY heard of him from time to time in Paris and always retained a respect for one who, while 'half a lunatic, half knave', managed to keep 'a proud head amid great poverty'.

THE NATIONAL LITERARY SOCIETY, DUBLIN, was the product of a campaign waged by John McGrath and WBY in the columns of *United Ireland* in the spring and summer of 1892, but in fact its roots went back to the 1840s when the Repeal Association's Reading Rooms served as literary and educational clubs throughout Ireland. A number of attempts to establish similar organizations, based now on the Young Ireland League, had been proposed in the 1880s but had come to nothing, as had an attempted amalgamation of such societies by JO'L (q.v.) and WBY in 1891. The publicity about the Irish Literary Society, London (q.v.), drew attention once more to Ireland's need for a national society, especially when the Unionist *Daily Telegraph* suggested on 7 March 1892 that London was the most appropriate venue for an Irish literary society since it was the real capital of Ireland. This provoked a debate in the correspondence columns of *United Ireland* under the heading, 'The Irish Intellectual Capital: Where Is It?', which culminated on 4 June with a letter from J. T. Kelly, late of the Southwark Irish Literary Club, announcing that plans for a National Literary Society were in hand. A meeting to initiate such a society had already taken place on 24 May, shortly after WBY's return to Dublin, and further discussions went on through the summer. As with the sister Society in London, a major ambition was to promote a series of Irish books, and there were also proposals for concerts, lectures on Irish literature, art, and music, as well as for a network of lending libraries throughout the country. These objects were not original: indeed, they closely resemble the programmes outlined at meetings of the Young Ireland League in 1885 and 1891. What was new, in the mood following the fall of Parnell (q.v.), was both the wide support enjoyed by the new Society—its provisional committee reflected the whole spectrum of Irish politics and numbered among its members writers, scholars, and journalists—and the importance which Irish literature had now assumed in the popular press and the public mind.

The Society was set up on a motion of WBY's at a public meeting on 9 June, and on 16 August George Sigerson delivered the inaugural lecture, 'Irish Literature, its Origin, Environment, and Influence'. Although relations in the Society were troubled by the disagreements between WBY and Duffy's supporters over the New Irish Library (q.v.), the lecture programme began a full season in November with 'The Necessity of De-Anglicising Ireland' by Hyde (q.v.); WBY spoke in this series on 19 May 1893 on 'Nationality and Literature', as well as reciting poetry and giving informal talks at social evenings.

Besides his work for the main Society, WBY was also appointed secretary of the Libraries Sub-Committee, with instructions to establish and supply circulating libraries in the country branches. He threw himself energetically into this work, soliciting books from many quarters, organizing (with MG's help) public meetings in various towns, and discussing with JO'L and J. F. Taylor the volumes to be sent out. However, his lack of method as secretary came under censure, and he later complained that the whole scheme had been sabotaged when the young men in Dublin misappropriated for the central Society books destined for a country branch.

Looking back on this period, WBY could recall little except bitterness, but thought that his efforts had struck the first of many blows for intellectual freedom in Ireland. Few provincial clubs affiliated with the National Literary Society, and it did not become the centre of an extensive organization, while the series of Irish books and the plans for country libraries were also a disappointment—its anticipated national role was in fact assumed by its own offshoot, the Gaelic League, which had more energetic organizers and a more tangible purpose. Nevertheless, it continued to flourish in Dublin well into the next century, first in its rooms in College Green and later at 6 St. Stephen's Green. It was middle-class in membership (which in 1900 totalled over 350) and non-political. If it failed to enhance the status of Irish literature in a single burst of energy, it did provide an agency through which cultural institutions and literary consciousness could develop. Most of the leading Irish writers, historians, scholars, and journalists lectured to it in due course, and in 1899 it acted as sponsor of the Irish Literary Theatre, an initiative from which the Irish dramatic movement grew.

THE NEW IRISH LIBRARY was the revival of a scheme first instituted in 1845 by the Young Irelanders under Charles Gavan Duffy's editorship (q.v.). A perennial lament throughout the nineteenth century (and beyond) was that the Irish were 'not a book-buying people', and in October 1844 Thomas Davis pointed out that there were ten counties in Ireland without a bookseller. The original 'Library of Ireland' tried to overcome these problems by issuing twenty-two monthly volumes costing 1/– and distributed, at least in part, through the Repeal Association's Reading Rooms. The series was a great success but only one further title was added after the collapse of the Young Ireland movement, and sporadic attempts to revive the idea later in the century failed through lack of the necessary organization to back them up.

The formation of influential Irish literary societies in London and Dublin in 1892 seemed to offer a new opportunity for such a scheme, and from early in that year we find WBY airing possible titles for a series he was projecting with his publisher, T. Fisher Unwin. Duffy also had plans for reviving his old series in a new form, and came to London in the early summer of 1892 to float it. Since Duffy had by far the greater public prestige and editorial experience his proposals overshadowed those of WBY.

Two problems stood in the way of the scheme; one was economic, the other ideological. In June 1892 Duffy and Rolleston (q.v.) planned with the Irish-born London publisher, Edmund Downey, a series of twelve monthly volumes at 1/– each, in editions of 5,000, to be issued by 'The College Green Publishing Co.' After his difficult negotiations in Dublin in July, Duffy realized that an Irish publisher would have to be associated with the books and proposed 'The Irish National Publishing Co.' This, however, ran into financial difficulties and Downey was asked to organize a 'General Publishing Co.' in London with a capital of £10,000 and

Duffy as its chairman. On closer investigation, Duffy and Rolleston decided that this plan would not be economically viable and proposed to issue only six books a year. Downey advised them that the overheads on such a small series would be prohibitive and that they should arrange for publication through an established firm. At this point, in October 1892, with Duffy's original scheme a non-starter in any of its various forms, Rolleston revealed that WBY had discussed with Unwin just such a plan as that suggested by Downey. He began negotiations with Unwin on Duffy's behalf and persuaded him to take up their proposals, so shutting out WBY, since the market could not possibly support two rival series.

WBY's anger at this turn of events was inspired by the ideological problems the scheme involved. The original Library of Ireland had modelled itself on a utilitarian and practical series organized by Lord Brougham in England and, while more nationalistic in its scope, had retained much of the same didactic purpose. And it was this purpose that Duffy emphasized in his lectures on the proposed new Library: the books were to be selected 'to fill up the blanks which an imperfect education, and the fever of a tempestuous time' had left among Irish people. WBY, as he made clear in his public speeches and in his letters to the newspapers, wanted not manuals but imaginative and well-written volumes that would educate the spirit and not merely the intellect.

These differences in outlook made collaboration between WBY and Duffy impossible, especially after the controversy in the *Freeman's Journal* of September 1892 (see pp. 310–14). At this time WBY still thought he could, if necessary, go his own way by playing the Unwin card. When he realized that Rolleston had trumped him, he found himself in a difficult situation: if he did not denounce Duffy's plans, the new Library would be saddled with inappropriate books and a great opportunity lost; but if he protested too vigorously, Unwin would take fright and drop the whole scheme. He therefore tried to persuade the London and Dublin Literary Societies (q.v.), on whose support any such series depended, to insist upon a voice in the choice of books. In this, despite acrimonious debates, he was only slightly successful. Although Rolleston and Hyde (q.v.) were appointed sub-editors, they had no control (nor did they seek any) over Duffy.

The first volume issued by the New Irish Library, Thomas Davis's aridly historical *Patriot Parliament*, confirmed WBY's worst fears about Duffy's editorial policy and exhausted much of the public good will for the project, which was never to have the cultural and financial success hoped for it. Nevertheless, twelve volumes were published, including books by O'Grady (q.v.), Todhunter (q.v.), and Ashe King, and most of the titles appeared in the Dublin best-seller charts listed in the *Bookman*.

STANDISH JAMES O'GRADY (1846–1928) was the son of a Church of Ireland rector in Cork. After attending Tipperary Grammar School he read Classics at Trinity College, Dublin, subsequently becoming a barrister and leader-writer on the ultra-Conservative Dublin *Daily Express*. Discovering books on Gaelic literature and history in the library of a country house, he was inspired to write a series of histories of Ireland that helped lay the foundations of the Irish literary revival by making Irish mythology and, later, Elizabethan Ireland, available to the rising generation.

His two-volume *History of Ireland*, published at his own expense in 1878 and 1880, gives a narrative account of bardic times, centring upon the exploits of Cuchulain and the Red Branch warriors. Although he knew no Irish, and even mispronounced the name of his hero Cuchulain, he managed to impose order upon his disparate sources and, despite some inaccuracies, interpolations, and bowdlerizations, he successfully communicates his immense enthusiasm for his subject. His classical interests, an evangelical background, and his admiration for Shelley and Whitman, all helped to form his style and outlook, as did the precepts of Carlyle—that history was an art not a science; that it should appeal to the imagination over the reason; and that it was the biography of great men. His stress upon the value of the imagination and his insistence upon the continuity of Irish history (or race feeling) found a ready response in younger writers such as WBY, AE (q.v.), and T. W. Rolleston (q.v.), all of whom regarded him as the father of the Irish literary revival.

Politically, O'Grady was a Conservative and an Imperialist, and borrowed much from Lord Randolph Churchill's platform of Democratic Toryism. Some of his most impassioned prose was directed towards urging an absentee or irresponsible Anglo-Irish Ascendancy to recognize its duties and opportunities. 'An active working ruling and controlling aristocracy is all I care about,' he wrote to JO'L. His writings never lose sight of these ideals.

O'Grady thought his chance to rouse the Irish landowners had come during the dispute with England in the mid-1890s over the supposedly excessive taxation of Ireland. In his book *All Ireland* (1898) he advocated an Irish Convention, made up of all Irish interests but led by the landlords and sitting in Dublin. When nothing came of these plans he resigned his post with the *Daily Express* and bought a provincial newspaper, the *Kilkenny Moderator*—hoping to gain a hearing for his ideas in rural Ireland. Unhappily, a libel action against the newspaper put an end to these plans and threatened O'Grady with ruin. In January 1900, however, he founded, edited, and wrote practically single-handed the weekly *All Ireland Review*, sold at 3*d*. to the rich and 1*d*. to those who could not afford more, which ran until 1908. His prose now began to take on an elegaic tone as he contemplated the inevitable decline of his class; in a series of articles entitled 'The Great Enchantment' he lamented the causes of the Irish landlords' chronic inaction. In 1918 O'Grady exiled himself from Ireland, settling first in France, then in Northamptonshire, and finally in the Isle of Wight, where he died in 1928.

O'Grady was the nearest thing to an Irish Carlyle, but if he lacked Carlyle's intellectual range, he also lacked his rancour, and to the end preserved innocence of mind even in the midst of vigorous polemic. 'Here was a man', as WBY wrote, 'whose rage was a swan-song over all that he had held most dear, and to whom for that very reason every Irish imaginative writer owed a portion of his soul.' It was after reading his books that WBY 'turned my back on foreign themes, decided that the race was more important than the individual, and began my "Wanderings of Oisin".' The recollection of O'Grady making a drunken speech at a public dinner— in effect he was prophesying the 1916 Rising sixteen years before the event—

remained with WBY throughout life and became one of his 'Beautiful Lofty Things'.

JOHN O'LEARY (1830–1907) exerted one of the most powerful influences on the young WBY because of his role in the struggle for Irish independence. Born in Tipperary on 23 July 1830, he seemed destined for a normal professional career. He studied law briefly at Trinity College, Dublin, and later spent a year studying medicine at Queen's College, Cork, followed by a further three years of medicine at Queen's College, Galway, and intermittent medical studies in Dublin, London, and Paris. However, he had taken charge of the finances of the Irish Revolutionary Brotherhood (later the Irish Republican Brotherhood) within a few months of its inception in 1858, and the fight for national liberation occupied him increasingly. From 1863 to 1865 he edited *Irish People*, the newspaper of the IRB, which openly advocated the overthrow of British rule. Along with the other leaders of the movement he was arrested in 1865 as part of a suspected conspiracy involving insurrection, tried on a charge of treason-felony and sentenced to twenty years penal servitude. In December 1865 he was imprisoned in Pentonville, where his punishment was to pick oakum; he was transferred in May 1866 to the Isle of Portland to serve at hard labour in the quarries. As part of a general amnesty he was released in 1871, but not permitted to return to Ireland until 1885. During the intervening years of exile he lived mainly in Paris. On his return to Ireland he settled in Dublin, his sister, Ellen, acting as his housekeeper. It was at this time that he met WBY, who was immediately deeply impressed by him, and later recalled: 'From these debates, from O'Leary's conversation, and from the Irish books he lent or gave me has come all I have set my hand to since.' Yet WBY recognized clearly the differences between them: 'I often wonder why he gave me his friendship, why it was he who found almost all the subscribers for my *Wanderings of Oisin*, and why he now supported me in all I did, for how could he like verses that were all picture, all emotion, all association, all mythology?' He felt disappointed in JO'L's *Recollections of Fenians and Fenianism* (1896), finding it 'unreadable, being dry, abstract, and confused; no picture had ever passed before his mind's eye'. Despite these reservations, WBY retained a strong sense of his symbolic importance, rendered most memorably in the refrain from 'September 1913': 'Romantic Ireland's dead and gone, / It's with O'Leary in the grave'.

In addition to his grief at the death of his sister Ellen in 1889, JO'L's later years were also impoverished in a more literal sense because of a bitter dispute between a landlord and his tenants in Tipperary in the years 1889–91. JO'L's income derived from rents in the district and with the withholding of rents by tenants he soon found himself in extremely straitened circumstances. He opposed all kinds of land agitation by his fellow nationalists and thus became estranged from many former colleagues. For a while he left Ireland to live in London, returning to Dublin at the time of the fall of Parnell (q.v.). He spent his last years isolated from the mainstream of Irish political activity, dying in Dublin on 16 March 1907.

CHARLES STEWART PARNELL (1846–1891) was born in Co. Wicklow, the son of a Protestant landlord and an American mother. After Cambridge, which he left without a degree following a fracas with the police, he settled down to the life of a country gentleman on his Avondale Estate in Wicklow. His interest in Irish politics had been roused by the execution of the 'Manchester martyrs' in 1867; in 1874 he stood unsuccessfully as a Home Rule candidate, and in 1875 was returned as MP for Meath. He associated himself with the more extreme faction in the Home Rule Party, and this brought him into conflict with Isaac Butt, whose leadership of the Party was weakening. In 1877 he ousted Butt as President of the Home Rule Confederation of Great Britain and he began to cultivate Fenian support. Although he did not assume control of the Irish Party immediately after Butt's death in 1879, he increased his standing in Ireland by leading the 'new departure', an alliance between the radical wing of the Party, the Fenians, and Michael Davitt's newly formed Land League, of which Parnell became president. These initiatives, together with the election of more of his supporters in 1880, brought him the leadership of the Home Rule Party, which he at once set about welding into a tightly-knit and organized group.

In August 1881 he acquired the weekly, *United Ireland*, which under the editorship of William O'Brien was outspoken in his support. In October he was imprisoned without trial and the Land League suppressed, but Gladstone, finding this policy counter-productive, negotiated the 'Kilmainham Treaty' in May 1882 whereby Parnell agreed to support Liberal policies in return for a widening of the terms of the 1881 Land Act. Although Parnell had used agrarian agitation to consolidate his power and bring pressure upon the British government, he had no great liking for the Land League and after his release from Kilmainham gradually replaced it with the 'National League', which was more directly under his control, and which put self-government before land reform.

In June 1885 Parnell helped bring down Gladstone's administration, and the Irish party held the balance of power in the new Parliament. At first this was exercised on behalf of the Conservatives, but following Gladstone's conversion to Home Rule Parnell sided with the Liberals. Gladstone's First Home Rule Bill was defeated in the spring of 1886 by an alliance of Conservatives and Liberal-Unionists, and in the ensuing election the Conservatives were returned with an overwhelming majority. In 1887 *The Times* published a series of articles, 'Parnellism and Crime', which implicated him in acts of violence. A Commission, set up to investigate the authenticity of these allegations, proved that they were based upon forgeries; Parnell was exonerated and his reputation soared in England as well as Ireland. The Irish Party and the Liberals were now in firm alliance, the so-called 'Union of Hearts', with a new Home Rule Bill as a fundamental plank in their policy.

Since 1880 Parnell had been having an affair with Katherine O'Shea. Her husband, Captain William O'Shea, knew of the relationship almost from the beginning, but not until December 1889, and then largely for pecuniary reasons, did he file for divorce, citing Parnell as co-respondent. The case did not come to court until 15 November 1890 and in the interim Parnell assured his followers that there was nothing to fear. Nevertheless, he did not defend himself, and O'Shea was not only awarded his divorce but also custody of Parnell's two daughters. In the immediate aftermath the Irish Party and press rallied to Parnell; the Irish hierarchy played a waiting game, but in England religious feeling was more decided, especially among the nonconformists from whom the Liberals derived much of their support. Gladstone, realizing that a continuing alliance with Parnell would split his party, asked Justin McCarthy to convey as much to the Irish members. This McCarthy unaccountably failed to do, and at a meeting on 25 November Parnell was re-elected leader. Stunned by this news, Gladstone made public a letter stating that he could no longer support the Irish Party if Parnell remained its head. By bringing this into the open (a course of action he had tried to avoid) Gladstone put the Party into a difficult position: if they now ditched Parnell they must do so in the full light of publicity and at the apparent behest of an Englishman. Parnell responded with a manifesto 'To the People of Ireland', which insisted that the Party should keep its independence, and also gave a contentious account of private conversations he had had with Gladstone. These revelations, which Gladstone repudiated, alienated a number of Parnell's followers. On 1 December, in an atmosphere of growing disquiet, the Party began to debate the leadership question in Committee Room 15 at the House of Commons; on 3 December the Irish bishops formally called upon the Irish people to reject Parnell, and on 6 December the Irish Party split when Justin McCarthy withdrew from Committee Room 15 with forty-four anti-Parnellites. Parnell was left with twenty-seven supporters.

Within a year Parnell was dead. In the interim he threw himself into electioneering campaigns, appealing especially to the more radical elements among the nationalists. In spite of his efforts he lost ground, three of his candidates were defeated at by-elections (including one at North Sligo during which George Pollexfen, WBY's uncle, met and talked with him). On 25 June 1891 he married Mrs O'Shea; on the same day the Irish hierarchy denounced him in uncompromising terms, and the hitherto loyal *Freeman's Journal* made his marriage an excuse to go over to the other side. His health was undermined by the physical and mental stresses of these months and he died in Brighton on 6 October 1891. His body was brought back to Ireland and buried at Glasnevin, an event which WBY did not apparently attend but which he was to make the theme of his poem 'Parnell's Funeral'.

Although he would have heard much in praise of Parnell when visiting KT (q.v.), WBY has little to say of him before his fall. His father's intense dislike of Parnell, and the O'Leary group's suspicions about his endorsement of the Land League and boycotting, probably had much to do with this. After the split, however, WBY came out firmly for him, seeing his struggle as a confrontation between single-minded integrity and compromising populist politics. In time this view hardened into a myth. Parnell became an ideal of the proud and lonely Anglo-Irish leader, who stood against all that WBY despised in Irish politics and character: the loose-lipped demogoguery, unscrupulous rhetoric, and clownishness typified, in his opinion, by 'the Great Comedian', Daniel O'Connell.

The most important and immediate consequence of Parnell's fall was that it forced thinking Irishmen, now confronted with rival nationalist parties, to question more deeply than hitherto what constituted their Irish character. In the 1880s national identity had been defined overwhelmingly in political terms; now, amid the wreckage of the political movement, it seemed that the cultural dimension might be more profound and important. WBY had 'the sudden certainty that Ireland was to be like soft wax for years to come' and set about helping to found literary societies and publishing enterprises which would help to stamp an imprint on the wax. Since it was a tenet of Parnell's last campaign that his faction, and not the McCarthyites, were the 'true' guardians of Ireland's separate political identity, the Parnellite press was particularly eager to support an independent literary movement, and WBY found allies among the journalists on *United Ireland* and the *Irish Daily Independent*.

THE RHYMERS CLUB of young poets, founded by WBY and Ernest Rhys (q.v.), flourished from early 1890 to 1894. It met weekly, occasionally at private houses, but usually in an upper room of the Cheshire Cheese, an inn with long literary associations in Wine Office Court, off Fleet Street. Membership was by election; regular attenders, besides WBY and Rhys, included John Davidson, Ernest Dowson, Edwin Ellis, A. S. Hillier, Selwyn Image, G. A. Greene, Lionel Johnson (q.v.), Richard Le Gallienne, Victor Plarr, Ernest Radford, T. W. Rolleston (q.v.), and John Todhunter (q.v.). Edward Garnett and Arthur Symons appeared at earlier meetings but less often thereafter; Oscar Wilde sometimes looked in when the gathering was at a private house. Guests were also permitted, and at various times WBY brought JO'L (q.v.), MG (q.v.), the artist Jack Nettleship, and Arthur Lynch (who gave a scathing account of the artificiality and self-satisfaction of the members and their proceedings).

WBY established the Club to meet the poets of his generation and so overcome his jealousy of them. He was also eager to formulate some agreed artistic manifesto, and in an early article proclaimed that the members were united by a rejection of French formalism, and by the desire to 'look once more upon the world with serious eyes and set to music . . . the deep soul of humanity'. In fact, his fellow Rhymers were deeply suspicious of all theories and, if they did share a philosophy, it was very loosely based upon certain Paterian ideas and the influence of Rossetti. Of more importance to WBY, as to the other members, was the Club's practical value: since most of them reviewed for the press they could notice each other's work regularly and, with occasional exceptions, in laudatory terms. They also read their verse aloud at meetings, and, although politeness tempered the criticism, this experience helped WBY to think more carefully about his poetic technique, and to 'learn his trade'. In this respect the Club was a necessary complement to WBY's Dublin experience: O'Leary's library had provided him with Irish models and themes, but many of the nineteenth-century Irish poets had lacked rigorous craftsmanship. Yet the Club also confirmed WBY's sense of himself as an Irish poet by revealing to him how far his provincialism and lack of education had cut him off from an English tradition available to his contemporaries.

The Club's two anthologies, published in 1892 and 1894, show the wide divergence of outlook and talent of the contributors, and much of the verse now seems faded and too obviously of its age. But WBY's 'The Man who Dreamed of Fairyland', 'The Cap and Bells', and 'A Mystical Prayer' (later 'The Poet Pleads with the Elemental Powers'); Johnson's 'The Dark Angel', and Dowson's 'Cynara', give the books a more lasting interest. The involvement of a few members with real poetic gifts is what distinguishes the Rhymers Club from the many other small literary societies that flourished at that time.

Although a third anthology was planned, the Club began to break up before it was published. In after years, when WBY found himself confronted by public hostility, he constructed a myth of the Rhymers—that true to their art but unable to sustain the Paterian intensities in a philistine world, they had preserved their integrity by a dissipation which led to suicide or early death. This poignant vision is, however somewhat lacking in truth. The deaths of Dowson and Johnson were indeed hastened by dissipation, and John Davidson did commit suicide, many years after the demise of the Club; but others survived to enjoy the solid, sometimes even stolid, pleasures of middle-class life, and a number actually outlived WBY. Challenged by Rhys for calling the whole group 'The Tragic Generation', WBY confessed that 'One begins to think of "the Rhymers" as those who sang of wine and women—I no more than you am typical'.

ERNEST RHYS (1859–1946) was born in London of Welsh extraction but, apart from a few childhood years in Carmarthen, grew up in Newcastle-on-Tyne. After a period as a mining engineer he decided, in January 1886, to seek his fortune in literary London. While eking out a precarious existence as a free-lance writer and journalist he was commissioned by the publisher Walter Scott to edit the Camelot Series of prose writing, and he decided to enlist the help of the younger literary generation, one of whom was WBY. The two had met in May 1887 at one of William Morris's Sunday evenings. WBY took immediately to Rhys, 'dreamy and amiable and weak of will', in the otherwise uncongenial atmosphere of London, and Rhys introduced him to 'Michael Field' and the Society of the New Life as well as asking him to compile *Fairy and Folk Tales of the Irish Peasantry* for the Camelot Series.

In February 1888 Rhys paid a six-month visit to the USA where he made the acquaintance of many writers, including Whitman and E. C. Stedman. On his return to England he asked WBY to edit a selection of William Carleton's stories as a Camelot book, and together they founded the Rhymers Club (q.v.) in January 1890. It was at a party given by WBY in the early summer of 1890 that Rhys met Grace Little, whom he married in January 1891. To reduce living expenses, he and his bride moved to a cottage in the Vale of Llangollen. In 1891 Rhys published *The Great Cockney Tragedy*, a sonnet sequence narrating the miseries and suicide of a Jewish tailor, illustrated by Jack Yeats, and this was followed later in the year by his book of lyrics, *A London Rose*. After the birth of his first child in October 1891, he began to write regularly for the *Pall Mall Gazette*, and was also placing poems and articles with New York and Boston papers. In June 1892 the family left Wales and settled in Hampstead, where a second child was born. Rhys, now acting as 'writer, editor and what not', helped J. M. Dent with a series of publishing enterprises. Under the influence of WBY and the Irish literary revival he sought inspiration in Welsh mythology, and in 1898 this bore fruit with his *Welsh Ballads*.

The birth of a third child and his wife's continuing ill-health aggravated his financial uncertainties and persuaded him to revive the idea of the Camelot Series.

He prepared a list of literary classics that could be published cheaply, and presented it to Dent who took up the project (christened by Rhys 'Everyman's Library') with enthusiasm. Rhys prepared 153 titles for publication in the first year of the venture and thereafter added monthly to the list: sadly, his commercial acumen did not match his literary enthusiasm and he, unlike Dent, made little from the project. At the outbreak of the First World War Dent dispensed with his services and thereafter he returned to free-lance journalism and editorial work, as well as publishing a novel and further books of verse (notably *The Leaf Burners* in 1918). He also travelled in Europe and called upon WBY during a trip to Dublin in 1925. In 1927 he made an extended lecture tour of the USA, where his wife died in 1929. The remainder of his life Rhys spent in London on various literary projects, producing two auto-biographies shortly before his death.

WBY remained a friend of Rhys's throughout his life and described him as 'a writer of Welsh translations and original poems, that have often moved me greatly though I can think of no one else who has read them'. Looking back on his early meetings with WBY, Rhys gave a modest but shrewd estimation of the difference between them: 'Yeats was destined to do for me more than I could then foretell. He was single-minded, while I was but an undecided visionary, trying to adapt myself to the fashions and imitate the men of the moment.'

THOMAS WILLIAM ROLLESTON (1857–1920) was born at Shinrone, near Roscrea, Tipperary, into Protestant Ascendancy stock; his father was a lawyer and his mother the daughter of Baron Richards, who had tried Gavan Duffy (q.v.) for treason-felony. After a distinguished career at Trinity College, Dublin, Rolleston went to Germany, largely on account of his wife's health, and developed an interest in German thought and literature; he was to help translate Whitman into German in 1889 and in the same year wrote a life of Lessing. He returned to Dublin in the mid-1880s and edited the *Dublin University Review* in which WBY's first publications appeared. In spite of his background, he came under the influence of JO'L (q.v.) and took up the nationalist cause—although, like JO'L, he was suspicious of the agrarian wing of Parnell's movement and in 1888 wrote a pamphlet against boycotting. It seemed for a while that he might be the successor to Thomas Davis.

In the late 1880s he moved to London where he joined the Rhymers Club (q.v.) and wrote regularly for a number of periodicals. He helped WBY found the Irish Literary Society (q.v.), his skill in organization proving invaluable, but in 1892 he revealed to Gavan Duffy, who then appropriated them, WBY's ideas for publishing a series of Irish books through Fisher Unwin. Since Duffy was in Nice for large parts of the year, Rolleston did most of the administrative work for the New Irish Library (q.v.) of which he became a sub-editor. On his appointment as Secretary to the Irish Industrial Association in 1893, he returned to Dublin and soon convinced himself that the success of the Home Rule movement depended upon economic development, and in particular upon economic co-operation between the north and south of Ireland. To this end he supported Horace Plunkett's agricultural co-operative movement and deplored the attacks upon schemes for economic amelioration by nationalist politicians. His first wife, Edith de Burgh, died in 1896, and the following year he married a daughter of Stopford Brooke. After some initial reservations, he became an enthusiastic supporter of the Gaelic League; in 1900 he published a pamphlet, 'Imagination and Art in Gaelic Literature', and in the same year co-edited with his father-in-law an important anthology, *A Treasury of Irish Poetry in the English Tongue*. From 1899 to 1905 he worked for the newly created Irish Department of Agriculture, under whose auspices he organized the Irish Historic Loan Collection to the Great Exhibition in St. Louis in 1904.

On leaving the Department Rolleston retired to Wicklow but, feeling too sequestered there, moved back to London to take up the editorship of the German section of the *Times Literary Supplement*. In 1910 he helped found the India Society, of which he became Honorary Secretary, and he also became a member of the Society for Psychical Research. In 1888 he had published *The Teaching of Epictetus*, and in 1908 issued his own philosophical speculations as *Parallel Paths: A Study of Biology, Ethics, and Art*; this was followed in 1909 by a book of verse, *Sea Spray*, and two books derived from Gaelic mythology: *The High Deeds of Finn* (1910) and *Myths and Legends of the Celtic Race* (1911). During the First World War he worked in the Censorship Department of the War Office (where, after 1916, he made use of his knowledge of Gaelic in censoring the letters of Sinn Fein prisoners), and later became Librarian at the Department of Information. As the political situation in Ireland deteriorated he wrote articles and pamphlets condemning England's lack of an Irish policy and urging economic aid as a way of improving the position.

Rolleston believed in WBY's poetic genius from the beginning and helped him with a number of literary enterprises. For his part, WBY was always hoping to set Rolleston to some significant Irish work, but became increasingly worried that his caution and gentility would stifle his creative and administrative energy. He never forgave him for divulging to Duffy the plans to issue Irish books through Unwin, and wondered whether he had done it out of 'a subconscious desire that my too tumultuous generation should not have its say'. After his appointment in the Irish Civil Service, Rolleston grew, according to WBY, 'more & more a country clergyman's daughter's dream of a perfect gentleman every day', a fastidiousness which, he thought, had sapped the vigour of Rolleston's writing. Yet WBY went on hoping that 'the old Rolleston, who really was a person of some conviction, may wake'. In fact, by birth and temperament, Rolleston had always been wary of the radical elements in Irish nationalism, and, as these forces became more influential, he withdrew into the patriotic neutrality of his work for the Department of Agriculture.

GEORGE WILLIAM RUSSELL, 'AE' (1867–1935), was born in Lurgan, Co. Armagh, but at the age of eleven moved to Dublin, where his father took a job in a firm of accountants. After attending the Metropolitan School of Art, where he met WBY, he became, in 1890, a draper's clerk, a post which he held until joining Horace Plunkett's Irish Agricultural Organization (IAOS) in 1897.

He had, from 1888, attended meetings of the Dublin Lodge of the Theosophical Society, and in April 1891 he moved in with a community of theosophists at 3 Upper Ely Place, where WBY occasionally stayed during visits to Dublin. His pseudonym was suggested partly by divination and partly by a compositor's error. Whereas WBY tried from the beginning to reconcile his mystical and national interests, there is little in AE's early poetry and prose to indicate that he was even conscious of living in Ireland: as John Eglinton comments, the 'event of 1891 was not, for Russell, the death of Parnell, but that of Madame Blavatsky'. In 1894 he published his first book of poems, *Homeward Songs by the Way*, and the following year he came under the influence of an energetic American theosophist, James Pryse.

From this time he started to take a greater interest in public life. His reading of Standish James O'Grady (q.v.) enabled him to see the Gaelic mythological cycle as an Irish expression of the universal religion, and in 1895 he joined the National Literary Society (q.v.). He began to prophesy the imminence of an Irish Messiah, and in 1897 turned pamphleteer with the intention of saying 'things in fierce print to make people's hair stand'; in fact, his pamphlets propose a spiritual and pastoral destiny for. Ireland if she will only throw off English commercialism, political dogma, and orthodox religion.

His work for the IAOS (he organized rural banks) gave a practical dimension to these ideas. Although he travelled widely throughout the country, Dublin was his base (he had married Violet North in 1898) and he saw a great deal of George Moore who settled there in 1901. In late 1901 he allowed the Fay brothers to rehearse his play *Deirdre*, and also persuaded WBY to give them *Cathleen ni Houlihan*; the performances of the two plays in April 1902 led to the formation of the Irish National Theatre Society of which AE became a Vice-President. He had by now gathered round him a new generation of Irish writers and in 1904 he edited *New Songs*, an anthology of their verse. WBY did not care for it. Indeed, the differences between the two men over what poetry should be extended also to drama. Although AE helped WBY reform the Irish National Theatre Society in 1905, turning it from a quarrelling group of amateurs into a more professional limited liability company, he soon afterwards resigned from it, preferring the cosy inclusiveness of amateurism.

In 1905 AE was appointed editor of the *Irish Homestead*, the weekly organ of the Irish co-operative movement, and he opened its pages to literary as well as IAOS contributions. In 1913, the year in which his *Collected Poems* appeared, he spoke out on behalf of the workers involved in the extended Dublin lock-out, writing open letters to Irish and English papers. He also tried to find a peaceful solution to Ireland's political troubles, inflamed by the Easter Rising, by taking part in the ultimately unsuccessful Irish Home Rule Convention from 1917 to 1918.

AE approved of the Treaty which ended the Anglo-Irish conflict, although he refused to become a Free State senator. In 1923 the *Irish Homestead* was merged with the *Irish Statesman* and he was appointed editor under the proprietorship of Sir Horace Plunkett. The new weekly was non-party but pro-Treaty and AE used it to denounce the die-hard Republicans. In January 1928 he made his first trip to the USA to raise funds for it, crossing the Atlantic again in June to receive an honorary degree from Yale. That autumn the costs of a libel case nearly ruined the *Irish Statesman*; it was saved by a public subscription, but the respite proved to be temporary and in April 1930 it ceased publication.

AE's wife was now seriously ill with cancer and in September 1930 he left on an extended tour of the USA to raise money for her treatment. He returned the following May, renewing his friendship with Moore on his way through London. In February 1932 his wife died; later that year he helped WBY set up the Irish Academy of Letters, becoming its secretary. The deaths of his wife and Plunkett, the election of de Valera, and the pietism roused by the Eucharistic Conference of 1932 prompted him to leave Ireland; in July 1933 he sold his Dublin house and the following month moved to London. In December 1934 he set out on his last trip to the USA where he lectured on rural reorganization; the tour was cut short by illness, and he returned to London in March 1935. In July he went to a nursing home in Bournemouth where he had an operation for cancer. He died on 17 July and his body was taken back to Dublin for burial.

After a close friendship in the 1890s, AE and WBY went different ways. WBY had been impressed by AE's gift for vision and by his religious temperament. He praised highly the early poetry written under these influences but gradually perceived that AE's moral enthusiasm drew him away from human nature and into abstractions, and his religion to an ideal that was too vague and remote. He recommended him for the IAOS post probably in the hope that this would give a more earthy quality to his verse. He also, and just as unsuccessfully, tried to interest AE in matters of technique, but by 1900 he had realized that they were 'the opposite of each other'. AE was democratic, endlessly tolerant, and lacking in passion, and WBY began to resent his influence in Dublin, especially his support for bad poets out of a religious impulse which led him 'to look upon all souls as equal'. There was a distinct coolness between them from 1905 to 1913, and even thereafter, though more amiably disposed, they found each other's company awkward. Part of this was a defence mechanism on AE's part, for in his last letter to WBY he confessed that he had always been afraid of becoming absorbed into his personality.

OLIVIA SHAKESPEAR (1863–1938) was the second child of Major-General Henry Tod Tucker, an ex-Indian Army Officer, and Harriet Maria Johnson an aunt of Lionel Johnson (q.v.). In December 1885 she married a London solicitor, Henry Hope Shakespear, also from an Anglo-Indian background. She later told WBY that her husband had 'ceased to pay court to me from the day of our marriage'; Their only child, Dorothy (who became Ezra Pound's wife), was born within a year of the wedding. OS first saw WBY early in 1894 at a literary dinner and engineered a meeting with him through her cousin, Lionel Johnson, shortly after 30 May 1894. WBY told her of his unrequited love for MG and the two corresponded (she told him later that his were 'unconscious love-letters') when he went to Ireland for the autumn and winter of 1894–5. Her first novel, *Love on a Mortal Lease*, was published in May 1894, followed by *The Journey of High Honour* in November of the same year. Shortly after his return from Sligo, in the early summer of 1895, WBY met her once again and, as he later put it, 'the conversation that was to decide so much in my life took place'. She apparently made some sort of declaration; WBY thought the matter over for a fortnight, decided that 'if I could not get the woman I loved, it would be a comfort even but for a little while to devote myself to another', and asked her to elope with him. In fact, they decided to postpone this step until after the death of her mother, and agreed to remain as friends rather than lovers until then. During the summer they met in art galleries, railway carriages, and the house of her confidante Valentine Fox. In the autumn WBY moved to Fountain Court, where the relationship could be continued more privately, and he wrote a number of poems to her, which were eventually published in *The Wind Among the Reeds*. Her mother's longevity evidently persuaded them to abandon their earlier resolutions and, on the advice of their friends, they planned to live together. Unexpectedly, however, Hope Shakespear was so distressed by the thought of a separation from his wife that OS thought it better to deceive him about the affair. WBY took rooms in Woburn Buildings early in 1896, which OS helped him furnish (there was 'an embarrassed conversation in the presence of some Tottenham Court [Road] shop man upon the width of the bed—every inch increased the expense'). After a failure on his part, caused by nerves, the affair was consummated. It continued for a year; then WBY met MG again and OS realized that his affections lay irrevocably elsewhere.

Their correspondence resumed in 1900, and Richard Ellmann states that the affair was renewed in 1903. It was OS who introduced Ezra Pound to WBY in May 1909, shortly after Pound's arrival in London, and in February 1911 her brother, Henry ('Harry') Tudor Tucker, married Edith Ellen Hyde-Lees, whose daughter by her first marriage later became Mrs W. B. Yeats. Both before and after his marriage WBY kept up a relaxed and lively correspondence with OS and called on her whenever he was in London. Hope Shakespear died in July 1923, and from 1926 until her death in October 1938 OS took charge of the upbringing of her grandson, Omar Pound.

When WBY heard of her death he recalled that for 'more than forty years she has been the centre of my life in London and during all that time we have never had a quarrel, sadness sometimes but never a difference'. When they first met she had just begun to write fiction seriously and was impressed by his play *The Land of Heart's Desire*, which she saw at the Avenue Theatre. Throughout their early relationship it was she who took the initiative; she 'startled and a little shocked' WBY with the passion of her first kiss. Later, her sympathetic understanding was to redeem the temporary sexual failure on his part that might otherwise have been disastrous. Yet, from the beginning, as WBY confesses in *Memoirs*, there was something lacking, and he 'could not give the love that was her beauty's right'. When he first met her he was desperately in need of a reciprocated emotional relationship: he came near to asking Eva Gore-Booth to marry him in November 1894 simply because she had pitied him. OS also listened sympathetically to his tales of MG, and he was moved by the desolation of her marriage, seeing in her beauty 'the nobility of defeated things'. WBY admired OS's 'profound culture' and her gentle, contemplative ways, numbering her as one of the three friends who had 'wrought / What joy is in my days'.

THE THEOSOPHICAL SOCIETY was founded in New York in September 1875 by HPB (q.v.), Colonel Henry Steel Olcott, and William Quan Judge, as a club for the discussion of occult matters, Olcott becoming President, and HPB Corresponding Secretary. The purpose of the Society was 'to collect and diffuse a knowledge of the laws which govern the Universe': the term 'theosophy' (literally, 'God-knowledge') was chosen after a hunt through a dictionary for a suitable name. The publication of HPB's *Isis Unveiled* (1877), a 1320-page syncretic treatise on occult belief, did not greatly clarify the rather vague aims of the Society, though it sold out within a few days of publication, despite a hostile press.

One of Olcott's Indian acquaintances put him in touch with the Arya Samaj, a Hindu movement for the restoration of a pure Vedic religion, and in 1878 the two organizations merged. This, together with dwindling numbers in the New York Theosophical Society, and a damaging public attack on HPB by her erstwhile colleague, the spiritualist D. Dunglas Home, persuaded the two leaders to sail for India in December 1878. They broke their journey in England, where they visited the London Lodge, founded by Charles Massey who had been present at the original New York meetings. In India they enlisted the help of A. P. Sinnett, editor of *The Pioneer*, and founded *The Theosophist* which HPB edited, but in 1880 alienated the Arya Samaj by taking Buddhist vows. In 1882 the Theosophical Society Headquarters were established at Adyar in Madras, and theosophical ideas gained wider currency with the publication of Anna Kingsford's *The Perfect Way* (1882), Sinnett's *The Occult World* (1881) and *Esoteric Buddhism* (1883), and Mabel Collins's *The Light on the Path* (1885).

In 1884, while HPB was on a visit to the European lodges with Olcott and the Indian theosophist Mohini Chatterji, she was accused of fraudulent mediumship by her Adyar servants, the Coulombs. She hurried back to refute the charges, which were already being investigated by Richard Hodgson on behalf of the Society for Psychical Research. His report was damning, and she returned to Europe, leaving Olcott to run the Adyar headquarters. In 1887 she established her own lodge in London. Anna Kingsford had already resigned from the Society because of its Buddhist leanings, and now there was ill-feeling in the London Lodge as HPB enticed away most of its members. Through the force of her personality and the generosity of her rich disciples, the Blavatsky Lodge soon gained ascendancy in London, and in 1890, on taking over new premises, declared itself the Headquarters of the Society in Europe.

In 1889 HPB had persuaded Annie Besant, the social reformer and one-time secularist, to join the Society, and after HPB's death in 1891 Mrs Besant proclaimed herself the new Corresponding Secretary on the authority of hidden Tibetan Masters. W. Q. Judge, however, alleged that these very Masters had appointed him as HPB's successor; in 1894 he was accused of having forged the communications upon which his claim was based (a charge that WBY suspected was true), and seceded from the Society, taking with him most of the American lodges and also the one in Dublin. Mrs Besant moved to Adyar with C. W. Leadbeater, formerly an Anglican clergyman, where, after the death of Olcott in 1907, she became President of the Society. Under her leadership the Society turned to Messianism. Jiddu Krishnamurti, the son of one of the staff at Adyar, was groomed for the role of spiritual leader, but, although he declared himself the new Messiah in December 1925, soon retracted his claims. Between 1891 and 1935 some forty-five branches of the Society were set up throughout the world; by the early 1930s, however, membership was shrinking rapidly, and after the death of Mrs Besant in 1934 the Society never regained its earlier strength.

The publication in 1888 of HPB's *The Secret Doctrine*, which differs considerably from the more thaumaturgic *Isis Unveiled*, showed that by drawing on a large number of sources, especially Buddhism and Hermeticism, she had managed to give some coherence to her ideas on the nature of theosophy. In it, she redefined the term 'theosophy' as 'Divine Science'—the study of the absolute truth which lay behind all religions and myths, as white light behind a prism. This truth, she argued, had been known to all the great teachers of the world and kept alive by esoteric cults. The immediate sources of HPB's wisdom were allegedly two Tibetan Masters who had vouchsafed her first-hand and telepathic knowledge of the ancient *Book of Dzyan*, upon which *The Secret Doctrine* was a commentary. The *Book of Dzyan* is, she maintained, predicated on three fundamental doctrines: (1) that the Deity is not anthropomorphic but an 'Omnipresent, Eternal, Boundless, and Immutable PRINCIPLE on which all speculation is impossible'; (2) that the law of periodicy, of flux and reflux, is universal; and (3) that each individual soul, being part of the Universal Over-Soul, has an obligation to progress through a vast number of incarnations in order to become reunited with it. The universe was not created but is in a constant state of evolution, and humanity, having evolved from the deity, is on its return path to it. The journey is a long one, for to complete the cycle the soul must pass through seven root races, each having seven sub-races which in turn have seven branch races. Each root race survives for 1,000,000 years and mankind has just passed the half-way mark in the fifth race.

Just as the macrocosm falls into seven parts, so does the microcosm, man himself, who is composed of three spiritual and four physical attributes. Only the physical parts become carnate, so that the enduring spiritual Ego is like an actor who in his time plays many different characters, these characters being its terrestial personalities. Yet the Ego is responsible for the good behaviour of its earthly manifestations, and an evil life will be punished, not in the recurring post mortem state, but in the next re-incarnation. It is, therefore, important that theosophists should behave ethically (HPB advocates a mildy ascetic and socialistic regimen), although they may take comfort in the thought that their sins will not lead to eternal damnation, but may be redeemed in a future existence.

WBY and his Dublin friends were much excited by theosophical ideas when they came across them in Sinnett's books in the mid-1880s. In 1885 they formed a Hermetic Society to discuss such matters, and the vist to Dublin, at their behest, of Mohini Chatterji, left a lifelong impression on WBY. In April 1886 Charles Johnston and Claude Wright obtained a charter to set up a Dublin lodge of the Theosophical Society, but WBY, while associating himself closely with it, did not join. Only when he came under her personal influence in London did he become a member of HPB's lodge, although he still entertained doubts about her Tibetan Masters and her own occult powers. In 1888, possibly to counter the attraction of the newly formed Golden Dawn (q.v.), HPB established an Esoteric Section—an inner order devoted to the 'occult sciences'—in her lodge, which WBY immediately joined. In return for magical knowledge and the development of latent psychic and psychological energies, members had to pledge themselves to abstinence, asceticism, good works, and to an unswerving faith in HPB and her Masters. WBY had difficulty with these last stipulations but managed to square his conscience. He pressed for more instruction in practical magic, and in December 1889 became a member of the Recording Committee for occult research. However, his over-enthusiastic experiments upset his timid colleagues and in 1890 he was asked to leave the Society.

Because of his doubts about HPB's Mahatmas, and about her manipulation of psychic phenomena, WBY was never an orthodox theosophist—he told JO'L (q.v.) that they were 'turning a good philosophy into a bad religion'—but the Theosophical Society had many attractions for him at this period of his life. The very verve and apparent erudition with which HPB expounded her anti-materialist arguments were a joy to someone whose innate religious sensibility had been perplexed by positivist ideas. Particularly appealing was her adaptation of evolutionary theory, her use of scientific terminology in refuting contemporary science, and her claim that esoteric tradition had long ago answered and transcended all modern questions and speculations. The fact that such knowledge came from secret and traditional sources, that theosophy was an unveiling and not a revelation, also delighted him, and encouraged him to look for similar truths amid the symbols and images of Irish myth and folklore. Indeed, Ireland seemed to be given a special importance by the doctrine of racial evolution for, as he wrote to JO'L, the Blavatsky Lodge looked 'to Ireland to produce some great spiritual teaching'. He also took readily to the belief in reincarnation, retaining it throughout life, while the suggestion that terrestial personalities are passing manifestations of an abiding spiritual individuality perhaps first turned his thoughts to the theory of masks. In its eclecticism, theosophy introduced him to many occult and mystic beliefs which he later traced back to their origins, so that much that appears in *A Vision* has affinities with what he learned from HPB.

JOHN TODHUNTER (1839–1916) was born in Dublin of Quaker stock. After some years in commerce he decided to enter Trinity College, four years after his great friend JBY (q.v.). At Trinity he won the Vice-Chancellor's Prize for verse three times in succession, but after graduating decided upon a medical career to ensure financial security. It was he who first encouraged JBY to submit his sketches for professional appraisal, and he later commissioned a number of pictures from him. In 1870 he married Katharine, sister of Robert Ball, subsequently Astronomer Royal, but she died in childbirth less than a year later. From 1870 to 1874 he was Professor of English at Alexandra College, Dublin, where he met Dora Digby, whom he married in 1879, after he had moved to London. He settled with his new wife in Bedford Park (q.v.), where he lived for the rest of his life. His first book, *Laurella and Other Poems*, appeared in 1876, followed by a version of *Alcestis* (1879), *A Study of Shelley* (1880), and in 1881 *The True Tragedy of Rienzi*, which WBY read with enthusiasm. As JBY told Todhunter in April 1885, 'Willie . . . watches with an almost breathless interest your career as dramatic poet . . . he has read everything you have written most carefully.' WBY did not see the production of

Todhunter's *Helena of Troas* in 1886, but accounts of its 'religious' staging greatly impressed him.

On his return to London, WBY saw a good deal of Todhunter, especially after they had become neighbours. He encouraged him to write poetry on Irish themes and acted as his intermediary with JO'L (q.v.) and KT (q.v.) who were compiling *Poems and Ballads of Young Ireland*. He reviewed *The Banshee and Other Poems* (1888) twice, as well as urging his friends to give the book publicity, but the work of Todhunter's which most impressed him was *A Sicilian Idyll*, performed at the Bedford Park Social Club in May 1890 with Florence Farr (q.v.) playing a leading role. WBY reviewed the play, a slight pastoral verse drama, four times, seeing in its simple lyricism and lack of rhetoric the promise of a revival of poetic drama and a new manner of stage production. His excitement over this play caused him, as he later confessed, to overrate Todhunter's work. He gave warm but qualified praise to *The Poison Flower*, produced in 1891, but *The Comedy of Sighs*, put on with WBY's *The Land of Heart's Desire* at the Avenue Theatre in March 1894, was a disaster, being jeered by the audience on the first night, and had to be quickly withdrawn.

After this fiasco Todhunter staged no more plays. In 1895 the New Irish Library (q.v.) issued his *Life of Patrick Sarsfield*, and his *Three Irish Bardic Tales* appeared the following year. He was a member of a number of literary clubs, including the Sette of Odd Volumes and the Omar Kayyám, but only published two further books, *Sounds and Sweet Airs* in 1905 and a translation of Heine in 1907. Several other works, including *Essays* (1920) and *Selected Poems* (1929), were published posthumously.

WBY described Todhunter as 'a tall, sallow, lank, melancholy man', who never developed into a major writer because he lacked emotional power and because 'with him every book was a new planting, and not a new bud on an old bough'. Nevertheless, he exerted a significant influence on WBY by alerting him to the possibilites of poetic drama: not merely to the potentialities of dramatic verse, but also to the value of chorus, stylization, staging, and verse-speaking. When he founded the Irish Literary Theatre, and later the Abbey, WBY was to develop many of the ideas and perceptions first suggested by seeing *A Sicilian Idyll* in Bedford Park.

KATHARINE TYNAN (1859–1931), was born in Dublin in 1859 (not 1861 as she always claimed), the fifth of the twelve children of Andrew and Elizabeth Tynan. Her father, a substantial farmer (the model for WBY's essay 'The Knight of the Sheep'), was an ardent Parnellite who nevertheless made money through British Army food contracts; he exerted the major influence on her early life. A plain but lively girl with poor eyesight, she attended a school for young ladies in Dublin and, from 1872 to 1876, Siena Convent, Drogheda. Her father encouraged her literary ambitions, and she published her first poem, 'Dreamland', in *Young Ireland* in 1875; in 1877 the *Graphic* printed her poem 'August or June'. Her work appeared frequently thereafter in *United Ireland*, the *Spectator*, and *Merry England*, and from 1880 in the *Irish Monthly*, whose editor, Fr. Matthew Russell, was her valued friend.

She was a fervent admirer of Parnell (q.v.) and, influenced by his sister Anna, joined the Ladies' Land League, although she later regretted this venture into agrarian agitation. In 1885 Wilfred Meynell, whom she had met through Fr. Russell, arranged for Kegan Paul to publish her first book of verse, *Louise de la Vallière*, at her father's expense. The volume was a success and went into a second edition. Although critics identified the influence of D. G. Rossetti in her verse, her style and themes derived more directly from Adelaide Proctor, whom she had read at school, and Longfellow, whose influence persisted until disparaged by WBY.

KT saw WBY for the first time in June 1885 when C. H. Oldham brought him out to Clondalkin to discuss plans for the *Dublin University Review*, and thereafter the two poets met regularly in Clondalkin, at the Yeatses' house in Rathgar where KT often stayed, at the studio of JBY (q.v.), who painted a sympathetic portrait of her, and at the O'Learys' 'at homes'. Under the influence of JO'L (q.v.) they encouraged each other to take up Irish themes, and it was KT who first suggested that WBY should attempt a play on an Irish subject. For KT, these discussions resulted in *Shamrocks* (1887) and *Ballads and Poems* (1891) two books of verse which are shaped by their Irish and Catholic inspiration.

While always convinced of his genius and grateful for his literary advice, KT found WBY exasperating in some respects and would send him off on imaginary errands when she wanted time to herself. Although WBY did not venture to address her by her first name until the autumn of 1889, the relationship began to trouble his youthful susceptibilities and he wondered 'if she was in love with me and if it was my duty to marry her. Sometimes when she was in Ireland, I in London would think it possible that I should, but if she came to stay, or I saw her in Ireland, it became impossible again.' There was belief in the Tynan family that WBY had in fact proposed but been rejected.

From 1887 KT's career as a free-lance writer and journalist prospered and she began to contribute articles, stories, and poems to American as well as Irish and English papers. During this time she reviewed—sometimes more than once—all WBY's publications, including the otherwise little noticed *Mosada*. A visit to England in the summer of 1889 cemented a number of literary friendships as well as opening up others, for she was indefatigable, if disarmingly obvious, in her cultivation of the famous and the titled.

On 6 September 1888 KT met Henry Hinkson, the son of a saddler of Dame Street, Dublin, then reading Classics at Trinity College; the two later became engaged but for social and religious reasons (he was a Protestant with Ascendancy pretensions) they were not married until 4 May 1893, and then in London; they settled down in Ealing. Although two sons and a daughter were to survive, their first child died after a few weeks and another was stillborn. Hinkson, a struggling barrister, tried his hand at writing novels and plays without great success and as their means grew increasingly straitened KT was obliged to turn her hand to pot-boiling novels, serials, and reviews. WBY's passing criticism of Hinkson's anthology, *Dublin Verses* (1895), caused a temporary coolness between him and KT.

After the beginning of 1892 WBY and KT corresponded less frequently, but the friendship survived. In 1906 WBY edited a selection of KT's poems and enlisted her help in a dispute with his sister over the editorial policy of the Cuala Press. In

1911 the Hinkson family returned to Ireland where WBY met KT on occasion, regarding her as one of the triumvirate (he and Lionel Johnson being the others) who had initiated the reformation of Irish poetry.

In October 1914 Hinkson was appointed Removeable Magistrate for Castlebar, Co. Mayo, where they lived until his death in 1919. In the following years KT travelled widely in Britain and on the continent, paying three long visits to Cologne, then under French occupation. She returned to Ireland from time to time and her daughter, the novelist Pamela Hinkson, recalled a meeting in the late 1920s between her, AE and WBY. This was probably the last time that she and WBY saw each other, for KT died on 2 April 1931 in London; she is buried in St. Mary's Churchyard, Kensal Green.

JOHN BUTLER YEATS (1839–1922), the poet's father, was born in Tullylish, Co. Armagh, a son of the Revd William Butler Yeats, and was educated at Atholl Academy on the Isle of Man, where he met Charles and George Pollexfen, later to be his brothers-in-law. By the time he entered Trinity College, Dublin, in 1857, he had lost his Christian faith, and turned, under the influence of Mill and Comte, towards sceptical positivism—a philosophical position he retained until his death. In September 1862, just before taking up law studies, he fell in love with Susan Mary Pollexfen on a visit to Sligo. That November JBY's father died, bequeathing him the heavily mortgaged Thomastown estate in Co. Kildare and a Dublin town house. In the following September JBY married Susan Pollexfen and the two set up home at 5 Sandymount Avenue ('Georgeville') in Dublin, near Sandymount Castle, the residence of his uncle, Robert Corbet. By his marriage into the silent and introspective Pollexfens JBY proclaimed that he had 'given a tongue to the sea cliffs' but the marriage was not a complete success; temperamental differences were aggravated on Susan Yeats's part by her husband's lack of financial success and the tribulations of running a household perpetually on the edge of indigence.

Their first child, WBY, was born on 13 June 1865 and the following January JBY was called to the Irish bar. August 1866 saw the birth of a second child, Susan Mary, at Enniscrone, Co. Sligo. JBY, finding the law little to his taste, abandoned it to enrol at Heatherley's Art School in London. He took a house at 23 Fitzroy Road, where a third child, Elizabeth Corbet, was born in March 1868. With Edwin Ellis, Sydney Hall, and later George Wilson, JBY formed 'The Brotherhood', an informal group of painters united more by personal friendship than by any aesthetic programme.

JBY had paid for his art training by taking out further mortgages on his property, but with few commissions for paintings, money grew short, especially after the birth of a fourth child, Robert Corbet, in March 1870. Moreover, feeling that he as yet lacked sufficient mastery of basic technique, he was rarely able to finish the paintings he had begun. On 29 August 1871 his fifth child, Jack, later to be an artist himself, was born. The following summer, to save money, JBY sent his family to stay with his in-laws in Sligo, Robert dying there in March 1873. That summer JBY spent some time in Sligo, and WBY, now aged eight, received his 'first clear image' of his father—a tall man with a 'very black beard and hair'. JBY executed some portraits in Ireland but in October 1874 the whole family moved back to London, taking a house at 14 Edith Villas, Kensington. On 29 August 1875 the last child, Jane Grace, was born but she lived only until June 1876; a few weeks after this JBY was called to his mother's deathbed in Dublin.

In 1879 the family moved to 8 Woodstock Road in the new development of Bedford Park (q.v.). Two years later, in the hope of more success in Dublin, JBY rented a studio there and, when the lease on Woodstock Road ran out, the family moved to Howth. Although this resulted in more commissions, they were not profitable; late in 1883 lack of funds obliged the Yeatses to take a house in the less pleasant surroundings of Harold's Cross. Not only was JBY not earning money, but the income from Thomastown steadily decreased and in 1886 he resolved to sell the property to his tenants under the government-assisted provisions of the Ashbourne Act. He moved back to London where the family joined him, at 58 Eardley Crescent, in the spring of 1887. Earlier that year he had been elected to Associate Membership of the Royal Hibernian Academy.

In the autumn of 1887 Susan Yeats suffered a stroke that was to leave her an invalid for the rest of her life. JBY, despairing of portrait work, turned his hand to illustrations for magazines and books, and even to writing stories. In 1888 the family returned to Bedford Park where they suffered a further financial blow when the proceeds from the Thomastown property turned out to be smaller than anticipated and were quickly swallowed up by debts. JBY was to look back upon this period of his life as one of 'incessant humiliation'. It was also a time when the house emptied: Jack Yeats had married in August 1894; in October 1895 WBY moved out to lodge with Arthur Symons; the following month Lily left to become a governess in France.

A further stroke in the mid-nineties left Susan Yeats more *distraite* than ever; on 3 January 1900, she died suddenly. Shortly afterwards, JBY was astonished to find that he still had £869 owing to him on the sale of the Thomastown land; he paid his debts and went on a fortnight's visit to France, followed by a long holiday with Jack and Cottie Yeats in Devon. In October 1901 a Dublin exhibition of his and Nathaniel Hone's pictures, organized by Sarah Purser, was an unexpected success, with John Quinn among the purchasers. JBY went over to Ireland for it and never returned to Bedford Park. The following year the two girls also moved to Dublin to help organize the Dun Emer craft industries, settling with JBY in Churchtown. The family was still short of money and both ECY and JBY asked for loans from WBY during his profitable tour of the USA in 1903–4. In May 1904 six of JBY's works were included in a London exhibition of Irish painting by Hugh Lane, and a visit by John Quinn in the autumn led to further commissions. In January 1905 his support of Hugh Lane's proposal for a Dublin gallery of modern pictures brought JBY into conflict with most of the other members of the Royal Hibernian Academy. During these years JBY painted portraits of Douglas Hyde (q.v.), Standish James O'Grady (q.v.), J. P. Mahaffy, J. M. Synge, and George Moore. In 1907 the last of the money from the Thomastown property helped pay off his debts. Hugh Lane had meanwhile organized a subscription to send him on a trip to Italy, but JBY decided instead to accompany SMY to an Irish Exhibition in New York where Dun Emer work was on show.

JBY liked New York so much that he stayed on when SMY returned to Dublin, moving in September 1909 into the Petipas sisters' boarding-house on West 29th Street, where he remained until his death. In February 1911 Quinn ordered a self-portrait of JBY, a commission that gave him an excuse to remain in America; he worked at the picture for the rest of his life without ever finishing it. He began to write regularly to WBY, sometimes twice a day, unfolding his ideas on life, art, and literature. The vigour and shrewdness of this correspondence impressed and delighted WBY, and helped him to a fuller appreciation of his father's ideas and intelligence. He saw him on his visits to New York in 1911 and 1914, and helped to support him by selling manuscripts to Quinn on a regular basis. Pound's selection, *Passages from the Letters of John Butler Yeats* (1917), received good reviews. JBY was knocked down by a car in January 1915, and in November 1918 an attack of influenza, followed by pneumonia, nearly proved fatal. Despite the efforts of Quinn and WBY to persuade him to return to Ireland he remained obdurately in America, meeting the new Mrs Yeats there when she accompanied WBY on his 1920 tour. Although he kept his intelligence and wit to the end, he went into a physical decline from the middle of 1921. He died in February 1922, with $14 in his bank account, and is buried at Chestertown, New York. In the year after his death the Cuala Press published his *Early Memories*.

JBY's intellectual curiosity, artistic integrity, and relish for dramatic literary readings had a great influence on WBY, but, seemingly incapable of pushing any work through to a conclusion, he was also important as an example to be avoided. He was for his part disconcerted by the rigour of his son's approach to art and life, seeing in it a ruthlessness foreign to his own nature; as he told Quinn, the 'weakness in my character is a distrust of any kind of personal success'. WBY summed up the differences between them in a letter written shortly before JBY's death: 'It is [his] infirmity of will which has prevented him from finishing his pictures and ruined his career. He even hates the sign of will in others. . . . the qualities which I thought necessary to success in art or in life seemed to him "egotism" or "selfishness" or "brutality". I had to escape this family drifting, innocent, & helpless, & the need for that drew me to dominating men like Henley & Morris, & estranged me from his friends.' Father and son differed on religious, philosophical, and artistic matters and, as was the way in the Yeats household, argued these points vigorously. JBY had recognized his son's poetic gift from the first, and understood the difficulty he had in social relationships, yet WBY remained always something of an enigma; as late as 1920 JBY wrote that he had never really known him and was 'quite as curious about him as is the great public of America and England'.

ADDENDA

The following letters came to light too late for inclusion in the main body of the text. The first should appear on page 368; the second on page 384.

To D. J. O'Donaghue, [c. 1 December 1893]

56 North Cir Road | Dublin.

My dear O'Donaghue

I had intended to cross over to night for the dinner[1] but a cold which I have been struggling with of late seems to have settled on my chest for the present. I must therefore stay at home. Would it be possible to let the 10/– which I sent for the dinner ticket go to the Rolleston testemonial? If so please let it do so.

Yrs ev
W B Yeats

ALS UCLA.

To W. E. Henly, [late March 1894]

THE IRISH LITERARY SOCIETY | LONDON |
BLOOMSBURY MANSION | HART ST. | W. C.

Dear M[r] Henley

I enclose article on 'Revival of Irish Literature'.[1] The subject was thorney & I fear I may not in making it suitable for my own purposes have made it suitable for you.

I hope you will be able to see my play.[2]

Yrs ever
W B Yeats

ALS Private.

---

[1] The Irish Literary Society, London, held a dinner on 2 Dec 1893 at the Criterion Restaurant to mark W. T. Rolleston's retirement as secretary since he was returning to Ireland to take up the post of managing director and secretary of the Irish Industries Association. *United Ireland* reported on 9 Dec (1) that 'Mr W. B. Yeats was . . . expected to be present and speak, but a cold unfortunately prevented his attendance'. After dinner Rolleston was presented with a gold watch and Mrs Rolleston with a copy in gold of the Tara brooch.

[1] The article was evidently unsuitable and did not appear in the *National Observer*.
[2] See p. 383.

INDEX OF RECIPIENTS

INDEX

Italic page-references indicate passages where the subject is particularly discussed.

Yeats, W. B., at Burnham Beeches, 3–5; early
love of boats, 5; at Howth, 5–6; at
Rathgar, 9; writes few letters, 10; moves
to lodgings in London, 11; on pleasures of
solitude, 11; moves with family to Eardley
Crescent, London, 12; homesickness for
Dublin, 12; attends Irish debate in Parliament, 13–14; meets Rhys, 15; visits
artists, 16; working habits, 17; approval of
'Michael Field', 18; on Sparling, 22; on
London men of letters, 18, 22; meets May
Morris, 22; supper at William Morris's,
23, 26; Socialism not his work, 23; dislike
of London Theatre, 24; moodiness, 26;
on the heroines of the 'neo-romantic
school', 29–31; visits Sligo, 33; on the
'Mitchelstown Massacre', 36; working on
'Wanderings of Oisin', 37; climbs Ben
Bulben, 37; mother and SMY ill, 38;
nervous collapse after finishing 'Oisin',
41; stays with Katharine Tynan at Clondalkin, 43; organizing subscriptions for
first book of poems, 44; returns to London, 45; at Mme Blavatsky's, 45; trying to
get regular employment, 48, 50, 51; need
for passivity and to break web of thought,
48; indifference at relation's ruin, 48;
meets Shaw, 50; views on Shaw, 50n;
correcting MS of *Oisin*, 53; submits it
to Kegan Paul, 54; offering poems to
American papers, 55; to move to Bedford
Park, 56; hopes for assistant librarianship,
56; writing articles not satisfactory, 56;
no faith in success or future, 57; at
Southwark Irish Literary Club, 58, 68, 71;